The Economics of **natural resource use**

The Addison-Wesley Series in Economics

Abel/Bernanke
Macroeconomics
Allen
Managerial Economics
Berndt
The Practice of Econometrics
Bierman/Fernandez
Game Theory with Economic Applications
Binger/Hoffman
Microeconomics with Calculus
Boyer
Principles of Transportation Economics
Branson
Macroeconomic Theory and Policy
Brown/Hogendorn
International Economics: Theory and Context
Browning/Zupan
Microeconomic Theory and Applications
Bruce
Pubic Finance and the American Economy
Burgess
The Economics of Regulation and Antitrust
Byrns/Stone
Economics
Canterbery
The Literate Economist: A Brief History of Economics
Carlton/Perloff
Modern Industrial Organization
Caves/Frankel/Jones
World Trade and Payments: An Introduction
Cooter/Ulen
Law and Economics
Eaton/Mishkin
Reader to accompany The Economics of Money, Banking, and Financial Markets
Ehrenberg/Smith
Modern Labor Economics
Ekelund/Tollison
Economics: Private Markets and Public Choice
Filer/Hamermesh/Rees
The Economics of Work and Play
Fusfeld
The Age of the Economist
Ghiara
Learning Economics: A Workbook
Gibson
International Finance
Gordon
Macroeconomics
Gregory
Essentials of Economics
Gregory/Ruffin
Economics
Gregory/Stuart
Russian and Soviet Economic Structure and Performance
Griffiths/Wall
Intermediate Microeconomics
Gros/Steinherr
Winds of Change: Economic Transition in Central and Eastern Europe
Hartwick/Olewiler
The Economics of Natural Resource Use
Hogendorn
Economic Development
Hoy/Livernois/McKenna/Rees/Stengos
Mathematics for Economics
Hubbard
Money, the Financial System, and the Economy
Hughes/Cain
American Economic History
Husted/Melvin
International Economics
Invisible Hand Software
Economics in Action
Jehle/Reny
Advanced Microeconomic Theory
Klein
Mathematical Methods for Economics
Krugman/Obstfeld
International Economics: Theory and Policy
Laidler
The Demand for Money: Theories, Evidence, and Problems
Lesser/Dodds/Zerbe
Environmental Economics and Policy
Lipsey/Courant
Economics
McCarty
Dollars and Sense
Melvin
International Money and Finance
Miller
Economics Today
Miller/Benjamin/North
The Economics of Public Issues
Miller/Fishe
Microeconomics: Price Theory in Practice
Miller/VanHoose
Essentials of Money, Banking, and Financial Markets
Mills/Hamilton
Urban Economics
Mishkin
The Economics of Money, Banking, and Financial Markets
Parkin
Economics
Phelps
Health Economics
Riddell/Shackelford/Stamos
Economics: A Tool for Critically Understanding Society
Ritter/Silber/Udell
Principles of Money, Banking, and Financial Markets
Rohlf
Introduction to Economic Reasoning
Ruffin/Gregory
Principles of Economics
Salvatore
Microeconomics
Sargent
Rational Expectations and Inflation
Scherer
Industry Structure, Strategy, and Public Policy
Schotter
Microeconomics
Sherman/Kolk
Business Cycles and Forecasting
Smith
Case Studies in Economic Development
Studenmund
Using Econometrics
Su
Economic Fluctuations and Forecasting
Tietenberg
Environmental and Natural Resource Economics
Tietenberg
Environmental Economics and Policy
Todaro
Economic Development
Waldman/Jensen
Industrial Organization: Theory and Practice
Zerbe/Dively/Lesse
Benefit-Cost Analysis

The Economics of natural resource use

SECOND EDITION

John M. Hartwick
Queen's University

Nancy D. Olewiler
Simon Fraser University

An imprint of Addison Wesley Longman

Reading, Massachusetts • Menlo Park, California • New York • Harlow, England
Dons Mills, Ontario • Sydney • Mexico City • Madrid • Amsterdam

Sponsoring Editor: Denise Clinton
Production Supervisor: Heather Garrison
Senior Marketing Manager: Quinn Perkson
Production Services: Ruttle, Shaw & Wetherill, Inc.

Library of Congress Cataloging-in-Publication Data
Hartwick, John M.
The economics of natural resource use / John M. Hartwick, Nancy D. Olewiler. — 2nd ed.
p. cm.
Includes bibliographical references and index.
ISBN 0-321-01428-6
1. Natural resources. 2. Environmental policy. I. Olewiler, Nancy D. II. Title
HC59.H3558 1997
333.7'13—dc21 97-8418
CIP

Printed in the United States of America.

5 6 7 8 9 10-MA-02 01 00 99 98 97

Brief Contents

Contents

Preface

This is a textbook on the economics of using natural resources, a subject that has been intensively refined and developed since the 1960s. The first edition appeared in 1986, at a time when the major concerns were energy use, forecasts of impending resource depletion, and the destruction of ecosystems. That edition captured these concerns by addressing basic resource use questions in chapters on nonrenewable, renewable, and environmental resources. In addition, we examined energy use, natural resource scarcity, limits to growth, and regulation of natural resources. The text provided a framework for analyzing a broad range of natural resource use issues with a graphical format and simple calculus accessible to undergraduate students who had taken an intermediate microeconomics course. This edition reflects our continued belief that complex issues of resource use can be presented so that upper-level undergraduates and beginning graduate students can not only understand the concepts and issues, but also develop analytical skills that will enable them to examine a wide range of economic problems.

In the 12 years since the publication of our first edition, we have faced many of the same natural resource and environmental issues as in the mid-eighties. Indeed, pressure on our natural systems has intensified around the globe. Fisheries worldwide are threatened by excessive harvesting and pollution from industrial activity and urban life. Inefficiently high rates of forest harvesting, particularly but not exclusively in tropical regions, are a major concern. While many regions have made great gains in the levels of environmental quality, rapid industrialization continues to threaten the quality of the air and water elsewhere. Concerns over the depletion of stratospheric ozone and over global warming have intensified since the 1980s. Depletion of soils and reduction of groundwater reserves remain serious problems. However, some issues of natural resource use are no longer as pressing as they were in the previous decade. Fears that we would run out of energy resources have abated as the economic system has responded to periodic shortages induced by weather, the actions of suppliers, and depletion of particular reserves. Energy supplies now consists of a broad spectrum of products, ranging from nonrenewable sources such as oil, natural gas, coal, and uranium to renewable energy sources such as solar and wind power and ethanol from plants. The economic system has generally worked well to induce substitution among energy inputs and to foster technological developments that reduce the amount of energy needed to produce our goods and services.

The biggest change in thinking about natural resource use since our first edition has been the widespread adoption of the concept of sustainability of our natural environment and economy. The 1987 publication of the report by Gro Harlund Brundtland, "Our Common Future," prompted a new look at how the economic system uses our planet's natural resources. The fundamental question the report asked was whether societies could sustain themselves over time without sinking below a subsistence level of consumption and without irreparably destroying the earth's environmental and natural resources. Since the late 1980s, everyone from politicians to presidents of large corporations has jumped on the sustainability bandwagon. However, it is a long way from rhetoric to actual policies. This edition devotes two chapters to sustainability. We provide an analytical framework with which to examine how the economy can generate a sustainable path of natural resource use.

We have extensively rewritten and reorganized the text for this second edition. We have benefited greatly from extensive suggestions for change offered by the many people who have used the first edition. Our goals are to provide a more user-friendly text for students with different economics backgrounds, to update policy sections and applications, to eliminate chapters that were not used extensively, and to retain what we feel is the key strength of the text—presentation of the core of natural resource economic modeling at a level that enables students to solve problems and to apply the analytical framework to a wide range of topics. Our chapters continue to rely extensively on graphical techniques combined with simple calculus to solve models. More complex analysis appears in chapters and sections identified as advanced. As in the first edition, each chapter contains applications of economic models to current policy concerns and illustrations of how the theory can be used to examine natural resource problems such as deforestation, depletion of fish stocks, national income accounting for sustainability, and water pricing.

The text is divided into three sections. Part I provides an overview of the microeconomic concepts used extensively in natural resource modeling and an introduction to sustainability and natural resource scarcity. Part II presents and develops models of natural resource use in a static framework. A static model can determine the socially efficient levels of land and water use, fish harvests, and pollution that can be sustained period after period. Static models are conceptually the easiest to work with and will be familiar to students who have taken first- and second-year economics courses. Part III turns to models of natural resource use in an intertemporal setting. In these models, the harvesting or extraction that occurs in one year will affect the amount that can be used subsequently. Our models cover nonrenewable resources such as energy and minerals, as well as renewable resources such as forests and fish species. We conclude with another look at sustainability, using the concepts developed in the preceding chapters.

HOW TO USE THIS BOOK

This book can be used for a variety of one-semester courses and for students of different backgrounds. For a course that focuses on both natural and environmental resources, we recommend covering Parts I, II, and Chapters 8 and 10 of Part III. For a course that examines natural resources exclusively, we suggest covering all chapters except 6 and 7. Courses with more emphasis on environmental economics should focus on Parts I and II and the sections on deforestation in the forest chapter. Chapters 9, 11, and 12 have material that requires somewhat more sophisticated analytical methods that would be of interest to advanced natural resource courses.

ACKNOWLEDGMENTS

Many people provided extensive comments on drafts of the manuscript. We are greatly indebted to them and apologize if we weren't able to incorporate all their suggestions. We thank Peter Berck, University of California, Berkeley; Clark S. Binkley, University of British Columbia; John B. Braden, University of Illinois; Jon Conrad, Cornell University; A. Myrick Freeman, Bowdoin College; Ken Hendricks, University of British Columbia; Charles W. Howe, University of Colorado; Charles Robin Lindsey, University of Alberta; Gabriel Lozada, University of Utah; Herbert Mohring, University of Minnesota; Andrew Muller, McMaster University; David H. Newman, University of Georgia; Peter J. Parks, Rutgers University; Steve Polasky, Oregon State University; Robert Rogers, University of Wisconsin, Stevens Point; Roger A. Sedjo, Resources for the Future; Robert Solow, Massachusetts Institute of Technology; Dale Squires, Southwest Fisheries Center; John Tilton, Colorado School of Mines; James Wilen, University of California, Davis; Elizabeth Wilman, University of Calgary; and Jennifer Wohl, University of British Columbia.

In addition, we thank Kelli Dawson for his extensive research assistance, and also those who provided reviews of the manuscript but wished to remain anonymous.

PART I

APPROACHING THE STUDY OF NATURAL RESOURCE ECONOMICS

In Part I, we set the stage for a detailed examination of natural resource use. Chapter 1 presents an overview of the concepts used throughout the book. Chapter 2 introduces the fundamental issues of sustainability and natural resource scarcity in the past and present.

chapter 1

Economic Concepts for Examining Natural Resource Use

INTRODUCTION

Global natural resource use has been an area of concern for economists since the simultaneous birth of modern economics and industrial society in the eighteenth century. Malthus was concerned with the choking off of population growth and the well-being of individuals by land and food constraints. Conservationists and the contemporary neo-Malthusians have addressed the same issues from perspectives that are not dissimilar. Today newspapers and public affairs television programs remind us regularly of the exhaustion of fish stocks, the increase of carbon dioxide in the atmosphere, the destruction of forests, reductions in oil reserves, the land constraints on world food production, and the rapidly growing populations and cities in developing countries.

Many of these issues form a backdrop to the discussion and analysis in this text. But we do not tackle these issues in sequence here; rather, we present a framework for analyzing and discussing them. Economics provides a means for dissecting certain social issues—for systematically analyzing the components of issues and how they are interconnected. For example, to try to understand the issue of oil depletion, we first need to know what determines the rate at which oil is pumped from the ground and whether exploration for new supplies is occurring. In this chapter, before we delve into the economics of natural resource use, we present some basic concepts.

Our *natural environment* contains the *natural resources* essential to life on earth. These include water, the atmosphere, and land. There are, as well, natural resources that lie within the water and on or under the land. These include aquatic and terrestrial plant and animal species, minerals, and energy resources. Natural resources provide inputs to our economic system—factors of production. Natural resources are combined with labor to produce an enormous array of goods such as lumber, food, metals, and fish. They also produce goods that endure over time—capital goods, such as machinery and structures. We can think of a natural resource as a unique factor input, but most natural resources have characteristics that make them very similar to capital. First of all, to be used for consumption or in production processes, most natural resources have to be extracted or harvested. Copper must be mined before it can be used to mint coins or produce wire. Forests and fish must be harvested and transformed into lumber and filets. So, like capital, most resources must be "produced" using other factor inputs such as labor. Second, like capital, natural resources yield productive services *over time.* A fish stock, forest, or mine is typically able to supply resources for long periods of time.

Time is a crucial component of the analysis of natural resource use. Time helps distinguish between different types of resources. A *renewable* natural resource is one that can supply productive inputs to an economic system indefinitely. A *nonrenewable* natural resource is one with a finite stock or supply that, once used up, is gone. But in a sense, all natural resources are renewable. They are distinguished by the length of time it takes a particular resource to be reproduced. Solar energy is an extreme case: The daily flow of solar radiation to the earth will be roughly constant and will continue for billions of years. Shrimp can reproduce by the billions each year. Oil deposits take billions of years to be produced by geological processes. For practical purposes, we separate natural resources into those that are renewable—fish, forests, solar energy, and environmental resources such as water and the atmosphere; and those that are nonrenewable—minerals, oil, and gas. There is, however, a caution regarding this distinction. Most renewable resources can be depleted or exhausted—that is, they can become nonrenewable. A fish population can be harvested to extinction. Forests can be cut and the soil remaining eroded to such an extent that no new trees will survive. Groundwater can be depleted by extensive irrigation of agricultural crops. Clean air and water can be destroyed by pollution. The link between renewable and nonrenewable resources is thus very close.

Figure 1.1 depicts schematically the fundamental connectedness between our natural environment with its natural resources and the economic system. We use natural resources to assist in the production of goods and services, to be consumed directly in the form of enjoyment of the natural beauty of ecosystems, and as a waste depository. But fundamental physical laws place constraints on how we can use these resources. The *first law of thermodynamics* states that matter is never created or destroyed; it simply changes form with use. The *second law of thermodynamics* says that as energy changes form, it degrades into components that have different characteristics from the original matter. For example, if we burn gasoline in our cars, the petroleum is used up, never to appear again in its original form. We are left with carbon dioxide, water, and other by-products of combustion such as sulfur oxides. The energy released cannot be used again. The only truly exogenous input into our circular-flow depiction of the natural environment is solar energy. Trees will be converted into paper; copper ore into copper wire. In the latter cases, the resource changes form but is durable for varying lengths of time. Copper wire may last for years; paper for hours. The key point is that as natural resources are converted into products, they will not return to their original state in the natural environment. This means that as natural resources are used up, the natural environment can be depleted over time. As we have noted, stocks of nonrenewable natural resources will decline over time if they are extracted and used. Renewable resources have the potential to regenerate new supplies to replace those used by the economic system (and by species other than humans).

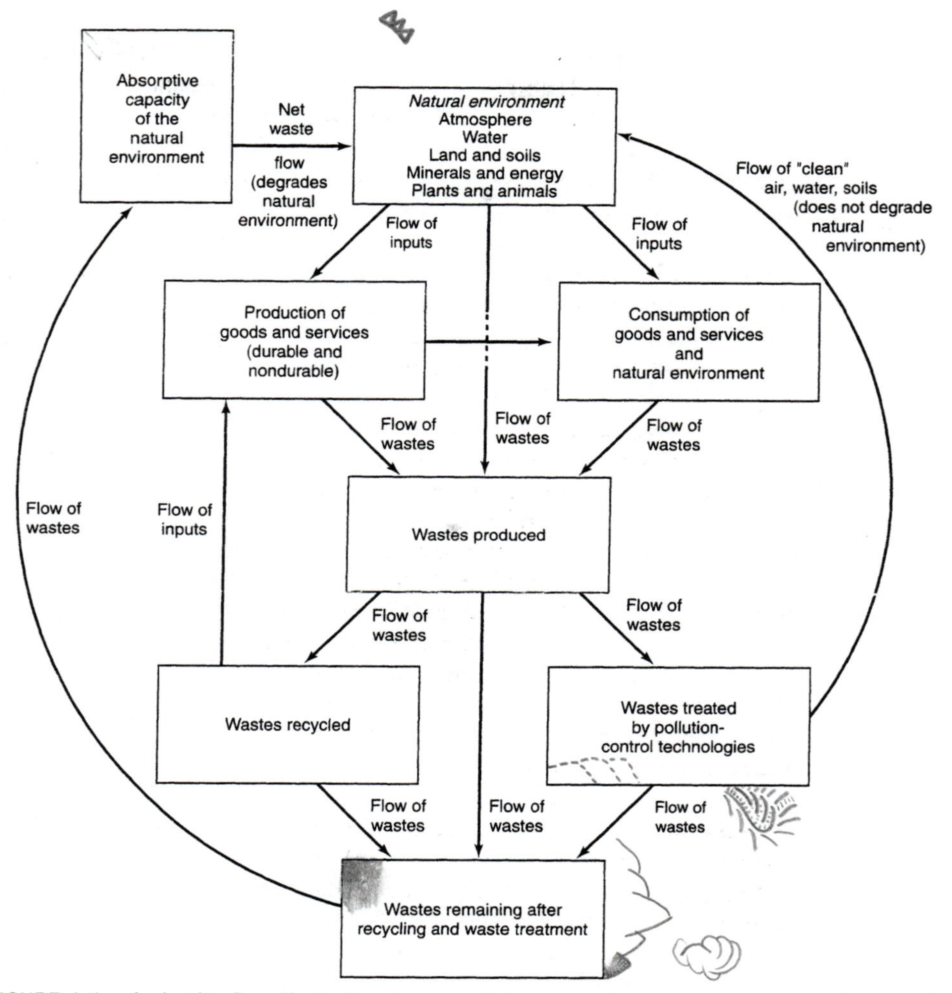

FIGURE 1.1 A circular flow illustrating the use of the natural environment and resulting waste flows. If flows of waste after treatment and recycling exceed the natural environment's absorptive capacity, the natural environment will degrade over time. This will ultimately lead to fewer inputs for consumption and production and hence fewer goods and services. This pattern is not sustainable.

As Figure 1.1 shows, there is also an inexorable flow of waste products emitted from production and consumption (and even the natural environment itself, e.g., volcanoes). If the flow of wastes into the natural environment exceeds the ability of the environment to absorb and neutralize the waste products, the life-support systems of the natural environment will decline over time. There are means of mitigating this decline, as the figure shows. We can invest in processes which reclaim wastes through recycling, reuse, and recovery of wastes. These activities can provide inputs into the economic system, lessening the demands on the natural environment. There are also pollution-abatement processes and equipment that convert more harmful wastes into less harmful products and beneficial products such as compost. But even after all this, there will still be waste released back to the natural environment. We really do not know whether it will be just a matter of time before the system is unsustainable, if human populations continue to grow, or whether our endeavors to develop technologies to conserve natural resource use and to reduce waste emissions will lead to a sustainable natural environment. These are all important issues that are addressed in this text. In each of the chapters that follow, we examine whether or not four economic system leads to sustainable natural resource use. If not, we look at policies and actions that help promote sustainability.

Economics is the analysis of how to allocate scarce resources among competing uses. How this is done depends not only on the endowments of factor inputs—natural resources in our case—but also on the state of technology of turning inputs into outputs and on the objectives of individuals and society as a whole. Economics has an extensive set of theoretical and empirical techniques that are used to analyze the actions of individuals, once these objectives are given.

We assume that individuals act in their own self-interest subject to a variety of constraints—consumers maximize utility, and firms maximize the present value of profits—and then evaluate the outcomes of this maximizing behavior. But economics cannot operate in a social vacuum. We must also specify criteria by which individuals or groups of individuals (including government) evaluate particular allocations of resources. Economists typically argue that social interests are maximized when resources and products are allocated to their most valuable uses. However, the value placed on alternative uses is not independent of the institutions and circumstances of each country.

The nature and distribution of property rights, wealth, and income affect the values placed on alternative uses of natural resources. How are income and wealth distributed? What are the property rights to particular resources? Are they held by individuals who can exclude others from using the resource, are they held in common, or is there open access with no individual or group rights? Although our focus is on the *allocative efficiency* of natural resource use, we will note distributive effects throughout the text, and especially their role in influencing government policy toward natural resources. Property rights are an important theme that we introduce in this chapter and elaborate on in subsequent chapters. We also look at the role of government and how to evaluate changes in economic efficiency under different market equilibria and types of government policy.

This may all sound like familiar material. Why do we study natural resources separately, and not as just another example in, say, production theory, capital theory, or public finance? We offer four reasons. First, a large set of policy issues of our day concern natural resources per se. An understanding of the economic principles behind resource use is an invaluable aid to informed discussions of these practical problems. Second, natural resources have unique features generally not found in other economic topics. One of these is nonrenewability; another is the problem of open access. Third, externalities are pervasive in the use of natural resources. Fourth, natural resource economics emphasizes economic *dynamics* and decision-making in an *intertemporal* setting. Certainly, all economic problems can be examined in a dynamic setting, but in many cases a very good approximation of the problem examined can be obtained with a *static* analysis. With natural resources, dynamics is essential. Static models typically fail to capture all the important tradeoffs in resource use that occur over time. We will make use of static models to introduce important concepts and show how analyzing the problem using dynamic techniques alters our conclusions. We have organized the text into chapters that examine natural resources in a static framework and chapters on intertemporal modeling of natural resource use.

In the chapters that follow, we will look at nonrenewable and renewable resources individually. We examine how in theory these resources can be extracted or harvested and whether the profit-maximizing decisions of firms yield an *efficient equilibrium.* We examine why individuals' behavior may not yield an efficient outcome and what can be done about this through government policies or other actions. We then look at a variety of practical issues associated with natural resource use. We believe strongly that theory and practice belong together. Theoretical material is presented first to provide a basis for analyzing particular real-world problems. We give examples of practical problems in "boxes" and case studies throughout the text. In these studies we make use of scientific information about natural resources—biological information about forests and fish, geological information about minerals, ecological studies on the environment and interactions among living things.

PROPERTY RIGHTS AND NATURAL RESOURCE USE

A *property right* is a bundle of characteristics that convey certain powers to the owner of the right. The owner may be an individual, a group of individuals (e.g., a firm), or the state (e.g., public lands). There are many different characteristics a property right can possess. To illustrate, let us consider a deed to a piece of land. The deed is a property right that typically gives the holder the power to use the land and to appropriate returns from the land. So, for example, crops can be grown and sold, and the proceeds go to the owner. An apartment building can be constructed and rented, with the rents paid to the owner of the land. The owner can also prevent others from using the land without permission. Thus, the deed is *exclusive* and *enforceable.* The owner of the land may be able to subdivide the property and sell or give others a portion. If so, the property right is both *divisible* and *transferable.*

Rights may also be constrained by restrictions imposed by governments or private individuals. An example of a government constraint is local zoning ordinances that prohibit certain uses of land. One cannot build a metal smelter in the midst of a residential community. Private constraints can be included in the deed, such as restrictive covenants that prevent construction of 10-foot-high fences in suburban neighborhoods. Other private restrictions may follow from custom—one keeps the grass cut so that neighbors won't complain.

The duration of the right is also an important distinguishing feature. For example, *freehold* title to land is an exclusive, enforceable, transferable, and generally divisible right that holds forever. A *leasehold* is also exclusive and enforceable and can be transferable and divisible, but it is of limited duration.

We cannot cover in detail all the different types of property rights that apply to natural resources, but we do want to make one very important distinction between types of rights and see what this implies about the economic analysis of natural resource use. The *exclusivity* of a right is an important distinguishing characteristic. A *private* property right gives the holder the power to the exclusive use of a natural resource. The holder does not have to share the natural resource with any others. A *common* property right is held by a group of individuals and excludes those not in the group. The group makes joint decisions about the use of the natural resource and distribution of the proceeds. These rights may be informal, as in some agrarian communities that share and jointly manage pasture lands. Common property rights may also be formalized into very specific share agreements, as in certain fisheries and agriculture. *Open access* is our final category. It represents a lack of property rights or ownership of any kind. No one can prevent another from using the natural resource and appropriating a share of the returns from the resources. Open access leads to the most serious problems in natural resource use. These include environmental degradation and overexploitation and potential extinction of fish stocks. We examine these issues in detail in Chapters 4 through 7. For more detail on different property right regimes, see Bromley (1991), Ostrom (1990), and Stevenson (1991).

Property rights regimes may have other important characteristics, but it is the degree of exclusivity that we emphasize. Private property is exclusive. It involves no sharing of natural resources. Common property has arrangements for sharing the natural resource with others in the designated group. Open access is completely nonexclusive—no one can be prevented from using or exploiting the natural resource. The presence or absence of exclusivity has an impact on many economic issues and on the role of government. With private property rights, markets for the production and exchange of natural resources typically exist. It is possible to obtain efficient allocations of resources without government intervention. To do otherwise results in losses due to a decline in the value of the natural resource. Natural resources that tend to be parceled out with private property rights are mines (both fuel and nonfuel minerals), private recreational sites, agricultural land, and forested land in many countries. We emphasize how an efficient allocation of resources is obtained for land use in Chapter 3, mineral extraction in Chapter 8, and forest operations in Chapter 10 through the profit maximizing behavior of firms. The emphasis is on the operation of markets, because in many cases these private markets function well. We do, of course, examine cases where private markets do not function efficiently for each of these natural resources. In general, our focus in these chapters is on the behavior of individual decision makers who have the exclusive power to use the natural resource.

By contrast, resources characterized by open access *cannot* achieve an efficient allocation of resources without some form of government intervention, the creation of a private property right, or both. Markets for the production and exchange of these natural resources either do not exist or operate inefficiently. Open access natural resources include many fisheries and environmental resources such as air and water.[1] We will show in Chapter 4 for fisheries and Chapter 6 for environmental resources that the equilibria obtained when individuals pursue their own self-interests are inefficient. We will thus devote considerable attention, especially in Chapters 5 and 7, to government attempts to promote efficiency in these sectors.

But why are land, forests, and minerals generally exploited under private property rights, while fisheries, air, and water are characterized by open access rights? We cannot give definite answers, but we examine some of the characteristics of the different natural resources and the emergence of property rights for these resources over time.

Private property rights for land and minerals have existed for hundreds of years and were created both by actions of governments (e.g., enclosure acts for land) and by actions of private individuals through litigation and the establishment of common law precedent. These rights tend to be either freehold or leasehold. Mineral rights are typically distinct from surface rights to land. In many countries, including Canada, the government (federal and provincial) reserves the mineral rights when land is sold to individuals. If you own property in Canada, in most cases you do not own the right to explore for oil or gold or to extract a mineral if it bubbles to the surface or your child strikes a vein of gold while digging in the sandbox. Those wishing to explore for and develop mineral deposits must first obtain the right to do so from the government. The right is then typically a lease which gives the individual (or firm) exclusive power to search for and then extract gold, nickel, oil, gas, or whatever over the life of the mine. Perhaps the reasons why land and minerals developed exclusive rights was their ease in delineation. These resources are generally immobile.[2] Some have also argued that private property rights will be established when the resource in question is highly valued, thus making exclusive ownership of sufficient benefit to overcome the costs of establishing and enforcing property rights.

Ownership arrangements related to water use have concerned legal scholars for centuries. Two polar cases are: (a) when my use does not interfere with your use, as when I swim in a river that runs through my farm; and (b) when my use interferes with your use, as when I divert large amounts of water upstream from your land. We have some comments on these matters and on water use in Chapter 3.

A mixed case is that of forestry. Trees are immobile and of value, so one would think that exclusive rights to forests would exist. Yet rights to harvest crops of trees over long periods of time typically do not exist independently. Rights for land and minerals are formal—deeds and agreements are drawn up. In forestry, however, the arrangements are more casual. Forests automatically accompany freehold title to land. Other forests are held on public land. But when rights to the trees (independent from the land) are granted by either the government or private landowners, they have tended to be restricted to the harvest of a particular "crop" of trees, not to successive crops of trees. There is no reason in principle why "tree" rights—rights to practice forestry operations over time—could not be granted. It is not obvious why the severance of tree rights has been slow to occur.[3]

Fisheries and environmental resources, by contrast, have remained as open access for long periods of time. Both the legal system and government have in general failed to produce private property rights for these resources until quite recently. Indeed, governments have even promoted open access. The Magna Carta, for example, abolished the authority of the English crown to grant exclusive rights to fish in tidal waters and replaced it with a public right—that is, open access to the fisheries. Why did this happen? There are a number of explanations, none totally convincing. Perhaps the simplest reason why private property rights have not emerged is that with fisheries and environmental resources—unlike minerals and land—it may be technologically or physically very difficult to achieve exclusion. Consider an ocean fishery such as tuna. Tuna can migrate over large distances. How is one to lay claim to a particular fish or population of tuna? Other open access resources such as air are consumed jointly by a large number of people. Dividing the resource up or obtaining payment for the use of these resources may be quite difficult. Another explanation is that it is optimal not to establish private property rights. Some argue that the costs—known as *transaction costs* of establishing and enforcing private property rights—are higher than the *benefits* (the value of an exclusive right). In particular cases this may be so, but as a general proposition it is dubious.

Whatever the explanation for the persistence of open access, it now appears that some changes are under way. In recent years, establishment of some private rights for open access resources has occurred through both legal and government actions. One explanation is that the value (both market and nonmarket) of these resources has now become so great that it pays to design more exclusive rights. Technological change may also play a role. For example, the development in the last century of barbed wire allowed ranchers to fence their land much more cheaply than was possible with wood fencing. This greatly reduced the cost of keeping others' cattle off one's land. It reduced the cost of exclusion. Certain fish species are now farmed, "corralled" in pens or in specific aquatic areas (for species that are relatively immobile). However, many open access resources are in danger of being exhausted even with various types of government regulation. A number of aquatic species—for example, the northern cod and many whales—have been harvested to the point of near-extinction. Our oceans have become dumping grounds for toxic wastes. The ozone layer shrinks each year by ever-increasing amounts, owing to the discharge of chlorofluorocarbons and other compounds. Government regulation for some of these open access resources has existed for many years. Many regulations have not been successful. In other cases, regulation has been virtually impossible because of the international dimension of many open access resources. Economic decision makers face many challenges with regard to the management of open access resources, and indeed all natural resource use. A major objective of this book is to examine the regulatory requirements and policy instruments available to governments for different natural resources.

WELFARE ECONOMICS AND THE ROLE OF GOVERNMENT

In the previous section, we noted that government intervention is necessary if an economy is to achieve an efficient allocation of resources when resources are characterized by open access. This is quite clearly not the only role for government in modern economies. Even if there were a full set of private property rights, certain *market imperfections* or *market failures* would still exist. Also, income might not be distributed equitably. Nonrenewable resources get used up too quickly; urban activity "eats up" agricultural land; trees are harvested too quickly. These are called market failures because the free interaction of individuals in the economy leads to inefficient outcomes. Some essential ingredient necessary for the efficient allocation of resources is missing.

Nonrenewable resources may be mined too quickly if, for example, firms discount the future at a higher interest rate than society discounts it. Trees may be harvested too slowly if exclusively biological considerations guide the harvester. Other examples of market failure include market structures that are imperfectly competitive (e.g., monopolies), failure of markets to exist for events occurring in the future, and of course the open access market failures that can lead to extinction of fish stocks, to air and water pollution, and to depletion of water supplies. We examine many of these market failures throughout the text.

To contrast and evaluate the difference between *socially optimal allocations of resources* and those achieved by private actions, we draw on a large body of work called *welfare economics*. Welfare economics, simply put, is the study of the level and distribution of individuals' and groups' well-being in the economy. Different allocations of resources are compared to see under which outcome society will be the best off. People may value alternative allocations differently. Some people may gain under a particular allocation while others lose. Therefore, some means of comparison, taking into account differences in individuals' preferences, income, and so on, has to be devised.

The technique used by economists is the creation of a *social welfare function*—a hypothetical relationship that weighs each individual's well-being or utility in some fashion, then "adds up" the utilities to obtain an aggregate function that is used to compare alternative equilibria. The eighteenth-century philosopher Jeremy Bentham expressed the view that such weights should be equal for all individuals. Hence we speak of a Benthamite social welfare function and characterize it as being egalitarian. Another way to look at this function is to assume that politicians are responsible for determining the appropriate distribution of income. Economists can then proceed by assuming that income has been redistributed so that the marginal utility of each person's dollar of income is the same for all individuals. The social welfare function can then "add up" individuals without assigning particular welfare weights. We will assume that distributional matters are resolved in this manner, but we recognize that in practice, problems of income distribution remain. As economists, we have no claim to being better at resolving these issues than other analysts. Indeed, social welfare can be defined in many ways that do not involve the adding up of individual's utility.

A social welfare function and its use can be illustrated easily using concepts familiar from introductory economics—production possibility frontiers and indifference curves. In Figure 1.2 we have drawn a production possibility frontier *(PPF)* that shows the maximum output obtainable of two goods—cars and clean air—from the economy's endowment of productive resources. Any combination of cars and clean air lying on or within the boundary of the *PPF* is obtainable. A set of social indifference curves represents society's valuation of the two goods. To achieve a socially or *Pareto* optimal allocation of resources, the highest social indifference curve tangent to the *PPF* should be chosen, as shown at point *A*. A socially optimal allocation is one in which it is not possible to reallocate resources and improve the welfare of any one person without making at least one other person worse off. If we assume that politicians are handling distribution of incomes, this condition implies that no allocation will lead to a higher net gain in welfare. This is a very simple representation. For a full social optimum, one must assume that consumers maximize utility, firms maximize profits, a full set of property rights exists, and all markets are efficient.

Producer surplus and *consumer surplus* are monetary measures of people's utility

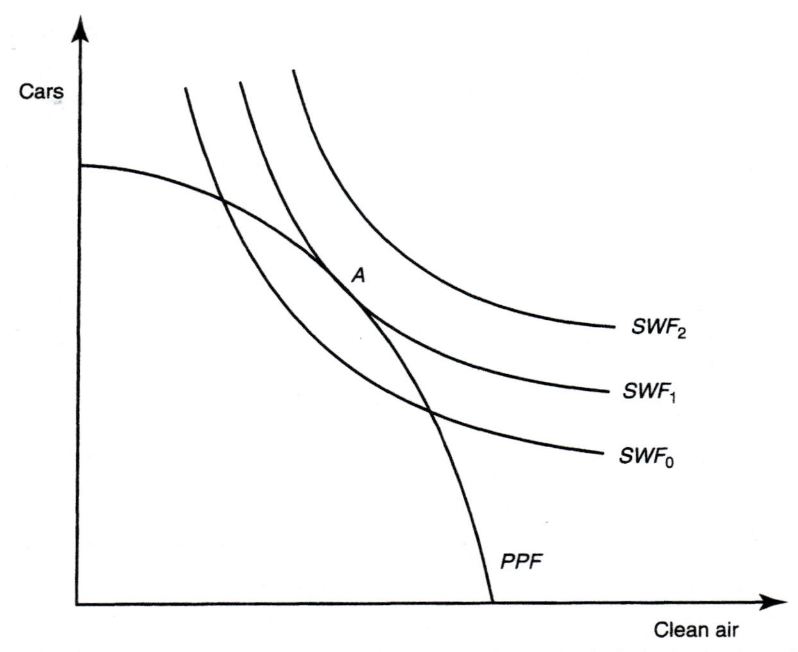

FIGURE 1.2 An optimal allocation of cars and clean air is reached where society's well-being is maximized. This occurs at A, where a social welfare function (SWF) is tangent to the production possibility frontier (PPF) for the two goods.

and firms' profits, which are used often as an approximation of social welfare. We follow this approach, which permits us to indicate optimal arrangements of resource use and to value different equilibria. Let us look first at the consumer and the valuation of different equilibria, given our assumption that matters of income distribution have been resolved.

Suppose we want to know how much "better off" a consumer would be if the price of gasoline fell from 40 cents per liter to 30 cents per liter. What measure would reflect the change in the consumer's well-being or utility? We can use the theory of demand to obtain an answer. Figure 1.3(a) illustrates the situation facing an individual—say, a woman—with a fixed income, who spends her income on one good, gasoline, and a market basket of other goods denoted Y. Assume that the price of these other goods equals 1. Then the Y axis reflects this person's income. Given gas prices, which are initially set at 40 cents per liter, and her income, the woman can consume any combination of gas (G) and other goods as shown by the budget constraint AB. Her utility-maximizing choice is where AB is tangent to her highest indifference curve between other goods and gas. In this case, the solution is point x on indifference curve I. Demand curves can be derived from this utility maximization representation, as shown in Figure 1.3(b). At 40 cents per liter, the woman will buy, say, 100 liters of gas *given* the price of other goods and her income. This is shown as point x' in (b).

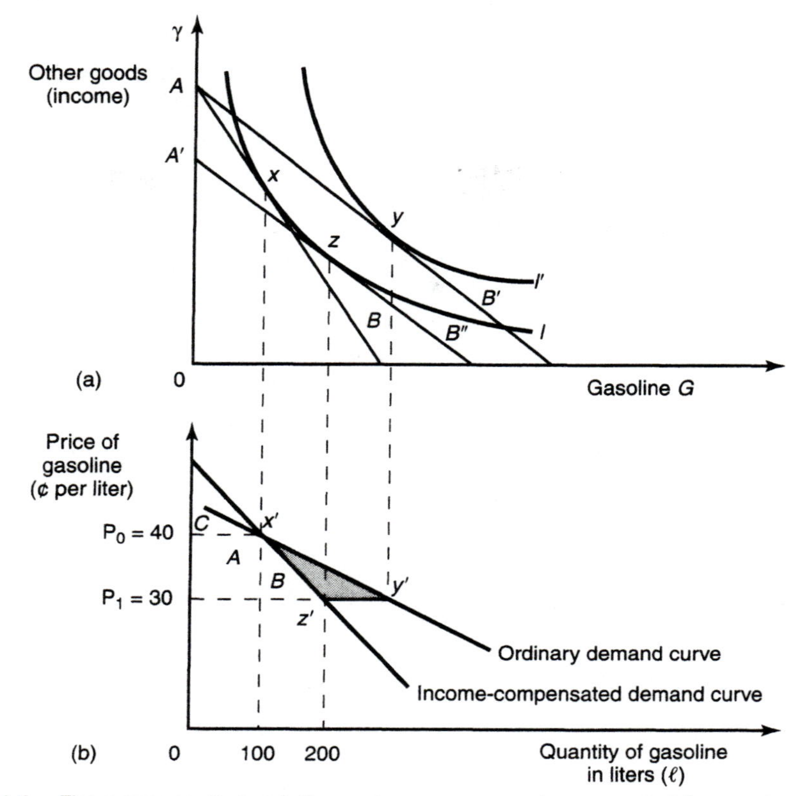

FIGURE 1.3 The compensating variation and consumer surplus generated from a decrease in the price of one good. When the price of gasoline falls from 30 to 20 cents per liter, a consumer benefits. Part (a) illustrates the increase in the quantity of gas consumed holding constant the price of other goods. Point *z* shows the increase in gasoline consumption holding utility constant on I. The initial equilibrium is x, the final equilibrium is y. In (b), the income-compensated demand curve links points x' and z', while the ordinary demand curve links points x' and y'. Compensating variation is the area under the income-compensated demand curve above the price charged for the good. When the price of gasoline falls from 40¢/l to 30¢/l, the compensating variation is areas A + B. Consumer surplus for the price change is measured under the ordinary demand curve and equals areas A + B plus the shaded area.

Now let the price of gas fall to 30 cents per liter, while all other prices are unchanged. The individual's budget constraint now shifts to *AB'*, allowing her to consume more of the other goods and gas at point *y* because her real income has risen and she can reach a higher indifference curve.

But we really want to know how much more gas this person would consume given a change in the price of gas without any change in her level of utility. Suppose her income is reduced just enough to keep her on indifference curve *I* facing the new set of relative prices. This amount of income is called a *compensating variation.* Her budget constrain then shifts to $A'B''$ and her utility-maximizing equilibrium is at z. Compensating variation measured in terms of other goods is then the vertical distance AA'. We can also measure compensating variation in terms of an *income-compensated* demand curve. The compensated demand curve shows combinations of prices and income that keep the individual at her initial utility level. The point z' in Figure 1.3(b) shows how much gas would be purchased—200 liters. This demand curve for gas is then derived holding the price of other goods and utility constant at I for different prices of gas. Note (and we will return to this) that the ordinary demand curve would link points x' and y' and thus lies above the income-compensated demand curve for price decreases (and below it for price increases).

Given the income-compensated demand curve, we can now measure the individual's compensating variation from the change in gas prices from 40 to 30 cents per liter.[4] Think about what has been gained. The consumer was willing to pay 40 cents per liter for 100 liters. That is, we can read off the demand curve what someone is willing to pay for any quantity of good. But this consumer no longer has to pay 40 cents, so she has saved or benefited by 10 cents per liter of gas consumed for the first 100 liters, or $10. This is the rectangle A or $(P_0 - P_1)100$. But in addition, the consumer is getting between 100 and 199 liters of gas for 30 cents per liter as well, but would be willing to pay more than 30 cents for these liters. So the consumer also "receives" as a benefit area B. If the demand curve is linear, we can measure area B, a triangle, by the formula 1/2(base times height). In this case, the base is $(200 - 100 = 100)$, the height is $(P_0 - P_1 = \$0.1)$, so area B is $1/2(100 \times \$0.1) = \$5$. The total gain to the consumer is the area $A + B$, the amount $15. This is the compensating variation for a price change from P_0 to P_1. Compensating variation can be thought of as the individual's maximum willingness to pay for the opportunity to purchase gasoline at the lower price.

Generally we approximate welfare changes by evaluating areas under the observed (or non–income-compensated) demand curve. The measure of welfare change under the ordinary demand curve is called *consumer surplus*. The gain in consumer surplus that results from the decrease in gasoline prices from 40 to 30 cents is the area bounded by 40 $x'y'$ 30. So far, we have assumed that there exists an income-compensated or Hicksian demand curve for each individual. But can we ever observe such a demand curve? We have an important conflict between theory and applied work here. The theoretical demand curve derived from utility maximization is not the same as the demand curve typically derived from statistical methods. The ordinary demand curve is typically an *aggregate* demand curve—it shows total demand by all consumers (or groups of consumers) for the good at various prices. There is no way to tell how much *each* consumer gains or loses from price changes unless each individual has identical preferences—an unlikely event. In addition, the measured demand curve is not an income-compensated curve but one that allows utility to vary with the price change. It is a demand curve similar to the one through points x' and y' in Figure 1.3(b).

The observed demand curve includes both income and substitution effects. If estimates of consumer surplus are made from the ordinary demand curve, they will not be a precise measure of consumers' willingness to pay for the good unless the income elasticity of all consumers is 0 (a 1 percent change in income leads to no change in consumption of all goods). This is an unlikely situation. But there are practical means of dealing with the problem—situations where using consumer surplus measured from ordinary demand curves will not lead to large errors in estimating willingness to pay. As a "rule of thumb," consumer surplus will be a good proxy for compensating variation if income effects are small or the good does not represent a large share of one's consumption bundle.[5]

In theory, producer's surplus is a less controversial measure of welfare changes to the firm, but again it can be difficult to estimate in practice. Consider the following example and Figure 1.4, which shows the cost curves of a perfectly competitive firm. Suppose the firm is in a short-run equilibrium facing price p_1 and producing output level q_1. The exogenously determined price for its goods now rises to price p_2. The firm sets price equal to marginal cost and produces at q_2. What are the compensating and equivalent variations for this price increase? If the producer can adjust its output, compensating variation is the amount of money that when taken away from the producer leaves it just as well off as if the price did not rise. This is shown as the shaded area in Figure 1.4. Equivalent variation is the amount of money that must be given to the firm if the price increase does not occur to leave it just as well off as if the price increase had occurred. Again, this is the shaded area. The shaded area is simply the *change in short-run profits* due to the increase in the price from p_1 to p_2. For situations where firms are producing an output level greater than zero and can adjust to price

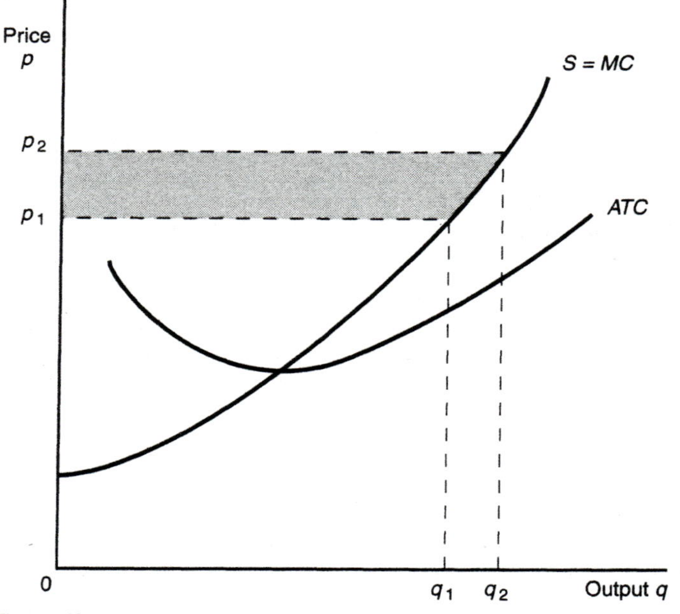

FIGURE 1.4 The welfare change associated with an increase in price for a firm's output is shown as the change in its profits due to the price change. This is the compensating and equivalent variation for the price increase and is shown by the shaded area.

changes, the change in its short-run profits is an appropriate measure of the welfare change due to the price increase.

A change in short-run profits will not be an appropriate measure of welfare change if the firm cannot adjust its production in response to a price change. Consider Figure 1.5. Assume that a policy is introduced by the government that prevents the firm from operating for 1 year. The initial product price is p_1 and output is q_1. What is the compensating and equivalent variation for this policy? Recall from microeconomic theory that a firm will continue to produce in the short run as long as price is equal to or greater than average variable cost. This is because a firm cannot avoid its fixed costs even if it shuts down. In terms of Figure 1.5, the firm will not cease production as long as the price of its product is at least equal to p_2. The firm therefore needs an amount equal to area A plus B to be just as well off with zero production as with production at q_1 when price is equal to p_1. This is the equivalent variation. In compensating variation, the firm would be willing to pay area A plus B to continue to produce q_1.

The term *producer surplus* has been used to depict the competitive firm's welfare change as the excess of total revenue above total variable costs. This is equivalent to saying that producer surplus is profit (area A) plus the total fixed costs (area B) the firm cannot avoid if it shuts down production. Graphically, producer surplus is the

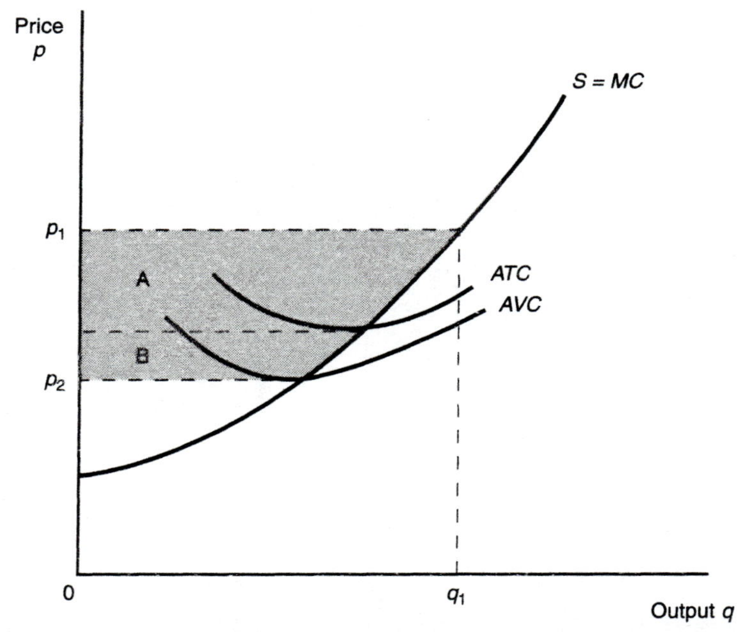

FIGURE 1.5 The producer surplus for a firm is shown as area A plus B—the area between the firm's short-run supply curve and below the price line. This is equivalent to saying that producer surplus is profit plus total fixed cost.

area between the firm's short-run supply curve and below the price line. This is the more general measure of welfare change for the producing firm.

Another way to think about producer surplus is as follows. In a competitive industry a firm's supply curve is its marginal costs of production lying above average variable cost (*AVC*). When a competitive firm is producing at the point where price equals marginal cost for the last unit sold, all previous units of output—the *inframarginal* units—are sold at a price greater than *AVC*. The firm earns a payment above the opportunity cost of producing all output to the left of its equilibrium output level. Note that in practice producer surplus may be difficult to measure, as it is difficult to obtain the data necessary to estimate the firm's marginal cost curve. Industry supply curves are easier to quantify, and producer surplus can be measured as the area between the industry's supply curve and the product price. However, industry supply curves will obscure the gains and losses to individual firms.

Now that we have defined and seen how to measure producer and consumer surplus, we return to the notion of a social welfare function and ask what is the optimal allocation of resources. In the chapters that follow, we assume that the social optimum or social welfare maximum is the equilibrium price and output level that *maximizes the sum of consumer plus producer surplus.* This is one traditional social welfare function. Its shortcomings have been extensively studied. (See, for example, Boadway and Bruce, 1984.) We show what this condition means for a single perfectly competitive market at a point in time in Figure 1.6. What price and output level would maximize consumer plus producer surplus? Where supply equals demand in a competitive market, consumer plus producer surplus is maximized. We can see this as follows.

At the equilibrium price P^* and output Q^*, consumer surplus is the area P^*ae, while producer surplus is the area P^*ed. Our argument is that no other combination of price and output can yield a larger sum of producer plus consumer surplus. Consider, say, a price P less than P^* (where P could be the result of a government-imposed price ceiling on gasoline). At P, the equilibrium quantity produced and consumed is Q, and there is excess demand for gasoline. Consumer plus producer surplus would be the shaded areas. Consumer surplus is area *Pabc*, while producer surplus is area *Pcd*. Consumers thus gain at the expense of producers, but the total surplus is less than under P^* and Q^*.

Or consider a price such as P' (due, say, to a price floor set for gasoline). By construction, the equilibrium output consumed is still Q, but there is now an excess supply of gasoline. The sum of producer plus consumer surplus is again the shaded area and thus less than the maximum total. But notice now that producers have gained at the expense of consumers. Consumer surplus has shrunk to area $P'ab$, while producer surplus has grown to $P'bcd$ compared with the previous case. We see that the net loss from a price of P or P' and output Q is the area *bce*. This is also known as a *deadweight loss*—an efficiency loss for an equilibrium other than that which maximizes welfare. Thus we see that only where supply equals demand and the competitive market clears do we have a social welfare optimum that maximizes the sum of producer plus consumer surplus. We will see different versions of this basic concept in the text. The basic concepts are the same as those developed here.

There are heroic assumptions to be swallowed in applying the central ideas in welfare economics. Ultimately, a social consensus is required. It is to the political process that we must finally turn for the emergence of the social welfare function. This political welfare function will in general be quite different from our social welfare function. Consideration of political issues takes us into the area of voting, vote trading, dissembling in voting, and so on, an area economists have analyzed at great length and in great depth.[6] Our approach in this book is that "government" is a separate agent acting in the social interest when activity by individuals fails to bring about a social optimum. There are limitations with this approach, but it permits us to abstract from the details of the political process as it relates to resource allocation in general and natural resource use in particular.

Two alternative approaches for analyzing the development of policies in the area of natural resource use are the historical and the comparative. In the historical approach, we analyze the evolution of a sector over time and try to arrive at policies that could improve the current situation. In the comparative approach, we analyze what is being done in other countries and try to design policies that would improve the situation in our own country. Although we do consider much institutional detail, we make little use of the historical or the comparative approach. Ours is basically a welfare economics approach. The merit of this approach to policy design is that it is based on a set of concepts that have been analyzed and refined over many decades. If a policy

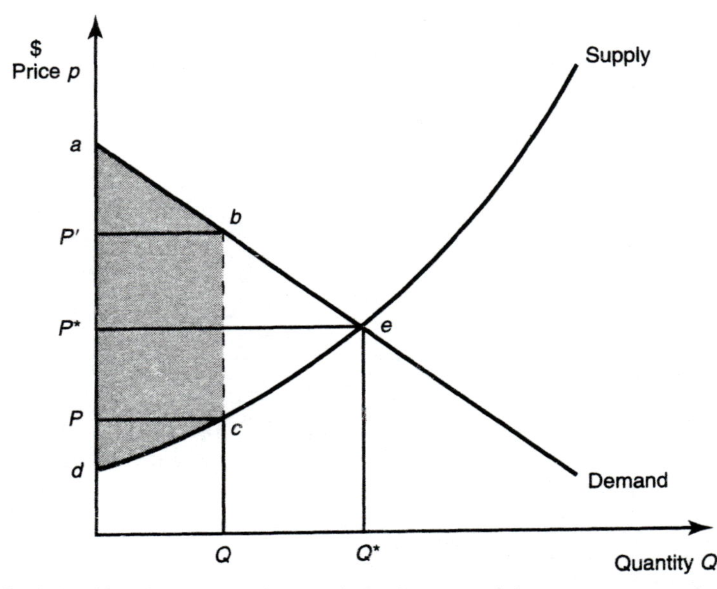

FIGURE 1.6 Social welfare is at an optimum where the sum of the consumer surplus plus producer surplus is maximized. For a competitive market, this will occur where supply equals demand and yields the equilibrium price P* and output Q*. For P* and Q*, consumer surplus is the area P*ae, while producer surplus is the area P*ed. Any other price and output combination, such as P and Q or P' and Q, will lead to a smaller total surplus.

seems wrong, we can dissect it into its components: who gains, who loses, by how much, at what prices, and over what period of time. There are natural efficiency criteria for better, best, and an improvement. This approach may not be easy to apply, since requirements for data are often severe, but it is a consistent and extensively analyzed approach turning ultimately on the notion of improving the welfare of individuals in society.

DECISION MAKING OVER TIME

Natural resource use involves decision making over time. How much gold should be extracted from a mine this year, how much next year, and so on, as long as the reserves of gold in the mine exist? Should salmon be harvested intensively this year, or not at all? The supply curve of a natural resource is always shifting, owing to depletion of nonrenewable resources and biological or physical changes in renewable resources. This is very different from, say, a shoe factory, in which demand and supply schedules can stay fixed year after year. A static framework is acceptable for analyzing some types of natural resource use. However, for others working with familiar supply and demand curves is not adequate, because the changes in natural resource supply over time must be part of the analysis. A dynamic framework is required. We make use of pairs of demand and supply diagrams—one diagram for period t and another for the next period, $t + 1$. *Intertemporal analysis* involves precisely relating the set of schedules in one period to the set in the other period. Some basic concepts are reviewed in this chapter. Part III examines intertemporal models, starting with the extraction of minerals.

Interest Rate

The interest rate is the crucial link between periods. Let us consider an example.

> **Should I sell my land in the country?** I have an offer of $100,000 now (period t). If I sell and put the proceeds in the bank at 10 percent interest, next year (period $t + 1$), I will have $100,000 plus the interest $10,000, or $110,000.
>
> Suppose I do not sell this year but sell next year (period $t + 1$), for a price of $112,000. This would mean that selling in period t and banking the money is a poorer strategy than selling in period $t + 1$. (Of course, if I will get only $104,000 if I sell in period $t + 1$, it is best to sell early (in period t) and put the proceeds in the bank.)

Owners of mineral deposits make such calculations every day. Substitute "another ton of ore" for "land in the country" in our example, and you have a decision about mine exploitation! The interest rate is the Hamlet in this little drama. It is always central to the unraveling of the action.

Recall the basics of interest rate arithmetic—*compounding* and its opposite, *discounting* or getting *present value*. We review these concepts now.

Compounding

Compounding is essentially letting the principal (say $\$V$) grow while interest is calculated on the interest earned period by period. After one year, $\$V$ becomes the original value plus interest on the original value:

$$V(1) = V + Vr = (1 + r)V$$

After two years, $\$V$ becomes the original value V plus interest for one year on V plus interest on interest on V plus V's interest for the second year:

$$V(2) = V + rV + rrV + rV = (1 + r)^2 V.$$

After 12 years, $\$V$ becomes $V(12) = (1 + r)^{12}V$. And so on for any number of years. We plot $V(t)$ against t in Figure 1.7. The points in Figure 1.7 each represent V compounded over a specific number of years or periods. The series represents the phenomenon of ***exponential growth*** (sometimes referred to as ***geometric growth***). It is V that is growing here.

The ***rate of growth*** is the change in $V(t)$ divided by the value of $V(t)$. For example, between years 11 and 12, the rate of growth is

$$\frac{V(12) - V(11)}{V(11)} = r$$

Thus, at a constant interest rate, V grows at the rate r. This is an important concept that will be integral to our analysis in Part III.

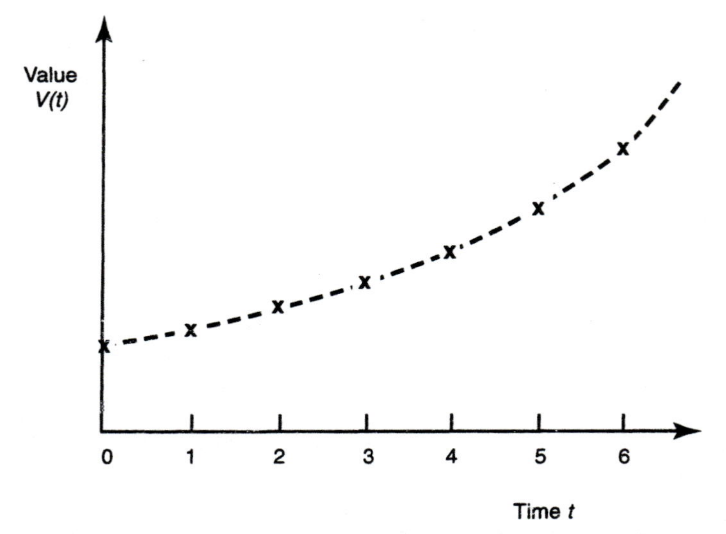

FIGURE 1.7 We illustrate the value of V(0) growing "by compound interest" or exponentially (or geometrically) at rate r.

Discounting or Getting Present Value

This is the "opposite" or "inverse" of compounding. The *present value* of V dollars delivered five years from now is

$$\frac{V}{(1 + r)^5}$$

rather than V multiplied by $(1 + r)^5$ as in compounding. We say that V is discounted back to the present (period 0). Discounting permits us to compare what are essentially apples and walnuts—values at two different points in the future. We discount both values to the present, and then they are perfectly comparable.

Very frequently we are interested in a stream of values into the future. Suppose you win a lottery that is worth $10,000, but the winnings are paid out to you in five annual installments of $2000 each. You get the first installment today, the next at the end of 1 year, and so on. The present value of this stream of payments is calculated by converting each payment to the present, then summing them up:

$$PV = 2000 + 2000/(1 + r) + 2000/(1 + r)^2 + 2000/(1 + r)^3 + 2000/(1 + r)^4$$

This is the discounted present value of a sum of future values. If r is, say, 10 percent, this sum equals approximately $8342. This is what your lottery winnings paid out over five years are worth today. Looking at this another way, you would be indifferent between earning $8342 today and $2000 per year for each of the next 5 years. Each term in the present-value formula tells us what $2000 earned in a specific year is "worth" today. For example, the $2000 paid in year 3 is worth $1504 today. If you put $1504 in the bank and earned 10 percent per year (compounded), you would have $2000 at the end of 3 years.

With a mine, profits often get smaller in the future as the ore thins out, so the stream of future values of concern to the owner would decline. With forests and fish, it has been traditional to arrange production to get a steady harvest into the future, and thus a constant stream is often seen in such problems. (We will see this in Chapters 4 and 8.)

We summarize in Figure 1.8. Let a stream of future payments be the points with x's. Each value can be discounted to the present, yielding a stream of o's. The sum of the o values is the discounted present value of the stream of future values. What does the present value stream of o's look like for the x's in Figure 1.8? It will be a horizontal schedule, with each term equal to V at time period 0.

How long does it take my $100 to double in the bank at 8 percent interest? This is an example of compounding: $100 becomes $108 after 1 year, $108 × 1.08 after 2 years, etc. We want

$$\$200 = \$100(1.08)^T$$

where T is the unknown. We find on a calculator that for $T = 9$, $(1.08)^T = 1.99900$, so that *9 years of compounding at 8 percent will double our money*. (It turns

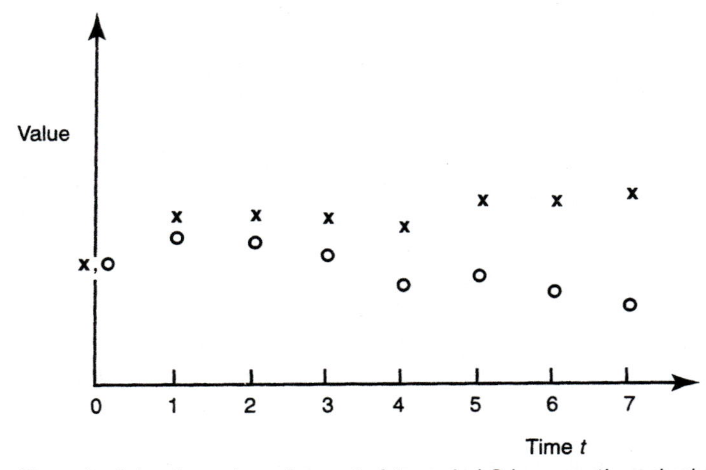

FIGURE 1.8 The schedule of xs when discounted to period 0 become the schedule of os. The sum of the zero values over time is the discounted present value of the stream.

out that if we divide 70 by the interest rate, we get a good approximation of the years it takes to double our money. This rule of thumb works well for any interest rate.)

What is $100 a year forever worth as a lump sum today if the interest rate remains at 8 percent per year? This is an example of discounting each future payment and summing up the discounted values to get the sum of discounted present values. That is, we want

$$\begin{aligned} Z &= \$100 + \frac{\$100}{(1.08)} + \frac{\$100}{(1.08)^2} + \frac{\$100}{(1.08)^3} + \frac{\$100}{(1.08)^4} + \ldots \\ &= \$101 + \$92.59 + \$85.73 + \$79.38 + \$73.50 + \ldots \\ &= \$1250, \text{ or} \end{aligned}$$

$$Z = \frac{V}{r} = \frac{100}{.08}$$

A note paying $100 per year forever at an 8 percent interest rate is worth about $1250 in a lump sum today. The discount factor, $1/(1 + r)^t$, is a geometrical progression that approaches zero as t gets large. For example, in year 20, $100 is worth around $21 in present value ($100/1.08^{20}$); after 50 years, $100 has a present value of slightly more than $2. In the limit then, the discount factor is ($1/r$). The interest rate used by individuals to discount streams of payments that occur in the future is called the personal rate of discount or personal *rate of time preference.*

The net benefits from building a water purification plant. In deciding the value or benefits from a public work like a water purification plant, which lasts for many decades into the future, assessors evaluate the dollar value of purified water year by year and the dollar value of the costs of construction and operation of the plant and arrive at a figure of V dollars of net benefits *per year*. To get the sum of benefits, these yearly figures must be added up. But of course $1 million of benefits in 1995 is different from $1 million of benefits in 2005. The net yearly benefits and costs should be discounted at some interest or discount rate r.

The computation of a present value is straightforward; which discount rate is the correct one is the problem. Low values of r in discounting make the sum of present values large, and high values of r make the sum of present values small. (Recall the example of receiving $100 forever. If r is 8 percent, then $100 forever is worth $1250 in present value, whereas if r is 4 percent, it is worth $2500 in present value.) Hence, individuals much in favor of a purification plant costing, say, $500 million will argue for a low discount rate when assessing the desirability of doing the project, and those opposed will favor the higher discount rates. There is considerable debate over what is the appropriate discount rate to use when evaluating projects financed by governments. Some economists advocate using an average of *market interest rates*—those rates that private firms would face in borrowing funds for large capital investment projects. Others argue that there should be a *social discount rate*—an interest rate that reflects the government's cost of borrowing (often less than that of the private sector) adjusted for risk and distortions in the economy such as income and commodity taxation. While we will speak of *the* discount rate, it is important to recognize that no single rate is agreed to by all policy analysts. We return to this issue in our discussions of sustainability in Chapters 2 and 12.

Techniques of Analysis

The definitions of compounding and discounting and the three examples are reference points. We use these basic concepts frequently in the analysis of different resources throughout the text. But the material that follows does not suddenly get more complex; our approach is to present the economic concepts of natural resource use by employing simple mathematical techniques. No analysis has been left out simply because it involves advanced economics or mathematics. Instead, we have put in material originally presented with advanced math and developed it with elementary college math used in many undergraduate economics programs.

For example, finding a program, sequence, or time path of outputs from a mine is a dynamic maximization problem usually analyzed with advanced mathematics. We analyze such problems with elementary maximization techniques, taking first derivatives. We do this consistently and present a diagrammatic exposition as well. Burying basic and exciting economic ideas under a mountain of mathematics is frequently unnecessary and can be a waste of time for the reader. Clearly, for good exposition of fairly intricate ideas in economics, we need a balance between mathematics and prose. Our approach has been to use graphic techniques and only differentiation in the text. We find maximums and minimums and analyze equilibria. We generally use discrete periods of time, and we present concepts using smoothly flowing continuous time only when the discrete model is explained fully. This permits us to stick to simple mathematics.

TABLE 1.1 **U.S. EMPLOYMENT IN NATURAL RESOURCE INDUSTRIES**

***Timber-Based Industries:* Employment (000s)**

	1970	1975	1980	1985	1990	1991	1992
Lumber and wood products	554	615	578	593	605	556	563
Logging camps and contractors	NA	74	71	67	70	64	76
Sawmills and planing mills	196	202	190	172	173	160	182
Millwork, plywood, and structural members	NA	166	164	195	211	189	245

***Mineral Industries:* Employment (000s)**

	1970	1975	1980	1985	1990	1991	1992	1993	1994
All mining	623	752	1027	927	711	689	635	611	605
Metal mining	93	94	98	46	59	56	53	50	51
Coal mining	145	213	246	187	148	136	127	109	114
Oil and gas extraction	270	329	560	583	394	393	353	351	339
Nonmetallic minerals except fuels	115	117	123	110	111	105	102	101	101

***Fisheries:* Employment, fishing craft, and establishments (000s)**

	1970	1975	1980	1985	1990	1991	1992
Persons employed	227	260	296	351	NA	NA	NA
Fishers	140	168	193	239	NA	NA	NA
Shore workers	87	92	103	112	72	73	72
Craft used	88	103	113	1230	95	NA	NA
Vessels 5 net tons and over	14	16	19	24	32	NA	NA

Source: U.S. Department of Commerce, Bureau of the Census, Statistical Abstract of the United States, 1982–83, Tables 1243, 1281, and 1256; 1992, Table 1172; 1994, Tables 1133, 1170; 1995, Tables 1180, 1164.

RESOURCES IN THE ECONOMIES OF THE UNITED STATES, CANADA, AND OTHER NATIONS

The importance of the natural resource sector to the economies of the United States and Canada is assessed in part by examining the sizes of the sectors measured in terms of employees. In the United States in 1992, forestry and wood processing had about 563,000 workers; mining, including oil and gas extraction, had about 605,000. In Canada in 1991, forestry had only 46,000 workers, a decrease of 10,000 from a decade earlier; mining remained fairly constant at 56,000 workers; and fishing employment had doubled over the last 15 years, to 40,000 workers (see Tables 1.1 and 1.2). Contrast Canada's employment figures for fisheries with those of Iceland, a fishing power. Employment in Iceland's fisheries was approximately 5,200 person-years in 1976 and 6845 in 1991, reflecting a gradual and continual increase over the 15-year

TABLE 1.2 **CANADA, EMPLOYMENT IN RESOURCE SECTORS (000S)**

	1975	1981	1984	1986	1989	1991
Fishing, hunting, and trapping	20	33	32	36	37	40
Forestry and logging	49	60	64	53	55	46
Mining and quarrying	53	78	63	61	61	56

NOTE: Data prior to 1984 were coded using the 1971 Standard Occupation Classification System. Data for 1986 and beyond used the 1980 System.

Source: Canada Yearbook (Ottawa: Ministry of Supply and Services), 1978–79, Table 8.5, 1990, Table 5.7, 1994, Table 6.6.

period.[7] As we will see in Chapters 4 and 5, large increases in employment in fisheries may be a signal of some serious problems in the management of a country's natural resources.

Consider the significance of natural resource sectors as proportions of gross domestic product *(GDP)* for a group of countries in Table 1.3 (figures for the United States and Australia were not available for all natural resource categories). Norway's 13.3 percent for mining reflects the oil deposits in the North Sea (98 percent of GDP attributed to mining is due to petroleum production). These figures reflect value added in the respective sectors, or primary factors such as labor, capital, and used in these sectors. A gross measure would reflect the direct and indirect uses of outputs from these primary sectors as intermediate goods in other sectors of the economy. Returning to the comparison of the fishing industries in Canada and Iceland, it is interesting to note how the importance of this industry in terms of GDP has changed over the 15-year period under discussion. The contribution of Canada's fishing industry to GDP remained unchanged from 1976 to 1991 at approximately 0.2 percent of GDP. In Iceland, however, the fishing industry's contribution to GDP rose from 5.5 percent in 1976 to 7.9 percent in 1991. Clearly, some very different factors are at work in these two countries. The models presented in Part II will help to explain why the experience in these two countries is different.

TABLE 1.3 **GROSS DOMESTIC PRODUCT BY KIND OF ECONOMIC ACTIVITY AT CURRENT PRICES, 1991, PERCENT**

	Australia	Canada	Greece	Norway	Sweden	United States
Agriculture and hunting		1.5%	13.4%	1.7%	0.9%	
Forestry and logging		0.5	0.2	0.5	1.2	
Fishing		0.2	0.5	0.7	0.1	
All of the above	3.1	2.1	14.1	2.9	2.2	2.0
Mining and quarrying	4.2	2.7	1.2	13.3	0.2	1.6

NOTE: Because of rounding, numbers may not add up.

Source: OECD, National Accounts, Detailed Tables, Volume II, 1981–1993.

SUMMARY

1. The economics approach to analyzing natural resource use draws on models in biology, ecology, geology, and geography. The efficiency of an allocation deals with the issue of whether more output (tons of coal, tons of cod, etc.) can be obtained by reorganizing the input into production. Welfare effects involve how much better off consumers are when more outputs can be produced.
2. Property rights crucially affect the types of outcomes and the efficiency of allocations in natural resource use. For example, open access arrangements are less efficient than private ownership arrangements.
3. Improving welfare involves assessing how much each consumer is better off and how much the aggregate of consumers is better off. A rough and well analyzed measure of "better off" is the increase in producer and consumer surplus.
4. Natural resource use often involves time paths of outputs and inputs in an essential way. Mineral extraction changes the supply schedule period by period. The intertemporal nature of these problems lead us to use discounting, compounding, and present value calculations very frequently. These adjustments are made to terms in different periods because the utility of a dollar today is higher than that of a dollar at a future period. (The reason is that with a dollar today, one can save it and have that dollar in the future, but not vice versa.)

DISCUSSION QUESTIONS

1. Suppose you are considering buying a gold deposit. It will cost $1 million per year to construct a mine so that gold can be extracted. The construction period lasts 3 years. In the fourth year, production starts. Each year the mine operates, it will yield a net return (total revenue minus total cost) of $500,000. What will you pay for the gold deposit if:
   a. Interest rates are 10 percent and gold can be extracted for 10 years?
   b. Interest rates are 5 percent and gold can be extracted for 6 years?
2. What are the important characteristics of a property right? Distinguish between a private property right and open access.
3. a. Explain the concepts of consumer surplus and producer surplus.
   b. Suppose the demand for nickel is given by $Q^D = 1.2 - 0.6P$, while the supply of nickel is given by $Q^S = 0.3P$. Compute consumer and producer surplus.
   c. For the problem in (b), suppose the government restricts the price to 1. Compute consumer and producer surplus in this new situation.
4. A new bridge is built, and a person now makes 35 trips per month to the center of town rather than his or her former 25 trips per month. The time cost of the trip plus wear and tear on the person's auto declines from $4.75 before the bridge to $3.75 per trip after the bridge. Evaluate the benefit in dollars per month of the

bridge to this person. (*Hint:* You might want to sketch the person's demand curve for trips to decide on how to calculate the dollar benefits.)

5. We indicated in the chapter that a stream of income of $100 per year forever into the future is worth in present value today 100/0.08 = $1250 when the interest rate is 8 percent per year. What will be the value of this stream if the interest rate were 16 percent per year? If the interest rate is 10 percent per year? Suppose it is known today that the interest rate will increase to 12 percent after 10 years and remain there forever. Would this raise or lower the present value of the income stream?
6. If you inherited an apartment building and were trying to decide whether to sell it and buy some federal government bonds now or keep the building for a few years and then sell it, how would you arrive at your final course of action?

NOTES

1. In developing countries, forests and agricultural land may be open access resources.
2. Oil and gas pools can flow underground when pressure differentials exist. Sharing rules have developed for these common pools.
3. There are examples where firms have been given (or sold) rights to manage forest land. But these rights are far more idiosyncratic and ad hoc than the standardized rights developed for oil and gas deposits. The holder has the right to harvest trees and to construct roads, ports, etc., to facilitate the harvest. But the rights are nontransferable and frequently have had limited durations, which are less than the time it takes to grow a tree to a harvestable age.
4. The point of going through the derivation of the income-compensated demand curve is that it is the demand curve required in theory to measure welfare gains or losses. Technically, consumer surplus can be derived from this curve. See Broadway and Bruce (1984) or Just et al. (1982) for more details on the theory behind the derivation of welfare measures.
5. See Just et al. (1982), Chapter 6, for details. In Figure 1.3(b) one can see the "error" of using consumer surplus from the ordinary aggregate demand curve to measure compensating variation. For the price change shown there, the error will be the lightly shaded area. For further discussion on consumer surplus, see Willig (1976) and Morey (1984). Just et al. also present a very detailed discussion of producer surplus.
6. See Hirshleifer and Glazer (1992), Chapter 16, for an introduction to economics and voting behavior.
7. OECD, *National Accounts, Detailed Tables*, Volume II, 1974–1986, p. 293; and 1980–1992, p. 311.

SELECTED READINGS

Anderson, T. L., and P. J. Hill (1975). "The Evolution of Property Rights: A Study of the American West," *Journal of Law and Economics*, 18.

Boadway, R. W., and N. Bruce (1984). *Welfare Economics.* Oxford: Basil Blackwell.

Bromley, D. W. (1991). *Environment and Economy: Property Rights and Public Policy.* Oxford: Basil Blackwell, Inc.

Hirshleifer, J., and A. Glazer (1992). *Price Theory and Applications*, 5th edition. Englewood Cliffs, N.J.: Prentice Hall, Inc.

Just, R. E., Hueth, D. L., and A. Schmitz (1982). *Applied Welfare Economics and Public Policy.* Englewood Cliffs, N.J.: Prentice-Hall, Inc.

Morey, E. R. (1984). "Confuser Surplus." *American Economic Review* 74, pp. 163–173.

Ostrom, E. (1990). *Governing the Commons: The Evolution of Institutions for Collective Action.* Cambridge: Cambridge University Press.

Stevenson, G. (1991). *Common Property Economics.* Cambridge: Cambridge University Press.

Willig, R. D. (1976). "Consumer Surplus Without Apology," *American Economic Review* 66, pp. 589–597.

World Commission of Environment and Development (1987). *Our Common Future.* Oxford: Oxford University Press.

chapter 2

Sustainability and Natural Resource Scarcity

INTRODUCTION

In Chapter 1, we introduced many of the analytical concepts that are used in this book. The present chapter provides an introduction to the notion of sustainability of our natural environment and economy. In a sustainable economy and environment, the use of resources today to meet present needs does not adversely affect the environment and the economy's ability to produce goods and services in the future.[1] We examine sustainability in a more rigorous fashion in Chapter 12. Here, we look first at the notion of sustainability, then turn to a more specific topic that has occupied the attention of many economists and ecologists—the measurement of natural resource scarcity. Natural resource scarcity can be an indicator of the sustainability of the economy and environment.

SUSTAINABILITY

Conceptual Issues in Sustainability

Sustainability is a difficult concept to define and put into practice. In our attempt to define sustainability, we will first focus on issues of *intergenerational* and *intragenerational* equity. We then turn to a more applied discussion of how to determine whether or not an economy is on a sustainable path.

The Brundtland report, *Our Common Future* (1987), singled out two sorts of potential losers in nonsustainable economies—poor people today, particularly those in third world countries, and members of future generations. There is a link between these groups. Because they are poor, people may part with their natural resources today at unfavorable terms in exchange for current income. In so doing, they can deprive their descendants of a valuable heritage, one that could make their lives more prosperous. A number of questions come to mind. Should economies with high standards of living transfer income to economies with low standards of living to reduce the incentive to "use up" resources in low-income countries? If so, how should the income be transferred? Can international agreements pertaining to resource use and environmental quality help? A notable example here is the Montreal Protocol of 1987—an agreement among many of the world's countries to phase out use of ozone-depleting chemicals. In this agreement, high-income countries must phase out their production and use of the compounds sooner than low-income countries. Also, the high-income countries are to contribute to a fund that is to be used to assist low-income countries in the transition from ozone-depleting to ozone-friendly compounds. These are examples of issues addressed in the field of *development* economics. Our focus in this chapter will be on the intergenerational question: How can current generations prosper and not deprive future generations of their own claim to a prosperous life?

Consider first some cases of sustainable economic activity. A fish stock could be harvested in such a way that it is not depleted over time. In Chapter 4, we will show in detail how this can be done. With a sustainable fishery, the next generation will have access to the same stream of harvests. The stock "producing" the harvest period after period remains intact. Similarly, a forest can be harvested in such a way that it renews itself at a rate allowing a perpetual constant harvest to be yielded. The time horizon for renewal will typically be very long compared with that of most fisheries. Sustainable forestry models are the subject of Chapter 10.

By contrast, consider some nonsustainable trends. Agriculture—sustainable as it seems relative to oil extraction—can in fact be responsible for the steady depletion of soil stocks and water supplies, and it can pollute water supplies and contaminate soils. Figures on aggregate soil erosion worldwide paint a gloomy picture. Wind, water, and agricultural practices cause topsoil depletion in sometimes subtle ways. A plowed field awaiting seeds is not a natural object. Many minor erosions in different places add up to a large loss of topsoil each year in many regions of the world. Worldwide it is estimated that 25.4 billion tons of topsoil are lost each year (Smith, 1992). Another form of depletability in agriculture involves the accumulation of chemicals and salts in the soil and in nearby streams and underground freshwater reservoirs. The chemicals are often washed from fields as residuals from pesticides and fertilizers. With irrigation, salts often leach from the soil. This is depletion of a freshwater stock by pollution rather than physical depletion. Depletion of aquifers through agricultural, industrial, and household use is another global concern. The continuous irrigation of crops depletes reservoirs in many parts of the world. Population growth in arid regions such as the southwest United States has led to a depletion of the underlying aquifers. We discuss water use in Chapter 3. Table 2.1 presents some data illustrating these nonsustainable trends.

In all these cases of nonsustainable trends, our reflex is to demand policies or incentives that will make the practices sustainable. One can think of charging users of water fees for use—fees set at such a level that irrigation no longer depletes aquifers. These fees will become a new cost of production and will have the side effect of driving some marginal producers out of business. On a large scale they will lead to increases in the prices of harvested crops and to increases in the prices consumers pay for food. This is a variant of an idea of long standing—the Pigovian doctrine, named for the economist A. C. Pigou, who wrote extensively about these issues in the 1930s.

TABLE 2.1 **INDICATORS OF NONSUSTAINABLE NATURAL RESOURCE USE**

I. Land Degradation, Late 1970s as Percent of Land Surface

Continent	Slight	Moderate	Severe	Total
Africa	60	23	17	100
Asia	56	28	16	100
Australia	38	55	7	100
Europe	69	25	6	100
North America	70	23	7	100
South America	73	17	10	100

II. Environmental Damages as Percent of GNP

Country and Year	Form of Damage	Annual Costs as Share of GNP (percent)
Costa Rica (1989)	Deforestation	7.7
Ethiopia (1973)	Deforestation effects on fuel wood and crop output	6.0–9.0
Hungary (late 1980s)	Pollution damage (air pollution)	5.0
Indonesia (1984)	Soil erosion and deforestation	4.0
Netherlands (1986)	Pollution damage	0.5–0.8
Nigeria (1989)	Soil degradation, deforestation, water pollution, erosion	17.4
Poland (1987)	Pollution damage	4.4–7.7

Sources: Lester R. Brown, ed. (1990). *State of the World, 1990,* New York: Norton. I: Table 4-1, p. 60. II: Selected countries from Table 1-1, p. 12.

Pigou, and other economists since, have argued that negative spillovers from many economic activities should be dealt with by inducing a scaling back of the offending activity through the use of charges (taxes and user fees) until the negative spillover equates the marginal damages from the activity to the marginal benefits created. Notice that the activity as a whole is scaled back in order to curtail the flow of the offending by-product. Alternatively, polluters could be required to reengineer their production process so that fewer negative by-products are generated. This often requires up-front costs in the form of new designs for the basic activity and new machines for the implementation of the newly engineered activity. We deal with all these issues in more detail in Chapters 6 and 7.

The objective of all these policies is to change production and consumption practices so as to move them from nonsustainable to sustainable. The Pigovian doctrine suggests curtailing the flow of negative by-products from production through the use of charges. Sustainability has the same goal, but the curtailment must be done so that there are no long-term negative effects. One does not simply curtail pollution of groundwater today. One arranges activities so that years from now, there will be no deterioration in groundwater quality. The *cumulative* negative impact is zero in the long run under the doctrine of *strict or strong* sustainability.

There is obviously some degree of rigidity in the doctrine of strict sustainability. Once certain practices are corrected, things will remain in a *steady state* into the indefinite future. A steady state is a sort of equilibrium that can be sustained indefinitely if there are no outside forces acting upon the equilibrium to upset it. This echoes the idea that we must use the planet in such a way that it resembles the state in which we inherited it. Clearly, though, this is an extreme view, since the planet looks very different today from 100 years ago. Are we supposed to wind the clock back to a "right" state, or to "the" sustainable state? In the past 100 years, the human population has more than doubled and there has been much accumulation of useful roads, factories, machines, houses, and knowledge. The standard of living has increased for a great number of people in response to better health care and nutrition, improved sanitary conditions, and water purification. The beneficiaries reside mostly in the developed countries. These changes have taken place at the same time that agricultural land has expanded and timbered land has been cleared, and oil stocks have been run down in places and opened up in others. Recent history exhibits patterns that are distinctly non–steady-state. Is there a correct pattern that can be a guide for the future?

One principle we might infer, in an attempt to link sustainability for the future to recent history, is to not allow renewable resource flows to decline: Preserve the environment that generates the harvest. For example, one should not harvest fish in a way that depletes the stock "generating" the harvest, or deplete soils so that crops cannot be grown in the future. This principle runs into many problems, however. For example, as a result of urban growth, cities expand onto land formerly used in agriculture. Rivers are dammed to generate electricity and to provide flood control and water for irrigation. Fisheries and agricultural lands are lost in the resulting flooding. The encroachment of cities on agricultural land and the damming of rivers had been upsetting many observers well before a concern for sustainability per se became widespread. These trade-offs have no simple solutions. However, the trade-offs would be less extreme if the human population stopped increasing. If this were combined with slow growth in per capita income, there would be much less pressure to expand urban areas, or to supply large new flows of electricity for homes and factories. Sustainability is often linked to a policy of slowing population growth. This is a second principle. Although intervention in decisions regarding family size has of course been very controversial, population growth is one force working against sustainable use of renewable resources. To feed more people, we press harder for harvests from fish stocks, and this drives the stocks down—an instance of nonsustainable development. But there are two other forces causing the pattern of economic development to be nonuniform in the longer term—technical progress and exhaustibility of essential inputs to the economy, such as oil.

Technical progress often works in favor of sustainability. It has been observed that the fraction of the price of many products occupied by the natural resource inputs has declined in the twentieth century. This makes knowledge, labor, and processed inputs larger fractions of the value of many commodities. Table 2.2 illustrates the decline in the use of natural resource inputs per unit output by focusing on energy intensities per unit GDP. As is illustrated, the use of energy per unit output has fallen for virtually all the countries examined, in some cases by very large

TABLE 2.2 **ENERGY INTENSITY OF GROSS DOMESTIC PRODUCT (GDP)**

	Energy Intensity		
Country	**1970**	**1985**	**Percent Change 1970–1985**
Canada	0.80	0.66	−20.5
United States	0.60	0.44	−27.4
Japan	0.38	0.27	−30.9
Australia	0.54	0.47	−12.6
New Zealand	0.48	0.63	32.4
Austria	0.49	0.41	−16.4
Belgium	0.72	0.53	−26.3
Denmark	0.49	0.32	−35.5
Finland	0.58	0.49	−16.3
France	0.44	0.37	−16.3
West Germany	0.53	0.41	−22.5
Greece	0.43	0.58	36.6
Ireland	0.61	0.48	−21.4
Italy	0.42	0.32	−23.1
Netherlands	0.55	0.48	−12.7
Norway	0.57	0.44	−21.9
Portugal	0.55	0.67	22.1
Spain	0.39	0.45	16.5
Sweden	0.58	0.52	−10.6
Switzerland	0.27	0.28	3.3
Turkey	0.49	0.79	61.0
United Kingdom	0.61	0.41	−33.1
OECD	0.54	0.41	−24.6

NOTE: "Energy Intensity" = Primary energy requirements per unit GDP (at 1985 prices and exchange rates, converted to U.S. dollars)
Source: OECD (1991). *Environmental Indicators: A Preliminary Set.* Paris: OECD.

amounts. Of course, one should remember that GDP has been rising, so that total energy use should also be examined. Unfortunately, for many countries total energy use has risen because GDP has grown faster than energy use has fallen. If energy intensities continue to decline, total energy use may begin to fall.

Technical change can, however, work against sustainability when new technologies of natural resource extraction are more productive. Consider the modern methods of finding fish and catching them: for example, global positioning units that track fish with the help of satellites, and oceangoing processing plants. The efficiency of these new technologies has made it easier for fishing fleets to "vacuum" up stocks and drive many close to extinction. Table 2.3 illustrates the change in harvests of fish stocks worldwide from their peak year to 1992. In all the world's oceans except the Indian Ocean, the harvests have declined. This is a very worrisome change that indi-

TABLE 2.3 **CHANGE IN MARINE FISH HARVESTS**

Region	Peak Year	Peak Harvest (million tons)	1992 Harvest (million tons)	Percent Change[a]
Atlantic Ocean				
Northwest	1973	4.4	2.6	−42
Northeast[b]	1976	13.2	11.1	−16
West Central	1984	2.6	1.7	−36
East Central	1990	4.1	3.3	−20
Southwest	1987	2.4	2.1	−11
Southeast[b]	1973	3.1	1.5	−53
Mediterranean and Black Seas[b]	1988	2.1	1.6	−25
Pacific Ocean				
Northwest	1988	26.4	23.8	−10
Northeast[b]	1987	3.4	3.1	−9
West Central	1991	7.8	7.6	−2
East Central	1981	1.9	1.3	−31
Southwest	1991	1.1	1.1	−9
Southeast	1989	15.3	13.9	−9
Indian Ocean				
Western	still rising		3.7	+6[c]
Eastern	still rising		3.3	+5[c]

NOTES: [a]Percentages were calculated before rounding off harvest figures. [b]Rebounding from a larger decline. [c]Average annual growth since 1988.

Source: United Nations, Food and Agriculture Organization, Fisheries Database (FISHSTAT-PC), Fisheries Statistics Division, 1994, as cited in L. R. Brown. (1995). *State of the World 1995.* New York: Norton, p. 22, Table 2-1.

cates declining fish stocks. Tree-harvesting technologies are another example. Capital has replaced labor in many ways in commercial forestry: Huge devices now grab trees and cut their trunks, replacing the lumberjacks with axes of days gone by, and even the simple chain saw itself is a very efficient tree-harvesting tool. Technical progress lowers the cost of producing existing products and results in a steady stream of new products. This inherent change runs counter to the tranquil steady-state world implicit in the strong view of a sustainable economy—a world with an unchanging pattern of commodities produced and consumed, in which production takes place with unchanging inputs and techniques.

Some inputs are derived from exhaustible stocks of natural resources. The flows from these resources have to shrink over time as the stocks are depleted. Oil is an example. Constant consumption cannot be sustained indefinitely, because the source is finite. A fixed reserve is being drawn from. This means that a steady-state economy is not possible when some essential inputs are derived from stocks that deplete as extraction from them occurs. Alternative inputs must be found through technical progress, or the inputs must be used in a way that circumvents their exhaustibility. For example, although oil stocks may be finite, they could yield a flow forever if the flow gets ever smaller and smaller. Such a pattern is called *asymptotic depletion* and, though not a practical approach to oil consumption, it provides a conceptual benchmark for guiding our thinking about exhaustibility. An example of asymptotic depletion would occur when the quantity used is halved each period. This means that use can go on forever, but the quantity used becomes vanishingly small very soon. Either substitutes must be found for the essential inputs from exhaustible stocks, or some approximation to an asymptotic pattern of use must be followed. An optimistic scenario has essential inputs from nonrenewable sources obtained in the future from renewable stocks such as fusion and solar and wind power.

Solow (1974) explored the implications of asymptotic depletion for a type of steady-state economy. He asked whether an economy could balance the declining use of oil in production with an increase in durable produced capital goods such as machines, factories, and infrastructure. This balancing depends upon substitutability between human-made capital and natural resource capital. Suppose that there is a finite stock of oil to draw from, but each year new capital goods are produced as part of the economy's annual output and the remaining output can be consumed. Solow wondered: (a) whether a fraction of each year's output could provide sufficient new capital each period to maintain enough output so that aggregate consumption need not decline to zero; and (b) if so, what level of consumption could be sustained at a constant level into the indefinite future. Alternatively, how much output must be invested each year to keep consumption constant or in a steady state? To make this possible, it is obvious that output cannot decline to zero over time and hence the growing capital stock must "take over" as oil use in production gets smaller and smaller over time. The stock of machines and other capital goods must be built up sufficiently fast that output does not decline as oil use becomes very slight.

A Cobb-Douglas production function of the form $K^a R^{1-a}$ where K is machine capital and R is oil input can yield a constant output level if $a > 1-a$. Note that in the Cobb-Douglas production function, one input readily substitutes for the other (the elasticity of substitution between inputs is unity). For this example, one can have steady-state consumption even when an essential input is being drawn from an exhaustible source. Technical progress is not required to keep consumption constant. People have to accumulate capital (through saving), and the technology of production has to allow capital to substitute for oil as oil use becomes extremely small over time. For this model, it was later discovered that the level of savings required to keep consumption constant was just equal to the value of oil used in production (oil rent), which in turn equals the decline in value of the stock each period. We discuss this model more formally in Chapter 12. Investment in capital offsets the decline in the value of the stock of oil. In a sense, the sum of the two types of capital is being held constant by having one form of investment offset disinvestment in the other sort of capital (namely, the oil remaining in the ground).

The balancing of the disinvestment in natural capital with investment in human-made capital can be made more general. The notion can apply to a group of natural capital stocks comprising, for example, oil, forest, fish, and so on. One then aggregates the value of investments, including negative values (disinvestments) and balances this with investments in human-made capital. When the balance is positive overall, some observers have defined the corresponding economy's path as sustainable; when the balance is negative, the economy is said to be on a nonsustainable path (Pearce and Atkinson, 1993). By this measure, Japan's economy, with its few natural resources and high rate of investment, will look highly sustainable, whereas some third world economies relying on natural resource exports and low rates of investment appear to be unsustainable.

Our brief discussion of Solow's constant-consumption model brings us a new concept of sustainability—the case of a society's consumption remaining in a steady state while its pattern of input use is always changing. Some call this concept *weak sustainability*. This is a significant departure from the view of an economy living, for example, on a steady harvest of fish or steady flows from renewable stocks. With weak sustainability, some stocks are growing while others are being depleted, but the society's possibilities for consumption remain unchanging. How well one form of capital can replace another in aggregate production is discussed below.

Sustainability in Practice: Adjusted National Accounts

The concepts we have been discussing may be theoretical, but practitioners are now looking at national economies and estimating their rates of growth, taking into account the sustainability of production. National accounting statistics for some countries now include estimates of the contribution of natural assets to income flows and the impact of production and consumption activities on resource stocks and environment quality. A measure of an economy's sustainability is its sustainable income or extended *net national product* (NNP). Extended net national product is a measure of total income from all sources in an economy *minus* depreciation of natural and manufactured or produced capital, where depreciation includes all costs associated with production and consumption activities, including environmental degradation and depletion of natural resources. As we have noted, a weakly sustainable economy requires the sum of investments in machine capital and knowledge capital and disinvestments in natural capital stocks to be greater than or equal to zero. Let's look more closely at the relationship between standard national income accounting and accounting for sustainability (or "green" accounting).

The national income and product accounts for a country measure the flow of products and incomes.[2] Consider the following simple example. Suppose there are two economies. Economy A has a national income growth of 5 percent per year, but its natural assets are declining at a rate of 8 percent per year without any appreciation of produced assets. Economy B has a growth rate of 3 percent per year, and its decline in natural assets is exactly balanced by a growth in manufactured assets. It is fairly obvious which economy is sustainable. Conventional national accounts do not provide the information necessary to see if an economy's growth is sustainable or not, for two fundamental reasons. First, the measures of income and output in the accounts exclude many of the services derived from natural resources and the environmental resources (as well as other nonmarketed services such as the value of household production, volunteer work, and nonpriced use of public infrastructure like roads). Second, the accounts do not incorporate changes in the stocks of natural and environmental resources.

Measurement of sustainable income requires the following modifications of conventional national income accounts. First, the definition of what constitutes income would have to be broadened to include the market (or imputed) values of all goods and services flowing from all sorts of capital, both produced and natural. This is a nontrivial task because it is very difficult to put values on the services flowing from many forms of natural capital and some types of produced capital. Some examples follow. Many nonmarketed services, such as the value of household production, are currently not entered in the national accounts. Many are difficult to estimate because they have only implicit prices and flows. And any input or output that is subsidized will have a market price that does not reflect the real resource cost of its use. The value of environmental services (for waste disposal, habitat protection, etc.) would require imputation or estimation by indirect means.

The second task in the computation of sustainable income is to broaden the measurement of depreciation of capital to include depreciation of all types of capital. At present, depreciation is measured only for produced capital, not natural capital. Many countries are currently working on measuring depletion of natural resources (minerals, oil, forests). Canada, for example, now has some estimates of the physical stock and value of its oil, natural gas, and coal reserves, and some of its forests. Work is in progress on other minerals, fish stocks, and parklands. The goal is to include the value of these natural assets in the national accounts by 1997. Once these assets are valued, annual depreciation can be calculated. Box 2.1 provides an example of the calculation of depreciation of oil reserves for Indonesia.

In summary, net national income or sustainable income is the amount of income left over after allowing for the depreciation through use or loss of all types of capital—natural (including human capital) and manufactured. Table 2.4 lists all the possible capital assets that should be included in a measurement of sustainable income or net wealth and whether they are or are not included.

Empirical work, of an exploratory sort, on "greening" the national accounts was done by Daly and Cobb (1989) for the United States and Repetto et al. (1989) for Indonesia. The idea was to net out negative outputs (pollution and congestion) from a measure of national product and to subtract off disinvestments in natural resource stocks from conventional investment. Repetto et al. focused on oil stock depletion and deforestation in Indonesia in an effort to measure disinvestment in natural capital. They ended up with about a 4 percent decline in green national product relative to the traditional measure of national product (net national product). In a subsequent study, deforestation in Costa Rica was treated as annual disinvestment. Meanwhile, teams combining researchers at the World Bank and the United Nations estimated disinvestment of national capital in Papua New Guinea (Bartelmus et al., 1993) and Mexico (van Tongeran et al., 1993). Net national product declined about 6 percent in Mexico with the loss of natural capital (disinvestment). This decline principally involved oil stocks.

Other projects pursed by many national accounting agencies involve measuring the value of natural stocks—as oil deposits underground, standing timber stocks,

BOX 2.1 Estimating Economic Depreciation of a Natural Resource: Oil Extraction in Indonesia

An early empirical study of sustainability was done for Indonesia by a team from the World Resources Institute (WRI) under the leadership of Robert Repetto. We will focus on the dissaving (economic depreciation) in the oil sector. Sustainability is measured by the sum of saving plus the economic depreciation (dissaving) of natural resource stocks. The WRI analysis neglected to distinguish between total rent (inclusive of producer surplus) and rent to the natural resource that emanated from the finite stock of oil reserves. It also neglected to incorporate gains accruing to Indonesia because oil prices were moving through time. Vincent, Panayotou, and Hartwick (1995) reworked the WRI study. First, the natural resource rent due to finite reserves turned out to be about one-quarter of the total rent reported as economic depreciation by WRI. In other words, the value of oil stocks used up each year (dissaving) was rather smaller than WRI indicated. Indonesia was experiencing steadily rising world oil prices in the period under study. Sustainability is easier because the value of exports relative to imports is rising. When these "capital gains" on oil exports were factored in the Indonesian oil study, they swamped the depreciation due to declining oil stocks. The export of oil did *not* reduce wealth! Indonesia could have consumed more than it produced each year between 1971 and 1984 and still have experienced sustainability (positive net saving). We should, however, also point out that real oil prices have been declining since the mid-1980s. This may mean that Indonesia could have negative net savings in recent years, and hence no longer be on a sustainable path.

oceanic fish stocks, and so on. This is measurement of *national wealth* or *natural capital* as distinct from current disinvestment or declines in natural capital. Measurement of wealth involves estimating unexploited stocks, generally of uncertain size. Disinvestment can be measured by observing current "harvest," estimating natural replenishments, and multiplying by unit value (current price minus the cost of the last unit extracted).

Sustainability in an Open Economy

The good news about having an approach to measuring the sustainability of an economy's current path must be tempered, since the measure has been derived in a closed economy—one in which all prices correspond to an equalibrium in the economy. Since no actual economy is without some trade or is uninfluenced by world prices or those set elsewhere, one must make revisions to the measure of sustainability in order to deal with (a) prices exogenous to the economy in question and (b) commodity flows in trade that incorproate natural resources.

Consider the sorts of revisions one must make in defining sustainability in an economy open to trade. If an economy such as Japan's is importing large amounts of natural resources from its trading partners and then reexporting those inputs in processed "final" goods, one should assess the impact that these flows have on the economy of the country running down its natural stocks. In an example of a two-country world, where one country is an importer of oil, the model suggests that the

TABLE 2.4 **A SUSTAINABLE NATIONAL INCOME ACCOUNT: ASSET MEASUREMENT**

Type of Asset	Services Provided	Current Treatment in Accounts
Manufactured Capital		
Tangible, privately owned	Services of business-owned plant and equipment to industry and commerce	Measured
	Nonmarketed intermediate inputs	Not measured
	Nonmarketed final services	Most not measured[a]
Tangible, publicly owned	Services paid for through user fees	Measured
	Factor services from public infrastructure to industry, commerce, and households	Not measured
Human	Services of labor paid for by wages and salaries	Measured
	Volunteer services	Not measured
	Nonpecuniary education services	Not measured
Natural Capital		
Environmental	Marketable permits for pollution	Measured where they exist
	Waste disposal fees	Measured
	Nonmarket waste disposal services for industry, commerce, and households	Not measured
	Value of environment for human and ecosystem health	Not measured
Renewable natural resources	Agriculture, forests, water, fish, and recreation paid for in market	Measured
	Nonmarketed services from resources (recreation, ecosystem)	Not measured
Nonrenewable natural resources	Energy, minerals, and water paid for in market	Measured
	Nonmarketed services	Not measured

NOTE: [a]An imputed value of owner-occupied housing is included in gross domestic product.
Source: Adapted from Congressional Budget Office (March 1994). *Greening the National Accounts.* CBO Papers.

importer should "overinvest" in machine capital in its country because it is in part depleting its partner's oil stock by importing oil. A different way of interpreting this scenario is that, looking at both economies together, the importer is facing a continually rising price of oil because oil is exhaustible. To keep its consumption constant, the importer must "overinvest" in machine capital in order to balance the increasing cost of oil. Symmetrically, the oil exporter benefits from a continually rising price of its exports and can "underinvest" in machine capital when it strives to maintain a constant consumption program. It appears as if the importer is assisting the exporter in balancing or offsetting the decline in the value of oil stocks in the exporting country. However, that is probably a misleading way of interpreting what is going on. If the importer wishes to keep consumption constant, it must deal with the continually rising price of its imports of oil relative to its exports. "Overinvesting" in machine capital does balance the negative impact on its economy of rising oil prices (negative terms of trade effects). Japan is both a major importer of raw materials, including oil, and also a country with a high rate of savings. Policy makers in both the public and private sectors work hard to protect the Japanese economy from potential jumps in the price of imports.

In practice, one is usually dealing with a single economy and the rest of the world. If a country is primarily an oil exporter and faces continually rising world oil prices, then it can "underinvest" in machine capital when it is pursuing a program of constant consumption. The amount of "underinvestment" is determined by the relative steepness of the path of future oil prices. Clearly, some estimate of this future price path must be obtained when one sets out to measure the economy's sustainability. If one made an adjustment for the large flows of oil and coal imported to Japan each year and their associated long-term upward price trend, Japan's net investment, adjusted for the future price increases for oil and coal, would be lower than it has been calculated to date.

Sustainability of a Region's Economy

A region can be viewed as a nation engaged in trade with its neighbors. The distinguishing feature of a nation is the use of a specific currency. If currencies are free to adjust, the difference between a region engaged in trade with its neighbors and a small open nation is relatively minor. Thus our comments on defining sustainability for a nation engaged in trade are very relevant for defining the sustainability of a region's economy. If a large fraction of a region's aggregate production is traded, then the rising prices of natural resource inputs in the calculation of net investment in the measurement of sustainability will be curcial. This implies that defining sustainability for the economy of a large region might be easier because price effects for traded natural resources might be relatively smaller and might cause fewer problems if approximate values are imperfect.

The economy of a region surrounding a mine will not be sustainable when investment in new capital is being done outside the region. This illustrates the folly of analyzing the sustainability of a region's economy when the definition of the region is small. We do not ask if a city is in balance-of-payments equilibrium on its current account, because the geographic specification is not very useful. Analogously, one should select the region whose sustainability is of interest with some care. An answer can be obtained, but will it be useful?

A major implication of Solow's concept of sustainability is that sector-by-sector sustainability is not a sensible goal of policy. One might consider a sustainable forestry policy desirable, but some depletion of forest stock is sensible in a broader view of an *economy's* sustainability. No one doubts that there have been appropriate times for clearing forests to make way for agriculture—although forest capital was depleted, agricultural land capital was built up. In recent years, we have come to recognize the value of forests as repositories of or banks for biological diversity. Their role in absorbing carbon dioxide has also become well understood. Heightened awareness and scientific revelations have led to demands that a high price be assigned to forested land and that agricultural activity must be able to meet the high price if forested land is to be cleared for new agriculture. Much clearing in the past was done when property rights on the forested land were not enforced and an implicit low price was charged (or a subsidy granted) to agriculture in the transformation of land from forests to crops. We continue in many parts of the world to make the same mistakes today by not adequately pricing many of our natural environments, such as wetlands, forests, and oceans.

A Sustainable Energy Scenario?

In an earlier age, economists calculated the maximum size to which the city of London could grow by the availability of wood for fuel in the surrounding countryside. Over a century ago, the great philosopher-economist W. S. Jevons wrote a book, *The Coal Question* (1865), that dealt with the question of when world economic activity would decline because of exhaustion of coal as an energy source. His advice to the governments of the time was to burn the coal because as it became more scarce, the economic system would respond by bidding up its price. This would create incentives to find substitute energy sources. Jevons did not know that oil, natural gas, and nuclear power would emerge as viable substitutes for coal, but his analysis of the economic system was correct. We continue, however, to ask the question posed by Jevons: Will economic activity begin to decline as a result of exhaustion of depletable energy resources and depletion of our ecosystem due to by-products of energy use such as carbon dioxide and sulfur oxides? A sustainable pattern of energy consumption must ultimately rely on renewable flows from winds, tides, the sun, and nuclear fusion. An "energy future" based entirely on renewable sources would be part of a sustainable economic path. At present, we are a long way from a sustainable pattern of energy use. Table 2.2 earlier in this chapter offered some good news about energy intensity. However, much of the world remains very dependent on fossil fuels and nuclear power for energy. The twenty-first century may be the period in which we see a major shift to renewable energy sources—to a sustainable path for both the economy and environment. There remain, though, many technological and engineering problems associated with power generation by renewable sources. If these problems are not resolved, we may enter an era of high energy costs. That would not be a time of widespread comfort or abundance. But the prospect of low cost and sustainably supplied energy is, in the 1990s, more than an optimist's fantasy. Harnessing nuclear reactions was considered fantasy as recently as 1938, when the uranium nucleus was split. We are less than six decades into that break with the past. Reasonably priced power from fusion technology may be in our future.

NATURAL RESOURCE SCARCITY

Our discussion of sustainable national income accounting and energy use suggests that in our quest to determine sustainable paths for our economy and environment, we may wish to monitor the stocks, consumption and production flows, and prices of our natural resources. *Natural resource scarcity* is the term that has come to represent these measurements, with scarcity defined and measured in a number of different ways, as we discuss below. The scarcity of resources may serve as a signal or indicator of sustainable or nonsustainable paths, and the measurement of scarcity has attracted many people. We sense that population pressure will rob civilization of its progress. We all probably think (though with varying degrees of conviction) that scarcity will catch up with us sooner or later. Ecologists have been expressing this view most vocally in recent years, but concern with the long-term supply of natural resources is now new; it dates back to the work of Malthus. In the 1950s and 1960s a number of studies were done to examine the availability of certain natural resources in response to the great consumption of these products during World War II. The report of the Paley Commission in 1952 and the very important work of Barnett and Morse in 1963 were done in this period. Barnett and Morse used constant-dollar market prices of natural resources as their indicator of scarcity and found little cause for alarm. For the period they examined, 1870 to 1957, only forestry indicated any apparent increased scarcity. The evidence for the agricultural and mineral sectors suggested that these resources were becoming *less* scarce. In an update of the Barnett and Morse's work to include data up to 1970, Barnett (1979), still found no relationship between real mineral prices and time.[3]

Some reasons why effective supplies of the mineral resources examined had increased over time are noted by Smith and Krutilla (1979). First, for many minerals such as copper, as high-grade deposits are depleted, the low-grade sources substituted are typically found in greater abundance. Second, as a mineral resource becomes more scarce, possible increases in the rate of appreciation of its price are dampened or offset by substitution of other resources. Third, increases in mineral prices stimulate exploration for new deposits and encourage recycling of nonfuel minerals. Fourth, technical changes reduce the costs of extracting and processing nonrenewable minerals and make previously uneconomic deposits practical.

Will these factors continue to affect resource supply favorably? We do not know. There is some evidence, for example, that the supply of various ores does not increase uniformly as their grade is reduced but follows a bimodal or more complex distribution. Who can predict technical change or the potential for continued substitution? Work on resource scarcity is based on past observations, present trends, and expectations about the future. But no one can foretell the future; we can only develop concepts that let us use information about the past to make predictions. Economists assume that this is what people do and also assume that the underlying structure of our predictive models does not change. See the papers in Smith (1979) for a survey of the important issues raised by natural resource scarcity.

What has happened more recently? In the early 1980s, the economist Julian Simon challenged the ecologist Paul Ehrlich to demonstrate that natural resource scarcity was upon us. Ehrlich carefully selected a key group of exhaustible and renewable resources, and Simon bet that a weighted average of prices would not display a rise over a 10-year period. Simon won the bet. Not one of the resources showed a real price increase. The inference we are to draw from this experiment is unclear. Is demand or population pressure not severe? Is the availability of natural resources abundant, or is the supply flowing abundantly? Are we witnessing a "fire sale" of natural resource products because of overexploitation due to weak property rights over their stocks? A view of the pressure of scarcity involves some notion of how the pressure of demand on supply causes prices to rise. Declining supplies could force up the price, or expanding demand might be the cause. In either case, net demand pressure forces prices up.

Measures of Natural Resource Scarcity

We turn now to a more detailed examination of some of the different measures of natural resource scarcity.

Changes in the Real Price of Resources

The price of commodities in the marketplace is what most of us think of as an indicator of the scarcity of a good or service. The great strengths of using resource prices adjusted for inflation as a measure of scarcity is that they are easy to compute and typically available over long time periods. There are a number of indexes with which to deflate the price. This is a forward-looking measure because expectations about future supplies, costs, technological changes, and so on will be reflected in the market price of the resource. However, one of the drawbacks is that the choice of the deflator or numeraire used to calculate real prices can have an influence on the results. Caution should also be used when prices are being observed for a short time period, or for selected years. Table 2.5 illustrates the difficulties. The impression one gets from comparing 1970 and 1980 is that, with the exception of copper and zinc, most real prices have risen substantially. This could be because stocks are declining through use and lack of new discoveries, or because there have been few cost-saving technological changes, or both. But look at the numbers for 1993. With the exception of phosphate rock, the deflated prices of all the nonfuel minerals are lower than their 1970 value. Did these minerals suddenly become less scarce than in 1980? Or were other factors, such as a major recession, significantly affecting these market prices? If we look only at selected years out of long-term trends, very different impressions of mineral scarcity emerge.

Did the minerals suddenly become *less scarce* from 1979 to more recent years? No. It takes time for any mineral supplier to respond to price increases. Capacity must be expanded, reserves brought onstream, and so on. Real interest rates in the United States were low in the 1970s. By the 1980s, a lot of new capacity did come onstream. But the early 1980s and early 1990s saw most of the world in recession. Mineral prices fell not just because supply rose, but because there was little aggregate demand for the products that use minerals as inputs (automobiles, steel, and so on).

TABLE 2.5 **CONSTANT DOLLAR PRICES OF SELECTED NONFUEL MINERALS, 1970, 1980, 1993**

Mineral	1970	1980	1993
Copper	$1.34/lb	$0.86/lb	$0.53/lb
Iron	$23.05/lb	$31.67/lb	$18.05/lb
Phosphate rock	$11.20/tonne	$20.01/tonne	$13.21 tonne
Lead	$0.29/lb	$0.36/lb	$0.12/lb
Zinc	$0.29/lb	$0.30/lb	$0.27/lb
Sulfur	$49.38/tonne	$77.15/tonne	$19.69/tonne
Aluminum ingots	$0.61/lb	$0.62/lb	$0.33/lb
Gold	$77.80/oz	$530.63/oz	$223.07/oz

NOTES: All prices are deflated by the United States producer price index for intermediate materials, 1982 = 100. Mineral prices are from the U.S. Department of Interior, Bureau of Mines, *Minerals Yearbook,* Volume 1, *Metals and Minerals,* 1993, 1989, 1985, 1981, 1977, 1969. A tonne is a metric ton.

One simply cannot look at selected years to make inferences about scarcity. Looking at real prices over a long period of time may be more meaningful, but there is still the problem that there may be no significant relationship between prices and time and that price movements reflect much more than scarcity. We will illustrate more fully what sort of links one can make between natural resource prices and scarcity by examining the case of oil.

The price of oil on world markets jumped in the early 1970s from about $3 per barrel to more than $30 in nominal terms. Though cartelization by OPEC sellers was the immediate "cause" of the price increase, it turns out that many producers were pressing against capacity constraints on their production. There was upward pressure on current price and anticipated excess demands in the future. In 1970 world consumption was 40 million barrels a day—double the figure for 1960. High prices led to conservation. The 64.5 million barrels consumed in 1979 were 3 million more than the amount consumed in 1981. A boom in exploration resulted from the high prices in the 1970s. But prices in 1995, adjusted for inflation, were only slightly above the low prices of 1970. The modern history of world oil prices represents a scenario that no informed observer predicted. Current data or the trends in recent figures failed to signal the sharp jump in oil prices in 1973–1974 and failed to signal the substantial declines after 1980. In retrospect, some measure of the pressure of current demand on current production capacity was a meaningful signal of subsequent price change. But the links from the signal or indicator to the price change were not tight. The question is still: Were the price changes a signal of impending natural resource scarcity?

If the demand curve for world oil is inelastic and someone announces convincingly that the world has 20 percent less oil in usable reserves than was thought up to that point, then a substantial jump in current prices could occur. A similar jump could occur if future consumption was expected to be rather more than was being expected before our particular date. The inelastic demand should suffice to generate a notable jump. An inelastic demand is associated with a condition in which there are few good substitutes for oil. A price jump can induce new conservation practices (a form of "elasticizing" the longer-run demand schedule) and can induce new exploration. Successful exploration implies that reserves are larger than was previously thought, and this alone can dampen or even depress current oil prices. Successful exploration has been associated with the term *more elastic long-run supply*. This suggests that successful conservation can be interpreted as *more elastic long-run demand*. Each case of an induced increase in elasticity worked, in the longer run, to counter the upward motion in the price of oil in 1973–1974 and 1979.

This scenario above can be summarized by a simple observation in economics: Long-run supplies and demands are more elastic than short-run supplies and demands. This is an important consideration. There are automatic countervailing forces that emerge in response to rapid increases in price. We would like matters to be more precise, of course. A price jump of x percent is always matched by a gradual decline from the peak of y percent within 10 years. For oil, x, the initial price hike, was about tenfold in 1973–1974. The price decline was interrupted by another jump in 1979, but the ultimate decline was also about tenfold and took place over about 15 years. This observation supports the notion that long-run elasticities of supply are larger than short-run elasticities—a technical way of saying that substitutes or alternative sources of supply are brought onstream in response to higher prices.

How is one to measure oil scarcity in such a situation? The initial rapid price increase indicates short-run excess demand—an obvious scarcity. The subsequent decline in price reflects excess supply in some sense. The two motions of price reflect complicated interactions of current demand and supplies and longer-run paths of demands and supplies. It is the paths, particularly equilibrium paths, that we focus on in Chapters 8 and 9 when we analyze models of using up exhaustible resources. Daily observations of oil market activity can be interpreted as deviations around some basic long-run equilibrium path. Knowledge of the long-run path will shed little light on the activity in the oil market day by day, since the nature of the deviations is only remotely connected to the factors shaping the long run path. An analogy with share prices on the stock exchange is valid. Day-to-day fluctuations in the share price of, say, AT&T are almost impossible to predict, whereas the long-run value of the shares (value averaged over many periods) will be determined by the profitability of the company. This analogy can be drawn more closely. The "fundamental value" of AT&T is determined by its expected future profits (discounted future profits), and the fundamental current price of oil reflects discounted future profits on the marginal barrel extracted. Given the possibility of exploration and discovery of new reserves, the fundamental current price of oil reflects the discounted future value of a marginal profit, which includes the marginal costs of discovering new reserves.

Since current observed price will be deviations from the fundamental scarcity value, it makes little sense to use short-term changes in observed prices as indicators of fundamental scarcity. Trends in moving averages of observed prices should pick up scarcity values better. Because world oil prices in 1995 are at about the same level as world oil prices in 1972, we should infer that fundamental scarcity in oil is about the same currently as some 20 years ago. But arriving at this inference in any year between 1974 and 1988 would have been problematic. In fact, in the late 1970s, experts were predicting real oil prices well above $60 a barrel for the 1980s and beyond. It is fair to say that informed observers underestimated the capacity of oil companies to discover new reserves and to bring them into production. Also, the capacity of oil consumers to conserve energy and switch to cheaper fuels was underestimated. Deregulation also took place. This is an important cautionary story about the pitfalls of inferring fundamental scarcity from current short-term price movements, reserve-to-use ratios, or both.

Let us recapitulate. True increasing scarcity should show up in a rising price trend for the relevant commodity. It is necessary to calculate this price trend using a moving average or smoothing procedure, since observed prices represent a combination of fundamentals plus shorter-run deviations. Price jumps induce supply expansions. This has been noticeable in oil prices in the past 30 years. Long-term price increases also induce supply expansions, demand reductions, or both. *When* the bite of fundamental scarcity will make itself clear is hard to predict, but when it does the prices of scarce commodities will rise relative to some index or average of all prices.

Costs of Discovering New Supplies of Resources

The current supply of a number of natural resources is dependent on finding stocks of these resources. Two obvious examples are energy and mineral resources. But the search for fish stocks could be another example. As noted earlier, one reason why fish harvests became quite plentiful in the 1970s and 1980s was the development of sophisticated satellite tracking devices that allowed harvesters to locate migratory species in oceans all over the world. There were not more fish—it was simply that more fish were found. For the case of oil, were there indicators available in the mid-1970s that hinted at the possibility of relatively low-cost "discoveries"? If the cost of discovering a barrel of new reserves (its *marginal discovery cost*) was not rising in, say, the 1960s, then one might have inferred that new reserves would be brought on-stream in the late 1970s and the 1980s. This suggests that a reliable estimate of marginal discovery costs is a good indicator of current fundamental scarcity. In many parts of the world, oil shale acts as a backstop supply. It is a substitute for the oil pumped from reservoirs underground, it does not have to be explored for, and it is hugely abundant. This places a ceiling on the marginal cost of discovering an extra barrel. Here *discovery* means processing oil shale to produce an extra barrel of oil. Also, Canada has oil-bearing "tar sands" that have actually been mined for oil. The problem with oil shale and tar sands as oil reserves is that the cost of producing a barrel from them has been above—though not hugely above—world prices for liquid oil from underground reservoirs. Thus oil scarcity means a shortage of supply from "conventional sources." High costs of discovery of additional oil from its "conventional sources" becomes less relevant, since oil shale will be mined when the reasonable-cost supply from conventional sources is exhausted. Actual marginal costs of discovery of new oil are obviously harder to obtain than oil prices. They should be somewhat less than marginal profit on oil currently extracted when producers are maximizing profit net of extraction and discovery costs. Marginal discovery costs will thus always be less than the true scarcity price of oil, since output price includes costs—costs of extraction and processing as well as costs of discovery. Average costs of discovery can, of course, be minuscule, since finding one more barrel may be associated with a huge new oil field "attached" to that one new barrel.

Possible supplies of exhaustible resources are reflected in the marginal costs of discovering new stock. The principle of equalizing marginal benefits or payoffs to marginal costs implies that marginal discovery costs should be reflected in the marginal profitability of extracting output from underground stocks. There is an imperfect link, however, between these two basic marginal values. The former is inside the latter but is not exactly reflected in the marginal profitability (rent) of current extraction. It is not inappropriate to say that the higher costs of discovery of additional stock will show up in price increases of output. Thus rising long-run prices reflect the rising marginal costs of discovery or the increasing cost of "creating" new supply. In the simplest view of the world (homogeneous stock, no uncertainty, demand and cost curves unchanging over time), profits on the marginal ton extracted do indeed rise at a rate equal to the interest rate. The *Hotelling*, or *r percent rule*, for rational extractors, implies this. We derive this rule formally in Chapter 8, and we introduced the basic concept in Chapter 1. One can combine rising price as a signal of increasing scarcity or impending exhaustion with rising marginal profit. Each indicator is rising, though each rises at a slightly different rate. However, a more realistic view of the world (with just the added assumption that stocks or reserves are being exploited in a sequence of declining quality) yields marginal profits shrinking over time, generally to zero, as "exhaustion" occurs. Thus it is inappropriate to link the trend in marginal profitability (output price minus marginal cost of extraction) to increasing scarcity. Some measure of rising price or marginal costs of "creating" new supply are reasonable measures of increasing scarcity.

Figure 2.1 shows hypothetical data that roughly illustrate the tenor of our remarks on the recent history of oil prices, rents, and marginal discovery costs. The run-up in price in 1973 opened up a large gap in rent, or in price minus marginal extraction cost. This high profitability of oil extraction induced a rush of exploration that drove up marginal costs of discovering new stock. Exploration companies could afford to search in unusual places because high rents meant that they coud pass discovery costs on to customers. The burst of exploration brought much new stock onstream, and prices, marginal profit from extraction, and exploration activity declined. A new price jump in 1979 led to a repeat of the episode of 1973–1975. A price jump meant a jump in rent per barrel, and this induced a boom in exploration. New discoveries caused reserves to expand and price and exploration to decline. Around 1987 real prices were only slightly above their 1972 levels.

Durable Resources, Backstop Technologies, and Resource Scarcity

We have used oil as an example to illustrate the difficulty of imputing increasing scarcity to simple current trends in key variables. But oil is actually a special sort of

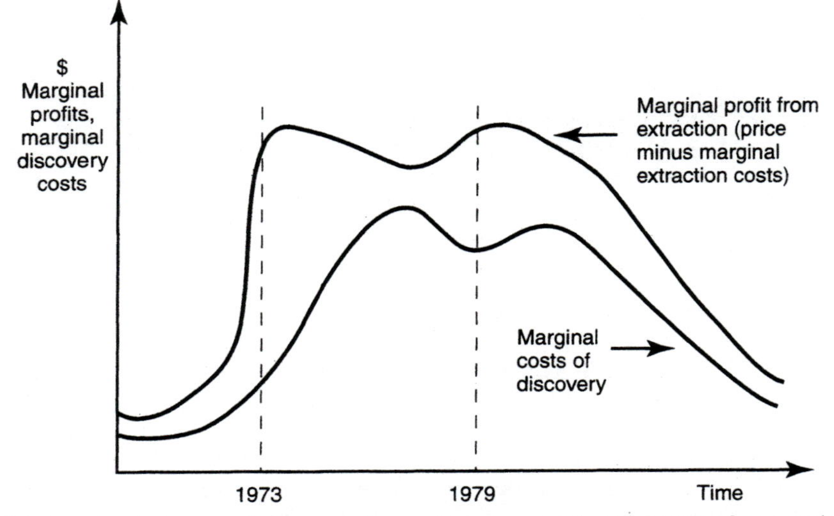

FIGURE 2.1 Marginal costs of discovering new stock rise rapidly with bursts of new exploration. Such bursts occur after prices increase and make rent or marginal profit in extraction large.

exhaustible resource. It is nondurable in the sense that use generally occurs shortly after extraction, and use involves the "disappearance" of the product. This contrasts with, say, copper—which once extracted can be used, possibly with recycling, for many future periods. Copper, gold, aluminum, etc., are examples of durable exhaustible resources or those resources that, once extracted, yield services for multiple periods. In contrast, oil, once extracted, yields services for one period and then is "gone." The durability of some resources leads to a form of market saturation, since as more output comes to market, it must compete with that already in the market and providing services. The effect is to put downward pressure on prices. For the case of an amost perfectly durable exhaustible resource, such as gold, we can expect prices to decline as extraction proceeds and the stock in use increases, unless the market demand curve shifts outward over time. For imperfectly durable resources, such as copper, with an unchanging demand schedule, we can expect decades of downward pressure on price as more and more product is brought to market from mines. But as the extracted stock "decays" because recycling can never be "perfect"—a percentage of the material degrades into a nonusable form with each round of reuse—there will be a gradual run-up in price. In any case, we should keep the "saturation effect" in mind when we reflect on price movements for exhaustible resources with some durability or some "uselife" over multiple periods. We present examples of the movement in mineral prices over a long period of time in Chapter 8. For example, Slade (1982) has examined long-term price behavior of a group of exhaustible resources, mostly semidurable, and found little evidence of upward price trends. Although increase in supply through the discovery of new stock and improved extraction technology are two persuasive explanations for these results, "saturation effects" should also be factored into the forces forestalling price increases.

If scarcity measures turn on the characteristics of price levels over time, it is reasonable to ask how those price paths are anchored. It is one thing to say that fundamentals imply a price moving in a particular fashion, but what determines the relative height of the path? Nordhaus (1973) emphasized that substitutes for, say, oil can be thought of as emerging at some future date—for instance, fusion power as substitute for oil in generating electricity. He called such substitutes *backstops.* If fusion power will generate electricity at $100 per kilowatt-hour, this represents a ceiling on what oil can sell for. If more than this is charged for oil, users will use fusion power exclusively. Fusion power is the theoretical substitute for oil and could be the backstop source of electricity. The $100 price is an anchor fixing the end of the price path for oil at some particular date in the future.

To see why this works, consider the possibility that it might suddenly become feasible to produce fusion power at a price equivalent to $20 a barrel for oil. This would cause panic among oil producers, since they would realize that the highest price they will ever receive for a barrel of oil is $20. Suddenly, all of the world's oil—which was going to be disposed of at prices ranging up to the equivalent of a $100 per kilowatt-hour—must be sold at much lower prices. This could lead to a huge drop in current oil prices because owners will compete with each other to dispose of their oil *today* at $20 per barrel. The resulting scramble for customers will start an auction in which each seller of oil shades the current price. Today's price will plummet in response to the arrival of a new, unexpected ceiling on price. The backstop is a particular kind of substitute, one downstream in the future which affects the level of the price of oil today. In contrast, a very high anticipated price for fusion power would act as a high ceiling on today's oil price. Poor substitutes mean that sellers can charge relatively high prices without experiencing an "invasion" of their markets by competitors with a substitute product. A difficulty here is, of course, that the future, including supply prices from backstop suppliers, is uncertain. This uncertainty is reflected in current energy prices. Price volatility is one reflection of uncertainty.

If backstops do indeed emerge for depletable resources, society's use of these resources will entail a phase of using exhaustible resources, followed by using renewable resources. The use of depletable resources represents a transition to an era of supply from the backstop source. The nature of resource use in the transition is hugely affected by the price of output from the backstop and the date at which the backstop is available as an alternative source of supply. If the oil extraction phase is the dog, the backstop may be the tail wagging the dog.

CONCLUDING COMMENTS

There are some difficulties with all measures of resource scarcity. Market prices will be inappropriate for open access resources such as many fisheries and environmental resources such as air, water, and natural environments because the market price will not reflect the scarcity value associated with the exploitation of these resources (see

BOX 2.2 Are Minerals Essential for Sustainable Growth?

Possibilities for substitution among resources may mean that minerals are becoming less important in the production of goods and services over time. Fiber optics are being used instead of copper wire in telecommunications. Cellular phones eliminate the need for wiring of any sort between users. Plastics are used instead of zinc in automobiles. Recycling of a myriad of products reduces the need to use raw materials. The industrial structure in developed economies is also changing. Demand for resources may fall over time once the aggregate capital stock of a country reaches a certain level and population growth declines. There are only so many factories, railway tracks, roads, houses, and so on needed when an economy is in a "steady state," with zero population growth. Machines and automobiles will have to be replaced when they wear out, but the demand for many resources is much smaller when they are used for replacement, as opposed to building up a country's capital stock. The decline in resource use per unit GDP may also reflect a shift in the composition of goods and services in an economy. The recent high growth in many countries worldwide has been in the service sectors of the economy, not sectors that are resource-intensive. At the same time, however, there is increased demand for the world's environmental and renewable resources, such as fish and forests—and these resources appear to be declining in both quantity and quality. Rates of population growth in many countries are too high to allow us to reach a sustainable steady-state equilibrium. This is why world attention has shifted from concern with the scarcity of nonrenewable resources, such as minerals in the 1970s and early 1980s, to concern over our renewable but depletable stocks of environmental and living resources.

Chapters 4 through 7 for a full discussion of these issues). Distortions in the form of noncompetitive markets and government policies can mean that market prices do not reflect the underlying scarcity of a resource. People cannot determine the future, but they form expectations about what will occur. These expectations will influence decisions about the extraction and use of nonrenewable and renewable resources, which will in turn influence the measures of resource scarcity. Often, our expectations are wrong, as the discussion of oil markets indicated. What was anticipated does not happen. Finally, none of the measures of resource scarcity incorporate social (nonmarket) valuations of resource exploitation and use.

Although much work has been done on resource scarcity using the measures described above, it is not clear to us (and others) that these measures are useful in deciding what actions to take if we agree that a resource is becoming more scarce. What we want to know is how scarcity affects our general welfare: What will happen to the goods and services we are able to produce and consume over time? This brings us back to the notion of sustainability. If a resource is becoming more scarce, does it mean that we will no longer be able to sustain production of certain goods and services? Will substitutes (other resources) be available, or will we have followed the Solow principle and invested in sufficient produced capital to allow for a continued supply of the commodities we need and want? Simply knowing that a resource is becoming scarcer does not tell us whether or not the well-being of society will change. It does not suggest that governments should, for example, attempt to conserve that resource.

In our discussion of sustainability and natural resource scarcity, the availability of substitutes for particular resources has been a vital consideration. If a resource has many good substitutes (and it is not valued for its own sake or its contribution to environmental sustainability), then do we care if we run out of it? There are many instances where one resource has been substituted for another to produce essentially the same product. There is growing evidence that many minerals are no longer needed in large quantities to produce the goods and services in great demand today and into the future (see Box 2.2). What all this suggests is that the focus should be on sustainability. This means that we need to know of possibilities for substitution and the importance of resources in our economy, not a measure of the scarcity of individual resources in isolation. Scarcity measures are a first step in the process of determining what is happening to natural resources over time.

SUMMARY

1. In a sustainable economy and environment, the use of resources today to meet present needs does not adversely affect the environment or the economy's ability to produce goods and services in the future.
2. A principle of sustainability is not to allow renewable resource flows to decline. This means that there must be a sufficiently large stock of the renewable resource (such as fish or forests) to generate a flow that can be sustained over time. Problems with this principle occur when these are population pressures. A second principle of sustainability is, therefore, to slow population growth.
3. Technical change works in favor of sustainability when it is resource-saving. Technical change works against sustainability when it lowers the cost of depleting resources. Examples are modern forestry equipment and computer-assisted fishing vessels.
4. To have a steady-state sustainable level of consumption over time, economies have to accumulate produced capital to offset any declines in nonrenewable resources. If the loss in natural capital is balanced by an accumulation of produced capital, and if the two types of capital are substitutes, consumption can remain constant even with declining stocks of resources. If there are no substitutes for the resource, a sustainable path may not be possible.
5. Sustainable income is the amount of income (broadly defined to include services from natural and produced capital) left over after allowing for depreciation through use or loss of all types of capital—natural (including human capital) and manufactured. Efforts are under way to measure sustainable income in many countries.
6. The real price of a resource can be used, with care, as an indicator of natural resource scarcity. An alternative indicator for nonrenewable resources is the cost of discovering new stocks of the resource.
7. Measures of natural resource scarcity are an indicator of the sustainability of our economy and environment. But even if a resource is deemed to be growing

"scarcer," society is not necessarily worse off if: (a) other inputs are good substitutes for the resource in question; (b) the goods produced with the resource have good substitutes.

DISCUSSION QUESTIONS

1. Is economic growth essential for raising the world's standard of living? Contemplate policies to reduce intragenerational inequities among the world's populations.
2. Will technology "save" us from a nonsustainable path of natural resource use? Discuss.
3. How might market economies ignore the interests of future generations? How could this be rectified?
4. Suppose that an economy's rate of growth of net national wealth is 1 percent per year, but the people in this economy have a personal rate of time preference (the rate at which individuals discount future values) of 3 percent. Will this economy have a sustainable growth path? Explain.
5. "To know what a high-cost-energy future will be like, we need only examine economies in those parts of the world where energy is scarce today." Evaluate this argument. Are there different valid interpretations of the word *scarce*?
6. "Price changes in basic inputs will guide the world economy away from sudden collapse." Evaluate this argument. Would the history of the price of wood burned for heat in England or Western Europe provide a guide to future prospects for a scarce essential input?
7. Suppose that the real price of a natural resource and its rental value are falling over time. Does this mean that the natural resource is becoming less scarce? Explain.

NOTES

1. There are many definitions of sustainability or sustainable development. Our definition follows that presented in the report of the Brundtland Commission (see World Commission on Environment and Development, 1987). This report drew worldwide attention to issues of sustainability.
2. For an excellent discussion of the relationship between standard national income measures and accounting for sustainability, see Congressional Budget Office (1994). *Greening the National Accounts*.
3. Smith and Krutilla (1979) make the important point that although the work of Barnett rejects the hypothesis of increasing natural resource scarcity over time for minerals, the statistical model used does not allow us to conclude that there is any statistically significant relationship between the relative price of resources (in terms of other goods or factors) and time. The relationship may vary considerably over time, and this instability means that the trend regressions between real prices of resources (the measure used by Barnett) and time may not be telling us very much.

SELECTED READINGS

Barnett, H. (1979) "Scarcity and Growth Revisited," in V. K. Smith, ed., *Scarcity and Growth Reconsidered.* Baltimore: Johns Hopkins Press.

Barnett, H., and C. Morse (1963). *Scarcity and Growth: The Economics of Natural Resource Availability.* Baltimore: Johns Hopkins Press.

Bartelmus, P., E. Lutz, and S. Schweinfest (1993). "Integrated Environmental Accounting: A Case Study for Papua New Guinea," in E. Lutz, ed., *Toward Improved Accounting for the Environment.* Washington, D. C.: The World Bank, chapter 7.

Brundtland, G. H. (World Commission on Environment and Development) (1987). *Our Common Future.* New York: Oxford University Press.

Congressional Budget Office (1994). *Greening the National Accounts.* CBO Papers, March, Washington, D. C.

Daly, H. E. and J. B. Cobb (1989). *For the Common Good: Redirecting the Economy toward Community, the Environment, and a Sustainable Future.* Boston: Beacon.

Jevons, W. S. (1865). *The Coal Question.* New York: A. M. Kelley (1965 edition).

Kneese, A. V., and R. U. Ayres (1971). *Economic and Ecological Effects of a Sustainable Economy.* Washington, D. C.: Resources for the Future.

E. Lutz, ed. (1993). *Toward Improved Accounting for the Environment.* Washington, D.C.: The World Bank. See P. Bartelmus, E. Lutz, and S. Schweinfest, "A Case Study for Papua New Guinea"; and J. van Tongeren et al., "Integrated Environmental and Economic Accounting: A Case Study for Mexico."

Meadows, D. L., et al. (1974). *Dynamics of Growth in a Finite World.* Cambridge, Mass: Wright-Allen.

Nordhaus, W. D. (1973). "The Allocation of Energy Resources." *Brookings Papers on Economics Activity* 3, pp. 529–570.

Paley Commission (United States President's Materials Policy Commission) (1952). *Resources for Freedom.* Washington, D. C.: U.S. Government Printing Office.

Pearce, D., and G. Atkinson (1993). "Capital Theory and the Measurement of Sustainable Development: An Indicator of Weak Sustainability," *Ecological Economics* 8, pp. 103–108.

Repetto, R., W. McGrath, M. Wells, C. Beer, and F. Rossini (1989). *Wasting Assets: Natural Resources in the National Income Accounts.* Washington, D. C.: World Resources Institute.

Simon, J. L., and H. Kahn (1984). *The Resourceful Earth: A Response to Global 2000.* New York: Blackwell.

Slade, M. E. (1982). "Trends in Natural-Resource Commodity Prices: An Analysis of the Time Domain." *Journal of Environmental Economics and Management* 9, pp. 122–137.

Smith, V. K. (1992). "Environmental Costing for Agriculture," Resources for the Future, Quality of the Environment Discussion Paper, No. 92–22.

Smith, V. K., and Krutilla (1979). "The Economics of Natural Resource Scarcity: An Interpretative Introduction," in V. K. Smith, ed., *Scarcity and Growth Reconsidered.* Baltimore: Johns Hopkins Press.

Solow, R. M. (1974). "Interregional Equity and Exhaustible Resources." *Review of Economic Studies,* symposium, pp. 29–45.

United Nations Development Programme (1994 and 1995). *Human Development Report, 1994 and 1995.* New York and Oxford: Oxford University Press.

Van Tongeren, J. S. Schweinfest, E. Lutz, M. Gomez Luna, and Guillen Martin (1993). "Integrated Environmental and Economic Accounting: A Case Study for Mexico," in E. Lutz, ed., *Toward Improved Accounting for the Environment.* Washington, D. C.: The World Bank, chapter 6.

Vincent, J., T. Panayotou, and J. Hartwick (1995). "Resource Depletion and Sustainability in Small Open Economies." Harvard Institute for Economic Development, Environment Discussion Paper, no. 8, forthcoming in *Journal of Environmental Economics and Management.*

World Resources Institute (1994). *World Resources, 1994–1995: A Guide to the Global Environment, People and the Environment.* New York and Oxford: Oxford University Press.

PART II

THE USE OF STATIC OR STEADY-STATE MODELS TO EXAMINE NATURAL RESOURCE USE

The five chapters in Part II introduce and develop models of natural resource use in a static or steady-state framework. These sorts of models assume that an equilibrium can be reached that is sustainable period after period if no exogenous variables change. Static models are a typical starting point for analysis because they are analytically less difficult than dynamic models. Renewable natural resources can be examined using static models because there is the potential to reach a steady state. The natural resources we examine are land, water, fish, and the natural environment. We derive socially efficient levels of use for these natural resources and show when these equilibria can be reached.

chapter 3

The Valuation and Use of Land and Water

INTRODUCTION

In this chapter, we examine two natural resources fundamental to life on earth—land and water. Land use and valuation was an important concern in the early decades of modern economics, beginning in the late eighteenth century. In a sense, the study of land economics was the beginning of the economics of natural resources. Land is clearly an important input factor into many economic activities—agriculture and forestry; residential, commercial, and industrial uses; and mineral exploration. It also supports an enormous variety of ecosystems. Land ownership was also for many centuries the key to personal wealth and social power. Our focus is on the economic principles surrounding the efficient use of land as a natural resource, the determination of the value of land, and how different types of ownership of land affects land use and value.

Water is an essential natural resource. Without it, all life on earth would perish. Introductory textbooks in economics often illustrate the principles of valuation of any commodity or input with a "paradox" involving water and diamonds: Why is water so inexpensive in many parts of the world when it is essential, while diamonds, a nonessential item for most people, are very costly? The answer lies in the abundance of water supplies relative to demand for it. We will address methods of determining the efficient use of water and how it is priced in its various uses. We then look at water pricing in practice, finding that in many instances, pricing is very inefficient. We examine the reasons for these inefficiencies and propose alternative pricing policies.

The objective of this chapter is to illustrate, using simple static models, how land and water can be efficiently priced and allocated to different uses. We emphasize the importance of marginal conditions for efficiency. We also illustrate the importance of property rights in land and water use. In Part III we focus on the valuation and use of natural resources over time—that is, in a dynamic setting. The dynamic models are typically more complex than the static models, which is why we begin with the simpler, fundamental concepts here. The principles established in this chapter will apply to all natural resources we subsequently study.

Land is fairly complicated to analyze because it is heterogeneous both in terms of intrinsic fertility (physical properties) and also in terms of its relative accessibility—its location relative to the point where the products obtained from the land are demanded. We examine homogeneous land first, and then land with different fertilities. In each case, our primary concern is to show how land is used efficiently and how the value of land is determined. As we will see, we can distinguish many natural resources by differences in their ownership arrangements. The different property rights will also have implications for the need for government policy. We also examine the relationship between land values and location. Land and all natural resources are heterogeneous not just because of differences in their physical characteristics, but because they differ in their location from markets using the resource. A piece of land used to grow carrots or a copper deposit located far from the markets where outputs are consumed will in general have a lower value than an identical piece of land or copper deposit located close to the market. We uncover some general principles about the relationship between land use, land value, and location.

It makes sense to analyze land varying in quality separately from land varying in location or accessibility. Ricardian (or differential) land rent is associated with variations in land quality. Ricardian rent can arise in the use of any natural resource. In the case of land, this rent arises from different quality or fertility of the land. Location or von Thunen rent is associated with variation in accessibility. Many basic issues in the analysis of land use and urban structure turn on the relative accessibility of sites to transportation arteries and to certain activities in highly dense locations.

Rent is a flow. Think, for example, of renting an apartment. The rent is the monthly dollar amount paid to the landlord. A farmer who owns his or her operation can be thought of as implicitly renting the farm to himself or herself. Thus there will be an implicit rent per month to untangle from other payments to factor inputs. However, durable assets like farms and apartments are bought and sold for a "price." Farms, houses, and land command a flow price or rent and a cumulative or asset price, the sale price of the entity. Needless to say, there is a close relationship between rent and asset price. A plot of land yielding high rents will be expensive to buy—it will have a high sale price or asset value. In this chapter, we will focus on the flow value of land, rent per unit of time, rather than on the sale price or asset value. In Chapter 8 we examine asset values in the form of mineral resources.

Rent can be viewed as a residual or surplus after payments to other inputs used with land have been netted out. The term *rent* can apply to any factor input that is fixed in supply. Many natural resources have this characteristic. The rent for a particular piece of land can vary depending on how the land is used. For example, an acre of land used to grow carrots may yield a rental value of $1000, whereas that same acre used to "grow" apartment buildings may have a rental value of $10,000.

To determine the most efficient use of land, a basic condition is that the rent generated from the use of the land should be a maximum. Thus, when deciding whether to use the acre for carrots or apartments, the values cited above say grow apartments. This condition of rent maximization can be formulated in terms of a rule stating that when there are two or more uses for a particular piece of land, the piece of land should be allocated among the uses until the *price or rent of a marginal unit of land is equal for each use*. If we have 100 acres of land and two uses—carrots versus apartments—we would construct apartments on each acre of land until the rental value of the land used for apartments (if it declines as the number of acres used increases) equals $100, the value of an acre used to grow carrots.

We discuss the basics of land valuation and the efficient allocation of uses to land. Decisions about land use will be the basis for developing concepts of natural resource or scarcity rent. We observe how accessibility of land affects its price how different fertility or quality of the land can lead to another form of rent—Ricardian or differential land rents. Changes in land use are an important topic. In recent years, the change in land use from forests to agriculture and to human settlement has been associated with phenomena such as global warming and a loss of biodiversity and many habitats, such as wetlands. We then turn to a discussion of water pricing and use. The focus is on how to price water in its various uses efficiently and how this differs from current pricing practices for different water uses.

THE CONCEPT OF ECONOMIC RENT

Rent is a surplus—the difference between the price of a good produced using a natural resource and the unit costs of turning that natural resource into the good. The unit costs include the value of the labor, capital, materials, and energy inputs used to convert the natural resource into a product. What remains after these factor inputs are netted out is the value of the natural resource itself—the land, water, or as we will see later, fish, minerals, forests, and environmental resources such as air and water. This is the definition of *rent per unit* (per acre or per hectare).

The rent per unit can be an average value, the difference between the price of the good and the average costs of the inputs used to produce the good; or it can be a marginal value, the difference between the price of the last unit of the good sold and the costs of the last units of inputs used to produce that marginal unit. In many cases, average and marginal rents will coincide because we make simplifying assumptions that the price of the good is constant and that factor inputs (other than the natural resource itself) are available in perfectly elastic supply at a given factor price.

In what follows, we are typically concerned with the rent on the margin, although in empirical measurements of rent for land and other resources, it is often difficult to obtain marginal measures. Average calculations must be made. We will also talk about *aggregate rent*. One must therefore be careful as to which concept is being used. We emphasize rent because it is an important concept in understanding the efficient and optimal use of all natural resources.

Rent on Homogeneous Land

In England as well as in other countries, up to the industrial revolution, land represented economic and political power. Explaining the nature of that economic power was high on the agenda of classical British economics, starting with Adam Smith in 1776. How is the ownership of land related to the high income of landlords? More narrowly, what is the relationship between the *value of land* and the *price* fetched by agricultural products grown on that land? How is the size of the labor force on the land related to the income of the landlord and the price of products grown on the land? These questions received much attention among economists in Britain in the first half of the nineteenth century.

The pivotal idea in the classical literature on rent and land use is the way the value of the product grown on land "spills back" into an income to the landowner. The threads were difficult to untangle. For example, there was serious and long-standing debate over whether the "high" price of land (land rent for the moment) made wheat expensive, or whether the "high" price of wheat made the value of land "high." Sorting these matters out took considerable time. Let us see what the arguments were. Consider first the case of *homogeneous* land.

Suppose a landlord owns 150 acres and employs 10 people on the land. The people use basic implements and seed to cultivate wheat. For simplicity, assume that the cost of these tools and seed is zero. The landowner can then harvest, say, 1800 bushels of wheat at the end of the season: see Figure 3.1. On the vertical axis, we show output per worker; on the horizontal axis, the number of workers. Each point on the graph then gives us the average product *(AP)* of labor. If the landlord employed 11 workers instead, 1900 bushels could be produced at the season's end. Employing another worker yields more output but will cost the landlord more in payments to the workforce. Notice that although total output rises when one more worker is employed, the *AP* of that additional worker declines. Land rent on the 150 acres is then the value of crops harvested less the cost of inputs—namely, the workforce here.

If a worker is paid 100 bushels a year, then the cost of labor with 10 workers is

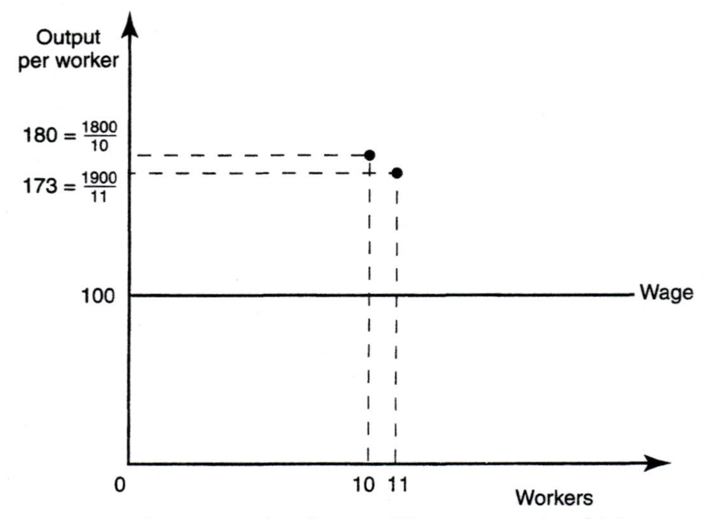

FIGURE 3.1 Average product per worker for two different amounts of labor on a fixed plot of land. Output per worker exceeds the wage per worker, which results in a residual income or rent left for the landowner.

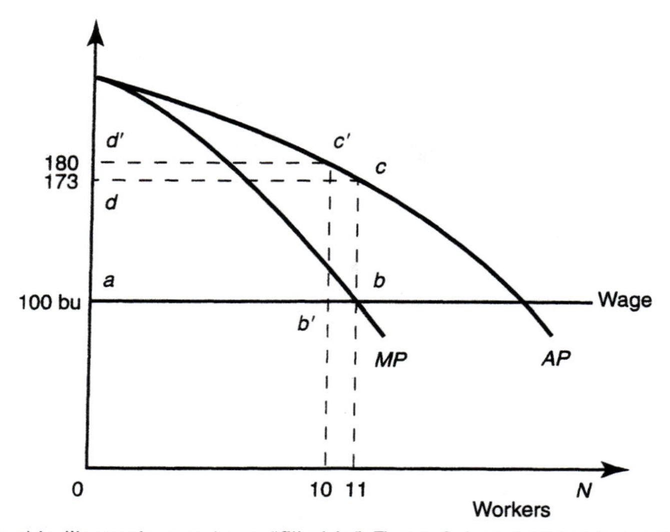

FIGURE 3.2 In this illustration we have "filled in" Figure 3.1 and added the marginal product schedule. Total rent (total product less total wages) is a maximum when the marginal product of a worker equals that worker's wage "cost" to the landowner. (Total product is *AP* times quantity of labor, or the area under the marginal product schedule *MP* up to the current amount of labor used in production.)

1000 bushels, leaving 800 bushels as land rent to the landowner. With 11 workers, the cost is 1100 bushels for the year, leaving total rent on the 150 acres again at 800 bushels. *The average product of labor* declines from 180 to 173 bushels. The *marginal product* of the eleventh worker is the change in total product resulting from the employment of that worker divided by the change in the amount of input, one worker. We have then $(1900 - 1800)/(11 - 10) = 100$ bushels as the marginal product of the eleventh worker. This is 73 bushels less than the worker's average product. The 100-bushel marginal product here equals the "cost" of the worker to the landowner, the annual wage of 100 bushels. The marginal product of labor, the variable input, is diminishing as more labor is used on the fixed supply of land.

We complete the schedules of Figure 3.1 in Figure 3.2. The condition for the landowner to maximize total rent on the 150 acres is to maximize total wheat produced net of payments to workers by choosing the optimal number of workers. That is, the landowner will maximize total rent, which equals total product minus (100 *bu* $\times N$), where N is the number of workers. Total product has two representations in Figure 3.2: First, it is output per worker, *AP*, times the total number of workers; second, it is the area under the *MP* curve up to the total workers employed. The condition for total rent to be a maximum is that the marginal product of one more worker equals the wage payment or $MP_N = 100$, where MP_N is the marginal product of the last added worker.

Total rent is a surplus, residual, or profit accruing to the landowner. It can also be viewed as the return to the input land, as a factor of production used to grow wheat along with the other inputs. Total rent is the area *abcd* in Figure 3.2; where the marginal product of labor equals the "price" of labor, this rent is maximized. The maximum rent *abcd* exceeds the rent that would be obtained if only 10 workers were employed (the rectangle *ab'c'd'*).

There is another diagrammatic representation of our argument: see Figure 3.3. We can put bushels or output on the horizontal axis and dollars per unit on the vertical axis. The *MC* schedule is the marginal cost of producing another bushel of wheat on the land. The rectangle *0pAq* is the total revenue (price times quantity) from the plot. Part of this total revenue, the area under the marginal cost curve (area *0Aq*) gets shifted back as payment to workers on the land in the form of wages. The residual, area *0Ap* above the marginal cost curve, is rent to land. With the fixed plot of land in the background, as more labor is added to the land, more output is produced.

Observe that if a government levied a tax of, say, 10 bushels per acre, then the landowner would still maximize total rent, but now net of 150 acres × 10 bushels = 1500 bushels tax payment at the outset. That is, the landowner would maximize rents by choosing the number of workers N, where the total product from the land minus the total cost of the workers is the greatest—or equivalently, where the marginal product of labor equals the marginal cost of labor. Total product minus (100 bu × N) − 1500 bu is the landlord's profit. Maximization yields the same optimal amount of employment N^* and the same output $Q(N^*)$ would be produced.

The tax simply reduces the rents received by the landowner by 10 bushels per acre regardless of how many bushels are produced. The landowner can do no better than to continue to produce where the marginal product and marginal cost of labor are equal. Thus a land tax is ***neutral*** in the sense that factor use and output remain unchanged before and after the tax.

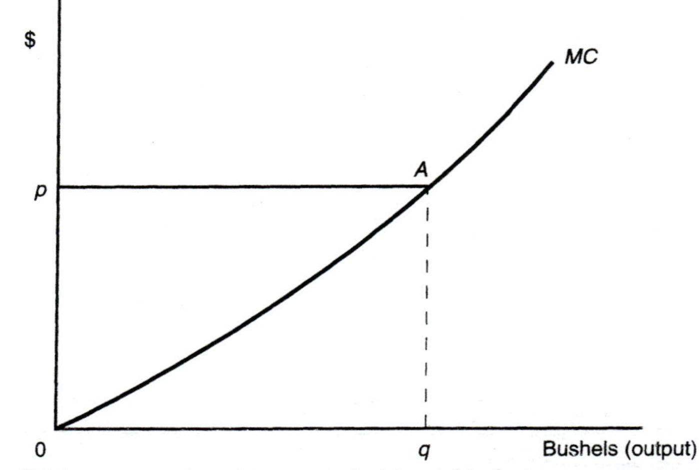

FIGURE 3.3 Total revenues comprise payments to variable factors—wages—and payments to fixed factors: rent.

A rise in the annual wage of 100 bushels to 110 bushels would lower rent to the landlord and lower the output and number of workers employed. A reduction in wages would raise employment, rent, and wheat production. The *share* of rent relative to total wages depends on the shape of the marginal product schedule and where the points of comparison are in the schedule. Of great political interest in nineteenth-century England was whether landlords or workers were increasing their respective share of total output as time passed. As with many such issues, it depends on certain elasticities. Here the concern is with the elasticity around the point on the marginal product of labor schedule where the equilibrium is. The *elasticity* of the marginal product curve is the percentage change in the marginal product divided by percentage change in N, the labor force. If labor increases by 10 percent and the marginal product of labor falls by 10 percent, the aggregate income to labor will be unchanged, but aggregate rent might rise or fall as labor increases.

In this reasonably general situation, note that we have been dealing with an aggregate income flow—rent as income to the landlord. There is no obvious way to translate this aggregate into rent per acre of land. We will pursue this point below and develop a somewhat different notion—rent per acre like a price per acre of land.

Plots of Differing Quality: The Ricardian Approach to Land Rent

Suppose there are two separate plots, A and B, each consisting of 150 acres. Plot A is very fertile; plot B is less so. The higher quality of plot A is reflected in its marginal product of labor (MP_A), which exceeds the marginal product of labor for plot B (MP_B). Does this difference in quality mean that only plot A will be farmed? Let us see. The rent-maximizing allocation of labor to land requires the product of the marginal worker on each plot to be the same and equal to the "cost" of the marginal worker. Making all the calculations in terms of bushels and proceeding with a constant wage of 100 bushels per year, we illustrate the equilibrium in Figure 3.4.

The horizontal axis shows the total amount of labor available to the two plots. As we move from zero to the right on this axis, labor used on plot A increases. Plot B has its horizontal axis reversed—more labor on B means moving from right to left. N_A and N_B are the rent-maximizing levels of labor on the respective plots. Given a constant wage, more workers will be employed on each plot as long as their marginal product exceeds the wage rate. An equilibrium is reached on each plot where the marginal product equals the wage rate.

Notice that workers are used on both plots of land, but relatively more are employed on plot A—the most fertile site. On plot A total rent is the area *abc* in Figure 3.4, and on plot B total rent is the area *bed*. If *ed* is relatively small, it means that the initial "dose" of labor used on plot B barely covers its cost. Land of marginal quality, or *marginal land*, has the property that its net product ($MP - MC$) is approximately zero. Productivity is essentially a technical datum depending on the skill of the workers and the fertility of the soil, assuming that other inputs are held constant.

In what sense does the rent on marginal land determine the rent on more productive plots of land? Suppose that the supply of labor is perfectly elastic at wage w.

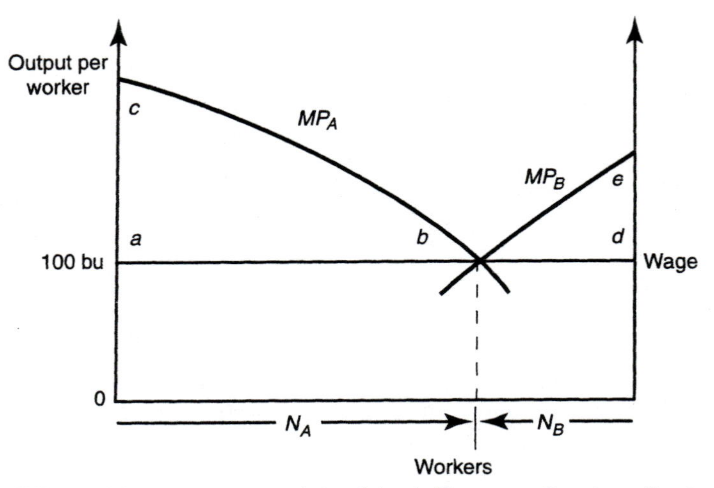

FIGURE 3.4 Efficient labor use on two plots of land. The sum of rent on the two plots is a maximum when labor is allocated to each plot until the respective marginal products of labor are (a) equal to each other and (b) equal to the wage rate for workers.

All workers can be thought of as identical. Suppose that we have a large number of plots of land, each of which has its own marginal product of labor curve that reflects the land quality, and hence the productivity of labor on the plot. Plot A has the highest quality, plot B the next, and so on. Figure 3.5 illustrates the marginal product of labor on each plot. The marginal product curves for plots A, B, and C are shown as MP_A , MP_B, and MP_C. We start each new plot at a different vertical axis, shown by the dashed lines. Plots will be brought onstream as long as the marginal product of labor is at least equal to the wage rate paid to labor. In Figure 3.5, the last plot what will be under cultivation will be plot M. The efficiency condition that marginal products of labor are all equalized for the last unit of labor hired is met. On plot A, N_A units of labor will be used; N_B will be used on plot B and N_C on plot C.

The marginal plot is depicted by plot M (for marginal). Note that its marginal product curve does not rise above the wage rate. This means that plot M will yield no differential or Ricardian rent. The total returns to the plot are paid to its workers. Plots A through C all earn total Ricardian rents equal to the area above the wage rate and below the MP curve for each plot. Note also that if plot C were the last unit of land available, then it would be the marginal plot and yet would still earn a differential rent. We have drawn the labor supply curve as perfectly elastic. If it were positively sloped, the wage rate would be determined where the marginal product of the marginal plot of land intersects the supply of labor curve. Then the marginal plot determines both the aggregate rent on the inframarginal plots of land and the wage rate. In our simpler model, only the aggregate rent is determined, as the wage rate is fixed at w.

A well-known nineteenth-century tenet was that the supply of labor is infinitely elastic at the *subsistence wage.* This principle was used as a basis of the Malthusian doctrine that population growth would outstrip the growth of the food supply. In terms

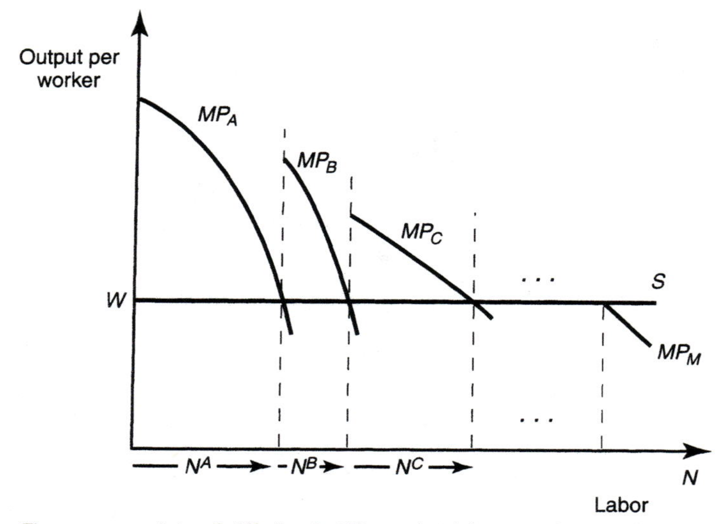

FIGURE 3.5 There are *m* plots of differing fertility and a rising supply curve for labor. More fertile plots (higher marginal product of labor) are brought into use first. The wage rate is determined by the intersection of the supply of labor and the marginal product of labor on the least productive plot. Total land rent will be the sum of areas under the marginal product schedules, less wage "costs."

of Figure 3.5, the subsistence wage is w. The quality of the marginal land still interacts with the cost of labor to determine the Ricardian rent on the intramarginal plots. The rent on the intramarginal plots is still differential rent and Ricardian rent in the same sense that such rents were defined for the case of a rising supply curve of labor. As an empirical matter, observers were unsure when population growth would push wages to subsistence and bring the genuinely marginal plots into production. In fact, the doctrine was slowly abandoned as industrialization and technical progress continually short-circuited the supposed decline in wages. New demands for labor arose, offsetting the effect of population growth in forcing down wages. As we saw in Chapter 2, these fears are rising again as a result of pressures from population growth on the world's natural resources.

Institutional Arrangements: The Role of Market Structure and Property Rights in the Determination of Rent

How much land is used productively and at what price is a function of the ownership arrangements and property rights in society. In our single-plot illustration, we had a single owner who varied the employment of labor until the rent or surplus from land was at a maximum. Suppose that the landowner operated in a competitive market—where there were many such plots of land. No distortions of any sort exist. How would the equilibrium obtained by the landowner compare with that of a government-managed property? If the land were controlled by a government planner charged with maximizing public welfare, we assume that the planner would maximize the consumer and producer surplus in the market for the wheat grown on each plot of land. (*Consumer* and *producer surplus* were defined in Chapter 1.) We can look at one plot in this competitive market and extend the result to all the other plots. The planner would choose a labor force N, such that the welfare function in equation (3.1) was at a maximum

$$W = B(q(N)) - p\ 100N \tag{3.1}$$

where W = aggregate consumer plus producer surplus

$B(q)$ = area under the demand curve for wheat at each quantity of wheat produced

p = equilibrium "price" of wheat; 100 bushels is the annual payment in wheat per worker

The function $q(N)$ shows how much output is obtainable with different numbers of workers; it is a simple production function. Maximizing W by choice of N results in $MP_N = 100$, where MP_N is again the marginal product of a worker.[1] This condition for hiring labor is the same as the one we observed for the case of a single private landowner. This implies an important principle: *Privately organized production on land yields the socially efficient outcome, given the assumptions of the perfectly competitive model.*

Suppose that there is no unique owner of a parcel of land, nor any government planner to allocate labor. If anyone is free to use the land however he or she sees fit, we have what has come to be known as an *open access* arrangement, as was discussed in Chapter 1. In this case each worker is concerned only with whatever he or she can "take" from the land. Since there is no landowner trying to maximize rent from the land, the landowner's "take" is available to be shared among the workers. Is each worker better off in this open access arrangement? If the supply of labor is perfectly elastic and everyone has open access to the land, the worker is no better off under open access than under private property arrangements. The first workers coming onto the plot will earn a return greater than their market wage. This surplus income to a worker above his or her market wage induces "outside workers" to come in to work the land and receive the going share of product. *If such entry by outside workers is unrestricted and product is shared equally among all workers who enter and work the plot, the return per worker will be driven down to the market wage of 100 bushels per year.* Aggregate employment will increase, but the return per worker will not. A new equilibrium emerges in which the average product of each worker equals the wage attainable in other sectors of the economy. This is an open access equilibrium (see Figure 3.6).

In Figure 3.6, the equilibrium under an open access regime occurs with labor at N_{OA}. Average product per worker equals the wage, and there is no surplus to go to the worker or to a landlord. Corresponding to N_{OA}, will be a total output of wheat $q(N_{OA})$ greater than that occurring with a single owner or under government management. The private property equilibrium utilizes N_{PP} workers and yields a rent *abc* to the landlord. Total output of wheat under private property is $q(N_{PP})$, which is less than $q(N_{OA})$. The open access solution leads to excessive use of labor and produces too

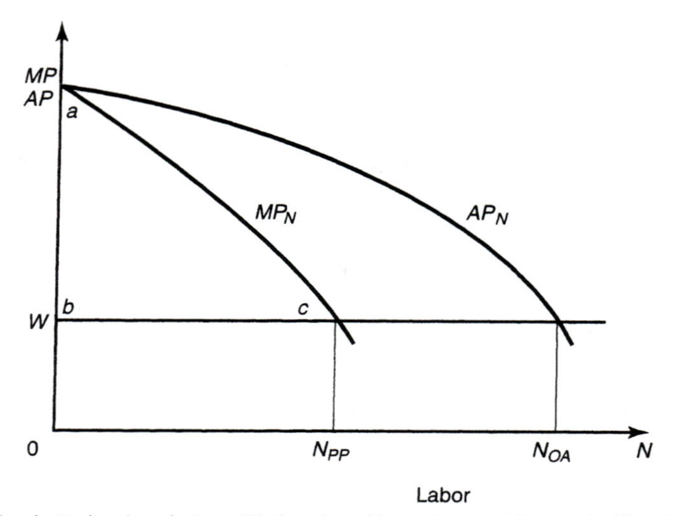

FIGURE 3.6 A private landowning equilibrium has N_{pp} workers on the plot of land and total rent or income to the landlord of area *abc*. In an open access situation, workers will enter until AP_N equals *W*. There will be N_{OA} workers on the plot in equilibrium and no income left for a landowner. Rent is said to be dissipated under open access.

much output compared with the efficient solution of the single owner, which we saw was socially optimal. Alternatively, for a given amount of labor, aggregate output on the land is not as large as it could be in the absence of a common property approach.

> **Example.** Suppose we have a plot of land. The production function relating labor to output is given by $q = 12N - 2N^2$ per day. Suppose the eage rate is \$8 per worker per day. Equating average product per person, $\frac{q}{N}$, to the wage yields the open access solution. We find that $8 = 12 - 2N$ or $N = 2$. With 2 workers, total output will be 16, and output per worker equal to 8.
>
> If the marginal product of labor, $\frac{dq}{dN}$, is equated to the wage rate, the private property solution is obtained. We find that $8 = 12 - 4N$ and $N = 1$. Total output is now 10 bushels, resulting in output per worker in the economy of 10 bushels as well. This illustrates the efficiency of the private property allocation of workers, which equalizes marginal products. The equity or fairness of distributing the total product among the workers is a separate issue.

Open access with free entry of "owners" involves excessive use of variable inputs and excessive output. Moreover, the workers are no better off; they receive the same wage, although more may be employed. This latter statement is not true if the *supply schedule for labor is rising*. When more labor is used, workers receive a higher wage. This is shown in Figure 3.7. Because the open access equilibrium results in higher levels of employment than under private property (as shown in Figure 3.7), each worker is better off under open access. Interms of an income distribution, the open access solution is advantageous to workers when the labor supply curve is upward-

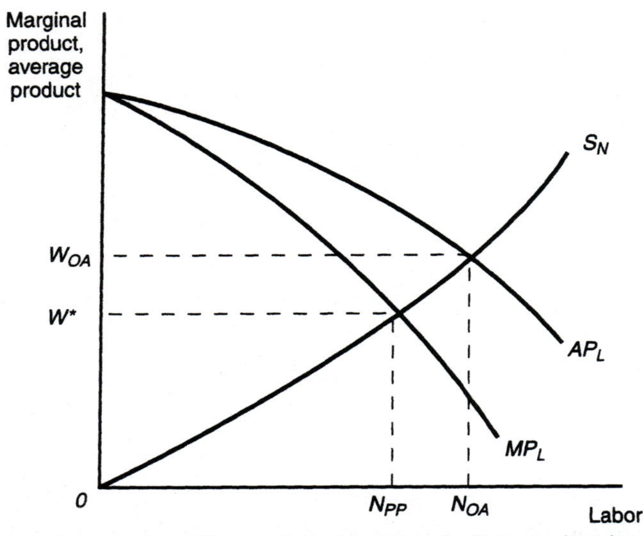

FIGURE 3.7 The open access equilibrium at N_{OA} has more workers employed and a higher wage rate than the private property equilibrium at N_{PP}.

sloping. If so, this advantage could motivate them to reorganize the institutional setting of wheat production. The reverse is also true. If one person can claim the land and hire workers, that person can earn rent. This may lead to a substantial reduction in the labor force. We return to these issues in Chapter 4 in our discussion of the fishery, a natural resource often characterized by open access.

LOCATION AND LAND VALUE[2]

Land Value and Accessibility

The economics of land use involves the pricing of land in its best use and the determination of economic activities to sites. This involves the determination of bid-rent schedules. Suppose we are examining a port city surrounded by homogeneous agricultural land. Output must be transported to the port for export at cost c per unit distance. At the port the output fetches price p dollars per delivered unit. At the production point (the farm), $p - cx$ is the relevant output price, where x is radial distance from the port. Let l denote acres of land input and n denote number of workers on the land. Then, given a production function, $f(n,l)$, efficient use of the inputs of land l and labor n satisfy:

$$(p - cx)\frac{\partial f}{\partial n} = w \tag{3.2a}$$

$$(p - cx)\frac{\partial f}{\partial l} = r(x) \tag{3.2b}$$

The term $\partial f/\partial n$ is the marginal product of labor, w is the wage ($ per unit of labor unit time), $\partial f/\partial l$ is the marginal product of land, and $r(x)$ is land rent ($ per unit of land per unit time). A zero profit condition

$$[p - cx]q = wn + r(x)l \tag{3.3}$$

given output level q, allows land rent $r(x)$ to be determined.

Under constant returns to scale we have $q = \left(\frac{\partial f}{\partial n}\right) n + \left(\frac{\partial f}{\partial l}\right) l$ and we obtain

$$p - cx = w/a_n(x) + r(x)/a_l(x) \tag{3.4}$$

where $a_l(x)$ and $a_n(x)$ are output per unit factor inputs for land and labor respectively at distance x from the port. If we solve equation (3.3) for $r(x)$, we obtain the equilibrium bid-rent schedule $r(x)$ that is sketched Figure 3.8. As is intuitively obvious, the rents decline as the distance from the port to the land increases.

A well-known special case of this model is named von Thunen, after the economist who contributed to these location models. Von Thunen showed that rent can exist even with land of homogeneous quality. In his model, the location of the site leads to rent. Hence we refer to *location* rent. Assume that there are fixed coefficients. This means that $a_l(x)$ and $a_n(x)$ are constant and independent of x. This sort of production function is called Leontief, after another famous economist. Leontief production functions have L-shaped isoquants for the inputs of labor and land in agriculture. The bid-rent schedule in Figure 3.8 becomes a straight line. Land can be viewed as a durable asset. The owner is satisfied only when she or he finds a use for the land that makes the asset value a maximum. Otherwise, the landowner would change activity

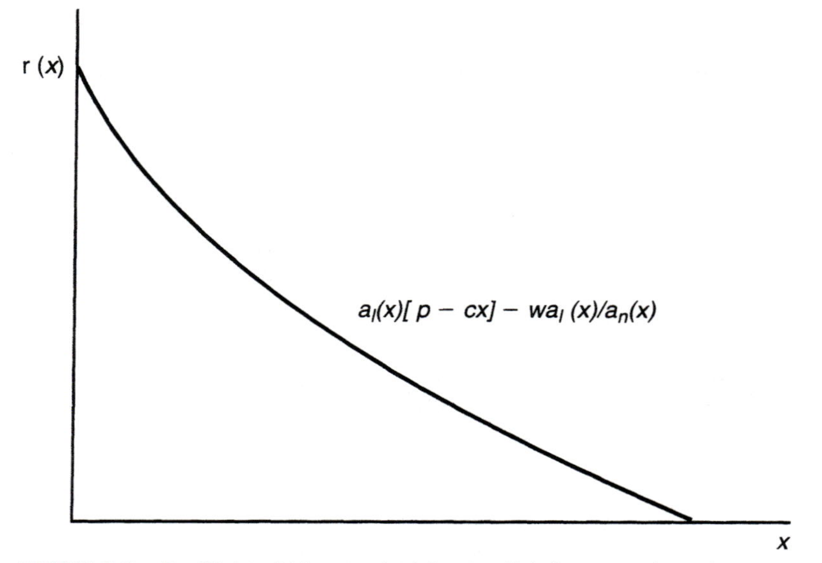

FIGURE 3.8 Equilibrium bid-rent schedule at radial distance x from the port.

on the land to increase the return (land rent) earned in each period t and asset value (land price). Under unchanging market conditions, asset value $V(t)$ equals the present value of land rent from time $t = 0$ into the future. Let i equal interest rate, and for simplicity, let the final time period T equal infinity. Then

$$V(t) = r(t) + r(t)/(1 + i) + r(t)/(1 + i)^2 + \ldots + r(t)/(1 + i)^T + \ldots \cong r(t)/i \quad (3.5)$$

Equation (3.5) holds true for any parcel of land at distance x from the port. We know from equation (3.4) and Figure 3.8 that closer plots (farms) command higher land prices (and rents) because they are less encumbered by transportation costs.

Competing Uses for Land: A Spatial Model

The allocation of the "correct" activity to land involves getting the land use on the site that yields the highest dollar return per unit time—the activity that can "bid" the most for the site. Consider a site at the spatial margin, distance x, defining a switch in activities on land. At the spatial margin x^*, a landowner will be indifferent between competing activities i and j. This means that the return to activities i and j is equal at distance x^*,

$$r_i(x^*) = r_j(x^*).$$

Activity i might be dairy farming with delivered price p_i, transportation cost c_i, and fixed input coefficients a_{li} and a_{ni}. Activity j might be potato farming with its respective delivered price p_j, transportation cost c_j, and input coefficients a_{lj} and a_{nj}. Then the equilibrium spatial margin x^* is defined by equal land rent bid at x^* or

$$(p_i - c_i x^*)a_{li} - wa_{li}/a_{ni} = (p_j - c_j x^*)a_{lj} - wa_{lj}/a_{nj} \quad (3.6)$$

When we substitute in equation (3.3) at distances other than x^*, one activity will bid more for land than the other. This is shown in Figure 3.9.

In Figure 3.9, we observe that at the spatial margin x^*, each activity bids the same for a site. On either side of x^*, one activity outbids the other for sites. These are intramarginal sites. Thus dairy activity outbids potato-growing activity close to the port and vice versa beyond x^*. We could derive the outcome in Figure 3.9 by an explicit profit maximization argument. Let the inside radius be x_i and the remote radius be x_j. Then in equilibrium, x^*_i and x^*_j maximize

$$\Pi = p_iQ_i + p_jQ_j - C_i - C_j - wQ_i/a_{ni} - wQ_j/a_{nj} \quad (3.7)$$

where

$$Q_i = \int_0^{xi} \pi x a_{li}\, dx$$

$$Q_j = \int_{xi}^{xj} \pi x a_{lj}\, dx \quad (3.8)$$

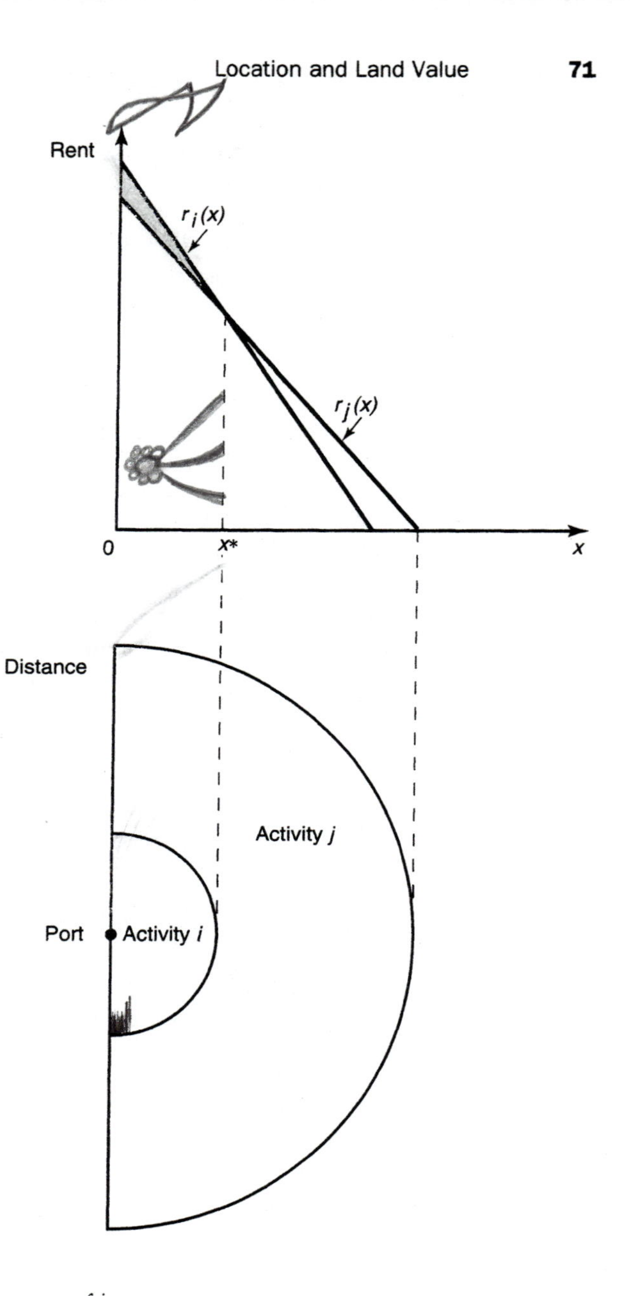

FIGURE 3.9 Bid land rent schedules are linked to land uses through maximizing bids for a site. The lower half of the graph shows that the location of the activities is confined to distinct distances from the port.

$$C_i = \int_{0}^{xi} c_i \pi x^2 a_{li} \, dx$$

$$C_j = \int_{xi}^{xj} c_j \pi x^2 a_{lj} \, dx$$

Q_i is aggregate production of commodity i, and C_i is aggregate transportation costs associated with getting output i to the port. Values x^*_i and x^*_j maximize net aggregate surplus, in the agricultural sector, which turns out to be aggregate land rent. When one does the maximization, one ends up with $r_i(x^*_i) = r_j(x^*_i)$ and $r_j(x^*_j) = 0$. These are the first-order conditions associated with surplus maximization. They are represented in the upper part of Figure 3.9.

Consider changes (comparative statics). If price p_i increases, the land rent associated with activity i increases and activity i encroaches marginally onto land devoted previously to activity j. Formally, we get dollar responses:

$$d\Pi/dp_i = Q_i \text{ and } d\Pi/dp_j = Q_j.$$

These expressions are uncomplicated because the first order conditions are in effect at the maximum rent position. Terms cancel out because of these conditions (an envelope result). Also, for the same reason, one obtains

$$\frac{d\Pi}{dw} = -\frac{Q_i}{a_{ni}} + \frac{Q_j}{a_{nj}}$$

These sections have provided a brief introduction to the economics of land use. We have seen how the location of land can influence the rent it receives and how to allocate plots of land to different uses.

Changes in Land Use: Market versus Nonmarket Valuations

Pearce and Moran (1994) present an analysis of the value of various types of land in its "natural use" versus in its "development use." Their focus is on the underpricing of land in its natural use because various benefits, external to the local owner, are not reflected in the owner's decision to switch "natural land" into "developed land." Developed land is usually in some form of commercial farming activity. Table 3.1

TABLE 3.1 **ECOSYSTEM: TROPICAL FOREST**

Present values \$/hectare (r = 5%, T = 20, sum discount factor = 12.5)

Benefit	Local	Global	Local and Global
Use value: direct			
Medicinal plants	250–750	12–250	262–1000
Tourism	20–1250		20–1250
Minor products	> 0–7000		> 0–7000
Use value:			1000–4000
indirect	0?	1000–4000	23
Carbon fixing	23		
Flood control			
Nonuse value	+	5	5+
Total*	> 293–9023	1017–4255	1310–13278

NOTE: Risks in aggregation are discussed in the text.
Source: David Pearce and Dominic Moran (1994), *The Economic Value of Biodiversity*, London: Earthscan.

(from Pearce and Moran's final chapter) summarizes their findings of complete value of land left in a tropical (natural) forest.

Note the distinction between values realized locally and those fully realized globally. The oxygenation function of plants and trees performing photosynthesis is an example of a benefit realized globally. A tree lives in a particular site, but the oxygen it gives off is deposited in the *world's* stock in the atmosphere. People scattered over the globe benefit equally from the oxygen given off at one site. Another feature of the land valuation table is the classification of benefits into direct-use values, indirect-use values, and nonuse values. Though direct-use values have a more local dimension, they can be difficult to realize by local owners without some innovation in market arrangements. The "letting" of forest for reconnaissance by manufacturers of medicinal drugs is a case in point. Contracts need to be developed to allow local people to benefit from the prospective marketable medicines that can be developed from plants in their forests. Merck, a large pharmaceutical company, has entered into an explicit contract in Costa Rica for such reconnaissance. The basic idea is, of course, that by benefiting from their forests, local people will value them more and will be less inclined, at the margin, to turn forested land into say ranch land.

A nonuse value corresponds to the value of a natural resource or natural environment to someone who does not directly consume the resource or its services. Nonuse value includes option, existence, and bequest values. Option value is like buying insurance against the event that the forest will be gone when one wishes to visit it. Existence value represents what one is willing to pay to be assured that, for example, the giant panda's habitat is not degraded in any way. Bequest values reflect one's wish to leave an "inheritance" of natural resources behind for future generations to use. We look at methods of assigning dollar values to these benefits in Chapter 7.

Table 3.2 (also from Pearce and Moran's concluding chapter), presents the estimated value (discounted future profit) of a plot of land in its developed use. The orders of magnitude ($1660–$5800) are similar to the values in "natural" use. Land in tropical forest can compete with the development alternative if it is fully priced. Full

TABLE 3.2 **PRESENT VALUES OF "DEVELOPMENT" OPTIONS**

(r = 5%, T = 20, sum discount factors = 12.5 $/ha)

Options	**Private**	**National**
Forestry	200–500 (sustainable) 1000–2500 (unsustainable)	NA
Crops		
General LDC,	2700–4630	1660–2320
United States, Japan, NICs	up to 100,000	5800
Livestock	large	negative to small

Source: David Pearce and Dominic Moran (1994), *The Economic Value of Biodiversity,* London: Earthscan.

BOX 3.1 **Drop by drop, southern Africa must embrace water conservation**

PETER MASER, *Southam News*

(HARARE) Rain. Sweet, blessed rain. When it returned to parts of Zimbabwe after an achingly long absence, the relief was almost palpable.

Gone were the heat and humidity, the waiting and wondering if the rain would ever come. Some people stood in the downpour and let it wash over them, a drenching gift from a black and rumbling sky.

In the following days tufts of green grass began to sprout. Insects emerged from a million hiding places. Fields came alive with the tilling of plots. Sweet, blessed rain.

Its arrival in late October was especially welcome news because there hasn't been much of it of late, either in Zimbabwe or the neighboring countries of southern Africa.

Indeed, in the last three years, the region has suffered two major droughts, both of which created severe shortfalls in food production.

Worse is the cumulative effect of no rain. Rivers and wells have gone dry. Shrinking reservoirs have forced restrictions on industry and residential users.

Harare probably has no more than eight or nine months of water left. Little wonder that people have been praying for rain and lots of it.

In the short term they may get it but the prospects into the next century are grim.

Annual rainfalls have been declining in southern Africa for more than a decade now, and the latest computer models suggest this is only the beginning of a 100-year drought.

A normal rainy season will come along every now and again but the long-term forecast points to a region that is both hotter and drier.

The impact of this will be devastating—lower food production, reduced industrial output, declining sanitation and greater disease. And to compound the problem, the region's population is growing about three per cent a year.

So what, if anything, is to be done?

A small measure of relief will come from the digging of more and deeper wells and the building of small dams.

Plans are also being floated for more major diversions that would take water from northern rivers and direct it south. This is of particular interest in South Africa, whose industry and population make it the largest consumer of water in the region.

It has already embarked on a multibillion-dollar project to divert waters from the tiny mountain state of Lesotho to the industrial heartland around Johannesburg.

Similar plans are mooted for rivers in South Africa itself, but the really big diversions would involve watercourses hundreds or even thousands of kilometres away.

The most ambitious—and unlikely—of these would start in southeastern Zaire and use a combination of pipes and canals to channel the headwaters of the Zaire River all the way to Johannesburg.

The second and more plausible operation would make use of the upper Zambezi River, re-routing its waters not only to South Africa but also to the thirsty regions of western Zimbabwe and eastern Botswana. This idea is not new; it was first discussed in the early 1930s.

Another option for these countries is making better use of the water it has.

The widespread practice of irrigation by flooding or spraying is horribly wasteful of water. Most of it evaporates or seeps into the ground without reaching the plants it's supposed to nurture.

Leaking water systems are similarly inefficient. A case in point is the black township of Soweto, which loses about half its daily supply through dilapidated pipes and theft.

The loss is significant—enough to fill 2,500 residential swimming pools every day.

The solutions to these problems lie in plugging leaks, recycling and drip irrigation, which takes the water right to the plants.

BOX 3.1 *(Continued)*

None of these is as glamorous as building a dam but they do save water. So, too, do realistic pricing policies, though they're not the norm in southern Africa.

As precious as it is, water generally sells for bargain-basement prices so there's little incentive to conserve.

Governments in the region are slowly turning their attention to these questions, but costs and competing issues mean they're not at the top of the agenda.

That could quickly change if the rains fail again this year. The season may have started well but it's only a start. Another drought and the situation will turn from bad to desperate.

Dispatches, an occasional feature of the editorial page on Monday, is written by Southam News foreign correspondents.

Source: Vancouver Sun, November 27, 1995, p. A10. Reprinted with permission of Peter Maser, Southam News Service.

price or full value involves explicit payment to local owners for the diverse benefits the natural land provides. It is in this realm that new institutions, facilitating transfers (payments) to owners, need to be developed.

WATER USE AND WATER VALUE

Water is a natural resource that can be renewable or depletable, depending on the source and on use. Water supplies comes from *surface waters* and *groundwater.* Surface water includes lakes, streams, and oceans. These are the renewable water sources, provided by the earth's hydrologic cycle. Groundwater has been accumulated over hundreds of thousands of years in underground aquifers that lie between layers of rock. Groundwater is primarily a depletable resource stock, although a small proportion (less than 5 percent) can be withdrawn each year and renewed by seepage of rainwater or snow melting into the aquifer.

While the total supply of surface and groundwater is quite large compared with current aggregate rates of use, there are many parts of the world where water is extremely scarce because of climatic conditions, geography, patterns of use, and water pricing policies. This is the case for the southwestern United States, parts of Africa, the Middle East, parts of Australia and Asia, and Latin America. The demographer Joel Cohen (1995) considers freshwater to be the key input constraining population increase. He estimates that 14,000 cubic kilometers of water are sustainably delivered by rivers and aquifers per year. Twenty percent gets allocated to agriculture. A benchmark case is a person who is a vegetarian and consumes 2500 calories per day. Assuming a 10 percent wastage of crops between the field and the plate, existing water flows constrain our planet's population to 10 billion. Box 3.1 illustrates the situation in Zimbabwe. Later in this section, we discuss some of the policy issues surrounding water pricing and use that are noted in the box.

The Efficient Pricing and Use of Water

Groundwater

Groundwater can be either a renewable or a nonrenewable natural resource. Aquifers are "recharged" through percolation of rainwater or melting snow. If the rate of groundwater use is less than or equal to the rate of recharge, water use from aquifers can be sustained indefinitely. If, however, withdrawals exceed the natural rate of recharge, groundwater is a nonrenewable resource. Groundwater may also be an open access resource if property rights have not been established. If no one "owns" an aquifer, there will be an incentive to sink a well and withdraw water before too many others begin doing the same. The result will be inefficient depletion of the aquifer over time. The early users will obtain water relatively cheaply because there will be large reserves in the aquifer and the cost of pumping the water out will be low. As a result of this, users will have an incentive to consume too much water relative to the efficient level. As users increase and the stock declines, pumping becomes more expensive for subsequent users, who may have much higher valuations of the water. If open access is not a problem, and we ignore regeneration, the determination of efficient use of the nonrenewable portion of groundwater is analogous to the efficient depletion of a fixed stock of minerals or some other nonrenewable resource over time. We examine this kind of intertemporal model in Chapter 8. The important concept is that withdrawals from groundwater today will reduce the supply available for tomorrow.

Surface Water

Some key issues must be addressed in determining the efficient pricing and use of water. These include: (a) provision for, and conflicts among, users with very different needs; and (b) accommodation of fluctuations in water supply due to climatic factors. We illustrate these issues using the simple model developed below. Because surface water can be a renewable resource, we can use a static model.

Figure 3.10 shows two demand curves for surface water. D_U represents the demand of urban users of water; D_R shows the demand of rural water users. We assume that urban use is more inelastic than rural use because agricultural users can adjust crop mix in response to water prices. Suppose that the rural users represent agricultural needs and the urban users represent household needs. D_U is drawn in the usual downward-sloping direction from left to right on the diagram. D_R is also to be interpreted as a downward-sloping demand curve, but it starts from the right-hand side of the diagram. The length of the horizontal axis indicates the total amount of water available for these two types of users. This is the amount OW.

This simple diagram can illustrate a number of important points about water pricing and use.[3] First, suppose that the price of water is zero; that is, no attempt is made to put a unit price on water. In this situation, the total demand for water will be $OU_O + WR_O$ which exceeds the available supply of OW. It is clear that this is not a sustainable situation, because the demands of both groups cannot be met. Some means of allocating the scarce water among the different users must be found.

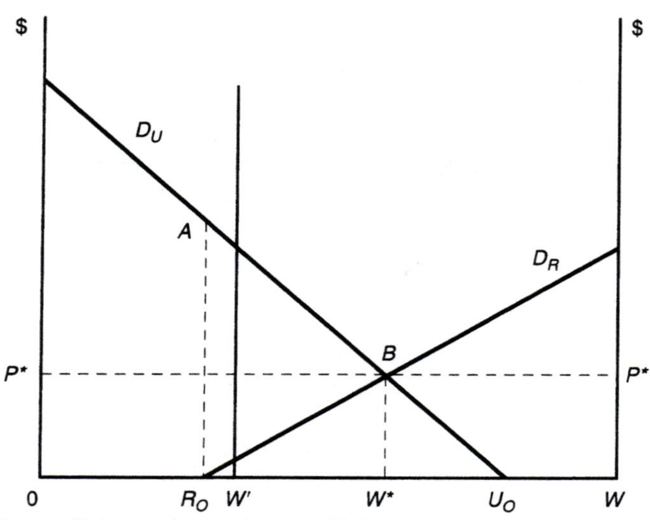

FIGURE 3.10 In an efficient water market, equilibrium is achieved where the marginal value of water to each user is equal. This occurs where D_U and D_R intersect at price P^*. When the total supply of water is W, rural users will consume W^*W amount of water and urban users OW^*. Any other allocation of water among the users leads to a loss in welfare.

There are a number of different ways in which the water can be allocated. We start with the economically efficient solution. Economic efficiency requires the marginal value of water to be the same for the two users for the last unit of water consumed by each group and equal to the marginal cost of supplying water. In this simple model, the supply of water is perfectly inelastic. Hence, demand determines the price. An efficient equilibrium occurs where $D_R = D_U$. The equilibrium price is P^*. At any other allocation of water among the users, the marginal value of one will exceed that of the other. This means that water could be reallocated from the low-value user to the high-value user and improve aggregate social welfare.

Very few systems for water distribution have efficient pricing of the sort illustrated. Why? First, there are very few examples of a competitive market in water supplied directly to households. (We are excluding here the market for bottled water, which could well be perfectly competitive.) To have a perfectly competitive market in water, a clear assignment of property rights must exist for the sellers and buyers of water. This means that buyers must be able to purchase water from any seller, and sellers have the right to sell to any buyer. Water rights don't work this way in many parts of the world. The doctrine of *prior appropriation rights* exists in many countries—for example, in the western United States. The first person to use the water acquires a property right that can often be traded. These rights contribute to economic inefficiency. Suppose that rural users have a prior right and are required to use the water available to them or else lose it. In times of a shortfall in water supply, prior appropriative rights indicate that those users who acquired rights first in time may draw on the supply ahead of subsequent users. This is the "first in time, first in use" principle.

The "use it or lose it" regulation can be illustrated using our simple model. Suppose rural users have a prior right. They will consume water until their demand for it is exhausted. They will use $R_O W$ amount of water, leaving only the amount OR_O available for the urban users (i.e., the rural users "lose" this amount of water). Economic waste occurs because the urban users have higher values of the water for amounts lying to the left of W^*. The value of the losses incurred by urban users for $R_O W^*$ water consumed by the rural users in the area $R_O AB$. When markets exist to trade these water rights, this sort of economic waste will not occur.

Governments control water supplies in many countries. These countries typically do not allocate water on the basis of economic efficiency but use other criteria. Fairness or equity may be a guiding principle. Suppose that rural users require the water for irrigation of crops. Governments may feel that irrigation is more important than household consumption by urban users. They may respond by charging rural users a lower price than urban users. This drives the solution away from an efficient outcome, and rural users end up consuming relatively more water than do urban users.

Efficiency may also be hard to obtain if water supplies fluctuate in response to climatic conditions. Suppose that there is a drought and the available water supply shrinks to W', as shown in Figure 3.10. Now there is no price at which $D_U = D_R$. To put this another way, the high-value users (urbanites) will be able to outbid rural users for all quantities of water available. Governments are unlikely to allow the market to reach an equilibrium where a group of people cannot afford water. Markets are therefore not necessarily the ideal mechanism for distributing an essential good such as water. One should distinguish market allocation systems from other systems. Below, we look at examples of how water is priced in many municipalities in North America and suggest ways in which efficiency could be improved by alternative pricing techniques.

The simple theoretical model indicates that economically efficient water use and pricing will occur when the marginal values of water of each user are equated and, in turn, are equal to the marginal cost of supplying water. This rarely happens in practice. Why? We have already noted that the type of property rights assigned to water may be an important factor in preventing efficient allocations. While governments in North America and elsewhere use the market system to allocate water in many cases, water markets are by no means ubiquitous. There are two major reasons. First, if water prices are set where aggregate demand equals the marginal costs of supplying the water, the supplier will earn a producer surplus or rent. This is shown in Figure 3.11 as the area P^*AB. Local governments are the principal suppliers of water in many countries. They are typically prevented by regulation from earning these rents. Second, market pricing may be very regressive. Low-income users may be unable to purchase water at the market clearing price, or they may be forced to spend a large proportion of their income on water. In Figure 3.11, suppose that the demand for water of a low-income household is shown by D_L. Equating D_L to the market-clearing price P^* would result in a very small amount of water consumption, W_L, and an expenditure of P^*CW_LO. This expenditure may be a large share of the household's income, and W_L may be insufficient to meet it's basic water needs.

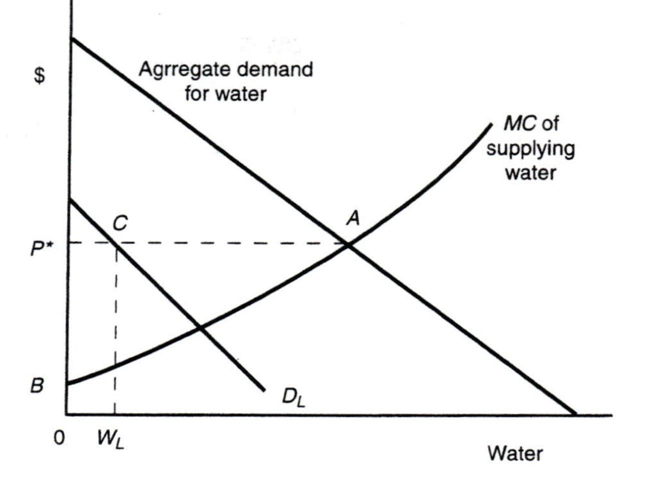

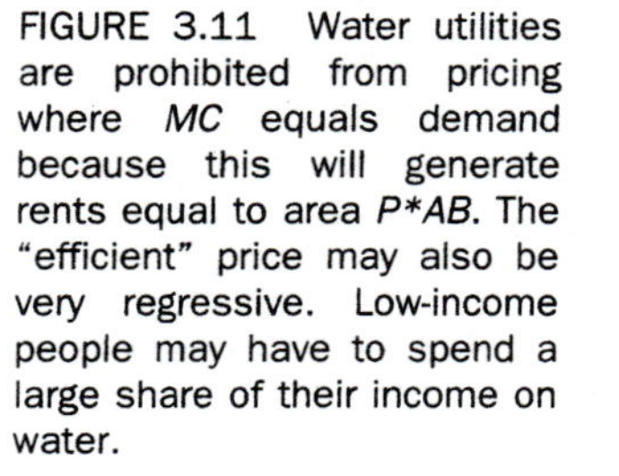

FIGURE 3.11 Water utilities are prohibited from pricing where *MC* equals demand because this will generate rents equal to area *P*AB*. The "efficient" price may also be very regressive. Low-income people may have to spend a large share of their income on water.

Allocating and Pricing Water in Practice

In the next section, we look at water pricing practices for household use. We then examine agricultural water use. Both categories are examples of *consumptive* water use. Water is withdrawn from its source. It will ultimately return via the hydrologic cycle, however the amount returned varies according to use. Agriculture consumes about 50 percent of the water withdrawn; urban users consume about 35 percent. Recreational water use is then looked at briefly. It represents a nonconsumptive use of water.

Household Use

The provision of water for drinking and household use requires the construction of considerable infrastructure. First, water has to be collected from a source (lakes, reservoirs, rivers, oceans). Governments typically own or regulate the use of such sources. Next, water requires purification. No doubt there are economies of scale in purification, although this idea is being challenged somewhat by the introduction of portable and relatively inexpensive water purification technologies available to individuals. Nonetheless, there is still a natural monopoly in the distribution of water to households. Water utilities are typically owned by government and are responsible for constructing and maintaining water pipelines. This complicates the pricing of water, because charges must cover the collection, purification, and distribution of water. In developing countries, purified water may be available only at public wells. A fee may be collected at the well. Households may also have their own private wells, drawing upon groundwater supplies. In this case, the household bears all the costs of obtaining the water. We confine our discussion to municipal water supplied by public utilities to households.[4]

For urban areas in North America, water is distributed by municipal utilities that are local monopolies. Two general types of pricing exist: flat rates, independent of the amount of water consumed; and unit pricing based on the amount of water consumed. In practice, neither of these pricing mechanisms provides for the efficient use of water.

Flat rates mean that consumers can use as much water as they wish without regard for the price. A household that uses 100 gallons will pay the same amount as a household that uses 1000. Clearly, this is extremely inefficient. The marginal price to the consumer of another gallon of water consumed is zero for all units consumed. The marginal price of water supplied by the municipality is certainly not zero (though of course it could be quite low). Studies have shown that municipalities that do not meter their water users consume at least twice as much water annually as in communities where households are metered. Rectifying this situation requires the installation of meters. The cost of doing this can be quite high. However, as populations grow and pressure is put on the existing networks for collecting, purifying, and distributing water, the lack of metering is an increasing problem and clearly contributes to non-sustainable levels of water consumption.

Municipalities that meter water commonly employ pricing policies that are also inefficient. As monopoly suppliers, municipalities face a dilemma in setting water prices. As noted above, they are typically prevented by regulation from earning excess profits or rents on the water sold. They also do not want to price water so high that low-income users cannot afford to buy it. The result is that prices per unit of water consumed are generally set below the marginal price that would clear a market in water (where marginal cost equals aggregate demand). A common practice is to set prices so that they cover the *average costs* of providing the water to users. Water is not assigned a value that reflects the opportunity cost of its use. Moreover, the average costs are typically based on historical costs of providing water. Historical costs will generally be much lower than the costs of increasing capacity or replacing worn-out water infrastructure and building new distribution networks to accommodate urban growth. These construction and replacement costs are then met by annual flat-rate fees levied on all users, by increases in local property taxes, by debt (if this is allowed at the local level), or by requests for subsidies from higher levels of government—which in turn leads to deficit financing, higher taxes, or both. Several inefficiencies result. Users who do not consume much water subsidize users who consume a lot of water, and future users subsidize current users. The general point is that prices that do not reflect the costs of providing water grant users a large subsidy and discourage conservation of water.

Another common pricing scheme is declining block prices. A high marginal price is levied for a specified initial volume of water consumed. Subsequent "blocks" of water consumed come with a lower unit price. This inefficient practice encourages overconsumption of water. Those who consume small amounts of water subsidize those who consume large amounts of water. As noted above, the cost of bringing on new capacity is also high in most regions. Given the cost structure of providing water, efficient block pricing would go the other way. That is, the price for a specified initial block of water consumed should be lower than prices for greater volumes.

Figure 3.12 illustrates an increasing block pricing schedule. This has a number of

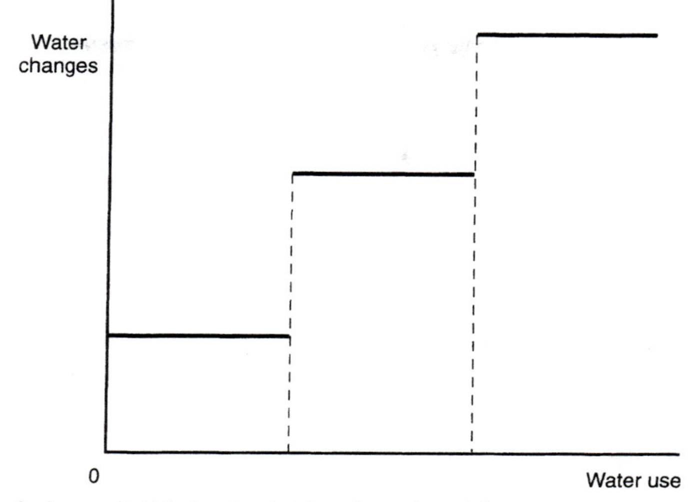

FIGURE 3.12 An increasing block rate structure for water pricing.

advantages over other schemes. First, it encourages more efficient use, as the marginal price of water increases from the first to subsequent blocks. Second, it could be adapted to deal with peaks in water demand. If, for example, auxiliary water supply is needed during dry summer months, a high block price could be charged. This would help cover the additional costs of supplying the water and would encourage conservation. In many municipalities, when seasonal demands are high, some form of rationing is used. Examples are mandatory cutbacks in allocations and bans on sprinkling lawns. These techniques do not allocate water to the highest-value user and clearly violate the equimarginal principle of efficient water use. A third benefit of increasing block pricing is that low-income users can be accommodated. The initial block can be based on "essential" water needs, and a price within the means of low-income users charged for it. One question: If increasing block pricing was implemented, why not go to full marginal cost pricing? Each unit of water would have its own price. This would be efficient, but the costs of implementing such a policy may outweigh the gains in efficiency.

Box 3.2 estimates the gains in aggregate welfare that can be obtained by moving from typical current pricing practices to marginal cost or peak-load pricing. The results suggest that installing meters (when these are not already in place) and switching to a more efficient form of pricing could lead to a gain in aggregate social welfare. However, this gain comes at the expense of residential households, which see their consumer surpluses fall because of higher water prices.

A final problem with water pricing is that governments typically do not differentiate between high-cost and low-cost users. High-cost users are, for example, those who live on hills and must have their water pumped up. Or they could be new users whose demands mean that reservoir capacity must be increased and new pipelines

BOX 3.2 The Welfare Effects of Reforming Municipal Water Prices

The city of Vancouver in British Columbia, Canada is used as an illustration of the efficiency gains that can potentially be achieved if inefficient pricing practices by municipal water utilities are replaced by more efficient methods. Renzetti (1992) has studied this case and has estimated the efficiency gains possible for Vancouver under different types of hypothetical pricing schemes that more closely reflect demand and supply conditions.

Vancouver is representative of many North American cities. It has water shortages in dry summer months, its per capita water use (160 gallons per day) is relatively close to the average in the United States (140 gallons per day), and the prices charged for water and marginal costs of its public utility are comparable to those in other major cities in Canada and the United States. In Vancouver, residential consumers face either an annual flat fee for water service (i.e., they are not metered) or an annual fee plus constant price per unit consumed if they are metered. Commercial, institutional, and industrial water consumers are charged an annual fee and face a declining block price schedule. These pricing policies have led to the types of inefficiencies noted in this section: the utility does not assign a value to the water, historical costs are the basis for average-cost pricing, and differences in demand among classes of consumers are not taken into account.

Renzetti calculates the marginal cost of supplying the water, along with residential and industrial demands for water. He uses these estimates in a simulation program that calculates the change in social welfare (defined as the change in consumer surplus for households and other users) associated with different types of water pricing. There are also costs of changing the pricing policy. These include the installation of water meters at households not currently metered and higher administration costs associated with the different pricing techniques.

The pricing schemes examined are a form of marginal-cost pricing, called Ramsey pricing, and peak-load pricing to reflect seasonal changes in demand. These sorts of pricing options are required because utilities are regulated industries that typically have declining average costs of production. This means that they cannot set price equal to marginal cost, because they would lose money. Regulations require utilities to break even. Price is therefore set above marginal cost in order to break even. Ramsey pricing is advocated as one means of dealing with situations in which marginal-cost pricing leads to a deficit for the utility. Under Ramsey pricing, the utility raises its price above marginal cost by a margin sufficient to offset the deficit. In a simple model with one output, the formula used is called the inverse elasticity pricing rule. Let p be the price of output, MC be marginal cost, η be the absolute value of the price elasticity of demand, and θ be a scalar that reflects the size of the markup in price. Then the Ramsey rule is: $(p - MC)/p = \theta/\eta$. An alternative to Ramsey pricing is to allow the utility to use more than one price. Renzetti examines two-part pricing. In the first part, p is set equal to marginal cost. The second part is an annual charge that apportions the deficit to each customer according to the formula $A = (C - R)/N$, where A is the annual charge, C the cost of supplying water, R water revenues, and N the number of consumers. This two-part pricing scheme is efficient as long as the annual fee does not exceed the consumer surplus of any customer whose marginal willingness to pay exceeds marginal cost. The two-part pricing rule can in turn be extended to deal with seasonal fluctuations in demand combined with fixed water capacity. The prices will then be as follows. For off-peak periods, price is equal to short-run marginal cost. For peak periods, price equates demand during that period to capacity, because the utility is capacity-constrained. If it were not, the peak price would be set equal to long-run marginal cost.

Renzetti's estimations for the city of Vancouver uncover some interesting numbers. Short-run marginal costs of supplying water range from a low \$4.35 per 1000 cubic meters (in 1986 dollars) in the winter (when there is a *very* plentiful supply of water) to a high of \$8.94 per 1000 cubic meters in the summer. Spring and fall prices are around \$6.

BOX 3.2 *(Continued)*

Household demands for water vary considerably with the season. Demand for water by households is very price- and income-inelastic in the winter, less so in the summer. The winter price elasticity is −0.0137, and income elasticity is 0.5515. Summer elasticities are −0.6487 for price and 0.9097 for income. Industrial demand cannot be estimated by season. Consequently only one estimate is given. Price elasticity is −1.913, and income elasticity is 0.785. The differences in these elasticities give rise to gains in welfare associated with efficient water pricing.

Renzetti's simulation measures the change in each group's consumer surplus under the different pricing schemes: the present system, average-cost pricing, Ramsey pricing, and the two variants of the two-part peak-load pricing. We report on the results for Ramsey pricing and the capacity-constrained peak-load pricing. Under peak-load pricing, residential consumers have a substantial increase in per-unit prices during both periods, but a decrease in their annual fee. Prices decrease substantially for industrial and commercial users during off-peak periods. Peak prices are now 15 to 20 times higher than nonpeak prices. Annual consumption rises by approximately 15 percent over the base case. Under Ramsey pricing, the results are quite different. Prices differ across seasons *and* across customer types. Aggregate output is 18 percent less than in the base case, and there are huge declines in water consumption during the third quarter of each year. Recall that with Ramsey pricing, there is no annual fee to cover deficits. Water prices must be above marginal cost; the amount by which they must be above is inversely related to a user group's price elasticity. Because residential demand is very price-inelastic (especially in the summer), residential users pay the highest premium of price over marginal cost. This is why their consumption falls by so much.

Changes in consumer surplus for the different users is shown in the accompanying table. Column (1) shows the change in residential users' consumer surplus, taking into account the new annual charge and the cost of metering. Column (2) again looks at residential consumers, but now nets out the changes in the annual fee plus metering costs. The figure in parentheses below each number shows the percentage change relative to the

CHANGES IN CONSUMER SURPLUS UNDER ALTERNATIVE PRICING RULES

Pricing Rule	(1) ΔCS_R(gross)	(2) ΔCS_R(net)	(3) ΔCS_T(net)
Peak-load pricing	−199.2	−1,332.9	2,091.0
	(−0.5)	(−3.4)	(3.9)
Ramsey pricing	−7,086.2	−8,770.1	−7,083.2
	(−18.6)	(−23.6)	(−13.3)

NOTES: **a.** All values are in thousands of 1986 dollars. **b.** ΔCS_R(gross) is the direct change in aggregate residential consumer surplus gross of changes in annual fees and gross of metering costs. ΔCS_R(net) is the change in ΔCS_R(gross) minus the change in the annual residential charge and metering costs. ΔCS_T(net) is ΔCS_R(net) + ΔCS_I(net) + ΔCS_C(net), where *I* and *C* denote industrial and commercial users respectively. **c.** Figures in parentheses are the percentage changes in consumer surplus compared with the base case (actual pricing policies).

Source: Adapted from S. Renzetti (1992). "Evaluating the Welfare Effects of Reforming Municipal Water Prices," *Journal of Environmental Economics and Management,* 22, Table V, p. 160.

(continued)

BOX 3.2 *(Continued)*

base cases. Column (3) adds the change in consumer surplus to the industrial and commercial users to that of net residential surplus in column (2). Very different results emerge with the alternative pricing techniques. Peak-load pricing, when the utility is capacity-constrained, yields an aggregate gain in welfare of 4.5 percent compared with the base case (existing policies). This increase amounts to $2.4 million per year (in 1986 dollars). What is happening here is that gains in industrial and commercial consumer surplus offset losses in consumer surplus to residential users. As can be seen from column (1), gross losses to residential consumers are not large (0.5 percent compared with the existing pricing policies), but this figure may hide some regressive impact. Ramsey pricing leads to a net decline in consumer surplus overall. The reason is that raising prices above marginal costs to cover the utility's deficit is not efficient. The annual charge employed by peak-load pricing is nondistortionary because it is assumed that the size of the market (*N*) is fixed. In a dynamic model with growth in users over time, this would not be the case.

These results suggest that water utilities could greatly improve the efficiency of water use by employing a peak-load pricing technique. This will reduce the consumer surplus of groups that have relatively inelastic demands. But of course, the elasticities may also change over time as consumers adjust to the new pricing technique. Whether efficient pricing is feasible politically remains an interesting question. Martin (1991) notes that when the city of Tucson, Arizona, first tried to implement a many-step increasing block schedule in 1976, the voters recalled the city council members who voted for the new scheme, arguing that "no-growth environmentalists" were responsible for this very unpopular price reform. A new city council chosen from the business community took over. In less than 6 weeks, the new council members voted in favor of even higher block rates. Increasing block rates have been in effect since 1976, with incremental increases in the rate structure imposed each year.

must be installed or old lines enlarged. Unless municipalities planned for new growth when the original pipelines were installed and built reservoir capacity commensurately, urban growth will mean, under prevalent pricing practices, that all users pay the same unit price. Old users will subsidize new users. People living in areas not requiring pumping subsidize people living in areas that do. To achieve efficient water pricing, new users and users with pumping costs should pay higher rates. Uniform average cost or block pricing to all users will make an area look cheaper to migrants that it really is in terms of their impact on the costs of supplying water. Consider the southwest part of the United States—Arizona and southern California. The marginal cost of supplying additional volumes of water to accommodate new residents there is very high. These areas depend on water from the Colorado and other rivers that are basically "used up." Water from the Colorado River never reaches the ocean, because it is completely pumped out. To increase water supply to these arid regions, water will have to be diverted from other rivers. This involves massive costs and potentially enormous environmental damage. Water prices have certainly risen in these regions, and developers do pay a charge for water access, but differential fees do not in general exist. Very expensive and controversial decisions about water supply are inevitable.

Agricultural Use

Large amounts of water are used in agriculture, primarily for irrigation. The price charged to agricultural users typically does not reflect the marginal cost of supplying the water to them. Agricultural water supply is subsidized by government programs to assist agriculture. Inefficient water use is exacerbated by the property rights systems in place. Water used in agriculture often generates adverse environmental effects—for example, salination of soils and eutrophication of water bodies due to runoff of irrigation waters laden with fertilizers. Box 3.3 notes the conflicts between irrigation and environmental quality. The subsidization of water has led to inefficient crop choices in agriculture. Arid regions of California grow water-intensive crops such as rice. If irrigation water was priced at marginal cost, rice would probably not be grown here. Distortions in crop choice arise when high-value crops are deprived of water because of prior allocations made to growers of low-value crops and subsidized irrigation waters. One study (cited in Colby, 1989, p. 521) estimated the short-run marginal value of water to different crops in Arizona. These ranged from $33 per acre-foot of water for grain sorghum to $157 for lettuce to over $1280 for dry onions. Efficient pricing of irrigation water would lead to a reduction in output from low-value water users and an increase in output from high-value users. Governments have recognized these problems and are slowly adjusting water prices and allowing some limited markets to operate. However, prices are still a long way from their efficient (full-cost) level. For example, it has been estimated (Gaffney, 1992, p. 76) that the wa-

BOX 3.3 **Irrigating Agricultural Land Sustainably**

About one-third of the world's crops are grown on land irrigated by human engineering schemes, a total of about 240 million hectares. About 70 percent of global water use is accounted for by agriculture. Irrigation can result in land that cannot sustain agriculture in the long term because of gradual salt accumulation in the soil. Salts are dissolved as ions in river water, and when the water evaporates or is drawn out by transpiration by plants, the ions are left behind as gypsum (calcium sulfate), salt (calcium chloride), lime (calcium carbonate), and other salts. Developing good drainage prevents salts from accumulating in the soil, but then the salts get deposited elsewhere—back in rivers or possibly in evaporation ponds. When drainage is not adequate, salinization of the soil builds up, ultimately creating desert conditions. It is estimated that about one-quarter of irrigated farmland is being damaged by salts. This is occurring in major irrigating nations such as the United States, India, China, Pakistan, Australia, and the nations that made up the former Soviet Union.

Israel is an exception, however. Its water scarcity has brought about very careful allocations and use patterns for agriculture. Drip and sprinkler technology optimizes the amount of water on crops and precludes large-scale evaporation as the water is delivered. Precise water allocations to crops and a forgiving geology have made salinization of soils a nonproblem in Israel. These techniques are being copied elsewhere. This shows that scarce water can be allocated in ways that improve crop yields without degrading the environment.

Source: Russell Clemings, "Mirage," *Earthwatch,* June 1991, pp. 14–20.

ter developed and distributed through the Gage Canal from the Santa Ana River to Riverside, California, costs $20 per acre-foot if it is used to grow citrus crops, and $240 per acre-foot at the wholesale level for municipal use. An estimate cited by Colby (1989, p. 523) puts the value of water by households for indoor uses at $326 per acre-foot. Gaffney puts the true social cost of developing and delivering the water to the marginal users at up to $2000 per acre-foot. Clearly, major distortions in water allocation result from such inefficient pricing.

Recreational Use

The discussion so far has focused on water that is withdrawn from its sources. Recreational users typically do not remove water from its source. This is called *in-stream* use. Examples are boaters, anglers, swimmers, hikers, and bird-watchers. These users clearly value the presence of the water as a habitat for other creatures, or to immerse themselves in or float on. The pricing problem here is that there are few mechanisms for charging recreational users a price that reflects their marginal valuation of the water. We examine this problem in detail in Chapter 7, where we look at techniques for pricing environmental amenities. Recreational use of water is an example of an environmental amenity. The basic problem is that markets may not operate, owing to open access to many water resources. Even in parks where entry requires a fee or permit, the prices charged are typically far below the user's valuation of the resources lying within the parks. This sort of pricing does not necessarily reflect people's willingness to pay for the enjoyment of the park. If people are willing to pay more than the entry price, this public good will probably be undersupplied. There are some exceptions to parks as public goods. In England, for example, individuals or associations may own rights to fish from particular streams. Anglers pay prices that reflect the costs of maintaining the streams and fish.

The difficulty of pricing recreational water use also means that water supplies to recreational sites may be threatened by increasing demands of consumptive users. Water allocation cannot be efficient when there is no efficient pricing of any use. Habitats will be destroyed when new reservoirs are constructed, when wetlands are drained for irrigation or for the construction of houses, and so on. This will reduce recreational use. In some instances, recreation may be the highest-value use, but there is no way to translate this implicit demand into efficient water use.

SUMMARY

1. Land and water are essential natural resources. Their value is derived from scarcity relative to use. The value of land appears as a surplus or residual, or a differential rent relative to the marginal unit of land that earns no surplus. Alternatively, the value of land can be thought of as the surplus or residual earned by intramarginal variable inputs—the marginal variable input producing output resulting in no surplus.
2. Scarcity rent emerges whenever the price of an input exceeds its marginal cost of

production for the last unit produced. Scarcity rent emerges when there is a finite supply of a natural resource. Ricardian or differential rent arises from different quality or fertility of the natural resource. If the quality of all resources with a finite total stock is homogeneous, there is no Ricardian rent; there is only scarcity rent.

3. The magnitude of the surplus or rent ascribable to land is important in measuring income shares of different groups in society. Different arrangements of property rights can affect the size of the surplus. In the case of open access to land, there will be no surplus, since the presence of any rents induces more people to take up the land that no one owns or manages.
4. Variable inputs will have the same wage under open access as with private property if the input supply curve is perfectly elastic. If the factor supply curve is upward-sloping, wages under open access will exceed those under private property. More variable inputs will be used with open access as all the rent from the land is dissipated.
5. For efficiency, different plots of land must have variable inputs working them until the marginal product of the input on any plot is the same.
6. Accessibility of land involves transportation costs, and higher-valued plots have lower transportation costs and more surplus or land rent. Each acre of land is generally at a different distance from a central node (a port or market). That makes even land of uniform fertility an essentially heterogeneous input. In an efficient land use arrangement, adjacent small plots in competing uses earn the same price per acre. As a result of this condition, aggregate land rent is a maximum.
7. Water can come from renewable and depletable sources. Groundwater is essentially a depletable resource, while surface waters are renewable. Governments are responsible for most water allocation and pricing because of their ownership of resources and the infrastructure to distribute water to users.
8. Efficient pricing of water requires that the marginal value of all uses be equal to the marginal costs of supplying the water. In practice, very little water is ever allocated in an economically efficient manner. There are a number of problems. Water rights that have evolved over several hundred years typically grant the initial users of water a prior right to all subsequent uses. This can impede efficient allocation when high-value users have no access to water. Governments do not price water efficiently to users. Households are typically charged an average price per unit consumed that does not reflect the marginal costs of supply. Some municipalities levy flat charges for water that do not vary with the amount consumed. The marginal price of this water is zero! Agricultural users are typically heavily subsidized, with prices far below the marginal costs of collecting and supplying the water.
9. Distortions and overuse of water result from inefficient pricing practices. Far more low-value agricultural crops are grown than would be the case if irrigation waters were not subsidized. Consumers have little or no incentive to conserve wa-

ter, and this leads to shortages in arid regions and regions with heavy seasonal demands. Population growth is exacerbating all these problems because new residents do not pay their marginal costs of obtaining access to water supply systems. Environmental problems can emerge from excessive water use in agriculture and as a result of diversions of rivers to areas with water shortages.

10. Increasing block pricing and pricing the full costs of water delivery (including all environmental costs) would alleviate many of the inefficiencies in water use. This would encourage conservation and reduce the subsidy high-value users pay to low-value users, thus leading to the allocation of water to its high-value uses. Low-income users would not be disadvantaged by this system, relative to one with a perfectly competitive market and a single market-clearing price.
11. Recreational users of water are not charged their marginal valuation of their in-stream uses for water. This can lead to insufficient allocation of water for recreational use, and to environmental degradation.

DISCUSSION QUESTIONS

1. One can think of office services as a commodity produced with the inputs floor space, location, and labor. To have floor space, one can have a low spread-out building or a high building with many stories. Does high-priced land result in tall buildings, or do tall buildings cause land prices to be high in cities?
2. Urban sprawl annoys many people. In Vancouver, British Columbia, urban development was stalled by a law that protected agricultural lands. Evaluate how such regulations can affect the long-term land use pattern—density and prices, beneficiaries and losers. (*Note:* To the north of Vancouver are steep mountains; to the west is the Pacific Ocean; the United States lies to the south. The prime agricultural lands lie to the east of the city, and to the border in the south.)
3. Suppose labor and fertilizer (another variable input) are used to produce crops from a piece of agricultural land. How much labor and fertilizer would the landowner use if the owner seeks to maximize land rent? Explain quantitatively the determination of the rent-maximizing solution.
4. How is rent determined on plots of land of different quality? Does it matter whether or not the supply of factor inputs used on the land are perfectly elastic? Suppose that the factor supply curve is perfectly inelastic. What happens to land rent on each plot of land?
5. Distinguish between private property management of land and open access to land with regard to the use of factor inputs on the land and the level of output produced. Will open success always result in more production from the land? What are the welfare implications of open access?
6. Why are bans on sprinkling lawns an economically inefficient way to control water use? What can be done instead to conserve water?

7. How could water pricing policies provide low-income people with essential water without jeopardizing water use?
8. Privatization of water markets is being advocated by a number of economists as the solution to inefficient water pricing and use. Discuss how a private market would operate and what impacts it could have on the allocation of water to different types of users. Also consider how property rights to water would have to be defined.
9. Could taxes be used to price water efficiently?

NOTES

1. Notice that $(dB/dq) = p$, the price of wheat. This indicates that a small change in gross consumer surplus (area under the demand curve) equals the price of the commodity in question.
2. This section contains more advanced material and can be omitted.
3. See Flatters and Horbulyk (1995) for an application of this model to conflicts over water use and resources in Thailand. Our model follows their framework.
4. In the United States, most water utilities are publically owned. About one-quarter, however, are owned privately and are regulated by local or higher-level governments. Water utilities either own their water supply or pay a fee or royalty to a water wholesaler, which in many cases is a government, for the water they purify and distribute to users.

SELECTED READINGS

Anderson, T. L., ed. (1983). *Water Rights: Scarce Resource Allocation, Bureaucracy, and the Environment.* Cambridge, MA: Ballinger.

Colby, B. G. (1989). "Estimating the Value of Water in Alternative Uses," *Natural Resources Journal* 29 (Spring), pp. 511–527.

——— (1990). "Transactions Costs and Efficiency in Western Water Allocation," *American Journal of Agricultural Economics* 72 (December), pp. 1184–1192.

Collinge, R. A. (1994). "Transferable Rate Entitlements: The Overlooked Opportunity in Municipal Water Pricing," *Public Finance Quarterly* 22 (January), pp. 46–64.

Cohen, J. E. (1995). *How Many People Can the Earth Support?* New York: Norton.

Flatters, F., and T. M. Horbulyk (1995). "Water and Resource Conflicts in Thailand: An Economic Perspective," International and Development Studies Working Papers, John Deutsch Institute for the Study of Economic Policy, Queen's University (August).

Gaffney, M. (1992). "The Taxable Surplus in Water Resources," *Contemporary Policy Issues* 10 (October), pp. 74–82.

Howe, C. W., D. R. Schurmeier, and W. D. Shaw (1986). "Innovative Approaches to Water Allocation: The Potential for Water Markets," *Water Resources Research* 22 (April), pp. 439–445.

Martin, W. E. (1991). "Water Price as a Policy Variable in Managing Urban Water Use: Tucson, Arizona," *Water Resources Research* 27 (February), pp. 157–166.

Pearce, D. W., and D. Moran (1994). *The Economic Value of Biodiversity*. London: Earthscan.

Reisner, M. (1993). *Cadillac Desert: The American West and Its Disappearing Water*, updated version. New York: Penguin.

Renzetti, S. (1992). "Evaluating the Welfare Effects of Reforming Municipal Water Prices," *Journal of Environmental Economics and Management* 22 (March), pp. 147–163.

Wahl, R. W. (1989). *Markets for Federal Water*. Washington, D.C.: Resources for the Future.

Weinberg, M., C. L. Kling, and J. E. Wilen (1993). "Water Markets and Water Quality," *American Journal of Agricultural Economics* 75 (May), pp. 278–291.

chapter 4

The Economics of the Fishery: An Introduction

INTRODUCTION

Fish can be a sustainable natural resource and have long been an important source of food and other products for people and animals. Table 4.1 shows the total landings and value of fish and shellfish in the United States from 1960 to 1994. Table 4.2 provides figures on employment and the value of the average product of fishers in the fishing industry in the United States from 1960 to 1993. Canadian landings and values for 1965–1993 are given in Table 4.3 These tables show that total landings have increased over time in both Canada and the United States. In the United States, this increase has been accompanied by a fluctuation in the deflated price of fish. In constant (1982–1984) dollars, the peak of the average price per pound landed occurred in 1965, the low in 1993. The price for the most recent year is the second-lowest price recorded. In Canada, deflated values for fish caught have generally risen steadily over the period. We also see, for the United States, that the average product of fishers has basically declined over the entire period shown because employment has risen proportionately faster than landings.

What explains these data? An obvious candidate as an explanation of falling prices is that harvests have risen. However, the aggregate figures shown may obscure significant changes going on in individual fisheries. The share of individual fisheries in the aggregate harvest has also changed over time. If harvests of high-value species are declining, while those of low-value species are increasing, average prices will decline. The hake and haddock fisheries illustrate these changes. The constant dollar price of Pacific hake (whiting) has ranged from 2 to 5 cents per pound from the 1970s to the 1990s. This is a "low-value" species. In the 1970s, hake harvests varied between 3 to 10 million pounds. From 1990 to 1994, Pacific hake harvests have grown from 21 million to over 500 million pounds. By comparison, haddock would be a relatively "high-value" species over the same time period. Its constant dollar price averaged 87 cents per pound over the period 1985 to 1994, and its average harvests have been steadily declining. The 1994 harvest was 724 million pounds; the harvest in 1990 was over 5 billion pounds; and the harvest in 1985 was 14 billion pounds. The model de-

TABLE 4.1. **LANDINGS OF FISH AND SHELLFISH, UNITED STATES, 1960–1994**

Year	Millions of pounds	Millions of dollars (current)	Average price per pound, cents (current $)	Average price per pound, cents (deflated)[a]
1960	4,942	$ 354	7	38
1965	4,777	446	9	43
1970	4,917	613	12	32
1975	4,877	977	20	37
1980	6,482	2,200	34	41
1985	6,258	2,326	37	35
1990	9,404	3,522	37	29
1991	9,484	3,308	35	26
1992	9,637	3,678	38	27
1993	10,467	3,477	33	23
1994	10,461	3,846	37	25

NOTE: (a) The average price per pound is deflated by the United States Consumer Price Index, 1982–84 = 100, *Survey of Current Business.*

Source: For all but deflated values: U.S. Department of Commerce, National Oceanic and Atmospheric Administration, National Marine Fisheries Service, *Fisheries of the United States,* annual, ASI 2164-1.

veloped in this chapter will help us understand generally what is happening to fisheries in North America and other parts of the world.

As noted in Chapter 1, fish are a renewable natural resource. However, they have the potential to be depleted if harvests continually exceed the ability of the fish popu-

TABLE 4.2. **EMPLOYMENT IN FISHERIES INDUSTRIES, UNITED STATES, 1960–1988**

Year	Number of fishers	Processing, wholesaling	Average Product of fishers[a]
1960	130,431	93,625	37,890
1965	128,565	86,864	37,156
1970	140,538	86,813	34,987
1975	168,013	92,310	29,028
1980	193,000	103,448	33,585
1985	238,000	112,310	26,206
1986	247,000	99,956	24,417
1987	256,000	103,072	26,938
1988	273,700	90,005	26,281

NOTES: (a) Average product of fishers is total landings from Table 4.1 divided by the number of fishers. (b) 1988 was the final year in which the number of fishers was reported. Data on processing and wholesaling employment are available for subsequent years.

Source: Fisheries of the United States, various issues, annual, 2164-1.

TABLE 4.3. **LANDINGS OF FISH AND SHELLFISH, CANADA, 1965–1993**

Year	Millions of pounds	Millions of dollars (current)	Average price per pound, cents (current $)	Average price per pound, cents (deflated)[a]
1965	2,407	$ 161	7	31
1970	2,675	204	8	30
1975	2,163	291	13	30
1980	2,955	741	25	35
1985	3,144	1,1057	35	37
1990	3,631	1,509	42	36
1991	3,340	1,487	45	37
1992	2,919	1,471	50	41
1993	2,540	1,438	57	46

NOTES: (a) The average price per pound is deflated by the Canadian Consumer Price Index for food, 1986 = 100. (b) All prices are in Canadian dollars.

Sources: Fisheries Prices Support Board, Canada, Annual Report, for 1965–1985, and Department of Fisheries and Oceans, Canadian Fisheries Statistical Highlights: 1990–1993.

lation to replenish itself through reproduction and growth. In the past 5 years or so, a number of fish populations have been threatened by overfishing, that is, by harvesting at levels that are too high relative to the ability of the fish stock to sustain itself over time. Fish populations in jeopardy include cod off the east coast of Canada, salmon off the west coast of North America, and numerous species worldwide. Box 4.1 highlights worldwide concerns over exhaustion of fish stocks. We will identify the conditions under which fish stocks are unsustainable in models of the fishery. In Chapter 5, we will look at examples of particular fisheries and what has happened to them in recent years. A complex mix of economic decisions, biological conditions, and government policy affects the harvest of fish and its impact on populations.

In the commercial fishing industries of most developed countries, the harvesting, processing, and marketing of fish do not represent a large share of GNP. However, commercial fishing can be an extremely important source of employment and income in particular regions. Although the fishing industry in the United States represents a very small proportion of total GNP, in states such as Alaska it represents over 10 percent of total state product. In Canada, until very recently about 20 percent of the gross domestic products of Newfoundland and Prince Edward Island originated in commercial fishing and fish processing. Anything that threatens the fish populations in these regions can therefore have a major impact on employment and incomes. The threats can be from pollution, as in the case of the Exxon Valdez oil spill off the coast of Alaska; or from overfishing and other effects on the fish stock, as is the case in Newfoundland.

In developing countries, fishing is typically even more important to the economy than in developed countries. Many fishing industries in developing countries involve individuals fishing on a small scale for personal consumption and limited sales. But as

BOX 4.1 **The Depletion of the Oceans**

From the end of World War II until the late 1980s, harvests from the world's oceans increased dramatically. By 1990, however, aggregate catches worldwide started to decline. While the decline so far is modest, the trend has many fisheries experts very worried. The Food and Agriculture Organization (FAO) monitors about 200 fisheries worldwide. Almost all of them are thought to be overexploited. What this means is that harvests exceed the ability of the fish stocks to replenish themselves. Fisheries are being depleted, not sustained. For years this depletion was masked by substitution of less valuable species for more valued ones. Harvests were reported in tons of fish, not value. But even the so-called "trash" species are beginning to decline. Fleets of fishing vessels worldwide are operating at a loss, estimated at $22 billion (U.S.) for 1989.

Why is this happening? The factors are many. First, technological change has greatly increased catches and reduced costs. The price of fishing nets dropped substantially with the introduction of nylon filament. Refrigeration has meant that large ships can be sent out to sea for months and process catches onboard. Satellites and computer technology have enabled vessels to pinpoint fish migrating almost anywhere in the world. Second, environmental factors are at work. Pollution and the loss of fish habitats due to economic development have led to a decline in the sustainable stocks. Estuaries are contaminated by effluent from agriculture, people, and industry. Wetlands have been filled in to make housing developments. Rivers have been dammed, reducing the populations of fish that spawn upstream of the dams. Third, stocks are depleted by high rates of fishing mortality due to the type of gear used to harvest fish. Fishing nets are not very selective. Anything trapped within the net is hauled in. Species not desired, called by-catches, are thrown back, but mortality is high. By-catches of nontarget species are thought to be very large for some fisheries. In the north Pacific, they represent an estimated 40 percent of weight of the harvests of gill-net fisheries. The ocean ecosystems are thus affected. Finally, regulation of fisheries has failed in most cases to prevent overharvesting. The most common form of regulation is the creation of an aggregate quota for the species. This has intensified the race to catch the allowed stock before others do so. Excessive amounts have been spent on equipping vessels that may sit in port for much of the year or may try to harvest other species. Harvests may go unreported to regulators, when quotas are exceeded. If so, estimates of the remaining stocks will be overoptimistic. The creation of the 200-mile limit for countries in 1976 has allowed these countries to have more control over who enters their waters, but it has not prevented the expansion of domestic fleets to take the place of foreign fleets.

Overfishing is a problem that can be solved. Fish stocks are an open access resource, and regulation is essential. There are tremendous gains to finding solutions. In the United States, it is estimated that the catch is perhaps half as valuable as it could be if the fish stocks could be allowed to recover. The European Union calculates that with better regulation, $2.5 billion more per year could be generated from fisheries. The FAO puts the annual loss from regulatory failure at $15 to $30 billion.

What can be done? The most promising schemes are to create some form of private property rights to the fishery that restrict entry of those not holding the right. These have been tried in New Zealand since the early 1980s. There have been problems with the introduction of the rights. Some quotas were initially set too high to sustain the fish stocks and had to be reduced. This necessitated a change in the rules for the holders of the quotas and led to lack of cooperation with the authorities. The situation is starting to stabilize. Now most quotas are set at some fraction of an overall quota that is determined by biological factors. The state of New South Wales in Australia has just created an elaborate scheme to give fishers shares in each fishery. The abalone fishery off Tasmania has operated with a limited-entry fishery for some years. Enormous rents have been created. (See

(Continued)

BOX 4.1 *(Continued)*

Box 4.3 in this chapter.) In Canada, individual rights for Pacific salmon and halibut fisheries have recently been created, as have individual rights for the surf clam and ocean quahog fisheries in the United States. For many fisheries, however, the only policy that will work to prevent exhaustion of the stocks is a moritorium on fishing. Fish farming is another response in markets where prices are high, the farming technology is favorable, and firms can set up operations. Aquaculture is growing at around 10 percent per year for species such as salmon and tuna. Shellfish are also farmed. But aquaculture is not without problems. Pollution of coastal waters and degration of coastlines can result. Breeding and nursery grounds for wild species may be threatened. Farmed escapees may also threaten the genetic integrity of wild fish stocks. Aquaculture isn't likely for many species. The FAO feels that aquaculture will account for only around 12 percent of world fish consumption by the end of the 1990s.

It is too early to see if better regulation will result from the growing awareness of declining harvests. It is difficult for governments and those in the fishery to accept policies that have long-term benefits but threaten employment and incomes in the short term. However, the cost of not changing regulation and dealing with excessive harvests, excess fishing capacity, and the environmental problems threatening the world's fisheries is high.

Source: "The Tragedy of the Oceans," *The Economist* (March 19, 1994), pp. 23–25.

noted in Panayotou (1982), these small-scale fisheries accounted for about *half* the world's marine catch used directly for consumption in 1980, and they employed about 10 million fishers. However, since the 1980s, large-scale commercial fishing operations are contributing an increasing share of total catch in developing countries as well as developed countries. Policy issues as well as the basic economic model we develop in this section are applicable to both small-scale fisheries of Southeast Asia, Africa, and Latin America, and larger fisheries of North America, Japan, and Europe. We will illustrate a number of interesting problems unique to the fishing industry, regardless of size and location.

We will be concentrating on commercial fishing, but note that in North America, as well as in many other countries, sport fishing is also an important industry. Sport fishing generates millions of dollars of revenue in industries supporting this form of recreation—boating, hotels, tourism. Indeed, the revenues from sport fishing may exceed those from commercial fishing in many regions.

There are two key issues: First, fish are living creatures, with their own biological "production function." Fish cannot be produced in the same way as a washing machine or a loaf of bread. People can influence, but not completely control, the reproduction and growth of fish populations. Their habitats—lakes, rivers, and oceans—are large areas which typically cannot be farmed in the same manner as agricultural land.[1] To understand commercial fishing industries, one must know about the biological characteristics of fish and their interaction with their habitat. But incorporation of biological characteristics into economic analysis is difficult because there are so many unknowns in the biology and ecology of fish populations. In the beginning, we must abstract from these complexities to build economic models that enable us to examine problems of interest.

The second major issue is the effect property rights have on the economics of harvesting a fish population. As noted in Chapter 1, fish are an *open access* resource. In the absence of regulation, a person is free to harvest as many fish as possible given his or her ability and the costs of fishing. Open access gives rise to a host of economic problems that threaten the sustainability of fish populations—overfishing, even extinction of fish species; inefficient use of factor inputs; low returns to fishing industries. These problems have led to extensive regulation of most fishing industries.

In this chapter we will examine and develop economic models of harvesting fish. This task requires incorporation of biological factors and an analysis of the open access problem. First, we develop the basic biological and economic model of the fishery. We examine issues such as what determines the size of fish population. Will open access to a fishery lead to an economic equilibrium different from the one reached if private property rights existed? Our discussion of fishing continues in Chapters 5 and 11: Regulation of fishing industries is the topic of Chapter 5. We look at policies that attempt to deal with the problems of open access. Examples of fishery policies in the United States and elsewhere are highlighted. Chapter 11 introduces the dynamic model of the fishery and presents some specialized advanced topics.

A MODEL OF THE FISHERY

A *fishery* consists of a number of different activities and characteristics associated with fishing, including the types of fish to be harvested and the types of vessels and gear used. There may be many species of fish being harvested by a variety of different vessels. Vessels may or may not be able to switch easily among different types of fish. To simplify our analysis, we assume that a fishery is a particular region where one type of fish, crustacean, mollusk, or sea mammal is harvested by homogeneous vessels all originating from a particular port.

There are many different types of marine animals—lobsters, salmon, halibut, whale, flounder, bluefin tuna. We will henceforth refer to all marine animals as "fish" regardless of whether they are fish, mammals, or mollusks. Biologists differentiate between two major classes of fish. *Demersal* or groundfish are those that feed on ocean or lake bottoms and typically do not range over a wide area, such as lobster, oysters, flounder, and cod. *Pelagic* species are the tourists—free-swimming fish that can migrate over a wide area in the ocean. Commercial pelagic species include tuna, herring, and sea mammals such as whales.

The distinction between demersal and pelagic fish is important not only in discussing fishing techniques, but also because property rights for the different species can be quite different. Demersal fisheries, because of their relatively fixed location, are frequently more amenable than pelagic fisheries to the imposition of private property rights. It may be possible to assign private property rights to species such as salmon, which migrate from saltwater to freshwater, during the period they are in freshwater, but not when they are in the oceans.

Because there are so many differences among fish that can affect the optimal economic harvest of each species, we will confine ourselves here to a simple model so that fundamental points common to all fisheries can be studied. Dynamic models and additional complexities—for example, the age distribution of the fish—will be discussed in Chapter 11.

Fish are living creatures that reproduce, grow, and die. This is what we mean by a *renewable* resource. There may be a limit to the number of fish that can be supported in a particular habitat at any point in time, but harvesting a fish and removing it from the population does not mean that the total stock of fish at the next instant in time will necessarily be smaller. Fish populations are potentially sustainable at a number of population levels.

But as with nonrenewable resources, it is important to distinguish between stocks and flows in the fishery. The *stock* or population of fish is either the number of fish or the *biomass*, the aggregate weight of the fish population measured at a point in time. There will be a number of fish of different ages, sizes, and weight represented in this biomass, but we do not distinguish among individual members of the stock. The *flow* is the change in the stock over an interval of time, where the change results from biological factors, such as the entry of new fish into the population through birth (called recruitment), growth of existing members of the population, and natural death; and economic factors, such as harvesting the species. Here is the difference between fish and nonrenewable resources: The stock of fish can be changing over time even if *no harvesting* takes place. The stock will grow in number or weight or both as new fish are born and existing fish increase in size. The stock will diminish as fish die naturally, are removed by predators, including humans, or are killed by environmental contaminants.

Before examining these concepts in a simple model of the fishery, we reemphasize one important similarity between renewable and nonrenewable resources noted in Chapter 1. Renewable resources can be fully exhausted or extinguished. If too many fish are harvested over some time period and their ability to reproduce is reduced, the stock may decline over time. When, for example, many females are harvested before they have a chance to lay eggs, the population falls. If harvesting is so great as to prevent *any* new births over time, the species will become extinct. Thus a sustainable natural resource can be turned into an unsustainable one by excessive harvesting.

Large harvests of blue whales (relative to their population) up until the 1960s drove them almost to extinction simply because there were so few whales that they had difficulty locating one another and reproducing. Other species are also under threat of extinction. We examine the conditions under which extinction can occur later in this chapter.

The model presented below will illustrate four important concepts:

1. The simple biological mechanics of a fishery
2. How harvesting affects the population

3. How conditions of open access affect the harvest and the fish population
4. A comparison of the private property harvest with the open access harvest

Fishery Populations: Biological Mechanics

Suppose we are examining a lobster fishery along the Maine coast. We have consulted a biologist about the reproductive and growth characteristics of the lobster. The biologist estimates that the region is capable of supporting a maximum of 30 million pounds of lobster each year. If the population begins to exceed that number, the lobsters will have to compete with one another (and other species) for scarce food supplies, and their numbers will decline. If no harvesting takes place in this fishery, we would expect to find approximately 30 million pounds of lobster residing off the coast at each point of time.

But we want to know more. We also need information about the growth of the species. For most fish species, including crustaceans such as lobsters, we typically assume that the growth rate of the stock taken as a whole depends on its size—the population or its biomass. This is a simplifying assumption, but it characterizes many species, especially demersal fish.[2] With small populations births will tend to outnumber deaths because of the large food supply. But as the biomass or stock size increases, deaths will begin to rise as food per creature diminishes. The growth rate will decline. The stock may ultimately get so large that deaths will equal births, and the growth rate will fall to zero. These biological features characterize a dynamic problem—fish populations are dependent on time. In this chapter we look at these biological dynamics very simply. Our concern is with steady-state populations—those that can be sustained indefinitely. To find these sustainable populations, we have to know a bit about population dynamics. Chapter 11 looks at dynamics more fully. We can summarize all this information graphically and with simple mathematical relationships.

Let $X(t)$ be the stock of fish at time t, which throughout this and the next chapter we measure as the biomass. How will this stock grow or change over time? Let $dX(t)/dt$ denote the change in the stock over a short interval of time, dt.[3] In the algebra that follows, for simplicty we will suppress the dependence of all variables on time. Let equation (4.1) describe the instantaneous growth of our lobsters before any harvesting occurs.

$$dX/dt = F(X) \tag{4.1}$$

$F(X)$ is the instantaneous rate of growth in the biomass of the fish population in question. It can also be thought of as a biological growth function for the fishery, or the biological mechanics. It indicates for each stock or biomass X the net increase over a small instant of time in the natural size of the population. This net natural growth (or relative rate of surplus growth, from Hannesson, 1978) is due to increases in the biomass—new fish entering the stock through birth, physical growth of the fish existing in the stock at each time t, minus decreases in the population through natural mortality. For a hypothetical population of identical members, it is number of births less number of deaths.

$F(X)$ is often represented with the logistic function, which yields a parabola when

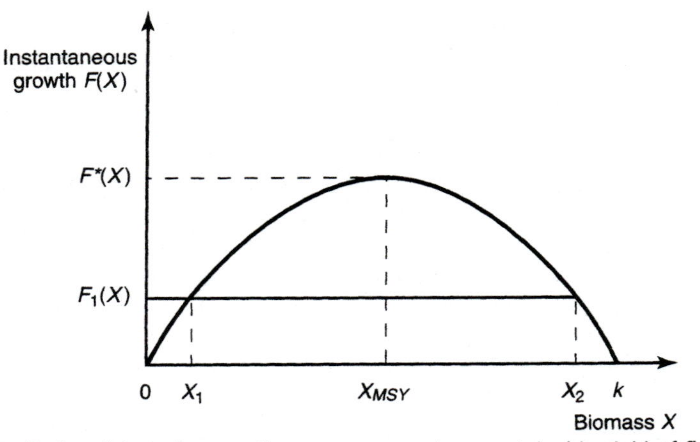

FIGURE 4.1. Each point on the growth curve represents a sustainable yield of fish for a given stock of fish, X. The point k is the equilibrium stock size that is reached without any human predation and is called the carrying capacity of the habitat. The point X_{MSY} is the stock size which corresponds to the maximum sustainable yield from the fishery. If the population were reduced to this level, the fish stock would grow at its maximum potential yield, $F^*(X)$.

$F(X)$ is plotted against X starting from a stock size of zero. The logistic function is illustrated in Figure 4.1 and can be represented mathematically by:

$$F(X) = rX(1 - X/k) \tag{4.2}$$

In equation (4.2), r represents the intrinsic instantaneous growth rate of the biomass and is equal to the rate of growth of the stock X when this stock is close to zero, while k is the *carrying capacity* of the habitat. We can think of k as the maximum population or biomass the habitat can support. We assume that r and k are parameters (fixed values) given to us by fisheries biologists. Although k is assumed to be fixed for our model, in more general models it would be sensitive to stochastic variables determined by a number of environmental factors, such as epidemic disease, oil spills, water temperature, and the presence of predators. Equation (4.2), then, reflects our earlier intuitive explanation.

Starting at a small but positive stock, the biomass will at first grow rapidly. Growth will reach a maximum, then decline until the biomass reaches its maximum carrying capacity. Notice that the net growth in the population can be identical at different levels of the stock. In Figure 4.1, we can see that a net growth rate of $F_1(X)$ can be obtained with a small population X_1 or a large population X_2. Intuitively what is happening is as follows: At X_1, births greatly outnumber deaths because the population is small and food is ample. The stock is small, though net births over deaths can be a large proportion of this stock. At X_2, births slightly outnumbered deaths, and the average size of the population is large.

Using Figure 4.1, we can find a biological equilibrium for the species. We define a *biological equilibrium* as the value of the fish stock X for which there is no growth in

BOX 4.2 Logistic Growth of Species

The familiar S-shaped curve is a time path showing the growth of individuals and numbers in a group. Growth is slow at the outset, with a few members of a group in existence, speeds up for an interval, and slows down at a "saturation level." The saturation level is referred to by ecologists as the *carrying capacity* of the environment. Growth is less than exponential (the biotic potential) because of *environmental resistance.* See the lower portion of Figure B4.1. Our familiar logistic growth function in the upper part of the figure has equation

$$\frac{dX}{dt} = rX\left(1 - \frac{X}{k}\right)$$

where k is the carrying capacity, r is the *intrinsic rate of increase,* and dx/dt is the instantaneous rate of growth corresponding to stock size X. If we integrate this equation, we get the time path of the biomass, X,

$$X(t) = \frac{k}{1 + ce^{-rt}}$$

where $c = (k - X_0)/X_0$. This is the S-shaped schedule of stock size plotted against time in

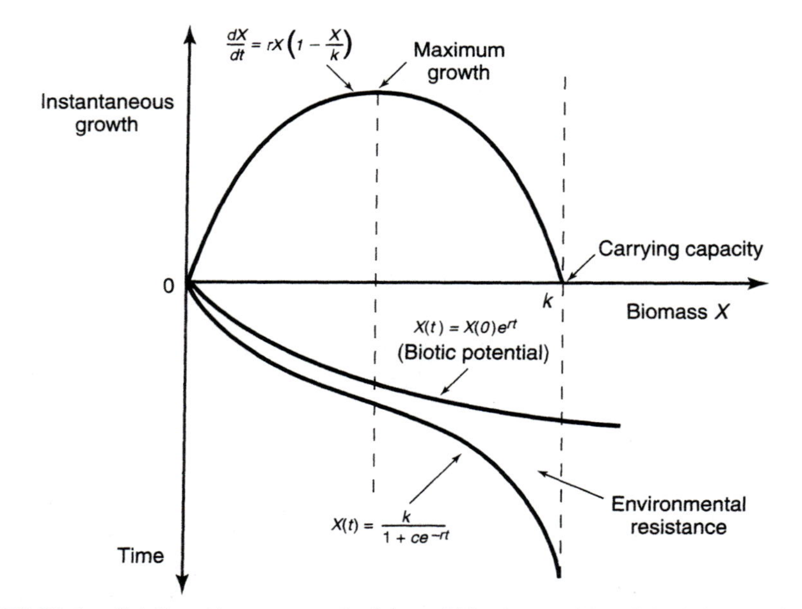

FIGURE B4.1. Relationship among schedules of (the inverted bowl) logistic growth function (the S-shaped curve) and biotic potential (explosive growth). The carrying capacity introduces a crowding or saturation element which constrains exponential growth from persisting beyond the very early stages of the growth in numbers of a species. ($c = (k - X_0)/X_0$). Note we have drawn the S-shaped curve for the initial population X_0 near 0. We could have made X_0 large and plotted a schedule of stock decline using our basic time path equation.)

(Continued)

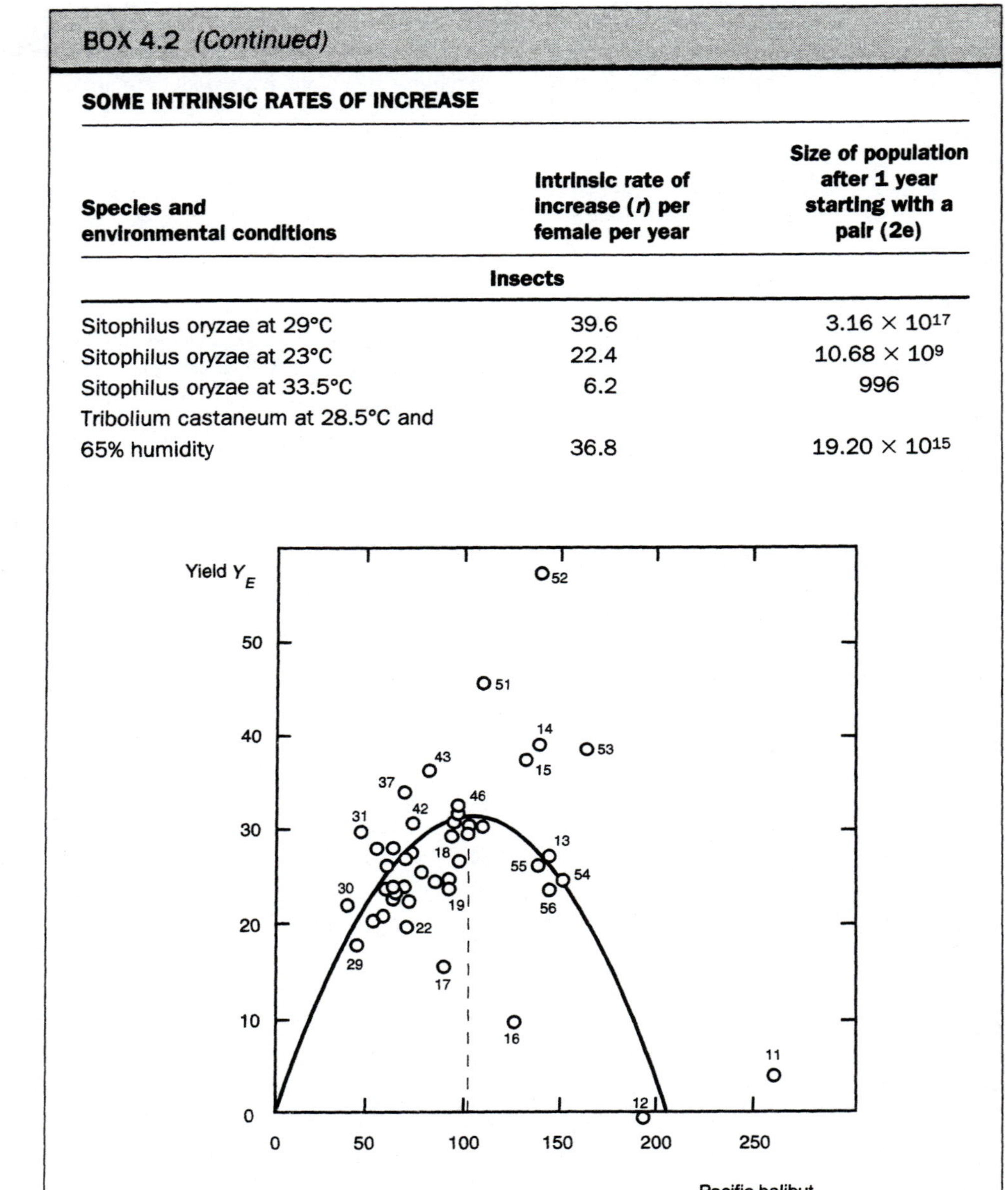

BOX 4.2 *(Continued)*

SOME INTRINSIC RATES OF INCREASE

Species and environmental conditions	Intrinsic rate of increase (r) per female per year	Size of population after 1 year starting with a pair (2e)
	Insects	
Sitophilus oryzae at 29°C	39.6	3.16×10^{17}
Sitophilus oryzae at 23°C	22.4	10.68×10^{9}
Sitophilus oryzae at 33.5°C	6.2	996
Tribolium castaneum at 28.5°C and 65% humidity	36.8	19.20×10^{15}

FIGURE B4.2. A fitted yield-biomass (stock) schedule for data on the Pacific halibut, years 1910–1957. We have yield plotted against current mean biomass. (*Source:* W. E. Ricker (1975), *Computation and Interpretation of Biological Statistics of Fish Populations,* Bulletin 191, Ottawa: Environment Canada, Fisheries and Marine Service, Figure 13.2, p. 324.)

BOX 4.2 *(Continued)*

SOME INTRINSIC RATES OF INCREASE

Species and environmental conditions	Intrinsic rate of increase (*r*) per female per year	Size of population after 1 year starting with a pair (2e)
Mammals		
Rat	5.4	442
Man	0.0055	2.011

Source: Roger Dajoz (1977). *Introduction to Ecology,* trans. A. South. London: Hodder and Stoughton, p. 180.

the bottom part of the figure. In the absence of a "saturation" or "negative feedback" from crowding or environmental resistance, the stock would grow exponentially at rate *r* along the line labeled biotic potential. Thus the time path equation combines in a subtle way exponential growth constrained by crowding effects induced by the carrying capacity being approached.

In the table we have the intrinsic growth rates of two types of insects (one breeding at three different temperatures) and two mammals. We also indicate the size the populations would grow to starting with two individuals in one year. In Figure B4.2, a yield-biomass schedule is presented for Pacific halibut.

the fish population or biomass—that is, the flow, $dX/dt = F(X)$, is equal to zero. Simply by examining Figure 4.1, we can see that there are two possible values of X for which there is no growth of the biomass. If X is equal to zero, there are no fish and therefore no growth occurs. The more interesting equilibrium is where the growth curve crosses the X axis at the point we have labeled k. As noted in equation (4.2), k is the carrying capacity of the habitat. The species will therefore be in a biological equilibrium whenever $X = k$. To see mathematically why this is so, simply set $F(X)$ equal to zero in equation (4.2) and solve for X. The notion of a biological equilibrium will be a reference point for our simple model with a homogeneous biomass comprising a single species. We will now add harvesting to the model, assuming that the fish population begins in a biological equilibrium at point k. The objective is to find a new equilibrium for the fishery.

Bionomic Equilibrium in a Simple Model

So far, we have not introduced any economic decision making into the model. We will now examine the role played by the economic activity of harvesting. We first as-

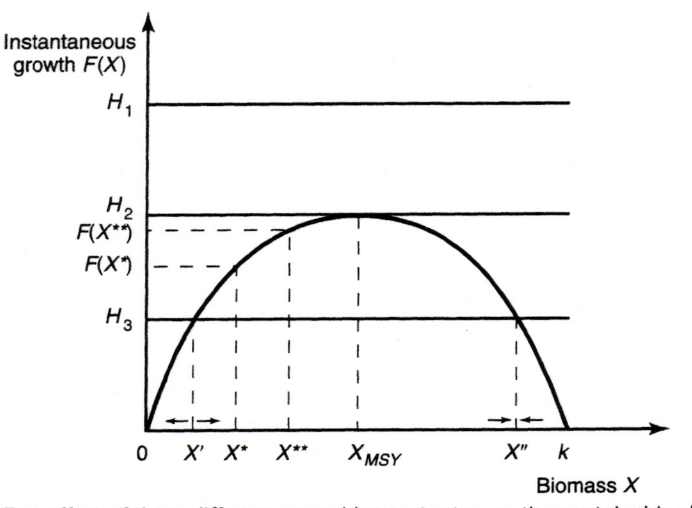

FIGURE 4.2. The effect of three different annual harvest rates on the sustainable yield from the fishery are shown. A harvest of H_1 will extinguish the fishery because H_1 is everywhere larger than the growth rate of the fish stock, $F(X)$. A harvest of H_2 leads to the maximum sustainable yield from the fishery. A harvest of H_3 results in two equilibriums, X' and X'', but only X'' is a stable equilibrium. This means that for any stock of fish to the right of X' if the harvest is H_3, the stock will reach X''. For any stock size to the left of X' given H_3, the species will be extinguished.

sume that harvesting is a costless activity. We do not yet worry about how harvest levels are chosen. We use this simple case to develop some important concepts that connect biological and economic factors. We derive what has been called a *bionomic equilibrium*—an equilibrium that combines the biological mechanics with economic activity. In Figure 4.2, three rates of harvest are shown. We will see how different harvesting rates will affect the fish population, given the biological mechanics postulated above.

The three different rates of aggregate harvest for an instant in time are shown in Figure 4.2 as H_1, H_2, and H_3. Assume that the lobsters are in a biological equilibrium at k. Consider catch or harvest levels of H_1 and H_2 pounds. As drawn, H_1 represents a level of harvest that lies everywhere *above* the biological growth function, $F(X)$. What this means is that more lobsters are removed at each point in time than are being reproduced. It should be obvious that no fish population can survive for long if more are harvested than are replaced by new births and growth of existing members of the population. The fish population will therefore decline to zero if this level of harvest is maintained season after season. This is an extreme example of *mining* the fishery—driving it to extinction.

Suppose now that the instantaneous rate of harvest is H_2. We can see that H_2 touches the growth function $F(X)$ at its maximum point. The value X_{MSY} is the maximum sustainable yield from the population, the point where the "net growth" or surplus growth is at a maximum. Given our logistic biological production function, we see that the *MSY* occurs at exactly one-half the carrying capacity, k. Suppose again that the population is initially at point k. Here the fish stock is in an equilibrium where there is no net change in its size. At each instant that follows, H_2 pounds of lobster are harvested. Because H_2 exceeds $F(X)$ for all levels of the biomass X from k to X_{MSY}, the stock will gradually fall to $k/2$, which is X_{MSY}. The remaining biomass of lobsters will grow at the maximum rate because food and space are more ample than at k.

At the *MSY* stock, the largest sustainable harvest can occur. That is, the process of catching H_2 pounds of lobster per unit of time can continue indefinitely (as long as no other exogenous changes occur), because the harvest removes exactly the amount of biomass that "grows" in that unit of time. In a very simple economic model, in particular one with no harvesting costs or discounting of future revenue from fishing, the *MSY* is the most desirable equilibrium for the fishery. This equilibrium generally is not an economic optimum, as we will see. Note finally that if the initial population were to the left of X_{MSY} initially, a harvest of H_2 would deplete the stock. If, for example, the stock were X^* when harvesting began at rate H_2, net growth would be less than the harvest. The population must then decline, because the population of X^* *cannot be sustained* at a harvest rate of H_2: The harvest exceeds the incremental growth of the biomass given by $F(X^*)$. At the next instant if H_2 is again harvested, the stock will decline further. If harvesting continues at rate H_2, the population would eventually be depleted.

A harvest set at H_3 pounds per season is an interesting case. There are two possible equilibriums for the fishery, the two points at which H_3 intersects the fishery growth function, $F(X)$, at X' and X''. Which one is likely to occur? Suppose harvesting has just begun in the lobster fishery. We are thus at point k, the habitat's carrying capacity. If the stock is initially at k and H_3 is taken at each point in time, the equilibrium point, X'', will be approached from the right. For stock sizes lying between k and X'' H_3 exceeds $F(X) = 0$ at k, and the population declines. That is, the harvest exceeds the net natural growth of the biomass.

But once the population reaches X'', there will be no tendency to move from this point because the natural growth rate exactly equals the harvest. The fishery will yield H_3 pounds of lobster each instant, while the stock size will remain at X''. This is another example of a *sustained yield* harvest; sustained, because H_3 can be removed at each point in time and the lobsters will remain at a population of X''. (Recall that the harvest of H_2 yielding X_{MSY} was the *maximum* sustained yield. The point X'' is simply a particular sustained yield, not the maximum.) The difference $(k - X'')$ is the reduction in the stock of lobsters from their biological equilibrium at k.

Now suppose that when harvesting begins, the stock is not at level k, but somewhere between X' and X''. What will the equilibrium be? Suppose, for example, that the stock is at the level X^*. The rate of harvest H_3 is now less than the natural growth in biomass at X^*, which is shown in Figure 4.2 as $F(X^*)$. The species will grow in size at the instant by the difference between $F(X^*)$ and H_3. At the beginning of the next instant, the additional lobsters will increase the stock from X^* to X^{**}, where $(X^{**} - X^*)$ is equal to $[F(X^*) - H_3]$. At X^{**}, the harvest rate of H_3 is again less than the biological growth, $F(X^{**})$, and again the stock will increase in size. This process continues until the equilibrium at X'' is reached. Thus any stock size that lies to the right of X' will ultimately yield an equilibrium at X''.

We call X'' a *stable* equilibrium. This means that if there is a slight movement in the stock size to the right or to the left of X'', the system will ultimately return to an equilibrium at X''. This is what we have just shown by seeing how the system behaves when the population is to the right or the left of X''. The arrows in Figure 4.2 that point toward X'' show that it is a stable equilibrium.

Suppose now that the population lies to the left of X'. This could be due, for example, to a toxic chemical spill that has wiped out much of the lobster population, or abnormally warm water temperatures that have interfered with their ability to spawn. If harvesting continues at rate H_3 per year, we can see that the species will be extinguished. The natural growth rate to the left of X' lies everywhere below H_3. Each period, fewer and fewer new lobsters enter the population because existing ones are captured before they get a chance to reproduce. Eventually all lobsters will be caught, and the fishery will cease to function.

Finally, what would happen at point X'? If the stock just happens to be X', given the rate of harvest H_3, this will be an equilibrium, but one which is *unstable* because a slight movement of the stock to the right or to the left of level X' will lead to a new equilibrium. If there is a slight increase in the stock, the equilibrium will eventually reach X''. If there is a slight decrease in the stock, the equilibrium will eventually fall to zero. To illustrate that X' is unstable, the arrows are directed away from it in Figure 4.2.

We can summarize the effects that harvesting has on the fish population over time in the following equation:

$$dX/dt = F(X) - H(t) \tag{4.3}$$

Equation (4.3) says that the change in the fish stock over a small interval of time will be given by the difference between the biological growth function and the amount of harvesting in that time interval. This equation can be solved for an equilibrium in which the fish stock does not change—that is, its growth rate to the rate of harvest. This is called a *steady-state bionomic equilibrium*. If we are given a harvest rate, say H_2 from Figure 4.2, the steady-state equilibrium will occur where $F(X)$ is equal to H_2. Thus, dX/dt will equal zero. Only when the growth of the stock is exactly equal to the harvest will there be no change in the size of the stock over time. In Figure 4.2, we saw that H_2 intersected $F(X)$ at the population level X_{MSY}. This is the steady-state maximum sustainable yield, a bionomic equilibrium.

Harvesting under Open Access

In the discussion above we arbitrarily picked three harvest rates to illustrate the principle of a steady-state equilibrium in the fishery when economic and biological factors interact. Each equilibrium derived above is a bionomic equilibrium. No assumption was made about the economic nature of the fishing industry or about how the harvest rate was chosen. Now we will derive the bionomic equilibrium when there is *open access* to the fishery, and then contrast the open access equilibrium with a socially optimal equilibrium. We continue to assume no discounting of the value of future harvests.

We first define a *harvest function* for the industry. We assume that the industry is perfectly competitive and each firm in the industry takes all prices, including factor prices, as given and constant over time. These assumptions mean that the demand curve for fish facing each firm is perfectly elastic, as is the supply curve of factor inputs. These simplifying assumptions can be modified readily, and we will modify them in later sections.

As before, let $H(t)$ indicate the level of harvest at time t. This is the output of an aggregate production function which we will call a harvest function. We assume that $H(t)$ depends on two inputs: $E(t)$ and $X(t)$. Mathematically,

$$H(t) = G[E(t), X(t)] \tag{4.4}$$

E is a variable known as *fishing effort.* Effort can be thought of as some combination of the familiar inputs in economics—capital, labor, materials, and energy. These inputs are combined to yield an aggregate measure of effort—for example, person-hours per trawler over 50 feet in length, or seiner nets per person per trawler. In other words, effort is an *index* of factor inputs. Continuing our example of the lobster fishery, here industry effort will be measured by the total number of lobster traps set.

The other factor input in the production function is the stock of fish at time t, $X(t)$. The harvest function is dependent on the stock of fish for the obvious reason that no fish can be caught if none exist, and that more fish will be caught with a given level of effort, the larger the stock in the region.

We can look at the interacton between E and X graphically in two ways. Again, we suppress the dependency of the variables on time. First, we can consider how the harvest changes when more effort is added to a fixed stock of fish. Then we can see how the harvest changes when we increase the stock of fish, keeping effort constant. Figure 4.3 shows a simple example. Suppose the stock of fish equals X. The harvest function is the curve $H = G(E, X)$. As more lobster traps are added to this fixed stock, the harvest will rise, but at an ever-decreasing rate. This is the well-known principle in economics of the *diminishing marginal product* of the variable factor (effort in this case) that is combined with a fixed factor (the stock of fish). The fixed stock of fish should be interpreted as a steady-state fish population discussed in the previous section—that is, one that can be sustained indefinitely at a particular level.

Now suppose the stock of fish is higher than X, say X'. At the higher stock, there will be a greater harvest for each unit of effort utilized.[4] This is shown in Figure 4.3 by the curve $H' = G(E, X')$. For a given level of effort, say E_0, H fish will be caught when the stock is X, and H' will be caught if the stock is X'. The marginal product of effort thus slopes downward given a particular fish stock, with slightly more effort resulting in proportionately smaller harvests. This concept will be useful in defining the equilibrium reached under open access to the fishery, and we will come back to it below.

Let us now see how a fixed level of effort combined with different stocks of fish affects the harvest. We can now determine the steady-state bionomic equilibrium. Figure 4.4 illustrates some possible cases. Suppose we take a given level of effort, E. The harvest will then be an increasing function of the fish stock. We assume for sim-

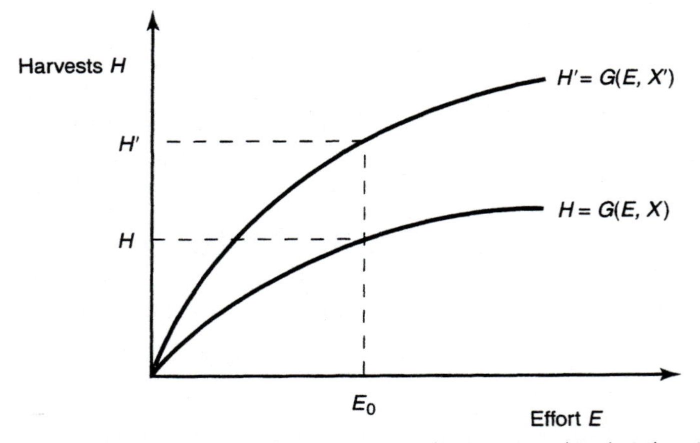

FIGURE 4.3. Two harvest functions for the fishery are shown, assuming that the stock of fish is held constant. The biomass caught depends on the amount of effort E and the fish stock X. If the stock of fish is assumed first to be X, the curve H shows the possible harvests as E increases. If we then have a larger fish stock X', the harvests as E rises are shown by H', which lies above H. This means that for a particular amount of effort, say E_0, the larger the stock available, the more fish can be caught.

plicity that this harvest function is linear. A particular amount of fishing effort will yield a larger harvest the larger the population of fish. The steady-state equilibrium will be, as before, where there is no change in the fish population, $dX/dt = 0$. This requires that $F(X) = H(t)$. Graphically, the equilibrium is defined where the harvest function, H, intersects the $F(X)$ function. The steady-state equilibrium is at a stock

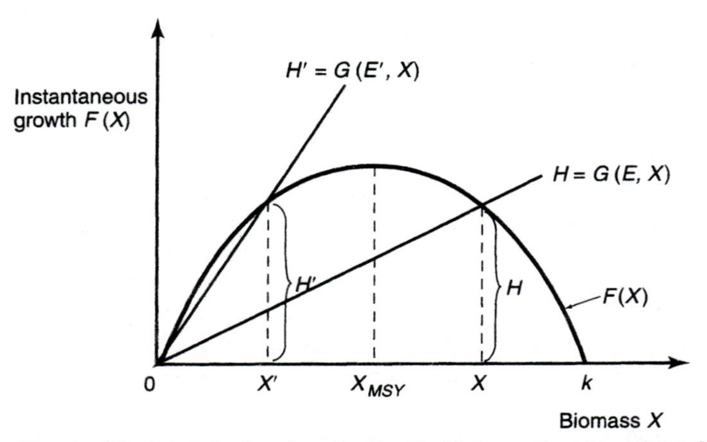

FIGURE 4.4. Steady-state harvests for given levels of effort as a function of the fish stock are shown. If effort is increased from E to E', the steady-state population falls from X to X', but the catch stays the same (H equals H'). Effort levels that give rise to a harvest function intersecting the biological production function to the left of X_{MSY} are inefficient in this model because the same harvest can be obtained with much less effort.

level of X, which yields a harvest of H. So far, the results are quite similar to those above. But now see what happens when we increase the amount of effort, say, by increasing the number of lobster traps set from E to E'.

The increase in the number of traps set causes the harvest function H to pivot upward to H'. Now the new harvest function intersects the biological growth function at a fish stock of X', which yields a steady-state harvest *exactly the same* as the harvest with only E traps. However, the fish stock, X', is *much lower* than the stock X. These results reflect the interaction of biological mechanics and economics. We will explain first intuitively and then more formally what is happening in this case.

Suppose the fishery starts in a biological equilibrium at k. There is no harvesting. Now some fishing firms enter, and traps are set. (We will discuss what determines entry of fishing firms more formally below). We are at a point such as X with harvests at H. Now more firms enter, and more traps are set. The harvest function pivots upward, and for a while more effort yields greater harvests. But notice that these increased harvests will decrease the stock of fish. Because of the shape of the biological function, harvests will increase until the steady-state equilibrium is where the stock of fish is at its maximum sustainable yield (imagine the intersection of a harvest curve at the top of the $F(X)$ function). Further increases in effort will pivot the harvest function until its intersection with the biological growth function is *to the left* of the MSY. The catch thereafter declines. As more fish are caught, the stock size falls, and it becomes more difficult to catch those remaining. The catch per unit of effort thus falls, and the total catch may decline for an effort level greater than E'.

Another way to look at the results is that if the stock size were larger, less effort would be required to catch the same number of fish (compare E with E'). *In a static model, it is clearly inefficient from an economic viewpoint for a fishing industry to operate to the left of the MSY stock level because more effort than necessary is used to catch a given amount of fish.*[5] The important question is whether an equilibrium would exist in this model to the left of the MSY biomass. We will see under what circumstances such an equilibrium would occur when there is open access to the fishery.

Suppose lobsters are an open access resource: No one has exclusive rights to harvest a particular quantity of lobsters or owns a stock of lobsters thought to reside on a particular section of the ocean bed. Anyone with a boat and lobster traps can attempt to capture lobsters. First, let's define the total revenues and total costs for the industry, and then see what determines industry equilibrium.

Suppose the unit cost of harveting lobsters is constant. It costs c dollars per unit of effort, where as before we measure effort by the number of traps set. In Figure 4.5, total costs are shown by the curve TC, which is linear with slope c (ignore for now the total cost curve TC'). Total revenues are given by the price of lobsters per pound times the number of pounds harvested *(PH)*. Let the price per pound be constant, and set equal to 1. This normalization of the price allows us to determine the steady-state harvest and stock of lobsters in an open access equilibrium as well as the equilibrium level of effort. Total revenue *(TR)* will simply be the harvest determined by equation (4.4).

Refer back to Figure 4.4. Suppose that we start at a biomass of $X = k$, with zero pounds of lobster harvested. As effort is introduced, the stock of lobsters falls.

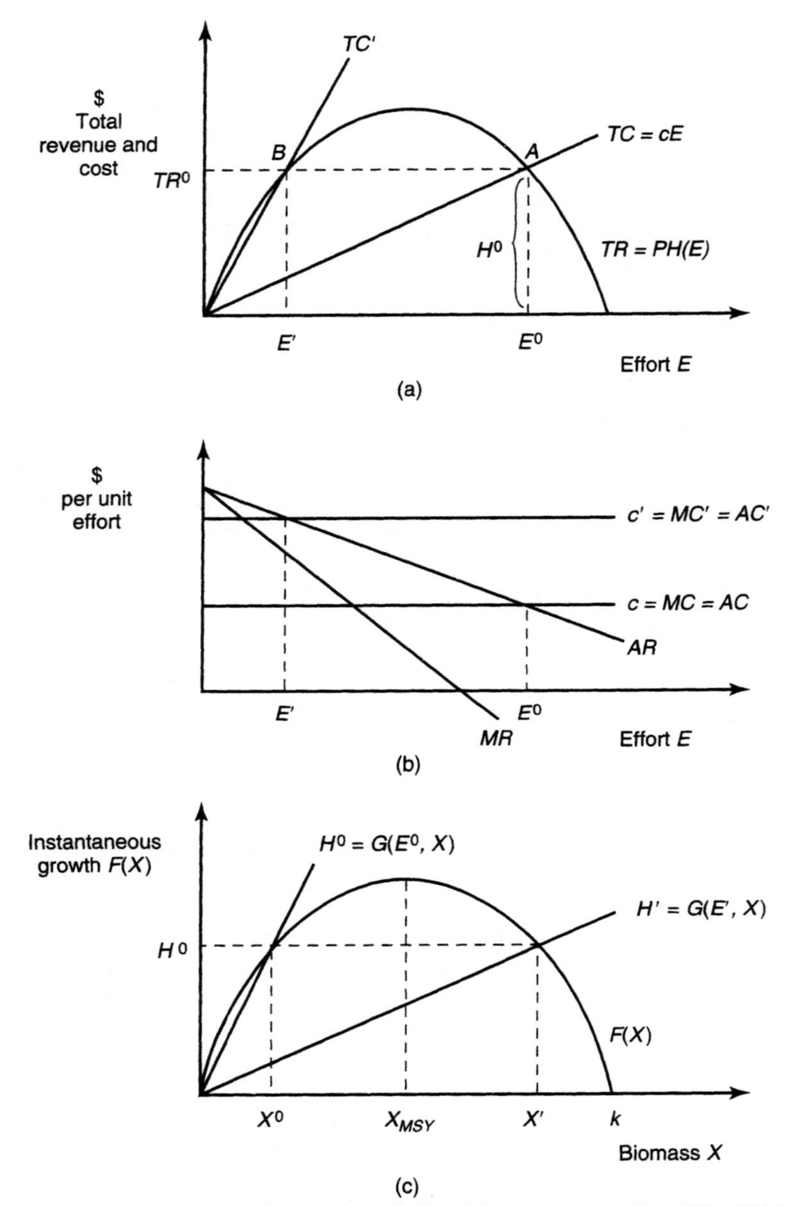

FIGURE 4.5. An open access equilibrium for a fishing industry occurs where $TR = TC$. Note in (a) and (b) that all curves are functions of effort (not harvest). If unit costs equal c, the equilibrium is at point A in (a). E^0 units of effort will be used, yielding a total revenue of TR^0. If the price of lobsters is normalized to 1, the total revenue is also the total harvest. Part (b) illustrates that the open access equilibrium is where the average revenues (as a function of effort) equal the marginal costs of effort and thus that marginal cost of effort exceeds marginal revenue. Part (c) illustrates the steady-state harvest in an open access equilibrium, H^0, that results in a steady-state stock or biomass of X^0. If unit costs rise to c', the open access equilibrium is at a point B in (a), with E' effort. This new equilibrium also yields a steady-state harvest of H^0, but with less total effort than when average costs $= c$. The sustained stock (c) is then X'. An open access equilibrium is economically inefficient because $MC > MR$. It can also be biologically inefficient if the equilibrium is to the left of the MSY stock.

Harvests at first rise as the industry moves up the biological production function. They reach a maximum, then fall again. The total revenue curve with $P = 1$ is thus *exactly the same* as the biological production function, $F(X)$. This means that once we know the equilibrium level of total revenue, we know the equilibrium harvests. Given the harvest, we can determine the steady-state stock that sustains these harvests.

The open access equilibrium for the lobster industry will be determined where total revenues equal total costs. For which stock is this so? Consider a level of effort such as E' in Figure 4.5(a). At E', total revenues exceed total costs, and excess profits or rents exist. Because there are no barriers to entry—no one in the fishery can exclude another from setting traps—firms will enter the fishery. Effort will rise. Entry will continue as long as total revenues exceed total costs and rents exist. When $TR = TC$ at point A in Figure 4.5(a), rents to the fishery equal zero, and economically rational firms will expend no effort beyond this point. No new effort will come into the fishery. The open access equilibrium for the fishery will employ E^0 units of effort.[6]

Another way to look at the open access equilibrium is shown in Figure 4.5(b). Here, we derive the industry's average revenue *(AR)* and marginal revenue *(MR)* curves as a function of effort from total revenues (AR is TR/E, while MR is dTR/dE). As explained before, both AR and MR are negatively sloped, with AR lying above MR. The open access fishery will be in equilibrium when AR equal MC. This is because each unit of effort earns on average what every other unit earns when there is no way to prevent entry into the fishery. With constant unit costs, MC simply equals c (and is thus also equal to AC). Notice that at the equilibrium level of effort, E^0, MR is less than MC and is negative. In the open access equilibrium, MR will always be less than MC and may be negative.

What is the open access harvest? With our assumption that $P = 1$, we can see in Figure 4.5(a) that harvests are given by TR^0, which equals a harvest of H^0. We now look at Figure 4.5(c), which illustrates sustained harvests at different stocks of lobsters. Measuring H^0 vertically, we find that H^0 in biomass can be taken at each unit of time at two different stock levels, X^0 and X'. Because the open access level of effort, E^0, lies to the *right* of the maximum sustainable total revenues, we know that the harvest function in Figure 4.5(c) must be to the *left* of the maximum sustainable yield in terms of biomass. Our harvest function is thus H^0. We see that more effort than is necessary is being used to harvest a biomass of H^0.

The same harvest could be achieved with E' units of effort. But as long as total costs equal TC, E^0 will be used leading to a harvest function such as $H^0 = G(E^0, X)$ in Figure 4.5(c). To achieve a steady-state harvest of H^0 with a lower level of effort, total costs would have to be TC' in Figure 4.5(a). Unit costs would then be c', which as shown in Figure 4.5(b), exceed c. The open access equilibrium would then be at point B, and E' traps would be set. Notice that TR and hence harvests are *exactly the same* at point B as at point A. Because unit costs c' exceed c, less total effort will be used in the industry. The open access equilibrium thus lies to the left of the maximum sustainable revenue. In Figure 4.5(b), AR now equals c'. And in Figure 4.5(c), we find that H' is the new harvest function which yields the same steady-state harvest as was the case with E^0 effort, but at a larger sustainable stock of lobsters, X'. What Figure 4.5 illustrates is that two levels of effort yield the same harvest. The level of effort chosen under open access depends on where $TC = TR$. For TC curves different from those shown in Figure 4.5(a), the harvest will of course change.

The open access equilibrium can also be defined in terms of average and marginal costs of harvest. This is quite simple. We know the *OAE* (open access equilibrium) is where $TR = TC$. Given our assumptions, the equilibrium condition can be written as $PH = cE$. Dividing by H, we see that $P = cE/H$—that is, price equals the average cost of the harvest. Firms will enter the fishery under open access as long as price exceeds average cost.

To summarize, two points can be made about the open access equilibrium in the fishery. First, the open access equilibrium occurs where $TR = TC$, which implies that AR = AC of effort. Thus MR is less than MC of effort. Second, an open access equilibrium may be both economically and bioeconomically inefficient. It is *economically inefficient* because efficiency requires that $MR = MC$, but we have just shown that $MR < MC$. *Bioeconomic inefficiency* can be interpreted as any equilibrium that is to the left of the maximum sustainable yield in terms of biomass (or to the right of the maximum sustainable total revenues). If an equilibrium occurs to the left of the MSY biomass, it indicates that the same harvest could be taken at a higher sustained biomass.

In terms of our example, if unit costs of effort are c, bioeconomic inefficiency will occur because the open access equilibrium lies to the left of the MSY biomass. If unit costs are c', the open access equilibrium is not bioeconomically inefficient. But all open access equilibria are economically inefficient. Let us also repeat: The equilibria described here are all steady-state in that they can be repeated indefinitely. When $F(X) = H$, additions to biomass are removed by harvests. But they are also static. Future revenues are not discounted, and we have not discussed the time paths of adjustment to equilibrium.

Socially Optimal Harvests Under Private Property Rights

One should suspect by now that the pursuit of private interests in the fishery will not yield a socially optimal allocation of resources. The reason is the lack of private property rights in the fishery. Because no agent has the *exclusive right* to the resource (or a portion thereof), a market failure exists. To examine the nature of the market failure, let us look more closely at the open access industry equilibrium derived above.

Our discussion thus far has focused on the behavior of an open access industry. In contrasting the open access equilibrium with the social optimum, we want first to look at the behavior of each firm in the industry. Given the assumption of constant costs of effort, we cannot predict the number of firms. If costs curves were U-shaped, a unique equilibrium could be defined, but there are problems associated with whether an equilibrium exists with U-shaped cost curves. There is, however, an important implication of the open access equilibrium for the fishing firm.

Under open access to the fishery, each firm receives the *average product* of the industry's total effort. That is, the catch per lobster trap is determined by the total harvest divided by the total number of traps set. A firm does not capture the marginal product of its effort; rather, it harvests the industry average product, which must lie above marginal product. But by harvesting the average product, each firm imposes *external costs* on every other firm. We can show this algebraically. Each firm treats the

BOX 4.3 Australian Abalone Millionaires

The creation of private property rights to harvest abalone off the shores of Tasmania has created a new group of millionaires. Abalone are harvested by scuba divers using only a sharp knife to pry the shellfish loose from the rocks they cling to. It is dangerous work: great white sharks frequent the waters looking for dinner, and divers also risk serious health problems created by working underwater for long periods of time. Until the beginning of the 1980s, the abalone fishery was open access. The stocks of abalone were quite high to begin with, and millions of dollars were made by the divers working in the area. By the early 1980s, stocks of abalone began to decline and the divers, worried about losing their livelihood, got together with the fisheries department to work out a solution.

The solution was the creation of individual licenses that gave the holder the right to harvest up to 28 units of abalone per year. A full license is 2.8 units, which can be divided and sold off as individual units, with each unit equivalent to 600 kilograms of abalone. There is an aggregate quota of 16.8 tonnes per year, which is thought to be sustainable. The units can be sold to anyone, but only a licensed diver can do the harvesting. The regulations also limited the total number of divers to 125. An annual fee for each licensed diver is collected by the Tasmanian state government. The regulations thus clearly limited effort in the fishery. Given the very simple technology, licensing people means controlling effort. The current market price for each unit of the license (i.e., the right to catch 600 kilograms of abalone) is around $100,000. The current price for a diving license is about $3 million (Australian dollars, or over $2 million U.S.). The Tasmanian government estimates that about 350 people currently hold rights to harvest abalone. The total annual value of the fishery is around $63 million (U.S.). A typical gross income for divers holding 28 units of a license is $420,000 (U.S.) per year, earned over 45 days, working 4.5 hours per day. Profitability in the fishery has increased about 400 percent in the last few years. The creation of private property rights with no new entry to the fishery has thus created substantial rents.

Is eveyone happy with this arrangement? The state government of Tasmania thinks that the public should share more in the rents created by the private property rights because the abalone are harvested in public waters. The government increased the annual fees for licensed divers from $20,000 to over $125,000 (Australian) at the end of 1993. It is also trying to introduce a system of 10-year contracts and a tax based on the market price of abalone. In early 1994, abalone prices were around $80 per kilogram, but they do fluctuate. The proposed changes have dampened the market price for licenses a bit and have meant that divers stay home when the price of abalone is relatively low. But this fishery, operating with private property rights, looks very different from those with open access. Even with the redistribution of the rents, the divers are still millionaires!

Source: "Australia's Larrikin Millionaires," *Sydney Morning Herald* (February 12, 1994), p. 7A.

stock X as exogenous when actually the action of firm, i, leads to a lower equilibrium stock *and* slightly higher harvest costs for every boat. This occurs because harvesting H pounds with a higher stock requires less effort than with a lower stock. From Figures 4.5 through 4.7, we know that the total harvest from the fishery will be equal to the average product of effort times the amount of effort used (with $P = 1$, average revenue equals average product). We write this relationship in equation (4.5):

$$H = AP_E \cdot E \tag{4.5}$$

Consider what would happen to the harvest with a marginal increase in effort—one firm sets an additional lobster trap. If we differentiate Equation (4.5) with respect to E (the marginal change), we find that

$$dH/dE = AP_E + E(dAP_E/dE) \tag{4.6}$$

The term dH/dE can be interpreted as the marginal product of effort (in the long run). Thus, equation (4.6) says that the marginal product of effort equals the average product of effort plus the term $E(dAP_E/dE)$. This latter term shows the change in the harvest per unit of effort due to the use of an additional unit of effort. It is negative because an increase in effort reduces the sustainable fish stock, X. The lower the stock (or biomass), the lower the catch per unit effort. All firms in the industry are then affected by the marginal change in effort.

But because the effect *per firm* is relatively small, each firm ignores the term $E(dAP_E/dE)$. Each firm perceives the marginal product of its effort to equal the average product before that increment in effort was added. The firm ignores the effect an increase in the number of traps has on the stock of fish and hence on the harvests of other firms. The term $E(dAP_E/dE)$ therefore reflects an externality we call the *stock effect*. In other words, for each increment in effort, firms actually receive the industry average product of effort *minus* the stock effect. But because the stock effect is felt by all firms, no single firm takes it into account when deciding how much effort to use. All firms act symmetrically. The industry equilibrium is where the value of the average product of effort equals marginal cost, not where the value of the marginal product of effort equals marginal cost. Marginal and average product differ by the amount of the stock effect. The stock effect is ignored in the steady-state open access equilibrium, and this is economically inefficient.

Another externality arises in our steady-stage model under open access in addition to the stock effect: congestion. In our simple model, harvesting costs per unit of effort were assumed to be fixed. What is more realistic is the general model where harvesting costs depend on the amount of total effort in the fishery and the stock of fish. For each additional unit of effort employed, harvesting costs generally rise because of congestion. Vessels have to line up in the fishing grounds. There can be conflicts among vessels with regard to equipment. Trawlers can tear the buoys off lobster traps or pots. Nets of different vessels can become entangled. In some instances, though, congestion can reduce costs. If fishers cooperate and radio each other when stocks are found, costs will decline. All congestion costs will be ignored in the open acess fishery. Under private property, they will not.

What is the socially optimal equilibrium for our model? Suppose the lobster grounds could be divided up so that each firm in the industry had the exclusive right to trap lobsters in a particular region. If there were a large number of firms, each with a private property right such that the industry behaved competitively (took all prices and factor costs as given), and no other imperfections of externalities existed, the assignment of private property rights to the lobster grounds would guarantee a social optimum.[7] We continue to assume that the discount rate is zero. A firm possessing private property rights will choose the level of effort that maximizes its long-run sustainable profits.

The profit-maximizing level of effort is where *marginal* revenue equals *marginal* cost; the difference between total revenue and total cost is at a maximum. If, for example, one firm "owns" the lobster fishing grounds, there can be no entry to those grounds without the firm's consent. The firm will then limit the number of traps set to that which maximizes its profits. The efficient amount of effort is E^*, shown in Figure 4.6(a) and (b), where $MR = MC$. The sole owner would choose E^* traps to maximize the rents from the fishery, where rents are the difference between total revenue and total costs. The fishery itself is now a factor of production that earns a return—rent.

We can compare the private property equilibrium (PPE) with the open access equilibrium (*OEA*) described in the previous section, maintaining all our previous assumptions (constant unit costs, $P = 1$, and PPE is competitive). In Figure 4.6, the *OAE* uses E^0 effort (setting $TR = TC$ or $AR = MC$). It is thus clear that with the *OAE*, more effort will be used than with a PPE, given the same cost and revenue curves: E^0 exceeds E^*. Given unit costs c, it also turns out in this case that the harvest under private property exceeds that of open access (H^* versus H^0). This need not be the case, of course.

With different *TC* curves, the optimal harvest could be greater or less than the open access harvest. The relationship between the private property and open access harvests depends on the location of the total cost curve. The lower the unit costs of effort, the more likely that the private property harvest exceeds the open access harvest. This is because low unit costs of effort will encourage entry into the open access fishery. If total costs equal total revenues to the right of the maximum harvest, as effort increases, harvest levels must decline. We can see from Figure 4.6(c) that the open access harvest is indeed biologically inefficient, while the private property harvest is not, given the same total cost curve for each ownership regime. The sustained stock under private property is X^*, which exceeds the open access stock, X^0. There is no stock externality under private property, because the sole owner fully incorporates the effect each increment in effort has on the biomass and hence the harvest. Under private property, the value of the marginal product of effort is set equal to the marginal cost of effort, where the *MP* includes the stock externality.[8]

Industry Supply Curve for Open Access and Private Property Fisheries

We can now use the model developed above to derive an industry supply curve for first the open access, then the private fishery.[9] The supply curves will be derived graphically. We then derive the supply curve algebraically. We want to know what will happen to the steady-state lobster harvests at different prices of lobster. In Figure 4.7(a), three total revenue functions are shown: TR_0 is derived assuming the price of lobsters is \$0.50 per pound; TR_1 assumes the price is \$1 per pound (as in Figure 4.5); and at TR_2 the price is \$2. We again assume that unit costs of effort are constant and equal to c and total costs given by the curve *TC*. The open access equilibrium can then be derived for each different price of lobster.

When the price is \$0.50 per pound, the open access equilibrium is at point *A* in

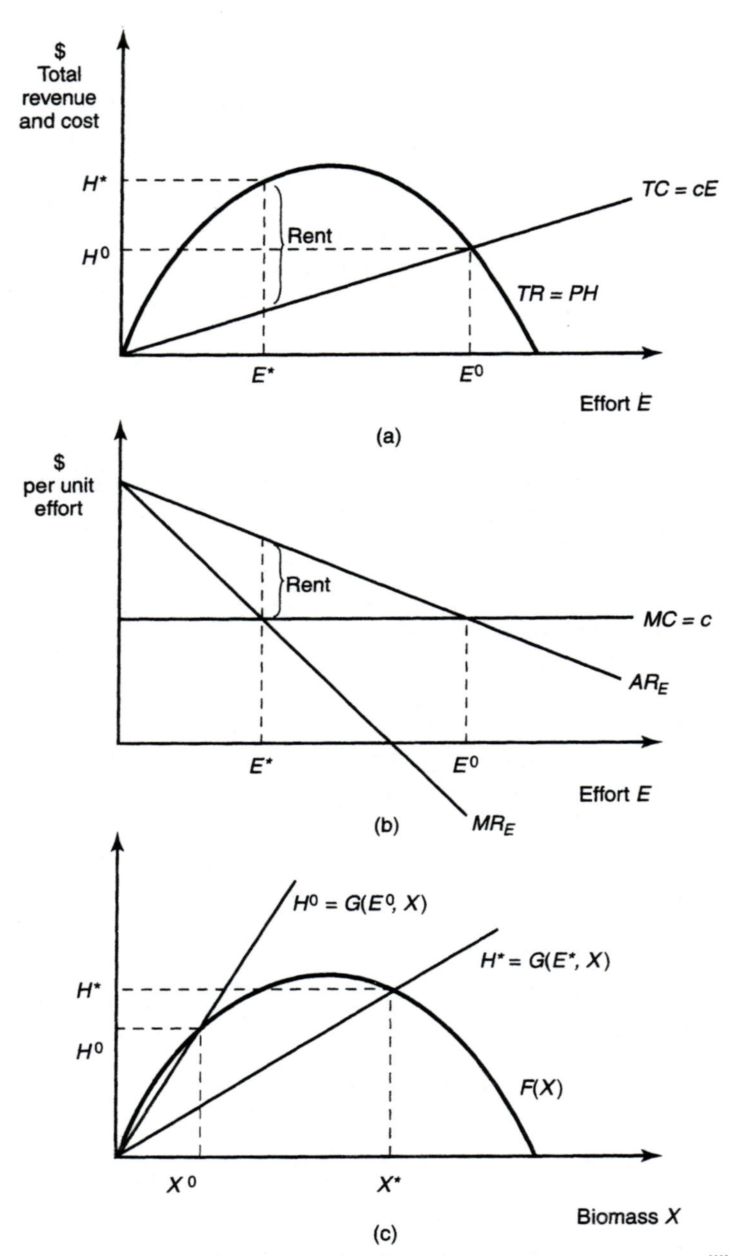

FIGURE 4.6. A private property equilibrium is compared with the open access equilibrium. If the fishery is managed by a sole owner, profits will be maximized where $MR = MC$. The private property equilibrium uses effort E^*, which is less than the open access effort of E^0. Given the total cost curve shown in panel (a), $MC = MR$ at a harvest level that exceeds the open access harvest. The two harvests are shown as H^* and H^0. Rent is maximized under the private property equilibrium and dissipated under the open access equlibrium. Total rent is shown in panel (a); rent per unit effort is illustrated in panel (b). The private property equilibrium is both economically and biologically efficient; the open access equilibrium is economically inefficient and may be biologically inefficient as well. In panel (c), the open access equilibrium is biologically inefficient because the sustainable biomass X^0 is to the left of the *MSY* biomass.

BOX 4.4 Lobsters

Can we use the simple model derived in this section to analyze a particular fishery? Bell (1972), using the Schaefer model presented in the text, has examined the New England lobster fishery. He estimated a harvest function for the open access fishery—the average product of effort as a function of parameters reflecting environmental carrying capacity of the fishery, a "catchability coefficient" which shows for each unit of E how much sustainable yield of biomass will be harvested, effort, and water temperature (an exogenous variable affecting lobster biomass). Bell found, using time series data from 1950 to 1966, that

$$\left(\frac{H}{E}\right)_t = -48.4 - 0.000024E_t + 2.13°F$$

$$(-1.43) \qquad (-3.37) \qquad (2.58)$$

$$R^2 = .96 \qquad D.W. = 2.05$$

where H is the annual landings of northern lobster, E the annual number of traps fished, °F the mean annual seawater temperature, Boothbay Harbor, Maine. The t statistics are given in the parentheses.

To use this average product of effort relationship to derive both the open access and private property equilibrium for the fishery, the average product equation is solved or normalized for a particular water temperature. Bell chose the temperature in 1966, as it was close to the average temperature for the past 65 years to 1966. Inserting this temperature (46°F) and multiplying by E, we find that

$$H_t = 49.4E_t - 0.000024E_t^2$$

This harvest function can then be used to solve for the open access and private property equilibriums. Assuming the industry's total cost curve is a linear function of effort, Bell calculated the average costs of effort for 1966 at $21.43 per trap (where effort includes measures of capital and labor used per trap). Bell assumes that demand for lobster is perfectly elastic at the 1966 price per pound of $0.762.

Given this information, we can now solve for the open access equilibrium. (Bell derives long-run marginal and average costs as functions of the harvest and solves for an *OAE* where $P = AC$, and for a *PPE* where $P = MC$. This is equivalent to our solution in terms of effort.) We know that the *OAE* for the industry is where $TR = TC$ of effort or the $AR = MC$ of effort. Substituting for all values, we find that

$$.762(49.4 - 0.000024E_t) = 21.43$$

and $E_t = 891{,}000$ traps in the open access equilibrium

Substituting this effort level, we find a harvest of about 25 million pounds of lobster. The actual number of traps set and the harvest in 1966 was 947,000 and 25.6 million pounds. The theoretical model thus fits reasonably well the observations in the fishery. It would seem that the lobster fishery off New England was approximately near an open access equilibrium.

What does the model predict the private property equilibrium would yield? To have a private property equilibrium, marginal revenue (as a function of effort) must equal the marginal cost of effort. Solving for the *PPE* using Bell's numbers, we find that the number of traps set would be 443,000, with a steady-state harvest of 17.2 million pounds. The open access equilibrium in 1966 thus used more than twice the number of traps than is efficient. Was the *OAE* biologically inefficient as well? No. Bell finds that both the *OAE* and *PPE* are to the left of the maximum sustainable total yield (the right of the *MSY* biomass). The *MSY* harvest is 25.5 million pounds with about 1 million traps set.

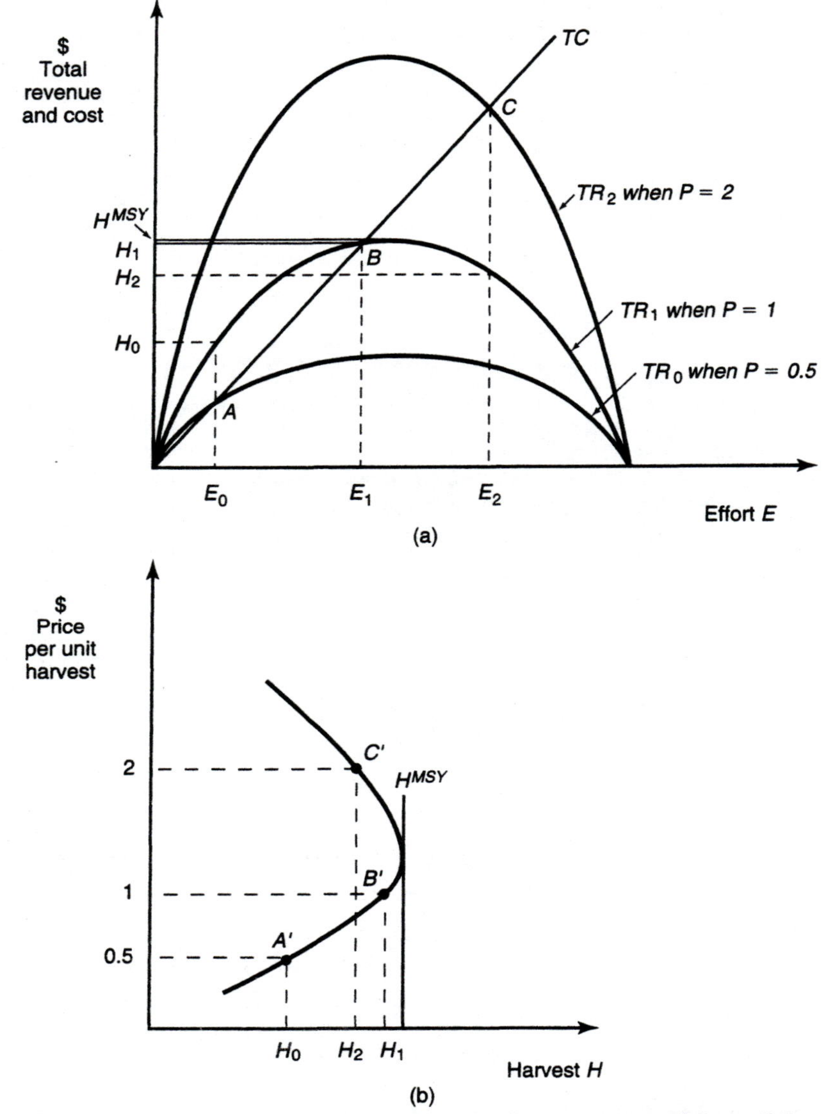

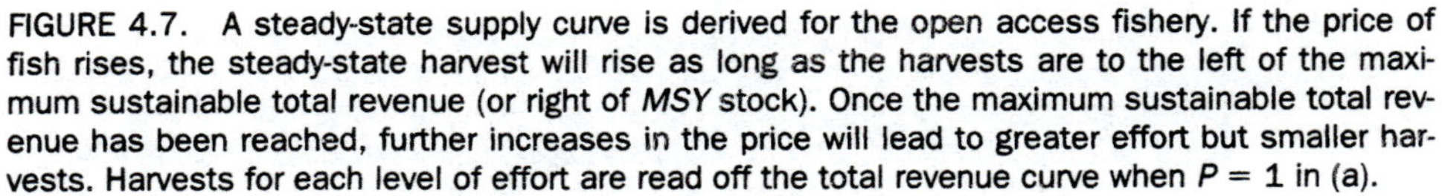

FIGURE 4.7. A steady-state supply curve is derived for the open access fishery. If the price of fish rises, the steady-state harvest will rise as long as the harvests are to the left of the maximum sustainable total revenue (or right of *MSY* stock). Once the maximum sustainable total revenue has been reached, further increases in the price will lead to greater effort but smaller harvests. Harvests for each level of effort are read off the total revenue curve when $P = 1$ in (a).

Figure 4.7(a), where E_0 traps are used. The open access harvest for E_0 traps is read off the TR_1 curve. Recall that when $P = 1$, TR also defines harvests uniquely. Therefore H_0 pounds of lobster will be harvested when the price per pound is \$0.50. In Figure 4.7(b), the industry supply curve is derived. The point A' corresponds to the open access harvest of H_0 at $P = \$0.50$. Similarly, when the lobster price is \$1 per pound, point B in Figure 4.7(a) is the open access equilibrium, E_1 effort will be used, and the harvest is H_1. In Figure 4.7(b), B' is the point on the supply curve representing this harvest at a price of \$1 per pound. Notice that the supply curve is positively sloped, as is the usual case over the range from A' to B'.

However, see what happens when price of lobster doubles yet again, to \$2 per pound. The open access equilibrium is at point C in Figure 4.7(a), with E_2 traps and a harvest of H_2. The corresponding point on the supply curve is C'. Notice now that the open access harvest of H_2 is *less than* that of H_1. The supply curve for lobsters harvested under open access is therefore *backward-bending*.

Can we determine where the supply curve begins to have a negative rather than a positive slope? The supply curve will bend backward for all harvests to the right of the maximum sustainable revenue (the left of the MSY biomass). This follows from the nature of the bionomic equilibrium. Once the MSY revenue is passed, moving toward the right from $TR = 0$, harvests fall as effort rises. Effort will rise when the fish price rises. So at high fish prices, it is most likely that the industry will be on the backward-bending portion of its supply curve.

We can now examine equilibria in the market for lobsters. Suppose our lobster market is in equilibrium where demand equals D_0 and supply equals S_0, as shown in Figure 4.8. The equilibrium price will be P_0 and the quantity sold H_0. Now suppose demand shifts to the right to D_1 because the incomes of consumers have risen. People now substitute lobster for chicken. The new equilibrium is at P_1 and H_1. Both price and consumption have risen. If incomes rise yet again and demand shifts to D_2, the market equilibrium will now occur to the left of the MSY harvest in Figure 4.8. The price of lobster will continue to rise, but the quantity harvested and hence sold falls. It is possible that the demand curve could continue to shift upward and to the right. Lobster harvests would continue to fall while the price rose, and the stock could be depleted to very low levels. But extinction is unlikely, because lobsters are by no means an essential good.

The industry supply curve for a fishery that has been allocated private property rights is derived analogously to that for the open access fishery. But as we will see, the shape of the supply curve is quite different, as are the possible market equilibria. We have previously assumed that the fishery is managed by a sole owner. To have a competitive market for the fish species, we must therefore also assume that many fisheries exist for the species, each with a sole owner. Alternatively, we can assume that there is one fishery, but private property rights have been distributed so that each fisher can exclude others from his or her fishing grounds, and there are no problems with enforcement. How ownership rights to fisheries might be allocated is discussed in Chapter 5. For a discussion in more depth of the nature and allocation of property rights to fisheries, see Scott, "Conceptual Origins of Rights Based Fishing" in Neher et al. (1989).

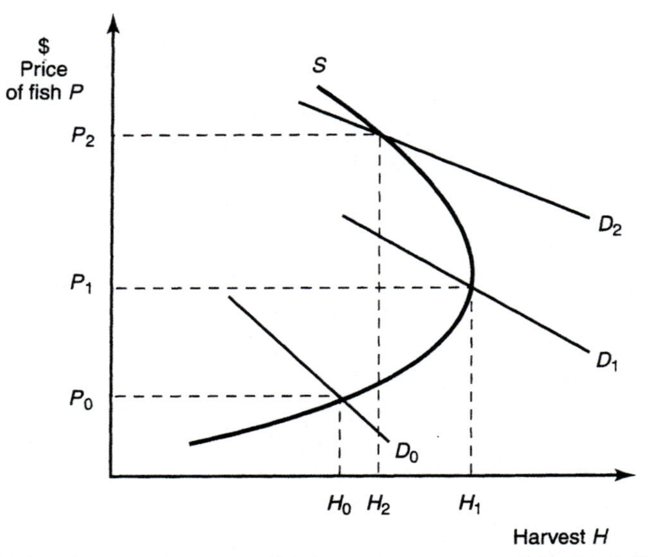

FIGURE 4.8. Equilibrium in a fish market with an open access supply curve. If demand shifts from D_0 to D_1, both harvests and the price of fish rises. But for shifts in demand beyond D_1, no further increase in harvest is possible. Therefore the price of fish will rise, but the catch will decline.

Figure 4.9 illustrates the derivation of the private property supply curve. Panel (a) shows the three total revenue curves for the fishery when the market price is \$0.50, \$1, and \$2 per pound. We assume that total costs are identical to those in the open access fishery. With a price of \$0.50 per pound, the private property equilibrium is at point A, with a harvest of H_0 and E_0 units of effort. In panel (b), the combination of the price of \$0.50 and H_0 is shown as point A' on the supply curve. Similar derivations for prices of \$1 and \$2 are shown as points B and C in panel (a) and B' and C' in panel (b). The shape of the supply curve is quite different under private property and open access. There is no backward-bending portion of the curve. The maximum harvest remains H_{MSY}, of course, but H_{MSY} is not reached: The supply curve approaches it asymptotically. The reason for this is that as long as unit costs are greater than zero, the private property equilibrium will always be to the left of the maximum sustainable harvest (experiment with different cost functions to see this for yourself). This means that the price of fish will rise continuously if demand shifts to the right, but that the amount harvested will only approach H_{MSY}. There is no backward bend of the supply curve and no risk of depleting the stock of lobsters in this steady-state model.

Table 4.4 summarizes the differences between the open access and private property ownership of the fishery in terms of the equilibrium conditions, levels of effort and harvest, and properties of efficiency. These results apply to the static model. Not all of them will carry over to the full dynamic model developed in Chapter 11.

TABLE 4.4. **OPEN ACCESS VERSUS THE PRIVATE PROPERTY EQUILIBRIUM FOR A FISHERY**

Category	Open Access Fishery	Private Property Fishery
Equilibrium condition	$TR = TC$ of effort $P = AC$ of the harvest	$MR = MC$ of effort $P = MC$ of the harvest
Economic efficiency	Inefficient, because *MR* of effort is less than *MC* of effort, and price is less than *AC* of harvest.	Efficient
Level of effort	Open access effort levels always exceed those of private property.	
Harvest	Ambiguous. Open access harvests can be greater, equal to, or less than private property harvests.	
Static economic rent	None	Maximized
Biological efficiency	Possible if effort is to the left of the *MSY* harvest.	Always, because effort cannot exceed the *MSY* harvest.

Algebra for Fishery Equilibria[10]

The open access equilibrium (*OAC*) and private property equilibrium (*PPE*) in a static model can be derived algebraically in two ways—in terms of effort and in terms of harvests. We now illustrate both approaches using the simple model presented in this chapter.

Suppose that the biological mechanics are given by

$$F(X) = aX - bX^2 \tag{4.7}$$

where a and b are parameters and X is the biomass. Equation (4.7) is thus a parabola. Let the harvest or catch be given by the steady-state harvest function

$$H = qEX \tag{4.8}$$

where q is a catchability coefficient and E is the index of effort inputs to the fishery. For simplicity, let $q = 1$.

A steady-state bionomic equilibrium requires $F(X) = H$; i.e., any increment in the stock is removed by harvest. We can therefore determine the steady-state level of effort, biomass, and harvest as:

$$\begin{aligned} E &= a - bX \\ X &= \frac{a}{b} - \frac{E}{b} \\ H &= E\left(\frac{a}{b} - \frac{E}{b}\right) \end{aligned} \tag{4.9}$$

Let $\alpha = a/b$ and $\beta = 1/b$. Then the steady state harvest is

$$H = \alpha E - \beta E^2 \tag{4.10}$$

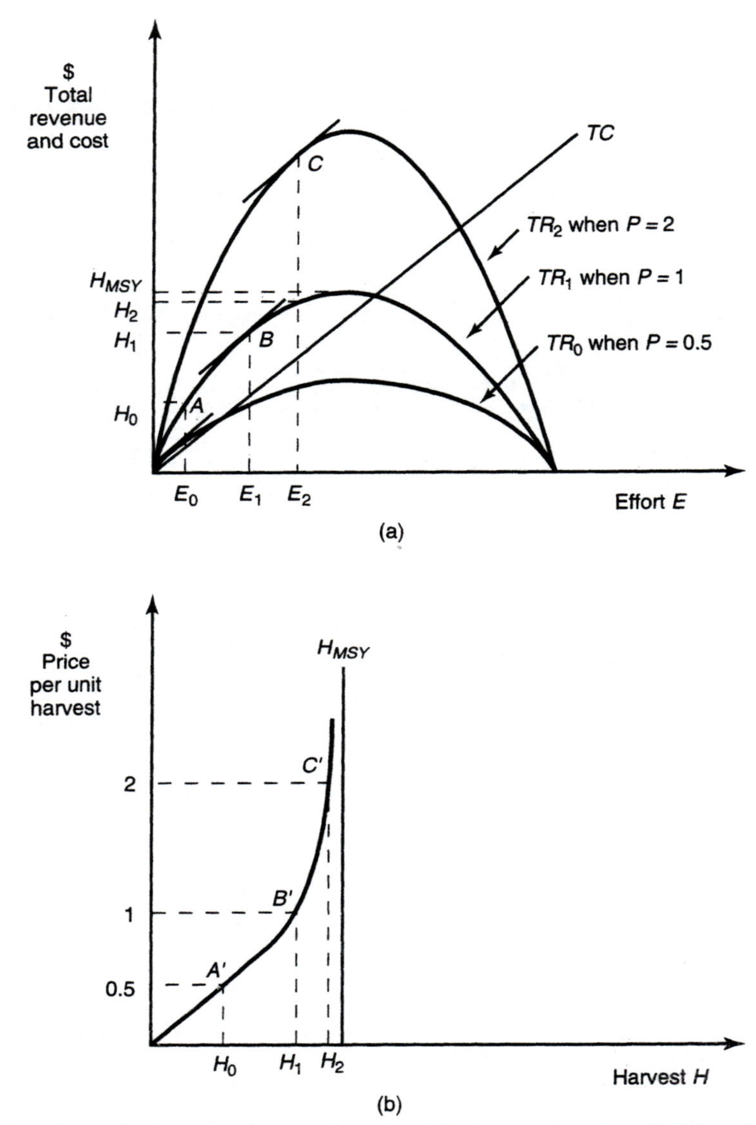

FIGURE 4.9. A steady-state supply curve is derived for the private property fishery in the same manner as the open access supply curve. As the price of fish rises, the steady-state harvest will increase. The harvest approaches the maximum sustainable yield but cannot exceed it. There is no backward bend to the supply curve.

which is again a parabola. Using equation (4.10), we can now solve for the *OAE* and *PPE*, in terms of costs and revenues first as a function of effort, then as functions of the harvest.

In the *OAE*, the industry will be in equilibrium where total revenues as a function of effort equal the total costs of effort. Assume that the price of fish is constant. Then $TR = PH$, and if $P = 1$, $TR = H$. Total costs are given by cE, assuming constant unit costs of effort $= c$. Substituting equation (4.10) for H, the *OAE* is where

$$\alpha E - \beta E^2 = cE$$

or

$$E = \frac{\alpha - c}{\beta} = a - bc \tag{4.11}$$

Equating $TR = TC$ is the same as setting average revenue per unit effort equal to the marginal cost of effort. With the assumption that $P = 1$, the open access harvest is

$$H = cE = c(\alpha - c)/\beta = ac - bc^2 \tag{4.12}$$

We can also solve for the common property harvest where the price of fish equals the average cost of the harvest, cE/H. This follows from:

$$TR = TC$$

$$PH = cE$$

$$P = cE/H$$

From equation (4.10), we can determine the cost of the harvest. Solving (4.10) for effort, we find

$$E = \pm\sqrt{-\frac{H}{\beta} + \left(\frac{\alpha}{2\beta}\right)^2} + \frac{\alpha}{2\beta} \tag{4.13}$$

Then

$$AC = \frac{2c}{\alpha \pm \sqrt{-4\beta H + \alpha^2}} \tag{4.14}$$

The *AC* curve is the backward-bending "supply" curve of the open access fishery derived graphically in the chapter. Equating *AC* to the price of fish yields the *OA* harvest.

What about the private property equilibrium (*PPE*) for the competitive firm? The *PPE* in terms of effort is determined where the marginal revenue of effort (MR_E) equals the marginal cost of effort (MC_E). The term MR_E is the change in total revenue due to a change in effort, dTR/dE; if $P = 1$, $MR_E = \alpha - 2\beta E$. Marginal cost of effort equals the change in total cost due to a change in effort, dTC/dE, which equals c. The *PPE* level of effort is then where

$$E^* = \frac{\alpha - c}{2\beta} \tag{4.15}$$

Comparing (4.15) and (4.11), we find that for this model, the *PPE* uses one-half the *OAE* level of effort. The *PPE* harvest is then $H = \frac{1}{4\beta}(\alpha^2 - c^2) = \frac{1}{4}\left(\frac{a^2}{b} - bc\right)$.

Solving the *PPE* in terms of harvests requires setting the price of fish equal to the marginal cost of the harvest, MC_H. The MC_H is found by differentiating the *TC* of the harvest with respect to *H*. Using the chain rule, $dTC/dH = dTC/dE \cdot dE/dH$, we know that $dTC/dE = c$. Then dE/dH can be found by differentiating equation (4.13) with respect to *H* (recall that (4.13) shows effort in terms of sustainable harvests). We obtain

$$MC_H = \frac{c}{\sqrt{-4\beta H + \alpha^2}} \tag{4.16}$$

This marginal cost curve is a monotonically increasing function of the sustainable harvest where marginal costs approach infinity as the sustainable harvest approaches the MSY biomass. Thus setting the price of fish equal to equation (4.16) yields the private property harvest.

Given the complex nature of the *AC* and *MC* of harvest curves, it is generally easier to derive equalibriums in the fishery in terms of effort. The cost curves in terms of the harvest are used in empirical work.

A VARIATION IN THE BIOLOGICAL BASICS: SALMON

We have focused on the classic logistic sustained-yield growth function thus far in this chapter. Clearly, there are many variations possible in the biological mechanics. Now, we discuss the case where a minimum stock size is necessary to ensure survival of the species. In this section we touch on a variation in the biological mechanics and how it can affect the optimal harvest.

Our model of the fishery developed in the preceding section is most applicable to relatively short-lived species where net growth depends on aggregate biomass rather than factors such as the age structure of the population, or exogenous environmental factors such as water temperature and currents. A number of models have been developed to analyze fisheries with different biological characteristics. The Beverton-Holt model, for example, looks at the age structure of fish population and can analyze the effect of different types of equipment (mesh size of nets) on the sustainable yield. The basic notion is that the sustainable yield relationship will change depending on the age class (or size of fish) harvested. The model applies to long-lived species such as cod and haddock, where a number of age classes are harvested simultaneously (see Beverton and Holt, 1957, and Hannesson, 1978, for more details).

In this section, we examine salmon, a species where the aggregate biomass is not a good predictor of growth over time. The number of salmon able to spawn is a better determinant of the growth of the population than biomass. In Chapter 11, we look at multiple-species fisheries and examine an interdependent species in a predator-prey relationship.

Weight or biomass has been our approximation of the stock of fish. We assumed that the net growth of the stock was dependent on the aggregate biomass. Any harvest from the stock then takes a mixture of age classes—fish of different sizes and weights. In the case of salmon, this type of population dynamics does not give a good approximation of the growth of the stock size over time. For salmon, age and the number of fish in different age classes (cohorts) is more important in determining the size of the stock over time than aggregate biomass. What is crucial to the growth of a salmon population is the number of fish able to spawn in each period. Biomass in period $t + i$ is not related to biomass in period t as precisely as the numbers spawning in period $t + i$ to the numbers spawning in period t, where i is the interval between birth of a particular cohort and its return to freshwater to spawn.

Escapement is the term given to the numbers of salmon that have survived the harvest in period t and will thus be able to spawn. In a fishery of this kind, maintenance of a steady-state population depends on the number left to spawn.

There are a number of different types of salmon. Our discussion focuses on the Pacific salmon, which consists of a number of species—sockeye, chum, pink, coho, and chinook. Each species has different biological characteristics and susceptibility to fishing equipment, but they all have the common characteristic that at a particular age (which varies by species) they return to the freshwater river or stream where they were born; there they spawn and then die. Atlantic salmon, by comparison, do not die after they spawn.

The key feature of Pacific salmon fisheries is that the stock is available for harvest for only a short period of time. The commercial salmon harvests occur as the fish are returning upstream to spawn. Harvests occur before spawning because the fish deteriorate rapidly in weight and commercial quality the closer they are to the spawning grounds. Typically, then, only one or two age classes will be exploited in a given season. The relationship on which to focus is between the number of fish that will spawn and the subsequent fish born from that age class that will return to spawn (and thus be available for harvest) in i years.

The relationship between spawning fish and new age classes is complex. See Crutchfield and Pontecorvo (1969) and Larkin (1966) for more details. Figure 4.10 is a simple illustration of the biological mechanics before harvesting occurs. The horizontal axis is the number of fish that can spawn in period t. These spawning fish are those born $t - i$ years ago that have survived life in the ocean to return to their spawning grounds. On the vertical axis is the number of fish born to those spawning in period t that are expected to survive all the rigors of their environment and return to spawn i years later (i ranges from 2 to 6 years). The curve $F(N)$ shows the relationship between the number spawning in t and the number returning to spawn in $t + i$. This curve rises, reaches a maximum, then declines again.

The biological reasons for the shape are as follows. If few "parents" spawn, of course, few fish will be born and survive to spawn again. The larger the spawning population up to a size of N_M, the greater the number surviving to an age of i. There will be a relatively large number of eggs laid and hatched, and a population substantial enough to survive the rigors of the environment. But once the population of spawning fish exceeds N_M, those of the next generation surviving decline. Although many eggs will be deposited and hatched, relatively fewer hatchlings will survive than when fewer eggs are laid. The reason is that spawning grounds become overcrowded, increasing the mortality of the new recruits as a result of scarcity of food and other causes of mortality that depend upon density. Hence, the $F(N)$ function has a maximum, then declines.

A 45° line has also been drawn. Along the 45° line the number of spawning fish

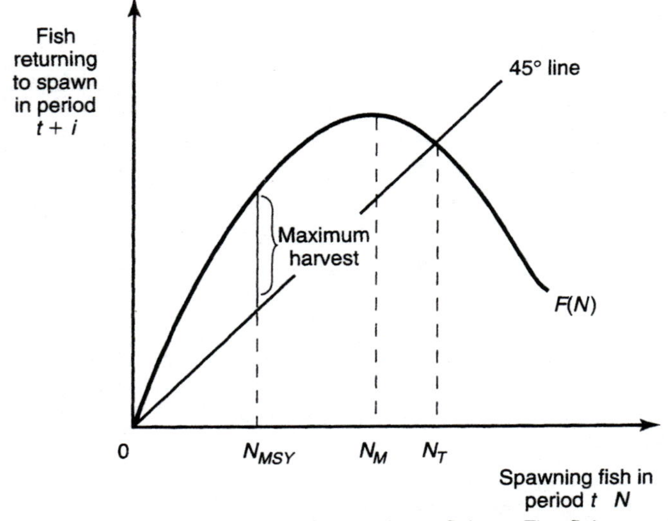

FIGURE 4.10. Simple biological mechanics for a salmon fishery. The fish spawning in period t determine the numbers which will return to the river to spawn in period $t + i$. The 45° line shows where the number of fish spawning in t exactly equals the number spawning in $t + i$. A harvest of the fish spawning in period t that yields no net change in the stock of salmon from t to $t + i$ is given by the distance between $F(N)$ and the 45° line. The *MSY* harvest is shown. This figure is the basis of the quadratic relationship between yield and effort for a salmon fishery.

exactly equals the number of fish returning in i years. The distance then between the 45° line and $F(N)$ lying above the 45° line is the number of fish that can be harvested in period t while still providing for replacement of themselves in period $t + i$. That is, the difference between $F(N)$ and 45° is the harvest that can be taken at different populations which yields a biological equilibrium with no change in the size of the stock. The maximum harvest (the *MSY* yield in physical terms) can be taken where the distance between the 45° line and $F(N)$ is the largest—where the slope of $F(N)$ equals 1. This occurs at a population of spawning fish equal to N_{MSY}. The same relationship can be repeated each year with different age classes of salmon.

Thus we have the same type of relationship between sustainable yield of a fish species and a measure of the stock of the species. The difference between salmon and, say, the demersal species represented by our aggregate biomass model is that we must talk about distinct age classes for salmon and spawning parents, rather than the aggregate biomass. But if we look at the relationship between a sustainable yield of salmon and the number of fish spawning, we obtain the usual quadratic shape seen with our simple biological mechanics. That is, the $F(N)$ curve from zero to N_T in Figure 4.10 lying above the 45° line shows the sustainable harvests possible for different numbers of spawning fish. This means that the relationship between the sustainable harvest and *effort* should look the same as in our simple model.

Figure 4.11 provides an illustration. Assuming that the price of salmon is con-

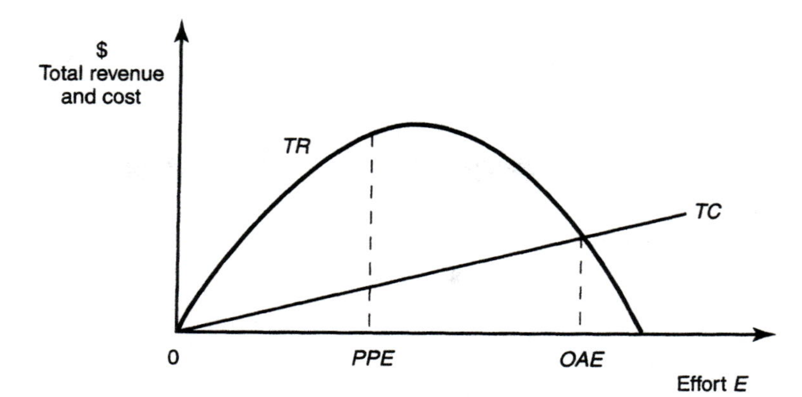

FIGURE 4.11. The *OAE* and *PPE* for a salmon fishery, assuming a constant price per pound of salmon and constant unit cost of effort. The fishery shown is for a particular age class, not the aggregate biomass of the fishery.

stant, the total revenue (*TR*) function is quadratic. Assuming that unit costs of effort are constant, total costs of effort (*TC*) are again linear. The open access and private property equilibria are shown in the figure, and the distinction between the two equilibria is the same as before. In the *OAE*, more effort is used than in the *PPE*, given the costs and price of fish.

In using a figure such as 4.11, we must interpret the relationships with care. We are looking at particular age classes of salmon available for harvest, not aggregate biomass. In addition, exogenous factors can have a big impact on salmon age classes. Salmon are affected by environmental hazards such as changes in food supply and the presence of predators, but they also must contend with human-made hazards. Hydroelectric dams may impede their travel upstream. Salmon habitats are threatened by pollution from residential areas and from industries such as mining and forestry. Thus there can be considerable variation in the actual population available for harvest in any given year. The yield-to-effort relationship is thought to be less stable than for fish species typified by the aggregate biomass model. These features of the salmon fishery thus create special problems for fisheries management.

We cannot go into detail on the various policies applied to open access salmon fisheries (see Crutchfield and Pontecorvo, 1969, and Pearse, 1982, for information on past and present policies). The basic management problem is that it is possible to harvest any particular age class very extensively because the fish swim through confined regions—rivers—to spawn. In theory, an entire age class of one or more species could be extinguished by putting nets across important spawning rivers. Earlier in this century, many salmon populations were destroyed or significantly reduced by the construction of hydroelectric dams and blockage of spawning rivers (before fish ladders were installed and perfected).

Regulation has generally come in three forms: restriction of the equipment used (size and type of nets, prohibition of particular items); area closures (high seas salmon harvests are prohibited to American and Canadian commercial fishermen); and time closures for the spawning rivers. British Columbia has also experimented with a licensing scheme for vessels. There are, in addition, a number of policies implemented by governments to protect the species and their habitats. These include the construction of fish ladders at dams and hatcheries.

The regulations have by and large led to economic inefficiency and high costs in harvesting salmon and have not prevented overfishing—harvests in excees of an economic optimum. Although damage to salmon habitats has taken its toll on the species, ineffective regulation of the fisheries and the resulting excessive harvests have reduced many spawning stocks far below their maximum economic potential. New policies have been recommended. It is too early, however, to predict the effect any of these policies might have on salmon stocks. Thus salmon represent a different type of biological mechanics and challenge to fishery management.

EXTINCTION OF FISH SPECIES

There is a large literature on extinction. See, for example, Clark (1973a, 1976), Smith (1977), and Hartwick (1982). In this section we highlight a case in which the extinction of a renewable resource is possible. In most such cases, extinction would occur only if the fishery was characterized by open access—that is, if lack of private property rights was the major problem. However, open access does not necessarily lead to extinction.

What are the critical features of a fishery that can cause extinction? We focus on two. First, the biological mechanics may be such that a species becomes extinct if the population sinks below a critical biomass or number of individuals. In our simple logistic model, extinction will occur only when the last fish is caught. It is hard to imagine cases where costs would remain constant as fishing firms search for that last fish (or pair of fish). For some species, extinction can occur if the population is reduced below some critical level. In these cases, survival of a sufficient number of individuals is required to ensure that enough new members are born to maintain the population. This type of biological mechanics tends to occur in species with few births per female—for example, sea mammals such as whales. For other fish, reproductive capacity is not the issue, as one fish can produce millions of offspring (shrimp, for example).

Second, extinction also depends on the economic characteristics of the markets for the resource and the technology of harvesting as Box 4.5 illustrates. Extinction is possible when the costs of harvesting are independent of the stock and the price of the fish increases significantly. In this situation a harvest function $H = G(E, X)$ can be tangent to the fishery production function $F(X)$ at the origin even without threshold effects. Entry of more and more vessels trying to catch ever fewer fish can lead to extinction of the species. Although the assumptions required for extinction in this static case are somewhat implausible, especially the assumption that costs are independent of the stock of the fish, the case does illustrate that cost and demand conditions are important in determining whether it can be privately profitable to keep on harvesting right to extinction.

To have extinction, it has to be the case that the price must always exceed the

BOX 4.5 **Extinctions: Past and Present**

Vernon Smith has made use of a version of the model of human predation of a species in analyzing the extinction of the megafuana some 10,000 years ago. He argues that the large herding animals such as mammoth, bison, camel, and mastodon, which become extinct, presented low hunting cost relative to kill value. The open access nature of these animal stocks removed an incentive to harvest conservatively. Wastage killing is evident in some ancient sites. The slow growth or long maturation of these animals also made them vulnerable to extinction. Small stocks did not grow rapidly once they were hunted intensively.

The commonly accepted cause of the extinctions was climate change and a consequent reduction in grassland areas. Smith contends, however, that human predation was the cause. There is clear evidence that humans hunted the animals in question; spear-

TABLE 1 **EXTINCTIONS OF SPECIES IMPLIED BY THE GLOBAL 2000 STUDY'S PROJECTIONS**

	Present species (thousands)	Projected deforestation (percent)	Loss of species (percent)	Extinctions (thousands)
	Low deforestation case			
Tropical forests				
Latin America	300–1000	50	33	100–333
Africa	150–500	20	13	20–65
South and Southeast Asia	300–1000	60	43	129–430
Subtotal	750–2500			249–828
All other habitats				
Oceans, fresh water, nontropical forests, islands, etc.	2250–7500		8	188–625
Total	3000–10,000			437–1453
	High deforestation case			
Tropical forests				
Latin America	300–1000	67	50	150–500
Africa	150–500	67	50	75–250
South and Southeast Asia	300–1000	67	50	150–500
Subtotal	750–2500			375–1250
All other habitats				
Oceans, fresh water, nontropical forests, islands, etc.	2250–7500		8	188–625
Total	3000–10,000			563–1875

Source: U.S. Council on Environmental Quality and the Dept. of State. *The Global 2000 Report to the President.* New York: Penguin, 1982.

BOX 4.5 *(Continued)*

TABLE 2 **RECORDED EXTINCTIONS, 1600 TO THE PRESENT**

Category	**Approximate Number of Species**	**Total Extinctions Since 1600**
Mammals	4,000	83
Birds	9,000	113
Reptiles	6,300	21
Amphibians	4,200	2
Fish[a]	19,100	23
Invertebrates[a]	Over 1 million	98
Vascular plants	250,000	384[b]
Total		724

NOTES: (a) Extinction totals are primarily representative of North America and Hawaii. (b) Vascular plants include species, subspecies, and varieties.

Source: W. V. Reid and K. R. Miller (1989). *Keeping Options Alive: The Scientific Basis for Conserving Biodiversity.* Washington, D.C.: World Resources Institute. Cited in W. V. Reid, "How Many Species Will There Be?" in T. C. Whitmore and J. A. Sayer, eds. (1992). *Tropical Deforestation and Species Extinction.* London: Chapman and Hall, Table 3.1, page 56.

heads have been found among the bones. Human migration to North America coincided with the extinctions. Lastly, Smith sees the types of spearheads discovered as being refined for big game hunting. Eighty genera in continental North America vanished about 10,000 years ago, and 49 of these had adult members weighing over 110 pounds. It was this group that Smith argues was hunted to extinction, like the passenger pigeon in our own era.

Direct human predation is today a small part of the phenomenon of species extinction. The problem now is one of having the habitats of species destroyed by the encroachment of settlement and forestry activity. For example, in East Kalimantan, Indonesia, logging was started in 1970 and the habitat of the orangutan is being ruined. In 10 years, the local human population jumped from 1000 to 8000. Much concern is focused on plant species today, and it is in tropical forests where diversity is greatest. It is estimated that less than half of the plant and animal species have been catalogued. But the diversity is thought to be important in ecological balance, and any major change in the balance involves unknown consequences for future human welfare. Natural preserves have been created in most areas of the world, but encroachment by squatters is a major problem. Politicians are reluctant to be severe with very poor families. The unquantified value of future biological diversity is not a practical point for rallying support from citizens for protecting natural reserves. This is an instance in which the beneficiaries of large-scale preservation of species are future generations, and their voices are not heard in current debates. UNESCO has encouraged the allocation of special areas to natural reserves by itself designating areas throughout the world as important in the drive to preserve species from extinction. More than half of extinctions since A.D. 80, the year the European lion died out, have occurred since 1900. Ten percent of the 22,250 plant species in the continental

BOX 4.5 *(Continued)*

United States have been listed as "endangered" or "threatened" by the Smithsonian Institution. Some recent projections are presented in Table 1 and Table 2.

Besides natural reserves protected by law, two other approaches to preserving species are (1) legal requirements that new projects must not result in a threat to a species, and (2) treaties outlawing trade in many species. With regard to the former, in the United States alterations to a project have often been worked out to preserve some threatened animal or plant. However, the difficulty with bans on trade in certain plants and animals is that many countries are not signatories to the principal treaties.

Sources: Erik Eckholm (1978). "Disappearing Species: The Social Challenge." Worldwatch Paper #22. Washington D.C.: Worldwatch Institute. V. Smith (1975). "The Primitive Hunter Culture, Pleistocene Extinction, and the Rise of Agriculture," *Journal of Political Economy* 83, 4 (August), pp. 727–756.

marginal cost of harvest. Under certain cost and demand conditions, it may be socially optimal to extinguish a species if society does not value the species for its own sake—that is, no social value is put on preservation of a species if it has no commercial value. Indeed, some species may have a large negative value to society—mosquitoes, parasites, and viruses. Extinction of these species would then be socially desirable. *Open access per se is not the cause of extinction in these cases.* We now examine an example of near extinction that illustrates the interdependence of the biological and economic features noted above: the blue whale.

Bioeconomics of Extinction in the Steady-State Model

Rather than assuming that the production function for the fish species is characterized by a smooth quadratic curve, we now consider a case where there is a minimum sustainable stock size, which we denote m. This is illustrated in Figure 4.12, panel (a). The left-hand side of the biological production function equals zero at m rather than at a population of zero, as before. If the biomass reaches m, there are not enough of the species for reproduction to exceed natural mortality, and it will gradually die out. This is shown by the production function dipping below the X axis until the population hits zero. Given these biological mechanics, if the fishery is characterized by open access, extinction becomes a likely outcome.

Panel (a) of Figure 4.12 also shows when extinction occurs for a species with a minimum stock threshold. Recall Figure 4.4, where we derived the steady-state harvests as a function of stock size for different levels of effort. We repeat this type of exercise in panel (a). Effort levels increase as we pivot the harvest function up and to the left. For any level of effort that exceeds $\hat{E}$, the species will be extinguished. Without the threshold, extinction would occur only with levels of effort large enough to make the harvest function tangent to $F(X)$ at its origin. Now, a much smaller level of effort yields a tangency of the harvest function with the $F(X)$ curve well to the right of the minimum stock size m.

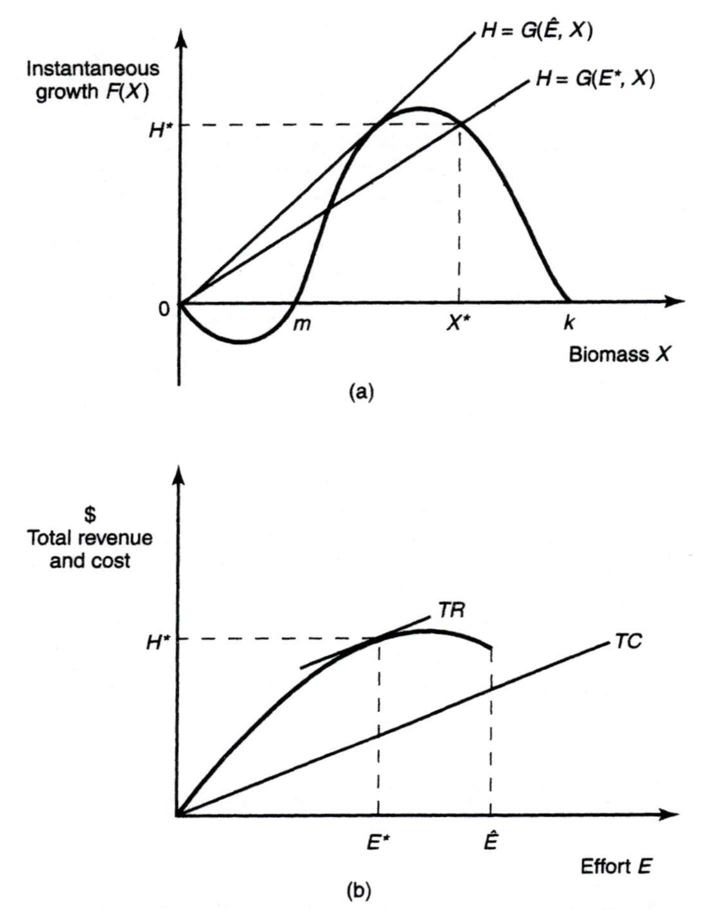

FIGURE 4.12. A biological production function when a threshold level of fish stock is essential for survival of the species is shown in panel (a). If the biomass falls below m, reproduction is less than natural mortality, and the species gradually dies out. If effort levels rise above $\hat{E}$, sustainable harvests are not possible. Panel (b) illustrates that total revenues are zero beyond effort level $\hat{E}$. Open access with low total costs of effort is likely to extinguish the fishery. A private property fishery will harvest H^* fish with E^* effort. It will not exhaust the fishery.

Why is open access more likely to precipitate extinction? Panel (b) of Figure 4.12 shows the total revenue function for a threshold fishery. It has the usual inverted-bowl shape up to effort level $\hat{E}$; beyond that, there is no sustainable total revenue. A total cost curve is shown that does not intersect the total revenue curve. For these unit costs and any unit costs to the right of a total cost curve that intersects TR at an effort level of $\hat{E}$, extinction will occur. Remember that with these steady-state pictures we are telling a dynamic sort of story. What we don't have in this situation is *any* steady state. With total costs as shown in panel (b), if there is any effort beyond $\hat{E}$, the harvest function will not intersect any point on the $F(X)$ function. The harvests will exceed the ability of the species to sustain itself. It will be driven to extinction.

Figure 4.12 shows that extinction is more likely if the fishery is characterized by open access *and* has low unit costs of effort. A possible scenario is as follows. An open access fishery starts out with a sustainable equilibrium, but then technological change lowers the unit costs of effort. In many fisheries there have been large technological advances that have reduced the cost of harvesting. Examples are the use of sophisticated capital equipment such as sonar. More recently, satellites are being used to track pelagic species, and information about the location of the fish is fed instantaneously to shipboard computers. These new techniques may offset the higher marginal harvesting costs that would normally result from a lower stock of fish. Harvesting continues, and the stock is ultimately extinguished. Rising demand for fish may also contribute to extinction of species. Rising incomes can cause demand to increase. The price of fish rises, harvests increase, and the fish population falls. If the demand curve shifts up enough, the open access equilibrium may again occur below the threshold, and the species will become extinct. (Prove this yourself by deriving the open access supply curve for the fishery with a minimum stock threshold.) Open access remains the key element, as we will see below in the case of the blue whale.

What happens under private property? If the fishery was managed under some form of private property, extinction would not occur in the steady-state framework. With total costs as shown in panel (b), the private property equilibrium uses effort E^*, which results in a sustainable harvest of H^*—shown in panels (a) and (b)—and stock size of X^*, as shown in panel (a). The private property equilibrium in a steady-state model with positive harvesting costs always leads to a biomass that is to the right of the *MSY* biomass. Thus, extinction will not occur. We caution that this result may not carry over to a fully dynamic model in which discounting of future harvests occurs. We revisit the question of extinction in Chapter 11.

The Blue Whale: A Case of Near Extinction

The blue whale is the largest creature in the world. It was harvested for many years, but the peak harvests occurred in the period from 1928 to 1938.[11] Up to 26,000 whales were caught in a single year in this period. Little whaling was done during World War II. The postwar catch declined steadily, until by the beginning of the 1960s the species was almost extinct. What factors led to near extinction of the blue whale? We focus on two: the minimum stock size of its growth curve, and the economics of whaling.

Whales are, of course, a pelagic species, and no property rights to the blue whale existed until 1964, when an international agreement among whaling nations prohibited their capture beginning in 1965. The question is this: Would open access lead to a sustainable stock of whales and thus a sustainable harvest? To answer this, the profitability of the whaling industry must be examined.

What happens to profits as the catch declines? One might expect that as the catch declines costs would rise faster than the value of the catch. Boats would then exit from the industry, and the species would recover. But whaling boats do not specialize by species. This is one reason why a number of whale species are endangered. Without regulation, whaling boats will go from species to species until the aggregate whale population is so low that costs cannot be coverd by revenues. The products of the blue whale—oil, blubber, meat—are all readily obtainable from other whale species. Thus, blue whales were harvested along with other species; they were the preferred catch because of their size. It is the costs of harvesting any type of whale that are important in the industry, not the costs of harvesting the blue whale alone. The economics of whaling did not protect the blue whale, and the biological mechanics are such that the species cannot survive unless sufficient numbers survive.

By the early 1960s, public attention was focused on this irreplaceable natural resource. An international agreement that prohibited the capture of any blue whales was signed. Their population was so low at that time that survival was in doubt. Thus the obvious policy response to preserve the species was to call a moratorium on the harvests. Was this the optimal economic policy?

Spence (1974) says "yes."[12] Even if we do not measure the social value of preserving the species, the economic optimum will correspond closely to the broadly interpreted social optimum. A calculation of the optimal economic harvest must incorporate both industry and biological mechanics. Spence computes the optimal steady-state population and the associated sustainable harvest. From his calculations, the steady-state stock with no harvesting at all is about 136,000 whales. The maximum sustainable yield (*MSY*) is 9890 whales at a sustainable population of 45,177. Given his assumptions, the optimal population would be about 67,000 whales, with a sustainable catch of 9000 per year. Notice that the optimal harvest is less than the *MSY* harvest, while the optimal population is larger.

What was the whale population in the 1960s, when international regulation began? Spence estimates that the stock of whales was about 1639 in 1960. Although the number of whales critical for survival was not known, most observers felt that the population at that point was very close to the critical threshold. What, then, was the optimal regulatory policy? A moratorium on whaling. The species had to be allowed to grow at its natural rate until the steady-state equilibrium was reached. *Any* harvesting of blue whales would drive the industry away from the steady state and toward extinction. Harvesting would reduce the value of the blue whale industry. Given estimates of the cost of whaling and the value per whale, Spence calculated that the harvest of blue whales would have to be prohibited for at least 9 years. That calculation was based on very sketchy information about the recovery rate of the species. Spence's model was overly optimistic about the net growth of the blue whale's population. His biological assumptions may also have been incorrect. The moratorium is still in place, owing to the fact that the recovery of the species has been slower than expected. A relatively recent estimate of maximum population is only 450 whales (International Whaling Commission, 1995). It is possible that blue whale harvests prior to the moratorium pushed this species below its critical threshold. Whether the population will ever recover remains to be seen.

The policy prescription for the blue whale—a moratorium—presents a difficult problem. What will happen to the factor inputs over the period when no harvesting is allowed? In the case of whaling, the vessels may just shift to other whale species. This creates another regulatory problem. If the other species are not protected, they too may be in danger of becoming extinct. Thus, regulations to deal with one case may merely shift the factors of production into another common property fishery. It is the lack of property rights that is the fundamental problem. Are there, however, cases where extinction will occur even with optimal management of the fishery?

Socially Optimal Extinction?

Are there any situations in which it is socially optimal to extinguish a renewable resource? There are combinations of values for the social discount rate, the price of the fish, the costs of harvest, and the reproductive rate of the population for which extinction is optimal, but it is very unlikely that all the necessary conditions will be met. If the social discount rate is very high, indicating that individuals do not care much about the future, the price of fish is high, and marginal harvesting costs are unaffected by declining stocks, it is possible that the optimal steady-state equilibrium occurs at a fish stock below the threshold necessary to sustain the population. However, we can think of no cases in which a commercially valued species was exhausted in a fishery managed by a sole owner or regulated by government. The assumption that marginal costs do not depend on the remaining stock of fish is simply not consistent with fact in most fisheries. It is also difficult to imagine cases where the social discount rate has been high enough to make the value of the fishery negligible in the future.

Extinction of many plant and animal species has occurred, largely as a by-product of economic activity that did not put a social value on these living things. These extinctions are classic examples of an externality for which social intervention is required. Extinction thus remains a phenomenon that is due to open access to the fishery.

SUMMARY

1. Fish populations are renewable natural resources that are often harvested under conditions of open access. This lack of property rights to the fish can lead to overfishing, inefficient use of factor inputs, low returns to fishing industries, and even the extinction of species.
2. To analyze the economics of the fishery, a biological production function for the species is needed. In a simple model, the stock of fish is assumed to grow over time according to a logistic function which relates the net growth of the population to its size or biomass. Each point on the biological production function shows a sustainable yield of fish. If no harvesting occurs, there will be a natural or biological equilibrium where the net increase in biomass is equal to zero. This equilibrium occurs at the maximum carrying capacity of the species' habitat. The biological production function has a maximum sustainable yield (*MSY*) at a population level of one-half the maximum carrying capacity for the model of logistic growth.
3. When harvesting is introduced, a steady-state bionomic (bioeconomic) equilibrium occurs when the net growth in the fish stock is exactly equal to the rate of harvest. The fishery can then continue indefinitely in this position of sustained cropping of fish.
4. Under conditons of open access to the fishery, an equilibrium will occur where the average revenue with respect to effort (where effort is an index of fishery inputs) is

equal to the marginal cost of effort—an economically inefficient equilibrium. This equilibrium gives rise to the following problems: (a) An open access equilibrium will use more effort in catching a given harvest than is socially optimal. (b) Economic rent from the fishery will be lost. (c) Fishing firms fail to incorporate the effects of their actions on the stock of fish (a stock externality) and on the harvesting costs of other firms in the same fishery (a crowding externality). A smaller sustainable stock of fish will typically exist in an open access equilibrium than in a socially optimal equilibrium. (d) Bioeconomic inefficiency may result if the open access equilibrium is to the left of the *MSY* biomass.

5. In the static model, the private property equilibrium occurs where the marginal costs of effort equal the marginal revenues from effort. It is economically efficient. Economic rent is maximized for the fishery. Biological inefficiency cannot occur because equilibriums must be to the right of the *MSY* biomass.
6. The biological mechanics for salmon should be based on spawning fish (escapement) rather than biomass. The biological relationship is then between spawning fish in period t and the age class that returns to spawn in period $t + i$, where i is the interval spent before spawning. Although the sustainable yield from the salmon fishery will look like that from our simple model based on aggregate biomass, the interpretation is different. Each year, one or more age classes are harvested as the salmon travel upstream to spawn.
7. Extinction of a fish species can occur when the population is reduced below a critical threshold or because of open access (or both). To have extinction, the price of fish must exceed the marginal cost of harvesting.

DISCUSSION QUESTIONS

1. Suppose that the biological mechanics for a fishery are given by the equation $F(X) = aX - bX^2$, where X is the biomass of the fishery, and a and b are biological parameters assumed to be constant. What is the *MSY* biomass? What is the biological equilibrium of the fishery when there is no harvesting? Suppose that harvesting of this species is always equal to H tons per instant of time, where H is less than the *MSY* biomass. Determine the bionomic equilibrium and explain how a steady-state equilibrium will be obtained: (a) starting from the biological equilibrium; and (b) starting from a point to the left of the *MSY* biomass.
2. Determine graphically the open access equilibrium level of effort and harvest for a fishery. Derive the industry supply curve for this fishery. Then show what happens to the supply curve (a) when the unit costs of effort rise; (b) when the unit costs of effort fall. (c) Show what happens to market equilibrium (supply equals demand) when demand shifts, say, owing to a change in tastes (people like fish more than they did in the past).
3. Derive the open access and the socially optimal equilibrium when the supply curve of effort is positively sloped (the costs of effort rise as more effort is required). Explain the difference between the open access and private property equilibria. Do any of the fundamental results derived for each equilibrium change? Explain.

4. Suppose the demand curve for flounder is given by $P = 400 - 3H$, where P is the price of flounder and H is the harvest in thousands of pounds. Let the *sustainable catch* given by $H = a_1E - a_2E^2 = 0.6E - 0.0015E^2$, where E is the level of effort. Unit costs are assumed constant and calculated to be about $200 per unit of fishing effort. Given this information compute graphically: (a) the open access harvest and level of effort; (b) the private property harvest and level of effort, assuming that a competitive firm owns the fishery; and (c) the private property harvest and level of effort, assuming that a monopolist owns the fishery. Show your solutions algebraically and graphically.
5. Under what conditions might a fish species be extinguished? Explain.
6. Use the data given below on harvests, prices, and effort to discuss what the bionomic equilibrium of the British Columbia salmon fishery might have been over the time interval given. Graphs and algebra may be helpful. Are the data more consistent with an open access or a private property equilibrium? Discuss what the biological equilibrium might be. Is the fishery in any danger of extinction? Is the fishery overcapitalized?

PACIFIC SALMON—BRITISH COLUMBIA, CANADA

Year	Landings (metric tons)	Average Price (per metric ton)	Effort (number of vessels)
1969	39,000	$2,700	6,100
1970	72,000	2,100	6,100
1971	64,000	2,500	5,800
1972	78,000	2,400	5,500
1973	86,000	4,200	5,100
1974	60,000	3,750	5,100
1975	38,000	3,900	5,000
1976	58,000	4,600	5,100
1977	69,000	4,200	5,100
1978	71,000	5,500	5,050
1979	60,000	7,300	4,800
1980	54,000	4,000	4,700
1981	79,000	3,400	4,600
1982	66,000	3,900	4,500
1983	75,000	2,500	4,500
1984	50,000	4,000	4,300
1985	108,000	2,900	4,350
1986	104,000	2,600	4,400
1987	67,000	2,100	4,400
1988	88,000	3,200	4,400
1989	89,000	2,500	4,500
1990	96,000	2,300	4,500

NOTE: Prices are in constant 1985 dollars.

NOTES

1. There are some fish "farms" in lakes and off coastal waters where certain species of fish are grown like domestic farm animals. For example, Norway has extensive fish farms, and in parts of the southern United States crayfish are grown in coastal regions. Oysters, a case we examine in Chapter 5, are also frequently farmed in well-defined "beds" off the coasts of the United States, Canada, and elsewhere. Salmon farming exists off Canada's east and west coasts.
2. This model was developed by Schaefer (1957) and is often referred to as the Schaefer model. Also see Gulland (1974) for more biological details. Obviously, many more complex features enter into the determination of the growth rate than are given in the simple model described here. However, biologists tell us that stock size is a major determinant of growth and can be used as a proxy for other variables that affect the species over time. The implicit assumption is that each member of the stock (as measured by weight) produces some offspring each season. The aggregate weight of the offspring thus depends on the aggregate weight of the current stock. Clearly, two stocks of the same weight could have different numbers of fertile members, and thus two seemingly identical stocks would have quite different net additions over time. Moreover, even two identical stocks could have different growth rates as a result of environmental factors. We return to these issues in Chapter 11; our simplified biological mechanics will be the working model for this chapter.
3. This is a continous time model. Alternatively, we could look at the change in X over a discrete period, say a year, as $X(t+1) - X(t)$. In practice, the discrete version makes more sense because fishing occurs over specific periods of time—a day, a week, or a fishing season. However, the continuous time version is easier to represent graphically and algebraically in most cases. Both yield approximately the same results, so in general we will use the continuous version here.
4. Mathematically, we assume for equation (8.4) that $G(0, X) = 0$, $G_E > 0$, $G_{EE} < 0$, $G(E,0) = 0$, $G_X > 0$, G_{XX} is uncertain, and G_{EX} also uncertain. In the figures relating harvests to stock size (for a given amount of effort), we assume $G_{XX} = 0$ for simplicity.
5. This result does not carry over to the dynamic model presented in Chapter 11.
6. In this example, with constant average and marginal costs, we cannot determine the number of firms in the industry. The problem is the same as that with any competitive industry facing constant costs.
7. Alternatively, we could have derived the social optimum from the government's maximization of the sum of consumer plus producer surplus. With no market imperfections, the private property equilibrium is the social optimum.
8. The graphic solution discussed above can also be shown using simple calculus. The objective of the sole owner is to maximize profits by choosing a level of effort, E^*, subject to the constraint imposed by the biological mechanics, $dX/dt = 0$. Mathematically, the problem is to

$$\max \text{social welfare} = pG(E,X) - wE + \lambda[F(x) - G(E,X)]$$

by choosing a level of E. To find the optimum, the equation above is differentiated with respect to E and X, and the resulting first-order conditions are set equal to zero. These first-order conditons are:

$$pG_E - w - \lambda G_E = 0$$
$$pG_X + \lambda[F'(X) - G_X] = 0$$

If an interior solution (nonzero) exists, then it requires that $dX/dt = 0$, or $F(X) = G(E,X)$, and that

$$G_E + (G_E G_X)/[F'(X) - G_X] = w/p$$

Now how does this equilibrium differ from that of open access? First, note that in a steady-state equilibrium that is socially optimal, the real wage, w/p, equals the marginal product of effort, G_E, not the average product of effort, as in the open access equilibrium. The term $(G_E G_X)/[F'(X) - G_X]$ represents the effect an additional unit of effort has on the steady-state stock on the growth of the fish population over time. It is the stock externality noted in the text. The open access equilibrium does not incorporate this stock effect at all. Because the stock effect is negative, the open access equilibrium must have a higher level of effort and lower level of the fish stock than is socially optimal.

9. This derivation is adapted from Hannesson (1978).
10. This is an advanced section and can be omitted.
11. Information on the blue whale is taken from Spence (1974) and some of the references cited therein.
12. See, however, a dynamic model of the blue whale in Hannesson (1978) based on a paper by Clark (1973b). The optimal stock is very sensitive to the discount rate. If harvesting costs are low due to versatility of whaling vessels, extinction is economically efficient if the discount rate exceeds 5 percent. This model ignores any social value of the blue whale—preservation for its unique position in the ecosystem.

SELECTED READINGS

Anderson, L G. (1977). *The Economics of Fisheries Management.* Baltimore: Johns Hopkins Press.

Beverton, R. J. H., and S. J. Holt (1957). "On the Dynamics of Exploited Fish Populations." *Fishery Investigations,* series III, vol. 19. London: Her Majesty's Stationery Office.

Clark, C. W. (1973a). "The Economics of Over Exploitation," *Science* 181, pp. 630–634.

Clark, C. W. (1973b). "When Should Whaling Resume?" Vancouver: Department of Mathematics, University of British Columbia, mimeo.

Clark, C. (1990). *Mathematical Bioeconomics: The Optimal Management of Renewable Resources,* 2nd ed. New York: Wiley-Interscience.

Crutchfield, J. A. (1981). "The Pacific Halibut Fishery." Technical Report No. 17, in *The Public Regulation of Commercial Fisheries in Canada,* Case Study No. 2. Ottawa: Economical Council of Canada.

Dupont, D. P. (1990). "Rent Dissipation in Restricted Access Fisheries," *Journal of Environmental Economics and Management* 19, pp. 26–44.

Gordon, H. S. (1954). "The Economic Theory of a Common-Property Resource: The Fishery." *Journal of Political Economy* 62, pp. 124–142.

Gulland, J. A. (1974). *The Management of Marine Fisheries.* Bristol: Scientechnica Publishing.

Hanneson, R. (1978). *Economics of Fisheries.* Bergen: Universitetsforlaget.

Hartwick, J. M. (1982). "Free Access and the Dynamics of the Fishery," in L. J. Mirman and D. F. Spulber, eds., *Essays in the Economics of Renewable Resources.* Amsterdam: North Holland.

International Whaling Commission (1995). *Report.* London: International Whaling Commission.

Larkin, P. (1966). "Exploitation in a Type of Predator-Prey Relationship," *Journal of the Fisheries Research Board of Canada* 23, pp. 349–356.

Munro, G. R. (1982). "Fisheries, Extended Jurisdiction, and the Economics of Common Property Resources," *Canadian Journal of Economics* 15, pp. 405–425.

Ostorm, E. (1990). *Governing the Commons, The Evolution of Institutions for Collective Action.* Cambridge: Cambridge University Press.

Panayoutou, T. (1982). "Management Concepts for Small-Scale Fisheries: Economic and Social Aspects." FAO Fisheries Technical Paper No. 228. Rome: Food and Agricultural Organization of the United Nations.

Pearse, P. (1982). *Turning the Tide: A New Policy for Canada's Pacific Fisheries.* The Commission of Pacific Fisheries Policy, Final Report, Vancouver, September.

Schaefer, M. B. (1957). "Some Considerations of Population Dynamics and Economics in Relation to the Management of Marine Fisheries," *Journal of the Fisheries Research Board of Canada* 14, pp. 669–681.

Scott, A. D., and P. A. Neher (1981). *The Public Regulation of Commercial Fisheries in Canada.* Ottawa: Economic Council of Canada.

Smith, V. L. (1977). "Control Theory Applied to Natural and Environmental Resources: An Exposition," *Journal of Environmental Economics and Management* 4, pp. 1–24.

Spence, A. M. (1974). "Blue Whales and Applied Control Theory," in H. W. Gottinger, ed., *Systems Approaches and Environmental Problems.* Gottingen: Vandenhoeck and Ruprecht.

chapter 5

Regulation of the Fishery

INTRODUCTION

The economic rationales for regulating the fishery are very clear. In Chapter 4 we saw that the open access equilibrium: (1) Was economically inefficient because the value of average, not marginal, product with respect to effort is set equal to the marginal cost of effort. Excessive amounts of effort are therefore used for a given harvest. (2) Could be bioeconomically inefficient with a steady-state stock of fish to the left of the MSY biomass. (3) Could lead to extinction of the species. (4) Dissipated all the rent to the fishery and could contribute to low incomes of workers in the fishery. Economic policies to remedy these problems should thus: (1) find methods of rationing the amount of effort in the fishery; (2) find methods of regulating the harvest to maintain efficient stocks of fish; and (3) recognize that any policy implemented may affect the distribution of income through the reduction of effort and by generating rents.

Regulation of a fishery is a complex task. We will focus on policies that in theory could improve the economic efficiency with which factors of production are utilized in the fishery. We note as well some of the practical issues of implementing policies and effects on the distribution of income and generation of rents. In this chapter we use the basic model presented in Chapter 4 to examine the possible ways in which the fishery can be regulated to achieve an efficient equilibrium. Then we examine policy objectives of governments, some regulations enacted, and the effects of these regulations on particular fisheries. In most actual cases, regulation has done very little to eliminate the inefficient use of factor inputs. The OECD supports this observation for its member countries. "Most stocks are over-exploited as traditional management measures used during the last decade have proved insufficient to cope with the problem" [of open access] (Organization for Economic Cooperation and Development, 1993, p. 7). Much existing regulation in the fishery has been designed to sustain the fishery and increase the incomes of fishers, not to reach a socially optimal equilibrium. There are bound to be conflicts of interest among different groups. What is beneficial to particular individuals in the fishery is costly to others; what is good for consumers may reduce incomes in the fishery. Governments have to be responsive to these interests. This is a major reason why it is so difficult to find cases where fisheries have been regulated so as to maximize social welfare.

How do we analyze the regulation of any fishery? First, we assume that a policy target must be set. Here we first assume that the target is to reach the optimal harvest and level of effort, and thus steady-state stock of a particular fish species. Later we look at actual cases where the target may be different. Second, methods of reaching the target must be found. We evaluate alternative devices in terms of their ability (administratively and in theory) to reach the optimum target. We examine taxes on the harvest or on effort, quotas on the catch or effort, licensing of vessels or fishermen, and the assignment of private property rights.

In each policy examined we assume that the regulators know the growth function of the species and how individuals in the fishery will behave. This is often not the case in practice. The ecology of fish species can be highly complex and not amenable to precise statistical analysis. It is hard to examine the interaction of different species and their habitat when everything happens below water. This is especially true for the pelagic species, which range over large tracts of the ocean.

In most regulatory environments, the growth function is estimated from the actual catch and the amount of effort used at different points in time. There are obvious problems with this technique, as we will see. But it is not just the stock of fish we have imperfect information about; regulators must also contend with the unpredictable behavior of the individuals working in the fishing industry. There are many examples of policies that looked good on paper but failed to reach their objectives because the individuals being regulated did not act as they were expected to.

ECONOMICS OF FISHERY REGULATION

We begin this section by defining the tax on the fishery that will convert an open access equilibrium to one that is socially optimal. As in Chapter 4, we concentrate on the static steady-state equilibrium.

Optimal Taxes on the Fishery

From Chapter 4 we know that under private property, the efficient fishing firm sets the value of the marginal product of effort equal to the marginal cost of effort. The open access fishery has firms setting the value of average product of effort equal to the marginal cost of effort. The difference between average and marginal products of effort we called the *stock effect*—the reduction in harvests for all firms due to an increase in effort by any one firm.[1] The stock effect must be incorporated into the equilibrium of any efficient fishery. Another way to express the efficient equilibrium is that the price of fish must be equated to the stock effect plus the marginal cost of harvests. Equation (5.1) expresses this relationship.

$$P = MC_H + E\left(\frac{dAP_E}{dE}\right) \tag{5.1}$$

As seen in Chapter 4, the industry harvest in an open access equilibrium will be set where the price of fish is equal to the average cost of harvest (which is equivalent to saying that the average revenue product from effort equals the marginal cost of effort), that is:

$$P = cE/H \tag{5.2}$$

The open access equilibrium (*OAE*) occurs because of the free access to the fishery and continued entry persisting when total revenues exceed total costs ($P > AC$ of harvest or AR of effort). Our problem is how to convert an open access equilibrium to one that is socially optimal.

One way is to impose a tax on the fishery. An *optimal tax*—one that is levied on the open access fishery to yield an efficient equilibrium—can be imposed on effort or on the harvest. In this section, we first note the components of such a tax on the harvest algebraically. We then illustrate optimal taxes on the harvest or effort graphically, using our steady-state static model. Compare equations (5.1) and (5.2). We see that they differ in two respects: The marginal stock effect is absent in equation (5.2), and price there is set equal to the average, not marginal, cost of harvest.

The reason the marginal stock effect is zero in the open access case is that fishers place no value on any harvests received in the future. Under open access there may be no fish to harvest in the future; therefore no individual in the fishery cares about the effect of harvests today on the growth of the biomass or the costs of tomorrow's harvests. This means that fishers operate with an infinite discount rate. By contrast, private property fishers in our steady-state model do not discount their future profits at all. In the absence of discounting or interest rate effects, the appropriate tax equates the marginal revenue product of effort to its marginal, not average, cost. Rent per pound harvested is made positive by this tax. Tax per unit harvested equals rent per unit harvested. This tax will reduce the value of the harvest to each firm. As total revenues decline, less effort will be employed in the fishery. Some factors of production will leave because they are not covering their opportunity costs. What this tax effectively does is to force fishing firms to incorporate the effect their actions have on the stock of fish—to prevent overfishing.

Figure 5.1 illustrates this tax. We have drawn marginal and average costs of harvesting fish as derived in Chapter 4. Suppose the price of fish is P. In the open access case the harvest will be H^0, but the optimal harvest is H^*, which is less than H^0 in this case. The harvest is too large under open access (but of course it could also be too small at a different initial price level). The tax on the harvest equal to $C' - cE/H$ means that each firm will be choosing a harvest *as if* it were on its marginal cost curve. For if we subtract $(C' - cE/H)$ from average cost, cE/H, we are left with marginal cost C'.[2]

Graphically, the tax can be interpreted as causing the firm's average cost curve to shift up to AC', where the vertical distance of the shift is equal to $C' - cE/H$ at the harvest H^*. With the constant price, the firms, still operating in an open access environment, will equate P to AC' and thus reach the optimal harvest H^*.

So far we have focused on the optimal tax on the harvest from an open access fishery. We turn now to a graphic examination of the different ways in which the optimal harvest and level of effort can be obtained. We will examine the steady-state equilibrium for taxes and quotas on both effort and the catch. Recall that although we

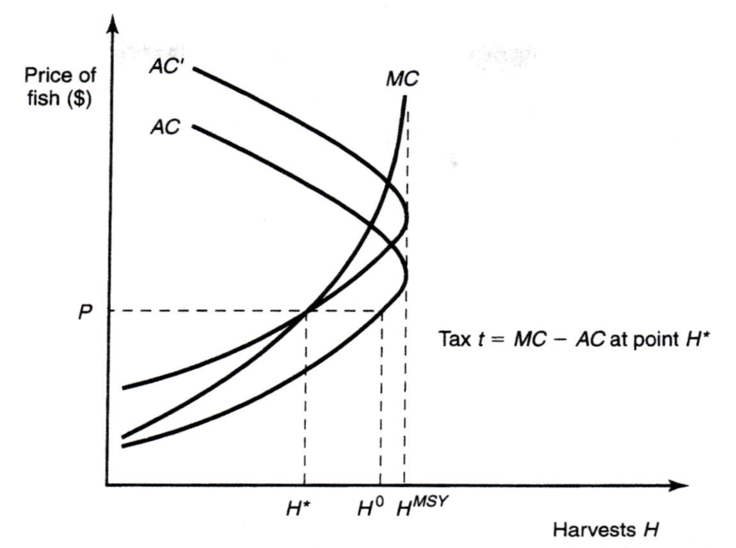

FIGURE 5.1. The optimal harvest is determined where the price of fish equals the marginal cost of the harvest. This occurs at a harvest of H^*. The open access equilibrium is where price equals the average cost of the harvest. This occurs at H^0. A tax equal to the difference between the marginal cost of the harvest and the average cost of the harvest at the optimal harvest will yield the optimal harvest in an open access fishery. The tax shifts the average cost curve from *AC* to *AC'* for the fishery. Setting price equal to *AC'* yields the optimal harvest H^*.

assume that the growth function for the fishery and the behavior of fishing firms are known, this is rarely the case in practice. Every policy studied below will be imperfect if these functions are not known. In some cases, the "cost" of an imprecise calculation of the optimal amount of effort and catch will be higher than in others. We will indicate when this is so.

A Tax on the Catch

The government fishery manager has just computed the optimal taxes discussed above in consultation with a fishery biologist, who has provided information on the growth function of the fish, $F(X)$. The government is prepared to levy a tax equal to the marginal stock effect plus the difference between marginal and average costs of harvest on the fishing firm. How will the manager impose the tax? Above, we noted that the tax would be levied on the harvests. One way to view the tax is that every pound of lobster that is landed now yields a price to the fisher net of the taxes.

In the preceding section, we illustrated the tax on the average costs of the harvest. Alternatively, we can look at the effect of the tax on effort. The tax on the catch reduces total revenue received for each unit of effort employed in the fishery. Figure 5.2 illustrates the situation. Before the tax, each firm in the industry faced a total revenue function given by $TR = PH$, where H, the harvest, is dependent on the amount

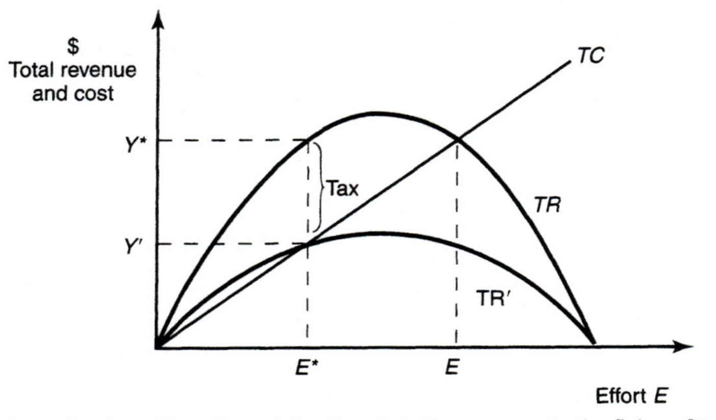

FIGURE 5.2. An optimal tax (t) on the catch will reduce the revenue to the fishery for each unit of effort employed. Before the tax, firms will enter an open access fishery until total revenues (TR) equal total costs (TC). The amount of effort used in the common property equilibrium is E. The tax reduces total revenue to TR', where $TR' = (P - t)H$. Firms now set $TR' = TC$, yielding the optimal amount of effort E^*.

of effort and the stock of fish. Total costs are dependent on the unit cost of effort, which is assumed to be constant, and the amount of effort used; $TC = cE$. The tax now means that for each fish sold, the price received is net of the tax, t, or $P' = (P - t)$. Total revenue is therefore $(P - t)H$. This is shown by the curve TR' in Figure 5.2.

Firms still equate total revenue to total cost (the open access condition remains), but if the tax has been set appropriately, the new equilibrium point will be at the optimal amount of effort, shown as E^*. The total value or rents from the fishery will be maximized. The value of the fishery is Y^* if effort is set equal to E^*. The government captures the rent in the form of the tax revenue equal to $(Y^* - Y')$. Fishing firms receive the amount Y'. Thus, the optimal tax generates the rent to the fishing ground that was lost under open access. But it need not improve the income of fishers; indeed, it may lower aggregate income from fishing, as we see below.

Notice that with a tax on the catch, the government is in effect sharing with the fishing firms some of the risks involved in fishing. A tax is levied only when fish are caught. There are no costs for the firm to pay "up front." Firms should incorporate the tax in their decision-making, but they will not incur any costs of this policy until they see their return reduced at the time of sale. The effect of the tax may thus be quite different from other forms of regulation—namely, license fees or quotas, which require payment before the harvest occurs.

The tax on the catch looks very appealing in theory. It allows fishing firms to act independently, it doesn't involve monitoring of fishing effort, and it can lead to the social optimum. Fishing firms still act as if they had open access to the fishery, but the tax forces them to reduce effort and harvests to the optimal level. In practice, however, we seldom observe taxes on the catch. Why? There are a number of administrative and political problems with a tax on the catch.

Suppose the tax is set at the wrong level. The government cannot determine the optimal tax and simply guesses at an amount that it thinks will decrease effort sufficiently to move the fishery toward the optimal steady state. If the fish species is in no immediate danger of extinction, the nonoptimal tax will still lead to a reduction in effort. This reduction may be too much or too little, but as long as the tax can be revised as data on the catch and the fish population are revealed, the system may ultimately reach the optimum. This is not to say that costs will not emerge. A tax set too high may create high unemployment in the fishery—a situation that has serious political implications and serious implications for income. If there is some uncertainty about the viability of the fish stock, an inappropriate tax may not reduce effort enough, and the species could be extinguished.

Note as well that the optimal tax will depend on exogenous variables such as the price of fish or, more generally, the demand for fish and the biological characteristics of the fishery. We have assumed that these exogenous variables do not change, but in practice they can fluctuate quite a lot. Over time, the demand for fish may rise owing to changes in income and tastes. Fishery population dynamics can be affected by environmental factors, changes in predators, and so on. The "optimal" tax must account for all these factors at each point in time. Altering the tax to incorporate changes in exogenous variables may be straightforward in theory; in practice, it is difficult to change any governmental policy, including taxes. What is optimal today may not be optimal tomorrow. This makes it very difficult to advocate taxes as a means of correcting an open access fishery. We will encounter this problem again in our discussion of environmental resources in Chapters 6 and 7.

A tax on the harvest could be very difficult to implement. Landed fish can be sold in a variety of different markets—to packers, to restaurants, to individuals from the backs of pickup trucks, and in different countries. It would be difficult for a government to make sure the tax was paid in each case. Fishing firms may have a big incentive to evade the tax and may find it easy to do so. Unlike other types of taxes (the retail sales tax, withholding tax on personal income), which are more difficult to avoid, a tax on the catch would be relatively difficult to collect in many fisheries. The tax may also interfere with the government's ability to formulate good fishery policies. This is because harvests are often the main source of biological and economic information and hence help determine the optimal tax rate. The regulator may think that the tax is working to reduce effort, when in fact the tax induces firms to underreport harvests and sell the unrevealed catch illegally.

A tax on the catch can create unemployment. Aggregate effort will typically fall if the tax is effective. Those remaining in the fishery are no worse off, but some will have to exit. If there are high costs of finding alternative forms of employment (whether these costs are real or perceived), these individuals will be worse off than before the tax was imposed. The government will be pressured not to impose the tax or, if the tax is implemented, to compensate those who lose. Recall that the government is collecting the rent from the fishery, so it is feasible to compensate losers by redistributing tax revenues received. But this may still not appease those displaced by the tax. In many countries, fishing communities have a lot of political power and may thus prevent the implementation of policies that threaten them. The commissioner investigating the West Coast salmon fishery for the Canadian government was heckled and

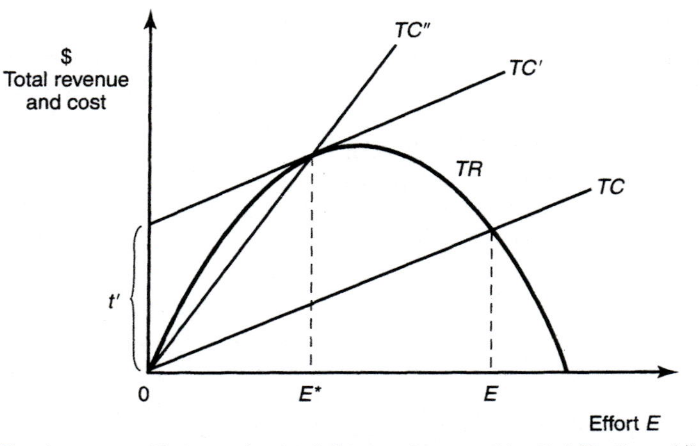

FIGURE 5.3. Two taxes on effort are shown. A license fee equal to t' shifts the original TC curve to TC', where $TC' = cE + t'$. Open access firms equate TC' to TR, and the optimal amount of effort, E^*, results. A unit tax on effort equal to t'' will pivot the TC curve to TC'', where $TC'' = (c + t'')E$. The optimal amount of effort is achieved where $TC'' = TR$.

booed by fishermen when he conducted hearings. His crime was to propose a tax on the salmon harvest. There are still no taxes on the salmon harvest in Canada. In the current political climate, taxes are very unpopular.

A Tax on Fishing Effort

Rather than tax fish as they are landed, suppose that the government decided to tax effort in the fishery. Would this form of tax lead to an optimal harvest? In theory, yes. Figure 5.3 illustrates two types of optimal tax on effort. The first is an *industry license fee*—a tax of a particular amount levied on each operator in the fishery. The industry must pay the government a particular sum if it wants to fish. The tax must be paid before any amount of effort is used in harvesting fish, but the tax is independent of the actual amount of total effort employed by the industry. There must then be some mechanism to distribute the industry license fee into a fee or tax per fishing firm. In what follows, we assume that each firm in the industry pays $(1/n)$ of the license fee, where n is the number of firms. Let's see how an industry license fee alters the industry's total cost function.

In Figure 5.3, before any taxes are levied, the industry has a total cost function that is given by TC, where TC is equal to cE, the unit cost of effort (c) times the amount of effort used. The open access equilibrium is originally at E (where $TR = TC$). The optimal amount of effort is E^*, where $MR = MC$. The optimal license fee equal to t' will shift the industry's TC curve to TC', where $TC' = cE + t'$. The industry still equates total revenue to total cost, but in this case they are equal where total costs, TC', are tangent to TR. Thus the tax has led to the optimal amount of effort, E^*. Notice that the fee must be levied in each period during which the industry operates. We are describing a steady-state fishery, and this means that the costs shown by TC'

must be repeated each period. If the license fee is paid only once, the cost curve will return to TC in the next period. The fee will have become a sunk cost that no longer has an effect on the marginal amount of effort employed in the fishery.

The second form of tax on effort is levied on each unit of effort employed in the fishery, in each period during which it is employed. With a tax equal to t'', the original total cost curve TC then pivots to TC'', where $TC'' = (c + t'')E$. The tax has no effect if no effort is used, so the total cost curve continues to pass through the origin (unlike the curve with the industry license fee). If the optimal tax is chosen, again the total cost curve will intersect the total revenue curve at the optimal amount of effort, E^*.

The most serious difficulty with any tax on effort is defining *effort*. We have talked about levying such a tax in theory, but how exactly is this tax to be imposed? Effort is an index of the capital, labor, and materials used by the fishing firm. When it comes to imposing a tax on this index in practice, how can it be done? It is not difficult to impose the tax on certain types of effort; government managers routinely license boats and even individuals. The problem is that unless all forms of effort are taxed, fishing firms have an incentive to avoid the effects of the tax by substituting types of effort that are not taxed for those that are.

Suppose that there is a tax on the boat. Clearly, we'd want to make this tax depend on the size of the boat, because it is generally possible to harvest more fish the larger the size of the vessel. But what if the equipment on the boat is not taxed? We would then see small boats top-heavy with electronic equipment, nets, and people. If individuals are licensed but vessels are not, large fleets owned by one person can result. If the government tries to tax all forms of effort, an incredibly complex and extensive set of taxes would be necessary. The government is likely to spend more than it collects in taxes trying to figure out what type of untaxed equipment fishing firms will substitute for taxed items each year. Meanwhile, neither the optimal amount of effort nor the optimal harvest is achieved.

The problem with taxes in general is that they may not have a predictable effect on the amount of effort in the fishery and hence on the harvest. They act on firms' *ex ante* decision making. That is, they represent a reduction in the firm's net returns ($TR - TC$) from fishing. In theory, this reduction in net returns should reduce the effort used by each firm. Mobility out of fishing generally has not been rapid; many individuals do not perceive alternative forms of employment to be desirable. If so, large taxes (which may mean that all firms take losses in the short run) would be necessary to induce these individuals to reduce their effort. Governments are averse to levying any tax, especially high taxes.

A Quota on the Catch and Effort

We turn now to the other type of regulation in the fishery—quotas or quantity controls on the harvest, on the amount of effort in the fishery, or on both. These are by far the most prevalent form of regulation in fishing industries.

Let's first consider a quota on the catch alone. Suppose the government has found that the fish stock is threatened. If harvests are not reduced to a particular level,

BOX 5.1 The Cod Fishery: Mismanagement or Biological Mystery?

In 1993, the cod fishery off the east coast of Canada was closed to commercial fishing. It remained closed as of 1996, with little hope of reopening in the near future. Harvests were holding in the range of 460,000 metric tons in the second half of the 1980s, but then they began to fall precipitously in the early 1990s. Canadian harvests fell over 60 percent, from a high of 510,000 metric tons in 1983 to 192,000 metric tons in 1992. Biologists had warned of signs that stocks were becoming dangerously low, but political pressures allowed commercial fishing to continue. The fishery provides jobs for a high proportion of people living in the Maritime Provinces of Canada. Over the past few years, the media have been full of articles indicating that the regulatory system was to blame. Total allowable catches were set too high. The figure below shows TACs and cod landings. While there is growing affirmation that TACs were set dangerously high, there is also evidence that biological factors were at least partly responsible for the depletion of the cod stocks.

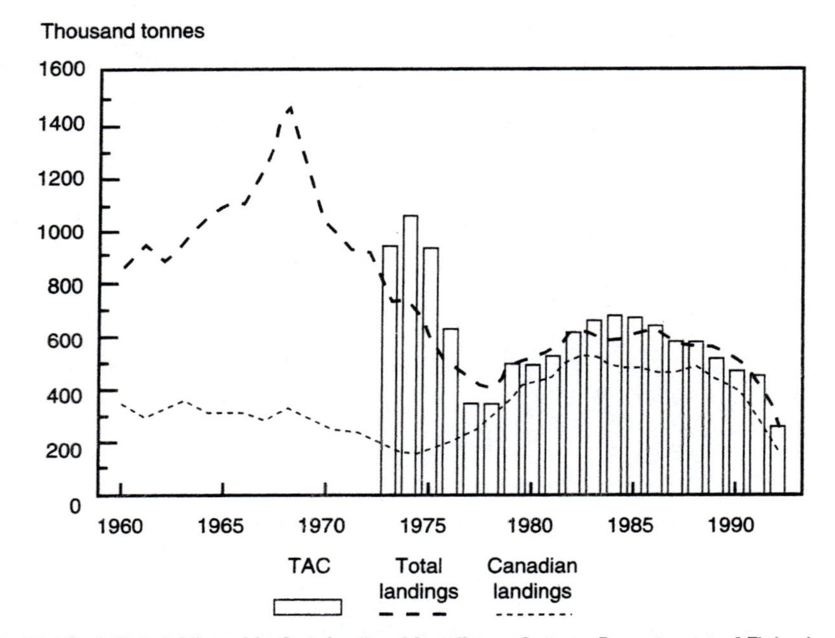

Atlantic Cod: Total Allowable Catches and Landings *Source:* Department of Fisheries and Oceans Canada, Biological Sciences Directorate, cited in Statistics Canada (1994). *Human Activity and the Environment, 1994,* Ottawa: Statistics Canada, Catalogue No. 11-509E, Table 4.14.4, p. 262.

Research on the groundfish off the east coast of Canada and the northern United States began in earnest when signs of plummeting stocks of these fish emerged in the 1980s. Before that time, the abundance of fish stocks meant that there was little interest in studying them. Since the early 1990s, Canadian researchers have been trying to find out what role natural phenomena play in influencing the size of the stocks. What they have

(Continued)

BOX 5.1 *(Continued)*

found so far is that something has affected all groundfish off the coast of northern Newfoundland and Labrador—commercial species as well as fish not harvested. These fish do not necessarily live in the same locations. Also, other species that were rarely found in large numbers, such as shrimp and crab, have flourished. The mystery is what is causing these large swings in fish populations.

The possible causes of the decline in fish populations include environmental contaminants, temperature, changes in predator-prey relationships, and fish genetics. Certain pollutants such as heavy metals, dioxins, and furans have been ruled out because no trace of these substances has been found in cod livers—where they would be concentrated if present. Temperature may be the culprit. The average water temperature in the region has declined from 0.5 degrees C to −1.0 over the past 30 years. The colder temperatures may have driven the fish out, or increased mortality, or both. Some people have blamed the ban on seal harvesting for the cod's decline. Seal prey on cod (and other species). But, again, the evidence is not conclusive. Finally, cod genetics may be at work. Scientists have found that some cod larvae starve themselves to death while there is plenty of food around. Why this occurs is not known. It could be connected to water temperature or other factors, unknown to scientists.

The challenge for fisheries regulators is daunting. The policy question is how to manage a marine fishery when biological factors are so uncertain. Estimates of fish stocks are based on data from harvests and fieldwork sampling the populations. The available data are fitted to biological models. If these biological models do not capture the underlying population dynamics, regulatory policies such as quotas, gear restrictions, and license fees may be aiming for the wrong target. This compounds the usual regulatory problems encountered in open access fisheries. The cod may or may not be back. In the meantime, those in the industry are not fishing.

Sources: Steven Strauss (1993). "The Mystery of the Missing Cod," *Globe and Mail* (July 10), p. D8. Statistics Canada (1994). *Human Activity and the Environment, 1994,* Ottawa: Statistics Canada, Catalogue No. 11-509E, Table 4.14.4, p. 262.

the species may become extinct and the fishery will vanish. This is a strong case for a quota on the harvest. Quite simply, the government limits the number (or biomass) of fish that can be caught in a given time period. In the case of the blue whale, as we saw in Chapter 4, the quota was zero: firms were prohibited from harvesting any whales. In 1993 a moratorium on harvesting cod off Canada's east coast was imposed to protect decimated cod stocks. Box 5.1 illustrates recent events in this fishery. Another example of a moratorium imposed to protect stocks was the Icelandic herring fishery in the early 1970s. Most fisheries are not in such an extreme situation, although these examples are by no means unique.

Typically, before the fishing season begins, a quota or total allowable catch (TAC) is established for the species. The TAC is based on information about the fishery in the past—the harvests and estimates of the remaining stock—and may also reflect biological and economic modeling. Factors such as expected recruitment for the period (or past period), water temperature, catches of related or predator species, and

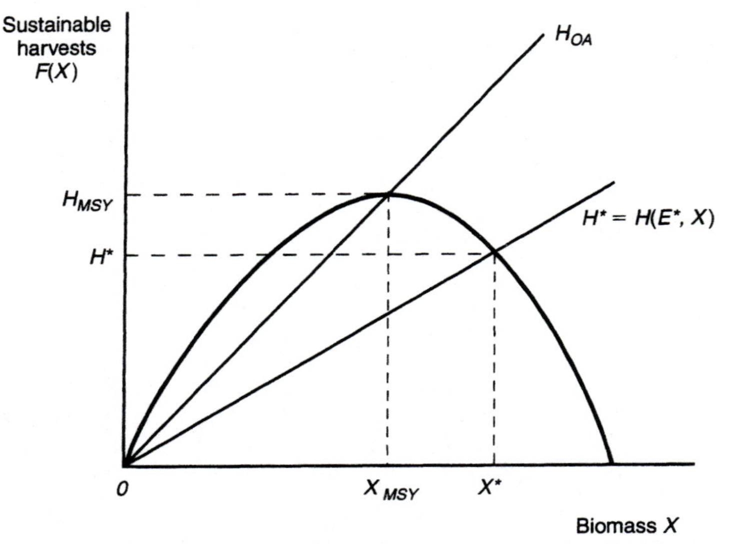

FIGURE 5.4. A quota on the total harvest from a fishery will not achieve the optimal amount of effort. Quotas on harvest are typically set at the MSY biomass, X_{MSY}. Effort will be expended until H_{MSY} is reached. The economically efficient harvest and level of effort are shown at H^* and E^*.

so on are taken into account. The TAC is often set at H_{MSY}, the maximum sustainable harvest. Then the fishery is opened up and boats are allowed to enter and harvest the species until the TAC is reached. Once the TAC is met, the fishery is closed.

A TAC quota will *not* lead to an efficient amount of effort in the fishery unless the quota is optimally rationed among individual firms. This can be shown quite simply. Figure 5.4 illustrates a biological production function, $F(X)$. Suppose that the government wishes to restrict the harvest each period to level H_{MSY}. Assume that $H^* = H(E^*, X)$ represents the economically efficient harvest. The value H^* is derived from the effort level that maximizes the difference between total revenue and total cost (recall our derivation of this condition in Chapter 4). The efficient harvest level is lower than that at H_{MSY}. With only the total harvest controlled—not entry—there is no way to prevent fishers from using large amounts of effort in an attempt to catch the allowed limit. Effort will rise. The harvest function will then pivot leftward until it intersects $F(X)$ at H_{MSY}. We call this harvest function H_{OA}, for open access equilibrium. Note that if the initial open access equilibrium were to the left of a TAC set at the MSY biomass, a quota on the catch would be completely ineffective and could lead to the destruction of the fish stock as more and more effort chases fewer and fewer fish. Fishers cannot even meet the TAC because of depletion of the fish stocks. Some observers suggest this is what happened to the Atlantic cod fishery off Canada's east coast.

A quota on the total harvest may in fact exacerbate the problems of open access. Suppose that the quota restricts the harvest, and the reduction in the harvest leads to an increase in the price of the species, as illustrated in Figure 5.5. In (a), with the fish-

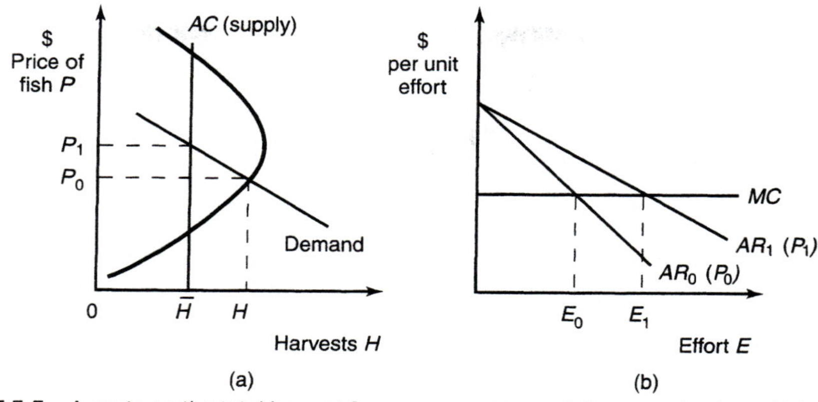

FIGURE 5.5. A quota on the total harvest from an open access fishery may lead to a higher price for the species. In (a), if the demand curve is downward-sloping, restricting total harvests to $\bar{H}$ will lead to an increase in the price of fish from P_0 to P_1. In (b), the rise in the price of fish from P_0 to P_1 will shift the average revenue curve as a function of effort from AR_0 to AR_1. The new open access equilibrium is then at a higher level of effort, E_1. The higher price thus induces more entry, which leads to greater congestion externalities and excess capacity in the fishery.

ery facing a demand curve D, the initial open access equilibrium yields a harvest of H at price P_0. If the quota restricts harvests to $\overline{H}$, price will rise to P_1. Vessels from other fisheries may then enter in response to the higher prices in the regulated fishery. This is shown in Figure 5.5(b). The rise in the price of the fish shifts the average revenue curve (as a function of effort) from AR_0 to AR_1. The OAE is then where the marginal cost of effort equals AR_1. This means that effort will rise from E_0 to E_1.

Fewer fish will be harvested with more effort. The quota may simply lead to a situation in which more firms fish for more valuable fish in a shorter period of time. Firms will race to catch the quota as quickly as possible to prevent others from getting the fish first. All the problems of open access occur as they did before the imposition of the quota—but in a shorter time period. Congestion externalities are likely to be rampant as vessels crowd in to get their share of the quota. Excess capacity in processing and retailing sectors may be needed to handle the large tonnages that are dumped on the market over a short time interval. The quality of the fish harvested may decline if boats stay out in the fishery for longer periods to try and catch as much as possible before the limits are reached. Clearly, a quota on the harvest can lead to many inefficiencies. The halibut fishery, discussed below, provides an illustration of the many inefficiencies resulting from a TAC.

The Individual Quota

What is needed is a means of allocating the quota among the fishing firms—in a sense, establishing a private property right to a particular harvest. A quota specific to a firm—an *individual quota* (IQ)—can lead to efficient use of effort within that firm. If each fishing firm has a guarantee that it can catch so many tons of fish each period, then the firm will act to minimize the cost of harvesting its allowable catch. Economic efficiency can be obtained. As long as the fish stock is abundant enough to ensure that each quota can be filled, no owner of a quota has any reason to put an excessive amount of effort into catching the fish. The open access character of the fishery is eliminated.

But simply assigning a quota to a firm does not guarantee that the most efficient firms are doing the harvesting. Whether economic efficiency occurs depends on how the quota is distributed, whether it is transferable and divisible, and how fishers respond to the specifics of the policy.[3] As we now see, there are two methods of allocating quotas—one by arbitrary administrative procedures and the other through market mechanisms.

First, assume that the government simply apportions the quota among the existing firms so that each is entitled to catch, say, h fish, where $h = H/E$. Alternatively, the government could apportion the quota on the basis of previous catches per firm. Those with historically large catches would be allowed a larger quota than firms which had caught relatively few fish. Some boats may not get a quota, or may get a quota so small that fishing does not pay. The arbitrary nature of such distribution schemes can politicize the fishery and create high administrative costs. If the quotas are nontransferable, economic efficiency will not in general be achieved. There is no guarantee that the firm receiving the quota is the one with the lowest costs of harvest. To see what may happen when a quota is distributed on an arbitrary or political basis, reflect on quotas on agricultural products and their documented inflation of food prices.

As noted above, an individual quota establishes a property right to the fish harvested. These rights will then have value. If quotas are divisible and transferable—in which case they are called *individual transferable quotas* (ITQs)—the holder of a quota would be able to capture some of the rents from the fishery. The firm could sell or lease part or all of the quota to another firm, just as it could a piece of land, and receive the discounted future profit from the use of the quota. This may mean that over time, an arbitrary distribution of quotas should lead to an efficient use of effort and harvest.

Firms with low costs could bid more for a quota than those with high costs. If the original holder of a quota was a high-cost firm, it would do better to sell its quota and move to another industry. Even if quotas are given away in an economically inefficient manner, if they are divisible and transferable economic efficiency may ultimately be achieved. If quotas are not transferabe, inefficiencies will persist. New firms with new and less costly technologies may be prevented from entering the fishery. Quotas may not benefit consumers. An effective quota will generally raise local prices consumers pay, and a decline in the industry will occur if the fish have good substitutes or foreign competition.

Another way to apportion quotas is to auction them off to the highest bidder. Firms will offer the present value of the potential profits from having the quota. If the quota restricts the total catch below what it would be under open access, these profits will be positive. They are the rent from the fishery, and the government will collect these rents from the sale of the quotas. They become public revenue or could be redistributed back to the fishery in some way. Auctioning should lead to an impact in the fishery per se similar to free distribution, as long as quotas are divisible and transferable and no imperfections exist in the market for fishing rights. Under auctioning, however, much of the rent is transferred to the government or the public domain. Under a free distribution scheme, the rents are captured by those lucky enough to acquire some of the quota initially. The income distribution effects are markedly different. Moreover, free distribution usually means that the political process is involved and fairness can get little attention. Obviously, there are many more complexities involved in the sale or free distribution of a quota, as we will see below.

Is there any rationale for the imposition of a quota on effort alone? An example of a quota on effort is the licensing of individual vessels. Let's first see how a quota on effort would achieve the optimal amount of effort and the optimal harvest. Suppose that an index of effort can somehow be accurately measured. The government fisheries board then solves for the socially optimal amount of effort, E^*. In Figure 5.6, E^* would be set where the slope of the total cost curve (the *MC* of effort) is tangent to the *TR* curve. No effort beyond E^* would be allowed in the fishery. This will yield the optimal harvest, because once E^* is achieved, the efficient harvest function is obtained.

Of course, this simple graphic representation omits all the difficult problems with a quota on effort. As with a tax on effort, the most severe problem is how to measure and then restrict each component of effort. Should the quota be placed on boats, people, equipment, or all of those? In practice, there are many different quotas on the various factor inputs that make up effort. Fishing firms have responded to quotas on one component by substituting factors that are not restricted. Government fisheries managers must then try to make the quotas as specific as possible. Regulations may be administratively very costly, and they must be altered frequently to reflect current conditions. There also remains the problem of how to implement the quota. Will it be sold or given to the firm? Will the quota be transferable and hence acquire a mar-

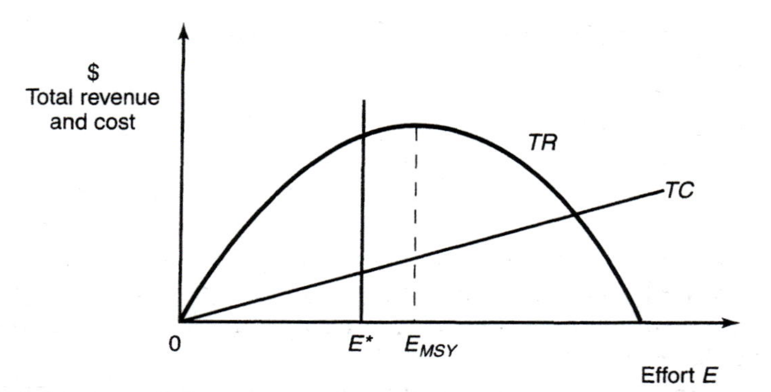

FIGURE 5.6. A quota on effort is imposed at $E*$, where $E*$ is determined by equating *MR* to *MC*. If effort could be measured, the quota would restrict effort to the efficient level and result in an efficient harvest.

ket value of its own (regardless of whether it was initially sold or given to the holder)? On what basis does the government restrict effort? These are the same problems taken up in the discussion of the quota on the harvest.

In practice, quotas on effort occur for a variety of reasons. Sometimes quotas are imposed because a specfic impact on the fish population is desired. For example, if the government managers wish to prevent the capture of a certain age class of fish (a cohort), restrictions on the size of the nets used in the fishery may be imposed to prevent the capture of fish below a certain size. This is an example of a *gear restriction.* All effort (and harvests) may be banned when biologists know that the species is reproducing. These restrictions may aid in the maintenance of the species, but they are difficult to design and enforce. Typically, they have no effect on the economic efficiency of the fishery.

Sole Ownership of the Fishery: The Cooperative

Before turning to our examples, we look at one further way in which an optimal allocation of resources to the fishery can be accomplished—turning the fishery over to a sole owner. We look at one example of government-backed sole ownership—the cooperative.

A *cooperative* is the self-administration of the fishery by the individuals doing the fishing. The government legally sanctions such organizations. The cooperative decides on quotas or other forms of control among its members, rather than taking orders from the government. To prevent overfishing, a government manager may set a total allowable catch each year and ensure that it is being met. The government biologist would also ensure that the total allowable catch is consistent with preservation of an optimal stock of fish.

The crucial decision of the cooperative is how many members to have and how to assign quotas to members. If the co-op is too large, each member would earn low profits. If the organization is too small, outsiders may be induced to demand compensation from the government for not being allowed to enter the industry. Cooperatives have been used in a number of fisheries—for example, the Bay of Fundy herring fishery.

FISHERY REGULATIONS IN PRACTICE

We turn now to fishery regulation in practice. We look at management objectives and activities in the United States, and then examine some specific fisheries in different parts of the world, looking at the type of regulations used and their impact on the fishery and the fishing effort.

Our objective in this section is to illustrate the impact of various regulations being used in different fisheries on variables of interest such as effort, the harvest, economic rent and incomes to workers in the fishery, the sustainable stock, and the quality of the harvest. We will, when possible, also indicate the costs of the regulations—their financial cost, and the costs in terms of potential misallocation of resources. We hope to give an indication of whether the benefits to society of regulating the fishery justify the financial and economic costs incurred in the regulatory process.

Before looking at particular cases, we discuss briefly the apparatus for regulating fisheries between 3 and 200 miles off the coast of the United States—the fishery management councils. We then consider in more detail three fisheries and how they are or are not regulated: (1) oyster fisheries off the Atlantic and Gulf coasts of the United States, (2) bluefin tuna caught by Australia and Japan, and (3) the Pacific halibut fishery of the United States and Canada. We need first to make some basic points about regulation in general.

First, regulation is costly. Governments must establish some sort of fisheries department with personnel to evaluate the fishery and design and implement the policies. Once the policies are in place, the fishery must be monitored to ensure that the regulations are being followed and to see if any changes must be made. Data from Canada suggests that large sums can be spent on regulation. In 1991, for example, the value of commercial fish landings was $1.3 billion (Canadian).[4] In that same year, Canadian governments spent over $350 million on various forms of financial support for its fisheries. To obtain the total financial costs of regulating the fisheries, we would have to add to this amount the costs of operating the fisheries bureaucracies. But even these costs do not measure the social costs of inefficiency that may result from particular types of regulation. It could easily be the case that the costs of regulation exceed the value of the commercial fisheries.

Are the expenses warranted? What is the value of the excessive amount of effort in the industry and perhaps excessively high harvest costs, the low harvests in many fisheries, and thus the forgone incomes that would be received under efficient management? We have no aggregate numbers, but some of the cases below will give estimates of forgone revenues and excessive costs when the fishery remains under open access or is regulated inefficiently, or both. (See Box 5.1.) In these cases, the costs of open access are much larger than the costs of regulation. A second point is that there is no guarantee that regulatory agencies will use economic criteria. This is clearly brought out in the case of the Pacific halibut and in the practices of some of the fisheries management councils in the United States.

Fisheries Management Councils in the United States

In 1976, the Fisheries Conservation and Management Act (FCMA, also referred to as the Magnusan Act), established the right of the federal government to manage the fish stock lying from 3 to 200 miles off all coastlines of the United States.[5] Fisheries within 3 miles are under state jurisdiction, and of course those outside the 200-mile limit are in international waters. Before passage of the act, virtually no management of fisheries beyond 3 miles had occurred.

The act established several objectives for the management of fisheries to be applied nationally. First, conservation and management measures were to prevent overfishing while achieving sustainable optimal yields. *Optimal* was interpreted as that yield which maximizes the country's benefits from food production and recreational fishing, as prescribed by the MSY biomass and modified by economic, social, and ecological factors. Fisheries were also to be managed to promote efficiency and minimize costs in utilizing the fish resources, but economic criteria were not to be the sole objective of management. At first glance, the objectives would seem to be very close to an economist's objective function for optimal fishery management incorporating distributional and ecological factors. However, because the stated objectives are qualified by the words "when practicable," some ambiguity is introduced into the interpretation of the act.

Eight regional fisheries management councils were established to implement the FCMA. Table 5.1 lists the councils and the fish species they manage. If a particular species is important in more than one area, the councils of the regions affected are to manage the fisheries jointly. The major task of the eight councils is to draw up a plan to determine the optimal harvest and how the harvest will be accomplished. The administrative procedures of the councils are complex. Other agencies, such as the Coast Guard, the State Department, the Department of the Interior, and the Commerce Department's National Marine Fisheries Service, are involved in the management programs. This has led to a fragmentation of responsibilities for fishery activities. For example, the Department of Commerce is responsible for data collection, research, management plans, and enforcement. But enforcement is also a responsibility of the Department of Transportation. The Office of Management and Budget covers fiscal responsibilities and operating procedures. The departments of State and Defense have authority over habitat quantity and quality. Coordination of all these agencies is supposed to be through each regional council. Some council members are appointed by secretaries for natural resources (or equivalent persons) from each state in the council's region (50 percent of membership); the remaining members are interested and knowledgeable members of the public (nominated to the council by the governor and secretary of commerce of each state). In practice, the "public" consists largely of representatives from the fishing industry and includes very few professionals such as economists or biologists.

Councils range in size from 8 to 16 people. Attached to each council is a professional staff that does include economists, lawyers, biologists, and so on. This staff may provide technical reports and assist the council in drawing up plans. Some councils also turn to outside consultants and universities for help in formulating plans, and still other councils use task forces or draw up the plans themselves. We cannot generalize about the nature of the plans or their impact on the fishery. However, we will make a few observations about the plans, then turn to some examples.

In principle, each council is to establish operational management objectives, then identify various means of implementing these objectives (harvests, effort allowed, and so on). In practice, Anderson (1982) notes that many plans look as if they were drafted first, and then objectives consistent with the plans were appended. In the plans developed thus far, it appears that distributional issues have been a more important objective than economic efficiency. This is slowly beginning to change owing to falling stocks of many species and continued problems of excess capacity in fisheries. In one case, though, economic efficiency was even ruled out by a council vote (cost minimization was not seen as a desirable objective). This is perhaps not surprising, given the strong representation of fishing firms on the councils. Economic efficiency is a fairly complex objective, requiring definition in operational terms (the optimal tax,

TABLE 5.1 **REGIONAL FISHERIES COUNCILS**

Council	States	Species
New England	Maine, New Hampshire, Massachusetts, Rhode Island, Connecticut	Atlantic groundfish, Atlantic herring, sharks, sea scallops, swordfish, redfish, billfish, hake, pollock, red crabs, American lobster
Mid-Atlantic	New York, New Jersey, Pennsylvania, Delaware, Maryland, Virginia	Surf clam and ocean quahog, Atlantic mackerel, butterfish, squid, sharks, bluefish, swordfish, scup, dogfish, billfish, other flounder, sea bass, tile fish, sea scallops
South Atlantic	North Carolina, South Carolina, Georgia, Florida	Billfish, coastal migratory pelagics, sharks, swordfish, corals, spiny lobster, tropical reef fish, calico scallops, sea scallops, shrimp, coastal herring
Caribbean	Virgin Islands, Puerto Rico	Spiny lobster, shallow water reef fish, swordfish, migratory pelagics, mollusks, billfish, corals, deepwater reef fish, bait fishes, sharks, rays
Gulf	Texas, Louisiana, Mississippi, Alabama, Florida	Groundfish, calico scallops, shrimp, coastal migratory pelagics, reef fish, corals, squids, spiny lobster, sharks, stone crab, sponges, billfish, coastal herring, swordfish, tropical reef fish
Pacific	California, Oregon, Washington, Idaho	Salmon, anchovy, groundfish, pink shrimp, billfish, herring
North Pacific	Alaska, Washington, Oregon	Tanner crab, Gulf of Alaska groundfish, king crab, high sea salmon, scallops, Bering Sea groundfish, Bering Sea clam, Bering Sea herring, Bering Sea shrimp, corals, dungeness crab, shrimp, snails
Western Pacific	Hawaii, American Samoa, Guam, Northern	Billfish, bottomfish, precious corals, seamount resources, spiny lobster

Source: L. G. Anderson (1982). "Marine Fisheries," in P. R. Portney, ed., *Current Issues in Natural Resource Policy.* Washington, D.C.: Resources for the Future. Copyright Resources for the Future, Inc.

the number and nature of individual quotas). People are often more comfortable working with physical objectives, such as restrictions on the total harvest and equipment. "Fairness" is also seen as an important objective, necessary to thwart any lawsuits by aggrieved parties losing out as a result of the management plan.

In 1990, the Assistant Administrator of Fisheries for the U.S. Department of Commerce was highly critical of the FCMA and the lack of success its councils have had in achieving sustainable yield and economically efficient policies. He noted:

> Preventing overfishing and allocating finite resources are two of the most critical fishery problems faced today. Virtually all of the important finfish stocks managed under the MFCMA [Magnuson Fishery Conservation and Management Act] off the northeastern, southeastern, and Gulf of Mexico coasts of the U.S. are

either overfished or on their way to that condition. It appears that the Pacific and Bering Sea fisheries will ultimately be depleted as well if the management practices under the MFCMA are not vastly improved. From the degree of overfishing, it is obvious that fishing effort and capital investments in vessels and gear are just too high. New and effective approaches are badly needed. (Fox, 1990, pp. 133–134).

One proposal by Fox to improve fisheries management is to create an arm's-length national fisheries board composed of experts on fisheries with powers to oversee the management and decisions of fisheries councils and make recommendations to the various government agencies for management activities. The Marine Mammal Protection Act has such a board, and—according to Fox—this has helped achieve the goals established by Congress under that act.

These concerns were echoed by a study of the FCMA in 1986 by the National Oceanic and Atmospheric Administration (NOAA; cited in National Research Council of Canada, 1993, p. 659). The NOAA found significant deficiencies in the implementation of the act. These included continued overfishing of certain stocks, lack of coordination between the councils and the National Marine Fisheries Service, failure to resolve conflicts among users, vulnerability of fisheries plans to delays and political influence, inconsistency in management measures across states, and adoption of unenforceable management measures. In general, the NOAA study found that the regional councils sacrificed resource conservation for short-term economic gains. Future interests of society were ignored.

To get a flavor of the types of plans implemented, let's look at two cases examined by Anderson (1982), and updated with various sources. The Mid-Atlantic Council established a plan for the Atlantic surf clam and offshore quahogs in the late 1970s. The surf clam was a heavily fished species, harvested under open access. The quahog had not been fished heavily at this time but presumably could be harvested with the same fleet that captured the surf clam. The plan established *annual and quarterly quotas* on the *total harvest.* Because the clam fleet was several times larger than that needed to harvest the total catch allowed, a moratorium on new vessel entry was imposed. There were no reductions in the vessels currently harvesting the clams. The plan also controlled the days per week and hours per day that vessels could harvest, and restricted harvests in areas where young clams resided.

Economic theory predicts well the impact of this type of management plan. The regulators found that the fleet harvested the allowable catch very quickly. Vessels were first allowed to fish 4 days per week. That limit was later reduced to 1 day (24 hours) per week. The fishery thus had considerable *excess capacity*, and firms were clearly not minimizing their costs relative to a more efficient management scheme. Without a reduction in effort (number of vessels), economic efficiency could not be obtained. The council considered individual quotas, but it could not implement them because of inadequate historical data on harvests. It considered basing individual quotas on harvests in a subsequent year but recognized that this would lead to excessive harvests on which to base the quotas.

All the problems of inefficiency (excess capacity, rent dissipation) finally resulted in a change in the management plans. In September 1990, an individually transferable quota (ITQ) was installed in this fishery—the first ITQ established under the Magnuson Act (OECD, 1993). A TAC remains for each fishery, but then a percentage of the TAC is allocated among fishers based on a formula involving historical catches and vessel size. The individual quota is transferable in minimum sizes of 160 bushels to anyone owning a documented vessel. It is too soon to assess the ITQ for this fishery, but we will have more to say about ITQs in this chapter. A segment of the snapper-grouper fishery and the wreckfish fishery in the south Atlantic had an ITQ approved in 1992. Other fisheries contemplating ITQs include western Pacific crustaceans, Alaska sablefish, Pacific halibut, Pacific groundfish, and Gulf of Mexico reef fish. Some fundamental changes in the regulation of fisheries in the United States may well be occurring.

In the New England Council, the management plan initiated in 1977 for groundfish such as yellowtail flounder, haddock, and cod also consisted of a quota on the total harvest of each species. It did not restrict entry to these fisheries. The groundfish fisheries to which these species belong are very complex. Different stocks of flounder and cod inhabit various locations. The fleet harvests a variety of different fish in addition to those mentioned above, and many of the species are biologically interdependent. To be fair to the council, devising management plans for these fisheries is difficult. However, its plan was a disaster.

With the annual quota, the harvest was taken early in the year and fishers were furious about the restriction on the catch. In the second year of the plan, the council allowed two harvests in response to these complaints (the quota was filled twice), but this was obviously not a long-run solution. Quarterly quotas on the catch were tried, with similar results. Then quotas based on vessel size were introduced. Thus the council shifted from a quota on the catch to a quota based on effort. The results were predictable: Boats incurred high harvesting costs because they frequently had to return to port before they filled their holds. As many of the costs of fishing (such as gasoline and time to fishing site) are relatively fixed, it meant lower profits, especially for large boats with quotas less than their capacity. Owners of small boats felt aggrieved because they were frequently affected by adverse weather and often missed filling their quota.

The quota was revised again and this time was based on the size of the crew. Large crews then appeared on each vessel. Additional regulations were then established for each type of fish and by size of boat. Finally, the whole regulatory system became so complex and unmanageable that it was abandoned. By 1981, these fisheries were regulated mainly by restrictions on the mesh size of the nets (to allow fish of a particular size to escape) and closed areas protecting juvenile fish. No taxes (except on foreign vessels) were used in these cases, nor were individual quotas used. These regulations did not eliminate open access to the fisheries.

Further evidence of the state of this fishery is provided by Crutchfield and Gates (1985), National Marine Fisheries Service (1993), and the National Research Council of Canada (1993). A very rapid increase of fishing effort occurred over the period from 1977 to the mid-1980s. In a very few years, the fishery went from being generally underfished to being overfished. Figure 5.7 shows the decline in landings and the

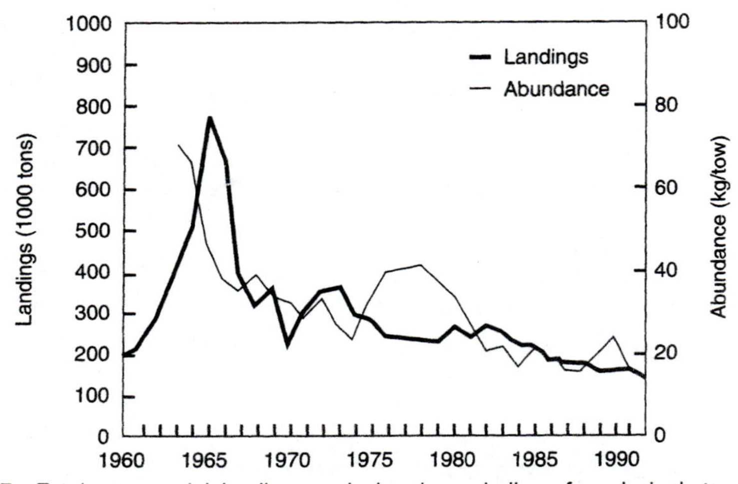

FIGURE 5.7. Total commercial landings and abundance indices for principal groundfish and flounders off the New England coast, 1960–1992. *Note:* Abundance indices are measures of mean weight in kilograms per tow taken in Northeast Fisheries Science Center autumn bottom trawl surveys. Species measured include: Atlantic cod, haddock, pollock, redfish, hakes, American plaice, and a variety of flounders. *Source:* National Marine Fisheries Service (1993). *Our Living Oceans: Report on the Status of Living Marine Resources.* Silver Spring, Md.: National Marine Fisheries Service, U.S. Department of Commerce, National Oceanic and Atmospheric Administration, Figure 1-1, page 36.

abundance of groundfish since the introduction of the fisheries councils. By 1983, the fleet size had reached 1423 vessels, up from 590 vessels in 1976, the year the Magnuson Act was passed. Vessel sizes also increased. Another measure of excess capacity is shown by the number of days fished per year. This has fallen by more than 40 percent over the same period. Catch per vessel fell by almost 45 percent (from 693,000 to 383,000 pounds) over the period 1965 to 1982. Revenue per vessel has declined by almost 38 percent from approximately $130,000 in 1965 to $81,000 in 1982 (in constant dollars). Crutchfield and Gates estimate that returns to vessels operating out of four ports (two in Massachusetts, one in Maine, and one in Rhode Island), became negative in all but one of the ports after 1979.[6] New regulations introduced in 1992 to cap multispecies groundfish permits and prevent their transferability, increase the minimum mesh size, and limit days spent fishing were introduced in an attempt to reduce fishing mortality. The conclusion remains that unless entry into this fishery is limited, all economic rent will be dissipated. However, employment and output have increased owing to exclusion of foreign vessels from United States waters within the 200-mile limit, gear restrictions, and the TAC. The trade-off between economic efficiency and creation of employment is illustrated by this case. Whether economic inefficiency is an acceptable "price" to pay for generation of employment in fishing communities is a value judgment, and ultimately a political decision.

The Oyster Fishery

Oysters are a sessile, benthic (bottom-dwelling) species. They are very well suited to management under private property rights. After a brief period in which the oyster larva are free-swimming, they settle down as adults and permanently fix themselves to material on the ocean floor, such as rock and shell deposits. The oyster lives in the intertidal zones off many seacoasts or in inland rivers and bays.[7] The productivity of an oyster bed is related to exogenous variables such as water temperature, salinity, and parasitic disease, as well as the size of the stock itself (which is, of course, affected by harvests), their predators, and the amount of suitable material on the seafloor. This material, called *cultch*, consists of rocks, shells, or anything to which the oyster can attach itself. Cultch can be treated as a variable input into the oyster fishery. If cultch is added to the fishery, more oysters find it a desirable home, and the productivity of the bed is enhanced. A barren seafloor can be turned into a thriving oyster bed with the addition of cultch. But a thriving oyster bed can also be reduced substantially if cultch is not maintained. Cultch is thus an input that can be controlled by humans.

In an open access oyster bed, there is no incentive for any firm or individual to add cultch to the bed. The fruits of that person's effort will be shared by all who harvest oysters from the bed. This is yet another externality that arises from open access which we have not yet examined. Agnello and Donnelley (1976) call this a "grounds quality" externality. Under open access, no individual has any incentive to invest in activities that increase the productivity of the fishery. Many more oysters could be harvested with the provision of more cultch, but less than the optimal amount of cultch is provided under open access.

The presence of this externality gives rise to the possibility that the optimal management of an oyster fishery *need not* result in a decline in the amount of effort used to harvest the oysters. One of the issues in regulating the fishery is that unemployment typically results. This can cause economic and political problems if the unemployed factors of production are immobile. But it is possible that, once an oyster bed is converted to private property management, an investment in cultch will be made, the productivity of the oyster bed will be increased, and no decline in effort will result. The increased output from the oyster bed eliminates the need to lay off factor inputs. The argument is simple and can be seen graphically in Figure 5.8.

Assume that there is an infinitely elastic supply of labor to the fishery at a real wage of w. For a fixed stock of capital (oyster equipment such as hand or power rakes and dredges), the average and marginal product of labor (the other effort input) can be derived in the usual fashion. Under open access, the average and marginal products of labor used to harvest oysters are shown as AP and MP. If the bed was then turned over to private property, cultch would be added. The average and marginal product curves would shift out. Each unit of labor will now catch more oysters than before because more oysters will attach to the added cultch. In Figure 5.8, the new curves are shown as AP' and MP'.

The use of labor will also change when the fishery is converted to private property. Under open access, the equilibrium would employ L individuals, given the wage rate w. The equilibrium occurs where the real wage rate intersects the AP curve. If no

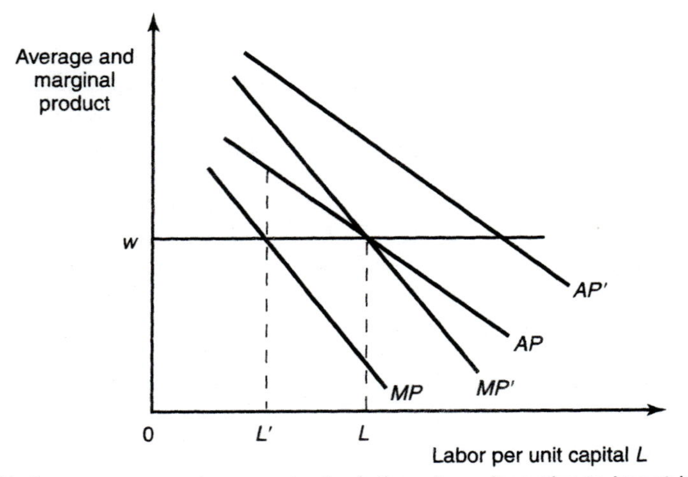

FIGURE 5.8. Under open access to an oyster bed, there is no incentive to invest in the productivity of the bed. The common property equilibrium with a real wage of w uses L units of labor per unit capital. When the oyster bed is managed by a sole owner, cultch is added to the oyster bed and the marginal and average product curves shift out, reflecting the higher productivity of the fishery. Under private property, the new equilibrium is where $MP' = w$, but again, L units of labor are employed. No decline in labor is observed in this example when the fishery changes from open access to private property management, because the productivity of the fishing grounds increases.

investment in cultch is made, the private property equilibrium would occur at point L', which is to the left of point L. The traditional result would then be reached: The rent-maximizing equilibrium leads to a decline in effort used in the fishery. But the addition of cultch may offset the decline in effort. If the AP and MP curves shift to AP' and MP', the private property equilibrium uses *exactly the same amount of labor* as the open access equilibrium. The curves shown in Figure 5.8 are not the only case that could occur, but they illustrate the point that the removal of the grounds quality externality mitigates the decline in effort that occurs when an open access resource is converted to private property.

What is the evidence in the oyster industry? Oysters are a good test case because they are harvested under both private property management and open access. Off the Atlantic and Gulf coasts of the United States, each state controls access to its oyster beds. There is a mix of property rights across the states. In some states, most of the oyster beds have been leased to individuals who basically have full control over the bed. In other states, most oyster beds are open to anyone.

Agnello and Donnelley (1976) attempted to estimate the average product of labor from an oyster bed under open access versus private property management to see if the argument above has any empirical validity. They estimated the average product of labor (total harvest per state/number of people harvesting) as a function of property rights and biological and economic characteristics. The property rights variable is a ratio ranging from 0 to 1 that shows the percentage of the oyster catch by weight harvested under private property to the total catch in each state studied. A value of 1 indicates that the entire harvest is obtained from private property beds. The property rights ratio ranges from a low of 0.04 in Mississippi and Texas to a high of 0.98 in Connecticut and Delaware. A biological characteristic—the presence of oyster parasites that periodically infest the beds—is incorporated by using a dummy variable. The economic variables are the capital intensity of the industry—an index of capital quality (the use of dredging vessels to total vessels), the amount of labor used, and the amount of seabed land used.[8]

A linear equation that fits the average product of labor to the economic and biological variables is estimated for a data set that pools a cross-section of 16 states with a time series over the period 1950 to 1972.[9] Their results for the variables of economic interest are shown in Table 5.2. The regression supports the arguments presented above. The property rights variable (*PR*) is positive and highly significant. The greater the degree of private property management of the oyster beds, the higher the average product of labor. Conversion of an oyster bed to private property may thus make it possible to produce more oysters and not create unemployment.

The other variables all have the signs expected in theory. Capital (*K*) is positive and significant. The biological disease variable is negative and significant. Labor and land have the right sign (positive) but are not significant. The authors of the study suggest that this is because the two variables are highly correlated with each other, very little variation in labor was observed over the sample (more support for their hypothesis?), and land was measured inaccurately.

TABLE 5.2 **REGRESSION RESULTS FOR THE AVERAGE PRODUCT OF LABOR IN OYSTER FISHERIES**

Variable	Coefficient	*t* value
PR	44.70[a]	2.94
K	7617[a]	3.76
MSX	−4032[b]	−1.75
L	−7.50	−0.94
A	1.71	0.53

NOTES: (a) Significance is at the 99 percent level; (b) significance is at the 95 percent level. Variables: PR is the property rights variable; K is the index of capital; MSX is a dummy variable for the presence of oyster parasites; L is the labor input fitted from a first-stage regression; A is the amount of land in the oyster bed.

Source: Agnello R. J. and L. P. Donnelley (1976). "Externalities and Property Rights in the Fisheries." *Land Economics* 52, pp. 519–529.

Because of statistical problems, Agnello and Donnelley cannot tell directly whether the oyster catch is larger under private property than open access, but they do solve for the increase in the value of output per person that results when the oyster bed is managed under private property. Their estimate is $995 (1976 dollars) per year. If the supply of labor to the fishery remains constant at 14,000 people per year, then the total output gain under private property would be over $13.9 million annually. Another estimate put the value of the actual loss in employment that would result from complete privatization of oyster beds at $667,000. So even if some decline in labor occurred, it is nowhere near the gains made. No figures are presented for the costs of the privatization method—leasing the beds to a sole owner—but it is hard to imagine that these costs would offset the gains in the value of the fishery under private management.

Unfortunately, in practice parts of the oyster fishery have not fared as well as Agnello and Donnelley predicted. Two problems are identified by Bosch and Shabman (1989)—MSX disease and the method of growing oyster "seed," the larvae that are planted on the seabed. From 1958 to 1988, total harvests of oysters from Chesapeake Bay in Virginia have declined from 5.7 million bushels to 600,000 bushels. The majority of the decline (90 percent) comes from private grounds. While MSX disease has contributed to the decline, Bosch and Shabman argue that the methods of harvesting oyster larvae have led to an increase in its real costs, causing profits in the industry to fall. Seed production is publicly managed in the area studied. The larvae are harvested by hand with tongs. The alternative technique is to use mechanical dredging, followed by returning clean cultch to the area. Mechanical dredging is much cheaper per unit seed harvested, but it employs far fewer people. For example, the average price paid in Virginia for seed harvested from public grounds using hand tongs was $2.10 per bushel in 1983–1984. Mechanically harvested seed from the Potomac River cost $0.50 per bushel over the same period.

Given the presence of MSX disease and the high costs of seed, oyster fishers in Virginia may well be behaving efficiently. Our steady-state model for a private property fishery predicts that an increase in costs leads to a reduction in effort, and a decrease in harvests. Profits will decline. Figure 5.9 illustrates the combined effects of the rising seed costs with MSX disease on the amount of effort and harvests in a private property fishery. This disease will reduce the sustained yield for all levels of effort. Hence the total revenue curve shifts in from TR to TR'. The MSY harvest is at a lower level and may also occur at a lower level of effort than in a fishery not affected by the disease. In the figure, E_0 shows the level of effort and H_0 the harvest in an initial equilibrium. If the only problem in the fishery is MSX disease, the new equilibrium is E_1 and H_1. But when the total cost curve shifts from TC to TC' as a result of higher seed costs, the level of effort and harvests falls to levels E_2 and H_2. Bosch and Shabman note that many of the privately held grounds have not been reseeded in recent years. Should the state, as manager of the seed beds, invest in better seed production technology to offset the depressed state of the fishery? Would profits in the fishery, effort, and, harvests all rise if both the oyster grounds and the seedbeds were managed privately? This question is raised but not answered in this study.

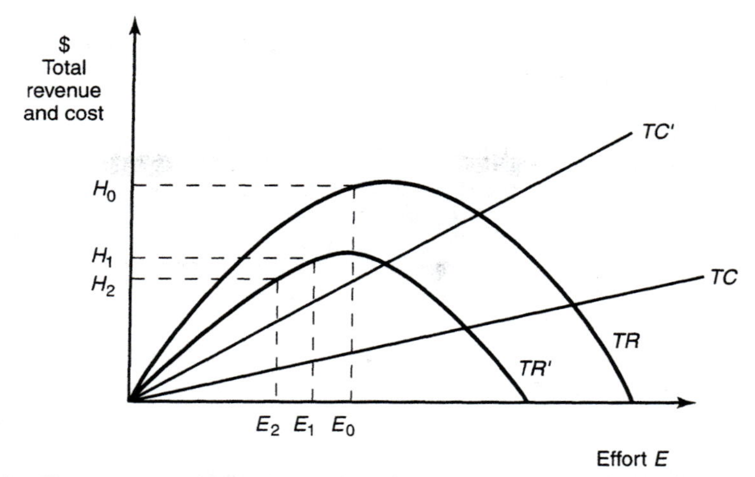

FIGURE 5.9. The presence of MSX disease in oysters collapses the total revenue curve to *TR'*. In the private property fishery, effort will fall to E_1 with harvests of H_1. The effect of rising cost of oyster seed pivots the total cost curve to *TC'*. The combined effects of MSX disease plus high seed costs results in harvests of H_2 with effort levels of E_2.

What does this example tell us? The oyster fishery is perhaps the most straightforward one we examine. Because oysters do not move, it is relatively simple and cheap to convert the open access resource to a private property resource. Well-defined beds can be enumerated, and each owner then farms the bed. There are no complex catch or equipment requirements. Each owner simply "pays" for the right to manage the resource. This comes as close to our optimal management objective and practice as we'll find in these cases. The other important point is that privatization need not result in a decline in the amount of effort in the fishery, if the productivity of the fishery rises. In this case, for at least some oyster beds, these rises in productivity have not occurred. But are private property rights feasible in a more complex fishery—say for a pelagic species? To examine this question, we turn to our second example, the southern bluefin tuna fishery.

Southern Bluefin Tuna

Kennedy and Pasternak (1991) examine the potential for generating rents in a pelagic fishery when two nations are harvesting the fish. Part of the fishery operates with an ITQ scheme. The fishery in question is the southern bluefin tuna, harvested in Australia's 200-mile limit and in open seas stretching from South Africa to New Zealand. This case illustrates how theory may be used to calculate different equilibria for a regulated fishery. Changes in ownership of the fishing rights, the age of the fish harvested, and the type of fishing gear used may lead to higher rents and harvest levels in this fishery.

BOX 5.2 **Measuring the Welfare Cost of Free Entry in a Lobster Fishery**

Estimates of the social cost of unrestricted entry to two lobster fisheries in eastern Canada were developed by Henderson and Tugwell (1979). They found these losses from unrestricted entry to be about 20 to 30 percent of the current market value of harvests in the areas. The loss was represented to a considerable extent by excess resources devoted to harvesting. While catch fell by 10 to 40 percent, effort or resources fell by 60 to 70 percent in the hypothetical switch from unregulated entry to optimally regulated entry. Let us observe the results for one area, Miminegash. Henderson and Tugwell found the stock-yield equation to be

$$X(t-1) - X(t) = X(t)[1.27024 - 0.00039X(t)]$$

and estimated a harvest equation as

$$H(t) - 2.51E^{0.48}X^{0.44}$$

where E is effort measured in hundreds of traps, $X(t)$ is the stock at time t, and $H(t)$ the harvest. The price obtained by fisher was $370 per 1000 pounds, and opportunity cost per 100 traps was $390. The results obtained are presented in the following table.

	Optimal solution	**Free entry**	**Observed 1959–1963**
Lobster stock (thousand lb)	2450	1125	1273
Lobster catch (thousand lb)	801	936	1094
Effort (traps)	122	365	—
Ratio: catch/stock	0.33	0.83	0.86
Shadow price of future stock	68	—	—
Optimal tax/thousand lb catch	225	—	—
Annual resource savings:			
Dollar value of traps saved			
Less value of diminution in catch	$180,470	—	—

Source: J. V. Henderson and M. Tugwell (1979). "Exploitation of the Lobster Fishery: Some Empirical Results," *Journal of Environmental Economics and Management* 6, pp. 287–296.

Japan is the major harvester of the southern bluefin tuna, followed by Australia. Small quantities are taken by New Zealand, Taiwan, Korea, South Africa, and Indonesia. The Australian fleet operates primarily within its 200-mile limit, harvesting juvenile fish ranging in age between 2 and 6 years. Thirty percent of the Japanese harvest comes from Australian waters, the rest from the open access oceans. The Japanese harvest mainly adult fish older than 6 years. Over the 20-year period from 1967 to 1987, the Japanese harvest has generally declined. Australian harvests gradually rose until 1983, then declined somewhat and have since leveled off. Figure 5.10 illustrates these trends in the harvest. Most of the fish caught are destined for the Japanese raw seafood market (sashimi).

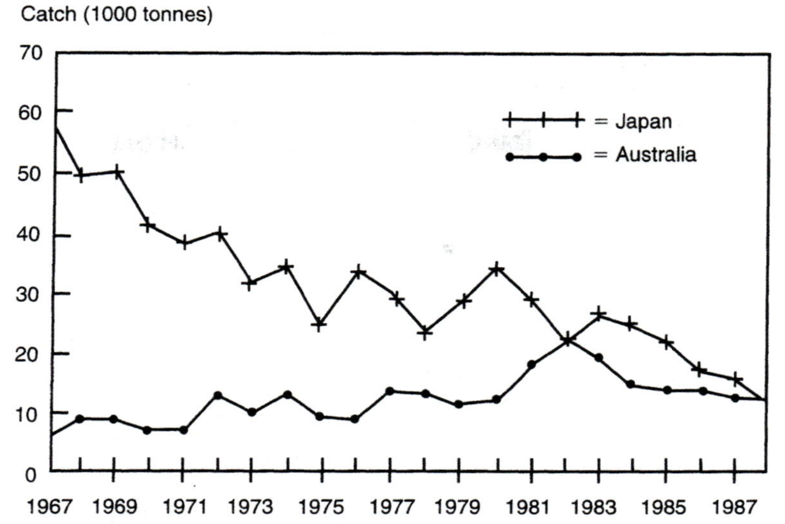

FIGURE 5.10. Historical harvests of southern bluefin tuna.
Source: Kennedy, J. O. S., and H. Pasternak (1991). "Optimal Australian and Japanese Harvesting of Southern Bluefin Tuna," *Natural Resource Modeling* 5, pp. 213–238.

The Australian government introduced an ITQ for the Australian fishery in 1984. Each individual holding a quota was entitled to a proportion of the TAC set by the government each year. The TACs have been reduced each year since 1984, owing to concern about the biological viability of the tuna stocks. By 1990–1991, the quota was about 23 percent of the quota for 1983. The TAC is divided between Australia, New Zealand, and Japan. For 1990–1991, the allocations were 6065 metric tons for Japan, 5265 for Australia, and 420 for New Zealand. There has been a reduction of over 50 percent in the number of vessels operating in the Australian tuna fleet since the introduction of the ITQ (from 44 to 20 boats by 1991). Current levels could be even lower. At the same time, the harvests have remained roughly constant at around 10,000 metric tons. The ITQ would seem to have achieved the objective of reducing effort in the fishery without affecting harvests. The question Kennedy and Pasternak ask is: Does the current situation maximize the rents from the fishery, or could the two countries do better? The answer depends on the nature of the competition between Japan and Australia, the type of fishing gear used, and the age of the tuna harvested. If Australia and Japan cooperate in their fishing efforts and maximize *joint* profits, rent from the fishery could be higher than in a noncooperative equilibrium. However, the distribution of rent between the two countries is very asymmetric. Using a simulation model of the fishery, Kennedy and Pasternak illustrate the possible outcomes.

A dynamic programming model is used to obtain solutions under different assumptions about the competition between Australia and Japan. Two scenarios are examined: In the first scenario the two countries operate as they do at present, both maximizing profits in a noncooperative duopoly; in the second they cooperate by maximizing their profits jointly. Japan fishes in two grounds—the open seas (ground

1) and within Australia's 200-mile limit, operating off Tasmania (ground 2). Australia fishes only within its 200-mile limit, but in different locations from the Japanese (ground 3). Australia can control the Japanese access to ground 2. Fishing effort will have different effects on the stock depending on the age of the fish caught and the type of gear used. Japan uses longliners, which are fishing lines with hooks spaced along them. This type of gear allows fish to be caught with minimum damage to the fish and the remaining stock. The tuna harvested by the Japanese are of high quality and command the highest prices in the raw fish market. Until recently, the Australian fleet harvested the younger fish from large surface schools using purse seiners and pole boats. This technique leads to lower quality of fish harvested, and it can have deleterious effects on the remaining stock. The tuna harvested by Australia are sold on the low-grade sashimi markets in Japan, receiving a price substantially below that of the price for high-quality tuna.

The authors develop a multicohort model of the fishery, looking at 19 different age classes of tuna. Demand functions for the tuna and harvesting cost functions for each country are estimated econometrically and combined with the fishery model to generate the possible equilibria under different industry behaviors. Under joint maximization for the two countries, the objective is to maximize the present value of the sum of annual social rents generated in each fishing ground. Social rent is defined as the social value of the catch minus harvesting costs and any costs for the fishing crews that are related to the value of the catch. If the two countries do not cooperate but instead operate as a duopoly, each country maximizes its own rents, given the impact of the other country's harvests on the tuna stocks. Japan gets rents from the harvest and also the consumer surplus from tuna sold in the Japanese market. Because Australian consumers do not eat the tuna, their rents include only those obtained from the harvest.

The modeling exercise has interesting implications for Australian fisheries policy. The type of equilibrium affects the harvesting profile for Australia significantly, although total harvests over the period examined change by less. Under joint maximization, the rent-maximizing solution requires Australia to close its fishing ground for 3 years. After that, harvests rise continuously over time until they level off at about 20,000 metric tons by the year 2008. Japan's harvests also rise throughout the period, from 9000 metric tons to about 20,000 metric tons. The present value of rents for this equilibrium are $81 million for Australia and $4.576 billion for Japan (in Australian dollars). Total social rents are thus $4.657 billion. Two duopoly equilibria are derived. In the three-ground equilibrium it is assumed that Japan continues to fish in open seas and within Australia's 200-mile limit. The two-ground duopoly has no Japanese vessels operating within Australia's 200-mile limit. Australian harvests are roughly constant over time under both duopoly equilibria at 7600 metric tons. The reason for this is that Australian harvesting costs are not sensitive to the stock of tuna. Japan's harvests again rise gradually over time to a maximum of 20,000 metric tons with three grounds and 17,500 metric tons with two. The big change comes in social rents to Australia under the duopoly cases. Its rents rise to $209 million with three grounds or $210 million with two. Either of these situations will more than double Australia's rents. Japan's rents fall in both duopoly cases, to about $4.4 billion in the three-ground situation and to $4.3 billion with two grounds. Total social rents are of course lower under the duopoly equilibria.

These results have a number of implications. First, while social rents would be highest under joint-profit maximization, this equilibrium is unlikely to be reached unless Japan redistributes some of its rents to Australia. Australia loses substantially under joint maximization. Duopoly with two or three grounds is clearly in Australia's interests. If Japan paid Australia to stop fishing for the 3 years, both parties could gain relative to either duopoly case. There is scope for a payment to be made. If Australia does not allow Japan to fish in its 200-mile limit, Japan loses over $500 million in rent, while Australia gains almost $120 million. Japan could fully compensate Australia for a 3-year moratorium and still be better off. Alternatively, Japan could be allowed to buy up some of Australia's ITQs for its fishing grounds and simply not use them for the 3 years. Australia would have to agree not to raise the quota allotments for its remaining fishers. The model also suggests that Australia gains very little from closing off ground 2 (Tasmania) to Japan. But it could extract some rents from the Japanese for the right to fish there. The difference in Japan's rents from fishing three versus two grounds is $307 million. The annual value of this sum is $36 million, according to the authors of the study. The actual fee Japan paid for access to tuna in Australia's fishing zone for 1989 was $4.6 million. The results also show that the tuna stocks are not threatened by the harvest levels under any of the equilibria. Under each equilibrium, tuna stocks rise from about 125,000 metric tons to between 300,000 and 340,000 metric tons between 1989 and 2007. However, the authors caution that these estimates are based on very uncertain parameter values for the biological model of the fishery. Finally, Australia might be able to increase its rents by switching to longline gear and harvesting adult tuna rather than younger ones. The divergence in the rents between the two countries suggests a potential for higher Australian rents if the gear and harvest strategy were altered. The authors do not investigate how the equlibria would change if this were done.

Tuna and oysters illustrate how private property fisheries generate economic rent, reduce fishing effort, and potentially increase harvests. However, until recently there have been few examples of fisheries managed with the objective of economic efficiency as well as protection of the fish stocks. There are many examples of regulatory failure. To illustrate what can go wrong with regulation, we next examine a fishery with a long history of regulation and problems resulting from regulation—the Pacific halibut.

The Pacific Halibut

Halibut have been commercially harvested off the west coast of the United States and Canada since the late 1880s.[10] The fishery originally extended from Santa Barbara, California, to Nome, Alaska. Over the years, the stock has been depleted in the southern portion of the region, so the fishery is now concentrated on the continental shelf off the coast of British Columbia in Canada and Alaska. Harvests peaked in the 1920s at around 70 million pounds, then decreased to about 30 million pounds in the 1930s, returned again to the 70 million pound level in the late 1980s, and are declining again.

Halibut are the largest flatfish. Their weight and, hence, their commercial value increase substantially over time. A 4-year-old halibut may weigh only 3 pounds, but a

20-year-old can weigh more than 100 pounds. Halibut reproduce only after the male is between 7 and 8 years and the female 12 or older. This makes the species vulnerable to overfishing. If a large proportion of juvenile halibut are harvested, the population can be reduced significantly. The long growing period means that it can take many years for the population to rebuild to commercially viable levels. Because the fishery has had open access until recently, it is not surprising that the stocks have been threatened with severe depletion.

The threat to the population was first recognized in the early 1920s. In 1923, a commission, first called the International Fisheries Commission and renamed the International Pacific Halibut Commission (IPHC) in 1953, consisting of both Canadian and United States participants, was set up to regulate the fishery. Its objective was to obtain the *MSY stock* and *harvest*. The initial regulatory device was a 3-month closure. But this policy was inadequate to protect the stock, so in 1930 the commission was given greater power to control harvests. Quotas on total harvests, equipment restrictions, and closure of nursery areas were implemented.

The quota on the total catch is still in place today in the United States, although its precise form has been somewhat modified. The quota is announced prior to the beginning of the fishing season each year and implemented by means of a limitation on the number of days that halibut can be harvested. The quota was first assigned to the entire fishery, but it has since been broken down into different seasonal openings in defined areas. In Canada, an ITQ was introduced in 1991. The United States ITQ began in 1995.

The equipment regulations stipulate that only longlines (fishing lines with hooks placed at different intervals) are permitted in the fishery. The commission had no authority to regulate entry. Any number of vessels of any type were permitted into the fishery, and there has been no licensing of boats or people until very recently. As we will see, these regulations did not protect the stock of halibut and have led to excessive amounts of effort used to catch a declining harvest. Before examining these effects more closely, we need some other facts about the fishery.

A large number of age classes are harvested simultaneously. This has meant that the harvests have tended to be more stable than, say, in salmon fisheries, where only particular age classes are harvested and therefore the catch is more sensitive to environmental factors that affect the stock. The vessels harvesting halibut range considerably in size, from small boats needing only one or two people to larger vessels with a crew of eight or nine. The number of small boats entering the fishery has increased dramatically since the early 1970s, owing to two factors. First, regulation in other Pacific fisheries—namely salmon—has released vessels to the halibut fishery. In the salmon fisheries in British Columbia, vessels must be licensed. Because the licenses are restricted and thus have a market value, owners who cannot afford the license shifted to the less restricted halibut fishery before the introduction of the ITQ. Second, the price of halibut rose considerably in the early 1970s as a result of increases in demand. Prior to this time, the industry had seen a gradual reduction in effort because of dwindling harvests and rising harvesting costs. But the increase in the price offset these factors, and entry surged. Table 5.3 shows the prices and harvests for 1965 to 1994, and a measure of catch per unit effort in the halibut fishery from

TABLE 5.3 **HALIBUT PRICES, HARVESTS, AND EFFORT, 1970–1992**

Year	Price per Pound[a]	Catch (millions of pounds)	Catch per Unit Effort[b,c]
1965	$0.32	63.2	NA
1966	0.34	62.0	NA
1967	0.23	55.2	NA
1968	0.23	48.6	NA
1969	0.38	58.3	NA
1970	0.37	54.9	NA
1971	0.32	46.7	NA
1972	0.64	42.9	NA
1973	0.74	31.7	NA
1974	0.70	21.3	NA
1975	0.89	27.6	64.2
1976	1.26	27.5	54.8
1977	1.31	21.9	62.6
1978	1.70	22.0	71.1
1979	2.13	22.5	75.7
1980	0.99	21.9	94.9
1981	1.02	25.7	110.3
1982	1.09	29.0	121.4
1983	1.13	38.4	172.7
1984	0.75	45.0	142.0
1985	0.89	56.1	138.9
1986	1.44	69.6	126.7
1987	1.58	69.5	NA
1988	1.28	74.3	289.5
1989	1.13	75.2	300.2
1990	1.37	70.5	278.6
1991	1.50	66.3	NA
1992	0.78	68.6	NA
1993	0.99	63.1	NA
1994	1.47	57.9	NA

NOTES: (a) Prices are average annual ex vessel nominal prices per pound. (b) Catch per unit effort is measured as pounds harvested divided by the number of skates used per day. (c) Effort is for both Canadian and United States fishers.

Sources: National Marine Fisheries Service (1990). *Fisheries of the United States,* selected years, International Pacific Halibut Commission, Annual Report.

1975 to 1990. Figure 5.11 shows estimates of stock biomass, recruitment, and a different estimate of catch per unit effort.

Compounding all these factors is one more problem in the halibut fishery: harvests of halibut by those seeking other fish. Fishing firms from both Canada and the

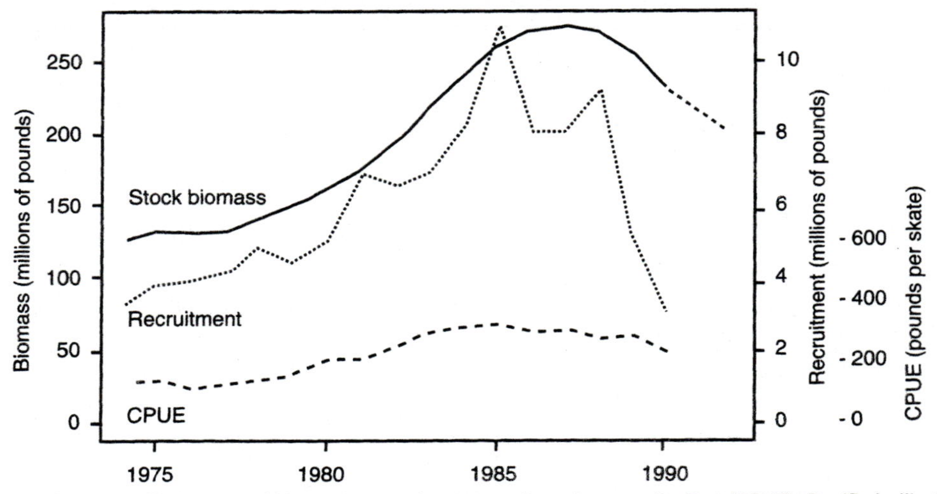

FIGURE 5.11. Estimates of biomass, recruitment, and catch per unit effort (CPUE), Pacific halibut. *Source:* International Pacific Halibut Commission (1990). *Annual Report.* Seattle, Wash.: International Pacific Halibut Commission, Figure 6, p. 28.

United States, as well as from Japan, fish for other species in the same waters. It is impossible to prevent the harvest of halibut by mistake, given the fishing techniques (trawling). These "bycatches" must be thrown back, but at least 50 percent of the halibut die in the process. Figure 5.12 shows estimates of bycatch mortality from 1960 to 1992. The bycatches have been significant relative to harvests, especially during the 1970s.

Bycatches can have an even more severe impact on the stock of halibut. In the early 1970s, foreign vessels were harvesting other species of fish in areas where juvenile halibut also lived. The mortality of these halibut had a much larger impact on the stock than would a bycatch of mature adults who had already reproduced. Biologists estimate that these bycatches were the most important cause of a significant decline in the halibut stock beginning in the late 1960s.

How have halibut regulations affected the fishery? Let's look first at the fishery before Canada's introduction of ITQs. Again, economic theory can predict the results. Recall that a quota on the catch alone will not reduce effort. This is exactly what happened in the halibut fishery, but the problem was exacerbated by the entry of more vessels from other fisheries. The economic impact of the regulations was considerable overcapacity in the fishery, high harvesting costs, and low incomes. After quotas on the total catch were first imposed over 50 years ago, the following chain of events occurred.

The catch was limited by restricting the time period in which halibut could be harvested. With no control over effort, the existing stock of vessels simply fished more intensively during the restricted season, then were idle or migrated to other

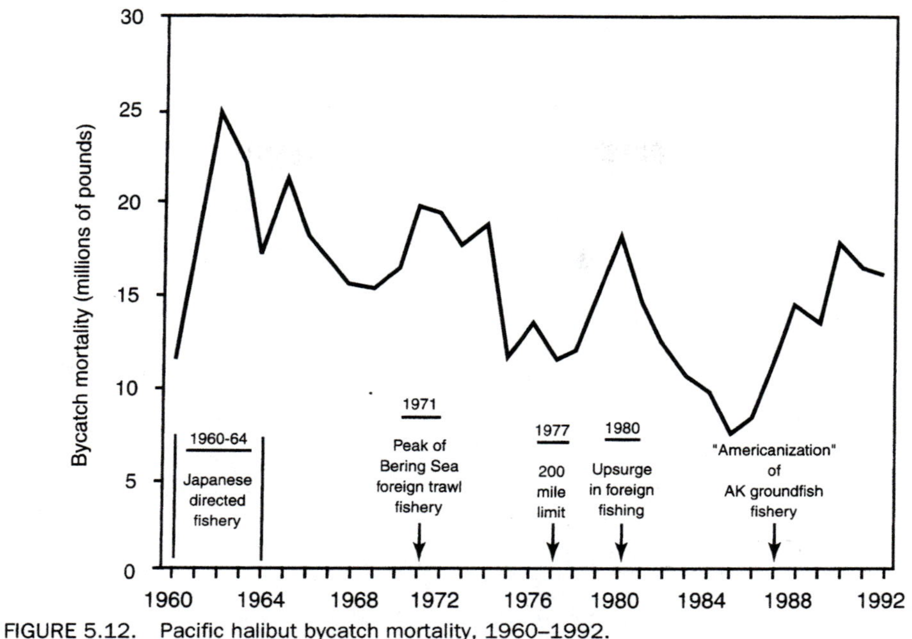

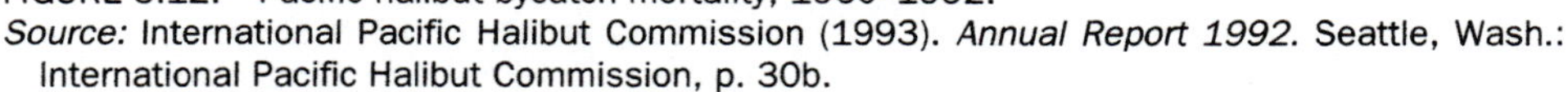

FIGURE 5.12. Pacific halibut bycatch mortality, 1960–1992.
Source: International Pacific Halibut Commission (1993). *Annual Report 1992.* Seattle, Wash.: International Pacific Halibut Commission, p. 30b.

fisheries in the closed season. But whenever the harvest was reduced (and demand for halibut was either constant or increasing), the price of halibut would rise, and the expected average return would rise. (When there is open access, firms are still setting average revenue from effort equal to the marginal cost of effort.)

Entry was encouraged. Boats would catch the quota more quickly, which then required a shortening of the season. The large increases in halibut prices, due both to declining halibut harvests and to increases in the price of other species in the 1970s, greatly increased the entry and required substantial reductions in the length of the season. Before 1977, a single fishing period lasting between 90 and 128 days was allowed. Beginning in 1977, there were three to five fishing periods spread over the season. The number of days allowed per period ranged from 5 to 19. Alaskan fisheries had the largest decrease in allowable fishing days, from a total of 73 days spread roughly evenly over the four open periods in 1977 to just one period of 5 days in 1983 (Quinn, 1987, p. 281). British Columbia fisheries were cut to approximately 1 week per yearly open season prior to the introduction of the ITQ. Figure 5.13 illustrates the large decline in fishing periods for one in the United States area.

Entry was also encouraged by the increased harvests over the period from the 1930s to the 1950s. The regulations did appear to increase the stock to about its MSY.[11] This increase in the stock, as we have earlier argued, decreases the average

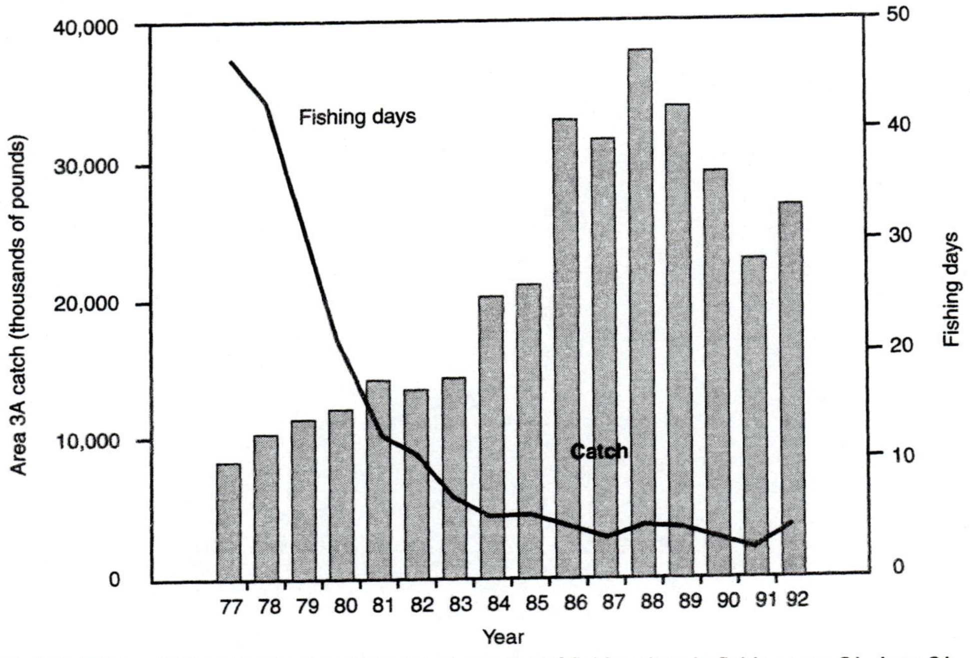

FIGURE 5.13. Halibut landings and regulated number of fishing days in fishing area 3A. Area 3A is off the coast of Alaska.

Source: International Pacific Halibut Commission (1993). *Regulations of the Pacific Halibut Fishery, 1977–1992,* Technical Report No. 27. Seattle, Wash.: International Pacific Halibut Commission, Figure 2, p. 20.

cost of harvests (more fish are around), which again encourages entry. A large influx into the fishery occurred by 1950. Effort rose from 384 regular boats (the larger boats) and 1903 people in 1931 to 820 regular boats with 4077 people in 1951. This represents an increase of over 100 percent in both boats and people over the period. The harvests rose as well, but by only 27 percent. Crutchfield (1981) estimated that two-thirds of this effort was totally redundant. That is, one-third of the vessels could have caught the entire quota in a season of 6 to 9 months.

If somehow entry could be limited to this number, many advantages would occur. With entry limits, the season could be lengthened. Boats and people would not have to be laid up or search for alternative useful activity. The fleet could be used far more efficiently. With the geographic quotas and limited seasons, the fleet is currently used inefficiently. Too many vessels crowd into an area during the season. With a season of less than 1 month, the problem is clear. Boats are scurrying out to catch as many fish as they can in the short period allowed. This not only increases the costs of harvest for each vessel (crowding externalities) but also increases the processing costs and reduces the quality of the fish.

Because the entire annual harvest is caught in a short period, large processing and storage capacity is required. If the harvest were spread over a long period, a far smaller (and less expensive) processing capacity would be required. Virtually all the halibut must be frozen and stored. The value of the catch is then lower than it would be if the harvest were spread more uniformly across the year. More fish could be sold as "fresh," commanding a higher unit price. The quality is reduced because vessels tend to stay in the fishery as long as possible; trips back to port take up precious time. With minimal storage capability on the vessels, fish spoils.

Returns to both labor and capital are also greatly reduced with a quota on the total catch, as the theoretical model predicts. No rents exist. Crutchfield estimated that labor was earning less than its opportunity wage in the late 1950s, and although no data are provided for the present, it is hard to imagine that any improvement has been made, considering the large influx of effort into the fishery in the 1970s. The return on investment in the vessels was between 3.9 and 4.8 percent before depreciation, hardly the opportunity cost of capital over this period. If an optimal number of vessels could be achieved, the return on capital would be approximately 8 to 10 percent, and the return to labor would double. Rents would then exist.

Costs of harvesting are also higher, no doubt because it is difficult to replace worn-out and technically obsolete capital with such a low rate of return. If effort were restricted, a more efficient fleet could be utilized. Equipment restrictions may also prevent the most efficient techniques from being used, although Crutchfield feels that the efficiency loss from the restriction to long lines is not too large.

Finally, and perhaps most important, there is no guarantee that the quotas have protected the stock of halibut. Mortality was high in the 1970s, especially because of the bycatches, and the continued survival of the fishery was in doubt. What had the halibut commission been doing all this time? Why has it taken so long to introduce policies that affect effort not just the TAC? There are some reasons. First, the goal of the IPHC was to achieve the MSY stock and harvest, not to achieve an economic optimum. As long as the stock was protected, the economic costs were not incorporated into the objectives of the commission. There is evidence that commissioners worried implicitly about economic factors but were hampered politically in doing anything about them. Crutchfield argues that the commission was afraid that if restrictions on effort were imposed, the IPHC would be seen as lackeys of the industry, imposing regulations to generate rents (profits) to the most vocal groups in the fishery that would be allowed to remain. Sticking to biological objectives is a much safer political strategy. When a fishery is international, it is difficult to enact policies to satisfy both countries.

But the whole halibut fishery has been changing since the imposition of the 200-mile limit. Up to 1978, Canadians and Americans were allowed to fish in each other's territorial waters. With the new limits, each nation has now prevented the other from fishing in its territory. United States fishermen were banned from Canadian waters in 1979, and Canadians exited United States fisheries by 1980. Because Canada took about two-thirds of its catch from United States waters off Alaska, the 200-mile limit has had a severe impact. However, each nation obtained exclusive rights to its respective halibut stocks and could limit entry. Pearse (1982) explains what has happened in the Canadian halibut fishery in the period after the imposition of the 200-mile limit.

The Canadian government implemented a license and compensation scheme in

1979 to deal with the displaced fishers. Halibut licenses were distributed to all vessels that had reported landings of at least 3000 pounds in 1977 or 1978. Licenses cost $10 annually and were transferable. Those fishing in United States waters who also had licenses to harvest other species were offered compensation for their halibut equipment and a vessel grant if they did not maintain their halibut license. Alternatively, they were given a vessel and equipment conversion grant to enter the sablefish fishery.

Fifty-four Canadian vessels were excluded from Alaska, and of these, 16 surrendered their halibut licenses while the rest received a license. In the British Columbia halibut fishery as a whole, about 331 vessels received licenses, and 400 fishers were excluded because they did not meet the requirements. Those excluded were largely part-time fishers who harvested in total less than 20 percent of the catch. Shortly after the licenses were issued, appeals were allowed on the grounds of financial hardship (and other factors). Many of these appeals were successful, and 100 more licenses were issued. Because of the minimal requirement for a license, by 1981 the British Columbia halibut fleet comprised 422 vessels. Prior to the introduction of "limited entry," 100 vessels operated in the fishery.

As well, the stock of halibut available in Canadian waters declined. The quota in 1982 was 5.4 million pounds and catch rates were very low, with no significant change in the landed price ($1.25 per pound in 1982). The fishery was therefore in dire straits: low harvests, overcapacity, and high operating costs. Pearse recommended the adoption of a system of transferable catch quotas assigned to areas and distributed to individual fishers now in the fishery. Equipment restrictions (no trawling) would still apply to protect immature fish. The fishing season was not to be curtailed; fishers are free to take their quota whenever they want. Pearse's suggestions were received with enthusiasm by halibut fishers and were implemented in 1983. In 1991, ITQs were finally introduced. The system in place is a cost-recovery program that generates funds to pay for the costs of administration and enforcement.

Using economic analysis, we can make some predictions about the effect of the individual quota on the operation of the fishery. First, the harvest should be taken much more efficiently. Each individual holding the quota now has a guaranteed catch (subject to the availability of halibut). There is no need to compete with hundreds of other vessels in a particular area over a short interval of time to get a share of the harvest. Factor inputs can then be arranged efficiently.

Transferability of the quota should ensure that the most efficient operators remain in the fishery. The quotas will quickly command a market value, and only those whose expected profits from fishing equal or exceed the market value of the quota should remain. Others will sell their quota. Of course, the original holders of the quota will receive a rent in the form of the market value of the quota. The cost-recovery feature of the ITQ absorbs some of these rents. Over time, the market for the exchange of ITQs could become imperfectly competitive if there is a substantial decrease in effort and accumulation of quotas by remaining fishers. Quotas may also have to be adjusted yearly if biological conditions warrant.

A potential problem is that those fishing for halibut may operate in other fisheries as well. Because halibut have been relatively unprofitable in recent years, there may still be some tendency to harvest one's quota in a short period of time, and then go catch other species. British Columbia also has an ITQ for sablefish (black cod), but other species could be threatened. Crowding externalities may still exist, along with problems with processing and storage. The problem of the bycatches from fleets trawling for other species also remains. Presumably, there is still an incentive not to report harvests in excess of one's quota. But owing to processing requirements, halibut cannot be sold "illegally" as easily as species such as lobsters. Given the enthusiasm of the fishers for the Canadian scheme and their role in the management and operation of the ITQ, they may play by the rules and not cheat on their quotas. Their understanding of the problems with open access so long endured in the fishery should provide an incentive to stick to their quotas.

While it is still too soon to provide a definitive evaluation of the ITQ policy for British Columbia halibut, it appears that the policy is working well.[12] Some measures of its success are that the fishery is now open over 200 days per year. Halibut are supplied fresh to their markets as a result of the more even distribution of landings over the year. British Columbia fishers can land halibut when the fresh market has relatively lower supply. This is in part why, since 1991, average prices for British Columbia halibut exceeded those in Alaska by amounts ranging from 20 to over 100 percent. Individual licenses have been transferable since 1993. Since then, the number of vessels operating in the fishery has begun to decline. This is what economic theory would predict. The overcapitalization of the industry should gradually decline. Employment will also fall, but for those remaining in the fishery, incomes and stability of employment should rise. Fishers in the industry generally feel quite positive about the ITQ. As noted in Casey et al. (1995), over three-quarters of licenseholders surveyed in 1993 felt they were "better off" under the scheme. The ITQs have also reduced bycatch mortality for Canadian fisheries to well below that of the United States. The IPHC estimates that only 16 percent of young halibut caught as bycatch fail to survive in Canadian fisheries, compared with 25 percent for United States halibut fisheries. Less bycatch mortality should help to increase halibut stocks. Finally, the ITQ system of the British Columbia halibut fishery is self-financing. Administration fees and a variable fee per pound of quota assigned each year generate revenues that cover the costs of monitoring and enforcement.

SUMMARY

1. Two types of government policy that can achieve an optimal steady-state harvest and amount of fishing effort are taxes on effort or harvests, and quotas on effort and harvests.
2. An optimal tax on the catch, levied when the harvest is landed, will reduce the total revenue to the firm. The firm operating under open access will still equate total revenue to total costs, but the total revenue curve faced by fishers will have shrunk until it is tangent to the total cost curve at the optimal amount of effort. An optimal tax is difficult to compute because of continuous changes in exogenous factors such as environmental conditions, demand, and costs, and difficult

to implement. Firms have a large incentive to evade the tax by landing their catch away from government tax collectors. The tax is rarely used to regulate fisheries.

3. Taxes on effort can be imposed as head (or entry) taxes or as taxes per unit of effort used in the fishery. The optimal effort tax will increase the total costs of fishing until they intersect the total revenue curve at the optimal amount of effort. The most serious problem with taxes on effort is ensuring that all components of effort are covered by the tax. If labor is taxed but not capital, firms can avoid the tax by substituting capital for labor. The optimal amount of effort will not be reached. Taxes on effort would be costly to administer because government regulators must attempt to keep track of all the components of effort.
4. A quota on the total catch will restrict harvests but will not lead to the optimal amount of effort in the fishery. A quota given to individuals or firms to catch a specified amount of fish can lead to the optimal amount of effort and harvest if the quota is transferable and divisible. Each holder of the quota has a private property right to the fish and can therefore choose a cost-minimizing amount of effort to harvest the allotment.
5. Since 1976, the United States has been regulating fisheries within its 200-mile limit through fisheries management councils. One objective of these councils has been to achieve an optimal harvest, where *optimal* suggests that economic efficiency is to be considered. Thus far, few actual regulations have been passed that are based on economic efficiency. Many still use inefficient quotas on the total catch and on various components of effort.
6. Oyster fisheries in the United States represent an example where assignment of property rights can increase the stock of the species by improving the productivity of the fishing ground. Under private management, firms have an incentive to invest in the grounds. Aggregate use of effort then need not fall, even when the fishery is managed optimally. The decline in effort that would occur under private management is offset by the increase in the productivity of the fishing grounds.
7. Southern bluefin tuna are managed by an ITQ for Australian waters. Japan also harvests these tuna. Cooperative fishing efforts between Japan and Australia would maximize social rents, but leave Australia with substantially lower rents than in a duopoly equilibrium. Japan could compensate Australia or buy its ITQs to obtain the rent-maximizing solution.
8. In the United States and Canada, halibut have been regulated by area quotas on the total catch since the 1920s. The quota has been unsuccessful in limiting entry to the fishery and has resulted in excessive amounts of effort (overcapacity), low returns to capital and labor, and no guarantee that the stock will not be depleted to levels that threaten viability. A quota on the catch assigned to individual fishers is the policy recommended to reduce effort, increase the returns to effort, and protect the stock from excessive harvesting. This type of individual quota was implemented in British Columbia in 1991 and is being considered in the United States.

DISCUSSION QUESTIONS

1. Explain graphically and verbally how a tax on (a) harvests and (b) effort yields a socially optimal equilibrium in the open access fishery. Explain some of the practical difficulties of imposing taxes on fisheries.
2. Explain graphically and verbally the effects of a quota on the total catch versus an individual quota for a portion of the catch on effort in a fishery.
3. What would be the effects of a quota on effort and on the harvest in an open access fishery?
4. If the demand curve for a particular species of fish moves out over time as consumer incomes and population increase, will costs of harvest generally rise, leaving no rent or high profit, or will the costs not rise significantly? What elements affect the trend in costs?

NOTES

1. Equation (4.6) in Chapter 4 illustrates this relationship algebraically.
2. Note if the price of fish is very high, the open access harvest is less than the optimal harvest. The tax will then increase the harvest by decreasing effort, so the equilibrium moves to the right-hand side of the MSY biomass (left of the MSY harvest). For each price, a different optimal harvest and hence tax per unit of harvest must be defined.
3. See Copes (1986) for an extensive discussion of difficulties in implementing and operating IQ fisheries.
4. By contrast, annual expenditures of goods and services related to recreational fishing in Canada for 1991 were between $2 and $3 billion. The source for these values is OECD (1993).
5. See the Fisheries and Conservation Act of 1976, Public Law 94-265 (amended by Public Law 95-354 and 96-61), Title III, Section 301(a). For a more detailed discussion of the act, see Anderson (1982).
6. The fishery with positive profits was the one in Rhode Island. Crutchfield and Gates suggest that its profitability may be due to the type of fish caught and to different management of the fishery. The principal fish harvested was the yellowtail flounder, whose stock was rising over the period examined. Also, a cooperative existed in this fishery and entry may have been limited in some manner.
7. This information is taken primarily from Agnello and Donnelley (1975). We also thank Jon Conrad for points of clarification.
8. Notice that they do not incorporate the biological mechanics directly. There is no stock effect in the relationship. The authors do not discuss this, but we suspect that the omission is due to lack of data on the stock of oysters.
9. Because of simultaneity problems, a two-stage least squares regression was performed. In the first stage, labor was regressed on production variables and a measure of the opportunity wage (the wage rate of production workers in manufacturing). The fitted labor variable from this regression was then used in the average product relation

$$APL_{it} = f(X_{it}, D_{it}, Z_{it}, e_{it})$$

where i is the state, t the year, and X the vector of production variables discussed above, except that the labor variable is from the first-stage fitted equation. The terms D and Z are binary shift variables for the cross-section and time series, respectively. These are necessary control variables in the pooled regressions. The final term, e_{it}, is the error term, which is assumed to have a zero mean and constant variance and to be independent across observations. No evidence of autocorrelation or heteroskedasticity was found.

10. Information on the halibut fishery is taken from Crutchfield (1981), Pearse (1982), and Stokes (1983), annual reports, technical reports, and statistical yearbooks of the International Pacific Halibut Commission.
11. There is some debate about this point, because of imprecise estimates of the stock in early periods. The stock was estimated from data on effort and harvests. Because effort was not measured accurately, some observers think the stock estimates in the 1930s were too low, making the estimates of the recovery of the stock by the 1950s too high.
12. See Casey et al. (1995) for additional information on the impact of the ITQ on British Columbia's halibut fishery.

SELECTED READINGS

Agnello, R. J., and L. P. Donnelley (1975). "Prices and Property Rights in the Fisheries," *Southern Economic Journal* 42, pp. 253–262.

Agnello, R. J., and L. P. Donnelley (1976). "Externalities and Property Rights in the Fisheries," *Land Economics* 52, pp. 519–529.

Anderson, L. G. (1982). "Marine Fisheries," in P. R. Portney, ed., *Current Issues in Natural Resource Policy*. Washington, D. C.: Resources for the Future.

Bosch, D. J., and L. A. Shabman (1989). "The Decline of Private Sector Oyster Culture in Virginia: Causes and Remedial Policies," *Marine Resource Economics* 6, pp. 227–243.

Casey, K., C. M. Dewees, B. R. Turris, and J. E. Wilen (1995). "The Effects of Individual Vessel Quotas in the British Columbia Halibut Fishery," *Marine Resource Economics* 10, pp. 211–230.

Copes, P. (1986). "A Critical Review of the Individual Quota as a Device in Fisheries Management," *Land Economics* 62, pp. 278–291.

Crutchfield, J. A. (1981). "The Pacific Halibut Fishery." Technical Report No. 17, in *The Public Regulation of Commercial Fisheries in Canada*, Case Study No. 2. Ottawa: Economic Council of Canada.

Crutchfield, J. A., and J. M. Gates (1985). "The Impact of Extended Fishery Jurisdiction on the Northeast Otter Trawl Fleet," *Marine Resource Economics* 2, pp. 153–173.

Fox, W. W. (1990). "Statement of Concerned Scientists on the Reauthorization of the Magnuson Fishery Conservation and Management Act," *Natural Resource Modeling* 4, pp. 133–142.

Henderson, J. V., and M. Tugwell (1979). "Exploitation of the Lobster Fishery: Some Empirical Results," *Journal of Environmental Economics and Management* 6, pp. 287–296.

Kennedy, J. O. S., and H. Pasternak (1991). "Optimal Australian and Japanese Harvesting of Southern Bluefin Tuna," *Natural Resource Modeling* 5, pp. 213–238.

National Research Council of Canada (1993). *Management of Marine Fisheries in Canada*. Ottawa: National Research Council of Canada.

Natural Marine Fisheries Service (1993). *Our Living Oceans, Report on the Status of Living Marine Resources*. Silver Spring, MD: National Marine Fisheries Service, U.S. Department of Commerce, National Oceanic and Atmospheric Administration.

Neher, P. A., et al., eds. (1989). *Rights Based Fishing*. Amsterdam: Kluwer Academic.

OECD (1993). *Review of Fisheries in OECD Countries, 1990, 1991*. Paris: Organization for Economic Cooperation and Development.

Parsons L. S., and W. H. Lear (1993). *Perspectives on Canadian Marine Fisheries Management*. Ottawa: National Research Council.

Pearse, P. W. (1982). *Turning the Tide: A New Policy for Canada's Pacific Fisheries*. The Commission on Pacific Fisheries Policy, Final Report, Vancouver, September.

Quinn, T. J. II (1987). "Standardization of Catch-per-unit-Effort for Short Term Trends in Catchability," *Natural Resource Modeling* 1, pp. 279–296.

Stokes, R. L. (1983). *Limited Entry in the Pacific Halibut Fishery: The Individual Quota Option*. Council Document No. 20. Anchorage: North Pacific Fishery Management Council.

Townsend, R. E. (1990). "Entry Restrictions in the Fishery: A Survey of the Evidence," *Land Economics* 66, pp. 359–378.

chapter 6

An Introduction to Environmental Resources: Externalities and Pollution

INTRODUCTION

Many natural resources are not exchanged in well-defined markets. The natural resources we examine are air, water, and the general state of the environment. We have already discussed in detail the case of the fishery exploited under open access. The distinct problem with the fishery under open access was the lack of property rights to the fish stock, which led to excessive use of factor inputs to exploit the stock and the possibility that the stock would be extinguished. As we will see, environmental resources also suffer from inefficient exploitation due to the lack of property rights.

As we pointed out in Chapter 1, there are few instances in which a property right to a particular environmental resource is assigned explicitly to an individual (or group of individuals). No one "owns" the air surrounding himself or herself; and many bodies of water—lakes, streams, and oceans—can be freely used as a waste depository. Our discussion will focus on the problems associated with inefficient use of these resources.

We first define an *external effect* or *externality* and show why it can arise. We then examine different types of externalities and illustrate the economic problems that emerge when externalities exist. In particular, we look at externalities that arise in the consumption and production of goods and services. Once the economic problems are identified, we examine methods of reaching an optimal allocation of resources. The tools we discuss include taxes, subsidies, and regulations governing outputs. In Chapter 7, we examine some actual environmental problems: what causes them, what can be done to eliminate the problems, and what has been done in practice.

DEFINING EXTERNAL EFFECTS

A *technological externality* can arise when two conditions are present:

Condition 1: For any two (or more) economic agents (consumers or firms) *i* and *j*, an externality is present whenever agent's *i*'s utility or production relationship includes variables whose magnitudes are chosen by the other agent or agents, *j*, without regard to *i*'s own preferences.

Condition 2: The *i*th individual or firm has no control over the variables chosen by *j* because the variables have no explicit exchange value. No markets (or imperfect markets) exist for the variables entering *i*'s objective function.

What these conditions signify is a technological interdependence among agents, which persists because no market mechanism operates to allow for the optimal pricing of the interdependent variables.

Let's consider some examples before examining externalities more completely. I like flowers but am too lazy to plant them in my garden. My neighbor loves to work in the garden and spends a lot of effort making it colorful. I walk by my neighbor's garden and enjoy its beauty without spending any of my time and energy to nurture it. This is an example of a positive externality, or an *external economy*. My neighbor's garden increases my utility, and I have not spent any of my own resources to obtain this enjoyment. My neighbor's garden is a variable in my utility function that my neighbor controls, but the garden nonetheless affects me. Furthermore, my neighbor's attractive garden can help me sell my house at a premium. A negative externality, or *external diseconomy*, arises when another agent's actions affect me adversely. I'm having a nice meal at a restaurant when two obnoxious people come in and start talking loudly. Their actions reduce the enjoyment of my meal.

Both types of externality involve no exchange through a market. In the case of the flower garden, my neighbor is not paid anything for the benefits others receive from the garden. In the restaurant, no one offers me a reduction in the price of my meal simply because I'm now too upset to enjoy it.

There is another type of externality called a *pecuniary externality* that operates through markets. Suppose we examine the market for compact disks (CDs). The supply curve of CDs is upward-sloping, indicating that the marginal costs of production are rising. The equilibrium price one pays for a CD depends, of course, on the intersection of this supply curve and the demand curve. Let this price be initially $12 per CD. Then suppose the demand curve shifts to the right because of a change in tastes: some people abandon their cassette tape players and switch to CDs. The equilibrium price of CDs rises, say, to $15 dollars per CD. All previous buyers are made worse off because they now pay $3 more per CD than before the change in taste. This is the pecuniary externality. It represents the normal operation of the market. If consumers do not like the new price of CDs, they can choose not to buy CDs, buy fewer CDs, and so on. The market will adjust to all sorts of changes in demand (and supply). With technological externalities, the affected parties do not have the option of influencing the market price through their own actions. The externality is determined by the actions of others. When air pollution surrounds my community, the actions I take to protect myself from it will have no influence on the quantity of pollutants that exist.

What then can be done about a technological externality? The gardening neighbor could erect a high fence around the garden and charge admission to see the flowers. If some payment or compensation is received for an externality, one is said to be *internalizing* the externality. The agent responsible for the externality now incorporates the effect its actions have on the utility or production function of the recipient. When the fence is built, if I choose to pay the admission price, that price will reflect my marginal utility from viewing the garden. The neighbor is thus compensated for the benefits received by passersby and may, in fact, plant more flowers. In the restaurant, some private action could be taken. I could complain to the restaurant and ask that the noisy people be asked to be quiet or to leave. I could leave as well. In these cases, an externality is likely to be internalized by private actions—actions taken by individuals. However, as we will see, most important examples of externalities cannot be internalized solely by private actions; some form of government intervention is required. To see why, let's examine more fully why an externality can persist.

In our study of environmental natural resources, most of the externalities we encounter are the negative kind. Air and water pollution are examples of external diseconomies—cases where individuals and firms discard waste products into the environment without acknowledging the damages these products cause to others. We know these externalities arise when some sort of technological interdependency exists (I am seated next to noisy eaters in the restaurant; toxic wastes are dumped on the land and in streams, adversely affecting people, animals, and plants).

Causes of Market Failure

Why do the external effects not get appropriately priced and allocated by the operation of market mechanisms? Alternatively, what are the possible causes of market failure? We highlight four.

Cause 1

Probably the most significant reason why externalities persist is that the natural resources affected are open access resources (air, oceans), and the externality generated is *nonappropriable.* The open access nature of the environment means that anyone can use it as a depository of pollutants. Nonappropriability means that any one agent's consumption of the externality (pollution) does not reduce the consumption of that same externality by others. My consumption of polluted air does not affect your consumption of polluted air. I do not in any meaningful way reduce the amount of air you breathe. When a resource or the externality that arises in the use of the resource is nonappropriable, it is very difficult—indeed virtually impossible—for private markets to function efficiently. We will show why in the next section.

Cause 2

Agents may lack information about the activities that are affecting them. This makes it very difficult for markets to work to internalize externalities. Information may also be asymmetric. That is, one agent may have more or better information than another. When this is the case, exchange through market mechanisms becomes quite difficult. For example, asbestos is now known to be a potent carcinogen. Asbestos fibers in the lungs can cause emphysema and a virulent form of lung cancer (mesothelioma). But these health problems can take decades to appear after the individual is exposed to the asbestos. Workers in asbestos mines (and others employed in the manufacture of asbestos products) did not know 30 years ago that their exposure to asbestos would result in debilitating disease and premature death. There is considerable debate about what the asbestos companies knew and whether they withheld information about the harmful effects of asbestos from their workers. But the point is that if you do not know what is affecting you, it is very difficult to take remedial action.

Cause 3

Markets may be too thin or too costly to operate. A market is *thin* when there are not enough traders to allow it to operate. If a "market" consists of just me and my neighbor with the garden, then it is unlikely that some formal exchange of money for the benefits of viewing the flowers will be established. This externality will probably persist because it does not pay the flower grower to erect a fence to get my fee every time I want to look at the garden. There are too few of us to make the establishment of a formal arrangement worthwhile. Another way to say this is that there may be transaction costs in operating a market. If the value of the item to be traded (viewing flowers) is much lower than the costs of establishing a mechanism to extract payment for that item (erecting a fence), no formal market will exist.

Cause 4

Finally, a market failure may persist when nonconvexities exist either in the operation of the market or in the technological interdependence among agents. A nonconvexity is present, for example, when the production possibility schedule (introduced in Chapter 1) fails to be everywhere bowed out; over some of its length, it is "punched" in. A nonconvexity in the market can be caused by setup costs—say, a large bureaucracy of some sort is needed to operate the market.

Externalities as Social Problems

When these market failures are present, external effects are likely to persist in economies where exchange occurs through the operation of markets governed by the private interests of individuals.[1] Are these externalities a social problem? Few people are likely to be bothered by the persistence of the flower garden externality. There may be too few flower gardens, but this does not represent a pressing social problem. Similarly, if I cannot resolve the problem with the noisy restaurant patrons, again there may be little social loss. But what about some major externalities—toxic chemical dumps or acid rain? The fact that these external diseconomies persist in all economies *is* a matter of concern to many individuals and a problem warranting government action.

Individuals, animals, and plants are harmed by these pollutants, and resources are being allocated inefficiently in the economy when these environmental externalities persist. Factor inputs and the output of certain goods are not priced according to their social value. That is, private valuations of inputs and outputs are different from their social valuations. If toxic chemicals are dumped into the environment, it is generally because the air, ground, and water sources onto which the chemicals are dumped are not valued by the firms doing the dumping. If these firms had to pay for the dump sites, far less (legal) dumping would be done. Without the incorporation of social valuations into the prices of these resources, too much toxic waste is spilled into the environment, and too few unpolluted areas remain. This is why many externalities are a serious social problem.

The question is: What do we do about these externalities? Some schools of economic thought argue that what exists is optimal. That is, if we see the persistence of certain environmental problems, that is because it is too costly to internalize the externality. They argue that any externalities we observe do not warrant any social concern. This view is not shared by others; their argument is precisely the opposite. The fact that we observe the persistence of a number of external effects means that the market is simply unable to cope with these problems and that another method of allocating resources is required. The solution advocated by many economists is to use the powers of government to impose a *price* on the external effect, so that agents are forced to include the external effect in their calculations of what goods to produce and consume. This concept has been called the *"polluter pays" principle*. Government policies can impose prices for pollution through the use of policies such as taxes, subsidies, user fees, and tradable emission permits. These are all examples of market-based incentives (MBIs). Alternatively, the government can use command-and-control (CAC) policies to address environmental problems caused by external diseconomies: CAC regulation involves the use of specific rules or procedures that must be followed, or a penalty will be imposed. Examples are emission standards and technology-based standards. Emission standards limit the discharges of specified pollutants. Technology-based standards mandate the use of particular pollution abatement equipment or processes. Thus CAC regulation focuses more on quantity controls, while MBIs provide price incentives. In this chapter, we examine MBIs and CACs theoretically. Chapter 7 looks at some examples in practice.

We want to emphasize that there is a difference in *belief* about the importance of externalities among economists and politicians. We do not accept the view that all relevant externalities are internalized by private markets and that the ones remaining are not relevant. We will follow the tradition that attempts to find ways through regulatory action to internalize externalities and will show why this may be in the social interest. As a first step, we distinguish between private and public externalities.

A TAXONOMY OF EXTERNALITIES

The emergence of an externality is the first part of the problem. We must then show why an externality persists in unregulated markets. Our objective is to show that there is no completely general model of why an externality persists. Markets fail for different reasons, and our analysis will highlight the different types of market failure and methods that may be appropriate for internalizing the externality in each case.

Public versus Private Externalities

We focus in this section on external diseconomies that affect natural resources—air and water. A *public* external diseconomy arises when a natural resource is used without payment, and the "consumption" of the externality by one agent does not reduce the consumption of the externality by others. There are many examples of public external diseconomies, notably air and water pollution. Air and (to a lesser degree) water are open access resources. Anyone is free to use the air in the way he or she sees fit. If it is used as a waste depository, no market price exists that reflects this use. Air pollution then emerges as a "public bad"—something consumed by a lot of people simultaneously. As we will see, the "jointness" in the consumption of the externality makes it difficult, if not impossible, to internalize it through private actions.

The nonappropriability in consumption of the externality is often accompanied by a large number of "producers" of the externality. For example, there are many emitters of the gases and particulates that make up air pollution. These include static sources such as electric generating plants and mobile sources such as automobiles. Thus, the externality is "public" in consumption, and it is also difficult to determine the degree to which a particular source is responsible for particular amounts of pollution. When many people are affected and consumption is the same (or very similar) for all, government intervention of some form is generally the only way the externality can be internalized.

A *private* external diseconomy is typically bilateral, or it involves relatively few agents. One party's actions affect the actions of another party, but there is no spillover of the externality to other agents. We will examine two-party cases in this section. The key characteristic of a private externality is that the external effect must be fully appropriated by the parties involved. If a company dumps toxic chemicals into a pond in a residential area, those who live around the pond must be the only ones affected.

Generally, there are more methods of internalizing a private externality than a public one. The role for private action through negotiation by the parties involved or the emergence of a market is much more likely when few agents are involved. Private externalities are a useful model for heuristic purposes, because they enable us to illustrate cases using simple graphic techniques rather than more cumbersome algebra. However, it is more difficult to think of actual cases in which an externality is private. There are typically some spillover effects and some degree of nonappropriability in most externalities. In addition, private externalities tend not to persist; they are more readily internalized than are public externalities.

The line between public and private is often hard to draw in practice. Our objective here is to present public and private externalities as separate cases, so that we can analyze the ability of market and nonmarket mechanisms to internalize externalities.

A Public External Diseconomy: Air Pollution

We turn now to an examination of a public external diseconomy.

Suppose we have a *public external diseconomy*—air pollution. Many agents produce the waste products that result in pollution. Also, large numbers of individuals "consume" the pollution by breathing air filled with particulates, sulfur dioxide, and oxides of nitrogen. Air is an open access resource. Because no property rights to air exist, those who generate air pollution are free to use the air as a waste dump without paying any fees. Each person affected might be willing to pay something to reduce the pollution, but if he or she did so, others who did not pay would also benefit.

Air pollution is thus quite different from ordinary goods in which consumption is fully appropriated or received by the individual purchasing the good. If I buy a television set and you do not, only I get to enjoy (or suffer from) the programming available on TV. But if I pay to have air pollution reduced and you do not, you get some benefits from cleaner air without any outlay of funds. Those who would benefit without any payment are called *free riders.* No decentralized market can handle a situation where those receiving the pollution (the demand side) are individually willing to pay nothing for the pollution or its cleanup because those who pay will benefit those who do not pay. On the supply side, producers of the pollution also face a zero price because they are able in an unregulated situation to use the air as a "free" waste depository. Thus, air pollution exists because no one is willing to pay for its reduction in an unregulated market, or for the right to use air for waste disposal.[2]

Let's see why the public externality cannot be internalized without government intervention. There are a number of ways to analyze this problem. We can view it from a perspective of the supply of and demand for "clean" air, which we can think of as a *public good* in that once it is provided (in this case by nature), all get to consume it equally. Person i may get more satisfaction from a public good such as clean air than person j, but they each get the same amount of clean air. Or we can start with a situation in which the air is already dirty because of the past failure of markets to lead to prices for the right to use the clean air. In either case, the same general principles will emerge. The precise equilibrium will, however, be different. This is a problem of the starting point. If we start with clean air and ask what people would be willing to pay to dirty it, we typically get an equilibrium different from what we get if the starting point is polluted air and we ask what people are willing to pay to clean it up. We will have more to say about this issue in Chapter 7.

Let's start with the case where the air is clean. Suppose we are given a stock of clean air. We want to abstract from any complex meteorology here. Air has both stock and flow characteristics, and there may indeed be a stock that can become polluted. But natural processes such as precipitation and movement of air masses tend to dissipate pollution over time. An appropriate model of air pollution thus requires analysis of the dynamic paths of pollution emission and air recovery. Rather than deal with these issues, we assume that there is simply a finite supply of clean air. Clean air is thus like a depletable resource.[3]

Figure 6.1 illustrates the "market" for clean air. In each of the three parts we show the supply of clean air as some fixed amount, Q. Supply is finite because there will always be some natural impurities human activity can do nothing to control (eruptions of volcanoes spill tons of particulates into the atmosphere). In (a), we show the demand curve of agent A (an individual or a firm) for clean air. The demand curve slopes down in the normal fashion because we assume that like any other good, clean air yields diminishing marginal utility as consumption increases. At the stock of air

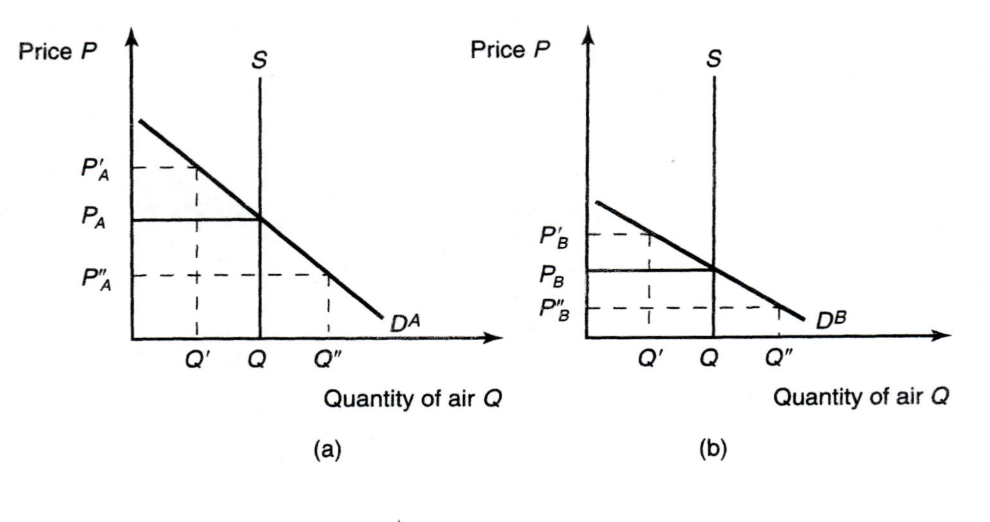

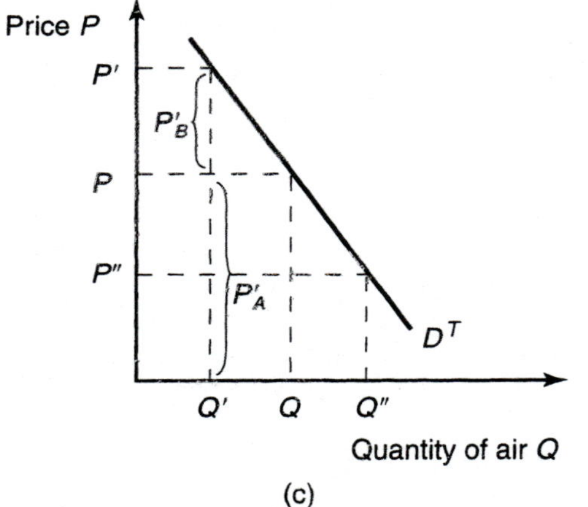

FIGURE 6.1. For a given stock of clean air, Q, each individual's willingness to pay for that air is shown by the individual's demand curve. If the stock of air is Q, individual A would be willing to pay P_A, while individual B would be willing to pay P_B. The "market" demand curve is obtained by the *vertical* summation of the prices each person is willing to pay for a particular amount of the clean air. If the stock of air is Q', the sum of these demand prices is P'. If the stock of air is Q, total demand sums to P. Finally, if the stock of air is Q'', the total willingness to pay is P''.

shown, Q, agent A would be willing to pay the price P_A for the air. Figure 6.1(b) shows the demand for clean air by agent B. As we have drawn agent B's demand curve, B is willing to pay less for any amount of clean air than A. With the stock Q, B is willing to pay P_B. So far, nothing is different from the case of consumer demand for an ordinary good. The difference between public goods (or bads) and ordinary goods comes in the determination of the *market demand curve.*

Because everyone consumes the same amount of air, we must aggregate individual demand curves by summing them *vertically* rather than horizontally, as in the case of an ordinary good. That is, we pick a quantity of air, say Q'. If that were the supply of air, it would be available to everyone. We then ask what each agent would be willing to pay for that amount. Agent A would be willing to pay P'_A, while agent B would be willing to pay P'_B (where P'_A exceeds P'_B). The sum of these two prices is shown in Figure 6.1 (c) as P'. A similar exercise for the stock of air at Q and Q'' leads to the determination of other points on the market or aggregate demand curve.

With the *quantity of the good fixed*, the only thing individuals' demand curves reflect is *the price they would be willing to pay* for the good. In the case of an ordinary private good, the individual typically faces a single price and chooses how much to buy. Addition of individuals' demands is thus done horizontally across quantities they are willing to purchase. In the case of the public good, there is no discretion over available quantities, so preferences are summed over prices.

What, then, does an equilibrium mean in a market with a public good? Suppose the stock of air is indeed Q. If air were a normal good, the equilibrium price of air would be P, as shown in Figure 6.1(c). With a private good, each person would then take P as given and decide how much of the good to buy. But with the public good, there is no choice over how much to buy: Q is the amount supplied; all individuals can do is reveal how much they would be willing to pay. But notice that the equilibrium price then has no meaning. Agent A is willing to pay P_A for an amount of air equal to Q, while agent B is willing to pay only P_B for that same quantity. It is difficult to see how a market that charges uniform prices could ever exist in this situation.

Suppose price P was in fact charged. At P, consumer A would be willing to buy Q' units of clean air, but B would buy nothing because P exceeds the maximum price B is willing to pay. Total sales would be Q', not Q. The equilibrium at P and Q is not feasible. This means that the equilibrium price and quantity cannot be decomposed into individual sales that are consistent with aggregate supply. Therefore, either one price must be charged to all, in which case individual demands are not recognized (consumer sovereignty is violated) and total supply does not equal total demand except by chance, or a multiplicity of prices must be charged. We have illustrated the demand curves for only two agents. In practice, there are many times this number of agents, which means that many different demand prices would exist for a given stock of air. No perfectly competitive market can exist to deal with all these prices.

But could a private market operate with a number of different prices? Suppose a monopolist was able to discriminate perfectly among all consumers with different demand curves for clean air. Each demander would then be charged a different price, and the monopolist could ensure that demand equals supply. But there are at least two problems with a discriminating monopolist. First, the monopolist receives all the consumer surplus from the market. This may not be desirable socially. Second, and more important, one of the essential requirements for perfect discrimination by a monoplist is that the monopolist must be able to prevent consumers from reselling their allotment of the good to others. When the good in question is clean air, prevention of resale is impossible: All get the same amount of air regardless of what they pay. The monopolist would be unable to charge different prices because it could not prevent one agent from consuming the air received by another agent who paid a lower price.

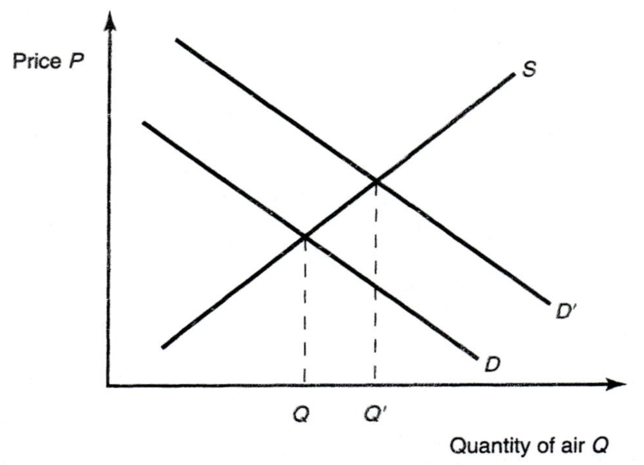

FIGURE 6.2. If people are charged a "tax price" based on their revealed demand for clean air, they will have an incentive to underreport their true willingness to pay for the air. The demand curve D results. The government will then supply Q units of clean air. If the "true" demand for clean air is represented by D', the desired supply of air is really Q'. Clean air is then undersupplied.

Indeed, it is difficult to imagine that any sort of contract made at different prices could be enforceable.

Can a public body do any better? In principle, governments have the ability to act as discriminating monopolists because they can force everyone to "pay" for the clean air by imposing taxes or some other sort of fee. No discriminating monopolist could operate unless the government gave it the right to collect payments for air (who would pay for something they can receive free?). Therefore, it seems more sensible to consider the government as the operator of the clean air "market." But the government will face the same problem a private monopolist would in determining what people are willing to pay for the clean air. Suppose that the government plans to levy a fee on each agent equal to what that agent says it is willing to pay for clean air. If agent i thinks that agent j is willing to pay less for clean air than i itself is, why should agent i tell the government it will pay a higher price, even if i values clean air more than j? Some individuals may be truthful and reveal their actual willingness to pay for clean air, but others will not. There is a strong incentive to cheat. If the government is unable to tell what your true preferences are, the result is that clean air will be underprovided relative to the "true" social optimum.[4]

Figure 6.2 illustrates this case. Suppose there is some "cost" to the government to provide clean air. We then allow the supply curve for air to be upward-sloping. To get more air, more expenses must be incurred per unit. If the government wishes to determine the optimal amount of clean air, it will equate supply with demand, produce the amount of air that is indicated by the equilibrium, and then charge everyone a price that reflects the demand curves the individual has revealed to the government. The problem is then evident. Agents will have a strong incentive to underreport their demand for clean air.

Suppose each individual reveals a demand curve that aggregates (vertically) to the "market" demand curve D in Figure 6.2. Each person would be charged a "tax price" derived from his or her individual demand curve. But some people would be willing to pay more than they reveal and would misrepresent their preferences in the hope that others will share more of the tax burden. Total demand is less than people really want. The supply of clean air will be Q. If they truthfully revealed their preferences and the market demand curve were D', the supply of clean air would be Q', which exceeds Q. The amount of clean air that then would exist is less than the optimal amount. People will in a sense be cheating themselves but, because of the nonappropriability of the clean air, will do nothing about it.

Suppose alternatively that the government asks people what they would be willing to pay but does not base the fee or tax it charges agents for clean air on the amount revealed. In this case, just the opposite result is expected. Agents will have an incentive to overreveal their willingness to pay for clean air. There will be a tendency then to have "too much" clean air relative to the social optimum. Such a result would occur if, for example, the government asks people their preferences for clean air and then charges everyone the same price (a flat tax) regardless of the response. Some people will pay more than they are willing to pay, and others will pay less. The equilibrium will not be optimal.

A final word on prices and markets for public goods. It is in theory possible to arrive at the right price each person should be assessed for consuming the commodity—the so-called personalized price—since this will vary from one person to another. But there is (a) no natural mechanism causing these correct prices to emerge (part of the free rider problem), and (b) if consumers got together to register their preferences, the transaction costs of getting together and deciding even if the correct preferences were to emerge would be very high. Thus we see that:

1. No private market can supply a public good such as clean air. Some form of government intervention is required.
2. Even if the government does regulate the supply of clean air and charges a tax to individuals for that air, it is quite likely that the supply will be different from the optimum because individuals have an incentive to hide their true preferences.

Note that the same type of result would occur if we viewed the problem from the standpoint of the demand for abatement of pollution. The demand for abatement would fall as the price of abatement rose. Those demanding abatement would have an incentive to underreveal their demand if the fee they were charged by the government reflected their stated willingness to pay. The amount of pollution would thus be higher in the equilibrium than is socially optimal because there would be too little abatement.

Externalities in Production

We turn now to an example of private externalities that arise from the production processes of firms. Many types of pollution fall into this category. In the process of producing a good, waste products (effluents) are emitted into the atmosphere, waterways, or ground. If no market valuation is placed on these environmental resources, they will be used excessively as depositories of wastes. In the process, other agents—consumers and firms—may find that their activities are adversely affected by the emission of the industrial effluent. In this section, we focus on a two-firm example. One firm discharges its waste products into a lake. Another firm is also located on the lake and uses the water in its production process.

Suppose the Creative Chemical Company discharges the by-products from the production of its chemicals into the lake. The Agrigoods Company is also located on the lake and uses the water to irrigate its major crop—apples. We will abstract from all the problems of who located first on the lake and whether each party was familiar with the production technologies of the other at the time it located there.[5] Suppose, for simplicity, that both firms have been located on the lake for a long time and have coexisted without any external effects until Creative began production of a new chemical which created wastes that adversely affected the quality of the water and reduced the production of apples by Agriproducts.

We illustrate algebraically and graphically the effect of the chemical effluent on apple production, then discuss possible means of internalizing the externality. We assume for simplicity that each firm needs only one variable input to produce its product. Both have fixed inputs (such as capital) that we are not concerned with, because this is a short-run model. The results would be fundamentally the same if multiple factor inputs were used, except if one of the inputs is some abatement technique that can reduce the amount of pollution emitted by the chemical company. Let each firm's short-run production function be given by equation (6.1):

$$\begin{aligned} Q^A &= f(x,z) \\ Q^C &= g(y) \end{aligned} \tag{6.1}$$

where Q^A is the output of apples and Q^C is the output of chemicals, x is Agriproduct's use of its major input water, and y is the chemical company's major factor input, say chemical compounds.

The term z is the effluent from the chemical company. It enters into the production function of the apple company in the same way as a factor input. The difference between z and the x input is that an increase in z reduces rather than increases the output of apples. Another way of saying this is that the partial derivative of A's production function with respect to z is negative. This is the external diseconomy. For an ordinary input, the change in output with respect to an increase in the use of an input would be positive. We assume that z is generated by the chemical company's use of input y. That is, z is some function (unspecified) of y, $z = h(y)$. The use and subsequent discharge into the lake of a particular compound in the production of chemicals is what adversely affects apple production.[6] The unpriced factor input in this case is the water. Neither the apple company nor the chemical company pays anything for the use of the water.

The effects of the emission of chemical effluent are now shown. We will examine each firm's profits in a static framework and assume no other agents are affected. This means that we are dealing with a partial equilibrium model and a private externality.

Each firm's profits are given by equation (6.2):

$$\pi^A = P^A Q^A - wx$$
$$\pi^C = P^C Q^C - wy \qquad (6.2)$$

where P^A is the market price of apples, P^C the price of chemicals, and w the unit price of the factor inputs x and y. We assume that the inputs x and y are available in infinitely elastic supply, and thus w is a constant. We also assume that apple and chemical input prices are identical. This assumption does not affect the results; it just simplifies notation. We then substitute each firm's production function, given by equation (6.1), into equation (6.2). This yields equation (6.3):

$$\pi_A = P^A[f(x,z)] - wx$$
$$\pi_C = P^C[g(y)] - wy \qquad (6.3)$$

Each firm then maximizes its profits independently of the other firm. For a profit maximum for each firm, we know that[7]

$$P^A f_X - w = 0$$
$$P^C g_Y - w = 0 \qquad (6.4)$$

where f_X is $\partial f/\partial x$ and g_X is $\partial g/\partial y$. In equation (6.4), the first term is the value of the marginal product of the factor input (x or y). Each factor input must thus be chosen so that the value of its marginal product is equal to the factor's marginal cost, which in this case is w. This is the normal condition for a profit maximum found in any industry. But there is a difference in this case: For the apple company, the marginal product of its input x also depends on the presence of z, the chemical effluent, where z in turn depends on the chemical firm's use of y. This means that the two firms are not independent of one another. When each firm maximizes its profits independent of the other firm, apple profits will not be at the highest level possible.

To see this, we note that in equilibrium, the change in profits with respect to a change in input use must be zero. This is what equation (6.4) requires. While this will be true for the chemical company, it will not be the case for the apple company. Whenever the chemical company increases its use of factor y by even a small amount, apple profits are reduced. Apple profits fall because either more water must be used to compensate for the decline in its quality, or apple production is reduced owing to the lower water quality. A marginal change in the use of factor y does have an effect on the apple producer. But for an efficient allocation of resources, a small change in y should not have an effect. The externality arises because the profits of A and C combined fall whenever y is increased (and conversely when y is decreased). An efficient use of inputs requires that there be no change in the profits of *both* companies with a very small change in the use of each factor input. To reach an efficient solution, the companies must *jointly* maximize their profits.

We now compare the equilibrium obtained above and a socially optimal equilibrium where the firms take into account the effect of the effluent, z, on the output of Agrigoods. To determine the efficient use of inputs, we must jointly maximize the profits of the two firms. This is the appropriate means of determining the optimal use of inputs for each firm because it accounts for the interdependence between them. The combined profits of the two firms are then given by equation (6.5):

$$\pi_{A+C} = P^A f[x, h(y)] + P^C g(y) - w(x + y) \tag{6.5}$$

where we have now substituted for the relationship between chemical effluent, z, and the chemical firm's use of the input y. Equation (6.5) is maximized with respect to both x and y (by differentiating with respect to x and y). The resulting conditions for a profit maximum are given by Equation (6.6):

$$\begin{aligned} P^A f_X - w &= 0 \\ P^A[(\partial f/\partial h)(\partial h/\partial y)] + P^C g_Y - w &= 0 \end{aligned} \tag{6.6}$$

We now want to compare equations (6.6) to (6.4). The first equation in (6.4) and (6.6) is identical. The value of the marginal product of input x is still equated to its marginal cost, as seen in the first equations of (6.4) and (6.6). But the second equations differ because of the presence of the term $P^A[(\partial f/\partial h)(\partial h/\partial y)]$. This is the value of the marginal damage done to the apple company by the chemical company's use of input y. It measures the reduction in output of apples resulting from a marginal increase in the use of y, which of course leads to an increase in pollution, z. The term in the expression, $\partial h/\partial y$, shows how much pollution results from a small increase in y (a positive amount), while $\partial f/\partial h$ shows how the pollution affects apple production (a negative amount). These terms are valued at the market price of apples, and the expression is negative.

Equation (6.6) says that the value of the marginal product of factor y net of the value of the marginal damage done by factor y should be set equal to its marginal cost, w. When the chemical company does not take into account the damage created by its production process, too much y is used. The efficient solution requires that y be reduced. Assuming that both firms operate in competitive product and factor markets, and using consumer surplus as a measure of social welfare, we can then say that the socially optimal amount of pollution requires that the marginal damage done by the chemical company be taken into account in its determination of the amount of input y to use in its production process. With the aid of a graph, we will now investigate methods of internalizing this externality.

Figure 6.3 illustrates the private market solution before any interdependencies among the two firms are recognized, and the social optimum. The diagram presented is commonly used in the analysis of externalities, but it must be interpreted with care. The curves drawn have particular meanings that correspond to the algebra we have just presented. Their shapes in actual cases of externalities might be quite different from the ones shown here. Recall as well that this is a partial equilibrium analysis.

In Figure 6.3, we have drawn the change in each firm's profits as the chemical firm increases the amount of input y it uses in the production of chemicals. The curve MB is the value of the marginal product of input y net of its marginal cost, as represented by the terms $(P^C g_Y - w)$ in equation (6.6). The curve MD is the value of the marginal damage to the apple company that results from C's use of input y, and it reflects the first term in the second equation of (6.6). We have drawn MB as negatively sloped. This is a reasonable assumption, because a variable factor input typically has a

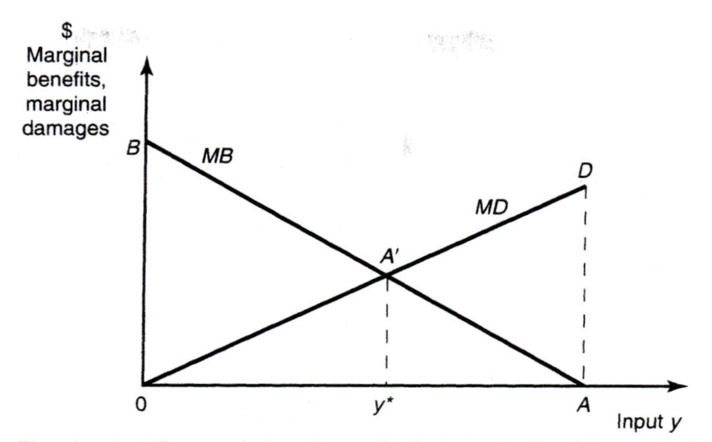

FIGURE 6.3. The chemical firm maximizes its profits independently of the apple firm where the marginal benefits from the use of input y are equal to zero at point A. This leads to the maximum level of pollution released. The apple firm suffers from damages AD. Internalization of the externality requires that the marginal damages be equated to marginal benefits. This occurs at point A' with y^* of the input.

diminishing marginal product as its use increases. We have drawn the *MD* function positively sloped to reflect a common assumption that marginal damages rise as greater amounts of y are used by the chemical company.

Most empirical studies of the effects of various effluents on production and consumption activities lend some support to the shape shown. Typically, when the use of the factor responsible for the effluent increases, so does the effluent; and as the effluent increases, so does the damage at the margin. Both *MB* and *MD* are drawn as linear functions of y. This is simply for convenience. Later we will look at the effects of different shapes of these functions on the determination of the optimal amount of the input that causes the externality.

In Figure 6.3, we examine the choice of input y from the viewpoint of the chemical company, because it is the firm that controls the amount of pollution emitted in a private market setting. If the chemical company does not take into account the effect its production process has on the apple company, it will simply set the net value of the marginal product of y equal to zero. That is, it will satisfy the second equation in (6.4). The equilibrium occurs at point A in Figure 6.3, where the *MB* equals zero. We can tell by looking at the figure that this is not a social optimum, because at point A the apple firm incurs a marginal damage equal to the amount AD. The total value of the input to the chemical firm is given by the triangle OAB, while the total damages to the apple company are shown by the triangle OAD.

To achieve the optimal use of input y requires that both the benefits to the chemical company and the damages to the apple firm be taken into account. The net gain to society will be the greatest where the marginal benefits to C equal the marginal damages to A. This occurs where *MB* intersects *MD* at point A'. The optimal amount of input y to use in the chemical company is thus y^*, not A. We can also see in this graph that the net benefits to society from the use of input y are the largest at point y^*. The chemical company loses total benefits (the value of the output) equal to the area y^*AA', but the apple company gains the amount (in terms of increased value of output) y^*ADA'. The gain to A exceeds the loss to C by the amount ADA'. Thus net benefits are maximized and equal ADA'. Because social welfare is measured by the consumer surplus from the consumption of both apple and chemical products, we are not concerned at this point about the distribution of the gains and losses among the companies. It is clear from our analysis above that if the chemical company is forced somehow to reduce its use of y without compensation, it will be worse off than it would be in an unregulated situation.

There are some important points to note. First, the optimum is reached where *marginal benefits* and *marginal damages* are equated. That means that in designing methods of achieving the optimum, we must know the shape of the *MB* and *MD* curves. Second, the *optimal amount of pollution is not equal to zero*. Because the optimal amount of input y is positive, the apple company will still have its production process affected by the chemical company's effluent. The effluent will be reduced, but not to zero. Again, this follows from the shape of our *MB* and *MD* functions. Both companies have outputs that are valued positively by society. Social welfare would fall if chemical production ceased. Under what conditions would the optimal use of y be zero? In this analysis, that would occur if *MD* intersected *MB* at point B. Think about what would happen to the optimal amount of y if the price of apples increased, the price of chemicals increased, or the pollution per unit of input y fell (owing, say, to a technological change). Try shifting the curves and determining the new equilibrium (see the problems for this chapter).

Pollution Control Mechanisms

We will look at two basic methods of internalizing the production externality just examined: private initiatives and government regulation of some sort. While all are capable of achieving the social optimum in theory, there may be reasons in practice why some types of regulation are more likely to succeed in optimally internalizing the externality than others. We begin with the market mechanisms.

Private Initiatives

Perhaps the simplest way of internalizing the externality conceptually is for the two companies to *merge*. One company purchases the assets of the other company and then has the power to control the operations of both divisions. This is called *unitization*. The optimum will be reached because the company will now maximize profits jointly, using the objective function presented in equation (6.5). As long as all markets remain competitive, merger yields the optimal use of both factor inputs, x and y, and the optimal amount of pollution, z. The new company then automatically equates *MB* to *MD* to achieve the optimal y^*. It is possible that one operation would be shut down. If, say, the marginal damage done to apple production is so large that it swamps the value of the marginal product of factors producing chemicals, then the company may cease chemical production if no effective means of controlling chemical wastes exists. Recall that we have not introduced methods of *abating* the discharge of effluent. There may be techniques that reduce the amount of effluent discharged (waste treatment plants for chemical effluents or scrubbers that remove particulates and sulfur oxides from power plants, smelters, and other manufacturing processes). If it is cheaper to use the abatement technology than to control inputs causing pollution or shut down operations adversely affected by the pollution, the company will use these techniques.

The advantages of merger are that it is done through market mechanisms. No costly regulatory process is required to impose restrictions on the polluter, no compensation of the afflicted party is necessary, no monitoring of pollution is required, and so on. There are, however, numerous difficulties. First, merger may reduce the degree of competition in the economy, which in turn may reduce consumer welfare. Second, if the externality "spills over" and affects other economic agents, merger of the two companies will not result in an optimal internalization of the externality for the bystanders. For example, people who use the lake for recreational purposes are not likely to find the marginal damage function of the apple division of the new company exactly the same as their personal marginal damage function resulting from the chemical division's use of the lake as a waste depository. If the marginal damage functions are not identical for all agents, merger between the generating party (the chemical company) and *one* of the afflicted parties (the apple company) will not lead to the optimal amount of pollution except by accident. Thus the more "public" the externality, the less likely merger is as a means of optimally internalizing the externality. Finally, there may be financial and legal impediments to merger that limit its use in controlling pollution in actual situations.

There is another general "market-like" solution—a series of negotiations and side payments between the agents involved. The direction of the payments depends on the property rights of the two firms with respect to the release of pollutants. Assume first that the chemical company has been polluting for some time and perceives that it has the right to continue to do so. The apple company will have to offer the chemical company compensation if it is to reduce pollution by lowering its use of input y. If the payment is equal to the value of the lost production from using less of input y, the chemical company will accept. To derive specific results, we assume particular functional forms for the parties. Let $MB = 12 - y$ and $MD = 2y$. Figure 6.4 illustrates some potential outcomes. Suppose that the apple company offers a payment of \$6 per unit of y reduced. The chemical company finds the level of y that equates \$6 to its MB curve. The chemical company reduces its use of input y to 6 units (\$6 $= 12 - y$, so $y = 6$). The chemical company receives a total payment of \$36 [(12 − 6)(\$6)]. It forgoes total benefits from the use of input y in the amount of \$18, which represents the area under its MB curve from 12 units of y to 6 units of y. The net gain to the chemical company is \$18. The apple company also gains. When the chemical company is producing using 12 units of input y, total damages from pollution are the area under its MD curve from 0 to 12 units of y, or \$144 in this example. When y is reduced to 6 units, total damages fall to \$36: at 6 units of y, marginal damages are \$12, and total damages are 1/2 (\$12)(6). The reduction in total damages is

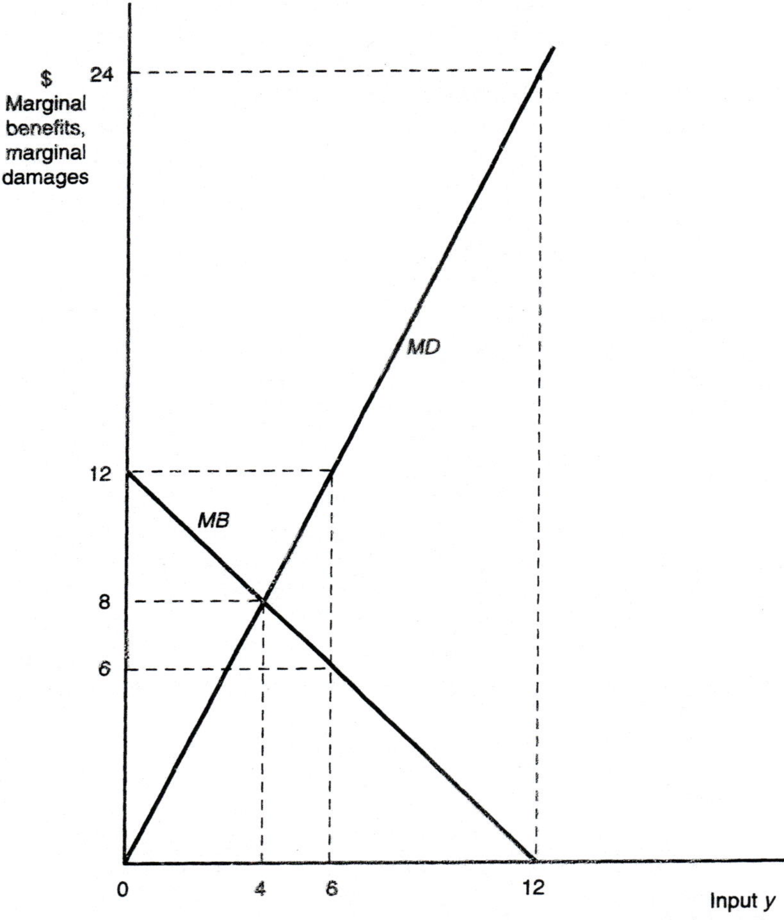

FIGURE 6.4. When the chemical company has the property right to pollute, the apple company must offer compensation for a decrease in input *y* that leads to a reduction in pollution. If the apple company offers $6 per unit *y*, pollution will fall to 6 units. At a payment of $8 per unit *y*, the socially optimal level of 4 units is reached. Both firms are better off after compensation is made, but the distribution of the net gains depends on the bargain achieved.

therefore $144 − $36 = $108. When the payment to the chemical company of $36 is netted out, the apple company is still better off by $72. The sum of the net gains to each party is $90.

Can the two parties do better than this? Suppose that in their negotiation process the parties find the efficient price that yields the optimal amount of input *y*, a payment of $8. Recompute the net gains of each party at this per unit payment. The chemical company will reduce *y* to 4 units. Its total benefits fall by $32 compared with its maximum use of input *y*, but it receives total compensation from the apple company equal to $64, for a net gain of $32. This amount is $14 higher than it received in the previous case, with a payment of $6 per unit *y* reduced. The apple company now has total damages of only $16, thus seeing a reduction of total damages of $128. The net gain to the apple company is $64 (equal to total damages forgone minus its compensation to the chemical company). The apple company is $8 poorer compared with the previous case. The sum of the net gains to each party is $96. Here we see one of the important issues in economics: the possible divergence between "social" and "private" gains. Society as a whole—in this case, apple plus chemical producers—is better off at the efficient equilibrium than at other locations, but individuals may be worse off. If all parties have perfect information about each other's function, they will not reach the socially efficient equilibrium unless a side payment is made, in this case from the chemical producers to the apple producers. If the chemical producer gives back $8 to the apple producer, the chemical firm will still have a higher net gain than in the case of the $6 unit payment. The apple producer will have its maximum payment of $72. *Side payments* are often necessary to ensure that an efficient equilibrium is reached.

Suppose now that a new law is introduced that requires the chemical company to compensate the apple company for any pollution damages. This changes the property rights to pollution. The chemical company now effectively faces a ban on polluting unless the apple company allows some pollution to occur. The apple company will allow pollution only if it is suitably compensated. Figure 6.5 illustrates this. Suppose now that the chemical company offers to pay the apple company $6 for each unit of input y it uses, remembering that input y leads to pollution, and that both parties know this technological relationship. The apple company will "allow" only 3 units of y to be used as it equates $6 to its marginal damage function of $MD = 2y$. The net gain to the apple producer is $9, which reflects the sum of the compensation it receives, ($6)(3) = 18, minus the total damages it incurs (the area under its MD curve from 0 to 3 units of y, $9). The net gain to the chemical company is the total benefit from being allowed to produce (the area under its MB curve from 0 to 3) of $31.50, minus its payment to the apple company of $18, for a sum of $13.50. The sum of the net gains to the parties is $22.50.

If the chemical company offers the socially efficient payment of $8 to the apple company, it will be allowed to employ 4 units of y. Net gains are now $16 to the apple producer and $8 to the chemical producer. The sum of the net gains to each party is $24. Again we see that total gains are maximized at the efficient equilibrium, but this leads one party to be worse off compared with another possible level of compensation. Side payments must again be made if this efficient outcome is to be reached. Now compare (1) the size of the side payment that is necessary to reach the efficient equilibrium in the case where the polluting chemical company has the property rights and (2) the side payment when the apple company has the property rights. If the apple company has the property rights, it can offer the chemical company a side payment of $5.50 to reach the efficient equilibrium. The apple company will still be better off than with compensation of $6 per unit. If the chemical company has the property rights, it has to offer a side payment of $8 to the apple company to reach this same equilibrium of 4 units of input y at a price of $8 per unit. Thus, while the efficient equilibrium is identical, the side payment necessary to reach it under a bargaining situation differs depending on who has the property rights. This difference may well influence whether or not the efficient equilibrium is reached. However, note that if the

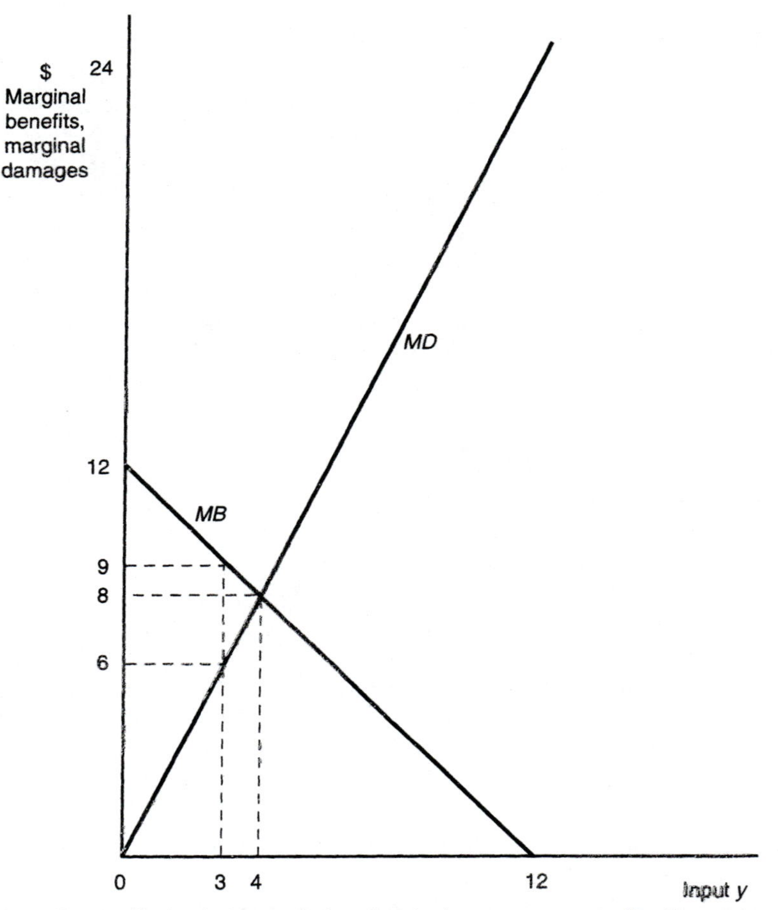

FIGURE 6.5. When pollution is banned, the chemical company must offer the apple company compensation if it is to produce. If the chemical company offers \$6 per unit y used, the apple company will allow 3 units. At the socially efficient price of \$8 per unit y, 4 units will be used. Whether or not social efficiency is reached depends on whether side payments are made and on the bargaining ability of each firm.

efficient allocation of resources is reached, it will be the same equilibrium in this simple model regardless of who has the property rights. This basic insight is called the Coase Theorem, after R. Coase, who published the fundamental paper that developed this result (1960) and later received a Nobel Prize in economics for this and other work.

These "bargaining" solutions involve no government intervention: Individual agents simply negotiate until a mutually agreeable solution is found. Bargaining thus has advantages similar to those of merger. When few agents are involved, it is a plausible means of internalizing the externality. However, as with merger, when the externality becomes more "public" in nature, bargaining generally will not internalize it. If large numbers of agents are affected and the external effects are nonappropriable, bargaining becomes extremely costly and generally unfeasible. Individuals who are concerned about pollution will be deterred from offering payments to polluters to reduce emissions by free riders who benefit from lower pollution levels but refuse to pay. If, say, we are talking about air pollution that comes from many different sources and affects many different people, it is hard to imagine them getting together and coming to some agreement. Could all the emitters and consumers of air pollution in Los Angeles County (millions of people) even find the means of negotiating, let alone agree on some form of payment? In the two-firm case above, it is quite likely that some sort of agreement would be reached. But cases like this one are rare. Indeed, one would not expect to observe them, because the externality would already be internalized. This is the situation in which those who claim that "all meaningful externalities that can be internalized" are accurate. If all externalities were private, we would expect some form of market mechanism to emerge that internalizes them. But the more pervasive and public the externality, the less able markets are to deal with them.

Government Policies

We turn now to methods governments can use to internalize the two-firm externality in production. Governments have two basic policies at their disposal—taxes and quantity controls (and combinations of these policies). While taxes, if set correctly, guarantee that the optimum will be reached, they are rarely used. Quantity controls can also reach the optimum but may lead to some inefficiencies.

A tax can be levied on the polluting firm in two ways. In the case of the apple and chemical firms, we assumed that the pollution flows from the use of input y through some sort of technological relationship between input y and pollution z (the h function). Either pollution itself or input y could be taxed. From the conditions for a social optimum given by equation (6.6), this means that the optimal tax on pollution would be equal to $P^A(\partial f/\partial h)$ while the optimal tax on input y would be $P^A[(\partial f/\partial h)(\partial h/\partial y)]$. Figure 6.6 illustrates t^*, an optimal tax on y. The chemical firm equates this tax to its marginal benefits of pollution, yielding the optimal input use, y^*. The chemical firm maximizes its profits subject to the tax and sets the value of the marginal product of input y net of the tax equal to zero. This occurs at y^*, the optimal amount of the input. It is important to note that these taxes must be evaluated at the optimum. Not just any measure of marginal damage works. The tax must be equal to MD at y^*. What this means is that the government must know the precise equation for *both* the marginal damage and the marginal benefit functions.

A quantity control that yields the optimal amount of pollution is also easily shown in Figure 6.6. Again, the government must know the equations for the marginal damage and marginal benefit functions. The optimal amount of the input causing the pollution is then calculated, and a restriction on the use of this input is imposed. In the example above, chemical firms would be prevented from using more than the amount y^* of input y. Alternatively, the government could restrict emissions of the effluent generated by input y. To do this, it must also know the functional relationship between input y and pollution z, the function we called $z = h(y)$. In practice,

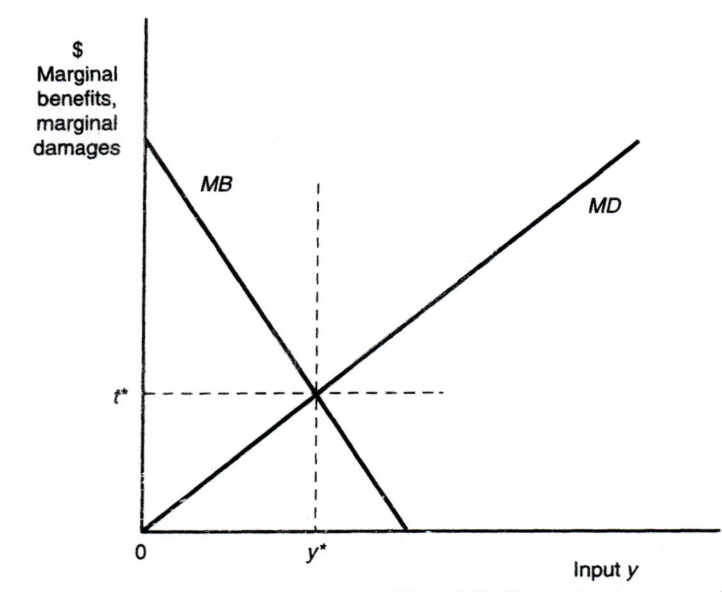

FIGURE 6.6. An optimal tax of t^* is set where $MB = MD$. The optimal standard is set at y^*.

regulations that restrict the use of pollution-causing inputs and the pollution itself are the most common forms of government control of externalities. But as we will see next, these forms of regulation may fail to satisfy an important efficiency condition—the equimarginal condition.

The Equimarginal Condition and Cost Efficiency

Standards are equivalent to taxes in terms of reaching the socially optimal level of pollution in a simple model with only one polluter and one "pollutee." However, there are important differences between the two policies when more than one polluter exists. Assume that marginal damages are the same for anyone who incurs them. Pollution comes from two types of firms: H and L, which stand, respectively, for high and low users of input y. To put the discussion in terms of pollution, further assume that one unit of input y used by either firm results in one unit of pollution z. That way, we can redraft our MB/MD diagram in terms of pollution. Now, MB and MD refer, respectively, to the marginal benefits from pollution and the marginal damages from pollution. Figure 6.7 illustrates the two MB curves for H and L, where

$$MB^H = 12 - y$$
$$MB^L = 6 - .5y$$

Note that the total pollution from the two firms is 24 units if there is no regulation of pollution. Suppose that the government has calculated the marginal damages from pollution and wants to reduce this level by 50 percent, from 24 to 12 units, by using

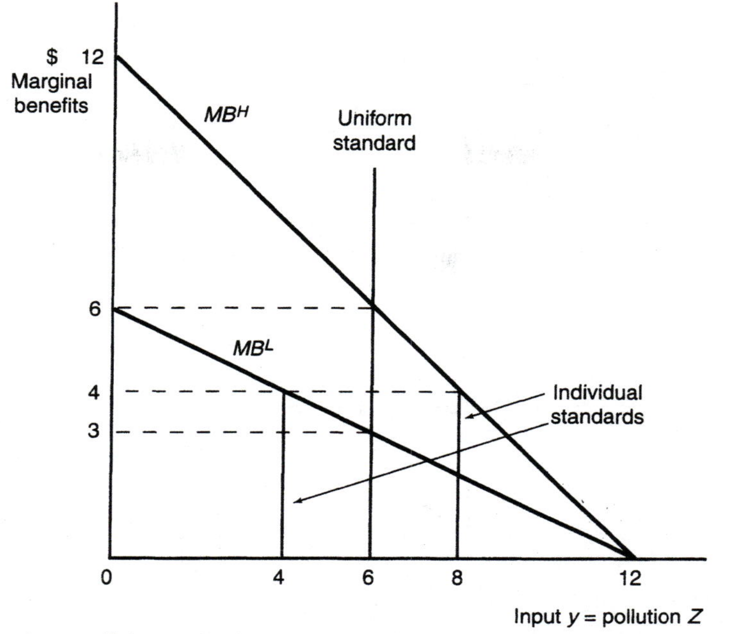

FIGURE 6.7. A cost-efficient policy is one that equates the marginal benefits of pollution. At $4, the marginal benefits of the *H* and *L* firms are identical. Individual standards set at 4 units of pollution for *L* and 8 units for *H* will be cost-efficient. The uniform standard set at 6 units of pollution is not cost-efficient.

either a tax or a standard. Once we introduce polluters with different production technologies, governments can use two types of standards. A *uniform* standard requires each polluter to release the same amount of pollution. In this case, the uniform standard would be set at 6 units. An *individual* standard allows the government to establish a specific level of emission for each polluter. Why might the government wish to do this? Here is where the equimarginal principle and cost efficiency enter.

Let's first see the effects on the polluters of the uniform standard. As Figure 6.7 shows, each polluter will end up with a different marginal benefit of pollution at the standard of 6 units of pollution. This is not economically efficient, because we could control the same amount of pollution at lower total costs to society if the standard was reallocated among the polluters. The gap between the two firms' *MB* of pollution means that these firms are not using input y efficiently. The low user of y could be asked to control more pollution than the high user. For example, suppose the *L* polluter was told to reduce its emissions by one more unit, allowing the *H* polluter to increase its emissions by one unit. Recall that this means changing their use of input y as well. The *MB* of pollution for *H* would fall while that of *L* would rise. Total pollution stays the same. If the government asks *L* to control one more unit of pollution, so that it is now emitting only 4 units while *H* emits 8, we see that total emissions are still 12 units, and that the two firms now have equated their *MB* of pollution at $4. Any further reallocation of emissions would move us away from this equality of marginal benefits.

The *equimarginal* condition states that pollution will be controlled at the lowest total costs to society if marginal benefits of pollution are equated across all firms. Any policy that achieves this equality of marginal benefits is said to be *cost-efficient*. Now let us prove all this. At a uniform standard of 6 units of pollution per polluter, each firm will forgo marginal benefits of pollution equal to the area under its *MB* curve from 12 units of pollution to 6. For the *H* firm, this amount equals \$18; for the *L* firm it is \$9—for a total opportunity cost of \$27. An individual standard set at the cost-efficient levels of emissions of 4 units of pollution for *L* and 8 units for *H* would cost the firms and society a total of \$24 (\$16 for *L* and \$8 for *H*). Less in total is forgone with the individual standard. The uniform standard is not cost-efficient, because it results in opportunity costs of controlling pollution that are higher than they need be to reach a given target. Try other combinations of reductions in emissions per firm to be satisfied that application of the equimarginal condition will lead to the lowest total costs.

The cost-efficient equilibrium can be determined quite readily algebraically. The two conditions that must be satisfied are:

1. Emissions from each firm must sum to the target level of emissions, or $z^H + z^L = 12$ in our case.

2. Marginal benefits of pollution must be the same for each firm, $MB^H = MB^L$. With the equations given, this means that $12 - y^H = 6 - y^L$.

Solving both equations simultaneously, we find that $y^H = 8$ and $y^L = 4$ and that $MB^H = MB^L = \$4$.

Is a uniform tax cost-efficient? Suppose that the regulator levies a unit tax of \$4 per unit *y* used by firms (which in this simple model translates into a tax of \$4 per unit emissions). Each firm sets the tax equal to its *MB* of pollution. The *H* firm will produce 8 units of pollution; the *L* firm, 4 units. Cost efficiency is achieved because the tax is set equal to marginal benefits; hence marginal benefits are equalized.

Cost efficiency need not imply that a socially optimal allocation is reached. The optimal allocation requires that the regulator equate marginal benefits and marginal damages. In this section, we have assumed that *MB* and *MD* are equated, but even if the regulator were to set a pollution target at an arbitrary level or at its "best guess" of the socially optimal level, cost efficiency would still be a desirable objective of any policy. Society will want to ensure that it reaches a target, however set, at the lowest possible total cost for the parties affected. With the saving in total costs, more of the goods society desires can be produced.

Marketable Permits to Pollute

There is an additional policy instrument that regulators can use to internalize pollution externalities—the marketable (or tradable) permit. The permit gives the holder a property right to release specified amounts of pollution. In this respect, the permit is like a pollution standard. The permit holder has a maximum emission level it must abide by. The innovative feature of the marketable permit is that these rights are tradable. The holder can sell its permits to a willing buyer at a mutually agreeable price. If there are enough buyers and sellers of permits, a market will be established, where, in equilibrium, there will be a market-clearing price that equates the supply of permits to the demand for permits. The market-clearing price becomes the "price for pollution." A polluter faces this price when deciding how much pollution to emit versus control.

The first question the regulator faces in initiating a marketable permit system is how to allocate the permits initially. There are two fundamental options—auction the permits or distribute them without charge on some basis. Assume first that the government auctions the permits. Let's see how the market price is obtained. Refer again to Figure 6.7, where there are two polluters: *H* and *L*. Assume that each polluter is initially at 12 units of pollution because there has been no prohibition against pollution. The target level of pollution is again 12 units in total (a 50 percent reduction), which means that a total of 12 permits with 1 unit of pollution allowed per permit will be auctioned. Suppose that firm *H* starts the bidding at $2 per permit. Each polluter equates the permit price to its *MB* of pollution. At $2, firm *H* will want to buy 10 permits and firm *L* will want to buy 5. This cannot be an equilibrium, because the total demand for permits (15) exceeds the supply (10). The permit price must therefore rise. Alternatively, suppose that the initial bid is $6 per permit. Firm *H* will want 6 permits and firm *L* will want none. Now there is an excess supply of permits, and their price will fall. The permit market, if there are enough buyers and sellers, will therefore operate just like any other market. Equilibrium will be established where the demand for permits is equal to the supply. In our example, equilibrium occurs at $4 per permit, with *H* buying 8 permits and *L* buying 4. Note that equilibrium in the permit market is cost-efficient. The equimarginal condition is satisfied.

For political reasons, governments may find it difficult to auction permits. The sale of permits will generate revenues. In the example given, the government collects $4 times 12 permits or $48 in revenue; in actual cases, the revenues could be substantial, leading to opposition for the scheme from polluters. Suppose therefore that the government simply distributes the permits without charge. Will the same cost-efficient equilibrium be achieved? If we look first at the short run, the answer is yes, provided the market has enough buyers and sellers to be perfectly competitive. Suppose the government gives each of our polluters 6 permits. The initial allocation of permits then looks exactly like the uniform standard discussion above. However, the firms will not hold 6 permits each, because they can benefit by exchanging the permits among themselves. Firm *H* has a higher *MB* of pollution than firm *L* at 6 permits ($6 versus $3). It offers to buy permits from *L*. Through bargaining, the firms will again reach the equilibrium price of $4 per permit (try other prices to convince yourself that this is the case). After this market reaches its short-run equilibrium, we see that firm *H* has paid firm *L* a total of $8 for its purchase of 2 permits from *L*. Thus there is a redistribution from *H* to *L*.

The government collects no revenue from this exchange. Thus the essential difference between an initial auction by the government and a "free" distribution of permits is in the generation of revenue. In the short run, the government collects the

BOX 6.1 Productivity Slowdown: A Cost of Environmental Regulations?

A study by Conrad and Morrison (1989) examines the relationship between pollution control expenditures on capital equipment and measures of productivity growth for the United States, Canada, and Germany for the period from the 1960s to early 1980s. Environmental regulation has been identified by a number of researchers as one factor that has contributed to the slowdown in productivity growth since the early 1970s. The argument is that investments in pollution abatement equipment are nonproductive, in the sense that they do not result in any increase in output. They also may crowd out other forms of capital investment that could enhance productivity. However, others have suggested that there may be some positive impact of pollution regulation on productivity in industries where it leads to accelerated capital turnover and modernization. Pollution control technologies may also be resource-saving or may promote recycling of inputs, thus saving firms outlays on variable factor inputs.

A wide range of studies have been done, and while most find that environmental regulation has had a negative impact on productivity growth, there is no clear consensus on the magnitude of the effect. Most of the studies do not look explicitly at the behavior of firms in response to regulation. Conrad and Morrison develop a model of a competitive firm that faces environmental regulation in the form of an emission standard. The firm must choose some level of investment in capital that abates enough pollution to meet the standard. They maintain the assumption that pollution capital is nonproductive; it has no positive effect on output and thus is not treated as a productive input. Conrad and Morrison then net out the costs of pollution abatement capital from total capital expenditures in estimating productivity growth. Firms are assumed to set product price equal to marginal costs of production when no distortion exists due to the requirement to invest in pollution abatement equipment. The traditional approach to measuring changes in productivity is inclusive of pollution abatement expenditures. If these expenditures act as a "drag" on productivity, one expects to see a lower measure of productivity growth when they are included in capital stock estimates than when they are not. This is what Conrad and Morrison test for econometrically.

Average productivity growth indexes for the periods 1967 to 1972 (or 1973) and 1972 (or 1973) to 1980 for the United States and Canada are shown in the accompanying table. German estimates are available only for the latter period. Canada shows a clear and large reduction in productivity growth from the earlier to the later period, independent of whether the dividing year is 1972 or 1973. Eliminating pollution abatement expenditures does increase the average annual values for each time period, but the adjusted index is much smaller in the second period (+0.05 to 0.06) than in the first period (+0.12). The divergence between the traditional and adjusted indexes for Germany is +0.12 to 0.13, in line with the early period for Canada. The indexes for the United States are quite sensitive to the year chosen for the interperiod comparison. If 1967–1972 and 1972–1980 are chosen, average annual productivity in the United States does not decline, whereas for 1967–1973 to 1973–1980 it does. These averages hide a substantial amount of year-to-year variation in the United States. Productivity growth was negative—substantially so—for the years 1966, 1970, and 1974, but positive and relatively large for 1972, 1973, 1976 and 1977. Nonetheless, productivity is higher in all estimates shown under the adjusted index. The adjustment ranges from +0.08 to 0.22.

Conrad and Morrison also estimate productivity indexes assuming that there were no environmental regulations. This allows them to test the overall impact of environmental regulation on productivity growth. They find for the United States that in periods of high growth of output and little investment (1971–1973 and 1976–1978), regulation has a de-

BOX 6.1 *(Continued)*

pressing impact on the change in productivity. The impacts are, however, quite small. Environmental regulation contributes to a reduction in productivity growth −0.003 to −0.14 percentage points. In many other years, environmental regulation appears to improve productivity growth by modest amounts ranging from +0.004 to 0.33. Environmental regulation depresses average productivity growth for the periods 1960–1967 and 1967–1972 (or 1973) by a small amount (−0.001 to −0.02), and increases it for the later period (+0.01 to 0.02). In Canada, a similar result occurs, although the size of the adverse impacts is often larger than that for comparable years in the United States. In Germany, in only 2 of the 10 years between 1972 and 1981 do environmental regulations adversely affect productivity growth.

What does one conclude from all these estimates? First, environmental regulation in Germany appears to have had a generally positive effect on productivity growth. The same cannot be said for Canada and the United States. Environmental regulations appear to have had a negative impact on productivity growth in each country for approximately half the years examined. Second, if pollution abatement expenditures are incorporated "incorrectly" in productivity calculations, the productivity measure will be biased downward. If these expenditures are believed to be unproductive, they should not be added to the estimate of the capital stock. More recent estimates are needed to see if the trends to 1980 have continued or changed.

PRODUCTIVITY GROWTH INDEXES FOR MANUFACTURING, PERCENT

Average Annual Growth	United States		Canada		Germany	
	Traditional	Adjusted	Traditional	Adjusted	Traditional	Adjusted
1967–1972	1.98	2.06	1.82	1.94	NA	NA
1967–1973	2.66	2.74	3.24	3.36	NA	NA
1972–1980	2.17	2.37	0.86	0.92	2.83	2.96
1973–1980	1.56	1.79	0.23	0.28	2.86	2.94

NOTE: Index is value-added productivity growth in percentages for the manufacturing sector of each country. Only one variable input, labor, is considered, so the indexes represent multifactor productivity growth for net output. The traditional measure incorporates pollution abatement investment in the capital stock figures; the adjusted measure exceeds the pollution abatement expenditures.

Source: Figures taken from Tables I, II, and III in Klaus Conrad and Catherine J. Morrison (1989). "The Impact of Pollution Abatement Investment on Productivity Change: An Empirical Comparison of the U.S., Germany, and Canada," *Southern Economic Journal,* 55, pp. 684–697.

"rents" from pollution permits if they are auctioned; individual firms collect these rents if there is a free initial distribution. This distinction will lead to different long-run equilibrium outcomes, depending on what the government does with the revenues it collects from permits when they are auctioned. The government could simply redistribute the revenue back to the polluters in a lump-sum fashion that does not affect the polluter's decision making. If so, the long- and short-run equilibria will coincide. The government could redistribute the permit receipts in a variety of ways that would probably affect polluting firms in a nonneutral way (e.g., by cutting taxes, increasing government expenditures). If so, the long-run equilibrium for polluters would probably differ from the short-run outcome described above.

In summary, marketable permits are a combination of the traditional policies of taxes and standards. They are like a standard in that the regulator specifies a maximum emission level for pollution. But they also provide a market-based incentive to reduce emissions because a price per unit pollution is created by the permit market. In this regard, permits create incentives on the margin to reduce emissions, as do taxes. Polluters are induced to equate the marginal benefits of pollution with the unit price of pollution. The price of pollution is the unit tax rate or the permit price established in the permit market. Marketable permits are cost-efficient because each polluter will equate the permit price to its *MB* curve. A key ingredient in the success of permit markets is that enough buyers and sellers exist to make the market competitive. In Chapter 7 we discuss some examples of permit markets in action and find that it may be difficult to have enough trades at any point in time to make the market competitive.

TOPICS IN THE THEORY OF ENVIRONMENTAL CONTROLS

In this section, we cover two additional topics. First, we consider whether subsidies to polluters to reduce their emissions—as compared with an equivalent tax—will yield the socially optimal amount of pollution. Second, we examine what happens when the government cannot determine the optimal tax because it lacks information about the nature of the marginal benefit or marginal damages from pollution. We see when quantity restrictions (standards) would be the preferred policy and when some combination of taxes and standards is indicated. This topic is of practical appeal, because until very recently most regulations were in the form of standards—limitations on the emissions of pollution.

Taxes versus Subsidies

To internalize an externality, a tax on pollution (or the factor responsible for the pollution) must be set equal to the marginal damage caused by the pollution at the point where marginal damages equal marginal benefits. However, suppose that those responsible for the pollution were simply offered a subsidy for each unit of effluent removed from the environment. Wouldn't this sort of subsidy also internalize the externality? No. Subsidies, even if equivalent to taxes on the margin, will not yield the socially optimal amount of pollution. We can show why with a simple model.

To show the difference between taxes and subsidies, we must be careful to distinguish between their effects on the firm versus their effects on the industry as a whole. This is the key to the difference between the two forms of pollution control. We will continue to assume that the pollution affects only two particular sectors of the economy—say, the chemical industry and apple growers. We maintain our partial equilibrium model. We begin with the firm: Suppose that each firm in the chemical industry produces z units of pollution for each unit of chemical output produced. For simplicity, we now drop the relationship between a particular input and pollution output and assume there is always a fixed proportion between output q and pollution z. The pollution adversely affects apple firms, as in the previous section. We assume that a large number of chemical and apple firms are involved and that they are dispersed throughout the country. Merger and bargaining solutions to the pollution problem are thus not feasible, by assumption.

The federal government seeks the socially optimal amount of pollution. The government first evaluates the effect on each chemical firm and the chemical industry of a tax set at rate t on each unit of pollution (where the tax rate is determined by the marginal damages to apple growers from the pollution). For simplicity, we assume that the chemical industry is perfectly competitive and faces a constant price p for each unit of output produced. We also assume that the total costs of producing the chemical product are given by the function $c(q)$. Then $\partial c/\partial q$ is marginal cost of production, which is denoted by c'. For now, we assume that the only way the firm can reduce the amount of pollution it emits is by producing fewer units of output.

Each chemical company will maximize its profits subject to the tax. The after-tax profits, $\hat{\pi}$, for each chemical firm are given by equation (6.7):

$$\hat{\pi} = pq - c(q) - tzq \tag{6.7}$$

Maximization of equation (6.7) yields the following condition for a profit maximum: $p - c' - tz = 0$. This condition says that the firm will equate the price of each unit of chemicals *net of* the *marginal* tax payments on each unit of output to marginal cost of production, c'.

Alternatively, suppose that the government considers a subsidy to polluters who abate. The subsidy would work in the following way. The government must first pick a benchmark amount of pollution, call it Z. This is the benchmark amount of pollution per unit output. Z is the level of emissions of each firm where no subsidy is paid—a maximum level. The government then offers to pay each firm amount s for *each unit* of pollution it emits below the benchmark. That is, the subsidy takes the form $s(Z - z)$. If the firm emits Z or more units of pollution, it receives no subsidy. If it emits less than Z, it receives a subsidy of s dollars times the difference between Z and z. Thus we see already a difference between the tax and the subsidy—the government must set both the rate of subsidy and the benchmark level, whereas in the other case only the tax rate need be determined.

When faced with the subsidy, the chemical firm will maximize its profits, taking the subsidy into account. If the firm does not reduce its pollution emissions, the subsidy becomes an opportunity cost—what the firm forgoes by not reducing its pollution. The profits for the firm are given by equation (6.8):

$$\tilde{\pi} = pq - c(q) + s(Z - z)q \tag{6.8}$$

Profits are maximized where $p - c' + s(Z - z) = 0$—that is, where price *plus* the subsidy payment for each marginal unit of pollution reduced is equal to marginal cost. Now if the tax rate t is equal to the subsidy rate s, the two government policies have *exactly the same effect on the margin*. Each firm is indifferent on the margin between the tax and the subsidy because the opportunity cost to the firm is the same. This is the

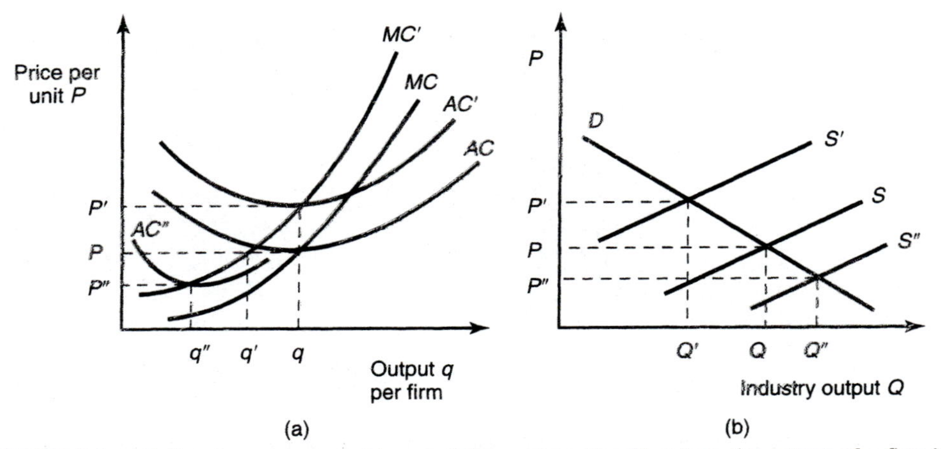

FIGURE 6.8. Both a tax and a subsidy set at the same rate will reduce the output of a firm in the short run, because both policies shift the marginal cost curve from MC to MC'. A reduction in output from q to q' results in a reduction in pollution. In the long run, the tax will lead to exit from the industry because at price P, firms cannot cover their average costs AC', which have risen because of the tax. The supply curve in (b) for the industry shifts from S to S'. The subsidy lowers average costs to AC''. In the long run, firms will then enter the industry. The industry supply curve would shift to S''. Industry output and aggregate pollution thus falls with the tax and rises with the subsidy.

amount $tzq = szq$. If pollution increases by 1 unit, the firm either pays the tax or does not receive the subsidy—the revenue forgone is exactly the same. What is the difference between the two policies? The tax and the subsidy have quite different effects on the incentives for firms to enter and exit from the industry, as we will see.

In Figure 6.8 we illustrate the effects of the tax versus the subsidy. In (a), the effects are shown for each firm in the industry; in (b), the effects on the industry supply curve are represented. Suppose each firm is initially in a long-run equilibrium with price equal to marginal cost at the minimum of the average cost curve AC. Initial output of the firm is q and price is P in Figure 6.8(a). In (b), we show the market equilibrium where aggregate supply equals aggregate demand for the good in question at price P. Total industry output is Q. The government then imposes a tax on pollution at rate t per unit of pollution emitted. The tax will shift up *both* the average and the marginal cost curves of each firm to, say, AC' and MC'. The output of each firm will fall *in the short run* to q', where MC' is equal to the market clearing price of P.

What are the *long-run* effects of the tax? Note that in (a), average costs, AC', exceed the price, P. Firms thus incur a loss for each unit of the good sold. Over time, then, some of the firms must exit from the industry as their capital is depreciated.[8] Exit is shown in (b) by the leftward shift of the industry supply curve from S to S'. A new long-run market equilibrium will be established at price P' with an aggregate output of Q'. At P', firms remaining in the industry are again in a long-run equilibrium. Thus, the effect of the tax in the long run is to *reduce the aggregate amount of pollution from the industry because the number of firms has fallen.* We do not know if in the long run pollution per firm falls unless we specify the precise position of the AC' and MC' curves. As illustrated, pollution per firm remains the same. But it is possible for pollution per firm to rise or fall, depending on the shape and location of the AC curve.[9]

Suppose now that a subsidy is granted to firms that reduce their pollution emissions below the established benchmark. The unit subsidy rate s is assumed equal to the tax rate t. Each firm will again see its *marginal cost* curve shift up to MC'. The marginal cost curve shifts by the same amount as with the tax because for each unit of additional output produced, the firm forgoes a subsidy identical to the tax payment under the alternative scheme. But the *average cost* curve of each firm shifts down to AC'' because the firm will receive compensation if output and hence pollution is lowered. Thus costs, on average, fall. The *short-run* equilibrium will again be where price is equal to marginal cost. This again occurs at an output level of q' for the firm. The effect of the subsidy on the output of the firm is *exactly the same* as that of the tax in the short run. But notice that the firm will now earn an *excess profit* with the subsidy; average costs are less than the price. This is a signal for *entry* into a competitive industry. The effect of the entry is shown in Figure 6.8(b).

Over time, as new firms enter the industry (and receive their subsidies for polluting less than the benchmark), the industry supply curve shifts to the right to S''. If the demand curve does not shift, the new industry equilibrium will occur at a price P'' and aggregate output Q''. The price falls from its initial level at P to P'', where zero profits are obtained for each firm and the long-run equilibrium is established. At this long-run equilibrium, the effect of the subsidy is to increase the amount of pollution. This occurs because although pollution per firm falls to q'', as shown in (a), the total number of firms in the industry has risen.[10]

The effect of the subsidy is thus counterproductive to the policy seeking a reduction in emissions of pollutants. Note as well that the subsidy may allow firms that are unprofitable to remain in the industry. Suppose that a firm had average costs slightly above that given by AC. The subsidy may then reduce these average costs so that the firm can stay in business. Eventually these inefficient firms will be driven out by efficient (lower-cost) firms, but the process may take some time. No such incentive for inefficient firms to remain in the industry exists with the tax.

There are some qualifications that must be made. First, the model is in partial equilibrium. If we allow for effects to spill over into other markets (factor and goods markets), the strong distinction between the effect of the tax versus the subsidy on aggregate pollution weakens.[11] Advanced analysis is necessary to determine the effects.

It is also unlikely that the government would introduce a subsidy in the precise form we assumed above. In our model, any firm that reduces pollution below the benchmark receives the subsidy, whether it is an existing firm or a new entrant. In practice, it is doubtful that the government would allow a new entrant to receive the subsidy. Actual subsidies are generally tied to the use of particular equipment that reduces pollution emissions.

We have also ignored the possibility that firms can reduce emissions of pollutants by introducing abatement technologies. Will the tax and the subsidy be equivalent if they are based on abatement equipment rather than pollution emissions? We cannot say for sure without more careful analysis. Subsidies will generally allow more firms to remain in the industry than would a tax. If the relationship between pollution emitted and abatement capital installed is the same for each firm, then again we would expect more pollution under the subsidy. Thus the tax remains the preferred policy to achieve both a reduction in pollution and an efficient use of resources.

But it is unlikely that the government could ever implement an optimal tax, simply because the information required to determine such a tax is quite high. We do not know the shape of the marginal damage function with any degree of confidence. Nor do we know the shape of the marginal benefit function. If the government must guess at the appropriate tax rate, it may indeed reduce rather than increase social welfare and end up with quite undesirable amounts of pollution.

Taxes versus Standards under Uncertainty

We turn now to a brief discussion of taxes versus quantity controls or standards under conditions of uncertainty.

Let's return to the case of a single firm that emits a pollutant as a result of the use of a particular input. We drew in Figure 6.3 a marginal benefit (*MB*) curve, which measured the value to the firm of using the input that generated the pollution. The curve was downward-sloping because it represented the value of the marginal product of the input. In this section, we assume that for each unit of the input used, one unit of pollution is emitted. We will therefore talk about the firm's emission of pollutants rather than its use of the factor input. We do this because pollution regulations often refer to individual pollutants rather than the inputs responsible for the pollutants. We continue to assume that the *MB* function is linear, as is the marginal damage function (*MD*), which measures the damages done by each additional unit of pollution emitted.[12]

Suppose that the government agency responsible for pollution control is trying to estimate this *MB* curve so that an optimal tax or standard can be calculated. Although the firm knows its own *MB* curve, the government does not. The government is uncertain about the location of the *MB* curve for the firm. The government makes an estimate of the expected marginal benefit curve, which in general will not be the actual curve, except by chance. For simplicity, we assume that the government is able to measure accurately the marginal damages (*MD*) from pollution. While this assumption is not realistic, it will not alter the fundamental results.

Figure 6.9 illustrates a case in which the government *underestimates* the marginal benefits of pollution to the firm, and what will happen in this case with the imposition of a tax or a standard set at the wrong level. Suppose the government's estimate of the marginal benefit of pollution to the firm is *MB*. Marginal damages are given by *MD*. The government then equates *MB* to *MD* to determine what it thinks is the optimal amount of pollution. The *MB* curve intersects the *MD* curve at an emission level of Z pollution. To obtain Z units of pollution, the government can impose a tax equal to $0t$ per unit of pollution emitted, or it can simply implement a standard that restricts emissions to Z. If the actual marginal benefit curve is *MB*, the two policies will be equivalent.

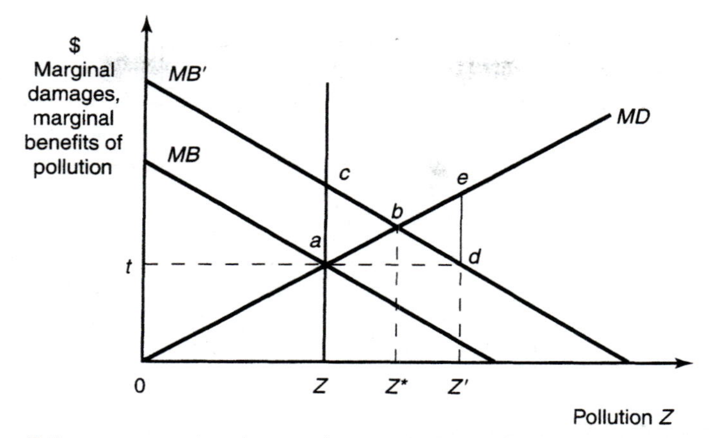

FIGURE 6.9. If the government estimates the marginal benefit of pollution (*MB*) to be *MB* but the true curve is *MB'*, both a standard and a tax will lead to an inefficient amount of pollution. A standard based on *MB* and set at *Z* leads to too little pollution and an efficiency loss equal to the area *abc*. A tax set at 0*t* leads to too much pollution (*Z'* rather than the optimal *Z**) and an efficiency loss of *bde*.

Suppose, however, that the actual marginal benefit curve is *MB'*, which lies everywhere above *MB*. That is, the government's estimate of the value of pollution to the firm is less than the actual value. Both the tax and the standard will then lead to nonoptimal amounts of pollution, but the amount of pollution will no longer be the same for each policy. The optimal amount of pollution is Z^*. With the standard set at *Z*, there will, of course, be no more than 0*Z* units of pollution emitted regardless of where the actual *MB* curve is. However, there will be a social or efficiency loss equal to the forgone benefits to the firm (the producer surplus) because *too little* pollution is emitted relative to the optimum. The cost to society of these forgone benefits is the triangle labeled *abc*. These net costs are the difference between the forgone value of production from the firm emitting pollution net of the reduction in damages due to the lower amount of pollution.

What then is the effect of the tax, which is still set at 0*t*? The firm will equate the tax to its actual marginal benefit curve and emit 0*Z'* units of pollution. *Too much* pollution is now emitted: Those who are harmed by pollution now lose, because pollution exceeds the optimal level. The value of the additional damage done by the pollution (forgone benefits of pollution abatement or loss in consumer surplus) is equal to the triangle *bde*.

What is the government to do when faced with uncertainty in its measurement of the *MB* function? Is it better to use a tax or a standard? In general, the government should choose the policy that minimizes the expected efficiency loss—the policy that minimizes the sum of the triangles over all possible realizations of the *MB* curve. We will look at particular examples where one policy is preferred over the other.

Consider Figure 6.10. In Figure 6.10(a), we have an *MB* function that is *flatter* (in absolute value) than the *MD* function. Let's compare the effects of the tax and the

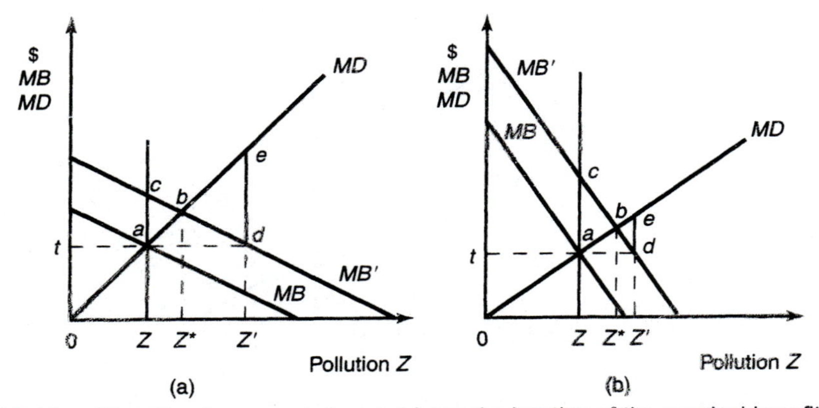

FIGURE 6.10. When the government does not know the location of the marginal benefit of pollution curve (*MB*) but it does know the slope of the *MB* curve relative to the marginal damage curve (*MD*), it can find the policy that minimizes the expected efficiency losses due to uncertainty about the *MB* curve. If the *MB* curve is flatter (in absolute value) than the *MD* curve as in (a), the standard minimizes the expected losses. The pollution emissions are closer to the optimum, and the efficiency losses are smaller than if a tax is used. If the absolute value of the slope of the *MB* function exceeds that of the *MD* function, the tax policy will minimize the expected losses from miscalculating marginal benefits.

standard when they are set at a nonoptimal level. Suppose that the actual marginal benefits of pollution are *MB*′, but the government has calculated them as *MB*. The tax is then set at $0t$ or the standard at *Z*. Under the standard, the firm will emit slightly less pollution than is optimal (*Z* versus *Z**), and the efficiency loss will be the small triangle *abc*. With the tax, the firm will emit far more pollution than is optimal (*Z*′ versus *Z**), which results in a large efficiency loss of *bde*. Thus, if the *MB* function is flatter than the *MD* function, a standard is the preferred second-best policy because it minimizes the efficiency loss resulting from the nonoptimal policy. Note that the government's uncertainty about the *MB* function must be in its location rather than its slope. If the government knows neither the location nor the slope of the *MB* function relative to the *MD* function, even these second-best policies become extremely tenuous.

The second-best policy is reversed when the slope of the *MB* function is steeper than that of the *MD* function. Figure 6.10(b) illustrates this case. Again, suppose that the optimal amount of pollution is *Z**, where the actual marginal benefit curve *MB*′ equals the *MD* curve. The government has estimated the marginal benefit curve as *MB* and thus implements either a tax of $0t$ or a standard of *Z*. Under the standard, the actual level of pollution will be far below the optimum, and the efficiency loss will now be quite high (triangle *abc*). Under the tax, pollution will be slightly above the optimum, and the efficiency loss will be relatively small (triangle *bde*). A tax would then be the preferred second-best policy because it minimizes the expected efficiency loss.

Can we give the same type of advice to governments about second-best policies when the uncertainty is about the location of the *MD* curve? The answer is no. Figure

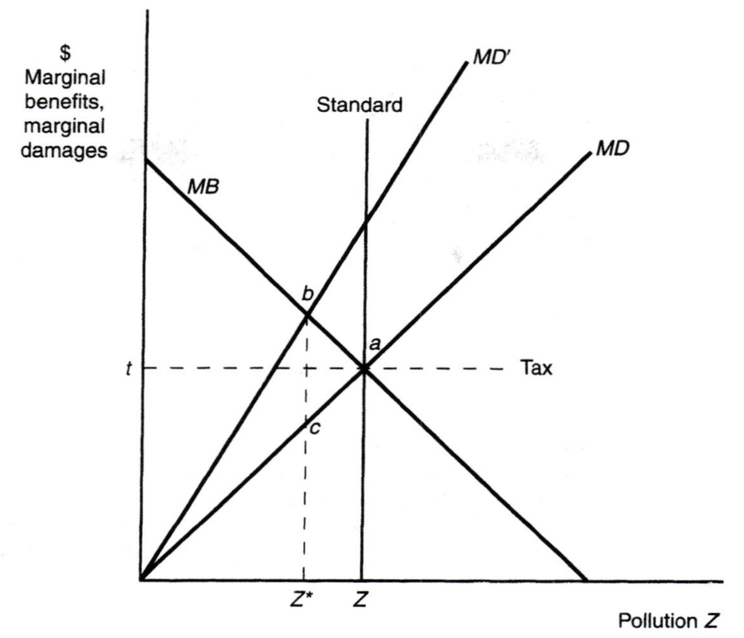

FIGURE 6.11. When uncertainty is about the location of the *MD* curve, information about the relative slopes of *MB* and *MD* will not assist the government in choosing a second-best policy. Pollutes equate *MB* to the inefficient tax at rate *t* or pollute at the standard of *Z*. The level of pollution is the same regardless of which policy is used.

6.11 illustrates this. The government estimates *MD*, but the true curve is *MD'*. The tax is set at *t*, the standard at *Z*. The polluter equates its *MB* to *t* or pollutes at level *Z*. There is no difference between the two policies as regards their impact on the level of pollution. Therefore, information on the relative slopes of *MB* and *MD* will not result in any change in social losses of being at the "wrong" equilibrium.

Marketable permits offer another means of dealing with the problems created by the uncertainty of the location of the *MB* curve. However, permits do not alleviate the need to know the relative slope of *MD* versus *MB*. The government must determine the number of permits to offer (either for auction or to distribute without charge). To determine the social losses from issuing permits, it will still need to know whether *MD* is flat or steep relative to *MB*. What marketable permits offer is information about the socially efficient equilibrium. Suppose that the government creates too few permits relative to the socially efficient level because it has miscalculated the *MB* curve. The market price of permits will rise in response to the excess demand for permits. Governments then know that the *MB* calculated is too low. More permits can be issued. Taxes also provide information about the *MB* curve. If the government has set the tax rate too low relative to the socially efficient level, it will collect more tax revenue than it anticipates because polluters will equate the tax to their "true" *MB* (which lies above the estimated *MB* in this case). They will pollute more than the government anticipated. The tax rate should then be adjusted upward until the anticipated tax revenues equal the actual tax revenues. This can easily be shown by using the diagrammatic analysis laid out in this section.

Obviously, cases of actual pollution will not be as simple as the examples presented here. Our model contains linear and continuous functions, models uncertainty very simply, has pollution damages well defined, and examines the behavior of one firm. If the firm is operating in a competitive market, increasing the number of firms presents no difficulty; the basic results are the same. Noncompetitive markets would require the use of game theoretic models—a topic beyond the scope of this chapter. We will not go into more complex models of uncertainty at this point, but we will examine what happens to the results when the functions are no longer continuous because threshold effects are present.

Figure 6.12 illustrates a case where a threshold exists in the damages inflicted by pollution. In (a), we present the total damages from pollution as its level rises; in (b) we show the marginal damage function. As pollution increases from zero to Z^+, total pollution damages increase monotonically and marginal damages are constant. At Z^+, however, the total damage function takes a large discontinuous jump upward and then again increases at a constant rate. Z^+ is the *threshold* where the impact of the pollution changes dramatically.

Many actual pollutants may have such thresholds. The existence of a threshold again means that the policy which minimizes expected efficiency losses under uncertainty depends on the shape and location of the *MB* and *MD* curves. Suppose the government knows the shape of the *MD* function—in particular, it knows where the threshold is—but it does not know where the *MB* function lies. If the government underestimates the *MB* function by assuming that the function intersects the *MD* function anywhere in the region from 0 to Z^+, it will set a tax equal to $0t$. If the actual *MB*

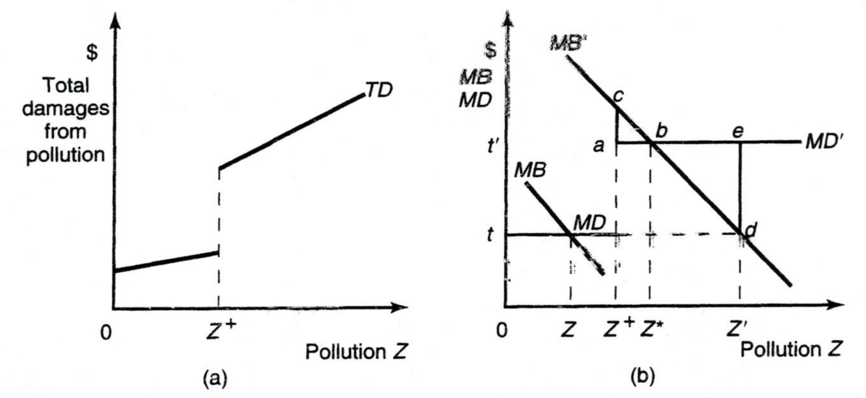

FIGURE 6.12. If the marginal damage function (*MD*) is discontinuous owing to the presence of a threshold effect in pollution damages, a combined policy using both a standard set at the threshold and a tax set equal to $0t$ will minimize the expected losses from miscalculating the *MB* function. If only a tax is used and marginal benefits are *MB'* rather than the estimated *MB*, the efficiency loss is *bde* and excessive amounts of pollution are emitted. If the standard is used alone, too little pollution is emitted and the efficiency loss is equal to *abc*.

function lies within this region, the optimal amount of pollution is emitted. The tax policy thus works well if the government knows that the *MB* function intersects *MD* to the left of Z^+. If, however, the government imposes a tax equal to $0t$ but the *MB* function intersects the *MD* function to the right of Z^+, the tax can lead to exessive amounts of pollution.

Suppose that the actual *MB* function is *MB'*. A tax of $0t$ will then yield Z' pollution rather than the optimal amount Z^*. Pollution at Z' greatly exceeds Z^*, leading to large efficiency losses (and of course large pollution damages). The loss-minimizing policy in this situation is then to impose a standard at the threshold level or a high tax, t which is equal to *MD* above the threshold. The standard ensures that pollution does not exceed the threshold but may result in efficiency losses (due to too little pollution) if the *MB* curve is actually *MB'*. The tax at t' will prevent excessive amounts of pollution emissions. If, however, the marginal benefit curve is *MB*, the high taxes will be punitive and lead to much too little pollution.

Perhaps the best policy when the location of the *MB* curve is uncertain is to combine the tax and the standard. Suppose that the standard is set at the threshold level of pollution and a tax is imposed equal to the lower portion of the *MD* function ($0t$). If the marginal benefit curve turns out to be *MB*, the tax is the binding constraint for the firm, and the optimal amount of pollution results. If the actual marginal benefit curve is *MB'*, the standard is the binding constraint. Pollution will be less than is optimal (Z^+ rather than Z^*), but the efficiency loss is much lower than would be the case if only the tax at rate t were operative. If the government does not know the shape of the *MD* function, again it would be prudent to set both a tax and a standard. An optimal policy will be impossible to find, but the risks of having far too much or far too little pollution relative to the optimum will be minimized with a combined policy.

SUMMARY

1. External effects or externalities arise because of technological interdependencies among economic agents that persist because of the failure of markets to price these external effects.
2. An external economy exists when the actions of one agent benefit another party; an external diseconomy exists when the agent's actions harm the other party. In each case, the affected party has no control over the actions of the agent generating the externality.
3. An externality is internalized when the external effect is incorporated into the objective function of both agents and a "price" is imputed for the external effect.
4. Markets may fail and externalities may persist when transactions costs are high or markets are thin; information is imperfect, asymmetric, or both; nonappropriability exists; nonconvexities exist.
5. Private externalities are bilateral or involve relatively few agents. One party's actions affect another party, but there is no spillover to other agents. Private externalities can generally be internalized by bargaining.

6. Public externalities typically involve natural resources that have open access and affect large numbers of individuals. "Consumption" of the externality by one agent does not reduce consumption of the externality by others. Private negotiations are generally incapable of internalizing a public externality, and some form of government intervention is required.
7. When an externality is public, individuals' demand curves, which reflect their willingness to pay for the internalization of the externality, must be summed vertically to obtain the aggregate demand curve. This is because the quantity supplied is consumed by all. Individuals cannot determine how much they consume; they can determine only the value they place on the amount supplied.
8. A government trying to internalize an externality and achieve the optimal amount of pollution through the use of taxes or fees that reflect individuals' willingness to pay for reduction in pollution will have difficulty determining the optimal tax. Individuals have an incentive to reveal valuations less than their true preferences if they think others are being honest. This is the "free rider" problem, and it can result in too much pollution relative to the social optimum.
9. Quantity restrictions on pollution can also internalize the externality, but they typically entail higher enforcement costs than the optimal tax.
10. A production externality that leads to pollution is internalized where the marginal benefits (*MB*) from pollution equal the marginal damages (*MD*) from pollution. The optimal amount of pollution is generally not equal to zero. If the externality is private, merger and bargaining can internalize it. If the externality is public, taxes, standards, or both are required.
11. Bargaining between polluter and "pollutee" can yield the same level of pollution, but the net gains to each party typically will differ. The socially efficient level of pollution may not be achieved unless side payments between the parties exist.
12. The equimarginal condition requires that marginal benefits of pollution are the same for the marginal unit of pollution emitted. This condition yields an equilibrium that is cost-efficient. Cost efficiency ensures that society is reaching any given pollution target at the lowest possible resource cost. A pollution tax, marketable pollution permits, and individual standards (if set appropriately) are cost-efficient. The uniform emission standard is not.
13. Marketable pollution permits are another example of a market-based policy. Once the government distributes the permits, either through auction or without charge, a market for the exchange of the permits will develop and a permit price will be established. This price will lead to the socially efficient equilibrium if the permit market is perfectly competitive.
14. A subsidy to polluters for reducing pollution emissions will encourage entry into an industry and lead to an increase in pollution over time, whereas an equivalent tax will lead to exit from the industry and reduce aggregate emissions.
15. When the government has imperfect information about the marginal benefit or marginal damage curves for pollution, it should use a quantity policy (a standard) if the *MB* curve is flatter than the *MD* curve and a tax if the reverse is true, if it wishes to minimize the expected efficiency losses from using a nonoptimal policy.

16. When the government is uncertain about the shape and location of both the *MD* and the *MB* curves, a policy that combines a standard with a tax will generally minimize both the expected efficiency losses from a nonoptimal policy and the costs of pollution control.

DISCUSSION QUESTIONS

1. Distinguish between private and public externalities and give an example of each kind. Why are public externalities difficult to internalize by private actions? Explain graphically and verbally.
2. Suppose the rock band High Noise practices in a garage adjacent to the home of a librarian. The band likes to blast its songs out over very large amplifiers—the more noise the better. The average reading near the garage is 120 decibels (well above the pain threshold for people with "normal' hearing). Derive graphically and explain verbally what the level of noise and net gains to each party will be in each of the following circumstances:
   a. The librarian and High Noise bargain to a mutually agreeable outcome.
   b. The librarian calls the police, who tell the band that their noise cannot exceed 90 decibels. High Noise and the librarian bargain after the noise limit has been imposed.
   c. The city council imposes a "tax" on noise equal to a tax rate of t per decibel. Noise monitors are installed on the outside of each house or apartment.
   d. High Noise moves out of the librarian's neighborhood and locates on the fifteenth floor of a 25-story apartment building. Everyone in the building now gets to hear the band practice. Would bargaining among the affected parties now lead to an optimal outcome? Explain.
3. The chemical dioxin, which is very toxic to plants, animals, and people, is occasionally released into Lake Ontario by accidental discharges from chemical companies located around the lake. Suppose that you work for an environmental control agency of a state bordering Lake Ontario. What policy or policies would you adopt to deal with this pollutant? Use graphic (or mathematical) analysis to support your prescriptions, and discuss the practical problems of implementiung the policy.
4. Consider the case of a town beach downstream from the pulp and paper mill emitting pollutants into the stream. If the factory was deemed the owner of the river, how much swimming and pollution would develop? What system of user fees would be likely to arise? If the town's beach users were deemed the owner, how much swimming and pollution would develop? What system of user fees would be likely to arise?
5. "Taxes on pollution are equivalent to subsidies paid to reduce pollution." Is this statement true, false, or uncertain? Explain your answer.
6. Suppose that there are two polluters: H and L. Each has its own marginal cost of abatement function. This function gives the marginal costs of reducing pollution. The functions are: $MC^H = 2A^H$, and $MC^L = 0.5A^L$, where A is the amount of abatement undertaken and translates into 1 unit of pollution not emitted. Each

firm is initially emitting 20 units of pollution. The target level of pollution set by the government is 20 units. Compute the socially efficient tax and standard, and discuss how a marketable permit scheme would work. Show numerically why a uniform standard would not be cost-efficient.

7. Suppose that you are designing policies to reduce water pollution for a government environmental agency. You have consulted industry experts who tell you the shape and location of the marginal benefit of pollution function (the function that shows the value to firms of using inputs that create pollution, or of using the waterways as a waste depository). Assume that this *MB* function is linear and all polluters are identical. However, you do not know for certain the shape or the location of the marginal damage function to those affected by pollution.
   a. Assume first that the *MD* function is linear. What policy would you advocate, and why?
   b. Suppose now that the *MD* function could be discontinuous. Does this change your policy recommendation derived in (a)? Explain.
8. "A standard always maximizes the cost of abating pollution." True, false, or uncertain? Explain your answer.

NOTES

1. We do not mean by this statement that externalities can arise only in market economies. Pollution, for example, is a problem in centrally planned economies as well. Whether decision making is done on a decentralized basis, as in a market economy, or by a central planner, an externality will arise whenever the interdependencies among agents are not taken into account in making decisions.
2. In Chapter 7, we examine government-organized markets that issue permits to pollute.
3. The alternative is to look at a steady state where pollution and recovery of the air are in some sort of balance.
4. There is a large literature on mechanisms the government can use to extract the true preferences of individuals for a public good. These include methods of determining from voting behavior what people want. See, for example, R. Boadway and D. Wildason, *Public Sector Economics* (1984) and J. Stiglitz (1988). The practical relevance of these preference-revelation techniques has not yet been fully ascertained.
5. These are complex issues of property rights and information. See, for example, Coase (1960), Demsetz (1967), Starrett (1972), Furubotn and Pejovitch (1972), Scott (1983), Ostrom (1990), Bromley (1991), and the references cited therein.
6. We could have the output of chemicals themselves as the variable that adversely affects the apple firm. The results will be similar. But the assumption that a particular factor input is responsible is typically more realistic and allows us to examine a richer set of corrective devices.
7. These results can be derived by differentiating each equation with respect to its factor input, x or y.
8. Alternatively, if abatement is possible new techniques may be installed that reduce pollution emissions per unit of output. Firms may then not have to exit.
9. If marginal costs are constant, for example, $MC = \alpha$, the imposition of the tax will lead to no decrease in output per firm in the long run. The total number of firms will decrease, so pollution falls. This is because marginal cost and average cost both shift up, by the same amount. Marginal cost equals $\alpha + tz$; average cost equals $(\alpha q + tzq)/q = \alpha + tz$.
10. Under the subsidy, output per firm must fall because the average cost curve shifts down and the marginal cost curve shifts up. Average cost equals $\alpha q - s(Z - z)$. Marginal cost thus equals average cost at a lower level of output.

11. See Mestelman (1981, 1982) for some discussion of qualifications to the results presented above.
12. We could alternatively label the *MD* function the marginal cost of pollution control or removal. The *MC* of abatement would typically be a positive function of the amount of pollution but need not be linear. Weitzman (1974) was one of the first to discuss the asymmetry of taxes versus standards in the context of uncertainty. His model is more complex than ours, but the basic results are similar. Morgan (1983) has a similar model with an *MC* of abatement or pollution removal curve. He is concerned with the problem of emission of heavy metals into sewage treatment systems. The linearity of the *MD* function is relaxed below in an example similar to that of Morgan.

SELECTED READINGS

Baumol, W. J., and W. E. Oates (1988). *The Theory of Environmental Policy*, 2nd ed. New York: Cambridge University Press, Chapters 1–4, 12.

Boadway, R. W., and D. E. Wildason (1984). *Public Sector Economics*, 2nd ed. Boston: Little, Brown.

Bromley, D. W., ed. (1995). *Handbook of Environmental Economics*. Cambridge, Mass.: Blackwell.

Coase, Ronald H. (1960). "The Problem of Social Cost," *Journal of Law and Economics* 3, pp. 1–44.

Conrad, K., and C. J. Morrison (1989). "The Impact of Pollution Abatement Investment on Productivity Change: An Empirical Comparison of the U.S., Germany, and Canada," *Southern Economic Journal* 55, pp. 684–697.

Cropper, M. L., and W. E. Oates (1992). "Environmental Economics: A Survey," *Journal of Economic Literature* 30, pp. 675–740.

Dales, J. H. (1968). *Pollution, Property and Prices*. Toronto: University of Toronto Press.

Demsetz, H. (1967). "Toward a Theory of Property Rights," *American Economic Review* 57, pp. 347–359.

Freeman, A. M., III, R. H. Haveman, and A. V. Kneese (1973). *The Economics of Environmental Policy*. New York: Wiley.

Furubotn, E., and S. Pejovich (1972). "Property Rights and Economic Theory: A Survey of Recent Litereature," *Journal of Economic Literature* 10, pp. 1137–1162.

Hahn, R. W. (1989). "Economic Perspectives for Environmental Problems: How the Patient Followed the Doctor's Orders," *Journal of Economic Perspectives* 3, pp. 95–114.

Mestelman, S. (1981). "Corrective Production Subsidies in an Increasing Cost Industry: A Note on a Baumol–Oates Proposition," *Canadian Journal of Economics* 14, pp. 124–130.

Mestelman, S. (1982). "Production Externalities and Corrective Subsidies: A General Equilibrium Analysis," *Journal of Environmental Economics and Management* 9, pp. 186–193.

Morgan, P. (1983). "Alternative Policy Instruments under Uncertainty: A Programming Model of Toxic Pollution Control," *Journal of Environment Economics and Management* 10, pp. 248–269.

Organization for Economic Cooperation and Development (1993). *Taxation and the Environment: Complementary Policies*. Paris: OECD.

Ostrom, E. (1990). *Governing the Commons: The Evolution of Institutions for Collective Action*. Cambridge: Cambridge University Press.

Scott, A. D. (1983). "Property Rights and Property Wrongs," *Canadian Journal of Economics* 16, pp. 555–573.

Starrett, D. (1972). "Fundamental Nonconvexities in the Theory of Externalities," *Journal of Economic Theory* 4, pp. 180–199.

Stiglitz, J. E. (1988). *Economics of the Public Sector*, 2nd ed. New York: W. W. Norton.

Tietenberg, T. H. (1985). *Emissions Trading: An Exercise in Reforming Pollution Policy*. Washington, D. C.: Resources for the Future.

Tietenberg, T. H. (1990). "Economic Instruments for Environmental Regulation," *Oxford Review of Ecnomic Policy* 6, pp. 17–33.

Weitzman, M. (1974). "Prices vs. Quantities," *Review of Economic Studies* 41, pp. 477–491.

chapter 7

Pollution Policy in Practice

INTRODUCTION

In this chapter, we examine two important aspects of environmental economics—the measurement of the benefits of improving environmental quality, and the methods of regulating the environment in practice. These include taxes, standards, and marketable permits. In Chapter 6 we determined the optimal level of pollution where the marginal benefits from pollution—the gain to emitters from using the environment as a waste depository—equal the marginal damages. Alternatively, we can define the optimal amount of pollution in terms of environmental quality. In this case, the marginal costs of abating pollution would be set equal to the marginal benefits of greater levels of environmental quality. If properly measured, the approaches yield equivalent emissions of pollutants at the optimum. In the first part of this chapter, we discuss methods of measuring the benefits and costs of improving environmental quality, and how policy makers can use this information to evaluate environmental investments and policies. This process is called cost-benefit analysis (CBA). A variety of techniques devised to estimate the benefits of an increase in environmental quality are examined. Examples are given.

Our emphasis in the second part of the chapter is on the actual practices used to internalize externalities. We explain and evaluate different approaches not just with regard to their connection to economic principles in achieving the optimal amount of pollution versus environmental quality, but to see which are administratively feasible, and to note the practical difficulties in carrying out environmental regulation. We keep the optimality conditions—equating marginal costs and benefits—as a basis for evaluation.

This second part of the chapter concludes with a more detailed examination of marketable permits. While economists have long advocated the use of a pollution permit that can be exchanged among polluters to minimize the costs of reducing emissions, it has not been until fairly recently in the United States that regulatory authorities have begun to change the law so that these permits might be used. We focus on air pollution and examine the different types of permit markets that could be used and how they might be implemented, along with the results of several studies evaluating different permit schemes with respect to their effect on emissions of air pollutants, costs of abatement, and the structure of the permit market.

EVALUATING THE BENEFITS AND COSTS OF IMPROVING ENVIRONMENTAL QUALITY

Cost-Benefit Analysis

Suppose a policy maker wishes to determine the optimal amount of environmental quality or pollution abatement and to evaluate alternative methods of obtaining these targets. The technique of *cost-benefit analysis* (CBA) is used. The fundamental role of CBA is to establish principles by which the costs and benefits of any public program are measured. Many of the components of costs and benefits are not exchanged in markets and thus have no well-defined prices. In addition, many markets contain distortions—taxes, subsidies, quotas, monopoly, monopsony—that make the market prices misrepresentative of the resource-scarcity or shadow price of the commodities exchanged.

We begin with a brief discussion of the elements of CBA: the decision rule and the calculation of the present value of net benefits. We turn next to a discussion of the measurement of the benefits from improving environmental quality. Space prohibits a discussion of the measurement of the costs of improving environmental quality. We refer the reader to Freeman (1993) for an in-depth discussion. We discuss the costs of alternative regulatory policies in subsequent sections of this chapter.

Cost-benefit analysis deals with two types of decisions: (1) whether to invest in a public sector project or (2) whether to implement a particular type of regulatory policy such as the taxes, standards, and marketable permits examined in Chapter 6. Examples of public investment projects for the environment are water and sewage treatment plants. The technique is used widely for all types of public investments and policies, not just for environmental concerns.

The decision rule most commonly used in CBA is called the *net present value* rule. Consider the following example. A local government is trying to determine what sort of procedure it should adopt to deal with the problem of contamination of groundwater reservoirs by nitrates. The nitrates come primarily from agricultural practices—the generation and use of animal wastes. The options for controlling the animal wastes, their annual costs, and the benefits of control for a 5-year period are shown in Table 7.1. We assume that there is no inflation over the 5 years. This means that we do not have to distinguish between real and nominal values.

The pattern of costs differs by project. Trucking wastes out of the district costs $50,000 per year indefinitely. This is an operating cost. The costs for reducing use of waste as fertilizer involve the substitution of alternative types of fertilizers that yield smaller amounts of nitrates per acre fertilized, and hence less nitrate contamination. The costs are initially higher than those for trucking but decline over time. The final option is to invest in containment facilities. This is an example of a capital investment project that involves large expenditures in the first year. Costs then decline over time to zero once the facility is complete. The benefits also differ among the projects.

TABLE 7.1. **COST AND BENEFITS OF CONTROLLING NITRATES FROM AGRICULTURE**

	Costs per year (thousands of dollars)				
Procedure	**1**	**2**	**3**	**4**	**5**
Truck animal waste out of district	50	50	50	50	50
Reduce use of waste as fertilizer	75	60	50	40	20
Construct waste containers at each site	200	40	10	0	0
	Benefits per year (thousands of dollars)				
Procedure	**1**	**2**	**3**	**4**	**5**
Truck animal waste out of district	60	60	60	60	60
Reduce use of waste as fertilizer	50	55	60	65	65
Construct waste containers at each site	10	20	80	100	150

Trucking yields a constant stream of benefits, but in the other two projects the benefits increase over time. We choose these cost and benefit streams to illustrate a number of points.

First, how should the government decide which is the "best" project? In Table 7.2 we show the present value of the net benefits for each project per year and the sum of these net benefits over the 5 years. Recall from Chapter 1 what present value is and the discussion of the choice of a discount rate. Suppose for this example that the discount rate is 3 percent. The present value of net benefits in each year t is then calculated by the following formula:

$$PV \text{ of net benefits} = \frac{(\text{benefits in year } t) - (\text{costs in year } t)}{(1 + r)^t}$$

where r is the discount rate. The sum of the present values over the 5 years is shown in the "total" column in Table 7.2.

Table 7.2 illustrates the different patterns of net benefits among the projects. For trucking of wastes, the undiscounted net benefits are always $10,000. This means that the present value of this stream will be gradually declining over time. Reducing wastes starts with negative net benefits and goes to positive numbers. The sum over the 5 years is less than that of trucking. Construction of waste containers costs the same amount as trucking in undiscounted dollars ($250,000 over the life of the project) but yields a very different stream of net benefits. The net benefits are very large negative numbers in the first 2 years but then become large positive numbers. The sum yields a total that exceeds the total net benefits of the other projects. This pattern of costs and benefits is quite representative for large construction projects.

The decision rule for the government advocated by economists is to choose the project with the *largest sum of the present value of net benefits.* Clearly, the construction of waste containers maximizes this present value.

Other important issues in cost-benefit analysis can also be illustrated with this

TABLE 7.2. **PRESENT VALUE OF NET BENEFITS FOR NITRATE REDUCTION**

	PV of Net Benefits (thousands of dollars)					
Procedure	**1**	**2**	**3**	**4**	**5**	**Total**
Truck animal waste out of district	9.7	9.4	9.1	8.9	8.6	45.7
Reduce use of waste as fertilizer	−24.3	−4.7	9.1	22.2	38.8	41.1
Construct waste containers at each site	−184.5	−24.4	64.0	88.8	129.4	73.3

simple example. The time period over which benefits and costs are computed may be very important. Suppose the government looked at these projects only over their first 3 years. Trucking would then be the project with the highest net present value. Another important issue is the choice of the discount rate. If a discount rate of 10 percent was used instead of 3 percent, again, trucking would be the "winner," with a present value over the 5 years of $37,900 compared with $25,100 for the construction project. This is because high discount rates effectively penalize projects with high initial costs and large net benefits that accrue in the future. As we noted, many public investment projects have this characteristic. This is why the choice of a discount rate is so important in public policy.

Another important technique related to cost benefit analysis is *cost effectiveness.* This approach focuses only on the cost side of potential projects or policies. It assumes that the benefits of each option are identical. Cost-effectiveness studies are done when there is little information about the benefits of improving environmental quality. In our illustration above, a cost-effectiveness study would compute the present value of the costs over the 5-year period. The decision rule would then be to choose the policy with the *lowest* sum of the present value of costs. Table 7.3 presents this information, assuming a discount rate of 3 percent. We see that the second project, waste reduction, is the most cost-effective. Note that if the government assumes that the benefits of each project are identical and they are not (as was the case above), it may choose the "wrong" project. The project with the lowest present value of net benefits is not necessarily the project with the lowest present value of costs. Cost-effectiveness studies should be used only when it is clear that benefits are identical for all projects examined. Box 7.1 presents an illustration of a cost-effectiveness study—an analysis of the fuel efficiency standards applied to new automobiles.

TABLE 7.3. **COST EFFECTIVENESS: PRESENT VALUE OF COSTS**

	Present Value of Costs (thousands of dollars)					
Procedure	**1**	**2**	**3**	**4**	**5**	**Total**
Truck animal waste out of district	48.5	47.1	45.7	44.4	43.1	228.8
Reduce use of waste as fertilizer	72.8	56.6	45.7	35.5	17.3	227.9
Construct waste containers at each site	194.2	37.7	9.1	0	0	241.0

BOX 7.1 **Corporate Average Fuel Economy Standards**

Economic theory predicts that uniform standards are not cost-effective in achieving environmental targets. Fuel economy standards in the United States provide an illustration of how cost-*in*effective a standard can be. Crandall (1992) contrasts corporate average fuel economy standards with a fuel tax and finds that the standards are between 7 and 10 times more costly in achieving comparable reductions in oil consumption.

The corporate average fuel economy (CAFE) standards were promulgated under the 1975 Energy Policy and Conservation Act. Standards were set for all new passenger cars, light trucks, vans, and sport and utility vehicles. The standard for passenger cars was 27.5 miles per gallon (mpg) and 20.2 mpg for light trucks at the time of Crandall's study. Each producer of motor vehicles gets a CAFE rating that is a weighted average of fuel-efficiency ratings for its vehicles. The U.S. Environmental Protection Agency (EPA) does the tests that establish the ratings. If producers exceed their CAFE standards in any year, they can carry forward or back 3 years to offset any deficiencies. Fines are levied for failure to meet the standards. The initial objective of CAFE standards was to reduce the United States' dependency on foreign supplies of oil—motor vehicles are responsible for 50 percent of oil consumption in the United States. Emphasis has since shifted to reducing the growth in greenhouse gases, since oil contributes 48 percent to annual carbon emissions in the United States.

Fuel efficiency of new cars increased almost 88 percent from 14.8 mpg in 1970 to 27.8 mpg in 1990; for new trucks, vans, and sport vehicles, the increase was approximately 52 percent (13.7 to 20.8 mpg). However, for all cars on the road, new and old, fuel efficiency over the same period increased by 55 percent for passenger cars and 35 percent for light trucks. The median age of registered cars has increased over this time period, slowing the impact of the CAFE standards on the motor vehicle stock. Fuel consumption by all vehicles has increased from 1970 to 1990 by 21 percent, although fuel consumed by passenger vehicles declined by 5 percent. The total number of vehicle miles traveled has increased by a whopping 93 percent. Had fuel economy stayed at its 1970 level for all vehicles, fuel consumption would have increased by 93 percent from 1970 to 1990. It appears that CAFE standards have had a dampening effect on total fuel consumption—but at what cost to society? Could fuel consumption be decreased in a more cost-effective way?

Crandall compares a fuel tax with CAFE standards. There are many differences. The CAFE standards take time to have an impact on fuel consumption (and hence on carbon emissions and air quality) and may have an uncertain impact. Several factors account for this. First, motor vehicles are durable assets. They are replaced as they wear out. New, more fuel-efficient vehicles will gradually become a larger share of the total stock of vehicles as consumers substitute the new cars for their old "gas guzzlers" over time. Fuel-efficient vehicles may be more costly and may have characteristics that differ from what the market likes at existing fuel prices. This may reduce the sales of new cars, contributing to a delay in trading in one's car for a new one. The median age for a registered automobile rose from 5.9 years in 1970 to 7.5 years in 1990, giving support to this scenario.

Second, people's driving habits are influenced by the cost per mile driven. If they do purchase more fuel-efficient cars, the cost per mile driven—marginal costs of driving—will fall. This may induce them to drive more miles per year. And of course, CAFE standards do nothing to affect gasoline consumption of older vehicles. Contrast this with a gasoline tax. A tax increases the marginal costs of driving all vehicles and should reduce the total miles driven. It should also accelerate the purchase of new, more fuel-efficient vehicles and the retirement of old vehicles. The impact of a gasoline tax on fuel consumption is dependent on its price elasticity of demand. Empirical studies put short-run elasticity at about

BOX 7.1 *(Continued)*

−0.5 and long-run elasticity at 1.0. It would seem that a fuel tax is likely to be far more effective than a CAFE standard at meeting environmental targets and targets for the use of energy. Why then use a standard at all?

The reasons put forth are not very compelling. One is political. The costs of the CAFE standard are concealed in the price of the vehicle, but fuel taxes are very visible and are not popular with voters. Fuel taxes are likely to be regressive, but it is not clear what the distributional impacts of CAFE are. If, as we argued above, higher prices for new cars lead people to postpone buying a new car, the price of used cars may rise. Low-income people are probably more likely to purchase a used car than a new one. The CAFE standards may thus be somewhat regressive. Some analysts feel that technological standards such as CAFE are necessary because people tend to underinvest in energy-efficient technologies. This may be the case, but raising the price of energy-intensive technologies would seem to be a logical response.

What are the social costs of the CAFE standard? Crandall provides estimates that are based on others' studies for the period from 1979 to 1989. The welfare costs consist of the loss in consumer surplus net of fuel savings (if any) plus the loss in producers' surplus. No measure is taken of the value of changes in environmental quality. The estimates range from a gain of $1.1 billion (1990 dollars) to a loss of $4 billion. In terms of costs per gallon of fuel saved (a measure of cost-effectiveness), the estimates range from $0.30 to $0.63 (depending in part on whether impacts on safety are measured). How does this compare with the welfare costs of a fuel tax? One study found that a gasoline tax of 2.4 cents per gallon would have achieved the same fuel savings as the CAFE standards over the period from 1979 to 1989, but at a welfare cost of only $0.08 per gallon of fuel saved. The adverse effects on safety of a fuel tax would be less than for CAFE because fewer miles would be driven with a tax and there would be less vehicle downsizing. Another study looked at CAFE standards of 34 mpg (the 1996 target) to 40 mpg (2001 target) compared with an equivalent tax that started at 3 cents per gallon and rose to 25 cents per gallon by 2006. The welfare costs of the tax were estimated to be 43 to 83 percent less than those of CAFE, excluding effects on safety. The fuel tax would thus appear to be far more cost-effective than a CAFE standard in reducing fuel use or meeting environmental targets.

Source: Robert W. Crandall (1992). "Policy Watch: Corporate Average Fuel Economy Standards," *Journal of Economic Perspective* 6, pp. 171–180.

The CBA decision rule—choose the project with the maximum sum of the present value of net benefits—can be linked to our notion of the efficient level of pollution versus environmental quality developed in Chapter 6. Recall from Chapter 6 that the efficient target is where the marginal benefits of pollution equal the marginal damages from pollution: more generally, the marginal benefits of an activity must equal the marginal costs of that activity. In the cost-benefit example, we are dealing with totals, not marginals. How are these two concepts related? Figure 7.1(a) illustrates a total cost (TC) and total benefit (TB) curve for different projects or policies as a function of the level of environmental quality. The slope of these functions gives the marginal values. Figure 7.1(b) graphs these slopes. Assume that all these values are present values. We can see from these figures that marginal benefits (MB) equal mar-

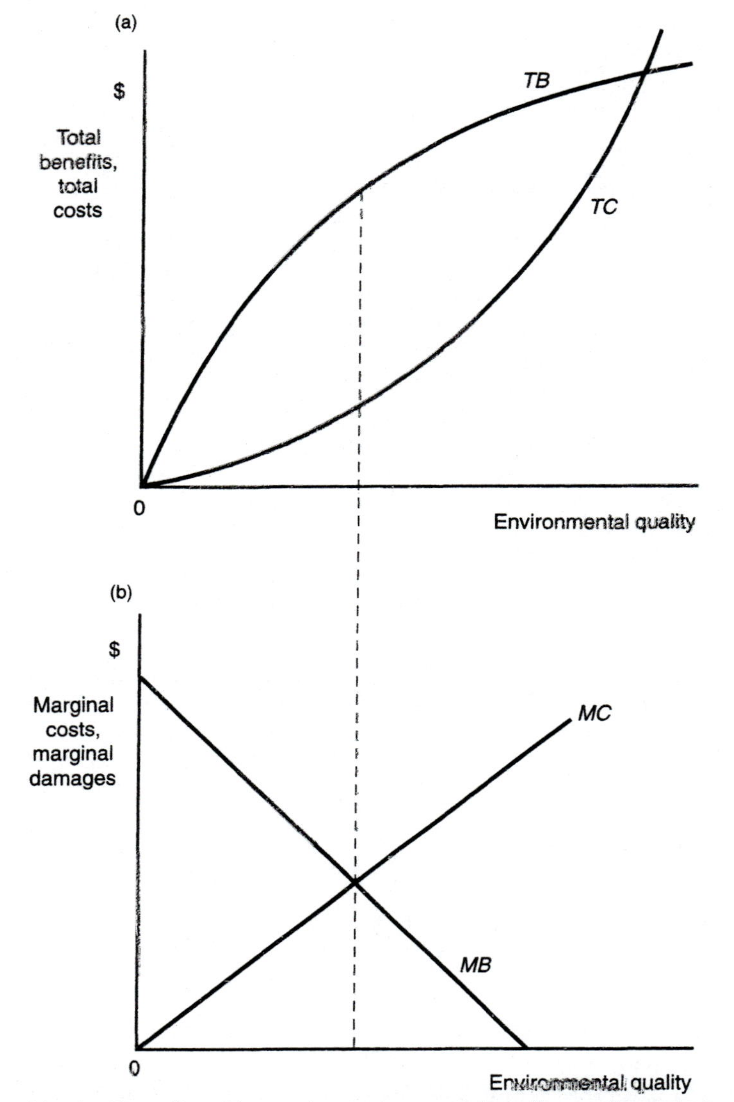

FIGURE 7.1. Marginal benefits of increasing environmental quality equal marginal costs where the difference between total benefits and total costs is at a maximum.

ginal costs (*MC*) where the slope of the *TB* curve equals the slope of the *TC* curve. At this point, the divergence between total benefits and total costs is at a maximum. The CBA decision rule that says to choose the maximum present value of net benefits is equivalent to being at the point where marginal benefits equal marginal costs. Policy makers can then measure total values, which are in general much easier to calculate than marginal values in evaluating projects and policies.

This concludes our brief overview of some of the important aspects of cost-benefit analysis. There are many other important issues that would be covered in a course focusing on CBA. Layard (1994) is an example of a text on CBA.

Measuring the Benefits of Improving Environmental Quality

Measuring benefits from improving environmental quality is difficult because most of these benefits must be *imputed* in some way. Some benefits routinely evaluated for cost-benefit studies of pollution are the value of life (mortality and morbidity), the value of intangibles such as the quality of life, the value of the natural environment (air and water quality), and property values.

Three relationships link any change in the emissions of a particular pollutant to the ultimate measurement of the benefits of reducing the emissions. Technical models that link the change in emissions to a change in ambient quality are required first. These models predict the path of the effluent from particular sources to zones surrounding the source. Meteorological factors and chemical processes are incorporated, and environmental quality is defined. For example, if one is measuring water quality, indicators that could be used include the biochemical oxygen demand of organic wastes as they are decomposed (BOD), suspended solids (SS), toxic chemicals, and heat.

It is not enough merely to define environmental quality; the change over time must also be noted. Can the elements be diluted or altered by complex chemical and biological processes? These analyses require extensive scientific expertise, and they are an area where much has been learned in the past 10 to 20 years. Prior to the mid-1970s, for example, many toxic chemicals that were present in waterways could not even be detected. We now have a much better idea of not only *what* pollutants are showing up in the environment, but in what *concentration;* for example, how many parts per billion (ppb) of a toxic chemical is in our water supply.

After the models that link changes in effluents to changes in environmental quality are determined, the next step is to see how the change in quality affects the flow of environmental services to individuals. Biological effects incorporate the impact on human health, effects on the economic productivity of natural resource sectors, and recreational uses of the ecosystem. One may also want to examine the overall health and stability of the ecosystem as the level of pollutants changes. Will plant and animal species become less able to deal with ordinary stress when their systems are also affected by pollutants such as toxic chemicals and noise pollution? Many different nonliving systems can incur economic loss from decreased environmental quality. Materials are damaged by air pollutants. Soiling, odors, reduced visibility, effects on production costs, climate, and weather (the greenhouse effect and the melting of the polar ice caps) are other effects.

Not only are there synergies or interdependencies between the effects of variations in environmental quality on living and nonliving systems, but what is beneficial to one component may be disastrous to another. Swimmers may not mind the effects of acid rain or thermal pollution on lakes because the water quality to them is enhanced—the lake is "cleaner" and warmer. But to the fish and those fishing, acid rain represents a substantial decline in benefits. The link between a change in environmental quality and its impact on environmental services thus combines science and social science.

The final relationship is that between the change in environmental services and the change in *economic welfare*, or the benefits of abatement. This is where the major focus of economic evaluation occurs (although economics plays a role in the previous two relationships as well). How are economic benefits measured? Economists typically use some type of quantitative technique—econometric analysis (regressions) and risk analysis; see, for example, Braden and Kolstad (1991), Freeman (1993), Johansson (1987), Smith (1986), Carson and Mitchell (1989), and the references within each. What we want to do here is look at the principles and various techniques involved in the measurement of the benefits derived from changes in environmental quality.

The foundation for the estimation of the benefits from a change in environmental quality is the willingness to pay (WTP) by an individual for an increase in environmental quality or the willingness to accept (WTA) a decrease in environmental quality. Both WTP and WTA depend on an individual's utility function and assume that utility is held constant. The WTP corresponds to compensating variation, defined in Chapter 1. However, we are dealing with quantity, not price changes, when discussing the level of environmental quality. Some economists refer to WTP as the compensating *surplus* in this situation. Higher levels of environmental quality are assumed to increase a person's utility. Thus WTP is the amount of money a person would be willing to pay to have a higher level of environmental quality. The WTA corresponds to *equivalent variation* or surplus. Equivalent variation measures the amount of money a person is willing to give up to hold utility constant after there has been an increase in the price of a good that person consumes. Refer back to Figure 1.3. Assume that the initial equilibrium is at point y on indifference curve I'. The price of gasoline now rises, pivoting the budget constraint in from AB' to AB. Equivalent variation is found by first constructing a budget constraint parallel to AB and finding its tangency with indifference curve I'. Then extend that budget constraint from this tangency to the income axis. The dollar amount from point A to that interception is the equivalent variation. In terms of environmental quality, WTA is the amount of money a person is willing to accept in compensation for a decrease in environmental quality. It is the equivalent surplus.

The challenge is to find practical methods of calculating WTP and WTA. That is the topic of this section. We examine two basic approaches: proxies and preference evaluation. Proxy approaches involve the use of market data that are connected to people's demand for environmental quality. The techniques examined are models of *averting behavior*, *revealed preferences*, *hedonic estimation*, and the *travel cost* approach. The other approach is to try to obtain direct information from individuals about their WTP for and/or WTA changes in environmental quality. These approaches include *contingent valuation methods* (CVMs) and experimental economics.

Proxy Methods for Estimating the Value of the Environment

Averting Behavior

Consider a community that is dependent upon a lake for its water supply. One day these people discover that their water is contaminated with a toxic compound. They

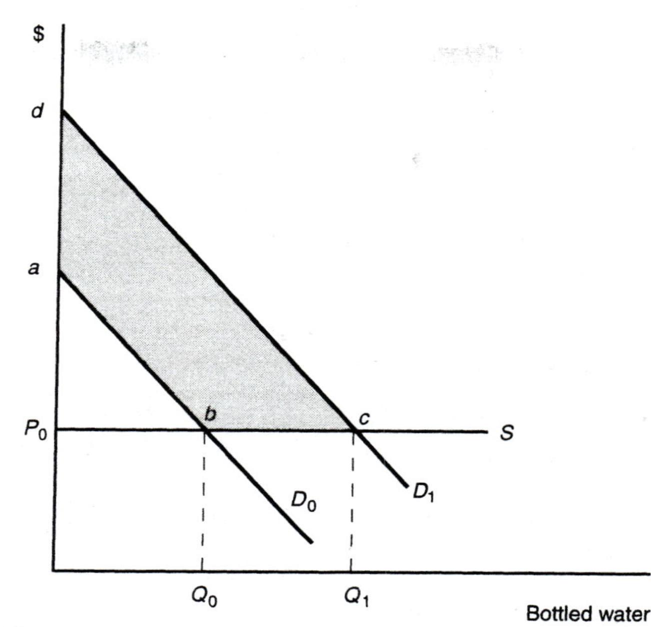

FIGURE 7.2. The market for bottled water can serve as a proxy for WTP for unpolluted water. Discovery of contaminated drinking water shifts demand from D_0 to D_1. The WTP for clean water is area *abcd*, the change in consumer surplus between the initial and the new equilibrium.

do not know the source of this compound. The community will be unable to bargain with anyone to reduce or eliminate the toxins because it does not know who is responsible for the emissions. It might seek help from a government organization, but this could take time, and the outcome would be uncertain. In the meantime, the community needs water. An obvious solution is to purchase uncontaminated water. In most parts of the world, there are well-defined markets for the exchange of drinking water. In North America, many people drink bottled water because of concerns about water quality. Thus, one way we could measure willingness to pay for higher water quality would be to try to estimate the demand curve for bottled water. We may be unable to obtain enough observations for one community of purchases of bottled water at different market prices. Hence, the approach taken is to estimate a market demand curve for bottled water. This demand curve could serve as a proxy for the demand for "clean" water in the community. It is a proxy because people may drink bottled water for reasons other than environmental quality.

Once this demand curve has been estimated using econometric techniques, it is straightforward to use information from the relationship to derive a WTP measure. Figure 7.2 illustrates this. Here, D_0 is the demand curve for bottled water before the contamination exists. We assume that the community is too small to influence the market price of bottled water, so it faces a perfectly elastic supply surve, S, and takes a price of P_0 as given in the market. Initial consumption of bottled water is quantity Q_0. The discovery of the contamination shifts the demand curve to the right, to D_1. With a constant price of P_0, the new consumption level is Q_1. Willingness to pay is measured as the *change in consumer surplus* between the old and the new equilibrium. This is shown as the shaded area *abcd*. The change in consumer surplus is a loss to individuals when water quality declines. That is, they are willing to give up area *abcd* to have drinkable water. If the toxic compound is eliminated, individuals would return to their lower level of consumption of bottled water, thus saving this consumer surplus. This amount could be used in a cost-benefit analysis to determine policies and projects to improve water quality.

This is an example of averting behavior. People make decisions about consumption, investment, or both to reduce their exposure to environmental contaminants. Other examples could include the purchase of air purifiers to reduce indoor air pollutants, consumption of organic vegetables, installation of insulating material to reduce noise pollution, and use of sun screens to reduce the risk of sunburn and skin cancer.

There are many advantages in using averting behavior as a measure of willingness to pay for improvements in environmental quality. Market prices are used, so there is no need to impute a price. Data may be readily available and reasonably inexpensive for researchers to collect. The approach is, however, limited by the number of possible markets in which to observe averting behavior. There may be many environmental situations for which no complementary market or no averting behavior exists. Also, the good consumed or the activity undertaken to avert the environmental deterioration may be inadequate and may not fully protect or compensate the individual for the loss in environmental quality. We do not know the exact relationship between the consumer surplus loss and a person's total willingness to pay for improvements in environmental quality.

Revealed Preferences

There are some markets for factors directly connected to the environment that involve not averting behavior, but positive links to the environment. Examples are people's purchases of fishing and hunting licenses, contributions to environmental organizations, and purchases of "environmentally friendly" goods (or shares in companies that are environmentally friendly). Again, the researcher estimates a demand curve for these environmental activities and uses consumer surplus as the measure of the marginal benefits of a change in environmental quality.

Hedonic Pricing

Environmental quality can enter into other important decisions made by individuals. The choice of a job and where to live may be influenced to some extent by environmental factors on the job and in the community. One's decisions about jobs and housing are obviously dependent on a large number of factors, not just environmental quality. In this sense they differ in degree but not in principle from the decision to buy bottled water or earplugs or sunscreen. The hedonic approach has been used to examine the contribution of environmental factors to these important decisions faced by individuals and families. Hedonic pricing is feasible and most meaningful when property markets are active, environmental quality is perceived by the population as a relevant factor in property values, the population perceives local variations in environmental quality or changes in environmental quality over time, and property markets are relatively undistorted, with transactions in these markets readily measured.

Many studies have been done on housing markets to determine the influence of environmental factors; fewer have been done for job markets. Let us examine an example to see how a hedonic model of a housing market could be used to derive estimates of the WTP for changes in environmental quality.

Brookshire et al. (1982) examine the effect of various types of air pollution on the housing market in California. They collected a sample of 634 house sales for the years 1978–1979. For each sale, information about the characteristics of the house were obtained. These included, for example, the size of the house, the number of bathrooms, and whether or not it had a swimming pool. Information about environmental quality—in this case, the concentrations of air pollutants at the site—was obtained from monitoring of air quality. Sales from across Los Angeles were collected to obtain a wide range of values for all variables. The air pollution variables can be called the *focus* variables. The hedonic technique allows us to determine to what extent these focus variables influence the price one is willing to pay for different levels of environmental quality, as represented by the purchase of a home. Other variables representing community characteristics are also collected. These include data on proximity to neighborhood amenities such as parks, schools, beaches, and transportation, as well as neighborhood *dis*amenities such as the crime rate.

A regression of the house price on all the variables collected is then performed. This yields an equation showing the contribution of each independent variable to the variability of house prices (the dependent variable) across the sample. The researcher then investigates the relationship between the price of the house and a measure of air quality. Figure 7.3(a) illustrates a possible outcome. We see that people are willing to pay more for higher levels of air quality. The graph shown is called the hedonic price equation. What we are interested in, for estimating the marginal benefits of increasing environmental quality, is the WTP for incremental changes in air quality. This information is obtained by finding the slope of the hedonic price equation shown in Figure 7.3(a), which can also be found by differentiating the price equation. This is shown in Figure 7.3(b). The vertical axis now shows the marginal value of air quality—willingness to pay for each level of air quality. The graph in 7.3(b) illustrates an implicit relationship, where the vertical axis shows the implicit price of the environmental characteristic. If the hedonic price equation is the shape shown, WTP will be a decreasing function of the level of air quality. We can then use this implicit price curve to obtain WTP calculations by finding the consumer surplus at different levels of air quality.

Table 7.4 illustrates the results of the hedonic regression done for Los Angeles. Two alternative nonlinear equations that gave the best fit were estimated using different measures of air pollution. In the first equation, the air pollutant measured was nitrogen dioxide (NO_2); in the second, it was total suspended particulates (TSPs). From these equations, the rent differentials associated with different levels of air quality can be calculated for each house in the study. The rent differential (our WTP measure)

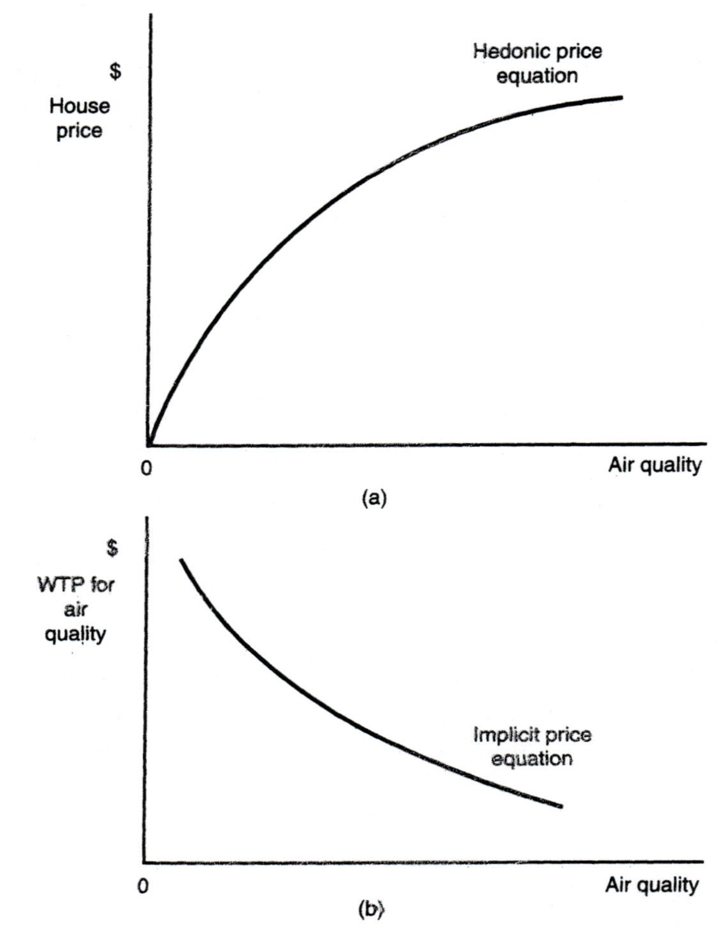

FIGURE 7.3. The hedonic price equation shows the relationship between house prices and environmental quality as measured by air quality, holding all other characteristics of the house constant. The implicit price relationship is the slope of the hedonic price equation and represents people's marginal valuation of air quality improvements—their WTP.

shows the premium a house buyer would have to pay to own a house with high air quality, holding constant all the other characteristics of the home. Brookshire et al. look at these levels of air quality—poor, fair, and good. These measures correspond to specific measured values of the air pollutants. For example, poor air quality has TSPs greater than 110 micrograms per cubic meter and levels of NO_2 greater than 11 parts per 100 million. A move from poor to fair and fair to good is associated with a decrease of about 30 percent in pollution levels. Using the coefficients from the NO_2 equation, and translating the value of a home into a monthly rental figure, the authors find that monthly rent differentials range from $15.44 to $45.92 for an improvement from poor to fair air quality, and $33.17 to $128.46 per month for fair to good. The

TABLE 7.4. **HEDONIC EQUATIONS FOR HOUSE SALES IN LOS ANGELES, 1977–78**

Independent Variable	**Nitrogen Dioxide**	**TSP**
Housing structure variables		
Age	−0.0182	−0.0214
	(−2.338)	(−2.815)
Living area	.00018	.00018
	(12.126)	(12.069)
Bathrooms	.1560	.1570
	(9.609)	(9.664)
Pool	.05806	.05840
	(4.630)	(4.652)
Neighborhood variables		
Log(crime)	−.08381	−.10401
	(−1.577)	(−1.997)
School quality	.00198	.00177
	(3.945)	(3.577)
Housing density	−.000067	−.000068
	(−9.128)	(−9.236)
Public safety expenditures	.00026	.00026
	(4.760)	(4.742)
Accessibility variables		
Distance to beach	−.01159	−.01161
	(7.832)	(7.782)
Air pollution variables		
log(TSP)		−.22183
		(3.824)
log(NO_2)	−.22407	
	(4.032)	

NOTE: The *t*-statistics are shown in parentheses below each coefficient estimate.
Source: Adapted from David S. Brookshire, Mark A. Thayer, William D. Schulze, and Ralph C. D'Arge (1982). "Valuing Public Goods: A Comparison of Survey and Hedonic Approaches," *American Economic Review* 72, p. 172. Not all of the independent variables examined by the authors are reported in this table.

method of translating a house price into a monthly equivalent rent is quite straightforward. When one buys a house, one is implicitly paying for the capitalized value of housing services over the expected lifetime of the house. This capitalized value is then simply the present value from our standard formula,

$$PV = \sum_{t=0}^{t} \frac{\text{annual value}}{(1+r)^t}$$

where t is the expected lifetime of the house. In this case, we simply solve for the annual value, since the present value is already known.

The results of the study by Brookshire et al. are representative of a large number of hedonic studies that have been done for housing markets across the United States. The environmental quality variable is usually some measure of air quality. In most of these studies, the researchers find that people are willing to pay for higher levels of air quality. The advantage of this technique, like that of averting behavior, is that actual markets are used to infer willingness to pay. Many studies have been done, and researchers have a good appreciation of the robustness of their estimates. However, any sort of econometric exercise will have to address a variety of estimation problems. We refer the reader to studies such as Graves et al. (1988) and Seller et al. (1985) for detailed discussion of these issues.

Other difficulties with these "market-based" approaches relate to the nature of the market and those in it. The researcher must be careful to have a market that is representative of people's preferences, not one out of equilibrium or capturing only certain income levels or ethnic groups in the population. The proxy techniques also typically specify an environmental quality variable that is objectively measured. Air pollution indexes are used, for example, not necessarily the buyer's perception of air quality at different houses. This is a potentially severe problem in hedonic wage studies where workers may be unaware of the environmental risks they face on the job. Their wage rates may then be totally unconnected to these environmental factors. These are illustrations of the types of issues researchers address in undertaking these types of WTP estimates.

Travel Cost Method[1]

Recreational use of water has significant economic value. Freeman (1979) cites a study done for the U.S. Environmental Protection Agency that estimated that the loss of recreational benefits due to water pollution was some $10.1 billion per year, or 60 percent of the total water pollution damages estimated. How does one estimate these sorts of forgone benefits when much water-based recreation does not have well-defined market prices? Many recreational sites have no entry fee, or a fee that is nominal and rarely fluctuates. Another proxy—the travel cost approach—attempts to place a value on the benefits consumers receive from recreation activities by examining consumption decisions made in related markets, specifically, the total costs the individual or family incurs traveling to a particular site.

Consider a simple model of consumer choice. The individual is assumed to demand recreational visits. Utility is derived from time spent at the site. The decision of how many times to visit a particular site is based on the characteristics of the site, the travel time to the site, one's income, and other socioeconomic variables (age, tastes in recreation, and so on). Environmental quality is a characteristic of the site that is commonly assumed to be a complement with the number of visits to the site. A demand curve for the individual can be derived from the maximization of a person's utility subject to budget and time constraints. The number of visits to the site will be a function of the price of a visit and the level of environmental quality. This price includes the monetary costs of the trip (e.g., fuel used, costs of on-route food and lodging) and the shadow price of the total time spent getting to the site and staying at the site. This shadow price of time could be the individual's wage rate or some value less than the wage rate. The wage rate would be used if the person could be working during the time spent getting to the site. Alternatively, if the person is using only leisure time, then his or her wage rate probably overstates the shadow price of time.

Econometric techniques are used to estimate the demand function for visits using data on rates of visitation and travel costs for different individuals. The hypothesis is that visits depend negatively on travel costs (so that demand curves slope down). It is also assumed that individuals respond to an increase in an entry fee to the site in the same way they would an increase in travel costs. The approach works something like this: Suppose we have two people who visit the site. The data gathered on these people is as follows:

Individual	Total travel costs	Number of visits per year
A	$1	10
B	2	7

Now assume that an admission fee of $1 is charged at the site. We want to see how this would affect the number of trips taken. The admission fee would raise the total costs of visiting the site for person A from $1 to $2. Thus A now has travel costs equal to those of person B. The usual assumption is that A will respond to the admission fee by behaving like person B, who lived farther away from the site and thus faced the $2 travel costs without any admission fee. They will then have the same visitation rates. Ideally, one would like to have actual data on the variation in trips with changes in travel costs, rather than an equation that is estimated using data on different individuals' separate trips, but this sort of data is typically not available. Travel cost data come from surveys administered to people at specific recreation sites.

The value of the recreational site is then the discounted present value of the flow of recreational services to the people who visit the site. This will be measured by consumer surplus, as the travel cost approach yields ordinary (uncompensated) demand curves. The travel cost approach determines the location of the demand curve. We need to know how the demand curve shifts in response to different levels of environmental quality. In principle, it is straightforward to incorporate water quality into a travel cost regression. Variables measuring water quality are estimated along with the other explanatory variables of the recreational demand function. The environmental quality variable should have a positive coefficient. Holding all else constant, if there is an improvement in water quality at a recreational site, it will lead to a rightward shift in the demand curve for visits to the site. The estimated value of the environmental quality coefficient will predict the extent of the shift in the demand curve. Refer back to Figure 7.2. The area between the demand curves, *abcd*, would represent the increment in consumer surplus due to the improvement in water quality.

This model is based on a number of simplifying assumptions. These include: (1) Individuals perceive and respond to changes in travel costs in the same way they would to changes in any admission fee to the site. (2) The sole purpose of the trip taken is to visit the site in question. If people visit more than one site, or stop off at the site en route to another destination, then the travel costs cannot all be allocated to the site. (3) All visits last the same amount of time. This allows us to measure site usage by the number of visits and makes the total travel costs the price of the visit and a parameter for the individual. If time at the site varies, the "price" of the visit will be endogeneous. (4) There is no utility or disutility involved in the travel to or from the site. If the trip is very scenic, for example, travel costs will be overestimated. (5) The wage rate or some fraction of the wage rate that is the same for all individuals is the appropriate opportunity cost of time. Much of the literature on travel costs examines each of these assumptions and finds ways of estimating demand curves even if the assumptions do not hold. See Freeman (1993) and the references in this source for full discussions of how to model and estimate recreational demand curves under more complex assumptions. Box 7.2 illustrates a simple travel cost survey.

In addition to the complexities introduced by altering some of the key assumptions above, the travel cost method suffers from some additional drawbacks. One is that it surveys only people who actually visit particular recreation sites. Nonusers are not identified. These people might be nonusers because their marginal valuation for the recreation site is less than the travel costs required to visit the site. If so, and if we extrapolate the WTP values derived from a sample of site users, we may overstate WTP for improvements in environmental quality. The travel cost approach is also basically limited to sites that are visited frequently, so that a demand curve can be estimated. For sites such as national parks and wilderness areas, people may spend quite a large sum of money to travel to them but go only once in a lifetime. This means that we cannot identify a demand curve. These sites may also be unique—is there a substitute for the Grand Canyon, Yellowstone, or Mount Everest? Despite these difficulties, the travel cost approach has been widely used and remains a valuable technique for measuring for benefits of improving environmental quality at water-based recreation sites.

WTP and WTA Estimates from Direct Approaches: Contingent Valuation Method and Experimental Techniques

The approaches discussed so far have all been indirect methods of obtaining information about willingness to pay for improvements in environmental quality. The basic feature of the next set of methods is that people are directly asked to state or reveal what they are willing to pay for environmental quality. The *contingent valuation method* (CVM) poses hypothetical situations to individuals in a survey. They are asked to state what they would be willing to pay (or willing to accept) for a change in environmental quality. Experimental studies involve the use of money, real objects, or both, which the subjects exchange in response to hypothetical situations. A very large

BOX 7.2 **Valuing Ecotourism in a Tropical Rain Forest**

Rain forests provide a host of aesthetic and ecological benefits. How can one value these largely nonmarket benefits? Tobias and Mendelsohn (1991) measure the ecotourism value to domestic users of the Monteverde Cloud Forest Biological Reserve in Costa Rica. The reserve consists of 10,000 hectares of primarily virgin rain forest. The site is relatively remote, so visitors have to incur travel costs to reach the reserve. Travel cost data were collected in 1988 by a survey of visitors who agreed to fill in a written questionnaire in exchange for a chance to win photographs of wildlife. Seven hundred fifty-five people participated. The distance between the domicile of each respondent and the reserve was calculated. A standard estimate of $0.15 per kilometer was used for each person's travel costs. (All dollar amounts are in U.S. dollars). No opportunity costs of time are included in the travel cost values.

One of the estimated demand functions for visits to the park was:

$$\text{Visitation rate} = \underset{(4.20)}{36.17} - \underset{(-2.77)}{0.121}\ \text{distance} + \underset{(2.76)}{0.008}\ \text{density}$$

$$R^2 = 0.145$$

where the figures in parentheses below the coefficient estimates are *t*-statistics.

The coefficients have the expected sign and are statistically significant, although the overall "fit" of the equation is not high. Distance to the site is the "price" term. Density measures the population density in the major urban area in which the respondent resides. Higher density results in more trips to the reserve. The maximum price per visit is $49. The regression implies that trips would fall to zero once the distance exceeded 328 kilometers from the respondent's home to the reserve.

Consumer surplus for each jurisdiction represented in the survey is calculated as the area under the demand curve between the maximum price people are willing to pay and the entrance fee. Summing across all jurisdictions, the annual consumer surplus is $97,500. Discounting this value in perpetuity at 4 percent yields a present value of domestic recreation of approximately $2.4 million. If this value is divided by the approximately 3000 visitors per year, the value of the site is estimated to be about $33 per domestic visit. These values can then be compared with the costs of conserving the rain forest and used as an aid in public policy decisions.

Source: D. Tobias and R. Mendelsohn (1991). "Valuing Ecotourism in a Tropical Rain-Forest Reserve," *Ambio* 20, pp. 91–93.

literature on both approaches exists. See, for example, Braden and Kolstad (1991); Freeman (1993); Mitchell and Carson (1989); Cummings, Brookshire, and Shultze (1986); and the papers by Portney, Hanemann, and Diamond and Hausman in the *Journal of Economic Perspectives* (1994) for a general discussion of these techniques.

The CVM approach is based on a very simple concept. People are asked to state their WTP for an improvement in environmental quality or their WTA compensation for a decrease in environmental quality in the context of answering a questionnaire that poses a specific change in environmental quality. Their response is their compensating variation if the question is about WTP and the equivalent variation if the question is about WTA. This direct measurement of a change in welfare differentiates CVM from the proxy methods that measure changes in welfare using consumer surplus as measured from ordinary demand curves, not compensating or equivalent variation.[2]

A number of steps are necessary in undertaking a CVM study. First, the researcher has to stipulate a hypothetical situation that involves individuals who buy some improvement in environmental quality or are compensated for a decrease in some environmental amenity. Next, a method of hypothetically extracting money from the respondent has to be decided. This is called the payment vehicle. Will the person be asked to pay higher user fees, property or sales taxes, or simply a dollar amount that is unconnected to an existing charge?

A key decision for the researcher at this point is whether the respondent will be given a range of values to choose among or be asked respond "yes" or "no" to a prespecified price set by the researcher. The first approach is a type of bidding or auctioning process. The respondents may be asked to state their WTP or may be given a range of values and told to pick the maximum WTP from the specified range. The "yes-no" option is called a dichotomous choice framework. This approach mimics most markets in North America. The buyer faces a given price for an item and must decide either to buy or not to buy. In the surveys, respondents are presented with different offering prices. Analysis of the data involves determining which variables, including the price faced, explains the percentage of "yes" answers given. The usual assumption that demand curves slope down is tested by seeing if the percentage of "yes" responses declines as the offer price increases. Again, there is a substantial literature on the merits of each of these "pricing" approaches. See, for example, Cameron and Quiggin (1994).

The researcher then must decide whether the survey will be conducted in person, by telephone, or by mail. Once the survey is carried out, analysis of the results typically relies on econometric techniques to estimate WTP or WTA for the group surveyed. The simplest approach is to compute the mean and median WTP and WTA from the survey. However, if socioeconomic information about the respondents is collected, or the survey offers a dichotomous choice, statistical analysis is performed. Box 7.3 illustrates a simple CVM survey.

The authors of a paper we examined above (Brookshire et al., 1982) also performed a survey of households' willingness to pay for improvements in air quality. These results can be compared with the hedonic price estimates derived from the study of home sales. During March 1978, 290 households were interviewed in 12 different census tracts in metropolitan Los Angeles. People living in areas of poor air quality were asked how much they would be willing to pay to have fair air quality; those living with fair air quality were asked their WTP to move to good air quality. The definitions of poor, fair, and good were the same as in the hedonic study. This was an open-ended survey, with no payment vehicle identified. The mean WTP for the regions in which respondents were asked for their valuation of an improvement to fair air quality ranged from $11 to $22.06 per month; while the bids for moving from fair to good ranged from $5.55 to $28.18 per month. The authors had conjectured that the hedonic estimates would be larger than the stated preferences in the WTP survey. They were correct for this study. However, the WTP estimates may have been biased downward by about 50 percent. This sort of empirical work comparing stated and revealed preference techniques is important in pinning down WTP estimates. Much research continues in this area. See, for example, Adamowicz et al. (1994).

BOX 7.3 **Willingness to Pay for Water in Nigeria**

A contingent valuation study (CVM) was carried out by Whittington, Lauria, and Mu (1991) in the rapidly growing city of 700,000 people in Onitsha, Nigeria, to estimate households' willingness to pay for drinking water. This type of study will help state water authorities in Nigeria supply water more efficiently. Water projects in developing countries have had difficulty establishing public water supplies that cover their operating and annualized capital costs. This is due to a variety of factors, including cultural and behavioral characteristics of the population, difficulty in getting pipelines to consumers, other infrastructure problems, and variability in water quality and water flows. Better information about consumers' willingness to pay could be helpful in the planning process.

Water for households in Onitsha comes from two sources—public supplies and private vendors. The delivery system is fairly complex, as shown in Figure A. Water sold privately comes from boreholes owned by individuals. Most of this water is carried by tankers and sold to households or businesses directly or through various types of distributors. Households buy water to store in drums or simply by the bucket for daily use. A modest amount of water comes from shallow wells. The private system provides just over 70 percent of the total daily flow of water. The public system supplies the balance.

The authors did extensive fieldwork to determine prices charged by private vendors. In the dry season, households paid approximately 120,000 Nigerian naira per day or about 0.04 Nigerian naira per British imperial gallon (4.546 liters). At these prices, private vendors were making a considerable rate of return on capital invested in their tankers. Public revenue from the water system existing at the time of the study amounted to about 5000 Nigerian per day, or about 0.003 Nigerian per gallon. Water quality from private sources was perceived by households to be of higher quality than public supplies.

Figure B shows the percentage of total monthly income spent by households on water.

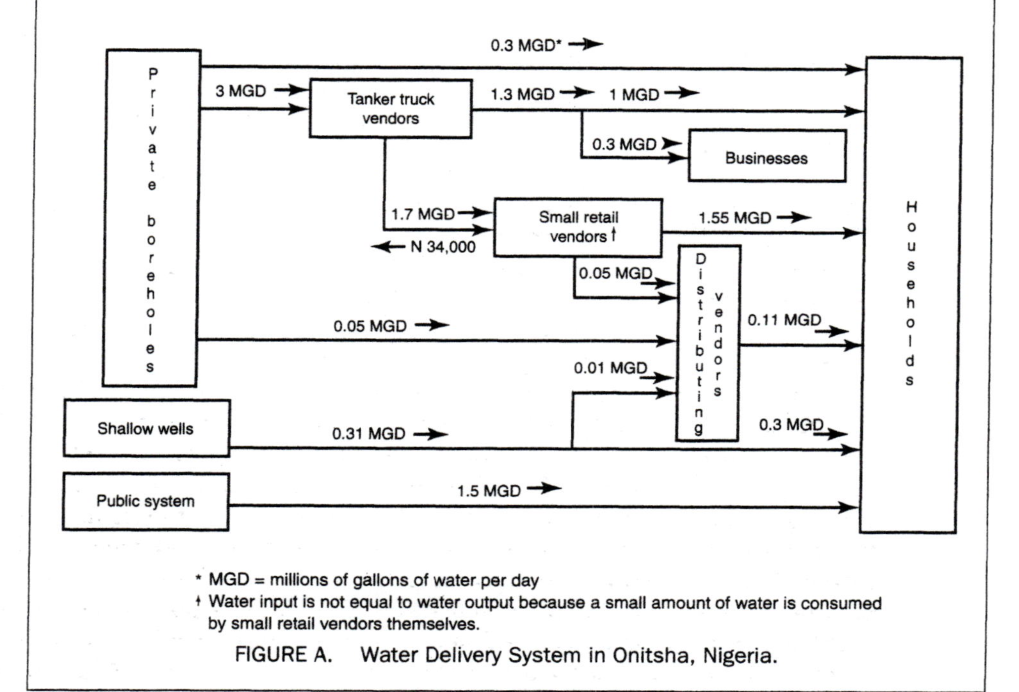

* MGD = millions of gallons of water per day

† Water input is not equal to water output because a small amount of water is consumed by small retail vendors themselves.

FIGURE A. Water Delivery System in Onitsha, Nigeria.

BOX 7.3 *(Continued)*

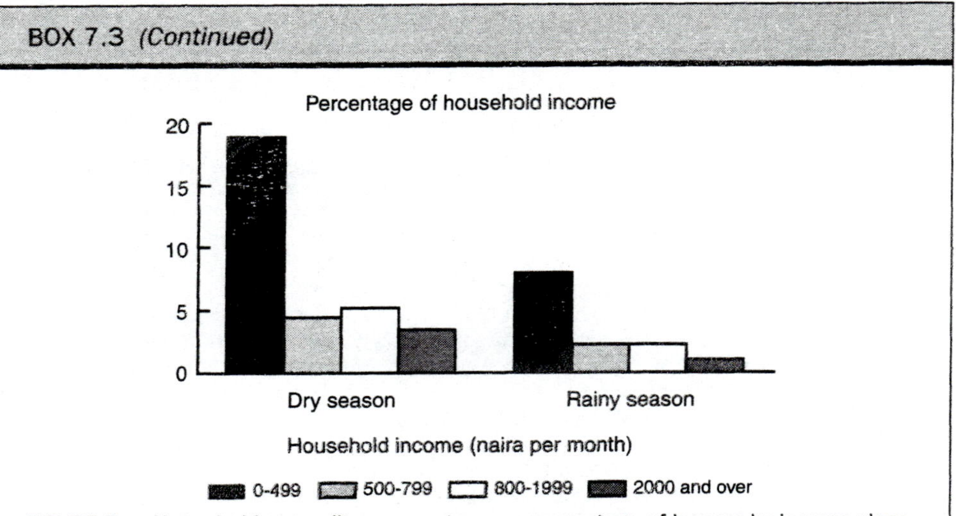

FIGURE B. Household expenditure on water as a percentage of income by income class.

As the figure indicates, the range of these income share numbers is considerable. It is the poor who spend the most—up to 18 percent of total income. One purpose of the CVM study was to see if water could be supplied publicly to meet the dual objectives of cost recovery and offer all households, especially the poor, water at prices that represent a lower share of total household income.

A "bidding game" was used to elicit willingness to pay; 235 households were interviewed in person and asked whether they would pay a specified amount for a "drum" of water. Respondents were very familiar with this unit of measurement from private water sales. If the respondent answers "yes," the price was raised; if "no," the price lowered. The exact questions asked are reprinted below. The authors had a good idea of the opportunity cost of water because they had computed the prices charged by private vendors. Thus, strategic behavior and other biases in the CVM study could be discerned.

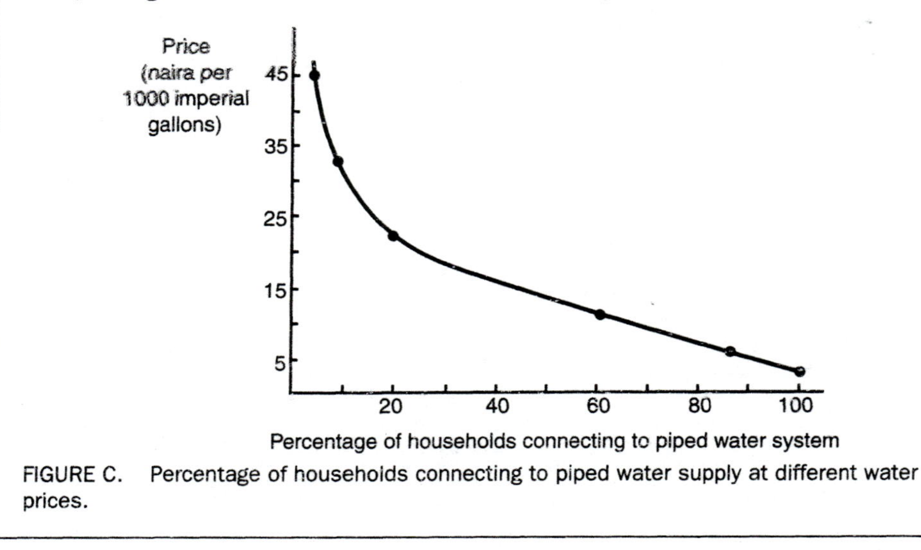

FIGURE C. Percentage of households connecting to piped water supply at different water prices.

BOX 7.3 *(Continued)*

WILLINGNESS-TO-PAY QUESTIONS FROM HOUSEHOLD QUESTIONNAIRE

Opening statement to bidding game

When the New Onitsha Water Scheme is commissioned and when distribution pipes reach your area, those households with private connections will have safe, reliable water — with good pressure — 24 hours per day, all year round.

The World Bank thinks every family wants its own water connection so that it can have as much water as it needs when it needs it. To be fair, each family should pay only for the amount it uses. Just as people who buy water from vendors only pay for the amount they buy, if you use a lot of water, you should pay more than if you use only a little. It would be up to the household to decide how much to use.

To achieve this, each family would have to have a meter installed on its connection, just like a meter is installed to measure how much electricity people use. Every month the meter would be read to determine how much water the household has used and how much the household would have to pay.

Of course, in some cases it will not be possible to provide a household an individual meter, at least for a long time, but assume that you could have a water meter. The decision on whether or not to connect to the New Onitsha Water Scheme and have a metered connection would be the household's or the landlord's. People would still be free to buy water from water vendors if they wished.

Bidding Game

(a) If the price you are charged for water is one naira per drum (or about 25 naira per 1,000 gallons) would you like to be connected to the New Onitsha Water Scheme and have a meter?

YES. . . . . GO TO (b).
NO. . . . . GO TO (d).
NOT SURE . . . . GO TO (d).

(b) If the price you are charged for water is two naira per drum (or about 50 naira per 1,000 gallons) would you like to have a metered connection?

YES . . . . Finished with this section.
NO. . . . . GO TO (c).
NOT SURE. . . . . GO TO (c).

(c) If the price you are charged for water is 1.50 naira per drum (or about 37.50 naira per 1,000 gallons) would you like to have a metered connection?

YES/NO/NOT SURE. . . Finished with this section.

(d) If the price you are charged for water is 0.50 naira — 50 kobo — per drum (or about 12 naira per 1,000 gallons) would you like to have a metered connection?

YES . . . . Finished with this section.
NO/NOT SURE . . . . . . GO TO (e).

(e) If the price you are charged for water is 0.25 naira — 25 kobo — per drum (or about six naira per 1,000 gallons) would you like to have a metered connection?

YES . . . . Finished with this section.
NO/NOT SURE . . . . . . GO TO (f).

(f) If the price you are charged for water is 0.12 naira — 12 kobo — per drum (or about 12 naira per 1,000 gallons) would you like to have a metered connection?

YES/NO/NOT SURE. . . Finished with this section.

Statistical analysis of the survey data (CVM responses and socioeconomic information collected by interviewers) was generally consistent with prior expectations. The households that: (1) have low income, (2) currently have poor water services, (3) are buying from small retail and distributing vendors, and (4) have toilets but no connection to a water distribution system are both able and willing to pay for an improved public water system.

Figure C shows the demand curve that links the percentage of households who would connect to public water supplies to the price charged. This demand curve was constructed from the CVM survey information. We see two regions identified—one fairly elastic range as price increases from 3 Nigerian naira per 1000 gallons to 20 naira; the other an inelastic range for prices above 20 naira per 1000 gallons. Using this information about elasticity, the total revenues the public authority could hypothetically collect is calculated. The authors find that total revenues reach a maximum at a price of 11 naira per 1000 gallons, assuming an average use of 20 gallons per capita per day. Total revenue is only one possible objective for public water supply agencies. Another is to provide high-quality water to as many people as possible. A trade-off between financial criteria (maximizing the difference between total revenue and total cost) and social objectives may result. Figure D illustrates this. The convex shape of the figure indicates that the same revenue can be obtained at a high or low level of household connection to public water supplies. The dual

BOX 7.3 *(Continued)*

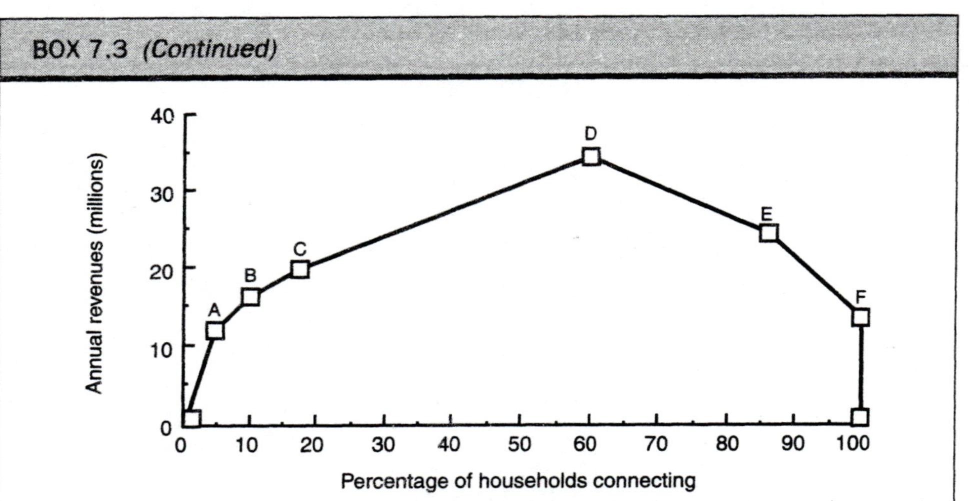

FIGURE D. Percentage of households connected to piped water system versus annual revenues of water utility (millions of naira); assumes average water use of 20 gallons per capita per day.

objective of fiscal responsibility and access could be met if the water authority can operate on the declining portion of the curve (the range from *D* to *F*).

The total cost of providing public water supplies (operating and annualized capital costs) for this project is about half what households are paying private vendors. The CVM work indicates that the public system could be constructed and social welfare increased by offering water at lower prices than the private alternative. Households can be charged a price that covers the costs of supplying the water and still be better off than they were buying from private vendors. Even those who cannot afford to have water piped to their residence may be better off, because the price of privately supplied water should fall once the public water is available. The CVM survey has provided the data that make these sorts of calculations possible.

Source: D. Whittington, D. T. Lauria, and X. Mu (1991). "A Study of Water Vending and Willingness to Pay for Water in Onitsha, Nigeria," *World Development* 19, pp. 179–198; Figures 1, 6, 7, 9; Questionnaire, p. 196.

Another way of eliciting WTP or WTA from individuals is through experimental techniques. Respondents are placed in a laboratory setting, are given hypothetical situations, and earn money for their efforts. Experimental economics is a relatively new field. It has been applied to a number of economic concerns in addition to the estimation of environmental benefits. Researchers are using experiments to evaluate various types of marketable permit schemes for pollution and are using experiments to look at noncompetitive behavior of firms more generally. Experiments have been used extensively to examine the divergence between WTP and WTA of individuals. See the work of Knetsch (1990), Kahneman and Knetsch (1992), and Shogren et al. (1994) for examples of experiments.

One of the key results coming out of this work is the discovery of a large divergence between WTP and WTA: WTA can be 3 to 10 times larger than WTA when the two measures of change in welfare are evaluated in the same study. This divergence has also been discovered in CVM studies. Economic theory predicts that WTP will be less than WTA because of income effects. If people are "buying" a good (in our case, buying environmental quality), the maximum price they are willing to pay is constrained by their income level. However, if they are asked what is the minimum price they are willing to accept to have something they already have taken away, there is no such income constraint. The questions that arise are why the divergence is so large and which measure—WTP or WTA—should be used to represent the value of changes in environmental quality. There has been a lively debate in the economics literature on these issues. Some economists believe that consumers' preferences are not continuous over all ranges of goods provided, because of a "starting point" problem. We have encountered the power of starting points in Chapter 6, in our discussion of property rights. In the case of WTP versus WTA, one hypothesis is that individuals' preferences are kinked or even discontinuous at the amount of the good they are currently consuming (their reference point, or the status quo). If you ask them their WTP for an incremental unit of the good, the answer is much less than their WTA—a decrease in that good by the same increment. People may be averse to losing something they already have. Figure 7.4 illustrates this agrument.

An alternative explanation is that people may perceive environmental quality differently from other goods and services. They may feel that there are no substitutes for certain aspects of environmental quality (what happens when there is no clean air to breathe?) and hence may respond with very large WTAs for declines in environmental quality. Hanemann (1991) developed an expression that predicts the divergence between WTP and WTA, based on a ratio between the income elasticity of the demand for the good and its elasticity of substitution relative to all other goods. However, even this may be questionable in practice. Knetsch (1990) and others have found that even when they are asking people to give up nonessential goods (with many excellent substitutes) such as chocolate bars and coffee mugs, the large divergence between WTP and WTA remains even when its predicted divergence would be much smaller. Another explanation is that people may express "protest bids" under WTA. People do not like the idea of having something taken away and so respond with deliberately inflated values.

Techniques for estimating the benefits of improving environmental quality using CVM techniques are imprecise. It is beyond the scope of this chapter to delve deeply into all the different problems in estimation of benefits. However, we focus on some key areas of concern and ongoing research. The necessary use of surveys in the CVM approach creates its own set of difficulties. There are all sorts of biases that can be introduced by the survey itself or the administrator of any surveying done personally. The choice of the payment vehicle can influence people's expressed WTP. For example, people may be very negative about any sort of tax increase. If the payment vehicle is an increase in sales taxes, WTP may be quite a bit lower than if people are asked to pay a user fee. If the market is an auction type with a closed range in the prices offered, starting-point bias can result. This means that respondents are influenced by

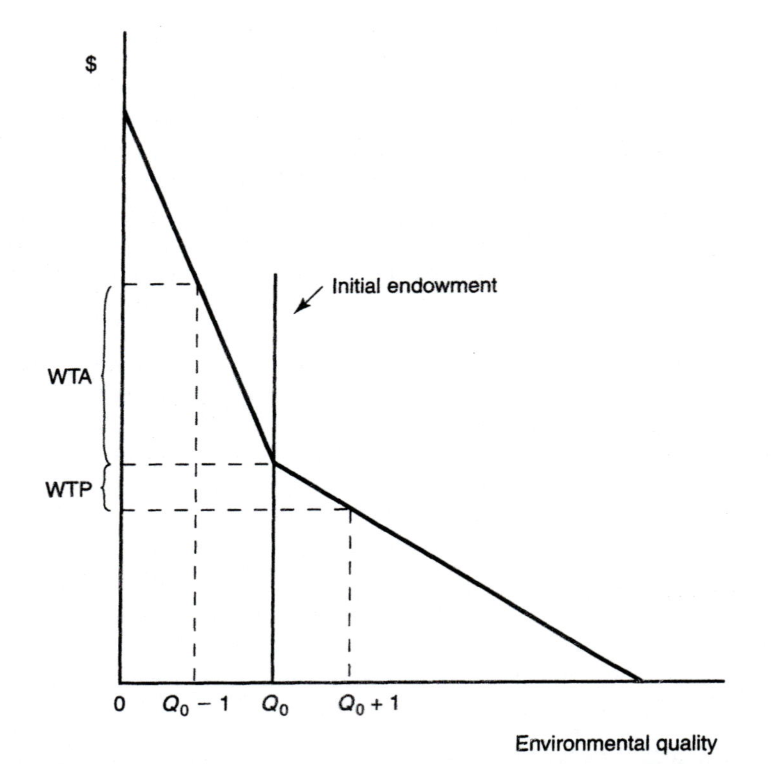

FIGURE 7.4. Individuals' preferences may be influenced by their current endowment of a good. This is illustrated by a possible kink in their demand curve at their endowment of Q_0. The WTP for a 1-unit increase in environmental quality is much less than the WTA for a 1-unit decrease.

the magnitude of the initial price. They may think that this conveys some sort of information about what their bid should be. The information provided in the questionnaire, or by those administering the survey, about the environmental problem at hand can also influence responses.

A major concern by critics of CVM is its hypothetical nature. The critics do not feel that people will respond honestly when their money is not really on the line. Respondents may try to behave strategically to influence political decision makers by overstating or understating their true valuations. Bids could be understated if people felt that the survey was going to lead to the introduction of new taxes or fees they would have to pay. They may overstate bids if they think this will encourage the government to improve the environment and then ask people to pay the average WTP discovered. Another problem connected to the hypothetical nature of the survey is known as the embedding problem. Many CVM studies have been done for a particular species or areas (saving spotted owls or snail darters or preserving a redwood forest). When respondents express a WTP, it may not be clear whether they have actually looked at all the possible things they could spend their incomes on, including all possible environmental goods, before deciding to pay, say, $20 to help preserve a spotted owl habitat. Perhaps the $20 represents their WTP for habitat protection everywhere, and the spotted owl survey is just serving as a proxy for this total WTP? This is a serious concern, because many CVM studies have found quite large values for WTP for specific environmental concerns. If embedding is a problem, it is difficult to know how to interpret the results.

Despite these problems, the CVM and other approaches to estimating benefits remain valuable tools in environmental economics. No single technique is likely to be "the" answer to determining environmental values. The alternative, doing only cost-effectiveness studies, is not very appealing. As the body of literature continues to grow, studies will be replicated and researchers will be able to put better boundaries on the values obtained. Benefit measures have been maligned by those who consider them useless because the numbers are so bad. This criticism misses the point of the exercise. If we have no numbers, no intelligent environmental policy can be designed. What is important is to provide as much information as possible about how the numbers are obtained, what assumptions are made, and how the results would be altered if slightly different assumptions were made. The estimate of the benefits of improving environmental quality is crucial to making informed judgments about environmental policy.

ISSUES IN THE PRACTICAL APPLICATION OF ENVIRONMENTAL POLICIES

In this section of the chapter, we look at examples of environmental policies in use. These include pollution taxes, standards, and marketable permits. Standards are the predominant form of regulation worldwide. Although there are now many types of tax incentives in use in different countries, few levy a fee that reflects the marginal damages from pollution. Most environmental taxes are motivated by revenue objectives. Our discussions will highlight some of the key features of actual policies in place in the United States and some other countries.

Pollution Taxes

Although taxes and fees have not been the predominant form of environmental regulation, their use has increased greatly in the past 10 years. In OECD countries, at least 50 environmental charges are levied on air and water pollution, wastes, and noise. See OECD (1995) for details on these instruments. Most of these taxes are designed primarily to raise revenue rather than to change behavior and reduce emissions. For example, in Denmark, environmental changes make up 7.3 percent of total tax revenues; in Finland, 5.4 percent; in the Netherlands, 6.1 percent; in Norway, 10.75 percent; and in Sweden, 6.3 percent. Damage estimates are not systematically linked to taxes. The revenues raised are sometimes tied to specific environmental initiatives. For example, the province of British Columbia uses a fee charged on all paint sold to finance reprocessing and environmentally safe disposal of used paint. Norway has a charge on fertilizers and pesticides. The funds from these charges are used for sustainable agriculture programs. In neither of these cases are the taxes high enough to discourage use of the good.

Some taxes have been imposed that are specifically designed to alter consumption. The United Kingdom and Canada had differential taxes on leaded versus unleaded gasoline to speed the conversion to unleaded gasoline. In Canada, a very small price differential was sufficient to induce most consumers to switch to unleaded gasoline well before the sale of leaded gasoline was banned. A number of other countries continue to sell leaded fuel and also have a differential tax. The United States introduced a tax on chlorofluorocarbons (CFCs) in 1989 with a similar objective—to phase out the use of these chemicals by the deadlines imposed by an international agreement, the Montreal Protocol. Another objective of the tax was to capture some of the windfall profits that chemical companies would earn when ever-decreasing supplies of CFCs led to price hikes. The CFC tax rate was to escalate over time, and the federal government expected to earn substantial revenues until substitutes for CFCs became widely available (and people switched from CFC-based technology to alternatives).

Perhaps the most controversial pollution tax under current consideration by many countries (and in place in some, such as Finland, Sweden, Norway, and the Netherlands), is a tax on the carbon content of fossil fuels. The so-called carbon tax is being contemplated as a means of reducing carbon dioxide emissions into the atmosphere and reducing the probability of global warming. A side benefit of any reduction in the use of fossil fuels is a reduction in other pollutants, such as sulfur dioxide (a local and regional air pollution problem), methane, and nitrogen oxides. There is now a large literature (see Cline, 1994, and the references therein) evaluating the potential impact of carbon taxes on economic activity. To meet a target of 50 percent reduction of carbon dioxide emissions from their 1990 level, rather substantial tax rates would have to be levied in most countries.

Macroeconomic and general equilibrium models trace the impact of these taxes on output, productivity, factor prices, and other economic variables. See Box 7.4 for an example of the simulated impacts of a carbon tax. Not surprisingly, most of these models predict a number of negative impacts on economic activity, especially in the energy-dependent sectors and regions of countries. One way to mitigate these adverse effects is to gradually increase the tax rate. This allows energy users to modify their technologies and capital equipment to reduce the use of fossil fuels. Although most studies find that the demand for fossil fuels is relatively inelastic in the short run, long-run elasticities are typically much higher. The success of a tax in affecting consumption is of course highly dependent on price elasticity, which in turn depends on many factors, including the availability of substitutes. At present, many governments are having difficulty imposing carbon taxes at rates high enough to significantly affect carbon emissions. One reason is political. Another is that the taxes are primarily designed to raise revenue, not to alter behavior. If the tax rate was set high enough to have a significant effect on energy consumption, revenue targets would not be met. This poses a potential dilemma for policy makers. Given the current political climate in the United States Congress, there is little support for pollution taxes of any kind.

Water Pollution Standards in the United States

Fragmentation, decentralization, and conflict characterize current water pollution policy in the United States. A common problem in all pollution regulation in the United States (and many other countries) is the division of authority between the federal, state, and local governments, and division of authority within each level of government. The federal government typically sets uniform standards for the entire country. The states and municipalities are then responsible for the implementation of these policies. In the United States, at least 27 different federal agencies have some degree of responsibility for water policy.[3] Add to this number the thousands of state and local governments, water supply districts, and pollution control authorities, and the problems of coordination, inconsistency in implementation and enforcement, and potential duplication and conflict of policies become apparent. We illustrate some of these problems through an examination of one of the federal laws governing water pollution.

There are three major laws that deal with water pollution in the United States: the Water Pollution Control Act, also called the Clean Water Act; the Safe Drinking Water Act; and the Resource Conservation and Recovery Act. Our focus in this section is the Clean Water Act, because it illustrates a number of important difficulties entailed by the imposition of standards. The act was passed by Congress in October 1972. It required the Environmental Protection Agency of the United States (EPA) to meet six deadlines:

1. By 1973, effluent guidelines were to be issued for major industrial categories of water pollution.
2. By 1974, permits were to be granted to all water pollution sources.
3. By 1977, all sources were to install the "best practicable technology" (BPT) for abatement of pollutants emitted.
4. By 1981, all major waterways in the United States were to be fishable and swimmable.
5. By 1983, all sources were to install the "best available technology" (BAT) to abate pollution.
6. By 1985, all discharges to waterways were to be eliminated.

This is an ambitious program, to say the least, and none of the deadlines have been met. We highlight the reasons why.

The initial deadline was the basis on which the remaining five depended. The guidelines were to be the standards for every major pollutant and the basis on which the permits were to be distributed. Each firm was to be given a permit (by 1974) that specified exactly how much it was entitled to emit. The task of determining guidelines and assigning permits to the over 200,000 industrial polluters emitting 30 major categories of pollution (and 250 subcategories) was simply impossible in the time period legislated, given EPA's insufficient human resources. Before any permits could be issued, information on the manufacturing process of each polluter, its discharges, technological options for abatement, and so on had to be determined and converted into guidelines within 1 year. EPA simply did not have the time to gather and evaluate the data, or sufficient research experience and personnel to complete the task.

BOX 7.4 On Taxing Emissions of Greenhouse Gases

Nordhaus (1991) reports a schedule of carbon taxes that could reduce emissions of greenhouse gases and slow global warming. The four greenhouse gases (GHGs) considered are carbon dioxide, methane, nitrous oxides, and chlorofluorocarbons (CFCs). Recent estimates of their presence are reported in figures below.

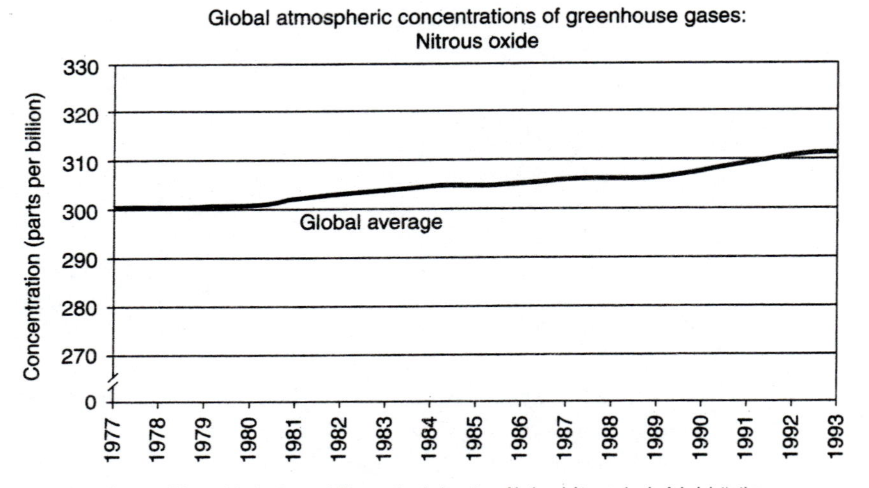

Source: Climate Monitoring and Diagnostics Laboratory, National Atmospheric Administration, Colorado, U.S.A.

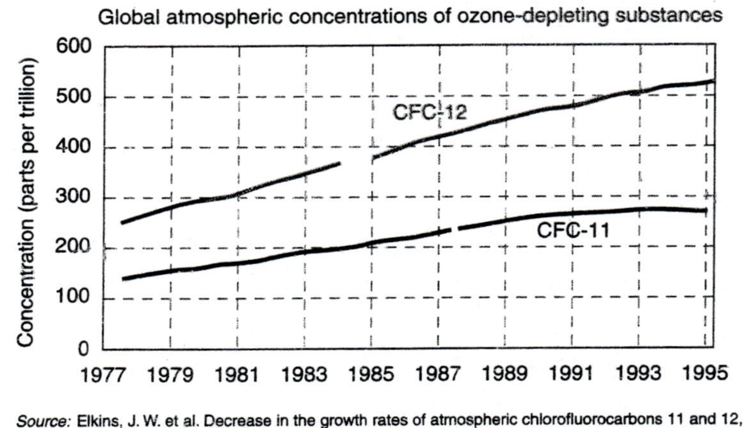

Source: Elkins, J. W. et al. Decrease in the growth rates of atmospheric chlorofluorocarbons 11 and 12, *Nature,* 364: 780–783 (August 1993).

Prepared by: State of the Environment Directorate, Environment Canada.

BOX 7.4 *(Continued)*

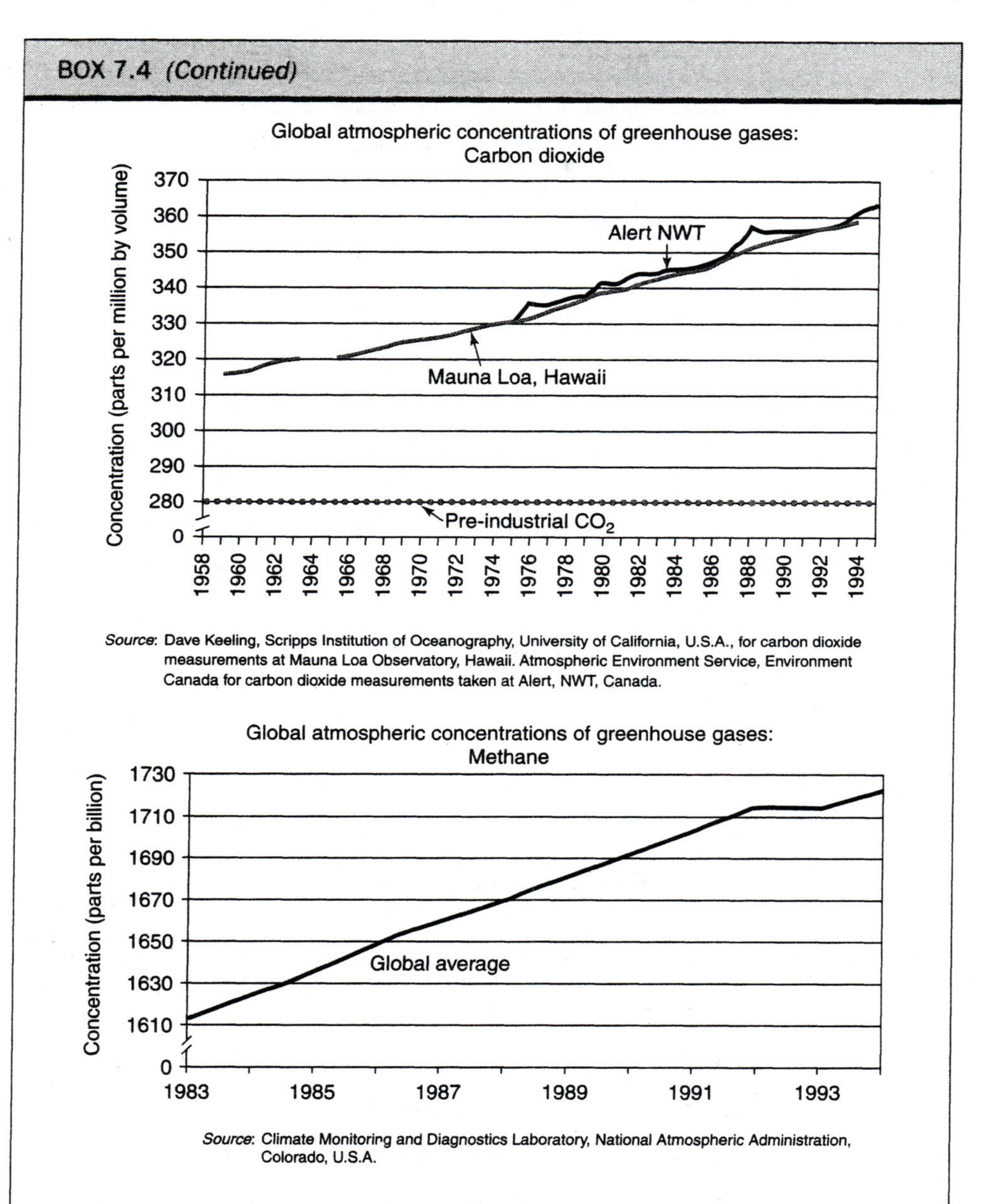

Source: Dave Keeling, Scripps Institution of Oceanography, University of California, U.S.A., for carbon dioxide measurements at Mauna Loa Observatory, Hawaii. Atmospheric Environment Service, Environment Canada for carbon dioxide measurements taken at Alert, NWT, Canada.

Source: Climate Monitoring and Diagnostics Laboratory, National Atmospheric Administration, Colorado, U.S.A.

Nordaus translates the GHGs into carbon equivalents. In particular, the carbon content of carbon dioxide by weight is 1/3.67. For the other gases, the equivalents are in carbon content per unit of global warming. Carbon taxes are intended to induce emitters of GHGs to cut back on their emissions in order to reduce their tax liability. Selective reductions in economic activities reduce GHG emissions, but other outputs produced as GHGs

(Continued)

BOX 7.4 *(Continued)*

ESTIMATED MARGINAL, TOTAL, AND AVERAGE GLOBAL COSTS FOR DIFFERENT LEVELS OF REDUCTIONS OF GREENHOUSE GAS EMISSIONS (1989 PRICES AND LEVEL OF GLOBAL ECONOMY)

Reductions of GHG Emissions (as percent of baseline)	Marginal Cost of Reduction ($ per *t C*)	Total Cost of Reduction (billions of $)	Average Cost of Reduction ($ per *t C*)
0	0.0	0.0	n/a
1	0.5	0.0	0.5
2	1.0	0.1	0.8
3	1.5	0.2	1.0
4	2.0	0.4	1.3
5	2.6	0.6	1.5
10	5.3	2.2	2.8
15	16.3	6.8	5.6
20	27.9	16.3	10.2
25	40.2	30.7	15.4
30	53.3	49.5	20.6
40	89.9	107.9	33.7
50	119.9	190.8	47.7
60	171.7	308.7	64.3
70	240.4	474.8	84.8
80	342.4	708.8	110.8

Note that these are cost estimates of making reductions by reducing or reorganizing economic activity to induce reductions in emissions. A different strategy is to adjust georganochemical activity to, for example, increase carbon dioxide absorption by the earth's ecosystem. Nordhaus discusses such policies in brief but does not consider yet them viable alternatives to "conventional" policies.

are also emitted. Alternatively, a selective reduction in economic activities of x dollars will reduce GHG emissions by y units. This is Nordhaus's way of measuring the cost of slowing global warming. Thus if world output is selectively reduced by $190.8 billion (1989 dollars), than a 50 percent reduction in emissions of GHGs could be achieved. This translated into a carbon tax per ton of carbon emitted of 119.9 dollars. See the table for these data, plus a complete schedule.

Source: W. D. Nordhaus (1991). "The Cost of Slowing Climate Change: A Survey," *Energy Journal* 12, 1 (1991) pp. 37–65.

Legal and political wrangles complicated the process. By May 1973, when the official guidelines were due, there existed only interim guidelines for 22 industrial categories. At that time EPA decided to begin issuing permits on the basis of the interim guidelines. This created a legal battle. As a result of its failure to establish final guidelines for all categories, EPA was sued by the National Resources Defense Council for delay in establishing guidelines. By January 1974, 38 guidelines for 30 different major categories and 100 subcategories were in place. Virtually no engineering or economic analyses were undertaken in setting these guidelines.

The EPA's permit scheme was thwarted by Congress, state water pollution authorities, and the companies receiving the permits. Congress was unhappy because EPA did not consult it prior to launching this scheme. The states thought EPA would supersede their own standards, passed in 1965. The polluters didn't want to reveal any information and did not submit the required applications for a permit. And even the environmentalists were skeptical that the scheme would reduce emissions. Then, EPA's actions were ended when a district court in Ohio found that each permit issued had to be supported by an environmental impact statement—a detailed evaluation of the costs and benefits of the action. Environmental impact statements are time-consuming and very costly. There was no way the EPA could evaluate each of the 50,000 operations for which it had permits. The program ended, but it did provide the EPA with information useful in establishing permits under the 1972 act.

Unfortunately, because the guidelines were not in place when many of the permits were issued (94 percent of the major sources of water pollutants had received a permit before the guidelines were released), there was much inconsistency between the permits and the guidelines. Permits and guidelines were established simultaneously by different offices within EPA using different information bases. The interim guidelines were also typically more restrictive than the guidelines ultimately issued. As a result, a slew of legal challenges to the permits occurred. Companies contested the permits because of inconsistency with the interim guidelines (in over 2000 adjudicary proceedings), then challenged the final guidelines themselves (in over 150 lawsuits). In these proceedings and suits, companies argued that the EPA did not have the authority to set an exact number for its guideline but could set only a range of numbers; that it had not obtained sufficient cost information on which to base the permit; that it failed to incorporate differences in discharges seasonally; that not enough subcategories were included; and so on.

What resulted from all this was extensive delay in establishing every component of the act. Clearly, the regulatory procedures established by the Water Pollution Control Act were not working very well throughout the 1970s and into the 1980s. Water pollution policy in general in the United States has had a history of rigid standards that are not met.

Even without the legal challenges and the difficulties the EPA had in establishing guidelines and permits, there are problems with the law. First, and very important, there are *no economic incentives.* Firms were given a permit that cannot be traded and required to abate all emissions by 1985. (This deadline has since been extended.) No calculation, however rough, was made of the marginal damages from water pollution versus the marginal benefits of pollution (or the marginal costs of abatement). It is most unlikely that it is in society's interest to remove *all* pollutants from waterways unless there is no intersection of marginal damage and marginal benefit functions at a positive amount of pollution. The requirement that all emissions be terminated has a detrimental effect on meeting even more modest reductions in emissions. Legal battles can tie up the regulatory procedure so completely that even the more moderate guidelines cannot be imposed. Note as well that legal battles are costly to both the private and the public sector.

It is instructive to contrast the experience in the United States with that of many European countries. The European method of standards plus charges may have initially led to greater than optimal discharges, but the policies were implemented and emissions were being reduced throughout the 1970s. Charges were established so that far fewer legal and procedural difficulties occurred than in the United States. The European countries are now able to further reduce emissions through higher fees, while the United States is still trying to figure out how to deal with water pollution.

Other features of the U.S. Water Pollution Control Act of 1972 also serve to increase the costs of pollution control and delay reductions in emissions. The notion of a uniform "best technology" is unreasonable, and, as we saw in Chapter 6, not cost-efficient. Within the same industry, there are large differences among plants. Imposing a uniform abatement technique is bound to increase greatly the total costs of pollution contol. Firms have a great incentive to challenge these technologies on the grounds that they are unfairly treated or that the technologies are not feasible to implement or are so costly that the firm cannot stay in business. The BATs do not allow for a tradeoff between pollution and economic activity. The effect of the abatement requirements may be to alter market structure as some firms are forced out of business or foreign firms facing much less severe pollution controls increase their exports to markets in the United States. These economic effects may make the standard a very costly means of reducing pollution. Losers in these situations who are not compensated can often exert great political pressure and discredit an otherwise good approach.

By the 1990s, more than 66,000 permits had been issued by the EPA to point sources, but the law is felt to be far from a success. Budget cuts over the past 10 years have taken their toll on monitoring and enforcement. It is alleged that many polluters violate their permits. Furthermore, nonpoint pollution remains a serious problem which is largely untouched by the permitting process. Recent amendments to the Clean Water Act give some regulatory authority over nonpoint sources to state governments. This devolution of powers to the states could make environmental regulations more cost-effective. On the other hand, state control could lead to a myriad of policies across the country, making compliance costly for companies operating in more than one state. If past performance of state governments is any indication, there may also be a large diversity in the intensity of regulation. Some states impose stringent policies, while others have weak or nonexistent regulation. A key problem is funding environmental protection activities. State governments may be given the power to regulate but lack the financial means to do so.

Some form of pollution control is very much in the public interest, but the methods required by the Water Pollution Control Act lead to a high-cost form of control that does not guarantee improved water quality.

Marketable Permits: The New Wave in Pollution Control?

We turn now to an alternative method of reducing pollution that deviates substantially from the dependence on the standard and lack of economic incentives—the marketable permit for pollution.

Economists have long argued that a government-organized market that trades in permits to pollute can be organized to internalize an externality. The government establishes a desired level of environmental quality or quantity of pollution emissions, then distributes permits which sum to that level. Government involvement is necessary to administer the market and ensure that emissions do not exceed permitted levels. As long as the market is competitive, the optimal amount of pollution should result from this scheme, with firms minimizing their costs of compliance.

Dales (1968) was one of the earliest proponents of the use of markets to deal with pollution problems. Montgomery (1972) proved that the market would lead to a set of efficient prices for pollution. Some states and the Environmental Protection Agency in the United States have begun to implement tradable emission permits for lead, sulfur dioxide, and water pollution that are traded in markets to deal with some significant pollution problems. The change in the legal and regulatory environment that has emerged in the past few years has given rise to a number of interesting economic analyses of marketable pollution permits. Our focus here will be on air pollution.

Characteristics of Marketable Permits

We developed a very simple model of marketable permits in Chapter 6. In this section, we look more deeply into the ways a market in pollution permits might operate. Permit markets should be designed to match pollution types. Following Tietenberg (1985), we group pollutants into two types: uniformly versus spatially distributed. Emissions of a *uniformly distributed pollutant* have the same impact on environmental quality regardless of where they are released. An example is chlorofluorocarbon (CFC) emissions. Release of CFCs from Bangkok will have the same adverse effect on stratospheric ozone levels as emissions from Paris. The effect of emissions of a *spatially distributed pollutant* on environmental quality depends on the location of the pollution source. A ton of sulfur dioxide emissions from an electric power plant in northern Ohio will lead to more acidification of New England lakes than that same ton would have if emitted from a power plant located in eastern Maine.

There are two generic types of permit schemes that correspond to uniformly and spatially distributed pollutants. The *emissions-based system* (EBS) regulates the total amount of emissions per unit time released into the environment. Permits allow emissions from each source to be traded one-for-one anywhere in the jurisdiction. The *ambient-based system* (ABS) sets total allowable emissions so that *concentrations* of the pollutants per unit time do not exceed ambient standards set for all locations. Permits will not necessarily be tradable one-for-one anywhere in the jurisdiction. Traders will have to prove to the regulatory authority that the exchange does not lead to emissions in excess of an ambient standard anywhere in the jurisdiction. Pollution from each source will have to be mapped in terms of its effect on the environment. This is done using technological relationships between emissions and environmental concentra-

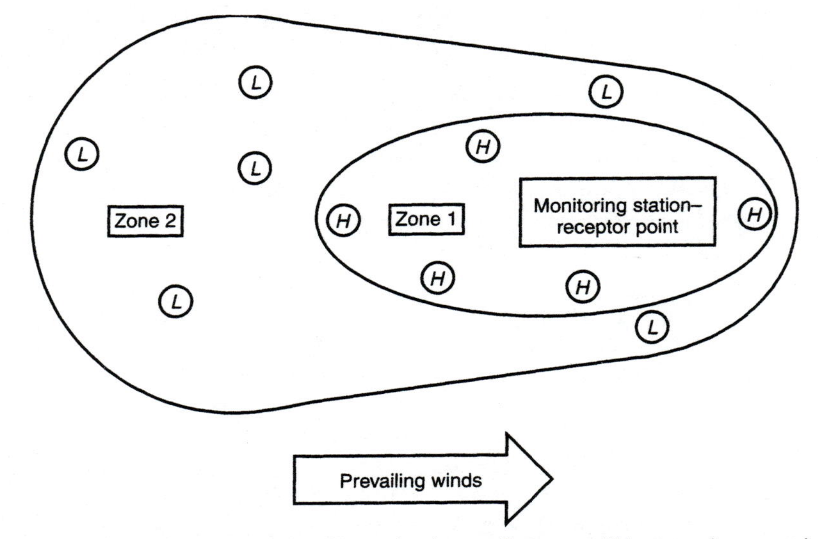

FIGURE 7.5. A spatially distributed pollutant is shown. Sources within zone 1 are marked *H* to indicate that their emissions will lead to high concentrations of the pollutant at the monitoring station–receptor point. Emissions from sources within zone 2, marked *L*, will yield low concentrations of the pollutant at the receptor.

tions. Figure 7.5 illustrates the concept. Emissions from sources far from a receptor point–monitoring station will typically have a smaller impact on pollution concentrations than emissions released close to the receptor. Geography, weather patterns, and the characteristics of the pollutant can all affect the dispersion of emissions and their impact on environmental quality at each receptor. These relationships are summarized by what is known as a *transfer coefficient.* The transfer coefficient tells how emissions from a source affect ambient environmental quality (concentrations of the pollutant) at each receptor point. Under an ABS, regulatory authorities would use the transfer coefficient to determine whether any particular permit trade between polluters is allowable, i.e., it does not violate ambient standards at any monitoring station. We now look at the ABS and EBS in more detail.

Ambient-Based System

To establish an ABS system of marketable permits, the government must first determine the receptor areas. This task requires the use of models predicting air diffusion from sources of pollution. Fairly sophisticated and reliable models exist. Then the total emissions permitted in each receptor area consistent with the ambient air quality standards must be determined. The setting of air quality standards ideally should be done with some computation of expected benefits net of costs of controlling pollution to particular levels. One would hope for some notion of establishing the "optimal" amount of pollution. But if this task is impossible, a reasonable standard can be set and altered over time.

Once the standard is determined for each area, the government issues the number of permits consistent with this total. The government can give the permits to existing polluters or auction them off. If the permits are given away, the government lets the market determine the final allocation of the permits and hence emissions among the pollution sources. No further regulation of the method of allocating permits among polluters is required, except to try to ensure that the market operates efficiently by encouraging a large number of trades. Finally, the government must enforce emission standards by determining if the source emitting the pollutant is in compliance with the number of permits it holds and penalize noncompliers. These monitoring and enforcement tasks are roughly comparable for all the permit schemes, so we will not comment further on this aspect of the scheme.

What are the advantages of the ABS marketable permits over other policies? First, an ambient-based system would be relatively simple and less costly to operate from the viewpoint of the regulator than any other type of pollution policy. The information requirements for establishing and operating the permit system are lower than what is necessary to impose taxes (fees) or to impose pollution standards on individual polluters. The government need not gather information about the abatement costs for each polluter. Nor must it attempt to compute marginal damages and marginal benefits of pollution, as was necessary in determining the optimal tax on pollution. Second, as we have noted in Chapter 6, the permit scheme does achieve the target at minimum cost. It also allows firms to pursue cost-reducing innovations in abatement technology (as would a tax).

There is one serious flaw with the ABS system, which makes it unlikely that it will be implemented: Polluters would find it extremely burdensome. Each polluter would have to have permits for every receptor area into which its pollution flowed. There would be as many markets as there were receptor areas, and firms might find it very costly to make transactions in a large number of markets. How costly these markets would be to firms is an empirical question.

Emissions-Based System

The EBS has been proposed as one alternative that eliminates the problem of multiple markets and permit prices per polluter. Permits are defined in terms of the level (or rate) of emissions from the source, rather than in terms of the effect of the emissions on the ambient air quality in all the receptor areas. Any emissions within a particular zone are treated as equivalent regardless of where they drift. The advantage of the system is that each firm would have to operate only in one market where its permit is tradable one-for-one within the zone. No trades across zones would be permitted.

There are, however, a number of problems with this approach. First, pollution can be concentrated within an area and yield "hot spots," locales within the zone that have pollution levels exceeding the standard. The hot spot problem can be reduced by defining the zones more narrowly, but then the system drifts closer to the ABS, with its problem of multiple markets for firms. Second, within the region polluters with very different transfer coefficients may be combined. Then the one-for-one trades will not reflect differences in the pollution concentrations of the emitters. The implicit price of emissions established by the market will not be the shadow price of the binding standard.

If pollution spills over a zone, there is no market to handle those transactions. Recall that with the ABS firms must have permits for wherever their pollution flows. The EBS works if the pollutant in question either is very local in impact or is quickly dispersed into the environment and affects large areas of the country equivalently. Another case in which the EBS may work is where the dispersion characteristics for emissions within a zone are relatively similar. If the zones where these characteristics are roughly the same can be defined, the hot spots and cost inefficiencies can be reduced. But even if there are no differences in the dispersion characteristics within a zone, the regulatory authority must still determine how many permits to issue per zone. This calculation requires far more data than the computation of the number of permits required in the ABS. The authority must solve the cost minimization problem. This means that it needs to have an air quality model and inventory of emissions, as before, also but it must know as well the source-specific abatement cost functions. It is unlikely to have this information, but if it did, marketable permits would hardly be required. Each source could then have the right number of permits or its own quota, and no market need function except to deal with entry and technological changes. What is more likely is that the regulatory authority will have limited information and thus run the risk that the permits issued fail to lead to the ambient standard established.

Air Pollution Policy in the United States: The Evolution of Marketable Permits

The primary regulatory apparatus for controlling air pollution is the Clean Air Act and its amendments in 1970, 1977, 1979, and 1990. Prior to 1970, state and local governments had primary responsibility for air pollution control other than automobile exhaust. In 1970, the Clean Air Act was amended to give federal jurisdiction over new sources of industrial pollution. The Environmental Protection Agency (EPA) was established in that year to determine and administer the new federal policies. The EPA was responsible for setting standards for new sources of pollution (the new-source standards), developing other standards, overseeing the states' plans to implement the new standards, and enforcing standards and monitoring air quality. The primary form of control was regulation, as in the case of water pollution. The EPA established ambient standards—targets for concentrations of air pollutants. Each state had to file with the EPA a plan showing how these ambient standards would be obtained for pollutants not classified as "new sources." The new-source pollutants were directly controlled by EPA through standrds.

One of the EPA's major tasks was to determine how to prevent deterioration of air quality in areas that are not heavily polluted. In the early 1970s, there was considerable concern over the degradation of areas of high air quality. Prodded by litigation that reached the Supreme Court of the United States (*Sierra Club* v. *Ruckelshaus*, 1972), the EPA responded with an amendment to the Clean Air Act in 1977 to prevent clean areas from becoming dirty. The country was divided into three types of regions with allowable increments in emissions designated for each type. Pollution increments were allocated to firms desiring to locate in any region on a first come, first served basis.

The difficulty with a nondegradation policy is that it becomes a deterrent to economic growth in regions with good air quality. This may lead to a loss in social welfare if the marginal value of the output from these potential entrants exceeds the marginal damages due to air pollutants. This is a basic problem with standards—marginal damages and marginal benefits of pollution are not equated at each point in time. Because pollution regulations act as a barrier to entry to firms in particular locations, they may give firms already existing in those regions some monopoly power and create economic rents. Consumers may be worse off because markets are less competitive.

However, the allocation of pollution increments may have been the first step in the move toward a system of marketable permits for controlling air pollution. In 1979, additional amendments to the Clean Air Act furthered the possibility that a market mechanism could be used. Two reforms in the transferability of implicit rights to pollute were made. The first was the introduction of an emission reduction scheme that has become known as the *bubble policy*. For a particular pollutant, the bubble allows an increase in emissions from one plant or firm (in a given area) *if* another source of the same pollutant in the same area reduces its emissions by the same amount. When first introduced in 1979, these trade-offs were allowed only within a given plant; the bubble has since been extended to different plants and even to different firms. All trades must be approved by the EPA.

The bubble represents a move toward a system of permits that are transferable, although in a very restricted sense. The transferability is crucial, though, as rights to pollute must be exchangeable if firms are to meet a given standard at minimum cost. The other significant feature of the bubble is that it moves the EPA away from its policies of imposing specific standards on each emitter. The advantage of the trading permit is that no information on abatement costs from individual firms is required, and no firm is restricted to a rigid individual standard.

The second component of the 1979 amendments was the *emissions offset policy*. Prior to 1979, if an area was not meeting its ambient standard, no new firms that contributed to air pollution were allowed to enter. Problems similar to those associated with nondegradation emerged. To allow for new entry into these areas, the EPA now allows new firms to enter if they succeed in getting existing firms to reduce their emissions by exactly the same amount as the expected emissions that will come from the new firm. Existing firms thus have a valuable property right for which they can extract payment. The EPA must again sanction these exchanges and ensure that there is no net change in total emissions. The EPA also requires new sources to meet the technical standards established for the region. Exchanges occur not through an organized market but as a result of bargaining among firms. However, it is not a big step from the offset policy to one of a pollution market with a fixed number of pollution permits per area.

The 1990 amendments to the Clean Air Act represented a major change in environmental policy in the United States away from command-and-control regulations and toward market-based initiatives—that is, a fully tradable emission permit. The 1990 amendments came after 10 years of acrimonious debate in Congress and opposition to environmental legislation from the Reagan administration. The target of the amendments of 1990 is to reduce annual emissions of sulfur dioxide by 40 percent from their level in 1980 of 25 million tons. The largest sources of sulfur dioxide are coal-fired electric utilities in the eastern United States. To prevent deterioration, yet still allow flexibility in meeting the target, the tradable emission permits were introduced. There are still limitations on trades: Nondeterioration requirements are imposed regionally. Electric utilities are given pollution allowances that are based on their previous and current emission levels, fuel type, and other factors. A polluter that has unused allowances can sell them anywhere in the United States.

As of this writing it was too soon to tell how well the amendments of 1990 were working. However, a number of concerns could be predicted from economic theory. Permits are tradable in a commodity market. There has been some concern that there are too few trades at one time. If so, this may mean that a competitive market has not been established. The efficiency gains, relative to command-and-control regulation, may not materialize, because of the thinness and potential lack of competition in the permit markets. One reason why few trades emerge could be the complexity of the trading rules established by the EPA. There are also potential "hot spot" problems because the permits are tradable nationally and are essentially an emissions-based system. This may mean that air pollution in the areas most severely affected by sulfur dioxide emissions (those areas suffering from acidic precipitation), may not see a dramatic improvement in air quality.

The EPA has estimated that the sulfur dioxide trading program of 1990 will save utilities and consumers between $700,000 million and $1 billion per year.[4] Two papers, the first by Atkinson and Tietenberg (1982), and the second by Atkinson (1983) simulate the impact of different types of trading systems. Obviously, neither paper examines the exact features of the amendments of 1990, but both papers offer some interesting results that might indicate the potential impact of the sulfur trading program.

Simulated Permit Markets

In Atkinson and Tietenberg's study (1982) of particulate air pollution in St. Louis, six types of marketable permit schemes are compared against each other and the program existing at the time of their study (the State Implementation Plan, or SIP). The six schemes considered include the ABS, as described above; a multiple-zone EBS with a rollback provision through which emissions must be reduced by a certain percentage at the worst site in the airshed; a simplified version of ABS called HAP (highest ambient permit), in which only one market exists for the permits, where these permits are defined in terms of the most polluted zone; and three other variations of zonal permits.

The simulation found that ABS involves the lowest abatement costs for all the standards considered, with HAP following closely behind (implying that restricting the market to one zone does not result in any significant increases in abatement costs), while the costs of the other schemes were markedly higher. A striking result was the high permit expenditures involved in the EBS system, both in terms of absolute amount and as a share of the total expenditure incurred through the scheme. Overall, permit shares of total expenditures fell for all schemes as the standards were made more restrictive, since abatement costs rise more quickly than the permit prices under high air quality standards. The ABS and HAP schemes removed the fewest tons of particulates per day, as expected. However, only the ABS was shown to guarantee that *ex ante* standards would be met *ex post*. No uniform ranking of the other schemes was possible in this regard. Finally, permit prices under the ABS were found to be highly unstable when standards varied. This implies a possibility of large transaction costs for firms under this system, thereby making it difficult to implement.

The authors conclude that the HAP looks like a reasonable policy for a relatively local pollutant such as particulates. Limiting the number of markets for which ambient permits are needed would greatly reduce the transactions costs incurred by firms, without increasing abatement costs much above their minimum level. The HAP would not work, however, when the pollutant was more global in its distribution. Air quality could decline in such a case. All the marketable permits are superior to the SIP in terms of their effect on abatement costs. However, all the systems except ABS can lead to hot spots.

Atkinson's study (1983) investigates an EBS, using a programming model similar to that used by Atkinson and Tietenberg to determine the effect of an emissions permit system for the Cleveland area. This region will be greatly affected by the amendments of 1990 because it contains many coal- and oil-fired electric utilities. The programming model indicates that the emissions permit is far more costly than either the ABS or the local SIP strategy to meet the ambient standard. An ambient permit system would be far less costly but would reduce the amount of abatement from the plants with tall stacks and increase the emissions of sulfur dioxide in the region relative to the local SIP and EBS, unless global restrictions on the transmission of the sulfur dioxide out of the region are imposed.

The EBS reduces emissions the most, but is costly ($158.2 million per year versus $144.3 million for the SIP and $112.9 for the ABS, where the numbers are based on abatement costs under a constraint on the long-range transmission of the emissions). There is also a problem of potential lack of competition in the market under either permit scheme. Only 8 of the 25 point sources that emit 95 percent of the sulfur dioxide from the region are owned independently. The electric utility plants generate 95 percent of the emissions from the group. Atkinson's results suggest that the marketable permits may meet the target set by the legislation, but at higher costs than expected. Marketable permits are not necessarily a panacea for environmental problems.

SUMMARY

1. Cost-benefit analysis is the technique used by economists to evaluate environmental policies and projects. The marginal benefits and marginal costs of pollution control will be equated by choosing the project or policy that has the maxi-

mum present value of net benefits (total benefits minus total costs). Cost-benefit analysis should measure all values in terms of shadow prices—prices that reflect resource scarcity.

2. A cost-effectiveness study assumes that the benefits of each project or policy are identical and compares the total costs of reaching some environmental target. The policy with the minimum total costs is the most cost-effective.
3. To measure marginal benefits from pollution abatement or improved environmental quality, three sets of relationships must be formulated and evaluated: (a) the relationship between changes in emissions to changes in the ambient quality of the environment; (b) how changes in environmental quality affect the flow of environmental services to individuals; (c) how the changes in environmental services affect economic welfare.
4. The basis for estimating benefits from a change in environmental quality is an individual's willingness to pay (WTP) for an increase in environmental quality or willingness to accept (WTA) a decrease in environmental quality, or both.
5. The techniques designed to measure the benefits of improving environmental quality include models of averting behavior, hedonic estimation, contingent valuation methods, and experimental approaches. The approaches differ in that some are based on revealed preferences of individuals and others on stated preferences. The objective of each approach is to estimate the WTP for improvements in environmental quality or the WTA for decreases in environmental quality. Each system has strengths and weaknesses. Many empirical studies have been done. Estimates are being widely used in government and for compensation after environmental damages have occurred.
6. Standards combined with fees have been used in several European countries to help finance water treatment facilities and to provide economic incentives to abate emissions to waterways. Until recently, fees have been too low to provide much incentive for emitters to abate at the source. However, with the fee structure in place, recent increases in charges may provide greater incentive for cost-reducing abatement in the future.
7. In the United States, pollution regulations have traditionally been command-and-control policies. Regulations imposed deadlines for the establishment by the Environmental Protection Agency (EPA) of standards for all important categories of emissions to waterways. Each major emitter of pollution was then to receive a permit by 1974 to discharge specified levels of the pollutants. By 1983, all sources were to install the best feasible technology. No choice over abatement techniques was to be allowed. By 1985, all discharges to waterways were to be eliminated. None of these deadlines have been met owing to EPA's lack of personnel in the early 1970s and to legal and political difficulties. The standards provide no economic incentives to abate pollution and can lead to very high costs of pollution control.
8. Marketable permits, which are now being used by the EPA for sulfur dioxide, are a means of achieving pollution standards at potentially lower cost than standards

imposed on each emitter. The SO_2 permits represent a modified emissions-based policy.

9. Other types of marketable permits are: (a) The ambient-based system (ABS), which is the cost-minimizing method of meeting a given standard. An ABS requires polluters to hold permits for all regions into which their emissions flow. The government regulatory authority determines the aggregate number of permits consistent with the standard (or level of environmental quality) for each region, distributes the permits to existing polluters (or auctions them), and allows firms to trade. The market "price" of the permits is then the marginal cost of abatement for the marginal firm in each region. (b) The emissions-based system (EBS) defines the number of permits for a given region consistent with a desired standard in that region. Polluters can trade only within the region. Emissions within the region are treated as equivalent, regardless of their effect on environmental quality at different points within the region.
10. Simulation exercises for St. Louis covering various types of marketable permits have led to mixed results. The ABS is the most cost-efficient system, as expected, and guarantees that the ambient standard is always met, but it may not yield stable market prices under different pollution standards or at different receptor points in the system. The EBS results in very high compliance costs and may not achieve a given standard. A modified ABS with trades limited to one zone achieves most air quality targets at a cost second to the pure ABS.

DISCUSSION QUESTIONS

1. The province of Ontario wants to know whether it should open up a particular wilderness site for recreational use or allow forestry firms to harvest trees there. It will choose the activity that maximizes net benefits to the province (benefits minus costs), where benefits and costs include any nonmarket values such as pollution from forestry operations or the value of recreational benefits. What would make up the costs and benefits for each use of the land? Briefly explain how you would measure these costs and benefits.
2. How would a "price" be set for a factor input that is used jointly by two firms, where once either firm uses the factor, the other also receives the factor's services without paying for them?
3. Suppose that there are two lakes in a municipality. The municipal government enacts a water pollution standard that improves water quality at one lake (lake A) but does not change water quality at lake B. Demand for recreational services at lake A rises, while demand for recreation at lake B falls. Suppose that the inverse demand curve for recreation at both sites before the change in water quality is given by $P = 100 - 0.5Q$. After the standard is imposed, demand at site A shifts to $P = 120 - 0.4Q$, while demand at site B changes to $P = 60 - 0.2Q$. There is no charge for using the lake. How would you measure the benefits of improved water quality for the municipality?

4. Explain graphically and verbally under what circumstances a market for the trading of pollution permits will minimize the costs of meeting a given pollution standard.
5. *a.* Explain the differences between the ABS and EBS systems of marketable permits for pollution, in theory.
   b. What are the advantages and disadvantages of implementing each type of system?
   c. Which system would you advise using, and why, for each of the following pollution problem? (a) Toxic chemicals dumped into rivers and lakes; (b) chlorofluorocarbons.
   d. Could a marketable permit system be used when emissions of a pollutant are the result of "accidents" such as oil spills from supertankers or radioactivity "spills" from nuclear power plants? Explain why or why not.

NOTES

1. This section draws primarily from Freeman (1993), Chapter 13.
2. A number of proxy studies use theoretical methods to infer compensating and equivalent variations from the data.
3. See Smith (1992). *The Environmental Policy Paradox*, Englewood Cliffs, NJ: Prentice-Hall, Inc. for a discussion of these and other issues of environmental policy.
4. These numbers are cited in Daniel J. Fiorino (1995). *Making Environmental Policy.* Berkeley: University of California Press, p. 185.

SELECTED READINGS

Adamowicz, W., et al. (1994). "Combining Revealed and Stated Preference Methods for Valuing Environmental Amenities," *Journal of Environmental Economics and Management* 26, pp. 271–292.

Atkinson, S. E. (1983). "Marketable Permits and Acid Rain Externalities," *Canadian Journal of Economics* 16, pp. 704–722.

Atkinson, S. E., and T. H. Tietenberg (1982). "The Empirical Properties of Two Classes of Designs for Transferable Discharge Permit Markets," *Journal of Environmental Economics and Management* 9, pp. 101–121.

Braden, J. B., and C. D. Kolstad (1991). *Measuring the Demand for Environmental Quality.* Amsterdam: North Holland.

Bromley, D. W., ed. (1995). *Handbook of Environmental Economics.* Cambridge, Mass.: Blackwell.

Brookshire, D. S., et al. (1982). "Valuing Public Goods: A Comparison of Survey and Hedonic Approaches," *American Economic Review* 72, pp. 165–177.

Cameron, T. A., and J. Quiggin (1994). "Estimation Using Contingent Valuation Data from a 'Dichotomous Choice and Follow-Up' Questionnaire," *Journal of Environmental Economics and Management* 27, pp. 218–234.

Clark, D. E., and L. A. Nieves (1994). "An Interregional Hedonic Analysis of Noxious Facility Impacts on Local Wages and Property Values," *Journal of Environmental Economics and Management* 27, pp. 235–253.

Cline, W. R. (1992). *The Economics of Global Warming.* Washington: Institute for International Economics.

Crandall, R. (1992). "Policy Watch: Corporate Average Fuel Economy Standards," *Journal of Economic Perspectives* 6, Spring, pp. 171–180.

Cummings, R. G., D. S. Brookshire, and W. D. Shultze (1986). *Valuing Environmental Goods: An Assessment of the Contingent Valuation Method.* Totowa, N.J.: Rowland and Allanheld Publishers.

Dales, J. H. (1968). *Pollution, Property and Prices.* Toronto: University of Toronto Press.

Freeman, A. M. (1979). *The Benefits of Environmental Improvement: Theory and Practice.* Baltimore: Johns Hopkins Press.

Freeman, A. M. (1993). *The Measurement of Environmental and Resource Values.* Washington, D. C.: Resources for the Future.

Graves, P., et al. (1988). "The Robustness of Hedonic Price Estimation: Urban Air Quality," *Land Economics* 64, pp. 220–233.

Hanemann, M. (1991). "Willingness to Pay and Willingness to Accept: How Much Can They Differ?" *American Econmic Review* 81, pp. 635–647.

Johansson, Per-Olav (1987). *The Economic Theory and Measurement of Environmental Benefits.* Cambridge: Cambridge University Press.

Journal of Economic Perspectives 8 (1994). See articles by P. Portney, M. Hanemann, P. Diamond, and J. Hausman in "Symposium on Contingent Valuation Methodology."

Kahneman, D., and J. Knetsch (1992). "Valuing Public Goods: The Purchase of Moral Satisfaction," *Journal of Environmental Economics and Management* 22, pp. 57–70.

Knetsch, J. (1990). "Environmental Policy Implications of Disparities between Willingness to Pay and Compensation Demanded Measures of Values," *Journal of Environmental Economics and Management* 18, pp. 227–237.

Layard, R. G. (1994). *Cost-Benefit Analysis.* New York: Cambridge University Press.

Luken, R. A. (1990). *Efficiency in Environmental Legislation: A Benefit-Cost Analysis of Alternative Approaches.* Boston, Mass.: Kluwer Academic.

Mitchell, R. C., and R. T. Carson (1989). *Using Surveys to Value Public Goods: The Contingent Valuation Approach.* Washington, D. C.: Resources for the Future.

Montgomery, W. (1972). "Markets in Licenses and Efficient Pollution Control Programs," *Journal of Economic Theory* 5, pp. 395–418.

Organization for Economic Cooperation and Development, OECD (1995). *Environmental Taxation in OECD Countries.* Paris: OECD.

Portney, P. R. (1991). *Public Policies for Environmental Protection.* Washington, D. C.: Resources for the Future.

Seller, C., J. R. Stoll, and J-P Chavas (1985). "Validation of Empirical Measures of Welfare Changes: A Comparison of Nonmarket Techniques," *Land Economics* 61.

Shogren, J. F., et al. (1994). "Resolving Differences in Willingness to Pay and Willingness to Accept," *American Economic Review* 84, pp. 255–270.

Smith, V. K. (1986). *Measuring Water Quality Benefits.* Boston: Kluwer-Nijhoff.

Smith, Z. A. (1992). *The Environmental Policy Paradox.* Englewood Cliffs, N. J.: Prentice-Hall, Inc.

Tietenberg, T. (1985) *Emissions Trading, An Exercise in Reforming Pollution Policy.* Washington, D. C.: Resources for the Future.

PART III

NATURAL RESOURCE USE IN AN INTERTEMPORAL SETTING

The five chapters in Part III introduce and develop models of natural resource use in an intertemporal framework. These sorts of models look at how a resource is used year after year. Decisions taken today will affect the amount of the resource available for the future. We look at both nonrenewable resources such as minerals and energy products and renewable resources such as forests and fish. This book concludes with another look at sustainability; in this final chapter, many concepts introduced throughout the text are brought together to see how our natural resources can be used over time to sustain the economy and its people.

chapter 8

Nonrenewable Resource Use: The Theory of Depletion

INTRODUCTION

Nonrenewable resources include energy supplies—oil, natural gas, uranium, and coal—and nonenergy minerals—copper, nickel, bauxite, and zinc, to name a few. These resources are formed by geological processes that typically take millions of years, so we can view these resources for practical purposes as having a fixed *stock* of reserves. That is, there is a finite amount of the mineral in the ground, which once removed cannot be replaced.[1] Nonrenewability introduces some new problems and issues into the analysis of production from the mine or well that do not arise in the production of reproducible goods such as agriculture crops, fish, and timber.

A mine manager must determine not only how to combine variable factor inputs such as labor and materials with fixed capital, as does the farmer, but how quickly to run down the fixed stock of ore reserves through extraction of the mineral. A unit of ore extracted today means that less in total is available for tomorrow. Time plays an essential role in the analysis. Each period is different, because the stock of the resource remaining is a different size. What we are concerned with in an economic analysis of nonrenewable resources is how quickly the mineral is extracted—what the *flow* of production is over time, and when the stock will be exhausted.

In this chapter, we determine the efficient extraction path of the resource—the amount extracted in each time period. First, we examine the behavior of the individual mine operator who must find a rate of extraction over an appropriate time interval. We then develop the extraction profile of a mining *industry*. In all cases, we assume that perfect competition prevails in every market. We derive the paths of mineral output, prices, and rents over time under varying assumptions about the nature of the mining process. We see that industry price rises as less and less quantity is brought to market as each firm runs down its stock. The intuitive result emerges—that exhaustibility must be associated with rising prices. Finally we focus on the issue of running out of stock, of true exhaustion and how this event is factored into the analysis of rate of extraction. We touch on the following topics: valuing mining firms when they are inherently shrinking in size (economic depreciation), taxation of mining firms, quality variation in the stocks held by firms, the effect of durability of the stock (a stock of gold being mined versus a stock of oil) on extraction paths, and the way substitute sources of supply, including "backstop" sources, affect rates of extraction.

Our initial model is very simple and abstracts considerably from reality so that we can identify and examine basic concepts. The assumptions are gradually relaxed so that we can deal with increasingly complex but more realistic models. In examining the mine's and industry's extraction decision, we also illustrate the effects on output and prices over time of changes in particular variables affecting the mining process. What will be the effect on extraction over time of, for example, a change in extraction costs, different qualities of ore, a change in the discount rate, the imposition of taxes?

THE THEORY OF THE MINE

We begin with a simple model of resource extraction from an individual mine or oil deposit that operates in a perfectly competitive industry. The mine owner will seek to maximize the present value of profits from mineral extraction in a manner similar to that of a manager of a plant producing a reproducible good. An output level must be chosen that maximizes the difference between total revenues—the discounted value of future extractions $q_1, q_2, q_3, \ldots$ etc., multiplied by price, p, and total cost—the discounted value of dollars expended in getting each q out of the ground. The presence of the finite stock of the mineral modifies the usual maximization condition; marginal revenue (MR) equals marginal cost (MC), in 3 fundamental ways.

First, suppose we compare farming with copper extraction. The owner of the copper mine faces an opportunity cost not encountered by the farmer. This is the cost of using up the fixed stock at any point in time, or being left with smaller remaining reserves. To maximize profits, the operator must cover this opportunity cost of depletion. For a competitive firm manufacturing a reproducible good, the conditions for a profit maximum are to choose output such that $p(= MR) = MC$. The nonrenewable resource analogue requires $p = MC +$ the opportunity cost of depletion. How then would the mine owner measure this opportunity cost? It is the value of the unextracted resource, a resource rent related to those discussed in Chapter 2.

The second feature that differentiates nonrenewable resources from reproducible goods concerns the *value of the resource rent over time.* Deciding how quickly to extract a nonrenewable resource is a type of investment problem. Suppose one has a fixed amount of money to invest in some asset, be it a savings account, an acre of land, a government bond, or the stock of a nonrenewable resource in the ground. Which asset is purchased (and held onto over time) depends on the investor's expectation of the rate of return on that asset—the increase in its value over time. The investor obviously wants to purchase the asset with the highest rate of return. However, in a perfectly competitive environment with no uncertainty, all assets must, in a market equilibrium, have the same rate of return.

To see how this is so, consider what would happen if the economy had two assets, one that increased in value 10 percent per year, an another that increased at 20 percent per year. Assume that there is no risk associated with either asset. No one would invest in the asset earning only 10 percent; everyone would want the asset earning 20 percent. The price of the high-return asset would then increase, and the price of the low-return asset would decrease until their rates of return were equalized.

What exactly is the rate of return to a nonrenewable resource? The marginal return to the mine is the resource rent—the value of the ore in the ground. When there is a *positive* discount rate, the rent is positive and rises in nominal value as depletion occurs. If the resource rent did not increase in value over time, no one would purchase the mine, because the rate of return on alternative assets would be more valuable. In addition, the owner of an existing deposit would attempt to extract all the ore as quickly as is technically feasible. Why should one hold onto ore in the ground that is increasing in value at a rate less than can be earned on, say, a savings account? Alternatively, if the value of the ore is growing at a rate in excess of what one could earn in an alternative investment, there is no incentive to extract at all. Ore left in the ground is then more valuable to the mine owner than ore extracted. To have mineral extraction, then, the rental value of the mineral must be growing at the same rate as that of alternative assets.

There is a third condition imposed on the mine owner that does not occur with reproducible goods. The total amount of the natural resource extracted over time cannot exceed its total stock of reserves. We call this the *stock constraint.*

Let us now draw these strands together. Suppose a mine owner has a plan of quantities extracted roughly worked out by a rule of thumb. It remains to make the extraction plan somewhat "tighter." Should the owner extract one more ton of ore in this year's liftings or leave it for next year's liftings? If the ore is *taken out this year* and yields $10 profit, that profit (rent) can be put in the bank at, say, 8 percent and return $10(1.08) = $10.80 next year. If the ore is left in the ground and *taken out next year*, the mine owner might get a different price and reap a profit (rent) of $11. If so, more money will be made by deferring extraction of the extra ton until next year. (If the owner were to get only $10.75 upon extracting next year, it would pay to extract currently and sell the ore this year.) By doing this calculation repeatedly the mine owner arrives at the best extraction plan year by year.

Let us now examine the important features of nonrenewable resource extraction in more detail.

EXTRACTION FROM A MINE FACING A CONSTANT PRICE

The Efficient Extraction Path

One of the earliest economic analyses of mineral extraction appeared in 1914 in an article by L. C. Gray. In Gray's model, the owner of a small mine has to decide how much ore to extract and for how long a period of time. To solve this problem, Gray made a number of simplifying assumptions. First, he assumed that the market price of a unit of the mineral remained constant (in real terms) over the life of the mine. The producer knew the exact amount of reserves in the mine (the stock) prior to extraction. All the ore was of uniform quality. Extraction costs are an increasing function of the quantity removed in each period.

We could view Gray's mine as a gigantic block of pure copper. Price per ton is constant forever, while the marginal cost of cutting off a piece of copper rises with the size of the piece cut off. If 1 ton of copper is cut off, it will cost $500 to remove. If 10 tons are cut off in a period, the extraction costs could be $10,000. Total extraction costs in each period thus depend on the ore extracted in that period.[2] The economic problem is to cut off appropriate quantities in each period in order to maximize the present value of profits available from the stock of the mineral. The model has practical appeal, because in many mineral markets we do observe relatively constant prices over long periods of time.

To determine the efficient extraction path for the mine, we start with a simple model. Suppose that the mining company owns a known stock, S_0 tons (say of oil). As extraction proceeds, the stock shrinks by current extraction of q_t tons.

$$S_t - S_{t+1} = q_t \tag{8.1}$$

This is basic accounting. How fast to extract? In such a way as to maximize profits to the firm. The *profit in one period* (year) is $pq_t - C(q_t)$ where p is price per ton extracted and sold and $C(q_t)$ is the total cost of extracting q_t tons. Profits over all periods of extraction are

$$\pi = pq_0 - C(q_0) + \left(\frac{1}{1+r}\right)[pq_1 - C(q_1)] + \left(\frac{1}{1+r}\right)^2 [pq_2 - C(q_2)] + \dots + \left(\frac{1}{1+r}\right)^T [pq_T - C(q_T)] \tag{8.2}$$

where r is the discount (interest) rate. Profits, π, are a familiar present value, essentially a weighted sum of profits in each period.

Maximization requires that *marginal profit,*

$$\left(\frac{1}{1+r}\right)^t [p - MC(q_t)],$$

be the same in each period. That is, $MC\,(q_t)$ is marginal extraction cost, $dC\,(q_t)/dq_t$. The firm must choose q_t in period t and q_{t+1} in period $t + 1$ so that

$$\left(\frac{1}{1+r}\right)^t [p - MC(q_t)] = \left(\frac{1}{1+r}\right)^{t+1} [p - MC(q_{t+1})] \tag{8.3}$$

This is a familiar principle of maximization: allocate your input (oil in the ground) to your activity (extraction) to equalize *marginal* profit in any part of your activity.[3] Each period must have its quantity selected so that the marginal ton in each period contributes equally to overall profit. Since $\left(\frac{1}{1+r}\right)^t$ cancels on both sides of the equality of marginal profit relation, we can write it as

$$\frac{[p - MC(q_{t+1})] - [p - MC(q_t)]}{[p - MC(q_t)]} = r \tag{8.4}$$

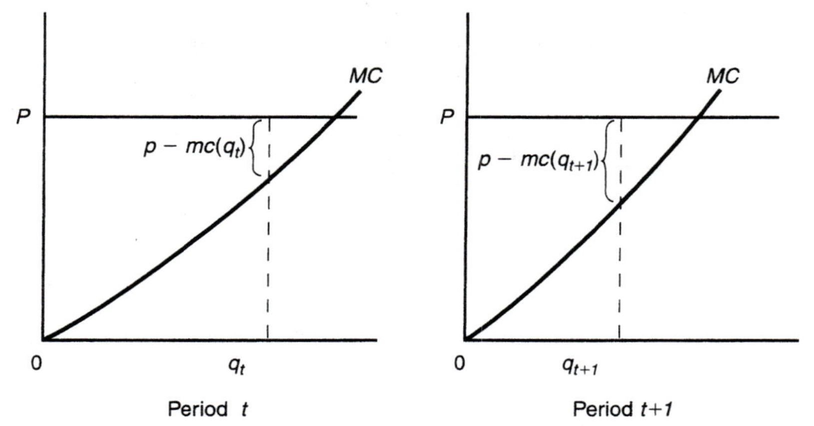

FIGURE 8.1. To maximize profits over all periods, rent $p-MC(q_{t+1})$ must be r percent larger than rent $p-MC(q_t)$. The firm will adjust quantities q_t and q_{t+1} to satisty this r percent rule.

Equation (8.4) is called the r percent rule of extraction. Equality of marginal profit across periods implies that, across two periods, $p - MC(q_t)$, is increasing at a rate equal to r percent. We illustrate this in Figure 8.1.

We seem to have solved the extractive firm's problem. How fast should it extract its stock S_0? At a rate $(q_{t+1} - q_t)/q_t$ so that $p - MC(q_t)$ is increasing at r percent. We know that any gap between price p and marginal cost is called *rent*. Hence our r percent rule can be read as: Rent on the marginal ton extracted in period t equals discounted rent on the marginal ton extracted in the next period. Rent in this case is referred to by various authors as *user cost*, *royalty*, *dynamic rent*, or *Hotelling rent*. Five names for the same thing! Rent exists here because overall supply S_0 is fixed and overall demand exceeds S_0. Price p exceeds marginal cost because supply S_0 is not expandable by production as it is in, say, the shoe industry. (In the shoe industry, price equals marginal production costs because more shoes get produced when demand exceeds supply). Finding extraction paths $q_0, q_1, \ldots q_T$, is thus a branch of profit maximization.

The next problem: How many periods of extraction should the mine operate to maximize the present value of profit? Obviously, mines cannot operate if they run out of stock S_0. We must therefore have any extraction program satisfying $q_0 + q_1 \ldots + q_T \leq S_0$. For this simple model, the operator will run out of reserves in the final period. But this leaves open the level of profits, $pq_0 - C(q_0)$, which is correct in the *first* period. If we had the correct q_0, then we could keep going with the r percent rule until the mine depleted the S_0 tons. Clearly the number of periods over which we extract the S_0 depends on the beginning level of extraction, q_0. But the correct q_0 cannot be chosen unless one knows "where" it will lead. Each value of q_0 implies a different path $q_0, q_1, \ldots, q_T$, spun out in accord with the r percent rule. The correct q_0 involves getting the *end* of the path correct. This is very basic to all economic decisions. For example, your career decision this year (being in college) affects how your life's activity will unfold. A good decision this year means good prospects in any future year, including your *end* years. Hence you allocate your time to an activity this year (going to college) that makes future rewards "optimal."

For our problem the marginal undiscounted profit in the final period, $p-MC(q_T)$, must be as large as possible,[4] as in Figure 8.2. Now the selection of the maximizing q_0 involves selecting q_T correctly (Figure 8.2) and applying the r percent rule backward until S_0 is used up. This is called backward induction. Get the end right and work back to see what getting the end right implies for actions today.

To summarize: For the firm to decide how to extract S_0 tons of oil, it must select a path $q_0, q_1, \ldots, q_T$ that maximizes the firm's profits. Since extraction occurs over many periods, it is the *present value* of profits that must be maximized. Maximizing the present value of profits involves (1) getting the rate of extraction $[q_{t+1} - q_t]/q_t$ to satisfy the r percent rule on rent $p-MC(q_t)$ in

$$\frac{[p - MC(q_{t+1})] - [p - MC(q_t)]}{p - MC(q_t)} = r$$

and (2) getting the number of periods of extraction to satisfy the END condition: $[p - MC(q_T)]$ is as large as possible.

The Value of the Mining Firm

Since any mine manager can work out the profit-maximizing way to use the mine's stock S_t tons remaining, there will be an agreed upon future extraction program

$$\overset{*}{q}_t, \overset{*}{q}_{t+1}, \ldots, \overset{*}{q}_T$$

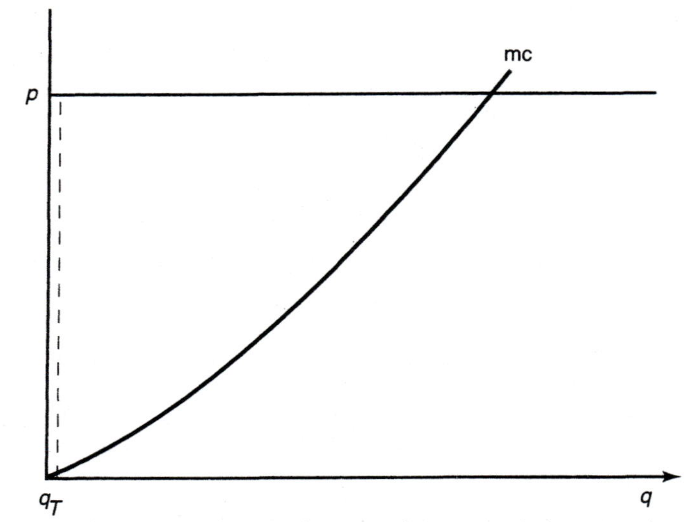

FIGURE 8.2. In the final period of extraction, quantity q_T extracted must make marginal profit, $p-MC(q_T)$, as large as possible.

at any date t. This implies an agreed upon current value of the firm with S_t tons remaining:

$$V_t = p\overset{*}{q}_1 - C\left(\overset{*}{q}_t\right) + \left(\frac{1}{1+r}\right)\left[p\overset{*}{q}_{t+1} - C\left(\overset{*}{q}_t\right)\right] + \dots + \left(\frac{1}{1+r}\right)^{T-t}\left[p\overset{*}{q}_T - C\left(\overset{*}{q}_T\right)\right]. \tag{8.5}$$

Thus the current value (selling price) Vt is discounted future profit along a maximizing extraction path. In the next period, the value V_{t+1} is less because $\overset{*}{q}_t$ tons were removed. V_{t+1} is the value of a mine with S_{t+1} tons remaining.

$$V_{t+1} = p\overset{*}{q}_{t+1} - C\left(\overset{*}{q}_{t+1}\right) + \left(\frac{1}{1+r}\right)\left[p\overset{*}{q}_{t+2} - C\left(\overset{*}{q}_{t+2}\right)\right] + \dots + \left(\frac{1}{1+r}\right)^{T-t+1}\left[p\overset{*}{q}_T - C\left(\overset{*}{q}_T\right)\right]. \tag{8.6}$$

The shrinkage in value V_t can be worked out easily by multiplying V_{t+1} by $1/(1 + r)$ and subtracting $V_{t+1}/(1 + r)$ from V_t. One gets

$$V_t - V_{t+1} \cong p\overset{*}{q}_t - C\left(\overset{*}{q}_t\right) + r\,V_t \tag{8.7}$$

This says: Value decline from extracting $\overset{*}{q}_t$ equals income from $\overset{*}{q}_t$ minus interest on value, rV_t. The "extra" rV_t term is present because a benefit from extraction is moving one period closer to future profits. Then equation (8.8)

$$\frac{p\overset{*}{q}_t - C\left(\overset{*}{q}_t\right) + \left[V_{t+1} - V_t\right]}{V_t} \tag{8.8}$$

is called the rate of return to the owners of the mine from mining $\overset{*}{q}_t$. Here $V_{t+1} - V_t$ is called *capital gains* (negative in this case) and $p\overset{*}{q}_t - C\left(\overset{*}{q}_t\right)$ is called current income from the mine (the asset). Asset management requires that the rate of return earned by the owners of the mine is equal to the market rate of return, r. The market rate of return is what V_t dollars invested in short-term government bonds will earn in one period.

A fundamental consequence of "correct" extraction for the firm is

$$V_t - V_{t+1} = \left[p - MC\left(\overset{*}{q}_t\right)\right]\overset{*}{q}_t \tag{8.9}$$

Or the decline in value of the firm from extracting $\overset{*}{q}_t$ is the *rent* associated with $\overset{*}{q}_t$.[5] Decline in value of an asset from "correct" use is called *economic depreciation*. Thus we have the *fundamental relation:* economic depreciation (decline in value of the mining firm) equals current rent associated with current extraction, $\overset{*}{q}_t$.

Economic depreciation and extraction is a subject with deep roots in history. For example, at one time the British monarch was assumed to own all mineral deposits. Mine operators had to lease their mines from the king. What is the appropriate change (royalty) the king should levy for the mine operator to "use" the king's mine?

The loss in value to the king is a reasonable answer. This loss in value is our $V_t - V_{t+1}$ or our economic depreciation. Hence the term *royalties* have been applied to our $V_t - V_{t+1}$. In modern times it is well understood that the taxing of current profit from a mine is unfair. It is unfair because the company is shrinking in value as its deposit is run down. Hence before taxes are assessed, the extractive firm should be allowed a *depletion allowance*. The "correct" depletion allowance or depreciation allowance is our $V_t - V_{t+1}$. We say correct because one can obtain (retrieve) the same extraction path with or without a tax on the extractive firm if deduction from gross profit for depletion effects is allowed by the government. The right depletion allowance restores the right extraction path. This is the feature of *neutral* taxation. In our case it means that rV_t becomes the *base* for taxation. This base is gross profit $p\overset{*}{q}_t - C(\overset{*}{q}_t)$ minus the depletion allowance $[p - MC(\overset{*}{q}_t)]\overset{*}{q}_t$ (equal to $V_t - V_{t+1}$). Using this economic depreciation as the depletion allowance implies neutrality with respect to the extraction path and value of the firm invariance (Samuelson, 1964). Getting depreciation or depletion right is of central importance in the taxation of extractive firms and also in the recent analysis of "greening" the national accounts (see Chapter 12). Economic depreciation of an oil reserve is literally current *disinvestment* in the reserve (the asset).

To summarize: The market value of the firm is the discounted profit remaining under profit-maximizing extraction. The market value declines as extraction proceeds because the firm has less remaining reserves to extract from. Decline in market value is reflected in current rent, $[p - MC(q_t)]q_t$, on the amount currently extracted. Decline in market value is the *economic depreciation* of the mine, or "depletion," as it is often referred to. The correct depletion allowance for an extractive firm leads to neutrality in the effects of taxation on the profit of the firm.

EXTRACTION BY A COMPETITIVE MINERAL INDUSTRY

In a competitive industry, such as the oil extraction sector, each firm is a price taker. But as extraction proceeds, the price of oil should rise. Each firm will see the same "industry price" rising as it extracts less from its stock period by period. Our earlier analysis, with output price constant, remains valid for a firm except that, in the extraction calculation, the firm's manager now uses a price schedule, $p_0, p_1, p_2, \ldots, p_T$ in place of the schedule $p_0 = p_1 = p_2 = \ldots = p_T = p$ that we used before. The firm's manager does not take any old rising price schedule; he or she uses a predicted future industry price schedule, and in equilibrium, each firm predicts the same schedule and the predicted schedule turns out to fulfill each manager's expectations (this is a form of perfect foresight and rational expectations). The predicted future price path is the observed future price path.

Two-Period Model for a Competitive Industry

A simple mathematical and graphical model will illustrate the derivation of an efficient extraction profile for a nonrenewable natural resource. The objective of the industry is to maximize the profits from extraction. Profits will be maximized when the rent obtained from extracting the nonrenewable resource is maximized. It is assumed that the industry operates for two periods, then closes. This is like our two-period model of the mine, except that now the price of the mineral is no longer constant but is determined by market forces for the mineral. As before, extraction in the second period will have an opportunity cost—the forgone rents (and interest paid on those rents) that could be earned if extraction had occurred in the first period. Thus, second-period rents must be discounted at the current interest rate. Maximization of rent requires the industry to maximize the present value of rent by choosing output in periods 1 and 2 subject to the constraint that the sum of extraction over the two periods equals the total stock of ore in the ground.

The problem for the industry can be defined mathematically as follows:

$$\underset{\{q_0,\, q_1\}}{\text{Maximize}}\ R = (B(q_0) - cq_0) + (B(q_1) - cq_1)/(1 + r) \tag{8.10}$$

$$\text{subject to:} \qquad q_0 + q_1 = S_0$$

where $B(q_t)$ is the consumer surplus from the extracted mineral during time period t ($t = 0, 1$), q_t is industry extraction in period t, c is the constant per unit extraction costs, r is the rate of interest, and S_0 is the initial stock of resources. The stock cannot increase in size over the two periods of extraction (there are no discoveries). This is a constrained optimization problem that can be written as one expression:

$$(B(q_0) - cq_0) + (B(q_1) - cq_1)/(1 + r) + \lambda(S_0 - q_0 - q_1) \tag{8.11}$$

where λ is a Lagrange multiplier.[6] Price, p_t, is $dB(q_t)/dq_t$, change in consumer surplus.

This problem can be solved in a manner analogous to that presented previously. The crucial distinction between the industry model and that of the single mine is that we must examine the demand curve explicitly and derive a unique price for the resource in each period the mineral industry operates. In the two-period model, the time to depletion is given (2 periods), whereas in the many-period model we examine below we must also determine how long the industry continues to extract ore (length of time T). We now derive the solution to the maximization of equation (8.11). The first-order conditions are:

$$\partial R/\partial q_0 = p_0 - c - \lambda = 0 \tag{8.12}$$

$$\partial R/\partial q_1 = (p_1 - c)/(1 + r) - \lambda = 0 \tag{8.13}$$

$$\partial R/\partial \lambda = S_0 - q_0 - q_1 = 0 \tag{8.14}$$

We are looking for values of q_0 and q_1 such that equations (8.12), (8.13), and (8.14) are satisfied. To help solve for these values of q, note that we can eliminate λ from equations (8.12) and (8.13) by solving each equation for λ, so that:

$$p_0 - c = \lambda \tag{8.15a}$$

$$(p_1 - c)/(1 + r) = \lambda \tag{8.15b}$$

Setting (8.15a) equal to (8.15b), we find

$$p_0 - c = (p_1 - c)/(1 + r) \tag{8.16}$$

Equations (8.15) and (8.16) are very important conditions for efficient extraction of a nonrenewable resource. Equations (8.15a) and (8.15b) require that price minus marginal cost in the initial period and the discounted value of price minus marginal cost in the second period must be equal to λ. What this condition says is that each owner would be faced with the following decision. We can call it a *flow* condition. Should I mine and sell a ton of ore this period and earn $(p_t - c)$ dollars of profit, or should I wait until the next period and extract, sell, and receive $(p_{t+1} - c)$ dollars of profit for the ton? If the prices p_t and p_{t+1} were such that equation (8.16) was satisfied—that is, $(p_t - c) = (p_{t+1} - c)/(1 + r)$—each owner would be indifferent between selling in this period or the next period. Since all owners and deposits are identical (there are no quality differences among mines), all are indifferent.

If there was a general tendency by sellers to wait until the next period, current output would fall and current price would rise. Sellers would then find it profitable to sell now and put their rents (or profits) into an asset earning r percent. If there was a tendency to sell a large quantity of ore in the initial period, the current price would fall, and mine operators would be reluctant to sell until future periods. Therefore, the flow condition will be met by each firm seeking to maximize profits to ensure extraction in each period, and the market forces of supply and demand will ensure that the condition is met.

Equations (8.15) also provide an interpretation of λ. It is the value of rent on the marginal unit of ore extracted when the industry is in equilibrium. This ***marginal*** rent is defined as the difference between the present value of price and marginal cost of extraction, as can be seen easily by equation (8.15b). In equation (8.15a), price and marginal cost are not discounted, because this is the initial period of operation.

Equation (8.16) eliminates λ by setting (8.15a) equal to (8.15b). It too has an economic interpretation: *Present value of rents must be the same in each period the mine operates.* Finally, the stock constraint is represented by equation (8.14).

A solution to the model can be illustrated with the aid of a numerical example. Suppose the fixed stock of ore is 2500 tons. Assume that demand for the resource is given by a linear inverse demand curve, $p_t = 700 - 0.25q_t$. The demand curve is assumed to be the same in each period. This is called a stationary demand curve. Unit cost of extraction is \$200. These are also marginal costs of extraction because of the assumption of constant costs (therefore marginal costs equal average costs). The rate of interest at which rents are discounted is 5 percent. Marginal rent in period 0 is found by substituting the values for price from the demand curve and marginal cost in equation (8.15a).

$$p_0 - c = (700 - 0.25q_0) - 200 = 500 - 0.25q$$

The present value of marginal rent in period one is found analogously using equation (8.15b).

$$(p_t - c)/(1 + r) = (500 - 0.25q_1)/(1.05) = 476 - .238q_1$$

The constraint expressed in equation (8.14) requires

$$q_0 + q_1 = 2500, \text{ or } q_1 = 2500 - q_0$$

We are now ready to solve the model for q_0 and q_1. Equation (8.16) requires

$$500 - 0.25q_0 = 476 - 0.238q_1$$

The resource stock constraint is met by substituting $q_1 = 2500 - q_0$ in the expression above,

$$500 - 0.25q_0 = 476 - 0.238\,(2500 - q_0).$$

This is an equation in one unknown, q_0, which is readily solved: $q_0 = 1268$. Once q_0 is known, equation (8.14) is used to derive $q1$, which is equal to 1232. Note that output in the second period is less than that in the first. Output declines over time.

From the information about q_0 and q_1, the market price for the extracted ore in each period can be found by substituting q_0 and q_1 in the demand curve for each period. We see that:

$p_0 = 700 - 0.25(1268)$ and $p_1 = 700 - 0.25(1232)$
$p_0 = \$383$ and $p_1 = \$392$

The nominal price of extracted ore in the second period exceeds the first-period price. *Market prices for the nonrenewable natural resource rise over time.*

Finally, the undiscounted value of λ in each period and its present value can be calculated using equations (8.15). Denote this undiscounted value by the symbol μ. Then $\mu_0 = p_0 - c = 383 - 200 = \$183$, and $\mu_1 = p_1 - c = 392 - 200 = \$192$. We see that μ rises in value over time. Equation (8.16) says that the present values of μ must be the same. Checking this, we divide μ_1 by $(1 + r)$ to obtain a present value of approximately \$183. *The present value of rent is constant over time.*

What happens to the value of resource rent over time in this simple model? We can find out by looking at the rate of change in μ, the undiscounted value of marginal rent, defined as $(\mu_1 - \mu_0)/\mu_0$. For the numerical example, this works out to be $(192-183)/183 = 0.05$. Expressing the right-hand side as a percent, we see that *undiscounted resource rent per ton "grows" at 5 percent*—the interest rate at which all assets, including this nonrenewable resource, are discounted. This is Hotelling's r percent rule.

If resource rents grow at rate r, at what rate do mineral prices grow? From our example, the rate of change in mineral prices is $(p_1 - p_0)/p_0 = (392 - 383)/383 = 0.023 = 2.3$ percent. As long as extraction costs are constant over time and per unit extraction, *mineral prices grow at a rate less than the interest rate.*

To summarize: In a two-period model of a competitive nonrenewable resource industry:

1. Mineral prices rise over time at a rate less than the rate of interest.
2. Undiscounted value of mineral rents rises at the rate of interest.
3. Present value of mineral rents is constant over time.
4. Quantity extracted per period falls over time.

The prices and amounts extracted in each period can be illustrated as in Figure 8.3. The horizontal axis is the total amount of the resource extracted in the two periods, 2500 tons. We read q_0 from left to right and q_1 from right to left. The left-hand vertical axis measures rent in period 0. The right-hand axis measures the present value of

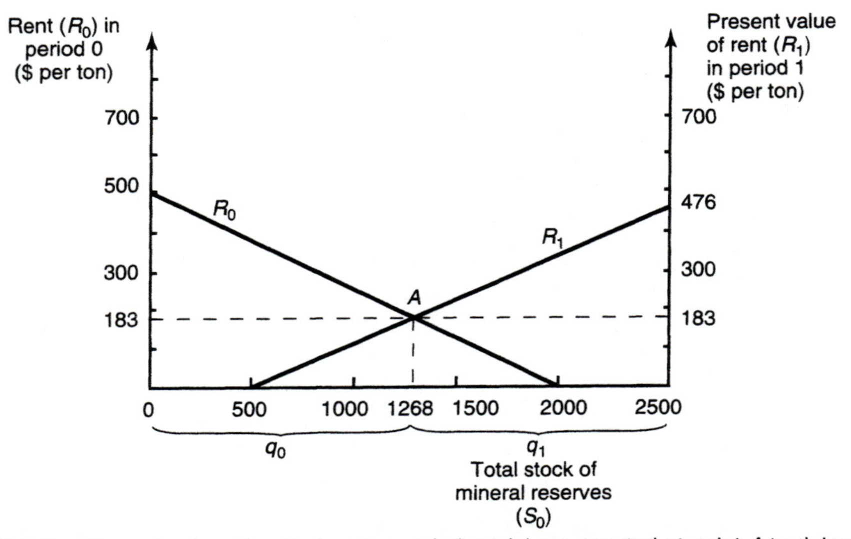

FIGURE 8.3. Present value of rents in a two-period model are equated at point A to determine output in period 0 (1268 tons) and period 1 (2500 − 1268 = 1232 tons).

rent in period one. Rent in period 0 as defined by equation (8.15a) is $500 - 0.25q_0$, a decreasing function of q. This equation is labeled R_0 in Figure 8.3. The present value of rent in period 1, denoted R_1, is $476 - 0.238q_1$.

Equation (8.16) requires that R_0 equal R_1. This occurs at the intersection of the two curves at point A. At this point, the sum of mineral extracted over the two periods is 2500, the total stock. From the figure, q_0 is 1268 and q_1 is 2500 − 1268, or 1232 units. The present value of rent is also shown on Figure 8.3. Reading across from point A to the right or left axis, we find the value of $\mu_0 = \mu_1(1 + r) = 183$.

In the multi-period case, each firm maximizes profit as before, but now a firm's $\{q_t\}$ schedule satisfies

$$\frac{p_{t+1} - MC(q_{t+1}) - [p_t - MC(q_t)]}{p_t - MC(q_t)} = r$$

The profit-maximizing condition is still an r percent rule, but output price varies across periods. Suppose that there are identical firms. Then in period t, each firm is extracting q_t tons and industry output is $nq_t = Q_t$ and price is $p(Q_t)$, as in Figure 8.4.

Note then that each firm's decision about quantity takes price as given because each firm is a small producer. But equilibrium industry price satisfies market clearing. Supply equals demand at price p_t.

We have, then, constructed an industry equilibrium comprising many small extractive firms. The new element is the endogenous future industry price in the calculation. A natural reaction is to say that each extraction manager cannot predict accurately into the distant future in order to make an equilibrium work. The analysis

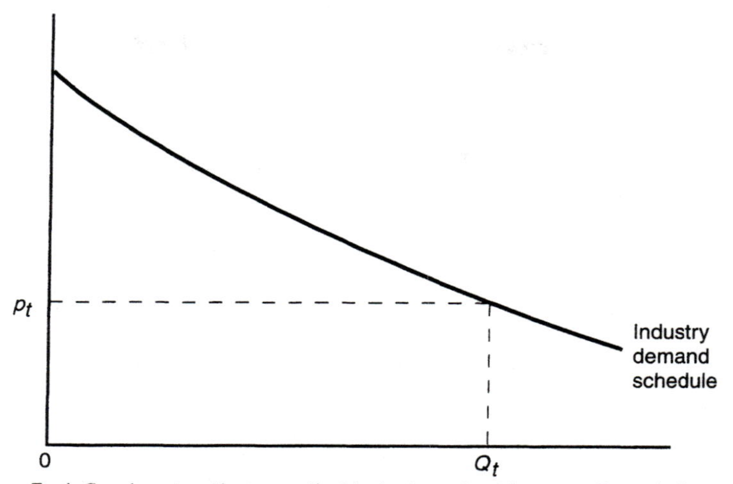

FIGURE 8.4. Each firm is extracting q_t so that industry output is $nq_t = Q_t$; and given the industry demand schedule, we have output price p_t.

requires extractors to behave in a superhuman fashion. Each manager forms a prediction of future industry price, independent of the decision-making activity of another extractor (they do not collaborate or communicate) and each ends up observing his or her prediction fulfilled. How is this possible? The answer is as follows: If an extractor does not predict and calculate well, his or her actual profits will be less than a maximum. An outsider can buy this manager out and increase the value of the firm—make more profit. The possibility of a buyout by an outsider forces managers to "get it right." Thus, though perfect foresight seems like an extreme assumption, the alternative—approximate foresight—implies a world of endless buyouts and rotating owners.

A central prediction of exhaustible-resource theory is rising output price. Each extractor mines less period by period, and industry price must rise, given a standard industry demand schedule. Exhaustibility means running out or severe output contraction, and price must rise. This was first made precise by Hotelling (1931). In his model each ton of output is owned by a separate firm. Each firm has the same cost c to extract its 1 ton. There is an industry demand schedule $p(Q)$, declining in Q. An industry equilibrium is represented by welfare maximization. Industry output Q_t in period t yields social surplus $B(Q_t) - cQ_t$ where $B(Q_t)$ is the area under the demand curve up to quantity Q_t. Thus $B(Q_t)$ is gross social-consumer surplus. Note that, by construction, $dB(Q_t)/d\,Q_t$ is $p(Q_t)$. Net social-consumer surplus in a period is $B(Q_t) - Q_t\,c$. The present value of surpluses for extraction schedule $Q_0, Q_1, Q_2, \ldots, Q_T$ is

$$W = B(Q_0) - Q_0c + \left(\frac{1}{1+r}\right)[B(Q_1) - Q_1c] + \left(\frac{1}{1+r}\right)^2[B(Q_2) - Q_2c] + \ldots + \left(\frac{1}{1+r}\right)^T[B(Q_T) - Q_T\,c]$$

For industry stock S_t we have $Q_t = S_t - S_{t+1}$ or the contraction in the (say) oil stock in the ground is current extraction Q_t. This is a materials balance requirement. With each firm owning 1 ton, Q_t currently extracted means that Q_t firms are extracting their 1 ton in period t. All firms are identical. A competitive industry equilibrium (and social welfare maximum) occurs when an extraction path $Q_0, Q_1, \ldots, Q_T$ maximizes W above. This maximization problem is of the same structure as that for our profit maximizing extractive firm. Thus W will be a maximum when marginal net surplus is equal across periods, i.e., when

$$\left(\frac{1}{1+r}\right)^t d\frac{[B(Q_t) - Q_t c]]}{dQ_t} = \left(\frac{1}{1+r}\right)^{t+1} d\frac{[B(Q_{t+1}) - Q_{t+1}c]]}{dQ_{t+1}}$$

and recalling that $dB(Q_t)/d\,Q_t = p(Q_t)$, this condition reduces to the Hotelling rule,

$$\frac{[p(Q_{t+1})-c] - [p(Q_t)-c]}{p(Q_t)-c} = r$$

which is an r percent rule in constant unit costs but varying prices. We illustrate this rule in Figure 8.5.

In Figure 8.5 we observe that rent $p_t - c$ must rise at r percent in a competitive industry extraction program. In each period Q_t firms bring their ton to market and each firm's profit on the ton is $p_t - c$. Since $p_t - c$ is rising at r percent, *each firm makes the same profit in terms of present value.* Hence each firm is indifferent as to the period when it extracts.

Since each firm makes the same profit $p_t - c$ in present value, what exactly is this unique level numerically? Make $p_T - c$ in the last period as large as possible, and this will be the profit level that each firm gets, valued in period 0, the beginning. The term p_T is the intercept of the demand curve (the choke price) with the price axis.[7] The value Q_T will be approximately zero or "jammed" against the vertical axis. Thus the complete solution $Q_T, Q_{T-1}, \ldots, Q_0$ follows from setting Q_T at zero and using the

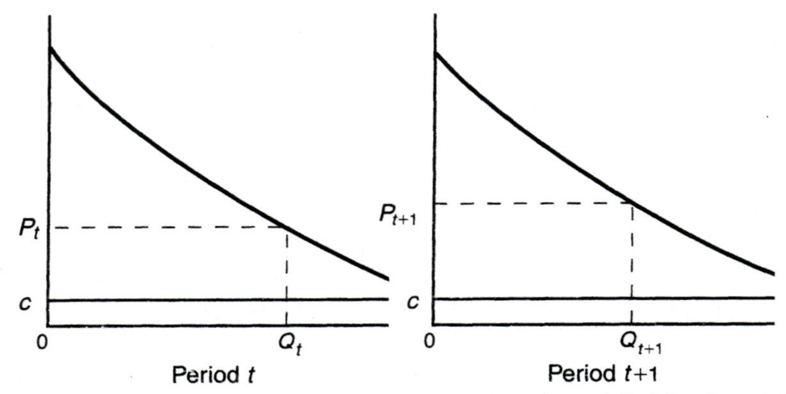

FIGURE 8.5. This competitive industry extraction program is satisfied by Q_t and Q_{t+1}. Thus $p_{t+1} - c$ is made r percent larger than $p_t - c$.

r percent rule to generate all preceding Q_t until the industry stock S_0 runs out. This exactly parallels the solution for the extractive firm. Here industry price and quantity are adjusted period by period. (For the problem with the extractive firm, marginal cost and quantity are adjusted.)

To summarize: In a competitive extractive industry with identical firms, each with a single ton of oil, industry price net of unit extraction costs rises at r percent. Each firm makes $p(Q_0) - c$ of profit in present value and extraction terminates with initial stock S_0 used up and $p(Q_T) - c$ at its largest value. In this final period Q_T equals zero.

Figure 8.6 puts together the components of the industry model: linear demand curve, stock constraint, flow and terminal conditions. In panel (a), a linear demand curve is illustrated. As usual, the curve has a negative slope and shows the relationship between the market price of the mineral in each time period and total quantity demanded. The price, $\bar{p}$, is called the *choke price*, and it reflects a feature of the linear demand curve: At some price, no one is willing to buy more of the mineral. Ideally, the industry (and each mine operator) would like to see the stock of the mineral go to zero at exactly the point that demand goes to zero. This will happen if the last unit of output for the industry is purchased at the price $\bar{p}$.

In Figure 8.6 (b), a *time path* diagram is presented. A time path shows the relationship between the value of a time-dependent variable and time. Here, we illustrate the time path of undiscounted mineral prices and can also derive the undiscounted mineral rents (μ) that arise from the efficient extraction of mineral. The current market price of the extracted mineral in each period is on the vertical axis; time (in years) is on the horizontal axis. Before we solve for the efficient extraction path, we can identify two values in this time path diagram. Choke price $\bar{p}$ can be drawn at the same level as it appears on the industry demand curve in Figure 8.6(a). Also, because we have assumed constant marginal costs of extraction, we can illustrate these as another horizontal line drawn at level c. If the price of the mineral is known, the current value of rent is illustrated as the difference between price and the marginal cost of extraction, c.

Figure 8.6(d) is another time path, the *extraction path*. Mineral output extracted in each period of time is given on the vertical axis; time is on the horizontal axis. Figure 8.6(c) has no economic interpretation. It is simply a 45-degree line for output (output is on both axes here) that allows us to translate output levels from the demand curve in (a) to identical output levels for the extraction path in (d).

We are ready to determine an efficient output path and from that derive efficient market price and mineral rent paths for the industry. It is important to remember that we are dealing with a competitive industry. Firms in this industry take the market price of the extracted mineral as given and maximize profits by choosing output. As we have noted, the appropriate way to derive the output and resulting paths is to start at the end of the extraction period, T, and work backward. An efficient industry will want to exhaust its stock of the mineral when the price of the mineral reaches $\bar{p}$. At this price and time, extraction equals zero, as shown in Figure 8.6(a) as $q_T = 0$. What should extraction be in the period immediately before T? We know from the flow condition that undiscounted mineral rents must rise at rate r from period to period.

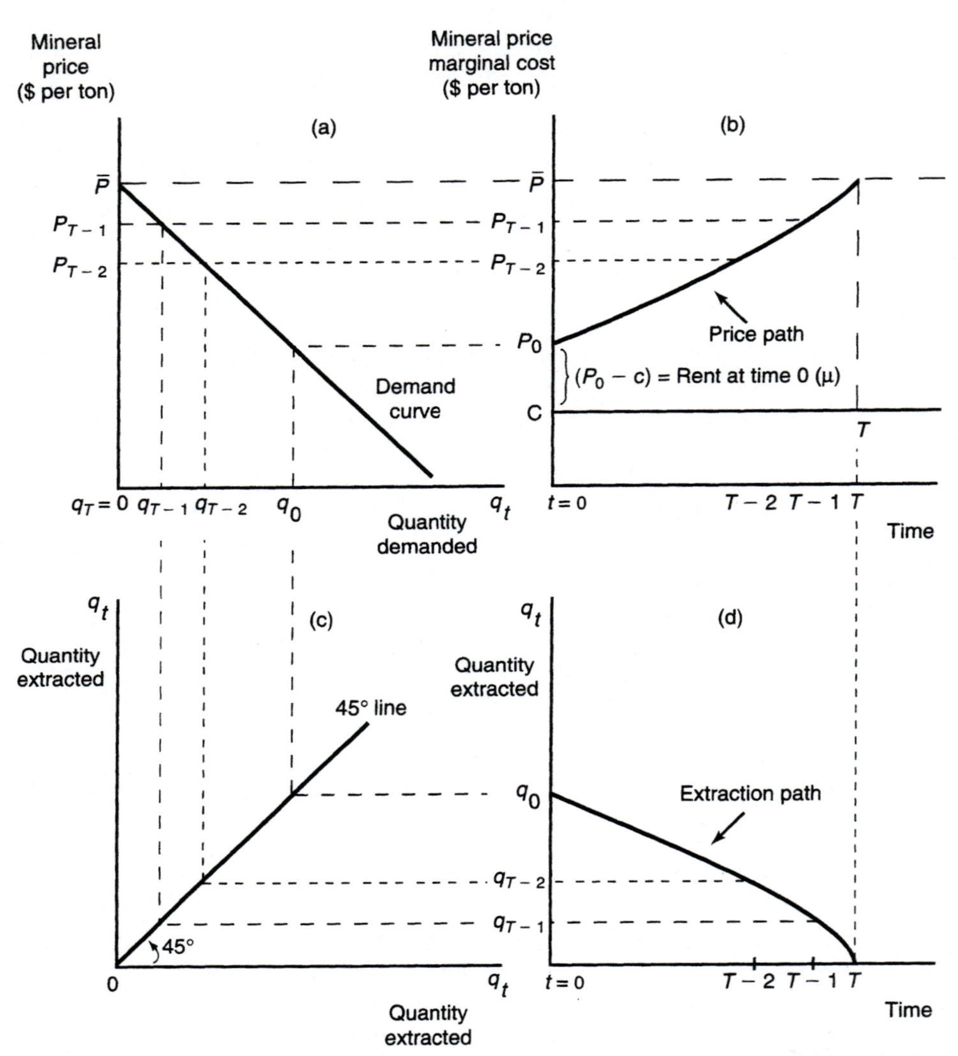

FIGURE 8.6. Given a market demand curve for minerals (a), the time paths of mineral prices and extraction are derived for the competitive industry in (b) and (d). Mineral extraction must decline over time to allow market prices to rise. With rising mineral prices, rents can increase at the rate of interest over time. The cumulative amount of extraction—the area under the extraction path in (d)—must exhaust the total stock of mineral reserves.

We can therefore work backward from T to $T-1$ by solving for p_{T-1} from equation (8.16), now expressed in terms of p_T and p_{T-1}:

$$\frac{(p_T - c) - (p_{T-1} - c)}{(p_{T-1} - c)} = r$$

This equation can be solved for p_{T-1} because we know that p_T is equal to $\bar{p}$, and c and r are given. Once we know p_{T-1} we can find from the demand curve the level of output that yields p_{T-1} and thus can identify a point on the extraction path. This process is repeated for all time periods back to zero. Notice that we have identified the time path of market prices in Figure 8.6(b). Mineral rents can be found for each period by subtracting marginal costs from the market price. We can ensure that rents grow at rate r (or decline at rate r from T) by inspecting the values of u in each time period.

So far, we have used the linear demand curve with its choke price and the flow condition to determine the time path of extraction. There may be a large number of time paths that could be drawn. But there will be only one such path that satisfies the flow *and* stock conditions (as well as the terminal condition). We can check the stock condition by inspecting Figure 8.6(d). The stock condition requires the cumulative amount of mineral extracted to be equal to its initial (and fixed) stock. The *area under the extraction path* is the cumulative amount of ore extracted. Thus there will be only one mineral price path that satisfied the flow condition and exhausts the total stock of ore in exactly T years. This path is illustrated in Figure 8.6(d).

How do we know that the path we have chosen is the one that maximizes the industry's rent from extracting minerals? Figure 8.7 shows the same four panels as Figure 8.6 and three possible paths of mineral output and prices. Path A is identical to what we have identified as the efficient path in Figure 8.6. Path B illustrates a higher rate of extraction than A after time O. If more ore is extracted in each time period than under path A, market prices will rise more slowly, and at $\hat{T}$ the industry depletes its total stock of reserves. The amount $\hat{q}$, is extracted in period $\hat{T}$, and this quantity exhausts the reserves at a price $\hat{p}$, which is below the choke price, $\bar{p}$. This path is inefficient because the industry is forgoing rents that could have been earned beyond $\hat{T}$ if it had extracted more slowly. The final price and quantity are illustrated in Figure 8.7.

With path C, less mineral is extracted in each period than with path A. In this case, the industry will reach the choke price before all the mineral is extracted from the reserves. Extraction will go to zero at time $\tilde{T}$ because there is no demand for the mineral. The industry will be left with unextracted mineral in the ground. No consumer will pay more than $\bar{p}$ for the resource. Again, this is inefficient because the industry is forgoing rents they could have earned under a faster extraction profile. The efficient path ensures that the terminal condition is met: Reserves, extraction, and quantity demanded all reach zero at exactly the same time.

An Empirical Test of the r Percent Rule

Suppose that we go the New York stock exchange and collect data on a group of oil extraction firms. For firm i, we will get reports on current reserves (stocks) S_0^i and on current extraction costs c^i and current market value V^i. The value V^i is equity value or discounted profit, net of debt and tax obligations. This value can be written as a present value of net profit in

$$V^i = [p_0 - c^i]\, q_0^i + \left(\frac{1}{1+r}\right)[p_i - c^i]\, q_1^i + \ldots + \left(\frac{1}{1+r}\right)^T [p_T - c^i]\, q_T^i$$

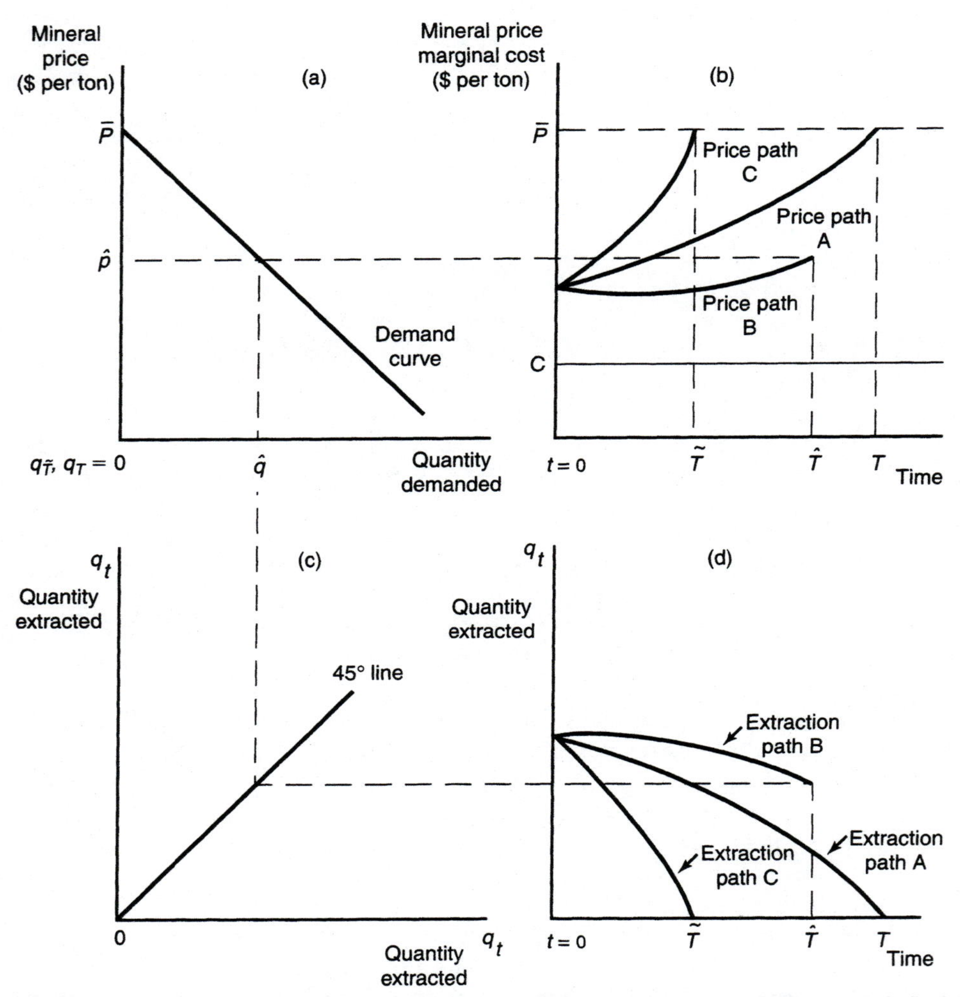

FIGURE 8.7. Inefficient extraction and price paths are compared with the efficient path A. Path B illustrates extraction that is too fast relative to the efficient path. More is extracted in each time period under path B than under path A. Mineral reserves are depleted before the choke price is reached if path B is followed. Path C illustrates extraction that is too slow relative to the efficient path. The choke price is reached before the mineral reserves are depleted. Paths B and C are inefficient.

Miller and Upton (1985) set this up and pointed out that $[p_0 - c^i]$ must rise at r percent in the competitive industry model. Hence V^i can be written as

$$V^i = \left[p_0 - c^i\right]\left[q_0^i + q_1^i + \ldots + q_T^i\right] = \left[p_0 - c^i\right] S_0^i$$

Miller and Upton regress, in a statistical fitting, V_i/S_0^i on $[p_0 - c^i]$ for a group of firms. If the r percent rule is operative, the estimated intercept for the regression should be zero and the slope (coefficient on $p_0 - c^i$) should be near unity. They find this to show up reasonably well with their data and conclude that the r percent rule is indeed governing increases for extractive oil firms.

Actually, for their agrument to work, very delicate assumptions are required on each firm's extraction costs relative to the other firms. In a Hotelling world, each firm has identical costs, and this assumption will work for Miller and Upton. But in the real world, variation in extraction costs among firms demands a more complicated formulation of an industry equilibrium. In fact, Adelman (1986) has argued that the Hotelling formulation cannot be relevant because the values of $p - c^i$ observed among oil extracting nations are quite different in any particular year. The short answer to Adelman's critique is that extracting units need to have more complicated and realistic cost structures specified before an industry equilibrium is derived. At a minimum, one should have extraction costs reflecting differences in the qualities of deposits among extractors and differences in qualities within each deposit. We turn to this topic next. Box 8.1 presents other empirical tests of the Hotelling model.

Quality Variation in a Deposit

Consider the case of a deposit being worked by a mining company in which the deeper the deposit is mined, the poorer is the quality of mineral. The simple way to represent this is to say that costs of extraction rise with depth or costs of extraction increase with cumulative extraction. The cost of extracting 10 tons is higher if 10,000 tons have been extracted than if only 1000 tons have been taken out. That is, $C\,(10;\,10{,}000) > C\,(10;\,1000)$ or generally $\partial C\,(q;\,S)/\partial S < 0$. Profit-maximizing extraction for the firm requires that

$$p - \partial C(q(t);\,S(t))/\partial q(t) = \left(\frac{1}{1+r}\right)\{p - \partial C(q(t+1);\,S(t+1))/\partial q(t) - \partial C\,(q(t+1);\,S(t+1))/\partial S(t+1))\}$$

We have a new term, $\partial C/\partial S$, in the next-period marginal profit, called a *stock size effect*—short for the effect of a change in stock size on extraction costs. We illustrate this in Figure 8.8.

Decline in quality means that current extraction q_t imposes costs on subsequent extractions in the sense that more extraction gets the mining company into poorer-quality ore faster. Thus one can view

$$p - MC_t + \left(\frac{1}{1+r}\right)\frac{\partial C}{\partial S}$$

as the net value of the marginal ton extracted today. The value of $\partial C/\partial S$ is negative and reflects future higher costs "caused" by current extraction. We will digress to

BOX 8.1 Tests of the *r* Percent Rule

A number of empirical tests of the *r* percent rule have been carried out for mines and nonrenewable resource industries. Many find that rents do *not* grow at the rate of interest in the economy. Sometimes the explanation for the rejection of the *r* percent rule is straightforward; for example, there are statistical difficulties and problems with data, or a more complex model is needed to explain the industry. A particular problem arises for certain mines and industries that produce more than one metal from an ore body. The *r* percent rule then becomes quite complex.

Halvorsen and Smith (1991) test the *r* percent rule adjusted for stock size effects in extraction costs with data from the Canadian metal mining industry over the period 1954–1974. Their data reject the rule. However, the data are aggregated over all firms in the industry as well as different types of metals. While the Hotelling model pertains to the industry level, it was not intended to cover a *range* of industries. Young (1992) uses data for firms extracting copper to test the *r* percent rule and, again, rejects it. Farrow (1985) uses data for a single mine over the period 1975–1981. The mine produces three joint outputs. Farrow examines the basic Hotelling model we have outlined plus some variations including cases with an interest rate that varies over time, a constraint on output, and specific types of price expectations. The empirical model is used to reveal the firm's implicit discount rate. Farrow finds this discount rate to be *negative.* One of the factors underlying this result could be the assumption of a constant grade for the mineral in the ore deposit. Even within a deposit, ore grades can vary as extraction proceeds deeper into the ground. More complex optimization rules result.

Though disquieting, these tests reflect the rejection of a particular version of the Hotelling model for the extractive firm or industry. Some form of profit maximization must be going on, or else the firms in these studies would be bought out by agents who do maximize profits. When more complex models are used, the simple *r* percent rule is no longer obtained.

A study by Su (1996) supports the *r* percent rule for the coal industry in Canada for the period 1949–1993. Note that this study has a longer time horizon than the others cited above. The model assumed that firms base decisions about extraction on expected prices, and that extraction costs can be a function of the stock of ore remaining in the deposit. Hotelling's rule for this framework is that resource rents will grow at the rate of interest minus the *stock effect* caused by rising extraction costs as depletion progresses. Su finds that the real discount rate implied by the data for the coal industry was between 3.6 percent and 4.4 percent. The real rate of return on all assets over this period was 4.43 percent.

Sources: S. Farrow (1985). "Testing the Efficiency of Extraction from a Stock Resource," *Journal of Political Economy* 93, pp. 452–487. R. Halvorsen and T. R. Smith (1991). "A Test of the Theory of Exhaustible Resources," *Quarterly Journal of Economics* 105, pp. 123–140. N. Su (1996). "A Test of the Theory of Exhaustible Resources: The Case of Coal," master's project, Simon Fraser University. D. Young (1993). "Cost Specification and Firm Behavior in a Hotelling Model of Resource Extraction," *Canadian Journal of Economics* 25, pp. 41–59.

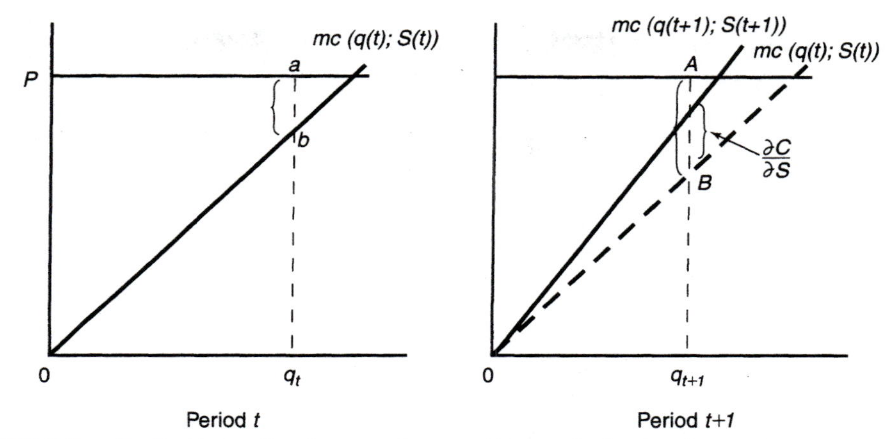

FIGURE 8.8. Decline in quality shows up here as the marginal extraction cost *rotates* upward over time. Costs within the deposit increase with cumulative extraction. Distance *ab* to distance *AB* increases by *r* percent. Distance *AB* comprises both *p-MC* and stock size effect $\partial C/\partial S$.

show how to derive our adjusted r percent rule, illustrated in Figure 8.8. We make use of the fact that $q_t = S_t - S_{t+1}$. Thus a firm's profits are

$$\pi = [S_0 - S_1]\,p - C(S_0 - S_1, S_0) + \ldots$$

$$+ \left(\frac{1}{1+r}\right)^{t+1} \{[S_{t+1} - S_{t+2}]\,p - C(S_{t+1} - S_{t+2}, S_{t+1})\}$$

$$+ \ldots + \left(\frac{1}{1+r}\right)^{T} \{[S_T - S_{T+1}]\,p - C(S_T - S_{T+1}, S_T)\}$$

Profit maximization requires that $\partial\pi/\partial S_{t+1} = 0$. This yields the adjusted r percent rule set out above and on Figure 8.8. This approach to determining the rule implied by maximization works for each problem, including the two above, in this chapter. It is a simple way to do dynamic optimization for a wide class of problems. One needs only elementary calculus and simple calculus arguments.

Durable Exhaustible Resources

Durable exhaustible resources such as gold, copper, etc. are extracted and used aboveground for many periods. This makes them different from oil and coal, which are extracted and consumed in a single period. There seems to be less "exhaustibility" associated with durable resources. This is true. Mining depletes the reserve underground but builds up a useful nondepleting stock above ground. One might argue that gold, once extracted, can be used indefinitely—it does not rust. One also thinks of the changing uses of some of these metals, such as copper, aluminum, and steel; changing uses is another dimension of recycling. In putting the extraction of durable resources into our framework, it suffices to use unit capital value for the price facing the extractor. Capital value is the discounted sum of single-period rentals. With nondurable resources, rental is the relevant revenue per unit facing the extractor. With durable exhaustible resources, discounted future effective rentals are the relevant unit revenues facing the extractor. Thus the relevant price for, say, a unit of copper is

$$v_t = y_t + \frac{(1-\delta)y_{t+1}}{(1+r)} + \frac{(1-\delta)^2 y_{t+2}}{(1+r)^2} + \ldots$$

where δ is the rate of "rusting," y_t is rental per period, and r is the discount rate. The profit-maximizing extraction rule for a homogeneous deposit is our familiar r percent rule, but with v_t as the extractor's unit revenue (see Levhari and Pindyck, 1982; and Hartwick, 1993). That is,

$$\frac{[v_{t+1} - MC(q_{t+1})] - [v_t - MC(q_t)]}{v_t - MC(q_t)} = r$$

At the level of the industry, extraction will tend to drive rentals and capital values down, because for low rates of "rusting" the material will accumulate in a larger and larger stock aboveground. Thus durability is a force causing downward pressure on prices of output; and some ultimate exhaustibility, after rusting and depletability become effective, drives prices up. One observes, for example, diamond sellers (the de Beers company) carefully controlling amounts supplied each year in order to prevent downward pressure on prices.

Deposits of Differing Quality

An intermediate sort of exhaustibility involves running out of a low-cost source of, say, oil (e.g., in shallow pools) and having to move on to a higher-cost source (e.g., offshore pools or shale). One can view the high-cost phase as a competitive industry equilibrium, which we have examined above, with another competitive industry phase grafted on as an earlier phase. Industry supply comes from the low-cost source in the first phase, and then there is a switch to a phase of extraction from the high-cost source. In phase 1 each small extractor has unit extraction costs c_1, and in phrase 2 each small extractor has unit costs c_2 with c_2 greater than c_1. The supply response is familiar—quantity paths are the outcome of rent, $p(t) - c_i$, rising at r percent in each phase. The new issue is how to link the two phases. The principles is: Price must not jump between phases. Otherwise, consumers will take advantage of the price jump to save money by waiting (if there is a jump down in price) or speeding up consumption (if there is a jump up in price).

We illustrate this in Figure 8.9. In Figure 8.9(a) we have the initial price $p(0)$ and the terminal price of phase I, $p(T_1)$. In Figure 8.9(b), we have the initial price $p(T_1)$ for phase II and its terminal price $p(T_2)$, the choke price for the demand schedule.

The industry stock sizes S_1 and S_2 complete the analysis of the duration of each phase. Careful analysis indicates than an exogenous increase in c_1 (technical regress, for example) leaves Figure 8.9(b) unchanged and *slows* extraction of S_1 in phase I. Analogously, if c_2 were to become higher its phase of extraction would lengthen and

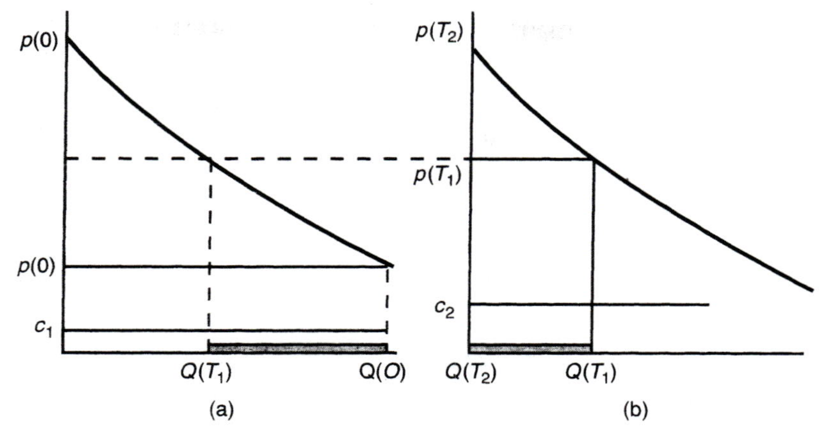

FIGURE 8.9. The high-cost phase is an ordinary competitive equilibrium (b). Rent $p-c_2$ rises at r percent, while price moves up from $p(T_1)$ to the terminal price $p(T_2)$. The low-cost phase is grafted onto the front. It ends with price $p(T_1)$, and rent declines at r percent until the stock runs out. In (a), $p(0)$ is the initial price.

its initial price would become higher. This will cause phase I to become shorter. We illustrate this in Figure 8.10. The dotted schedule is the price schedule after c_2 has increased.

In Figure 8.10, the effect of the increase in c_2 is to move T_1 to T_1' (lengthen phase II) and to move T_O to T_O' (shorten phase I). Note that in these comparative statics analyses, it is easier to do the analysis by working backward. The end is the anchor, so to speak.

The analysis of c_2 increasing illustrates an important point. Current exhaustible resource prices depend on future anticipated supply, including the supply of substitutes. The increase in c_2 indicates that future supply will be more expensive. This causes today's price $p(0)$ to increase to $p'(0)$. Conversely if a new technology is developed to make shale oil cheap to extract, then today's price will decline. In general, many and subtle future supply dimensions are capitalized in today's price of oil. This is also true for other products derived from mining activity.

Exhaustion and Backstops

A choke price (the point where the industry demand schedule hits the price axis) indicates that above a certain price, quantity demanded declines to zero. Demand is choked off by higher prices. Thus when oil supplies are run to exhaustion and price rises to the choke price the soundest inference is that at high prices, some other source of supply has taken over. Exhaustion becomes a relative term—one form of supply may be exhausted but another form of supply takes over. Moreover, in this view exhaustion is not some ultimate ending, but the mark of a transition to a new phase. Energy supply from hydrocarbon sources is replaced by energy supply from, say, nuclear sources. Fusion power is thought to be a limitless source of thermal

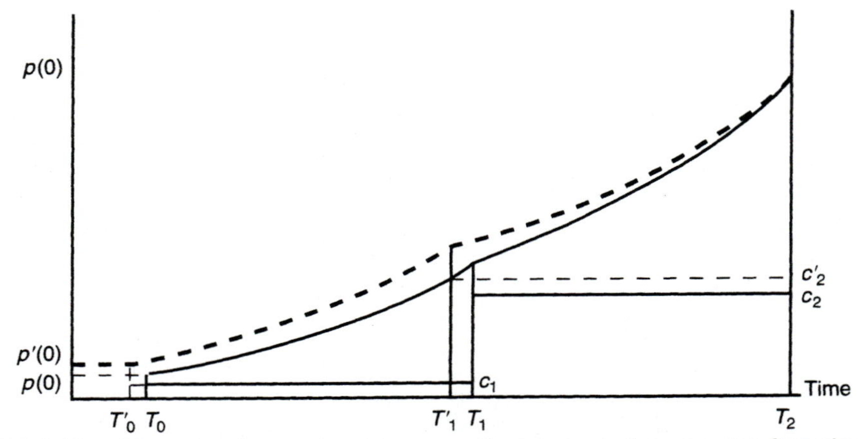

FIGURE 8.10. After extraction cost c_2 increases, the price schedule changes from the solid scalloped line to the dotted line. Phase II lengthens and phase I contracts. Initial price rises. (Solving backward from T_2 is much easier.)

power, though it is a technology awaiting perfecting for introduction to the marketplace. Resource economists have labeled fusion power a *backstop supply*—a substitute energy source that will come on line when cheaper sources are exhausted. Thus there is a close connection between the pace of depletion of, say, oil, its price, and the availability of the backstop.

Given a backstop (a constant cost source of supply at a "high" cost) exhaustion of oil can be viewed as an intermediate or transition stage until the backstop supply is brought on stream. There is the basic idea that if a price moves sufficiently high, someone will find it profitable to develop a substitute for the product with the high price. High prices provide an umbrella under which a substitute, expensive at first, can be developed. Once developed, the prices of new products generally decline as improvements are introduced and economies of scale in production can be taken advantage of. People have argued that the United States government could manipulate world oil prices by changing the volumes of money allocated to fusion research. Early reasonably priced fusion power could encroach on the market for oil in generating thermal power.

We illustrate this in Figure 8.11. In Figure 8.11, we observe that backstop supply of energy at price c_f creates a ceiling on oil prices. With oil rents rising at r percent, we can work back from c_f and observe, given world oil stocks, current oil price p_0 in units of energy. A lower backstop price c_f will cause a lower current price to be observed. In this view the exhaustion of oil defines a transition phase until the backstop source of supply takes over.

A more traditional view is that hydrocarbons represent an ultimate source of supply. Given an unchanging demand schedule, prices will rise as the stock is run down. Rent rises at r percent or a variant of the r percent rule. And prices keep on rising as stocks dwindle. Asymptotic exhaustion has output from stocks getting smaller and

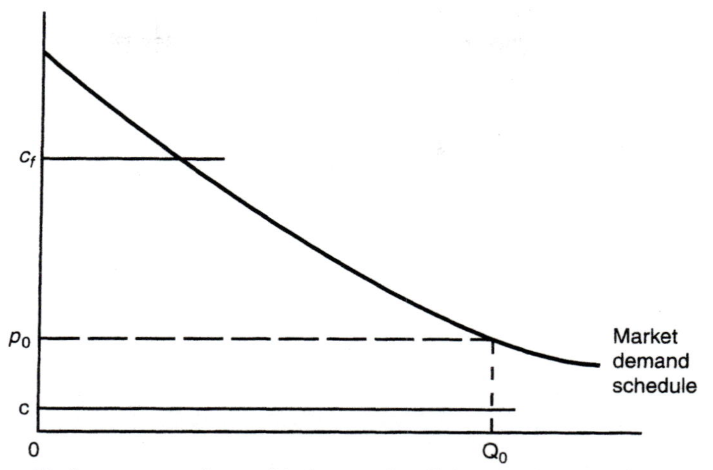

FIGURE 8.11. We have energy demand being met by oil "production" at prices of electricity below c_f. Above c_f, fusion power can provide energy for price c_f.

smaller as prices move ever higher. This process never terminates under asymptotic depletion.

SUMMARY

1. Nonrenewable resources differ from reproducible goods because they have a fixed stock of reserves that, once removed, cannot be replaced. A unit of ore removed today means that less, in total, is available for extraction tomorrow.
2. The economic theory of extraction explains the flow of production over time and how quickly the resource stock is exhausted.
3. The finite stock of a nonrenewable resource alters the condition for efficient production from a competitive industry in three ways: (a) price equals marginal costs of extraction plus resource rent; (b) the present value of resource rent must be constant for each period the mine operates; and (c) the total amount of the resource extracted over time cannot exceed the total stock of reserves.
4. In a mine facing a constant price, a positive discount rate, and extraction costs that do not increase as the stock of ore is depleted, extraction decreases in each period during which the ore is removed.
5. Extraction from a mineral industry facing a negatively sloped demand curve and constant costs of extraction will be socially optimal if resource rent per unit extracted rises continuously at the rate of interest. This is known as Hotelling's rule, and it is met if all mine operators have perfect foresight, with industry output declining over time.

6. Low-cost deposits will be exploited before high-cost deposits, leading to a scalloped but continuous price path.
7. A nonrenewable resource with a backstop technology will be extracted until the price of the resource reaches the choke price, that price at which the backstop becomes profitable to produce. If no substitute (backstop) is available, the price of the resource keeps rising over time.

DISCUSSION QUESTIONS

1. If the interest (discount) rate is zero, what is the value of resource rent over the extraction profile of the mine?
2. Using Gray's model, derive for a two-period case the extraction path of a mine's output assuming the following:
   a. Extraction costs (average and marginal costs) are linear and upward sloping.
   b. The market price of the mineral rises; the market price falls.
3. Suppose that a mine has two different ore qualities in its stock of reserves. Call them block A and block B. How would the mine owner efficiently extract the total stock if the costs of extraction are constant per unit within each block but differ between blocks? Use the Gray model.
4. For the numerical example of the two-period model of the competitive industry, derive graphically or mathematically the effect on extraction in each period, mineral prices, and mineral rents of:
   a. Decrease in extraction costs from $200 per ton to $150 per ton.
   b. Decrease in interest rates from 5 percent to 2 percent.
   c. Increase in the initial stock of mineral resources from 2500 to 3000 tons.
5. In the many-period Hotelling model of the industry, extraction cost per ton was constant. In order to reflect, say, diminishing returns to the extraction facilities in the industry, let cost per ton rise with the amount extracted in a period in the industry (as in the simple Gray model of the mine). Compare two programs of quantities extracted: one with constant costs and one with extraction cost per ton rising linearly with quantity extracted in a period.
6. Explain and show diagrammatically that a price path that does not reach the choke price in the basic industry model is nonoptimal and will not occur under perfect foresight.
7. In the basic Hotelling model of the industry, with constant unit extraction costs and a negatively sloped industry demand curve, technological progress in extraction can be approximated by a decline in the value of the constant extraction costs period by period. Outline how the program of quantities extracted with a 2 percent decline in unit extraction costs period by period compares with the program of quantities extracted when unit extraction costs remain constant.
8. Derive the effect on a mineral industry's output and price path if, at some point along an optimal path, the costs of extraction rise and:

a. The increase in costs is fully anticipated (foreseen) by the industry.
b. The cost increase is completely unanticipated.

9. What are the effects on a mineral industry's output and price path of a fully anticipated:
   a. Increase in the total stock of ore reserves.
   b. Fall in the choke price (cost of backstop technology).
   c. Technological change that decreases the cost of extraction over time.
   d. Rightward shift in the demand curve.
10. How would the price path for a competitive industry differ if it faced an isoelastic rather than a linear demand curve?

NOTES

1. Seabed nodules are an exception to the finite stock of minerals. Minerals such as nickel, copper, manganese, and molybdenum have been found on the ocean floor and might be growing over a time period much shorter than the millions of years required to produce hard-rock minerals, oil, and gas on land.
2. In a more complex model, extraction costs could depend on the *cumulative* amount of ore extracted to that date. This is not the case in the Gray model or other models we examine in this chapter.
3. For two periods, the problem reduces to maximize $\pi(q_0) = \left(\frac{1}{1 = r}\right)\pi\left(S_0 - q_0\right)$ by choice of q_0.
   In period *I*, profit is $\pi(q_i)$. This yields the first-order condition $d\pi\ (q_0)/dq_0 = \left(\frac{1}{1 + r}\right) d\pi\ (q_1)/dq_1$, where $q_1 = S_0 - q_0$. We look at the two-period model more fully below.
4. This is an instance of the more general rule: Marginal profit $p - MC(q_T)$ must equal average profit $[pq_T - C(q_T)]/q_t$ in the last period. In fact, this condition holds exactly only for cases in which periods are infinitesimally small in continuous time and holds only approximately for discrete time problems. See Lozada (1993).
5. A demonstration of this result requires results in the theory of dynamic optimization. One needs to insert Hotelling's rule in a large framework. Hartwick (1989) presented this result, and Lozada (1995) has explored it in considerable depth.
6. The Lagrange multiplier allows us to apply similar first-order conditions as in an unconstrained optimization problem. If the constraint binds, we can be sure that extraction in period 0 plus extraction in period 1 exactly uses up the total stock of ore. The term $\lambda(S_0 - q_0 - q_1)$ then vanishes regardless of the value of λ. The way to ensure that the constraint binds is to treat λ as another variable in deriving the first-order conditions. The present value of rents is differentiated with respect to q_0, q_1, and λ.
7. More generally, marginal surplus $d[B(Q_T) - Q_Tc]/dQ_T$ must equal average surplus $B[(Q_T) - Q_Tc]/Q_T$ in the final period. This implies $Q_T = 0$ for our problem. In fact, this end-point condition is exact for continuous-time problems but is only approximate for our discrete-time formulation.

SELECTED READINGS

Adelman, M. (1986), "Scarcity and World Oil Prices," *Review of Economic and Statistics* 68, pp. 387–397.

Farrow, S. (1985). "Testing the Efficiency of Extraction from a Stock Resource," *Journal of Political Economy*, 93, pp. 452–487.

Gray, L. C. (1914). "Rent Under the Assumption of Exhaustibility," *Quarterly Journal of Economics* 28, pp. 466–489.

Halvorsen, Robert, and Tim R. Smith (1991). "A Test of the Theory of Exhaustible Resources," *Quarterly Journal of Economics* (February), pp. 123–140.

Hartwick, J. M. (1993). "The Generalized *r* percent Rule for Semi-Durable Exhaustible Resources," *Resource and Energy Economics* 15, pp. 147–152.

Hartwick, J. M. (1989). *Non-renewable Resources: Extraction Programs and Markets*, London: Harwood Academic.

Hotelling, H. (1931). "The Economics of Exhaustible Resources," *Journal of Political Economy* 39, pp. 137–175.

Levhari, D., and R. Pindyck (1981). "The Pricing of Durable Exhaustible Resources," *Quarterly Journal of Economics*, 96, pp. 365–377.

Lozada, G. A. (1993). "Existence and Characterization of Discrete-Time Equilibria in Extractive Industries," *Resource and Energy Economics* 15, 3 (September), pp. 249–254.

Lozada, G. A. (1995). "Resource Depletion, National Income Accounting and the Value of Optimal Dynamic Programs," *Resource and Energy Economics* 17, 2 (August), pp. 137–154.

Miller, M. H., and C. W. Upton (1985). "A Test of the Hotelling Valuation Principle," *Journal of Political Economy*, 93, pp. 1–25.

Polasky, S. (1992a). "The Private and Social Value of Information: Exploration for Exhaustible Resources," *Journal of Environmental Economics and Management* 23, 1 (July), pp. 1–26.

Polasky S. (1992b), "Do Oil Producers Act as 'Oil'igopolists?," *Journal of Environmental Economics and Management* 23, 3 (November), pp. 216–247.

Samuelson, P. A. (1964). "Tax Deductability of Economic Depreciation to Ensure Invariant Valuation," *Journal of Political Economy* 72, pp. 604–606.

Young, Denise (1992). "Cost Specification and Firm Behaviour in a Hotelling Model of Resource Extraction," *Canadian Journal of Economics* (February), pp. 41–59.

chapter 9

Nonrenewable Resource Use: Departures from the Competitive Case and from Fixed Stock Size

INTRODUCTION

In this chapter, we depart from the case of competitive extraction with known, fixed stocks of reserves. We examine monopoly extraction first. Monopolists attempt to keep output price high and thus tend to slow extraction relative to the case of a competitive regime.

We next examine duopoly extraction. This requires assumptions about strategic interactions between firms. In simple cases, each firm treats its rival's extraction path as fixed. A case of asymmetric duopoly involves a fringe group of competitive extractors facing a cartel that behaves like a monopolist. Another form of duopoly involves a cartel extracting in the face of a high-priced backstop supplier. Manipulation of cartel extraction by the owner of the backstop technology is an extension of this model.

We then relax the assumption that stock size is given. We consider costly finding of mineral stocks and the possibility that the amount to be found is uncertain.

EXTRACTION BY A MONOPOLIST

Monopoly is associated with high prices. The essence of monopoly profit is in charging the buyer a price in excess of the costs of production. It is this desire for high prices that causes our monopoly producer to extract a fixed deposit S_0 more slowly than the corresponding group of competitive producers. The monopolist puts a small amount on the market each period in order to keep the price relatively high. A sequence of small quantities from a fixed stock implies a relatively long interval to exhaustion. Extraction from a monopoly producer will command a price greater than the costs of extraction. Marginal revenue minus marginal extraction cost defines marginal profit, i.e., profit on the marginal ton extracted. The difference between market price and marginal extraction cost is, of course, marginal revenue, $MR(q_t)$. Marginal revenue plays the key role in the monopolist's optimal extraction program.

In each period, the monopolist's profit is $Q_tP(Q_t) - C(Q_t)$, where $P(Q_t)$ is the inverse market demand schedule, Q_t is the amount extracted and sold in each t time period, and $C(Q_t)$ is the cost of extracting the Q_t tons. The profit on the last (marginal) ton extracted in the period is:

$$MR(Q_t) - MC(Q_t) \tag{9.1}$$

where $MR(Q_t) = P(Q_t) + Q_t(dP/dQ_t)$ and $MC(Q_t)$ is $[dC(Q_t)/dQ_t]$. To maximize the sum of discounted profits over many time periods, the profit on the marginal ton extracted in each period must be the same. This condition is:

$$MR(Q_t) - MC(Q_t) = \frac{1}{1 + r}[MR(Q_{t+1}) - MC(Q_{t+1})], \tag{9.2}$$

for two consecutive periods. The sum of profits is:

$$\pi = R(Q_0) - C(Q_0) + \left(\frac{1}{1 + r}\right)[R(Q_t) - C(Q_t)] + \left(\frac{1}{1 + r}\right)^2[R(Q_2) - C(Q_2)] + \ldots + \left(\frac{1}{1 = r}\right)^T[R(Q_T) - C(Q_T)]$$

where $R(Q_t) = Q_tP(Q_t)$. The term $R(Q)$ stands for total revenue from the sale of a particular quantity, Q. We illustrate the fundamental marginal profit condition in Figure 9.1.

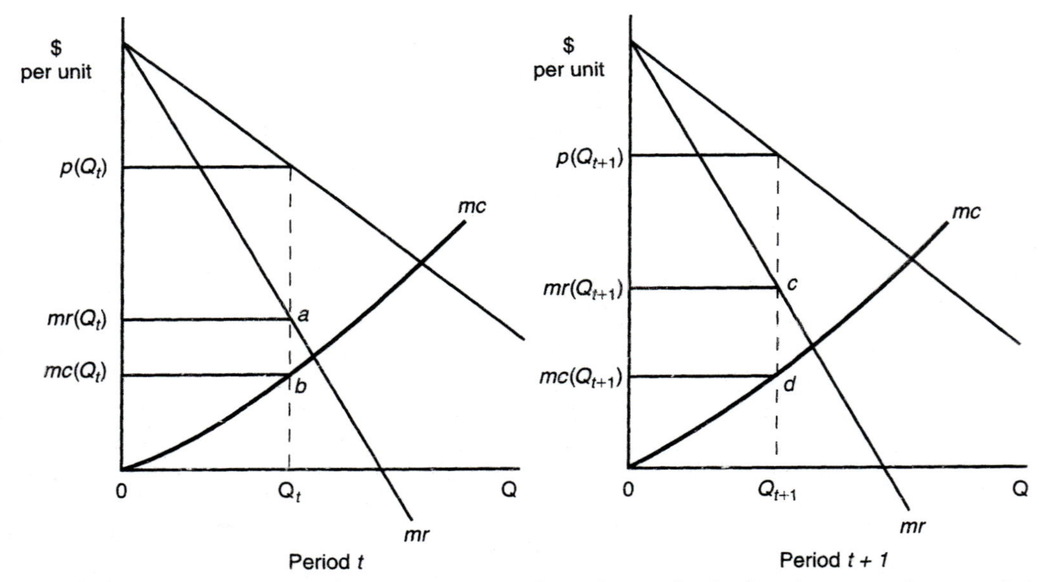

FIGURE 9.1. The monopolist maximizes profit on its stock of mineral reserves by arranging quantities Q_t and Q_{t+1} so that distance *cd* is *r* percent larger than distance *ab*.

Note that price minus marginal cost involves two components: marginal monopoly profit, $MR(Q_t) - MC(Q_t)$, plus a markup, $P(Q_t) - MR(Q_t)$. In a static problem, the monopolist maximizes profit by setting price high enough that marginal revenue equals marginal costs. Extraction thus involves an extra wedge: marginal revenue above marginal extraction cost in each period. And it is this marginal profit, or value of an "extra" ton in each period to the monopolist, that the monopolist makes equal across periods—equal inclusive of discounting.

The equal marginal profit condition above can be written as:

$$\frac{[MR(Q_{t+1}) - MC(Q_{t+1})] - [MR(Q_t) - MC(Q_t)]}{[MR(Q_t) - MC(Q_t)]} = r \qquad (9.3)$$

This is an r percent rule for a monopolist. It has marginal revenue in place of the price we observed for competitive extraction in the previous chapter. One gets the sense from Figure 9.1 that quantities must be relatively small in order to keep prices relatively high in the monopoly case. These smaller quantities per period lead to a longer interval for depleting a fixed stock than is observed in the competitive case. This result becomes obvious when we look at extraction near the end of the time horizon for the monopolist.

In the last period, given the upward-sloping marginal extraction cost schedule, we see that Q_T has declined to zero. This sort of condition for profit maximization was discussed in Chapter 8. The general condition is: Average profit on Q_T extracted in the last period must equal marginal profit. With our declining marginal revenue schedule and rising marginal cost schedule, this condition implies a Q_T of zero. For our schedules, quantities in each period will decline as extraction proceeds, and the optimal termination occurs when Q_T is just zero. Thus the complete solution involves starting with Q_T at zero and letting $MR(Q_t) - MC(Q_t)$ shrink by r percent each period, working backward in time, until the stock is used up. Or, to get the initial extraction right, one must work back from the correct end point.

It is in working back that one observes that a monopolist is extracting more slowly than a competitive group of producers. Suppose that each case involved termination at the same calendar date, period T. For each case Q_T is zero. In the case of the monopolist, $MR(Q_T) - MC(Q_T)$ is the relevant value that is decreasing, whereas for the competitive industry it is $P(Q_T) - MC(Q_T)$. Each shrinks by r percent to yield Q_{T-1}. We illustrate this in Figure 9.2. Here Q_{T-1} is bigger for the group of competitive extractors. Hence, the monopolist is extracting less near the end of the life of the deposit. One can jump to the inference that, working backward, the monopolist extracts less period by period. Given the same stock size for the two cases, the monopolist must take longer to deplete it. This phenomenon of slow extraction by the monopolist led Hotelling to call the monopolist the "friend of the conservationist." Stiglitz (1976) and others were intrigued by this phenomenon and came up with a counterexample. If the demand for the mineral has constant elasticity throughout (i.e., $Q = aP^{-\epsilon}$), marginal revenue is a constant fraction of price. Hence, with no extraction costs, a monopolist and a competitive industry will extract at the same rate. This is clearly a curiosity.

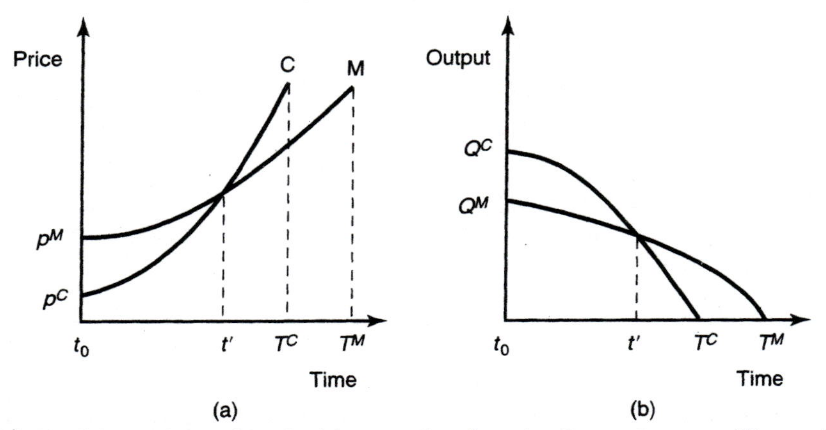

FIGURE 9.2. Price and quantity schedules over time for extraction under competition and under monopoly for a linear demand schedule and zero extraction costs. Monopoly extracts the same stock over a longer horizon. The monopolist produces less for all periods up to t' and charges a higher price. For periods after t', monopoly output exceeds competitive output and monopoly price is lower. The price path of the monopolist is flatter than that of the competitive industry exploiting the same stock.

DUOPOLY EXTRACTION

There are two versions of duopoly, differing in the strategic actions each extractor takes in response to its competitor. In the simplest case, each producer treats its rival's extraction *path* as given and arranges its own extraction to maximize profit, given the rival's extraction path. This resembles static Cournot duopoly in which each seller treats the current output of its rival as fixed or given. For this simple case, we get:

$$\frac{[MR^1(Q^1_{t+1} - Q^2_{t+1}) - MC^1(Q^1_{t+1})] - [MR^1(Q^1_t - Q^2_t) - MC^1(Q^1_t)]}{[MR^1(Q^1_t + Q^2_t) - MC^1(Q^1_t)]} = r \quad (9.4)$$

and

$$\frac{[MR^2(Q^1_{t+1} + Q^2_{t+1}) - MC^2(Q^2_{t+1})] - [MR^2(Q^1_t + Q^2_t) - MC^2(Q^2_t)]}{[MR^2(Q^1_t + Q^2_t) - MC^2(Q^2_t)]} = r \quad (9.5)$$

as two r percent rules defining a pair of extraction paths. The marginal revenue is $d[Q^1P(Q^1 + Q^2)]dQ^2$ for seller 1, and $P(Q^1 + Q^2)$ is the inverse industry demand curve. This solution is easy to write down and to interpret but would be difficult to work out because each producer's path is entwined with the other's. One can see that the solution resembles the case of two monopolists sharing a market, and thus we can obtain the result that this duopoly case lies between pure monopoly and pure competition. Thus its average output price would be lower for duopoly compared with the case of monopoly. Total stock would be extracted faster under duopoly than under monopoly.

The flaw in the above duopoly equilibrium is the assumption that each seller treats the *path* of its rival as fixed when the seller works out its best extraction path. A more realistic assumption is that each seller will reopen competition with each new period. This form of solution is called closed-loop. Each seller takes account of its rival's reoptimization as each period opens. Solutions with a new round of competition at each date are generally *dynamically consistent*—a seller does not deviate from an earlier commitment to a particular extraction path. Maskin and Newbery (1990) present a closed-loop dynamically consistent analysis of an oil importer selecting a schedule of tariffs in the face of an offshore monopoly supplier. Eswaran and Lewis (1985) also present some examples of duopoly extraction.

A Competitive Fringe of Extractors

The Organization of Petroleum Exporting Countries (OPEC) is an organization that produces a relatively large proportion of the world's oil supply. For a period during the 1970s and early 1980s, OPEC set the world price of oil. Economists were curious as to how price-setting behavior by a cartel would affect non-OPEC oil production. Duopoly models of a cartel extractor operating with a "competitive fringe" of price-taking extractors were developed. A number of possible extraction paths can be generated depending on the assumptions of the model.

Suppose that all producers have identical extraction costs and similar-sized reserves of oil. In this case, an equilibrium is obtained with the fringe extracting and exhausting first. The rent on each barrel of oil rises at r percent during this period. Once the fringe has exhausted its reserves, the cartel takes over and produces with its marginal revenue minus marginal cost rising at r percent until it exhausts at a later date. This is the solution because during the fringe phase, the cartel's marginal revenue minus marginal cost is rising at *more* than r percent. This is the signal to hoard reserves. Hence, the cartel waits until the fringe exhausts its reserves. Each takes the other's extraction path as fixed. This is not a closed-loop equilibrium. It is a type of Cournot duopoly solution. We illustrate this equilibrium duopoly solution in Figure 9.3. A key feature of the equilibrium in Figure 9.3 is that output price is rising sufficiently rapidly in phase I that it pays the cartel to hoard its stock during this phase.

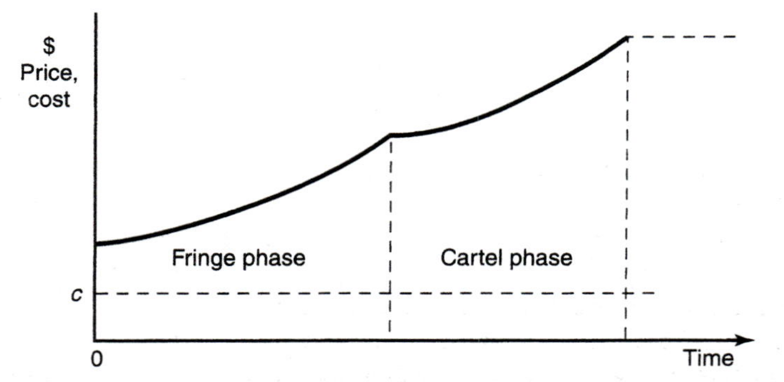

FIGURE 9.3. During phase I, the fringe extracts and price minus marginal cost rises at r percent. When the fringe's stock is exhausted, the cartel extracts as a monopolist. Marginal revenue minus marginal cost rises at r percent.

Consider a variant of this solution. It turns out that in some cases the cartel can increase its present value of profit by selling some of its reserves of oil in the early phase while acting as a small competitive extractor. Though it makes less profit from this stock sold early, it can shorten the early phase by driving average prices down. This is a sort of loss-leader action. What is lost on the stock sold early is made up for by eliminating the fringe extractors more rapidly. This solution can be set up with each group accepting the other's extraction path as fixed. It is a solution in which each maximizes its profits at the beginning by selecting the best path and sticking to it.

Within this loss-leader solution, there is obviously also a more aggressive course of action for the cartel. It can agree to the above solution at the outset of extraction and thus get the fringe to extract along its competitive path, taking the cartel's path as given. Then when the fringe has exhausted its stock, the cartel is free to renege on its commitment to sell some stock in phase I. It can renege because its competitor (the fringe) has been eliminated. See Newbery (1980) for more detail on this case.

We learn two things from this analysis. First, competitive interactions between a dominant seller and a fringe are hard to represent using basic extraction theory. Models predict that the cartel (monopolist) will wait until the competitors exhaust their stocks. This is not observed in practice. Second, basic duopoly theory leaves the solution vulnerable to manipulation by the dominant player. A more subtle, plausible, and durable solution is required. Indeed, closed-loop and dynamically consistent solutions were developed in order to remove the possibility of manipulation of the so-called equilibrium. An equilibrium is not a true equilibrium if it falls apart as soon as it is implemented.

The Manipulative Backstop Supplier

How is a dominant (cartel or monopoly) extractor affected by the price of the backstop? Suppose the backstop supply is some sort of renewable energy source such as fusion power. Oil extractors will be obliged to supply at prices less than the price charged by the suppliers of fusion. Fusion power will sit, waiting to be turned on, while oil suppliers use up their reserves. They will supply in such a way that marginal revenue minus marginal cost rises at r percent because they behave as a monopolist. They are cartel suppliers. The market price of oil will rise while the cartel depletes its stock. When the price rises to the backstop supply price, c_f in Figure 9.4, marginal revenue will be below c_f. If the cartel has stock left—as it will have in a profit-maximizing strategy—its new demand schedule and marginal revenue schedule will be flat at price c_f. Hence, marginal revenue "jumps up" to c_f when output price reaches c_f. The jump in marginal revenue is like a windfall profit. The cartel keeps supplying stock at a price just below c_f until its stock is exhausted. Each period it supplies quantity Q_f until exhaustion occurs. Then the fusion power supply takes over and continues to supply Q_f at price c_f indefinitely.

The delicate decision on profit maximization facing the cartel is the division of its stock between phase I, the rising-price phase (marginal revenue minus marginal cost rising at r percent), and the flat-price phase (phase II). The solution must have the cartel indifferent as regards between shifting a marginal barrel of oil from one

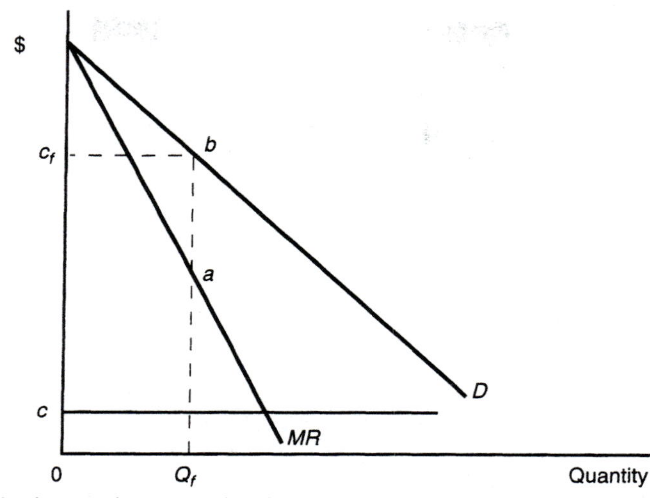

FIGURE 9.4. As the cartel extracts oil, price rises. When it reaches price c_f, the backstop supply price, the cartel's marginal revenue jumps from a to b. Then the cartel sells its remaining reserves at price c_f, supplying Q_f each period.

phase to the other. This will be satisfied when the present value of the profit on the last barrel extracted and sold in phase I, that is $MR(Q_0) - MC$ (marginal revenue minus marginal cost at the beginning of phase I), equals the present value of $c_f - MC$, the marginal profit on the last barrel extracted. This last barrel must have its present value of profit discounted back to the beginning of phase I. We illustrate this in Figure 9.5.

This setup intrigued observers because they wondered about the possibility that the United States government could manipulate the cartel's extraction by speeding up or slowing down research on fusion power, the backstop supply. Perhaps the United States could credibly commit to having fusion power available at some date τ in the future at a price of c_f. If the cartel believed in the commitment, it would respond with its profit-maximizing extraction path. If much of the cartel's oil was being used by American consumers, the United States government would want a cartel extraction program which did not harm American consumers excessively and a fusion development program that did not have to be rushed to completion. Rapid development of fusion power is more costly than a more gradual program of development.

Our analysis indicates what would happen if a crash program were undertaken and fusion power were ready today. Suppose that the day fusion was perfected was delayed a small amount. The cartel would stick with the same extraction program because when the oil price rose to c_f, fusion power would be ready to go. Thus, the United States could delay up to the date when the price of oil rose to c_f in Figure 9.4, and still have oil suppliers with the same cartel extraction program. Since delay of development is cost-effective, this hypothetical date is the earliest the United States

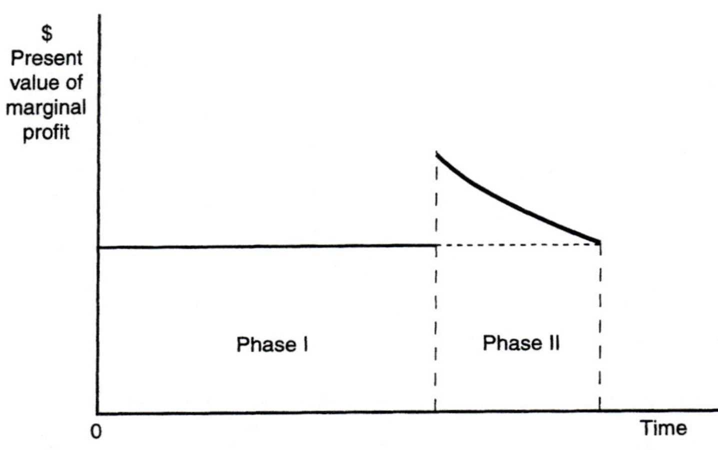

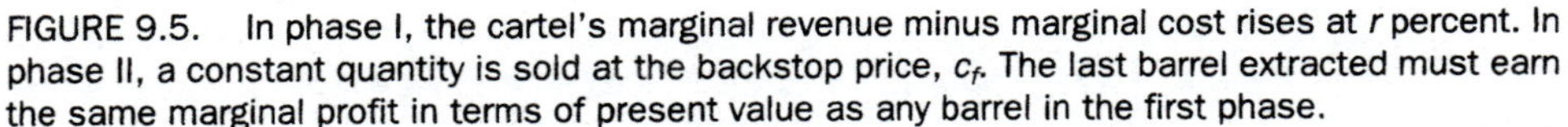
FIGURE 9.5. In phase I, the cartel's marginal revenue minus marginal cost rises at r percent. In phase II, a constant quantity is sold at the backstop price, c_f. The last barrel extracted must earn the same marginal profit in terms of present value as any barrel in the first phase.

government would ever make fusion power available, given its desire to "manipulate" cartel extraction in favor of American consumers.

On the other hand, a very late arrival of fusion power leaves the cartel with a long interval in which to charge prices well above c_f. It turns out that the best action for the United States government is to let the cartel have a short period of prices above c_f and then to have fusion power in readiness, making c_f an effective oil price ceiling with a bit of delay. For details on this model, see Dasgupta, Gilbert, and Stiglitz (1983) and Gallini, Lewis, and Ware (1983). It is true that the above analysis is valid only if: (1) the cartel believes what the United States government says about its plans for developing fusion power, and (2) the announcement by the United States government comes first and then the cartel responds. Relaxation of these assumptions leads to a different equilibrium in the competition between the cartel and the United States government.

FINDING MORE STOCK

Many mining companies explore as well as extract. They are in the business of adding to their stocks by exploration as well as being in the business of extracting and selling. Clearly, finding more stock is quite different from saying that exhaustion will not occur because more will always be discovered. Discoveries delay exhaustion but do not eliminate it. Extraction paths will therefore be greatly influenced by discoveries, but the issues associated with exhaustion of the reserves do not disappear once new stock is allowed to come on stream. Let us consider two simple cases.

The extractor knows that there are S_0 tons below the surface, but it costs money to locate the ore body or to turn it into usable reserves. This model was investigated by Pindyck (1978) and Hartwick (1991). The solution will have exploration and extraction take place simultaneously. It is too expensive to do all the discovery first, while earning no revenue from sales, and then to do the extraction. One hears of extraction companies keeping a particular percent of current sales in discovered reserves. When reserves are run down, exploration is accelerated. For the case of discovery costs independent of the stock of ore remaining, a straightforward r percent rule governs the simultaneous action of extraction and exploration. Equation (9.6) gives this rule:

$$\frac{[P - MC(Q_{t+1}) - MC(D_{t+1})] - [P - MC(Q_t) - MC(D_t)]}{P - MC(Q_t) - MC(D_t)} = r \qquad (9.6)$$

where $MC(Q_t)$ is the marginal cost of extraction from discovered reserves and $MC(D_t)$ is the marginal cost of discovering another ton to be placed in reserve. This model assumes that the firm owns the stock it is searching for. In an *open access* case, firms rush in to find a deposit before others can discover it. In the absence of regulation, open access leads to racing and a duplication of exploration activity. The legal institution of staking claims is intended to mitigate excessive duplication of exploration activity.

A large unexpected discovery will drive down current prices and hence inflict a capital loss of all owners of resource reserves. Thus one might presume that existing suppliers would hope that no competitor finds more stock. A duopoly version of this line of inquiry was taken up in Hartwick and Sadorsky (1990). There, an extractor worries not only about its competitor's extraction program but also about the rival's exploration program.

Another line of analysis of exploration involves uncertainty as to the amount to be discovered underground. Two cases come to mind. The firm could spend to explore up front, or it could simply start extracting and see whether the deposit ends up being small, large, or in between. Clearly, if a mine has to be built before any extraction occurs, there are benefits to knowing the size of the ore body being worked.

We proceed by introducing some uncertainty about stock size into a firm's extraction problem. In Figure 9.6, path *ab* is the rent path for a firm facing constant, price P, an upward-sloping marginal extraction schedule, and a fixed, known stock, S_0. Suppose this known stock is equal to 122 tons. Path *ab* is a standard schedule of rent rising at r percent to a terminal rent value of b. Mining occurs in two phases. In phase I, 90 tons are mined. This leaves 32 tons for extraction in phase II. We now introduce some uncertainty over stock size. In the second phase, instead of 32 tons, let 40 tons be in place with a probability of 0.8, and 0 tons be left with probability of 0.2. This leaves a certain 90 tons in the early phase. If 40 tons are present, a rent schedule of *ef* is realized. If 0 tons are all there is, then extraction ends at d, and no more rent is earned by the firm. The principal result in this problem is that schedule *cd*, phase I extraction under uncertainty, lies above schedule *ab*. Uncertainty causes the firm to slow its extraction in the early phase and in a sense to delay finding out whether 40 more tons are present or not. Formally, profits on a path are concave in stock size associated with the relevant path. This implies that expected profits beyond date τ in Figure 9.6 are less than profits for a certain path (32 tons extracted in phase II). The firm responds by "pushing" phase II beyond τ into the future or by slowing down early ex-

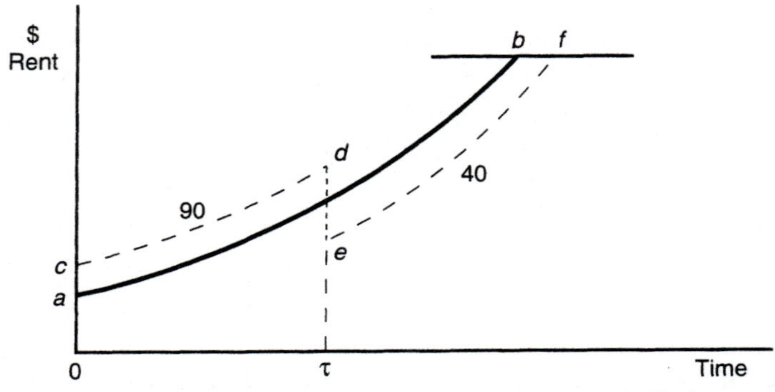

FIGURE 9.6. Rent schedule under certainty is shown as line *ab*. Under uncertainty, *cd* is the rent schedule for phase I of extraction. Uncertainty slows extraction as compared with the case where the total stock of reserves is known.

traction. See Kemp (1976), Gilbert (1979), Loury (1978), and Hartwick and Yeung (1985) for more details on these models.

Information is valuable. Our firm in Figure 9.6 could earn higher profits by knowing early on whether 40 more tons are present. Suppose that for an expenditure of $\$K$ at date τ^*, the correct answer becomes available. If $\$K$ is not too large, the firm will spend it at a date that balances the value of knowing against the expenditure of $\$K$. This is a form of costly exploration activity. See Dasgupta and Heal (1979). Polasky (1992) introduces costly learning by an extractor about stock size. This occurs before extraction takes place. The value of information causes the decentralized solution to differ from a planner's solution.

SUMMARY

1. In this chapter we have taken extraction theory into the area of noncompetitive behavior. A monopoly extractor strives to keep output price higher in order to expand profit. This leads to a slower extraction rate than is observed under competition.
2. Duopoly extraction displays an intermediate speed of extraction. Duopoly forces us to analyze strategic interactions between extractors. Issues of commitment and dynamic consistency must be dealt with.
3. The case of a cartel extractor and a competitive fringe is an extension of the duopoly model. In general, the fringe group will be induced to exhaust its stock first, in a two-phase sequence.
4. When competition is between the owner of a backstop source of supply and a cartel, jumps in the cartel's marginal profit schedule emerge. Strategic timing of development of the backstop turns on the trade-off between expensive early develop-

ment of the backstop versus later development and less "discipline" on the part of the cartel extractor.

5. The discovery of new stocks of reserves can involve costly exploration activity or can be a "free" by-product of extraction. Extraction paths are affected by the possibility of discovering stocks of ore. A case is examined in which uncertainty about stock size induces a firm to slow extraction.

DISCUSSION QUESTIONS

1. Consider two scenarios: (a) Earth must make do with fossil fuels for all time. (b) Fusion power, a constant-cost perpetual supply, becomes available in the year 2020. Compare the price of oil today if (a) is true and if (b) is true.
2. *a.* Derive and explain the price and output paths for a monopolistic versus a competitive mineral industry facing identical constant unit costs and a linear demand curve. Which will exhaust its ore reserves first? Explain why.
   b. Derive the price and output paths assuming that the monopolist begins extraction before the competitive industry. What will be the relationship between the monopolistic and the competitive price over the extraction periods?
   c. How will your results change from case (a) if the demand curve is isoelastic?
3. "Uncertainty about the date of arrival or the cost of a backstop technology will always raise the initial price of a nonrenewable mineral over its price under certainty." Is this statement true, false, or uncertain? Explain your answer.
4. Explain why, when the size of a nonrenewable resource stock is uncertain, the optimal price path is scalloped (there is a discontinuity at the date the uncertainty is resolved), and why the initial price of the resource is greater than the price that would prevail without the uncertainty. Will the private market obtain this price path?
5. There are two deposits of copper, one with a known total reserve of 1 million tons, the other with an unknown total reserve. From which deposit is ore extracted first, and why? Does it matter what the extraction costs are for each deposit?

SELECTED READINGS

Dasgupta, P. S., R. J. Gilbert, and J. E. Stiglitz (1983). "Strategic Considerations in Invention and Innovation: The Case of Natural Resources," *Econometrica* 51 (September), pp. 1439–1448.

Eswaran, M., and T. Lewis (1985). "Exhaustible Resources and Alternative Equilibrium Concepts," *Canadian Journal of Economics*, 18, pp. 459–473.

Gallini, N., T. Lewis, and Roger Ware (1983). "Strategic Timing and Pricing of a Substitute in a Cartelized Resource Market," *Canadian Journal of Economics* 16 (August), pp. 429–446.

Gilbert, R. (1979). "Optimal Depletion of an Uncertain Stock," *Review of Economic Studies*, 46, pp. 47–57.

Hartwick, J. M. (1991). "The Non-Renewable Exploring-Extracting Firm and the r % Rule," *Resources and Energy* 13, pp. 129–143.

Hartwick, J. M., and P. Sadorsky (1990). "Duopoly in Exhaustible Resource Exploration and Extraction," *Canadian Journal of Economics* 23, pp. 276–293.

Kemp, M. C. (1976). "How to Eat a Cake of Unknown Size," in M. C. Kemp, *Three Topics in the Theory of Internationl Trade: Distribution, Welfare and Uncertainty*. Amsterdam: North Holland.

Loury, G. (1978). "The Optimal Exploitation of an Unknown Reserve," *Review of Economic Studies* 45, pp. 621–636.

Maskin, E. S., and D. M. Newbery (1990). "Disadvantageous Oil Tariffs and Dynamic Consistency," *American Economic Review* 80, pp. 143–156.

Newbery, D. (1980). "Oil Prices, Cartels, and the Problem of Dynamic Inconsistency," *Economic Journal* 91 (September), pp. 617–646.

Pindyck, R. S. (1978). "The Optimal Exploration and Production of Nonrenewable Resources," *Journal of Political Economy* 86 (October), pp. 841–861.

Polasky, S. (1992). "The Private and Social Value of Information: Exploration for Exhaustible Resources," *Journal of Environmental Economics and Management* 23, pp. 1–21.

Stiglitz, J. E. (1974). "Monopoly and the Rate of Extraction of Exhaustible Resources," *American Economic Review* 66 (September), pp. 655–661.

chapter 10

Forest Use

INTRODUCTION

In economic terms, a forest is a form of capital, like a mineral deposit or a stock of fish. It is a renewable resource that relies on both natural regeneration and replanting by forest managers to produce new generations of trees. Many species of trees are very long-lived and may take over 100 years to reach their maximum size. Land covered by forests can provide a sustained flow of marketable products. These include timber, fruit, latex, oils, genetic materials, pharmaceuticals, rattan, and grazing for farm or game animals. Some of these products—fruit, oils, grazing, and latex, for example—can be sustainably harvested over relatively short intervals of time. Others, notably timber, may require long intervals between harvests. Forested land can also be put to a host of other uses and provide many other benefits that may or may not have easily measured value to individuals or society in general. These include recreation, habitats for a variety of plant and animal species, climatic impacts, watersheds, and soil erosion protection.

The focus of this chapter is on the optimal use of forest resources. We begin with a brief discussion of the biological basics of forests, then turn to an examination of timber harvesting. We look at how timber production is undertaken on land that is bare initially, then see how our results are affected when there is an existing forest with trees of different ages and species growing on the land. In some cases, selective cutting of age classes or types of trees will be the most profitable strategy. In other cases, a forest will be clear-cut. We also briefly consider situations in which a forest is cleared to make way for other activities.

Unlike the steady-state fishery, in timber harvesting the stock and that year's increment—the entire tree—are harvested after a period of time, not just the increment. On a plot of land used for growing timber, a cycle is observed: trees cut, trees grown, trees cut, trees grown, and so on. The period between one cut and the next is often called the *rotation interval* and is the center of analysis in the economics of timber production. What is the optimal rotation interval, and why and how does it vary from place to place and time to time? We take up these matters in this chapter. We also discuss how the optimal rotation interval is affected by the inclusion of ***nontimber values.*** These are uses other than timber production to which forested land can be put.

We then review the links between a price-taking firm in forestry and the industry price and quantity. Since separate plots are harvested in cycles, there can be large quantities somewhat suddenly delivered to market. Intermediaries or the use of inventories of forest products may be required to bring about smooth flows of timber for market demanders. Alternatively, a monopolistic, vertically integrated forestry operation, or a manager of large tracts of public forests, might arrange for smoothing of deliveries. The large firm or managers of public forests would control many plots of land on which marketable timber was grown. They could affect the total quantity delivered per unit of time and thus affect the price. The determination of the efficient rotation period on the many plots of land would be affected by the market conditions and method of smoothing deliveries.

Government policy instruments—taxes and subsidies to the forest industry—are examined next to see how they affect optimal rotation intervals. We then discuss the impact of property rights on the management of the forest. This section of the chapter serves as an introduction to the final topic: the role played by government policies in deforestation. Insecure property rights and a host of tax, trade, and other policies

BOX 10.1 **Forest Resources**

In 1990, the world contained an estimated 3.4 billion hectares of forests. Tropical forests covered 1.76 billion hectares. Forests in industrialized countries extended over 1.43 billion hectares. During the period 1981–1990, tropical forests had been lost at a rate of 15.4 million hectares (0.8 percent) per year. Net annual deforestation during this period exceeded 2 percent in 10 countries. *Deforestation* refers to the clearing of forest lands for agriculture and other land uses such as settlements, mining, and construction of infrastructure. Brazil and Indonesia accounted for the largest extent of forest area lost. Temperate forests increased moderately. Table 1 provides information on forest extent, logging activity, and deforestation for regions of the world.

Logging of tropical broadleaf forests during the 1980s averaged 5.6 million hectares, which was 0.5 percent of the total broadleaf forest area. Eighty-four percent of this occurred in forest not previously logged. Table 2 provides several measures of logging activity for regions of the world. Production of roundwood (all wood in the rough, whether destined of fuelwood or industrial uses) increased 19 percent between 1979–1981 and 1989–1991. The region of highest increase was Africa, where most of the wood cut (about 90 percent) was for fuelwood and charcoal, not for industrial uses such as paper production and construction materials. Globally, in 1989–1991 about half of the roundwood produced was used for heating and cooking.

Trade in roundwood was highest in Asia, and Japan was the world's largest net importer of roundwood during 1989–1991. Regions that are net exporters of roundwood saw an increase in trade over the decade. *(Tables continued on the next 2 pages)*

Source: Data collected by the Food and Agriculture Organization and Economic Commission for Europe, both United Nations agencies as cited in World Resources Institute (1996). *World Resources 1994–1995.* Washington, D.C.: World Resources Institute.

TABLE 1 **FORREST RESOURCES**

	Extent of Natural Forest (000 ha)		Annual Deforestation		Annual Logging of Closed Broadleaf Forest, 1981–1990		Plantations (000 ha)	
	1990	1980	1981–1990 Extent	Percentage	Extent (000 ha)	Percentage	Extent 1990	Annual Change 1981–1990
Africa								
North Africa	X	5,490	X	X	X	X	X	X
West Sahelian Africa	40,768	43,720	295	0.7	6	0.2	251	21
East Sahelian Africa	65,450	71,395	595	0.8	4	0.1	762	32
West Africa	55,607	61,520	591	1.0	312	2.0	445	14
Central Africa	204,112	215,503	1,140	0.5	571	0.4	175	11
Tropical Southern Africa	145,868	159,322	1,345	0.8	9	0.1	1,057	47
Temperate South Africa	X	1,421	X	X	X	X	X	X
Insular Africa	15,782	17,128	135	0.8				
Asia								
Temperate and Middle East Asia	X	186,084	X	X	X	X	X	X
South Asia	63,931	69,442	551	0.8	62	0.2	19,758	1,480
Continental South East Asia	75,240	88,377	1,314	1.5	304	0.5	3,197	140
Insular South East Asia	135,426	154,687	1,926	1.2	1,721	1.5	9,156	482
The Americas								
Canada	247,164	X	X	X	X	X	X	X
United States	209,573	299,154	X	X	X	X	X	X
Central America and Mexico	68,096	79,216	1,112	1.4	90	0.4	273	17
Caribbean Subregion	47,115	48,333	122	0.3	42	0.1	442	23
Nontropical South America	X	52,540	X	X	X	X	X	X
Tropical South America	802,904	864,639	6,174	0.7	2,445	0.4	7,922	333
Brazil	561,107	597,816	3,671	0.6	1,982	0.5	7,000	279
Europe*	140,207	126,210	X	X	X	X	X	X
Soviet Union (former)	754,958	918,930	X	X	X	X	X	X
Oceania**	50,909	185,988	X	X	X	X	X	X

NOTES: *Figures for Europe 1980 do not include Iceland, Italy, Norway, and Sweden. **Figures for Oceania 1990 do not include Fiji and Solomon Islands. Figures for Oceania 1980 do not include New Zealand. X = not available.

Source: Food and Agriculture Organization of the United Nations, as cited in *World Resources, 1994–1995* (World Resources Institute), table 19.1, p. 30.

(Table 2 on the next page.)

TABLE 2 **WOOD PRODUCTION AND TRADE**

	Roundwood Production						*Average Annual Net Trade in Roundwood (000 cu meters)*	
	Total		*Fuel and Charcoal*		*Industrial Roundwood*			
	(000 cu meters) 1989–1991	% Change Since 1979–1981	(000 cu meters) 1989–1991	% Change Since 1979–1981	(000 cu meters) 1989–1991	% Change Since 1979–1981	1979–1981	1989–1991
World	3,462,348	19	1,801,216	23	1,661,131	15		
Africa	513,545	34	455,760	36	57,785	15	−5,286	−4,098
Asia	1,071,682	19	817,437	22	254,245	11	37,310	49,527
North and Central America	749,939	20	147,280	14	602,659	22	−19,116	−25,974
Canada	179,004	15	6,834	40	172,170	15	−473	1,179
United States	508,200	22	90,300	8	417,900	26	−18,728	−27,129
South America	343,918	24	238,304	22	105,614	28	−922	−5,836
Brazil	262,439	25	186,477	24	75,962	29	−97	21
Europe	366,822	10	52,594	3	314,228	12	16,856	17,526
Soviet Union	375,400	5	81,100	2	294,300	6	−14,993	−15,898
Oceania	41,043	21	7,742	22	32,301	20	−8,299	−10,825

NOTES: (1) *Roundwood production* refers to all wood in the rough, whether destined for industrial or fuelwood uses. (2) *Fuel and charcoal* covers all rough wood used in cooking, heating, and power production. (3) *Industrial roundwood* comprises all roundwood products except fuelwood and charcoal. (4) *Average annual net trade in roundwood* is the balance of imports minus exports. Negative numbers indicate that imports exceed exports.

Source: Food and Agriculture Organization of the United Nations, as cited in *World Resources, 1994–1995* (World Resources Institute), table 19.3, p. 311.

appear to be contributing to the conversion of forested land to other uses and to wasteland.

SOME BIOLOGICAL BASICS OF TREES AND FORESTS

As a tree grows, the amount of wood usable for commercial harvests changes over time. The typical schedule of the tree's growth over time is sketched in Figure 10.1. We have the volume of wood per unit area (for example, cubic feet per acre or cubic meters per hectare), $V(t)$, growing over time, until a maximum is attained at date t^e. Time here is interpreted as the age of the forest. Beyond this point the trees begin to decay from old age, disease, insect predation, fire, or wind, and eventually collapse. Wood volume develops slowly in the early stages, as the trees take root, and then up to age t^x speeds up. It slows toward date t^e, when the maximum volume is achieved. This yield function measures wood volume net of mortality.

This volume-age schedule can be altered by arranging for the optimal density of trees on a plot, by fertilizing the land, and by other activities such as thinning trees and repressing pests. The schedule can shift in a variety of ways in response to human intervention. This is part of forestry cultivation and management, also known as *silviculture.*

Figure 10.2 shows the relationship between timber volume and age for a stand of Douglas fir in a particular region up to 160 years. Beyond 160 years, these trees may continue to grow very slowly. Some stands have reached an age of 400 years. The data generating the curve shown in Figure 10.2 (and subsequent figures on the Douglas

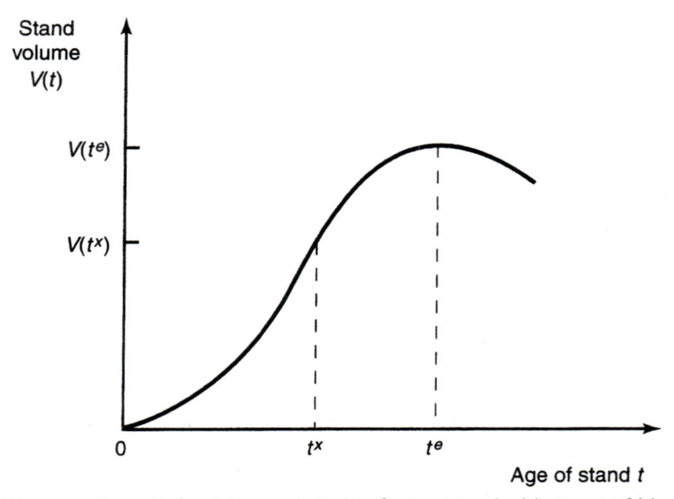

FIGURE 10.1 The growth cycle for a representative forest stand with trees of identical age. The maximum wood volume is obtained when the stand is t^e years old. Beyond t^x, the growth rate slows.

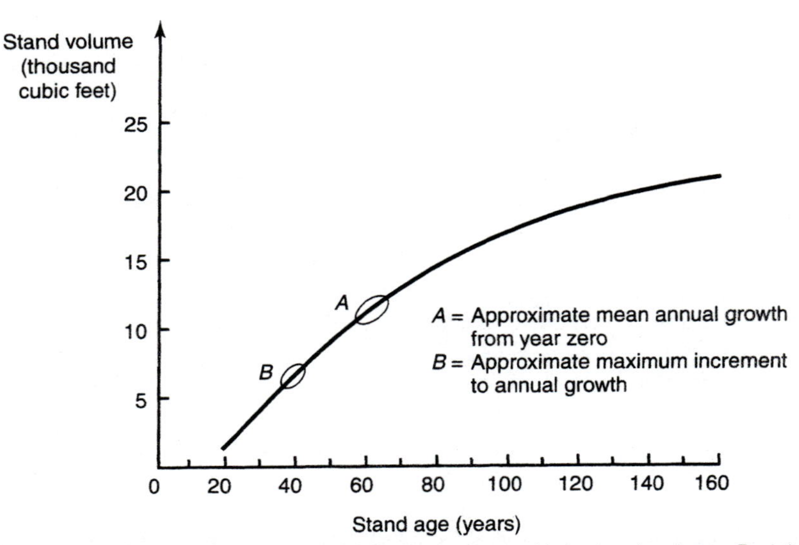

FIGURE 10.2 Volume of standing timber 5.0 inches or more d.b.h., by stand age, Douglas fir, in a particular site. *Source:* Clawson (see Table 10.1).

fir) are shown in Table 10.1. As the stand ages, mortality rises. In one example, a stand of Douglas fir at age 40 had 1,233 stems per hectare and 492 stems at age 80.

The volume-age schedule in Figure 10.1 can be *rewritten* in terms of the annual increase in volume schedule in Figure 10.3. Figure 10.3 resembles the yield-biomass schedule in the discussion of the fishery. The increment in volume is a maximum at wood volume $V(t^x)$ and age t^x. Note, however, that commercial forestry involves harvesting the tree and replanting if profitable, not harvesting the increment in the volume (or mass), as was the case with the sustained-yield fishery. The increment in the volume or stock of fish represented new standard-sized fish in our basic model, whereas here the increment in the volume of a tree represents a slightly larger tree. One does not harvest timber by shaving off part of a growing tree.

The same type of relationship for an actual stand of Douglas fir is shown in Figure 10.4 in the solid curve labeled "annual increase in volume in preceding decade." This curve has also been called the *current annual increment* (CAI), where the annual increment is the average annual increment taken over the 10-year intervals in Table 10.1, column 2. The CAI curve here shows the marginal changes in the volume of timber in the stand from one decade to the next. The data for the curve are derived in column 4 of Table 10.1. The CAI is thus an incremental growth relationship as a function of time. The maximum of the CAI, which occurs at around 40 years, is shown as area *B* in Figure 10.2. Area *B* thus reflects the maximum slope of the age-volume relationship.

Precise measurement of growth relationships in forestry is not possible because many factors can affect tree growth. But around the peak of the growth relationship (CAI), the tree volume changes very little, so that approximations of the growth rela-

TABLE 10.1. **TIME-GROWTH-VOLUME RELATIONSHIPS FOR DOUGLAS FIR, SITE CLASS II, SITE INDEX 180[a]**

Age (years)	Volume standing trees over 5.0 inches d.b.h.[b] (cu ft)	*Mean annual net growth to age*[c]		Change in mean annual net growth over decade (cu ft)[d]	*Increase in standing volume over preceding decade*		
		Volume (cu ft)	As % of volume at age		Total[e] (cu ft)	Average annual volume (cu ft)[f]	As % of volume at end of decade[g]
	(1)	(2)	(3)	(4)	(5)	(6)	(7)
20	1,190	59.5	5.0	—	—	—	—
30	3,600	120.0	3.3	+60.5	2,410	241	6.69
40	6,400	160.0	2.5	+40.0	2,800	280	4.38
50	8,850	177.0	2.0	+17.0	2,450	245	2.77
60	11,050	184.2	1.7	+ 7.2	2,200	220	1.99
70	12,850	183.6	1.4	− 0.6	1,800	180	1.40
80	14,500	181.2	1.2	− 2.4	1,650	165	1.14
90	15,900	176.7	1.1	− 4.5	1,400	140	0.88
100	17,100	171.0	1.0	− 5.7	1,200	120	0.70
110	18,000	163.6	0.9	− 7.4	900	90	0.50
120	18,800	156.7	0.8	− 6.9	800	80	0.43
130	19,450	149.6	0.77	− 7.1	650	65	0.33
140	20,000	143.6	0.71	− 6.0	650	65	0.32
150	20,650	137.7	0.67	− 5.9	550	55	0.27
160	21,150	132.2	0.63	− 5.5	500	50	0.24

[a]Fully stocked acre, trees of same age: volumes are stem volumes, exclusive of bark and limbs, between stump and 4-inch top; stump height equals d.b.h. for trees up to 24 inches d.b.h., and 24 inches for larger trees. Figures rounded to nearest 50. Management at "natural" level—fire control, but no thinning, no fertilizing. [b]d.b.h. means diameter breast-high. [c]Column 2 is column 1 divided by age; column 3 is column 2 as percent of column 1. [d]Column 4 is difference between volumes in previous and current age in column 2. [e]Column 5 is difference between volumes in previous and current ages in column 1. [f]Column 6 is column 5 divided by 10, to put decade differences on an average annual basis. [g]Column 7 is column 6 divided by column 1.

Source: Basic data in column 1 compiled by P. A. Briegleb, Pacific Northwest—Forest Range Experiment Station. All other figures derived from these data, as cited in M. Clawson (1977). *Decision Making in Timber Production, Harvest, and Marketing.* Washington, D.C.: Resources for the Future, Research Paper R-4. Clawson is also the source for Figures 10.2 and 10.4. Reprinted by permission.

tionship are possible. The tree can be harvested over a fairly long interval of time without the time elapsed significantly affecting its volume. A number of possible management schemes for a given tract of land are thus possible, as we shall see.

The dashed curve in Figure 10.4, called the mean annual growth to age, is ob-

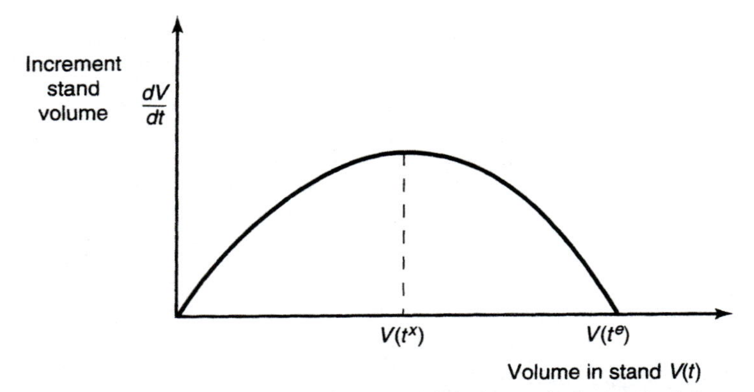

FIGURE 10.3 This schedule is derived from Figure 10.1. Instead of age, the increment in wood volume at different ages is plotted against the volume of wood in the stand of trees.

tained from column 2 of Table 10.1. This curve is also known as the *mean annual increment* (MAI). The MAI measures the average increase in timber volume from one decade (or year) to the next. The maximum of the MAI is called the *culmination of the mean annual increment* (CMAI). Note that the CMAI occurs at around 60 years and that the CAI intersects the MAI at this point. This relationship can be shown mathematically. The MAI is equal to $V(t)/t$. If we then maximize MAI with respect to t, we obtain $V'(t)t - V(t) = 0$, where $V'(t)$ is the derivative of $V(t)$ with respect to t, $(dV(t)/dt)$. Rearranging this expression yields $V'(t) = V(t)/t$. Hence, the MAI is at a maximum when it is equal to the CAI. The CMAI is also shown in Figure 10.2 at area A, approximately where the slope of a line from the origin to the age-volume relationship is the steepest. In economic terms, we can think of the CAI as the marginal product of time as the input and the MAI as an average product of time.

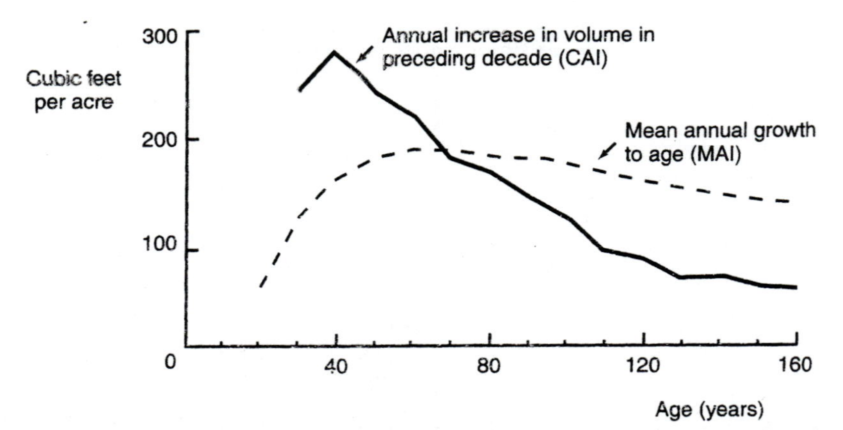

FIGURE 10.4 Annual growth by age and in relationship to standing timber volume, Douglas fir, in a particular site. *Source:* Clawson (see Table 10.1).

THE EFFICIENT ROTATION PERIOD FOR THE FIRM

To obtain the economically efficient sequence of rotations, the objective is to organize the forest to maximize the present value of a stream of net benefits. The key question is what constitutes these net benefits. In this section we focus on timber values only. That is, the benefits of forests are derived from the production and harvest of timber. This is a narrow view because, as noted earlier, forests also provide non-timber values (NTVs). After examining optimal rotations of timber, we will recast the model to include NTVs. Maximizing the net benefits from the forest requires in all cases that we maximize the present value of the land used to grow the trees. Land is vital to the calculation because it has opportunity costs—the other ways it could be used (if for nothing else, for the next crop of trees). If we don't take into account the next best alternative use of the land—be it for recreation, building houses, or supporting wildlife—we will not make the most efficient use of scarce resources. We will see the role of land values in the calculations below when we contrast efficient rotations with other decision rules.

When is the best time to harvest a tree or stand of trees? In practice, it depends on many factors, such as the final use of the harvested trees; whether we begin with bare land or a mature forest; cost, productivity, and demand conditions; and leasing or ownership arrangements. If, for example, a forest is to be used for pulp to make paper, the size of the stems and trunks is not important, but the volume of wood is. If the product is large timber beams, then the trees must be large enough in dimension to yield these beams. Larger trees also fetch a higher price per board foot than do smaller trees.

Timing of a Timber Harvest

We will abstract from these complications for the moment and concentrate on the timing of a timber harvest, beginning with a tract of land on which trees must first be planted. We begin with an economic model of the optimal time to cut a stand of trees of uniform age and growth characteristics. Once the stand is harvested, saplings will be replanted and the cycle begun again. We seek the economically efficient rotation period over an infinite number of cycles of planting, harvesting, replanting, and harvesting. We then contrast the efficient rotation period with an alternative method of managing the forest: the single-rotation model. It may not be economic to replant the stand. Second growths of timber may be too slow or costs of reforestation may be too high relative to the price of timber. Alternative uses of the land may have a higher present value than can be obtained by harvesting trees for timber products. We assume initially that replanting is economic to the producer of timber.

Determining the economically efficient sequence of rotations involves choosing a date to harvest and replant time after time. The interval could be varying or constant. We assume that the harvesting and replanting occur within the same period of time—say 1 year. Present value in this model is the dollar benefit from a series of plantings, harvestings, plantings, and so on into the infinite future. The objective is to maximize the present value of the land in growing trees. If the land is to be used for, say, houses 50 years hence, a different optimal forestry plan is required.

Two types of direct costs are associated with maximizing the net present value from the forest. First the costs of planting, silviculture, harvesting, storage, transportation to market, and so on—the actual costs of managing a forest. The second cost is the interest forgone while waiting to harvest the trees—the money that could be obtained if the trees were cut sooner and reinvested either in growing more trees on the land or in alternative enterprises. The value of the land on which the trees grow is an indirect cost. Land receives the residual income—the rent—from raising and marketing the forest, the income remaining after all planting, maintenance, and harvesting costs have been paid.

In our central model, we incorporate costs of clearing and planting the site, harvesting, and later delivery. By working with present discounted values, we have incorporated costs of delaying cutting. Land or site rent will be the residual. We want to ensure that the rotation interval chosen maximizes this land rent.

Suppose, then, that it costs a fixed amount, $D, to plant a unit of land (say an acre), and $c per cubic foot of wood to harvest the trees.[1] The cost in present value of the first "round" in the infinite cycle is

$$D + cV(T_1 - T_0)e^{-r \cdot (T_1 - T_0)} \tag{10.1}$$

where T_0 is the date of planting and T_1 the date of harvesting. The term $e^{-r \cdot (T_1 - T_0)}$ transfers harvests costs from the harvest date back to the beginning of the "cycle," or back to planting date T_0. Let p be the revenue per cubic foot sold upon harvesting, which we assume is constant in this competitive forest industry. Each forest manager faces a perfectly elastic demand curve that is stationary over time. Then the profit in present value (landowner's benefit) from planting and harvesting is

$$(p - c)V(T_1 - T_0)e^{-r(T_1 - T_0)} - D \tag{10.2}$$

Note that we have removed the multiplicative symbol (•) in Equation (10.2) and subsequent equations to avoid clutter.

After harvesting, the land is replanted at cost D and a new round is undertaken, then a third round. We have then the complete present value

$$\begin{aligned} W = {} & [(p - c)V(T_1 - T_0)e^{-r(T_1 - T_0)} - D] \\ & + e^{-r(T_1 - T_0)}[(p - c)V(T_2 - T_1)e^{-r(T_2 - T_1)} - D] \\ & + e^{-r(T_2 - T_0)}[(p - c)V(T_3 - T_2)e^{-r(T_3 - T_2)} - D] \\ & + \cdots \end{aligned} \tag{10.3}$$

Now we can assert that the intervals $(T_1 - T_0)$, $(T_2 - T_1)$, $(T_3 - T_2)$, and so on *must be the same* provided p, c, and $V(T)$ remain unchanged over time. The reason is straightforward but subtle: Once T_1 is arrived at, the remaining problem can be made identical to the original problem by relabeling dates. Once one cycle is completed, the problem is the same as before. This is because the horizon is always infinity. Let the intervals between planting and harvesting be written now as I. We call this the ***rotation interval***. Equation (10.3) becomes with these intervals, I,

$$\begin{aligned} W = [(p - c)V(I)e^{-rI} - D] &+ e^{-rI}[(p - c)V(I)e^{-rI} - D] \\ &+ e^{-2rI}[(p - c)V(I)e^{-rI} - D] \\ &+ e^{-3rI}[(p - c)V(I)e^{-rI} - D] \\ &+ \cdots \end{aligned} \tag{10.4}$$

Factor out the term e^{-rI} from the second term and each subsequent term of equation (10.4) and leave the rest of the discounting terms inside the brackets. This yields

$$\begin{aligned} W = [(p - c)V(I)e^{-rI} - D] &+ e^{-rI}\{[(p - c)V(I)e^{-rI} - D] \\ &+ e^{-rI}[(p - c)V(I)e^{-rI} - D] + e^{-2rI}[(p - c)V(I)e^{-rI} - D] + \cdots\} \end{aligned}$$

We see then that after the first term, we have exactly the same infinite sequence we had before, except that it is discounted one rotation interval. We can then substitute W for the infinite sum represented by the second term. This gives

$$W = [(p - c)V(I)e^{-rI} - D] + e^{-rI}W$$

We now solve in terms of W and obtain

$$W = [(p - c)V(I)e^{-rI} - D]\left(\frac{1}{1 - e^{-rI}}\right) \tag{10.5}$$

The forest manager then maximizes W, the value of the forest land, as represented by equation (10.5), by choosing a rotation interval I. The manager sets $dW/dI = 0$. This yields the condition

$$(p - c)V'(I) = r(p - c)V(I) + rW^* \tag{10.6}$$

where again $V'(I)$ is the derivative of $V(I)$ with respect to I. The left-hand side of equation (10.6) is the value of the marginal product of the timber if it is held another period. Over the period, the stand "grows" V' in physical volume and each unit of that volume is worth $(p - c)$ dollars. The right-hand side of equation (10.6) represents two opportunity costs that measure what the landowner gives up if the trees are not harvested and the land is not replanted at each interval of time. The term $r(p - c)V(I)$ is the interest on the money the landowner would earn if she or he had cut the timber in the stand and put the money into a bank to earn interest at rate r. The term rW^* is the opportunity cost of the land—the interest earned if the land is sold for its optimal timber production value, W^*. This optimal value is also called *site value*, and it represents the greatest amount that could be offered for the unforested land if it is used to grow timber. The rW^* represents the *site rent.*[2] Figure 10.5 shows a typical relationship between W and stand age for three different interest rates: 3, 5, and 8 percent. For each interest rate, there is a unique stand age at which W is at a maximum. The figure illustrates that as interest rates increase, the site values at all stand ages diminish. We can then use these maximum values of W to help determine the optimal rotation interval.

Figure 10.6 illustrates the determination of the optimal rotation interval using equation (10.5) and optimized values for W^* at interest rates of 3 and 5 percent. The optimal rotation interval in each case, I^*, is found where the left-hand side of equation

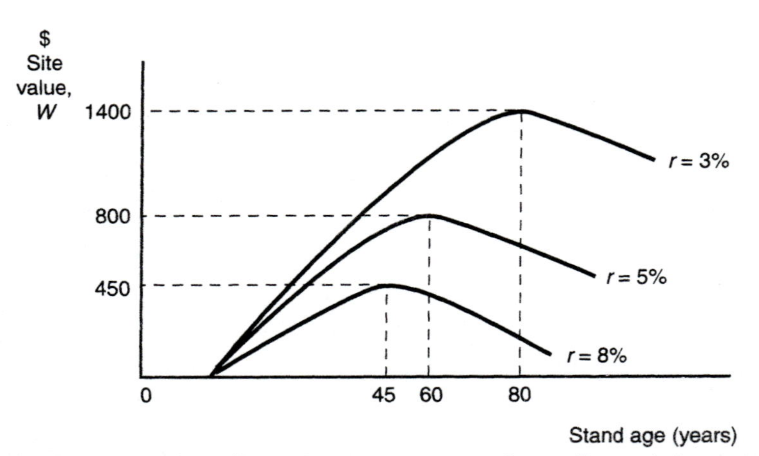

FIGURE 10.5 Site values for different interest rates are shown. For each interest rate, r, a unique maximum value of forested land, W, is found. Higher interest rates mean lower site values.

(10.5) is equal to the right-hand side. A typical value of the marginal product of the forest in growing timber, $(p - c)V'(I)$, is shown for the left-hand side of equation (10.6). Call this the VMPT curve. The timber has no market value until it is at least 25 years old. From that point on, the marginal product rises. Notice, however, that VMPT begins to get relatively flat after a stand age of 70 years. The right-hand side of equation (10.6) represents the two opportunity costs: $r(p - c)V(I)$ plus rW^*. We call this curve TOC, for timber opportunity costs. The intercept of this equation is rW^*. From the information in Figure 10.5, at $r = 5$ percent, rW^* is \$40; at 3 percent, it is \$42. The TOC curve then rises as $V(I)$ increases over the stand's age at rate r.

The optimal rotation interval, I^*, is determined where the VMPT equals TOC. In Figure 10.6, this is shown at a stand age of 60 years if interest rates are 5 percent and 80 years if they are 3 percent.

Let's now contrast this rotation interval with other possible outcomes and decision criteria. Suppose first that there is no discounting of future returns or costs: $r = 0$. In this case, the landowner wishes to maximize the undiscounted annualized stream of revenues. If regeneration costs are ignored ($D = 0$), the efficient rotation interval is where the CAI equals the MAI, $V'(I) = V(I)/I$. As we noted above, this is the maximum sustained yield of the forest. This is the preferred rule because it yields higher annual average revenues than will the maximization of total volume from a single stand. Even though the discount rate is zero, there is still a physical opportunity cost associated with the lowered physical growth that occurs while the stand is approaching maximum volume. Note that the efficient solution in this case does not depend on prices or harvesting costs. If there are replanting costs, the efficient rotation is no longer where CAI and MAI are equal, because timber prices and harvesting and replanting costs are included in the solution. The solution becomes $(p - c)V'(I) =$

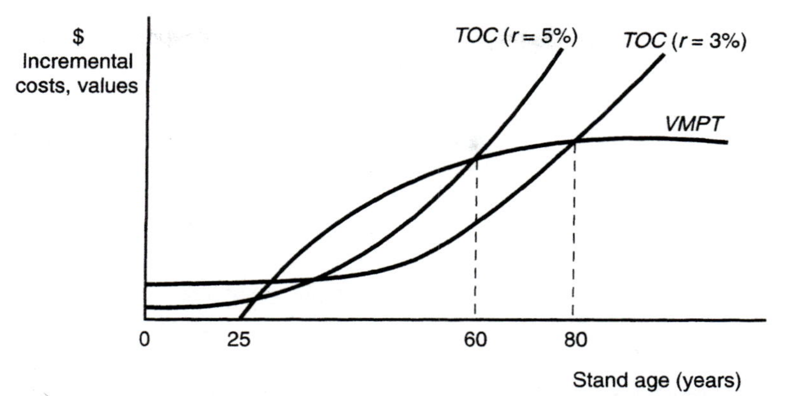

FIGURE 10.6 Optimal rotation interval is 60 years if $r = 5\%$. At this stand age, the value of the marginal product of growing timber, *VMPT*, equals the opportunity costs of deferring the forest. If $r = 3\%$, the optimal rotation interval is lengthened to 80 years.

$[(p - c)V(I) - D]/I$; and while the efficient solution with positive interest rates is generally shorter than when interest rates are zero, this is not always the case. See Binkley (1987) for a discussion of the possible cases. The Appendix to this chapter looks at the effect on the efficient rotation interval of changes in parameters of the model. These exercises are helpful in obtaining a greater understanding of the mechanics of the efficient model and can also be helpful in the analysis of public policies.

Suppose now that r is greater than zero, but $W^* = 0$. This means that land has no inherent value; its return or site value will be zero. Site value could be zero if unlimited land was available. Then from equation (10.6), we see that $V'(I) = rV(I)$. There will be no intercept in our line reflecting opportunity costs of deferring the harvest. In terms of Figure 10.6, imagine the *TOC* line dropping down. The efficient rotation interval rises. This result is equivalent to the maximization of the value of the forest over one rotation. For a single rotation, the problem is to choose I to maximize $e^{-rI}(p - c)V(I) - D$. The rotation interval that maximizes this expression must satisfy the optimality condition $V'(I) = rV(I)$. The single rotation does not take into account the net benefits of future harvests—the revenues from subsequent harvests grown on the land. The single-rotation decision rule is inappropriate for a timber firm that does not have an infinitely elastic supply of land on which to grow and harvest trees.

Efficient Harvests in a Mature Forest

The notion of efficient rotations can seem at odds with actual timber management, where there may be stands well past the age for the profit-maximizing rotation. We can see using planned rotations in a cultivated forest, but somehow not in a natural setting. One reason is that the first cut may involve trees of different sizes, ages, and species. In later cuts, perhaps, the forest has regenerated itself or has been cultivated as a planned forest. But the first cut involves a distinctly unplanned forest. Does this make the analysis of the efficient rotations irrelevant? Suppose the forest is to be clear-cut.

The first cut in clear-cutting a forest results in a net revenue of $\$K$, presumably positive, and is independent of rotation time. This $\$K$ is a fixed value at the beginning of the problem and does not affect subsequent marginal decisions. That is, after clear-cutting, the forest is managed in the same way as our bare land model covering an infinite series of rotations. We can incorporate this initial "messiness" into the framework of efficient rotations without amending our model or our general concept of a planned planting and harvesting cycle. However, if the original forest is thinned and gradually adjusted to an efficient program with selective cutting, a very complex planning problem emerges.

Selective harvesting of certain trees can bring a forest toward some sort of long-run equilibrium from a historically given setting. We might never get to a clear-cutting rotation cycle on the plot; for example, we might obtain an equilibrium with many ages of trees growing simultaneously and selective harvesting of those at the efficient age being the efficient policy. People have inquired into these issues in formal models and have found that some long-run equilibria involve maintaining a plot of land in trees of different ages that are harvested selectively rather than clear-cut. See, for example, Kemp and Long (1983) and Chang (1981).

Costs obviously play an important role in the strategy chosen. Clear-cutting may be the least-cost alternative if leaving some trees makes removing others quite costly. An example is a coniferous forest in which most of the species are commercially usable. In other forests, however, selective cutting may be highly cost-effective. Selective logging is typically practiced in forests that are very heterogeneous, with a significant portion of the wood volumes not merchantable. Almost all commercial timber harvesting in the tropics and in mixed-species and temperate hardwood forests is selectively logged. The redwoods of the American west have always been selectively cut. Machinery and technologies now exist that make selective cutting of some small trees cost-effective. Selective cutting may also minimize erosion of soils and ensure continued productivity of certain forest types over time. The efficient harvesting strategy will depend on soil conditions, terrain, the feasible harvesting technology, susceptibility to fires, and other factors.[3]

When may it pay to harvest a stand and not replant or reuse the land for growing more timber? Under an efficient rotation plan, we referred to rW^* as the opportunity cost of the land or its site rent. If there are alternative uses for the land, the correct way to compute the efficient rotation for an existing stand of timber is to substitute the value of the land in its highest use for W^* in equation (10.5). It could be that if the plot of land was cleared of timber and used for agriculture or housing, a surplus W that exceeds W^* could be obtained net of clearing costs. In this case, it makes economic sense to harvest all the existing trees (clear the land) and use the plot for agriculture or another activity. Obviously not all treed land has timber production as its best use. In the United States, the area of forest land was cut about in half as a consequence of land conversion to agriculture. During the late 1880s, the rate of deforestation in the United States exceeded by an order of magnitude the current rate in South America.

Socially Optimal Rotation Intervals: Timber Harvesting and Nontimber Values

We have not yet said anything about the socially optimal rotation interval for harvesting timber versus the rotation interval resulting from private management of timber resources. There are a number of possible cases. If social and private discount rates coincide and there are no externalities present in timber harvesting, and no imperfect competition, then an equilibrium such as 80 years (with $r = 3$ percent) is socially optimal. If, however, private discount rates exceed social discount rates (e.g., 5 percent instead of 3 percent), the rotation interval for the private firm would be shorter than is socially optimal (compare 80 and 60 years in Figure 10.6).

Also, timber harvesting firms and society may place different values on land. Society may wish, for example, to incorporate recreational use and wildlife and ecological preservation into its valuation of the land, whereas the private enterprise may not. Incorporating these nontimber values (NTVs) may affect the rotation interval: It may increase, decrease, or not change very much when the *multiple uses* of the forest are incorporated into decisions about timber harvesting. Some NTVs are higher when the forest cover is young or newly harvested. For example, deer do better if trees are cut at a young age because this allows more light to penetrate the forest and encourage growth of new vegetation that they consume. Alternatively, many birds must have old growth and undisturbed forests for nesting. This suggests a longer rotation interval than if NTVs were not present. It could also be the case that the value of land used to grow trees that are never harvested exceeds the value of the land used to grow and harvest timber. A social planner would then not allow the harvest of timber from the forest. This could happen if the NTVs are large and adversely affected by timber harvesting—for example, if plant and animal habitat are destroyed and the social value of these ecosystems exceeds the market value of the timber (over an infinite number of potential rotations).

There are a number of difficulties with evaluating NTVs. Many uses of the forest do not have well-defined market values. Determination of socially optimal forest use thus requires imputation of values for nonmarket uses such as the preservation of species habitats. We discussed techniques for measuring nonmarket values in Chapter 6. Leaving these difficulties aside for now, let us see how the efficient rotation interval might be affected by the inclusion of NTVs. Hartman (1976) and Calish, Fight, and Teeguarden (1978) were among the first to examine rotation intervals when NTVs are incorporated to arrive at an optimal rotation interval. Our discussion is based on Hartman's work and that of Bowes and Krutilla (1989).

Assume that we start with bare land and plant the entire plot within one time period, so that all the growing trees will be of the same age. Assume further that the benefits from NTVs are also a function of the age of the stand. Let the dollar value of the benefit flow be given by $N(t)$ per acre of forested land at any stand age t. The present value from NTVs is then

$$B = [N(T_1 - T_0)e^{-r(T_1 - T_0)} + e^{-r(T_1 - T_0)}[N(T_2 - T_1)e^{-r(T_2 - T_0)} + e^{-r(T_2 - T_1)}[N(T_3 - T_2)e^{-r(T_3 - T_2)} + \cdots \quad (10.7)$$

The same logic applies to equation (10.7) as to (10.5): that all the rotation intervals will be of the same length and we can factor out an e^{-rI} from (10.7) and substitute a B, to obtain

$$B = [N(I)e^{-rI}]\left(\frac{1}{1 - e^{-rI}}\right) \tag{10.8}$$

The social planner then maximizes the total value of the forest, F, in producing timber and nontimber benefits, where $F = W + B$, with W defined from equation (10.5) and B from (10.8). Maximizing F with respect to I yields the condition that I must satisfy

$$V'(I) + N(I) = rV(I) + rF^* \tag{10.9}$$

where F^* is the optimal value of the land including both timber and NTVs. Equation (10.9) can be interpreted as the optimal multiple use of the forest. The optimal rotation will again be at a stand age that equates the value of a marginal increase in stand age (the left-hand side of equation 10.9) with the opportunity costs of delaying the harvest—the forgone interest on the timber harvested plus the forgone land rent on delaying the rotation (the right-hand side). Thus NTVs enter in two ways—through $N(I)$ and rB^*. There is no reason to expect $N(I)$ to be increasing or decreasing throughout its range as I increases. This means that the socially optimal rotation interval for multiple-use forest management may be longer than, shorter than, or virtually identical to the efficient rotation interval for timber harvests. It is of course also possible that if $N(I)$ is very large, there will be no rotation interval at which equation (10.9) is satisfied, i.e., the timber is never harvested. In general, however, we expect the socially efficient rotation interval under multiple use to be somewhere between the timber management rotation and the stand age that maximizes the present value of the returns from NTVs alone. The solution depends on the total NTVs versus the present value of the timber harvests and on the separate rates of growth of the NTVs and timber values. If NTVs rise with stand age, the multiple-use rotation will be greater than the timber-harvest-only rotation. However, NTVs could fall with stand age, and this will lower the rotation interval. Some of the empirical work to date finds that land-use specialization is the best way to provide the multiple outputs from the forest. See Swallow, Parks, and Wear (1990), Swallow and Wear (1993), and Vincent and Binkley (1993) for examinations of optimal multiple use of forests. Box 10.2 illustrates some possible rotation intervals under multiple use management.

BOX 10.2 **Nontimber Values and Optimal Rotation Intervals**

Calish, Fight, and Teeguarden (1978; hereafter referred to as CFT) investigated some of the multiple uses of a forest and how their values changed over the age of the stand. Although the empirical data on which these values were based are limited, they are suggestive of the possible impacts NTVs could have on optimal rotation intervals. CFT compiled indices of NTVs for game species such as deer, and for water flows and aesthetic values, and then combined these with the value of the marginal product of timber over the stand age to see how optimal rotation intervals might change with the addition of NTVs. Figure 1(a)–(d) is adapted from Bowes and Krutilla's discussion (1989) of CFT's work.

BOX 10.2 *(Continued)*

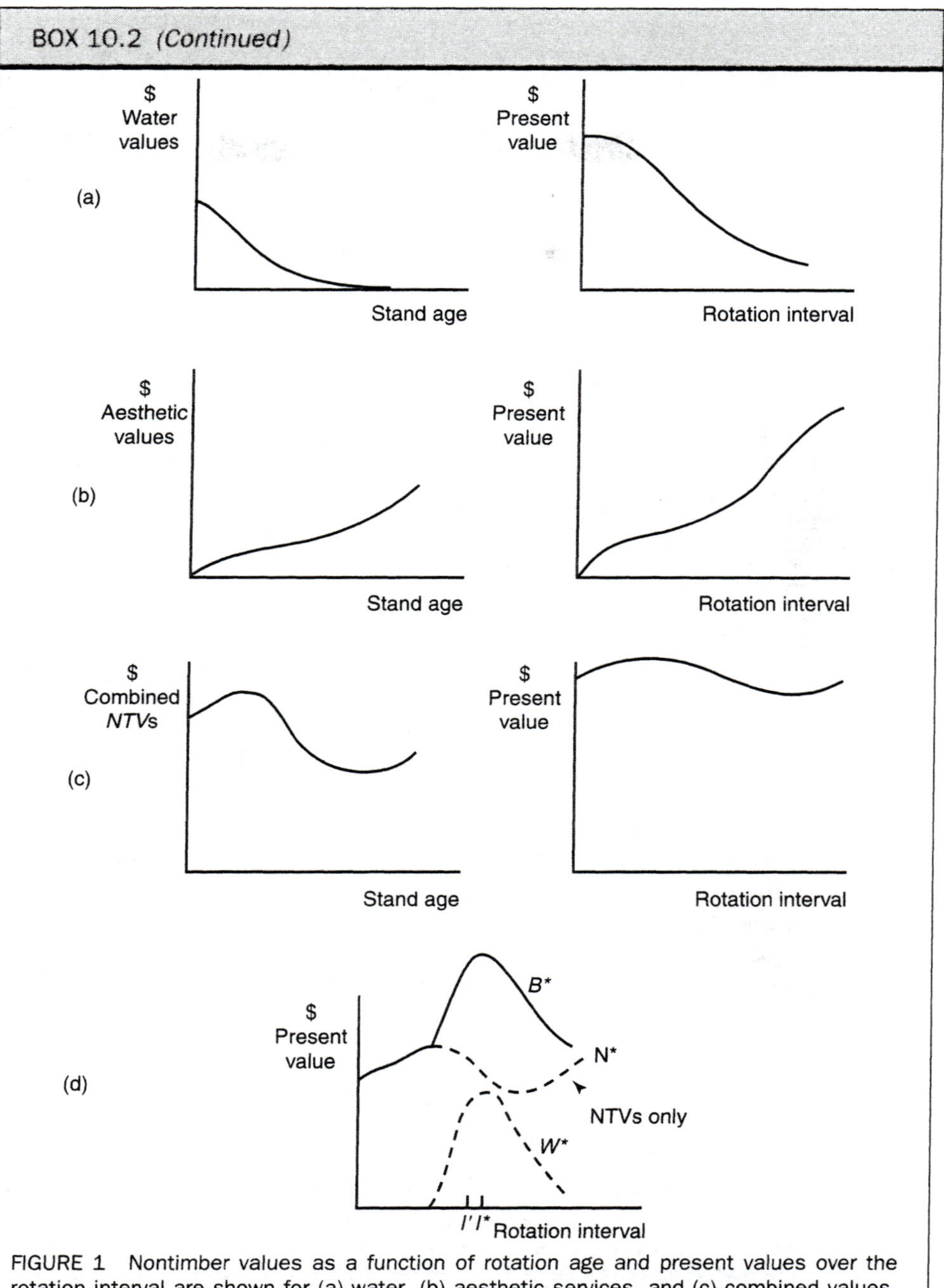

FIGURE 1 Nontimber values as a function of rotation age and present values over the rotation interval are shown for (a) water, (b) aesthetic services, and (c) combined values. (d) Shown here are combined present values of timber plus NTVs (curve $B*$) and timber alone (curve $W*$). The optimal rotation interval is slightly shorter when NTVs are included: I' versus $I*$.

BOX 10.2 *(Continued)*

Figure 1(a)–(c) show the NTVs as a function of the age of the stand and their present values over the rotation interval. In (a), the value of water flows decline with stand age; hence, its present value declines as the rotation interval increases. In (b), NTVs rise for aesthetic services of the forest as the stand ages and present values rise as the rotation interval rises. When these NTVs are combined—in (c)—and NTVs for hunting wildlife are also added, the resulting NTV and present value first rise, then decline. However, if the graph were extended to longer rotation intervals, the rising value of aesthetics could eventually lead to an increase in the present value of all amenities combined.

Figure 1(d) illustrates the present value from timber harvests over the rotation interval (W^*), the present value of NTVs (N^*), and the combined multiple-use present values (B^*). The maximum of W^* indicates the efficient timber harvest excluding NTVs; the maximum of B^* is the optimal multiple-use rotation interval. The multiple-use optimal rotation interval is slightly shorter than the optimal rotation for timber harvest excluding NTVs. This is because for CFT's empirical work, the combined effect of the NTVs is relatively flat over the rotation interval.

Bowes and Krutilla undertake their own investigation of NTVs for subalpine lodgepole pine forests in Colorado. These forests are not economic for timber production because the cost of constructing logging roads exceeds the value of the timber. If the timber is managed jointly with programs for augmenting water flows in the region, the optimal multiple-use management of timber and water combined can yield positive net benefits. Table 1 presents their data on one management area. In this example, Bowes and Krutilla assume

TABLE 1 **PRESENT VALUES PER ACRE BY ROTATION AGES, SUBALPINE LODGEPOLE PINES, COLORADO**

Rotation age, years	Timber value	Water value	Roading costs	Total value
10	$-74	$415	$281	$ 60
20	−18	415	248	149
30	−1	390	237	152
40	4	362	242	124
50	6	343	239	111
60	49	331	237	143
70	46	322	238	130
80	42	313	237	118
90	38	311	237	113
100	36	308	237	107
110	33	306	237	103
120	31	304	237	98

NOTES: Data are for the Fraser-Colorado, assuming a discount rate of 4 percent, moderate slope, seasonal roads (permanent construction, open except for seasonally bad conditions) and 5.5 miles of access road per square mile. Fifty percent of the area is harvested initially. The remainder, thinned to half its volume, is then not harvested again.

Source: Bowes and Krutilla (1989), table 5-10, p. 171.

BOX 10.2 *(Continued)*

a 4 percent discount rate and assume that 50 percent of the management area is logged initially. This area is then reharvested periodically. Timber on the other 50 percent of the management area is thinned to half its volume initially but then remains unharvested thereafter. The table shows the values of timber and water flow as well as the costs of road construction for rotation intervals ranging from 10 to 120 years by decade. The table clearly shows that no timber would be harvested if there were no water values. For all rotation intervals, the roading costs exceed the timber values. However, once water management is added, the total value of the forest is maximized at a rotation interval of 30 years for the timber on the plot.

This result leads to a potential problem with multiple-use management: capturing the returns from NTVs. If the forest were owned privately, how could the water benefits be priced and sold? This may be impossible if the water flows enter open access waterways. The harvesting would be undertaken only because of benefits from water flows, but the private landowner cannot capture the value of these benefits. Public management of the forest may be necessary to realize the net benefits from multiple use. This becomes even more likely when we consider recreational, ecological, and other uses of the forest whose values are generally not determined through markets. However, where these goods and services are marketed, landowners typically respond by managing their forests efficiently for multiple uses. Examples are forests in Germany and parts of the southern United States where returns from managing the wildlife exceed returns from timber harvests. The forests are thus managed for wildlife benefits.

Obvious conflicts arise in trying to implement multiple-use management, as has been highlighted in recent years by the case of the spotted owl in the Pacific northwest forests. It is an endangered species, and under the Endangered Species Act of the United States its habitat cannot be disturbed. This has led to the withdrawal of millions of acres of forested land from potential harvesting. Whether or not the decision to eliminate harvests on these tracks is socially optimal is very difficult to determine and has given rise to a major conflict between conservationists and timber producers. There is a lot of rhetoric on both sides, but unfortunately little in the way of systematic economic analysis.

THE FOREST INDUSTRY: PRICE DETERMINATION WITH MANY DIFFERENT FOREST TYPES

Our discussion so far has focused on a plot of land in which someone is maximizing the return from the plot, given a fixed price for output and a known cost structure. The scale of the operation is by assumption small. A lumber industry would involve many plots being worked by many owners. If the plots were controlled by a single owner, a monopoly situation would prevail, and the monopolist would control the price of output as well as the phasing of rotations over all plots. An important industrywide issue is how the smoothing of the delivery of wood over time is arranged. We assume that all plots will not be harvested on the same date. Prices of timber today and into the future (expected prices or contracted futures prices) will govern harvesting decisions.[4] Inventory holdings can also be used to smooth out the quantities for sale relative to deliveries from plots. Intermediaries can do this coordination, or for a few large firms, smoothing can be done within coordinated land management. It is not unlike coordinating sales and harvests of agricultural products—a difficult but not impossible task.

The price at the industrywide level of analysis will then be *endogenous*, and its level will depend on: (a) how the coordination of harvests and sales is handled, and (b) how concentrated or monopolistic those controlling supply are. Industry models that examine the coordination of harvests and sales are generally more complex than the optimal rotation model applied to the owner of a small plot of forest land; see Hyde (1980), Johansson and Lofgren (1983, 1985), and Binkley and Dykstra (1987). Now we consider the question of supply more generally, in terms of plots of different fertility in different locales.

Relative Profitability of Forestry Use in Different Locales

The relative accessibility of forests to markets and their soil fertility can make the surpluses accruing to landowners involved in commercial foresting quite different. If we envisage a world market for a particular type of delivered wood, some suppliers can be earning relatively high rent per delivered ton and others, conceivably, zero. The former would be supplying timber from very accessible or relatively fertile areas. It will be the marginal area that will, roughly speaking, determine the price in the market. Assuming there are no regeneration or reforestation costs, that supply point will have zero rent, and that intramarginal areas will have positive rent per delivered ton. We illustrate in Figure 10.7.

Figure 10.7 shows three regions in the world with different fertilities of soil but identical accessibility characteristics. The differences in fertility are represented by different harvesting costs per region, again, assuming zero regeneration costs. In region 1, timber can be harvested at an average cost of e; in region 2 at a cost of f; and in region 3 at a cost of g. The area used for forestry differs among regions, and amounts of delivered marketable wood differ. In Figure 10.7, we assume that the marginal region produces quantity cd and earns zero rent, so that price per ton, p, equals average cost per ton, g. The most profitable and most fertile area produces quantity ab and earns rent per ton delivered of price p minus cost e per ton. A region of middle fertility produces quantity bc with positive rent per ton $(p - f)$. In our analysis of optimal rotation periods in the Appendix to this chapter, a plot with lower fertility has a longer rotation period and lower aggregate rent than an otherwise identical region with a higher level of fertility.[5] A similar relationship would be observed for regions with differing accessibility to the main world markets. The marginal region will have zero rent, and intramarginal regions will have positive rent per ton delivered. A key point is that if land markets are competitive, then those who want to grow timber will have to pay a higher price for more productive land than for less productive land. The return on investment in timber production will therefore be equalized regardless of soil fertility.

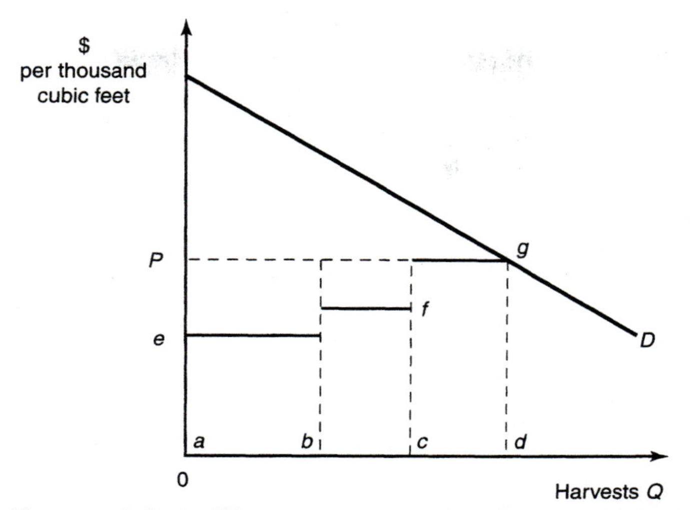

FIGURE 10.7 The steps indicate different average costs for different plots of timber in different regions. Cost can differ because of differences in soil fertility, accessibility, or both.

Government Policy and Optimal Timber Rotations

We now consider briefly various types of taxes and subsidies that the forest industry faces. Our objective is to see the effect of these policies on the rotation period of a forest plot and resulting harvests. These results will also be useful in our discussion of deforestation below. If the value of the forestry activity on the plot of land is positive (that is, W^* is positive), there is a surplus that is potentially taxable. Different types of taxation will have different effects on the activity on the plot. Clearly, a sufficiently high rate of taxation will make the operation unprofitable and end commercial forestry on the site. Let us consider some intermediate cases, which we assume do not take the activity from a profitable to a loss position.

Tax per Ton Harvested

This type of tax is commonly called a royalty or severance tax. This is, in terms of our simple model, equivalent to an increase in harvesting costs. Costs rise from c to $c + t$, where t is the tax per ton. An increase in c leads to a longer interval between planting and harvesting. More heavily taxed regions will have, other things being equal, longer rotation periods for the stand of trees grown. Total tax revenue, in present value, will be $tVe^{-rI}\left(\frac{e^{rI}}{e^{rI}-1}\right)$ if the policy is carried on in perpetuity. A larger quantity of wood will be harvested over all forest tracts per unit of time because of the increase in the interval I. This occurs because the efficient rotation interval is typically shorter than the maximum sustained yield rotation (MAI = CMAI).[6] Therefore a lengthening of the rotation interval will increase the average annual harvest. The yield tax is paid as a percentage of the value of timber when harvested. This tax has the same effect on the rotation interval as the royalty.

Site-Use Tax

A government might levy a tax per acre each time land is brought into forestry use. This would be equivalent to an increase in our setup costs, D. The effective setup cost would become $D + T$, where T is the total site-use tax. The effect of an increase in D was to increase the profit-maximizing rotation period. Hence the site-use tax causes the interval to increase, and again, per unit of time, less wood would be harvested though more wood per acre will be cut at each harvest date.

If the tax on site use is levied at harvest time, the total tax revenue will be $Te^{-rI}\left(\frac{e^{rI}}{e^{rI}-1}\right)$ rather than $T\left(\frac{e^{rI}}{e^{rI}-1}\right)$. The qualitative impact will be the same. The interval between planting and harvesting will be increased, and less wood per unit of time will be harvested in perpetuity.

Profit Tax

A tax on profits of t percent will not change the optimal rotation interval. Since "profit" here is the residual income ascribable to land in forest production, this "profits" tax can be viewed as a tax on the income accruing to landowners. The tax cannot be shifted by altering the rotation interval.

A License Fee for Foresting on the Land

An outright license fee per acre is the same as an increase in our setup costs, D. We saw above that a rise in D for all rotations lengthened the interval between planting and harvesting. If the license fee is levied *per year* rather than per rotation, it can be viewed as F dollars per unit of time, which amounts to a fixed cost of F/r for the perpetual forestry use program. Hence the present value of profits falls from W^* to $W^* - (F/r)$ when the annual license fee is imposed. *The optimal rotation interval is unaffected.* This is because the license fee is related neither to the amount harvested nor indirectly to the planting-harvesting interval.

Property Tax

An important tax in the United States that is applied at the state level is *current use valuation* for property tax purposes.[7] Forested land would be valued at W^* rather than its market value in other uses. Its value in other uses could well be higher than in growing trees. If so, this improves the after-tax value of land in forest use relative to alternative uses that are more highly valued and therefore more highly taxed. If we let τ represent the annual property tax rate, the after-tax value of land in forest is W^* minus $(\tau W^*/r)$ or $[(1 - \tau)/r]W^*$. The efficient rotation is not affected by this transformation of equation (10.6). The after-tax value of the forest will be less than in the case of no tax, but it will be less than the property taxes on alternative uses of the land. This sort of tax is frequently used to favor rural uses of the land such as agriculture and forestry over alternative uses such as for residences, commercial enterprises, or manufacturing. The incentive to stay in forestry or agriculture is even stronger when the tax authorities impose a "rollback" tax—payment of the taxes the property would have incurred in its highest use—if the property is converted to these other uses.

So far we have focused on the effects of taxes on a single plot of land devoted to forestry. Taxes obviously affect the relative profitability of different types of plots, possibly in different locations, and of forestry activity relative to other types of economic activity. Profits do not have to become negative in order for commercial forestry activity to cease; they need only fall below a threshold set by the profitability of other lines of economic activity. Tax increases can lead to "flights of capital" from one sector to another or one region to another.

Another way to say this is that the level of taxes will determine the extent of activity in the sector in question. Is there an optimal level of activity? A so-called first best approach would have no taxes and a maximum of net consumer and producer surplus generated. However, if the government must raise X dollars from the forestry sector or must levy charges on timber cut from public lands, different types of taxes will "take" more or less consumer and producer surplus while generating those X dollars of tax revenue. An *optimal tax* generates the X dollars of revenues and reduces consumer and producer surplus least. The corresponding intensity of forestry activity one might refer to as the *optimal extent of forestry use.* It is, however, based on the notion that X dollars of revenue must be raised in the forestry sector. How this level of X dollars is arrived at involves trade-offs at the level of the economy, not just the forestry sector.

Subsidies

Countries subsidize their timber producers in a variety of ways. In the United States, for example, there are two major federal government subsidy programs: the Forest Incentive Program and the Conservation Reserve Program. The Forest Incentives Program subsidizes a portion of the reforestation costs (our parameter D). The effect on the efficient rotation interval is thus identical to a reduction in D: The rotation interval will be shortened. This result is intuitive. The lower the reforestation costs to the timber producer, the higher the value of land in forest use, W^*. A fall in D implies that the second rotation and subsequent rotations are worth more because these fixed planting costs have risen. The response should be to hasten the time to the second and subsequent rotations.

The Conservation Reserve Program subsidizes establishment cost of a timber-producing property through a lump-sum payment and the opportunity cost of land purchases through a 10-year series of rental payments. The program is designed to convert marginal agricultural land to other uses (including timber production). This subsidy program has a more complex impact on rotations. The reduction in establishment costs is like a fall in D, and again, this should shorten efficient rotation intervals. The subsidy to land acquisition should increase the value of the land in growing trees and—analogously to the current use valuation scheme discussed above—should not affect the rotation interval.

Property Rights and the Management of the Forest

Government policy also influences property rights to the land, to timber growing on both publicly and privately held land, or to both. We examine two important issues in public ownership: sale and the duration of leases. And, for all forest lands, public and private, we look at security of the property rights.

Concessions of Public Forest Lands

For publicly held lands, a major policy concern is how to lease public forest lands. The term frequently used to describe the terms under which the rights to harvest timber or manage the timber-producing land within a specific period of time is called a *concession*. In determining concessions, governments must consider how to issue them (through grants, bidding processes, etc.); their duration; the extent of rent capture; and other features of a contract. The terms of the contracts between the government and the leaseholder can affect rotation intervals, the nature of the harvesting, the treatment of nontimber values, depletion of the forest, and more. There are a number of concerns with the types of policies that have been used. We first look briefly at how concessions are sold.

A key concern in many countries is whether or not concessions to harvest public forested lands are being sold for a price that reflects the present value of the harvests (our term W). Evidence from the United States and developing countries suggests that concessions are sold or leased for "below-market value" and, in some cases, below the costs of producing timber.[8] In the United States, timber harvesting rights are auctioned, but there are often too few buyers for each plot being auctioned to generate the "correct" price for the concession. One of the difficulties is the large transportation costs to get logs to market relative to their market value. See Rucker and Keffler (1988, 1991) for discussions of federal timber sales contracts in the United States. There has been considerable controversy in the United States over "below-cost timber sales." Environmental groups have argued that timber harvesting should be restricted and that national forest land should be protected because sales below cost are not in the public interest. The forest products industry argues that the sales are not really below cost because not all the costs associated with a harvest have been included in the measurement, and that critics have focused on one sale at a time rather than on the context of management plans. An economist would typically take a broader view than either of these. As Bowes and Krutilla (1989, p. 295) note, "a timber sale is economically justified if the expected net present value of the overall multiple-use benefits from the national forest are higher with the planned sale than they would be for any production plan without the sale." This requires investigation of areas larger than individual timber sales and computation of intertemporal multiple-use benefits. See Bowes and Krutilla for an illustration of how planning models could be applied to forest management.

The length of tenure a private firm is given over public forest lands is a very important policy issue. Leases typically last for less time than the rotation interval. In British Columbia, for example, leases are typically updated every 5 years and may run up to 20 to 25 years. There is the possibility that at the end of the period, the lease will be terminated. In Indonesia, the typical duration of a lease is 10 to 20 years. Most commercial timber species have rotation periods well in excess of 25 years. Hyde and Newman (1991, p. 34) cite the case of Sabah, Malaysia, in which "half of all concessions are for 21 years, most of the remainder are for ten years, and five percent are for one year. The full timber rotation, in contrast, exceeds seventy years. Concessionaires . . . may harvest gradually over a 21-year period, but with disregard for any residual growth or reforestation in that time."

The problem with short-term leasing arrangements relative to the growing cycle of the forest is that they introduce *uncertainty about tenure*. This creates an incentive for firms to cut more quickly than if they had secure tenure, if restrictions on cutting rates are not imposed or enforced. It also discourages investment in silviculture, reforestation, and other methods of increasing the productivity of the forest. Firms may therefore treat the forest as if only one cut were available, not as a sustainable resource. This may mean that harvests are high initially, but then will decrease over time as forests fail to regrow to the same wood volume as in their original mature state.

Security of Property Rights

Government policy can affect the security of a concession over public land and ownership of private forest lands. If governments cannot provide secure property rights to land, forest practices may not be socially optimal—in terms of rotation intervals, reforestation, and other practices. If property rights to the land are poorly defined and enforced, owners will be less likely to undertake the long-term planning and investment essential for optimal forest use. This can affect both timber and nontimber uses of the forest. As Deacon (1994, p. 421) notes, owners of land used to grow timber or allowed to go fallow between harvests of nontimber forest products (latex, rattan, oils, etc.) will be less likely to wait the optimal length of time between harvests if the land and its forest cover might be confiscated by the government or taken over by other parties. In fragile tropical ecosystems, harvesting without investment in regeneration may turn productive forests into degraded ones. Timber volumes will then fall over time.

Deforestation may occur if ownership is insecure because the current owner wants to take a "sure" harvest of timber or forest products now, rather than wait and run the risk that the timber may be confiscated by someone else. Tree poaching is found in many parts of the world, including developed countries such as Canada. Some species are so valuable that individual trees are felled on private property or leaseholds and stolen. It is impossible to trace these trees once they are milled into lumber products.

In some developing countries, such as Ghana, governments have taken over the forests from traditional communities. This has made these forests vulnerable to open access problems because the traditional communities often had their own customs and laws governing the use of the forest. Unless governments impose new policies—that is, new property rights to replace such customs—there can be less control over forest utilization than there was in the past. Governments in developing countries often do not have the resources needed to manage their forest lands or to enforce any leasing arrangement they impose. The local community that originally had the property rights to the forests finds its authority usurped and no longer has the same stake in managing it sustainably. Open access to the forest may result. If the forest becomes an open access resource, deforestation will continue until the net price $(p - c)$ is driven to zero. Box 10.3 examines the links between deforestation and security of property rights.

DEFORESTATION: THE ROLE OF GOVERNMENT POLICIES

In recent years there has been much concern over the state of the world's forests. It is feared that many forests, especially tropical and temperate rain forests, are being harvested at rates that are not sustainable over time. Harvesting practices may be destroying the soil's ability to sustain future timber crops. Conversion of land from forest to other uses is also seen as a major factor in deforestation.[9] In addition to the concern over timber values, there is also fear that a rich diversity of nontimber values—pharmaceuticals, other crops, homes for indigenous people, and the forest as carbon sink, to name a few—will also be lost. Our objective in this section is to examine the role governments have played in the management of their forests and their contribution to deforestation and potential loss of unique ecosystems. We examine examples from the developing world as well as industrial countries. Two classes of government policy are examined: (1) policies directly related to forestry and forest products; and (2) other government policies, such as income taxation and trade policy, that may have a bearing on the exploitation of the forest. We also see how governments can alter their public policies to maximize the net benefits from the forest, including nontimber values.

Government Forestry Policies

Governments in many countries own most of their forest land. This is the case in many developing countries and in developed countries such as Canada and the western United States. In developing countries, over 80 percent of forest area is public land (Repetto and Gillis, 1988). Governments play a key role in determining how the forest is to be exploited. It is important to remember that a socially optimal use of the forest requires whoever owns the forest to manage it in a way that maximizes the present value of the net benefits from the forest. This includes timber as well as nontimber uses. Governments in all countries frequently ignore NTVs in their forest policies. This leads to nonoptimal utilization of the forest, especially if the NTVs are

BOX 10.3 **Deforestation and Property Rights**

The empirical contribution of economics to understanding issues contributing to deforestation is growing. Deacon (1994) provides an empirical examination of three factors that might affect the extent of deforestation: population pressure, growth in income, and insecure property rights. Insecure property rights are proxied by government instability and inability to enforce ownership (general lawlessness and frequent constitutional changes) and absence of government accountability (type of government executive, frequency of political purges, and existence of an elected legislature).

Deforestation is a reduction in the land area covered by forests, using definitions of forested land from the Food and Agriculture Organization of the United Nations. Forest biomass is considered capital for purposes of the empirical investigation. Deforestation is then defined as a change in land use from a more capital-intensive to less capital-intensive activity. This simplified view will be inaccurate when forest land is converted to capital-intensive agriculture, as could be the case in developed countries. In these cases, deforestation may result in an increase in the value of capital per acre. But this sort of situation is unlikely in regions undergoing rapid forest conversion. These regions are often in developing countries where forest conversion means burning the biomass. This clears the land and releases nutrients to the soil to support labor-intensive subsistence agriculture. As better data become available, a more complex model could be examined.

The causes of deforestation are not widely understood. Popular discussions often mistake cause and effect. In developing countries deforestation has been attributed to slash-and-burn agriculture, logging, and demands for fuelwood, fodder, and forest products (Deacon, p. 415). But these demands are also seen in developed countries that are generally not undergoing rapid forest depletion or land degradation. Data for the period 1980–1985 from the 120 countries listed in Table 1 are used to test for the influence of three factors listed above on deforestation.

Population growth is often cited as the single most important cause of deforestation (see, for example, World Bank, 1990). Deacon tests this hypothesis and finds that the strongest association between deforestation in 1980–1985 and population growth is found with population growth 5 years earlier. In his simple model, a 1 percent increase in population during 1975–1980 is associated with a reduction in forest cover of 0.24 to 0.28 percent in 1980–1985 for the sample as a whole. A somewhat surprising result is found when the sample is separated into high- and low-income countries. For a given rate of population growth, a higher deforestation rate is found for high-income than for low-income countries.

Deforestation is also attributed to growth in national income. This factor underlies concerns about national economic development plans. Deacon finds a *negative* association between growth in measured income and deforestation. That is, rapid deforestation accompanies slow or negative measured economic growth. This is true for both high- and low-income countries. One problem with this finding is that measured income growth does not properly reflect a country's use of its natural assets (recall our discussion of net national wealth in Chapter 2). Deacon may simply be confirming that some growth in measured income is actually consumption of a country's forest capital. On the other hand, this may indicate that any consumption of forest capital is offset by an increase in the demand for forest preservation that is associated with higher levels of national income. Or there may be some other factor that is positively related to income growth and maintenance of forest cover. One such factor could be property rights.

The main hypothesis being tested is that poorly defined property rights favor conversion of forested land to non-capital-intensive permanent agriculture or degeneration to wasteland. Deacon finds support for this hypothesis. All of the coefficients for political at

(Continued)

BOX 10.3 *(Continued)*

TABLE 1 **PROPERTY RIGHTS AND DEFORESTATION: COUNTRIES IN SAMPLE**

High Deforestation	Low Deforestation		
Low- and Middle-Income Countries			
Afghanistan	Albania	German D. R.	Papua New Guinea
Costa Rica	Angola	Ghana	Paraguay
Cote d'Ivoire	Argentina	Greece	Peru
Ecuador	Bangladesh	Guatemala	Philippines
El Salvador	Benin	Guinea	Poland
Gambia	Bhutan	Guyana	Portugal
Guinea-Bissau	Bolivia	Hungary	Romania
Haiti	Botswana	India	Rwanda
Honduras	Brazil	Indonesia	Senegal
Iraq	Bulgaria	Iran	Sierra Leone
Jamaica	Burkina Faso	Kenya	Somalia
Lebanon	Burundi	Korea, North	Sudan
Liberia	Cambodia	Korea, South	Swaziland
Malawi	Cameroon	Lao P. D. R.	Tanzania
Nepal	Cent. African Rep.	Madagascar	Togo
Nicaragua	Chad	Malaysia	Trinidad and Tobago
Niger	Chile	Mali	Tunisia
Nigeria	China	Mauritius	Turkey
South Africa	Colombia	Mexico	Uganda
Sri Lanka	Congo	Mongolia	Uruguay
Syria	Cuba	Morocco	Venezuela
Thailand	Czechoslovakia	Mozambique	Vietnam
	Dominican Rep.	Myanmar	Yugoslavia
	Ethiopia	Namibia	Zaire
	Fiji	Pakistan	Zambia
	Gabon	Panama	Zimbabwe
High-Income Countries			
Israel	Australia	F. R. Germany	Spain
	Austria	Ireland	Sweden
	Canada	Italy	Switzerland
	Cyprus	Japan	United Kingdom
	Denmark	Netherlands	United States
	Finland	New Zealand	
	France	Norway	

NOTES: Excludes countries with fewer than 500,000 population. See text for definitions.
High deforestation = loss of more than 10 percent of 1980 forest cover during 1980–1985.
Low deforestation = loss of less than 10 percent of 1980 forest cover during 1980–1985.
Source: Deacon (1994), p. 419.

BOX 10.3 *(Continued)*

TABLE 2 **DEFORESTATION, POPULATION GROWTH, AND POLITICAL ATTRIBUTES (OLS REGRESSION COEFFICIENTS)**

Sample	**All Countries**		**Low- and Middle-Income**	
Population growth, 1975–1980	.1744	.1860	.0704	.1247
	(1.84)	(2.21)	(0.60)	(1.27)
Guerrilla warfare, 1980–1985	.0539	.0462	.0451	.0392
	(1.75)	(1.66)	(1.34)	(1.32)
Guerrilla warfare, 1975–1979	−.0297	−.0156	−.0141	−.0024
	(1.00)	(0.63)	(0.43)	(0.08)
Revolutions, 1980–1985	.0313	.0606	.0415	.0662
	(0.95)	(2.10)	(1.16)	(2.19)
Revolutions, 1975–1979	−.0536	−.0597	−.0579	−.0636
	(−2.00)	(−2.38)	(1.92)	(2.34)
Constitutional changes, 1980–1985	.0200	—	.0122	—
	(0.32)		(0.18)	
Constitutional changes, 1975–1979	−.0339	—	−.0357	—
	(0.81)		(0.79)	
Military executive, 1980–1985	.0220	—	.0192	—
	(0.66)		(0.55)	
Military executive, 1975–1979	.0017	—	.0029	—
	(0.06)		(0.10)	
Executive is not a premier, 1980–1985	.0177	.0168	.0227	.0207
	(1.25)	(1.29)	(1.42)	(1.43)
Investment residual	.0154	—	.0200	—
	(0.21)		(0.25)	
N	106	118	86	98
R^2	.21	.20	.19	.19

NOTE: Absolute values of *t*-statistics in parentheses.
Source: Deacon (1994), p. 428.

(Continued)

BOX 10.3 *(Continued)*

tributes during the period 1980–1985 are significant. The coefficients indicate the percent change in deforestation over this period due to the presence of each explanatory variable. For example, the presence of revolutionary activity during this 5-year period is associated with deforestation rates that are 6.8 to 10.5 percent higher over the period than in countries without revolutions. For the same period, constitutional changes are associated with deforestation rates 10 to 12 percent higher than in countries without constitutional changes.

The property rights variables that were correlated with deforestation are then combined with the population growth to examine the combined effects of these factors. Table 2 presents Deacon's results. The signs on all the explanatory variables remain unchanged. However, the elasticity and significance of deforestation with respect to lagged population change (changes over the period 1975–1980) are reduced. The overall explanatory power of the regressions is fairly low. This may be due to the exclusion of variables that Deacon cannot measure. The results should thus be viewed as preliminary support for the hypothesis that insecure property rights contribute significantly to deforestation.

Sources: Robert T. Deacon (1994). "Deforestation and the Rule of Law in a Cross-Section of Countries." *Land Economics* 70, 414–430. Also: World Bank (1992). *World Development Report 1992: Develoment and the Environment.* Oxford: Oxford University Press.

impaired or destroyed by timber harvests. Timber harvests have typically been seen as the *only* benefit. This is changing in some countries as governments recognize that NTVs may exceed timber values. But even if we focus only on timber values, many inefficiencies exist as a result of government policy. In this section we examine the types of timber policies governments are using and what their effects are on timber harvests and forest use.

Harvesting Policies

In some regions, governments prescribe the amount of harvesting that can occur each year. Some publicly managed tracts in British Columbia and on United States national forests are assigned production quotas each year. Even though many of these policies are referred to as sustained yield, the allowed cuts may bear no resemblance to what a profit-maximizing firm would harvest. If so, social losses will occur. Either too much or too little timber will be harvested on a given tract. If too little timber is harvested per plot, harvesters may seek timber elsewhere. This can contribute to timber harvests over a more extensive land area than is socially optimal.

In developing countries, similar biological rules for determining sustained-yield harvests have been used. One example is the "selective logging system" in Indonesia. This is essentially an allowed annual cut (AAC) allotted to each harvester by the Indonesian forestry department. The AAC specifies that harvests should be limited to "large stems" of the commercially desirable species. This can be a socially optimal selective logging regime if smaller trees remain behind to mature for future harvests and to ensure adequate vegetation of the site to minimize erosion. However, problems may arise with the policy. Concessionaires who have uncertain property rights to future harvests may "high-grade" the forest. High-grading is a forester's term that describes the practice of removal of high-value timber, leaving behind a degraded residual stand (Hyde and Sedjo, 1992, p. 343). In the case of Indonesia, low yields have been obtained from the forest. As few as 3 to 5 trees are harvested per hectare, representing about 1 percent of the 310 to 350 harvestable trees per hectare (Repetto and Gillis, 1988, p. 64). More extensive use of forested land has occurred.

Royalties and Fees

The basic problem here is that most governments are not charging royalties that reflect the rent generated by the forest. In Indonesia, a uniform royalty per unit applies to all logs regardless of species. This policy fails to capture differential resource rents and may encourage high-grading.[10] In countries such as Canada, fees are based on the volume of timber harvested and the market value of the timber, but still have been calculated in a way that is not consistent with maximizing the value of the forest. The fee is based on the difference between the price of timber sold and the opportunity costs of production and harvest. This is the economic rent if the costs are those borne by each harvester. But in British Columbia, the costs of production are not those of each harvester but averages for "efficient" operators in the industry. There is, as well, a minimum level of the fee. This average fee may be administratively simple, but it means that most operators will pay a rate that is not based on their rent from harvesting; instead, they pay too much or too little, depending on their costs. The fee does not promote efficient management of the forest. If governments are collecting rents for the use of their forest resources that are too low, society is not making the best use of these resources.

Reforestation

As managers of forest resources, governments also have an obligation to ensure that harvested tracts are regenerated. Given the insecurity of tenure in many countries, private firms will have no incentive to reforest unless required to do so by governments. Many governments have not done well at ensuring that reforestation occurs. In Canada, even though efforts to reforest have been substantial in the recent past, there remains a sizable proportion of potential forest lands that are "not sufficiently reforested." Over the period 1986–1992, approximately 6.8 million hectares of forested land were harvested, while 3.2 million acres (less than 50 percent) were seeded and planted (Statistics Canada, 1995, p. 105). Canadian provincial governments have historically been somewhat inconsistent in their requirements for reforestation and, in particular, who will pay for it—the government or the harvester. Reforestation is now typically required as part of the leasing arrangements. The record is not better in other countries. In Indonesia, for example, reforestation on both public and private lands amounted to just over 50 percent of all the hectares harvested over the 10 years from 1974 to 1983 (Repetto and Gillis, 1988, p. 62). Since then, there have been efforts to increase reforestation. But in Indonesia, as in many other timber-producing countries, even if 100 percent of harvested lands are reforested, there is little likelihood that the forest will contain the same volume of timber as in the original harvest. Repetto and Gillis argue that this is because of a loss in soil productivity and other environmental factors. There is thus reason to be concerned about the sustainability of forest resources over time.

Other Government Policies that Affect Forest Utilization

A variety of government policies can affect forest use, in addition to those specifically addressing forest management. These include trade, tax, agricultural, and industrialization policies. For developing nations a particularly important issue is land resettlement and development. We look briefly at each of these categories.

Trade Policy

A number of countries have used trade policy to try to influence their timber industries. One common policy is to restrict the export of unprocessed logs in an attempt to encourage domestic processing, thereby creating jobs and domestic value added. In British Columbia, for example, all unprocessed logs require a license for export. To obtain the license, the seller must show that the logs are surplus to the needs of the province. To prove that logs are surplus, they must be advertised for sale. If no domestic buyer comes forward with a competitive bid, the seller can apply to a log export committee for permission to sell the logs abroad. This whole process is expensive and time-consuming for the sellers. It ensures that only a small percentage of unprocessed logs will actually be exported.

To see the effects this type of policy can have, we turn to another example—Indonesia's export taxes on timber. Until 1985, the tax rate was dependent on the degree of processing done to timber. For example, the tax rate on logs was 20 percent over the period 1977 to 1984, while that on plywood was zero. The export tax structure created a high rate of effective protection to the wood-processing industry, greatly increasing the number of mills. These mills have been very inefficient at recovering wood value from logs made into plywood. This means that there is very little value added in the processing. Gillis estimates that domestic value added from plywood processing was about 9 percent (Repetto and Gillis, 1988, p. 70). Exporters saved taxes of 20 percent on each unit of wood not exported as logs. This means that the government gave up tax revenues more than twice the value added in wood processing.

There are real costs to the forest in addition to forgone rents, from these differential export taxes. The tax differential allows domestic processors to have production costs that are much higher than competitors in other countries, who must import their logs from Indonesia. A mill operating in Japan that buys its logs from Indonesia would have to pay the export tax of 20 percent. To match a price set by an Indonesian mill that pays no such tax, it must have much lower average operating costs. The Indonesian mill can thus produce inefficiently, compared with foreign competitors. Other countries, such as the Philippines, Ivory Coast, and Ghana, have similar schemes. What does this mean for the forest? If domestic processing of timber is inefficient, it will take a lot more logs than necessary to produce a unit of plywood. Gillis estimates that Indonesian plywood mills use 15 percent more log feed stock per cubic meter of plywood output than mills elsewhere in the region (Repetto and Gillis, 1988, p. 71). This means that over time, much more timber will have to be cut, exacerbating problems of deforestation. These trade policies effectively subsidize domestic processing, which in turn increases the pressures to harvest forests more quickly and extensively than is socially optimal. The situation in Indonesia worsened in 1985, when all log exports were banned.

Tax and Industrial Policy

Countries may offer tax incentives to encourage companies to invest in the forest industry. Examples include tax holidays for corporate income taxes during the first few years of operation, accelerated depreciation on capital equipment, and reduced property taxes. Brazil, for example, gave firms who set up wood-processing operations in the Amazon tax credits of up to 50 percent of their total tax liability and 75 percent of the total costs of investment in a project (Repetto and Gillis, 1988, p. 28). Recall our discussion of the effects of government policies on rotation periods. Any policies that treat the forest industry more favorably than other sectors subsidize the industry relative to other sectors. This tilts the rotation period to the present. Firms will harvest more quickly than is optimal to maximize the present value of the tax break. The public's share of the rents from forest lands is also reduced. As in the case of export taxes on logs, subsidies can encourage excessive exploitation of forests.

Land Development and Deforestation

Governments of a number of developing countries, notably Brazil, have implemented policies which have led to significant deforestation. Land resettlement schemes and a variety of subsidies to agriculture have contributed to massive deforestation over the past 20 years. Many developing countries have looked for solutions to problems of population pressures, high rates of unemployment, and low wages by subsidizing people to move from the urbanized to the rural regions of their countries. These subsidies can take different forms. In Brazil, for example, the government essentially gives people title to forested land if they clear it and establish a farm of some sort. The landowner then becomes eligible for further subsidies through agricultural credits. Governments also subsidize development by constructing the infrastructure—roads and rail lines—necessary to get people to these more remote areas and products back to markets. Cattle ranching has been a major beneficiary of these programs in Brazil. Enormous areas of forested land have been converted to pasture that is supporting inefficient cattle production. By 1980, conversion of forests to pastures accounted for 72 percent of the deforestation in the Amazon of Brazil (Repetto and Gillis, 1988, pp. 34–35). Repetto notes that "many of the ranches that were established have been uneconomic, and probably would not have been established without heavy subsidies and the hope of speculative gains in land prices. Unproductive and deteriorating pastures far from markets have not supported enough cattle to justify the costs of establishing and maintaining them. Many of these deforested lands have been sold or abandoned, while new lands are cleared for the tax benefits they offer" (p. 34).

Land resettlement has been a major policy initiative in countries such as Indonesia. The purpose was to move people from densely populated regions to the more remote islands. It is estimated that the Indonesian government spends about $10,000 per family for relocation (Repetto and Gillis, 1988, p. 77). The ultimate objective is to relocate 15 million more people by the end of the century. It is estimated that relocation programs will cause more deforestation than all other sources combined. It is difficult to estimate the net benefits of these programs, but agricultural use of the land has not met with much success, because of the fragility of deforested soils.

Policies to Improve the Utilization of Forests

There will always be competing uses for forest, or any land. The question is how governments can alter their public policies to maximize the net benefits from the forest, including nontimber values. Here, focus first on changes to policies that would increase the efficiency of timber production and promote sustainable harvests on forested lands. The more efficient the operation, the smaller the land area needed for commercial forestry operations for a given volume of wood.

Timber Policies

As noted above, many governments often value their timber resources below market prices when royalties or fees are assessed. Reform of these policies would entail increasing the fees. This should not only redistribute the forest rents to governments, and hence to the public, but—more important—reduce harvesting on uneconomic lands. Second, countries that encourage high-grading (e.g., diameter-limited cutting) and extensive forestry operations should revise these policies to ensure that maximum use is made of wood fiber per tract.

Leasing arrangements need to ensure more secure tenure over the land. This means increasing the period of the lease to more closely match the rotation period of the tree species harvested. Auctions of leases would improve the efficiency of forest management if a competitive market could be established. If this is done, governments must still ensure that efficient management occurs. This means that firms leasing the land must reforest or assist natural regeneration (or both) and invest in the sustainable productivity of the forest soils. Reforestation could be supported by requiring the firm to post a bond covering the costs of reforestation or regeneration at the time the lease is undertaken. To ensure efficient management, governments may still have to exert some control over harvesting practices. While there is still much to be learned about sustainable tropical forestry, it is clear that more intensive forestry will have to be practiced to avoid even further deforestation. This might entail more plantation planting of timber crops, which could lessen the demands on natural forests, allowing them to be used at their highest social value (which could be nontimber uses). Better information about the size of nontimber values would also encourage more socially efficient use of the forest. This is where developed countries could assist developing countries by providing research support. Expenditures of this sort would help compensate for the worldwide positive externalities that result from preserving tropical forests. The indigenous peoples of the forest often have considerable knowledge about nontimber values and sustainable use of the forest. Their expertise should be utilized.

Nontimber Policies

It is obvious that subsidies to activities that lead to deforestation are inimical to the sustainable use of the forests as well as being costly and contributing to inefficient economic activity. Socially optimal use of the forest requires the termination of these policies. This applies to distortionary trade policies as well as resettlement programs and subsidies to agriculture. Allowing market forces to work would reduce the inefficiencies. But there is still a need for government involvement in land use. As long as some nontimber values provide benefits, private markets will not lead to socially optimal land use. Population growth is also an important factor contributing to deforestation and remains a thorny public policy issue.

Policies for Developed Countries

Developed countries provide some of the markets for timber products from developing countries and may also compete with developing countries for a share of the world timber market. Trade barriers erected by all countries are partly responsible for inefficient timber harvests. Eliminating these barriers may help reduce the inefficient investment in timber processing and extensive harvests of tropical forests. International aid agencies have in the past contributed to forest exploitation by providing funds for infrastructure development (roads, dams, etc.), without regard to optimal forest use. This is now changing, and these agencies should be encouraged to continue to incorporate multiple uses of the forest in their assessment of where to support investment projects in developing countries. People all over the world share to some extent in the many benefits of the forests. The developing countries should not have to bear the total costs of preserving their forests.

SUMMARY

1. A forest is a renewable resource that is a form of capital, in that it can provide a sustained flow of products over time. The land covered by forests can provide marketable products such as timber, fruit, latex, oils, genetic materials, pharmaceuticals, rattan, and vegetation for grazing. Some of these products, notably timber, require long intervals between harvests. Forested land can also provide recreation, habitats for plants and animals, climatic impacts, watersheds, and protection from soil erosion. These benefits may be much more difficult to value.
2. The optimal timber harvesting of a plot of bare land requires maximization of the stream of net social benefits from the forest. This occurs where the value of the

marginal product of timber allowed to grow for one more period, $(p - c)V'(I)$, is equal to two opportunity costs that measure what the landowner gives up if the trees are not harvested during that period and the land is not replanted for future harvests. These opportunity costs reflect the interest on the money the landowner would earn if the timber had been harvested and sold and the money invested, $r(p - c)V(I)$, and the interest earned on the land if it was sold for its optimal timber production value, W^*.

3. If there is no discounting of future timber production from the forest, and if costs of regenerating the forest are zero, the optimal rotation interval is $V'(I) = V(I)/I$. This is the maximum sustained yield from the forest.
4. If land is available in an infinitely elastic supply so that $W^* = 0$, the optimal rotation interval for timber harvesting is found where $V'(I) = rV(I)$. This result is equivalent to maximization of timber harvesting over one rotation.
5. If a timber producer starts with a forest of standing trees rather than bare land, the optimal rotation interval is unaffected if the trees are clear-cut. If selective cutting and thinning practices are undertaken, a much more complex planning problem emerges. Costs, technologies, species, soil type, and other factors play a key role in determining whether to clear-cut or selectively cut a forest.
6. The inclusion of nontimber values (NTVs) in decisions about timber harvesting can affect the optimal rotation interval. No general results arise, as rotation intervals may be lengthened, shortened, or unaffected by the inclusion of the multiple uses of the forest. It is possible that timber harvests will be terminated and the forest left in its "natural" state, or that the value of the land is higher in an activity that requires no trees to be left standing.
7. Government policies such as taxes and subsidies can affect optimal rotation intervals. Intervals may be lengthened or shortened.
8. Property rights to land or to the timber growing on it can have a major impact on the use of the land. The sale and length of timber concessions are important policy issues. Insecure timber concessions and insecure private ownership of forest lands have contributed to deforestation worldwide.
9. Excessive harvests and conversion of forested land into wasteland are important concerns in many regions of the world. Government forestry policies, trade restrictions, taxation, and land development are seen as factors contributing to deforestation.

DISCUSSION QUESTIONS

1. For an infinite-period model in which the optimal rotation period for a forest is determined, explain the economic intuition for:
   a. Condition that determines the year (or time) the trees are cut
   b. Why each rotation period is the same length of time
   c. Role of the discount rate

2. *a.* How does the optimal rotation period change when:
   (1) Planting costs fall.
   (2) A tax on the volume of wood harvested is imposed.
   (3) A license fee is imposed for using the land.

   b. Suppose there are two plots of land, one more fertile (produces more wood volume per acre) than the other. Explain the optimal rotation period for each plot.
3. Air pollution has been observed to retard the growth of trees in forests in, among other places, the eastern part of the United States. Must we redevelop our model of optimal tree management and cutting, or is this matter of "atmosphere" a part of the existing model? Discuss.
4. "To maximize the volume of wood harvested, a forest should be cut when the mean annual increment reaches a maximum." True, false, or uncertain? Explain your answer.
5. Ontario's Algonquin Park was populated with very large conifers in the nineteenth century, as old photographs indicate. Now it is thickly forested with smaller conifers. Was a mistake made in harvesting all the very large trees? What characteristics should a forest display for an observer to know that it is being used properly for tree harvests?
6. Many observers lament the clearing of forests in third world countries to make new land for farming. Are the private decisions of these landowners at odds with the social value of the land with forest remaining on it? Was England, for example, stripped of its forests at the wrong pace and date?

NOTES

1. Ledyard and Moses (1977) made planting costs vary with the amount planted, rather than associating these costs simply with clearing the site and planting on it, as we have done. Their model involves two choice variables: how many resources to devote to planting and how long to work the crop from planting to harvesting. Their analysis is much more complicated than the familiar one-variable models of which ours is a representation. See also Hyde (1980) and Chang (1983).
2. The terms *site value* and *site rent* are taken from Pearse (1990), which is also the basis for the diagrammatic treatment in this section.
3. From an ecological viewpoint, most coniferous forests are subject to fire, whereas natural hardwood are much less so. Clear-cutting conifers mimics the periodic nature of fires in that much of the land is "cleared" at one time. Selective cutting mimics the much less pervasive fire disturbance in the hardwood stands.
4. To see how price expectations affect harvesting decisions in a forestry model, see Berck (1979).
5. Fertility differences may arise from the type of trees planted. For example, selective planting is being vigorously pursued in the southern part of the United States. The first generation of the selected trees planted commercially today are expected to grow 10 to 15 percent faster than the trees they replaced. Forest industry officials expect wood volumes on plantations to be double their 1980 levels by the year 2010.
6. Efficient rotations are shorter than the maximum sustained yield rotations unless the discount rate is very high. See Binkley (1987) for a comparison of rotation intervals under different models.
7. We thank Peter J. Parks for the information for this section.

8. See Bowes and Krutilla (1989) and the references therein for a discussion of below-cost timber sales in the United States.
9. See Sandler (1993) for an overview of the factors contributing to deforestation.
10. See Vincent (1990) for further discussion of the inefficiency of timber royalty systems in tropical countries. He emphasizes the importance of basing taxes on resource rent rather than other bases.

SELECTED READINGS

Berck, P. (1979). "The Economics of Timber: A Renewable Resource in the Long Run." *Bell Journal of Economics* 10, 447–462.

Binkley, C. S. (1987). "When Is the Optimal Economic Rotation Longer Than the Rotation of Maximum Sustained Yield?" *Journal of Environmental Economics and Management* 14, 152–158.

Binkley, C. S., and D. Dykstra (1987). "Timber Supply," in M. Kallio, D. Dykstra, and C. S. Binkley, eds., *The Global Forest Sector: An Analytical Perspective.* Chichester, England: Wiley.

Bowes, M. D., and J. V. Krutilla (1989). *Multiple-Use Management: The Economics of Public Forestlands.* Washington, D.C.: Resources for the Future.

Calish, S., R. D. Fight, and D. E. Teeguarden (1978). "How Do Nontimber Values Affect Douglas Fir Rotations?" *Journal of Forestry* 76, 217–222.

Chang, S. J. (1981). "Determination of the Optimal Growing Stock and Cutting Cycle for an Uneven-Aged Stand." *Forest Science* 27, 739–744.

Chang, S. J. (1983). "Rotation Age, Management Intensity, and the Economic Factors of Timber Production: Do Changes in Stumpage Price, Interest Rate, Regeneration Cost, and Forest Taxation Matter?" *Forest Science* 29, 267–278.

Deacon, R. T. (1994). "Deforestation and the Rule of Law in a Cross-Section of Countries." *Land Economics* 70, 414–430.

Hardie, I. W., and P. J. Parks (1996). "Reforestation Cost-Sharing Programs." *Land Economics* 72, 248–260.

Hartman, R. (1976). "The Harvesting Decision When the Standing Forest Has Value." *Economic Inquiry* 14, 52–58.

Heaps, T. (1981). "The Qualitative Theory of Optimal Rotations." *Canadian Journal of Economics* 14, pp. 686–699.

Hyde, W. F. (1980). *Timber Supply, Land Allocation, and Economic Efficiency.* Baltimore, Md.: Johns Hopkins University Press for Resources for the Future.

Hyde, W. F., and D. H. Newman with R. A. Sedjo (1991). "Forest Economics and Policy Analysis, An Overview," World Bank Discussion Paper 134. Washington, D.C.: World Bank.

Hyde, W. F., and R. A. Sedjo (1992). "Managing Tropical Forests: Reflections on the Rent Distribution Discussion." *Land Economics* 68, 343–350.

Johansson, P.-O., and K. G. Lofgren (1983). "Six Different Results on the Properties of the Timber Supply Function," in Å. E. Andersson, M.-O. Olsson, and U. Zackrisson, eds., *Forest Sector Development: Issues and Analysis.* Sweden: University of Umeå.

Johansson, P.-O., and K. G. Lofgren (1985). *The Economics of Forestry and Natural Resources.* New York: Basil Blackwell.

Kemp, M. C., and N. V. Long (1983). "On the Economics of Forests." *International Economic Review* 24, 113–131.

Ledyard, J., and L. N. Moses (1977). "Dynamics and Land Use: The Case of Forestry," in R. E. Grieson, ed., *Public and Urban Economics.* Lexington, MA: D. C. Heath.

Pearse, P. H. (1990). *Introduction to Forestry Economics.* Vancouver: University of British Columbia Press.

Perrings, C. A., et al. (1994). *Biodiversity Conservation.* Dordrecht, Netherlands: Kluwer Academic.

Repetto, R., and M. Gillis (1988). *Public Policy and the Misuse of Forest Resources.* Cambridge: Cambridge University Press.

Rucker, R., and K. Keffler (1988). "To Harvest or Not to Harvest? An Analysis of Cutting Behavior on Federal Timber Sales Contracts." *Review of Economics and Statistics* 70, 207–213.
Rucker, R., and K. Keffler (1991). "Transactions Costs and the Efficient Organization of Production: A Study of Timber Harvesting Contracts." *Journal of Political Economy* 90, 1060–1087.
Sandler, T. (1993). "Tropical Deforestation: Markets and Market Failures." *Land Economics* 69, 225–233.
Statistics Canada (1995). *Environmental Perspectives, Studies and Statistics*. Ottawa: Statistics Canada.
Swallow, S. K., P. J. Parks, and D. N. Wear (1990). "Policy Relevant Non-Convexities in the Production of Multiple Forest Benefits." *Journal of Environmental Economics and Management* 19, 264–280.
Swallow, S. K., and D. N. Wear (1993). "Spatial Interactions in Multiple Use Forestry and Substitution and Wealth Effects for the Single Stand." *Journal of Environmental Economics and Management* 25, 103–120.
Vincent, J. R. (1990). "Rent Capture and the Feasibility of Tropical Forest Management." *Land Economics* 66, 212–223.
Vincent, J. R. (1992). "The Tropical Timber Trade and Sustainable Development." *Science* 256, June 19, 1651–1655.
Vincent, J. R., and C. S. Binkley (1993). "Efficient Multiple-Use Forestry May Require Land-Use Specialization." *Land Economics* 69, 370–376.

Appendix to
Chapter 10: Efficient Forest Rotation Periods

RESPONSES TO CHANGES IN [illegible]ERS

In this Appendix, we exam[illegible] rotation interval of changes in some of the parameters of [illegible] look at how increases or decreases in planting costs (D[illegible]he interest rate (r), and soil fertility (a) affect the time b[illegible]ng the trees. To obtain the effects on the efficient rotatio[illegible] change, one at a time, the underlying parameters of our basic mo[illegible]ed to begin with the first-order condition for the efficient rotation interval, as shown in equation (10.6). To facilitate the comparative statics, we rewrite equation (10.5) as

$$\frac{dV(I)}{dI} = rV(I) + \frac{r}{p - c} = W^* \tag{A10.1}$$

where W^* is the optimal value of the program of planting and harvesting for the efficient rotation interval in perpetuity, and is equal to $[(p - c)V(I)e^{-rI} - D]\left(\frac{1}{1 - e^{-rI}}\right)$ by equation (10.5). An envelope result is that $dW^*/dI = 0$.

INCREASE IN PLANTING COSTS, *D*

This is the simplest case to examine. *A rise in planting or clearing costs in our basic model implies a longer rotation cycle.* Intuition works well here. Consider the first rotation. When reforestation costs, D, rise, the value of land in forest use, W^*, must decline. A rise in D implies that the second rotation and subsequent rotations are worth less because these fixed planting and clearing costs have risen. The response should be to delay getting to the second and subsequent rotations. (There is no way to avoid incurring the costs in the first rotation.) This intuition is confirmed by the mathematics. To determine the effects of an increase in planting costs, we totally differentiate equation (A10.1) to obtain:

$$\frac{\partial\left[\frac{dV(I)}{dI} - rV(I)\right]}{\partial I} dI = \left[\frac{r}{p-c}\right]\frac{\partial W^*}{\partial D} dD$$
$$= \left[\frac{r}{p-c}\right]\left[\frac{-e^{rI}}{e^{rI}-1}\right] dD$$

Both sides are negative, so

$$\frac{dI}{dD} > 0$$

as we argued in the text.

INCREASE IN INTEREST RATE, *r*

Now let r rise. Intuitively, we associate a higher r with more impatience or a desire to get results sooner. This intuition is correct for our basic model. *An increase in r implies a shortening of the efficient rotation interval.* The opportunity costs of holding the forest in uncut timber rise. Because W^* is a present value, a higher r means a lower value of the forest land for all time periods. Entrepreneurs will want to harvest more quickly. The forgone interest on timber that could have been harvested is also higher, so the term $r(p - c)V(I)$ also increases.

To prove this, totally differentiate the first-order condition of equation (A10.1) to obtain

$$\frac{\partial\left[\frac{dV(I)}{dI} - rV(I)\right]}{\partial I} dI - V(I)dr = \frac{W^*}{p-c} dr + \left(\frac{r}{p-c}\right)\frac{\partial W^*}{\partial r} dr$$

$$\frac{\partial\left[\frac{dV(I)}{dI} - rV(I)\right]}{\partial I} dI = \frac{W^*}{p-c}\left[1 - \frac{rI}{e^{rI}-1}\right] dr + V(I)\left[1 - \frac{rI}{e^{rI}-1}\right] dr$$

The left-hand side is negative and the right-hand side is positive, so we have $dI/dr < 0$.

CHANGE IN NET PRICE OF THE TIMBER $(p - c)$

The term $(p - c)$ is the price net of harvesting costs per unit biomass sold. If p rises or c falls, this net price increases. An increase rise in the net price will increase the value of the marginal product of the timber, $(p - c)V'(I)$, as well as increase both of the opportunity costs of delaying the harvest. In terms of Figure 10.6 in the text, the *VMPT* curve shifts up, as does the *TOC*. This leads to a shorter rotation interval, as forest owners shift their harvests to the present to take advantage of the higher net price. *A rise in* p *or a fall in* c *decreases the efficient rotation period.* To see this mathematically, let $t = (p - c)$. Totally differentiating the first-order condition yields

$$\frac{\partial\left[\frac{dV(I)}{dI} - rV(I)\right]}{\partial I} dI = \frac{-rW^*}{t^2} dt + \frac{r}{t}\frac{\partial W^*}{\partial t} dt$$

$$= \frac{r}{t}\left\{\frac{-tV(I) + e^{rI}D}{(e^{rI} - 1)t} + \frac{V(I)}{e^{rI} - 1}\right\} dt$$

$$= \frac{rD}{t^2}\left[\frac{e^{rI}}{e^{rI} - 1}\right] dt$$

The left-hand side is negative and the right-hand side is positive, so we have

$$\frac{dI}{dt} < 0$$

or

$$\frac{dI}{dp} < 0 \text{ and } \frac{dI}{dc} > 0$$

A rise in the price shortens the efficient rotation period, whereas a rise in costs of harvest lengthens the rotation period. This case can also be interpreted as a difference in the accessibility of forest plots to markets. Plots located farther from markets will have higher harvesting costs if we include transportation expenditures with the costs of harvest. Ledyard and Moses (1977) investigated this in considerable detail, using a slightly different model. They let both the rotation period and the resources devoted to planting be choice variables for a landowner or planner. In their more complicated model, they discovered that indeed the optimal rotation period would be longer for less accessible regions or plots. They also solved for the differences in site values between regions of differing accessibility and determined that site value per acre would decline with distance and the rent-distance function would have the familiar convex shape.

Our model also yields a convex rent-distance function. Suppose our cost per unit of wood harvested, c, comprises a cutting and processing cost of \$1 per pound plus \$1 x, where x is distance to the market for the lumber. The \$1 represents the cost of moving the lumber a unit of distance and getting the equipment back to the site for another delivery. Costs then become \$1 + \$1 x. Solving for W^* for different values of x indicates the price of land used in forestry at different distances from the central

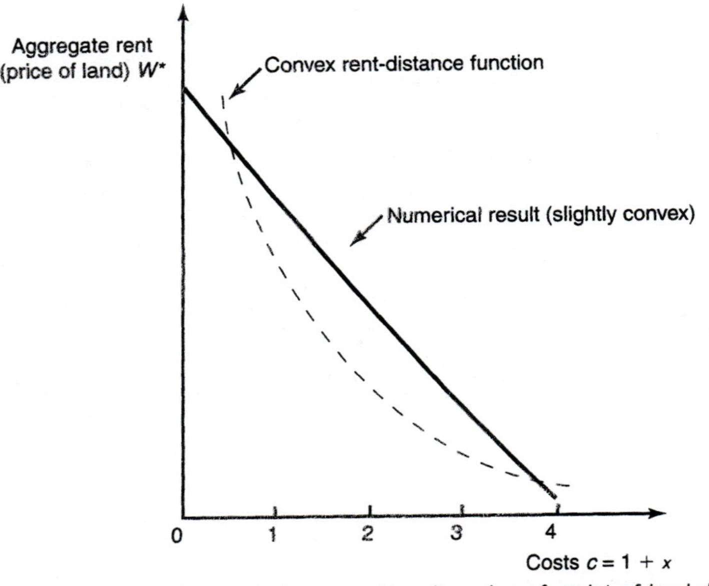

FIGURE A10.1 As transportation costs increase, the site value of a plot of land dedicated to forestry declines in our basic model. (This is an actual numerical example.) There is slight convexity in this land value–distance schedule. For different transportation costs, there is a distinct optimal interval for rotating the forest. For our basic model this optimal interval increases with transportation costs.

market (rW^* is land rent corresponding to those distances). We plot aggregate rent (the price of land) against constant harvesting and processing costs plus variable distance costs in Figure A10.1. Our choice of parameters has resulted in only a slight curvature to the land price-distance function.

The issue of how I^* varies with accessibility was reanalyzed by Heaps (1981) in a model that allowed for declining average costs of harvesting. He discovered that there could be cases in which I^* declined with distance from processing plants or that Ledyard and Moses's basic result could be reversed. We see that the specification of the model influences the comparative forest rotation results when parameter values change.

INCREASE IN FERTILITY OF THE SOIL, *a*

This case is slightly more complex than the previous ones. The reason is that a change in soil fertility affects the $V(I)$ function and will typically also change $dV(I)/dI$, the change in the biomass as we increase I. Suppose that two areas have land of different fertility. A planting-harvesting cycle will be shorter in the most fertile area. To see

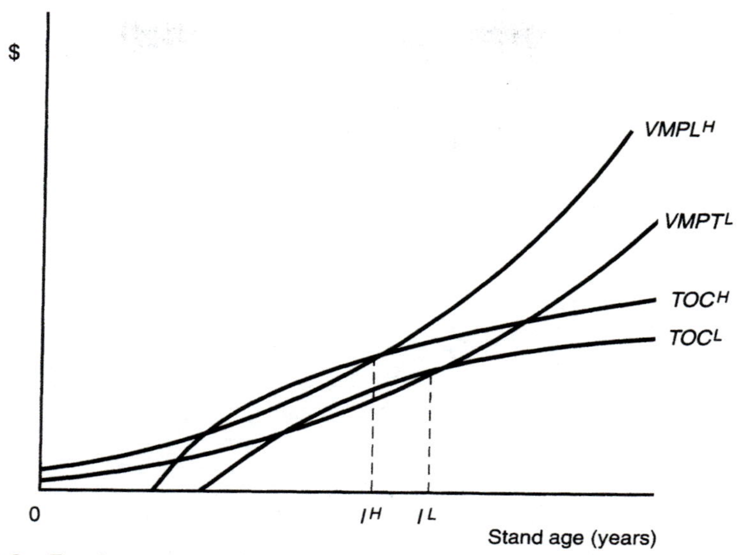

FIGURE A10.2 Two forests with different soil fertility are shown. L is the tract with low fertility; H has high fertility. Each tract has its own *TOC* and *VMPT* function. The more fertile forest has a shorter rotation interval than the forest with low fertility.

why, consider Figure A10.2, which shows a likely situation. In Figure A10.2, there are two *VMPT* functions: $VMPT^H$ is the land that has high soil fertility; $VMPT^L$ is the land with low fertility. Improved fertility means that for every age I, the value of the marginal product of timber on more fertile lands will exceed that on less fertile lands. Soil fertility will also affect the opportunity cost line. Here TOC^H lies above TOC^L because the value of the more fertile land, W^{H*}, is greater than that of the less fertile land, W^{L*}. The efficient rotation intervals are I^H and I^L. *The least fertile land is harvested later than the more fertile land.* Intuitively, what is happening is that trees grow more slowly on less fertile land. They must be allowed to grow for a longer time period before harvest. Because the growth is slower and the value of the land lower, the opportunity costs of holding the trees uncut is lower. Thus, I^H is less than I^L.

To reinforce this intuition mathematically, we need an expression for $V(I)$. Let $V(I)$ be the standard logistic growth equation:

$$V(I) = \left[\frac{a}{b + \left(\frac{a - bV_0}{V_0}\right) e^{-aI}}\right]$$

This is a function similar to that seen in the fishery. It is a complex expression that is difficult to sign without actual numerical values. We typically expect $dI/da < 0$, which means that the rotation interval is shorter for land of higher fertility.

SUMMARY: APPENDIX

Our results can be summarized in the following table:

Parameter change:	$D\uparrow$	$r\uparrow$	$p-c\uparrow$	$a\uparrow$
Rotation interval:	$\uparrow$	$\downarrow$	$\downarrow$	$\downarrow$

It is important to remember that these results depend on the prices, costs, and yields that define the efficient rotation in equation (A10.1). If any of these features of the timber management problem change, the efficient rotation interval could also change.

chapter 11

Dynamic Models of the Fishery

INTRODUCTION

In this chapter we introduce a positive discount rate into the analysis, examine the resulting steady-state equilibrium assuming the fishery is optimally managed, and compare this *dynamic* equilibrium with the *static* open access and private property equilibriums derived in Chapter 4. We also introduce more complex assumptions about the way in which fishing firms enter and exit the industry. In Chapter 4, we looked at the steady-state fishery and did not examine the adjustment of the fish stock, effort, or harvests over time. Now we look at an open access equilibrium under a specific assumption about the entry and exit of firms. We also analyze paths toward a possible steady-state equilibrium and revisit the issue of extinction.

In the first section we discuss aspects of *getting to an equilibrium*, not simply different types of equilibria. We will discuss all concepts verbally and graphically, and provide a numerical example. We then present an example of dynamic analysis for a fishery. Of significance is the derivation of a bionomic equilibrium when harvests occur over a number of years. The value of each future harvest will be discounted back to the beginning of the plan for harvesting. Before beginning the analysis, we discuss intuitively the effect discounting has on the steady-state harvest and the fish stock.

This chapter also introduces some special topics in fisheries economics. It builds on the previous material on fisheries, but in some sections the arithmetic manipulations are more complex than before. Three additional topics are examined. Biological conditions can greatly complicate fisheries management policies. Failure to incorporate biological conditions may lead to disaster in a fishery, as we illustrate with the case of the Peruvian anchovy fishery. In addition to differences in the biological mechanics for many species, there may also be complex interactions among species. For example, a "trash" species may be preying on a commercially desirable species. In this case, it may pay to harvest the trash species to improve the growth and hence the harvests of the desired species. We examine the optimal equilibrium in a fishery with this type of predator-prey relationship.

In the final section, we examine international disputes concerning a fish stock.

When two nations separately plan to exploit a single fishery, they must form conjectures about the reaction of one to the other. This means that a game-theoretic structure may be an appropriate tool in the analysis of these fisheries. We present a simple illustration of international competition and cooperation in the exploitation of a single-species fishery. An example of this in practice is the "cod war" between Iceland and Great Britain.

OPTIMAL FISHERY MANAGEMENT

The model of the optimally managed fishery in Chapter 4 assumed that no discounting of the revenue and costs of future harvests was made. One period was assumed to be identical to the next. This assumption means that individuals are indifferent between receiving a dollar today or a dollar tomorrow. Or, in terms of the fishery, one dollar of profit from fishing is valued the same whether it is earned this year or next. Although there are some who argue that the appropriate social discount rate is zero, most economists assume that a preference for dollars received today rather than tomorrow should be reflected in the computation of a socially optimal policy. It is the inclusion of the discount rate that distinguishes the *static* steady-state equilibrium from the *dynamic* steady-state equilibrium. What are the effects on the optimal fishery equilibrium when the discount rate is positive?

Let's first see what the inclusion of the discount rate means under open access and private property ownership. Under the open access fishery, the discount rate is effectively infinite. Long-run profits would increase in the fishery if entry could be reduced today to let the fish stock rise. But no single firm has any incentive to reduce its effort, because if it did, other firms would reap the benefits without incurring any loss in current revenue. Other firms might also increase their effort and thus offset the positive effect on the stock. When there is an infinite discount rate, all the static and dynamic equilibria coincide.

In a private property equilibrium where dynamic effects are considered, the discount rate will typically lie between zero and infinity. Throughout this section we will assume that the discount rate used by holders of a private property right will be equal to the social discount rate. This need not be true in practice, but it enables us to argue that the PPE will be socially optimal. When the discount rate is positive, the static and dynamic private property equilibria will not coincide.

With a positive discount rate, the owner of the fish stock faces an intertemporal trade-off. Harvests tomorrow are simply worth less than profits today. A firm may not be willing to operate with a large fish stock and low harvests today in anticipation of rising future harvests. The higher the discount rate, the more impatient the individual is for harvests today. Therefore, the larger the discount rate, the less the difference between the open access equilibrium, OAE, and the private property equilibrium, PPE. The sharp distinction between the OAE and PPE derived in the static model becomes less sharp in a dynamic model with high discount rates.

We now present a dynamic model of a fishery that is being managed optimally by a government agency or a competitive sole owner. We note briefly how a monopolist would behave. Assume that the objective function of society is to maximize the present value of the *net benefits* from the fishery by choosing a harvest rate $H(t)$ that maintains a steady-state biomass or fish population X. There are three ingredients to this problem. First, let $U[H(t)]$ be defined as the total benefits derived from the harvesting of fish. This function can be interpreted in a number of ways, depending on who is maximizing the net benefits from fishing.

If we are talking about a government maximizing social welfare, $U[H(t)]$ can be interpreted as the gross consumer surplus. Net benefits are then $U[H(t)]$ minus harvesting costs. If a sole owner is exploiting the fishery, where the owner may be operating in a competitive market or as a monopolist, then $U[H(t)]$ is the benefit (revenue) from harvests for the owner. We will concentrate on the optimal harvest from the viewpoint of *a government doing the maximizing*. The results will be identical for the competitive sole owner with private property rights, so we can compare the results in this section with those in Chapter 4. We will note the difference in the solution for the case of the monopolist.

Next, we have to specify what the harvest, $H(t)$, depends on. We assume, as in Chapter 4, that the harvests are a function of fishing efforts, E, and the stock of fish, X. Thus, $H(t) = G(E,X)$. In this model, $H(t)$ need not be a steady-state or sustainable harvest. If the harvest exceeds the sustainable yield from the fishery, the stock of fish will decline over time. If the harvest is less than the sustainable yield, the population will rise over time. We examined this situation in our simple model in Chapter 4.

The next ingredient is the cost function for harvesting fish. We assume a very general cost function. The cost curve is assumed to depend on the amount harvested, $H(t)$, and the stock of fish, $X(t)$. We have then $C = C[G(E,X),X(t)]$. Thus effort enters the cost function through the harvest function. We further assume that harvesting costs rise when there is an increase in the harvest ($\partial C/\partial H > 0$), while harvesting costs for a given H fall when there is an increase in the stock of fish ($\partial C/\partial X < 0$). The latter condition follows from our biological model, where we argued that the larger their stock, it is easier and thus cheaper to catch $H(t)$ of fish.

Finally, the biological mechanics must be incorporated into the problem. We require that in equilibrium the fish population must be sustainable—the change in the fish stock, dX/dt, must be equal to zero. When there is harvesting, the net growth of the stock over time must be exactly equal to the harvest over the same interval. As before, we assume the biological mechanics $F(X)$ can be represented by a logistic function. Thus, $dX/dt = F(X) - H(t) = 0$ is an equilibrium condition for the planning problem. Let us instead work now explicitly with distinct time periods.

We examine the fishery from one period, say a year, to the next. The two approaches are the same when we let the discrete periods get smaller and smaller. Let us then rewrite the biological mechanics in a discrete form as

$$X(t+1) = X(t) + F[X(t)] - H(t) \tag{11.1}$$

Equation (11.1) can then be rewritten in terms of $H(t)$ to obtain

$$H(t) = F[X(t)] - [X(t+1) - X(t)] \tag{11.2}$$

That is, the harvest in period t must equal the difference between the growth in the fish population at t, $F[X(t)]$, and the change in the stock from one period to the next. If the fishery is in a steady-state equilibrium where $X(t + 1) = X(t)$, $H(t)$ will equal $F(X)$. If the stock changes from one period to the next, the harvest will not be equal to the growth of the stock. Equation (11.2) simply specifies mathematically what we have argued verbally earlier.

The determination of the optimal fishery equilibrium can now be stated.[1] We assume that the government manager seeks to determine a sequence of harvests, $H(t)$, where $t = 0,1,2, \ldots n, \ldots \infty$ which maximizes

$$W = U[H(0)] - C[H(0), X(0)] + (1/1 + r)\{U[H(1)] - C[H(1), X(1)]\} + \cdots + (1/1 + r)^n\{U[H(n)] - C[H(n), X(n)]\} + \cdots \quad (11.3)$$

subject to

$$H(t) = F[X(t)] - [X(t + 1) - X(t)]$$

for

$$t = 1, \ldots, n, \ldots \infty$$

Notice that now we are solving for an optimal harvest and steady-state stock, not for effort as we initially did in determining the open access and private property static equilibria. To solve this problem, we can substitute the constraint representing the biological mechanics into the objective function for each t, then differentiate the expression with respect to the stock of fish in each period. To find the optimum, each derivative is then set equal to zero. The resulting equilibrium condition for any two periods, t and $t + 1$, is

$$\frac{U'(t + 1) - C_H(t + 1)] - [U'(t) - C_H(t)]}{U'(t) - C_H(t)} + \frac{[U'(t + 1) - C_H(t + 1)] F'[X(t)]}{U'(t) - C_H(t)} - \frac{C_X[H(t), X(t)]}{U'(t) - C_H(t)} = r \quad (11.4)$$

The term U' is the additional benefit received from harvesting an additional fish or pound of fish in period t or period $t + 1$. This derivative will be equal to the price of fish if a government manager or competitive sole owner is operating the fishery. (It is equal to marginal revenue if a monopolist is managing the fishery.) The term C_H is the marginal cost of harvesting an additional pound of fish in period t or $t + 1$. $F'[X(t)]$ is the marginal product of the fish stock, or the change in the biomass in the period t. C_X is the marginal cost of harvest due to a change in the stock of fish in period t. Finally, r is the social discount rate.

Equations (11.2) and (11.4) together govern the time path of the stock of fish, $X(t)$, and the time path of the harvest, $H(t)$, and determine as time extends far into the future the optimal steady-state equilibrium values of the harvest, H^*, and the fish population, X^*. We will interpret equation (11.4), then show how it simplifies for the case of our harvested fishery in a steady-state equilibrium. This dynamic steady-state equilibrium will be compared with the static one. We then show how the equilibrium changes under different assumptions about the discount rate and harvesting costs. We will examine possible paths to a steady-state equilibrium for two specific examples—the North Pacific fur seal and Spanish sardines.

Equation (11.4) can be interpreted as a "rule" that, combined with equation

(11.2), governs how X and H (and costs and benefits) evolve over time. Given a historical value of the stock $X(0)$, there will be a unique initial harvest $H(0)$, which will result in the fishery evolving to its steady-state or bioeconomic equilibrium. At the steady state, harvests and stock size remain at their equilibrium levels indefinitely, period by period. Let us examine each term in equation (11.4). (It is analogous to the Hotelling rule from Chapter 8.)

The first term in equation (11.4)

$$\frac{[U'(t+1) - C_H(t+1)] - [U'(t) - C_H(t)]}{[U'(t) - C_H(t)]}$$

is the percentage capital gain (or loss), the increase in net benefits or profits received from the fishery from periods t to $t + 1$. The capital gain is measured as a percentage of the net benefits to the fishery. The capital gain or loss term will be nonzero when the fishery is *on a path moving toward or away from the steady-state* values of H and X. If there is a capital gain (the value of the fish "asset" is increasing over time), it will pay the operator to shift harvests to the future—that is, to decrease harvests today to allow the stock to build up and reap larger gains in the future. This procedure is like mining where ore is kept in the ground if the rental value of the mineral is growing at a rate in excess of the interest rate. Here we are keeping fish in the ocean. If there is a capital loss, the value of the fishery falls from this period to the next. Harvests today should therefore rise, and the stock will decline.

If there is neither a capital gain nor a loss, we will have a steady state. There is no change in the net benefits from one period to the next when there is no change in the amount harvested from one period to the next. In the steady state, the numerator of the expression is zero and the term disappears. Let us define $V(t + 1)$ be equal to $[U'(t + 1) - C_H(t + 1)]$ and $V(t)$ be equal to $[U'(t) - C_H(t)]$; then in the steady state $V(t + 1) = V(t)$. For a government fisheries manager $U[H(t)]$ is the area under the demand curve and $U'[H(t)]$ is price per unit harvested. For the owner with private property rights, $U' = P$. Then $V(t) = P(t) - C_H(t)$ is the *rent* per unit of harvest.

Rent for the government manager or sole owner is the difference between price and marginal cost. For the monopolist, $U' = MR$, and rent is the difference between marginal revenue and marginal cost. Rent in the fishery is like rent in the mine. For nonrenewable resources, the percentage capital gain term was crucial and never went to zero because the stock and "harvest" (extraction) changed period by period until the reserves were depleted. The same sort of thing occurs in the fishery along the optimal path. The difference between the mine and the fishery is that in the fishery a sustainable steady state can exist where the harvests and stocks of fish remain constant over time. For the mine, no such steady state exists because ore is steadily depleted until reserves are exhausted.

The second term

$$\frac{[U'(t+1) - C_H(t+1)][F'(X(t)]}{[U'(t) - C_H(t)]}$$

is the value of an additional unit of biomass recruited to the fishery. The term $F'[X(t)]$ shows the growth in the fish stock in physical terms if the population is at X in the period t. This term is weighted by the ratio $V(t + 1)/V(t)$, to put it into dollar terms and thus make the physical change comparable to the net benefit measure of the first term. We call this expression the *marginal stock effect.* It reflects that effect the fish population has on the future growth of the fishery, valued by the net returns to the fishery. If the fishery is on a path to the steady state, as before $V(t + 1)$ will not equal $V(t)$. The fish stock will be increasing or decreasing. At the steady state $V(t + 1) = V(t)$ the stock is constant, so the weighting factor will simply be equal to 1, and the term reduces to $F'[X(t)]$. Note that this marginal stock effect is different from the stock effect discussed in Chapter 4. In the static model, $r = 0$.

The third term

$$\frac{-C_X[H(t), X(t)]}{U'(t) - C_H(t)}$$

captures the stock externality described in Chapter 4. If an additional unit of the fish stock is harvested, the marginal cost of harvesting rises. Conversely, if the stock is larger, the marginal costs of harvesting are reduced. Recall that in the social optimum or competitive equilibrium with private property rights, the effect of the stock on the costs of harvest will be incorporated into the analysis. This is the term that does it. This cost is again weighted by the net benefit in period t, $U'(t) - C_H(t)$, or simply $V(t)$. Note that the stock externality will be present whether the fishery is on the path to the steady state or at the steady state.

Equation (11.4) thus says that along a potentially optimal path, a rate of harvest must be chosen such that the sum of the capital gain plus the marginal stock effect minus the stock externality must be set equal to the interest rate. When the fishery is at a steady-state, equation (11.4) reduces to

$$F'[X(t)] - \left[\frac{C_X(t)}{V(t)}\right] = r \tag{11.5}$$

where $F'(X(t)$ is the marginal biological productivity of the stock of fish can be either positive or negative; $C_X(t)$ is the stock effect on fishing costs and will be negative; and $V(t)$ is the rent or net surplus on the marginal quantity harvested at t.

Let's examine the steady-state equilibrium. In particular, we will see how the equilibrium changes for different values of the discount rate and different costs.

Equation (11.4) cannot tell us exactly where the equilibrium stock of fish will be without having quantitative estimates of the terms in the equation. To see this, we rewrite equation (11.4) as

$$V(t) = \frac{C_X(t)}{F'[X(t)] - r} \tag{11.6}$$

where $V(t)$ is the difference between price and marginal harvest costs for the optimally managed fishery or competitive sole owner, or the difference between marginal revenue and marginal cost for the monopolist. Price will exceed marginal cost in the steady state because the fish stock will generate a rent. Thus the right-hand side of equation (11.6) must also be positive in the steady state.

We know by assumption that $C_X(t)$ is negative. Increases in the stock decrease the cost of harvesting a particular catch. The interest rate is positive. Thus to have the right-hand side of equation (11.6) be positive, it must be the case that r is greater than $F'[X(t)]$. The term $F'[X(t)]$ is the slope of the sustainable yield curve (the biological production function). This value can be positive, negative, or zero. *So it is possible that the steady-state equilibrium can be to the right or the left of the MSY,* given our introduction of discounting or interest rate effects. Another interpretation of equation (11.5) is that

$$\left[\frac{F'(X) - C_X(t)}{V(t)}\right]$$

can be thought of as the resource's internal rate of return. At the bionomic equilibrium, this expression is equated to the rate of return (r) on other investment in the economy.

Now let's compare the dynamic steady state with the static steady state. The comparison is straightforward. In the static case, the discount rate is zero. We could thus solve equation (11.3) with r equal to zero, or simply note that r vanishes from the steady-state condition in equation (11.5). The steady-state condition then becomes

$$V = \frac{C_X}{F'(X)} \tag{11.7}$$

where the ts have been dropped for simplicity. Remembering that $V = P - MC_H$, equation (11.7) implies for the sole owner or the government that the price of fish equals marginal costs of harvest plus the marginal stock effect. For the monopolist, marginal revenue equals marginal costs plus the marginal stock effect. This was our condition for rent maximization in Chapter 4. We know that the *static* steady-state equilibrium must therefore be at a fish population that is to the right of the MSY stock. Price or MR is positive; C_X is negative, and therefore $F'(X)$ must be negative. The equilibrium must lie on the decreasing portion of the biological production function. One error in doing the static analysis where r exceeds zero is that we rule out the possibility of an optimal equilibrium to the left of the MSY stock of fish. When is this error likely to be large? The higher the interest rate, all else equal, the greater the possibility that $F'(X)$ can be positive.

Now suppose we let r more toward infinity. In this case, the right-hand term of equation (11.6) vanishes, and we are left with the condition that $U' = C_H$. *This is the open access equilibrium,* where no stock effects are incorporated into the determination of the optimal harvest and stock of fish. The condition for a steady-state dynamic equilibrium is thus the general case. The static private property equilibrium is a special case with $r = 0$, while the open access equilibrium is a special case with r equal to infinity. Before turning to a discussion of the paths to the steady state, let us consider another simplification.

Suppose we return to the assumption made in our preliminary static model that *the costs of harvesting fish are independent of the size of the fish stock.* If we maintain the assumption that r is positive, we can see that the steady-state equilibrium must now lie to the left of the MSY population. Refer back to equation (11.5), where the term C_X is now zero. The equilibrium condition now becomes simply that $F'(X) = r$. If r is positive, then $F'(X)$ must be positive, and the steady-state equilibrium must occur to the

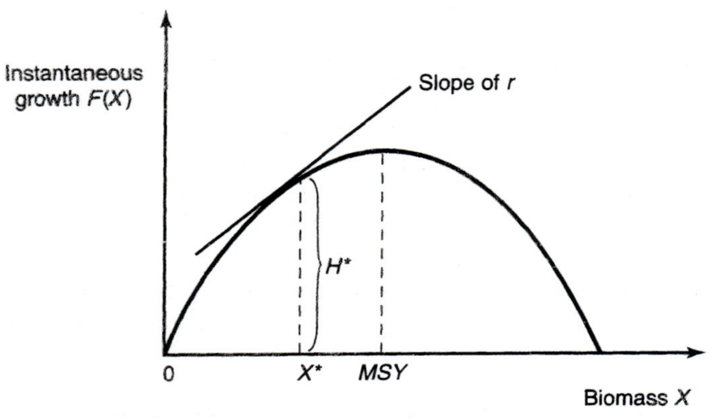

FIGURE 11.1 The steady-state equilibrium when the marginal costs of harvest are independent of the stock of fish. The equilibrium requires $F'(X)$, the slope of the biological production function, to be equal to r, the discount rate. If r is positive, then $F'(X)$ must also be positive, and the equilibrium must be to the left of the *MSY* biomass (and harvest).

left of the MSY. Figure 11.1 illustrates this case. We simply set the slope of $F(X)$ equal to the interest rate. The steady-state equilibrium is thus independent of both the price of fish (or marginal revenue) and the cost of harvest.

Notice that in the cases examined above, where r is not infinite, price (or U' or MR) is never set equal to marginal cost of the harvest. This is because of the stock effects involved in harvesting fish—the harvest affects the stock of fish, and the stock of fish in turn affects the cost of harvest. Two terms reflect the stock effects—$F'(X)$ and C_X. The optimal management of the fishery over time must incorporate these effects.

A Numerical Example

We will illustrate some of the cases examined above with a numerical example. We solve for the socially optimal equilibrium assuming a positive but finite discount rate, then show what happens when the discount rate is equal to zero or approaches infinity.

Suppose that the demand curve for flounder is perfectly elastic at a price p. Let the total cost of harvesting flounder be given by $C = wH/mX$, where w is the unit harvesting cost per firm per season, H is the harvest, m is the technology of harvesting or the "catchability coefficient," and X is the stock of flounder. Total costs thus increase as the harvest rises and the stock of flounder falls. The biological mechanics, as in equation (11.1), are given by

$$X(t + 1) = X(t) + F[X(t)] - H(t)$$

In this example, we let $F[X(t)] = X(t)\{a - b[X(t)]\}$, where a and b are parameters. This is the logistic growth relation for the stock. Our steady-state relation requires that $F(X) = H(t)$. This will occur where $X(t + 1) = X(t)$. We then take our steady-state value equation, (11.5):

$$F'(X) - [C_X/(P - C')] = r$$

where for this case $F'(X) = a - 2bX$, $C_X = -wH/mX^2$, and $C_H = w/mX$. We find in the steady state that

$$(a - 2bX) - (-wH/mX^2)/[p - (w/mX)] = r$$

Substituting for $H = F(X) = X(a - bX)$ in this expression, we obtain the quadratic equation

$$2bX^2/a + (r/a - 1 - wb/apm)X - rw/apm = 0$$

Let us now solve this expression for the steady-state solution, given some hypothetical values for the parameters in the problem. For $a = 0.5$ and $b = 0.1$, the stock corresponding to the maximum sustainable yield (X^{MSY}) is 2.5 tons, while the biological equilibrium stock (X^E) in the absence of harvesting is a/b, which is equal to 5. We now examine three cases with harvesting.

Case A

The socially optimal harvest, X^*, where we let $p = 1$, $w = 6$, $m = 4$, and $r = 0.05$, is equal to $(1.2 + 1.62)/0.8 = 3.12$. Hence, X^* exceeds X^{MSY}. This is what we expect when harvesting cost depends on stock size. In our cost function above, total costs and marginal costs fall as stock size rises. Therefore, larger stock sizes will increase the present value of the harvest.

Case B

Under open access to the fishery, the equilibrium conditions change from our steady-state equation above to $p = AC$, where $AC = w/mX$ for this example. For the same parameter values, the open access equilibrium stock, X^C, is 1.5, which is less than the MSY population. The open access equilibrium is thus in the biologically inefficient range of the stock size. We can also see that in the socially optimal solution, as the interest rate approaches infinity we obtain the common property equilibrium. Intuitively what occurs with r very large is that the future is irrelevant and optimization is done myopically, period by period.

Case C

Suppose now that the price of flounder approaches infinity. The optimal stock, X^*, would then approach $(a - r)/2b$. Now if r equals zero, the optimal stock is $a/2b$, which is the MSY. If the discount rate is positive, the optimal stock will be less than the MSY. In other words, in that case, with high prices the presence of discounting ($r > 0$) leads to steady-state stocks on the biologically inefficient branch, but not too far down the inefficient branch if r is relatively small. A positive r implies that harvests "today" are more desirable than harvests "tomorrow," and this impatience leads to the setting of X^* below X^{MSY} when price is high.

Our example shows that two factors typically prevent the optimal harvest from being at the maximum sustainable yield—the discount rate and stock effects on harvesting costs. If these terms are not zero, an MSY harvest is most unlikely. However, in case C we saw that the MSY harvest is socially optimal when the price of fish is very high and the discount rate is zero. Intuitively what is happening is that very high prices (large demand) make the cost effects of the fish stock insignificant. At lower prices, harvest costs are more important. Because the marginal cost of harvesting fish depends on the steady-state stock of fish, it is generally desirable for the firm to operate where there is a stock of fish higher and a harvest lower than the MSY. The value of having a large harvest is offset by the high marginal costs of having a low population. The lower the price of fish, the bigger the impact of the cost effect on the fishery.

The optimal steady-state equilibrium involves the interest rate and cost effects working simultaneously. In some cases, only one effect will be dominant. The interest rate effect tends to lead to an equilibrium to the left of the MSY, whereas the cost effect pulls the steady-state equilibrium to the right of the MSY. But unless both effects are absent or they just offset each other, the MSY is not the optimal steady-state equilibrium.

We turn now to two illustrations of fisheries equilibria in a dynamic model—fur seals and sardines.

DYNAMIC PATHS IN THE FISHERY

Let us return to equation (11.4), the condition for a steady-state equilibrium in our dynamic model and the condition that must be satisfied along a path that leads to the steady state. We will examine the paths to a possible equilibrium. Again, let $V(t) = U' - C_H$. We will proceed by treating time as a continuous variable. When $t + 1$ and t are separated by an "instant," we can look at the change in V over this instant by taking the derivative of V with respect to time, $dV(t)/dt$. Let us define this derivative of V as $\dot{V}(t)$. Then the change in $X(t)$ over an instant of time is given by $\dot{X}(t)$. We can then rewrite our basic dynamic value equation (11.4) in continuous time as

$$V[F'(X)] - C_X = rV - \dot{V} \tag{11.8}$$

If we solve for $\dot{V}/V$ to find the percentage change in V, we find

$$\dot{V}/V = r - F' + C_X/V \tag{11.9}$$

We have suppressed the time subscripts to avoid clutter.

It is equation (11.9) that must be satisfied at each instant along the optimal path to the steady-state equilibrium. Equation (11.9) should look familiar; recall the condition for the optimal extraction path of the nonrenewable mineral as given by Hotelling's rule (equation 8.9). In that expression, the percentage change in rent had to be equal to the interest rate at each point in time for there to be optimal extraction of a nonrenewable resource. Equation (11.9) is a generalization of the simple Hotelling rule which allows for the possibility of a growing resource stock rather than one that simply diminishes over time. We can see why this is so.

The fundamental distinction between renewable and nonrenewable resources is that for the latter, $F'(X) = 0$. There is no growth of the fixed stock (except perhaps over millions of years). The term C_X, the change in marginal harvesting costs due to a change in the stock of fish, will be present in the case of minerals when extraction costs per ton vary with location in the deposit.[2] With the terms $F'(X)$ and C_X set equal to zero, we have $\dot{V}/V = r$, which is identical to Hotelling's rule.

The North Pacific Fur Seal

Let's now examine some possible paths to the steady-state equilibrium. Rather than examine a general model, we illustrate a particular example taken from Wilen (1976). The model Wilen uses simplifies much of the complexities of the fishery, but it clearly shows the interaction of the biological mechanics with the dynamics of entry and exit of firms. The industry in this case is one of historical interest, the north Pacific fur seal fishery.

Wilen's model examines seal harvests from the late 1800s to the early 1900s. The fishery existed in the Pacific Ocean along the northwest coast of North America. Harvesting of fur seals occurred in two phases of the seal's annual migratory and reproductive cycle. Fur seals migrate relatively long distances, going up the west coast of North America from mainland United States to the Bering Strait. They also settle on land to mate. Harvesting that occurs when the seals are on land was long governed by regulations of both the Canadian and the United States governments. When harvesting occurred during the migratory phase, a common property situation generally existed. A number of countries, including Canada, the United States, the Soviet Union, Japan, and Great Britain, took part in the harvests. Our concern is with these pelagic harvests.

In the period from the late 1880s to the early 1990s, there was virtually open access to the pelagic seal fishery. A large number of vessels entered the industry at the beginning of this period, and at first large catches were made. After a few years, catches plummeted and vessels began exiting the fishery. By 1898, the Canadian fleet had shrunk to half its size in 1896. At this point, the Canadian fleet owners made an effort to save the industry. They formed a single firm, the Victoria Sealing Company, to exploit the fishery as a monopolist. The United States' fishing effort was withdrawn by the end of the 1800s because of a ban by the United States federal government on pelagic sealing. From 1901 to 1910, a single Canadian firm had almost complete control over the fishery. However, the Japanese entered the fishery in increasing numbers, and by 1909 the fishery was thought to be in danger of collapse. An international agreement signed by Canada, the United States, Japan, the Soviet Union, and Great Britain in 1911 prohibited all pelagic harvests and allowed only males to be harvested on land. The treaty is still in force today.

A number of interesting economic questions arise from the fur seal industry. We will look at the period from 1880 to 1990 using a dynamic bioeconomic model. The objective is to use the model to predict the steady-state equilibrium when there is open access to the fishery and to trace possible dynamic paths to that equilibrium. The question asked by Wilen is whether or not the fishery would have collapsed under open access. This involves two questions. First, does a steady-state equilibrium exist that involves both positive seal stocks and positive fishing effort? Second, without government regulation, would the industry find the dynamic path that leads to this steady-state equilibrium? Would it follow an efficient path, such as the one described by equation (11.9)? This exercise thus compares inefficient open access dynamics and socially optimal dynamics. We emphasize that open access cases cannot be optimal. Wilen's work asks whether or not open access leads to the collapse of the fishery.

To answer these questions, Wilen developed a simple model of the seal fishery. The biological aspect of the model is virtually identical to the approach taken in this chapter. The economic portion focuses on the conditions for an industry equilibrium with open access—that an equilibrium will occur when there is no incentive for firms to enter or exit. This will occur when there are zero rents from the fishery.

The seal population is assumed to have a quadratic growth function, $F(X)$, that looks like our biological model developed in Chapter 4. The equation for this function is given by

$$\dot{X} = F(X) = X_t(a - bX_t) \tag{11.10}$$

In this equation, a and b are parameters that represent the natural growth rate and net reproductive capability of the species. Equation (11.10) is again our logistic equation for the fishery. With harvesting, the change in the population is again given by $\dot{X} = F(X) - H(t)$, as we have assumed throughout this chapter and in Chapters 4 and 5. A very simple harvesting relationship is then assumed:

$$H_t = AE_tX_t \tag{11.11}$$

A is a technological parameter, and E_t is again effort, which in Wilen's model is represented by the number of sealing vessels in the industry.[3] Substituting equation (11.11) in the condition for the steady state, we find that

$$\dot{X} = aX_t - bX_t^2 - AE_tX_t = 0 \tag{11.12}$$

There will be an equilibrium if $X_t = 0$ (extinction) or if there are *no* harvests (the natural biological equilibrium), in which case E_t equals zero. To have a steady-state equilibrium with positive seal stocks and harvests requires an interior bionomic equilibrium where $\dot{X} = 0$, which implies that $F(X) = H(t)$. Solving equation (11.12) for X_t, we find this equilibrium stock at:

$$X_t = (a - AE_t)/b \tag{11.13}$$

Examining equation (11.13), we see that a sustained population and thus a sustained harvest depend on the parameters a, b, A, and the level of effort, E_t. We now have to determine the *number of vessels* that will exist in the industry. This is where economic assumptions enter.

Wilen assumes that an economic equilibrium occurs when there is no entry into or exit from the fishery. The condition for entry or exit is given by

$$\dot{E} = s(PH_t - TC_t - \alpha_t)/E_t \qquad (11.14)$$

The variables are defined as follows: P is the unit price of a harvested seal, and is assumed to be constant in each period; TC_t is the total industry operating costs of harvesting seals, assumed to be equal to cE_t; α_t is a cutoff rate of return for the industry, where this cutoff is equal to the opportunity cost of capital, r, multiplied by the number of vessels in the industry (E), so $\alpha = rE_t$. The term s is an industry response parameter that indicates how quickly effort (vessels) responds to excess profits. Quite simply, then, whenever the right-hand side of equation (11.14) is positive, positive profits per unit of effort (per vessel) exist, and more vessels enter the fishery.

When excess profits are negative, vessels exit. Note that the discount rate appears in equation (11.14) in the form of the opportunity cost of capital (r). If asset markets work perfectly, then we expect r to be equal to the private discount rate used by owners of fishing vessels. It is what these individuals forgo when investing in their vessels rather than alternative forms of capital. But there is no reason to expect r to be equal to the social discount rate. The analysis examines the common property equilibrium, not the social optimum. Incorporating all the assumptions listed above into equation (11.14), we obtain

$$\dot{E} = s(PAX - c - r) \qquad (11.15)$$

Industry equilibrium occurs when there is no entry or exit—that is, $\dot{E}$ is equal to zero. Setting $\dot{E} = 0$ in equation (11.15) and solving for X, we find

$$X = (c + r)/PA \qquad (11.16)$$

We now have an equation for the level of seal population that will lead to a steady-state equilibrium in the industry. Note that this population depends only on the parameters, c, r, P, and A, not on the number of vessels. This follows from the simple assumptions in the model. However, as we will see, the model is still powerful enough to explain much of the behavior of the industry and the seal population. We should also note that in a more complex (and more realistic) model, both P and c are not likely to be constant. If this is so, the dynamics become more complex.

The two equations necessary to solve for a steady-state bionomic equilibrium and to indicate the possible paths to this equilibrium are equations (11.13) (biological equilibrium) and (11.16) (industry equilibrium). Figure 11.2 graphs these two equations as functions of X_t and E_t. The diagram in Figure 11.2 is called a *phase* diagram. The curve $\dot{X} = 0$ shows combinations of vessels E and seals X for which there is a bionomic equilibrium where $F(X) = H(t)$—the net growth of the biomass equals the harvest. The curve $\dot{E} = 0$ shows combinations of E and X where there will be no entry or exit from the industry—the number of vessels will be constant. Notice that X_t is a decreasing function of E_t in the biological equilibrium, which we would expect. In the industry equilibrium, X_t is dependent on the ratio of c to P but is independent of E. The location of the two curves depends on the parameters identified previously.

The steady-state equilibrium for the seal fishery is where the two curves intersect. This is shown as point F in Figure 11.2. A steady-state equilibrium exists where there are positive levels of seals and vessels. It is possible, however, that the curves do not intersect in the interior of the phase plane. For the seal fishery over the period in

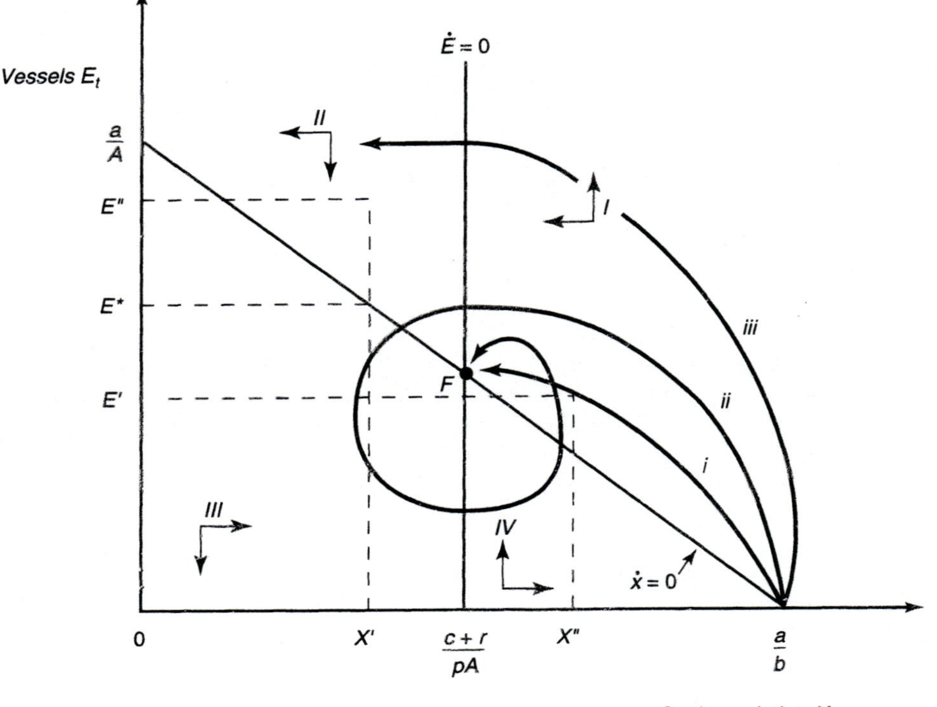

FIGURE 11.2 A steady-state equilibrium for the fur seal fishery and an illustration of possible dynamic paths. Paths *i* and *ii* converge to the equilibrium, but path *iii* does not.

question, the values for the parameters are such that an interior solution does exist. Using Wilen's numbers, in the open access phase of the fishery the steady-state equilibrium would have occurred at slightly more than 582,600 seals, with around 90 vessels actively fishing. This implies a maximum harvest of about 79,000 to 89,000 seals.

The question is whether the industry would have reached this common property equilibrium or whether the fishery would have been extinguished by excessive entry of vessels and overfishing before the equilibrium was reached. Recall that open access outcomes are not socially optimal. To answer this question, we need to examine the possible paths to (or away from) the steady-state equilibrium. We must describe the simultaneous motions of X_t and E_t when they are not at their steady-state values. This motion of X_t and E_t can be described mathematically, but we will explain intuitively what is happening.

The arrows in Figure 11.2 tell us how X_t and E_t will tend to change when the fishery is not on the steady-state equilibrium curves. Let us first examine the movement of X_t when it is not on $\dot{X} = 0$. Suppose the fishery is at X'. At X', E^* vessels would be needed to have the net natural growth of the seal population equal to the harvests. Suppose there are only E' vessels. Then the biomas harvested is less than the net growth of the seals over the time period in question, and the seal population will rise. The horizontal arrow below $\dot{X} = 0$ points to the right to indicate this increasing stock of seals. Conversely, if the fishery is at X' but there are now E'' vessels harvesting seals, the stock of seals will fall over time because the harvest exceeds the growth of the stock. The horizontal arrows above $\dot{X} = 0$ thus point to the left.

Now suppose that there are E' vessels fishing. To have a steady-state industry equilibrium, the fish stock must equal $(c + r)/PA$ seals. If, however, there are only X' seals, not enough will be caught for the industry to cover its costs (including the opportunity cost of capital). Exit from the industry will occur. This is shown by the vertical arrow pointing downward to the left of the $\dot{E} = 0$ line. Conversely, if the population of seals is X'', firms will be earning excess profits and entry will occur. This is shown by the vertical arrows pointing upward. In the figure, then, we have four different sets of arrows. Each set describes the movement of the variables X_t and E_t when not at the steady-state equilibrium. We have labeled the quadrants I, II, III, IV. Let's now see what happens out of steady-state equilibrium.

Suppose that the fishery starts in a steady-state with no harvesting of seals. We begin at point a/b on the X_t axis. Now fishing vessels enter. We illustrate possible dynamic paths emanating from the point a/b. In path i the industry converges smoothly to the steady-state equilibrium. Path ii shows an oscillating path that ultimately reaches the equilibrium. In this continuous time model, if $PA > 0$, open access can lead only to paths such as i or ii. If we have a discrete-time model, there will be a lag between the determination of rent in period t and the response of effort in period $t + 1$. In such a model, a third path labeled iii is possible. Wilen's empirical work is based on a discrete-time framework. He can test to see if path iii arises. Path iii leads to the extinction of the seals. Which path will occur? It depends on the values of the parameters in the model.

Path i will occur whenever s and b are relatively low or a is relatively high (or both). This means that the response of the industry to profits or losses is relatively sluggish, but the seals have low mortality rates and reproduce lustily. Path ii would tend to occur when both s and a are relatively high. The industry responds very quickly to excess profits or losses, but the seal population is very resilient. There will be large swings in both X and E, but these ultimately dampen, and the equilibrium is approached.[4] Finally, path iii could appear when s is high but a is low (relative to b), PA is high, and $c + r$ is low. This means that the $\dot{E} = 0$ curve will be quite close to the origin. When vessels first enter the fishery in response to the high profits, their harvests so deplete the seal population that recovery is impossible. The seals cannot reproduce fast enough to sustain their population, and extinction occurs.

What actually happened in the Pacific fur seal fishery in the late 1800s? Wilen calculated values for the parameters and predicted that path ii would result. He then looked at the actual figures for E_t and X_t for the period 1882 to 1990.[5] The path that resulted is shown in Figure 11.3. The actual path looks very much like the theoretical path shown as path ii. We will never know if the industry would have reached this equilibrium, because the Canadian firms were monopolized at the turn of the century. Again note that the steady-state equilibrium is not an optimal equilibrium; it is still the open access solution.

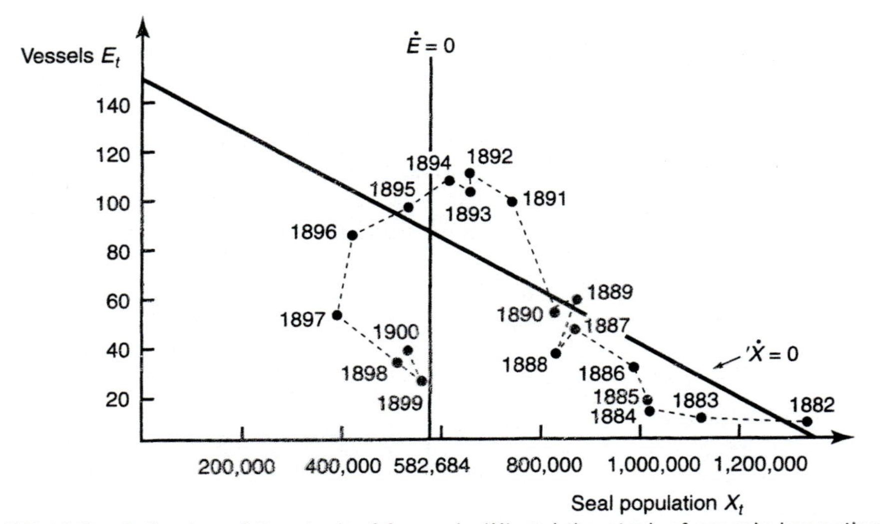

FIGURE 11.3 Estimates of the stock of fur seals (X_t) and the stock of vessels harvesting the seals (E_t) over the period 1882 to 1900. Notice that the path taken by the two stocks is very similar to the path labeled (ii) in Figure 11.2. It appears as if the path may have been converging to the steady-state equilibrium. *Source:* Wilen (1976).

Wilen computes the rents that were forgone as a result of open access to the fishery. They were substantial, and this suggests that monopolization of the fishery would pay off. It also suggests that some form of government intervention would be required if the monopoly solution was socially unacceptable (we know that monopolists generally produce less and charge more than is socially optimal). But what Wilen's analysis does indicate is that extinction is not an inevitable outcome under open access.

What, then, do these dynamic models tell us? A dynamic steady-state equilibrium and paths to that equilibrium (if they exist) can be defined under any property rights scheme. Values of parameters essential to industry and biological equilibrium are required. The parameters of the model will also help determine what sorts of regulations will expedite the movement to the steady-state equilibrium. Static models cannot determine the paths to the equilibrium and may give an inaccurate picture.

In a static model, effort in an open access equilibrium is always greater than is socially optimal. In a dynamic model, the PPE and OAE levels of effort might be quite close when interest rates are high. Effort may have to fluctuate in a dynamic model to achieve efficiency. This does not occur in a static model. One must therefore be careful in prescribing policies for the fishery based solely on static analysis. However, it is often difficult to obtain enough information about the fishery to do a thorough dynamic analysis. The gains from doing dynamic analysis may not be large if not enough is known about the fishery.

Spanish Sardines

This case was investigated by Gallastegui (1983). It illustrates the way in which a dynamic model of the fishery may be used to calculate the optimal equilibrium for a particular fishery, contrasts the optimal equilibrium with the existing open access equilibrium, then shows how the optimum can be reached. The study shows the costs of open access exploitation and the way in which a tax on the harvest (or effort) could be used to eliminate these costs. We do not know the costs of regulating the fishery, or whether the taxation schemes evaluated would be administratively feasible. But the study does indicate the potential gain from taxation in a fishery that is not amenable to the imposition of private property rights because the sardines (small herring) are pelagic.

The fishery in question is in the Gulf of Valencia on the eastern coast of Spain. The sardines move around the area but apparently do not venture far outside the region. All the sardines harvested are landed in two ports. Sardines are harvested only at night from March to December, and only when there is no full moon. No harvests occur on Sundays. This means, in effect, that harvests occur about 24 days per month in the season. The data used in the fishery pertain to the period from 1956 to 1969, when there was open access to the fishery. Gallastegui used a dynamic model of the fishery to calculate the optimal harvest and amount of effort.

Effort in this fishery is measured in terms of candlepower per dark day, because one of the most important inputs is the light potential of the equipment used to attract the sardines to the boats. The other major inputs are sonar equipment (if present), and of course time spent fishing. The author has assumed that the entire night is used, even if the time is spent searching for the fish. This seems reasonable, as one effect of open access would be that the smaller the population, the more time would be spent looking for fish. We know already that under open access populations typically will be smaller than those under optimal management.

The harvest and stock of sardines are determined under open access and then recalculated for a regime of optimal management. The model used is similar to that presented in this chapter. No data on the sardine stock are available, so the author calculated the stock from data on the amount of effort and the catch. Suppose that the harvest function is given by $H_t = F(X_t, E_t)$. If the harvest and the effort values are known, a point on the biological production function $F(X)$ is found. For different harvests and catches, the production function can then be mapped out. In Gallastegui's paper a more complex harvest function is presented, but the concept is the same.

Obviously, there are a number of difficulties with this approach. There may not be enough variation in harvests and effort fully to map out the biological function. The data on H and E may also be poor. Fishing firms may not reveal accurate information to government authorities. Estimates of the biological mechanics may have to be revised as the data change. The technique nonetheless provides a way by which numerical calculations of the stock can be made. And it is a method used frequently by government fisheries managers to calculate $F(X)$.

The author then uses data on the sardine fishery in an econometric model to de-

TABLE 11.1 **STEADY-STATE EQUILIBRIA IN A SARDINE FISHERY IN SPAIN AT DIFFERENT DISCOUNT RATES: THE SOCIALLY OPTIMAL CASES VERSUS THE OPEN ACCESS EQUILIBRIUM**

	Optimal equilibrium discount rates			
Variable	**0%**	**3%**	**8%**	**Open access**
Stock (tons)	35,065	34,415	33,450	17,750
Harvest (tons)	7,927	8,088	8,321	10,624
Effort (candlepower units per day)	390	403	425	886

NOTE: Each case above assumes that the unit of effort is 11.84 pesetas, the instantaneous rate of growth of the marginal product of effort is 0.000523, and the scale parameter estimated from the fishery production function is 0.6103. Numbers have been rounded up to the nearest unit.

Source: Based on C. Gallastegui, (1983). "An Economic Analysis of Sardine Fishing in the Gulf of Valencia (Spain)." *Journal of Environmental Economics and Management* 10, 138–150.

termine the steady-state harvest, stock, and amount of effort under optimal management. The values depend on three unknown terms: the social discount rate, the real unit cost of effort, and a parameter that reflects the rate of growth of the marginal product of effort. The author uses different hypothetical values for these terms. The open access harvest, stock, and effort are determined from the open access equilibrium (the average product of effort equals the real unit cost of effort). In Table 11.1, the open access equilibrium is contrasted with optimal equilibriums at different discount rates and a particular marginal product of effort. Table 11.2 shows how these values change at different unit costs of effort, and Table 11.3 lists the actual historical data.

These tables illustrate a number of points about the fishery under different forms of ownership. First, as is not surprising, the open access equilibrium always uses more effort and has a lower stock than the optimum. The higher the discount rate, the larger the optimal harvest and amount of effort and the lower the optimal stock. Why is this true? Under open access, the discount rate is effectively infinite. As the discount rate increases, the optimal equilibrium approaches the open access equilibrium. However, for this sardine fishery the discount rate would have to be substantially higher before the optimal equilibrium was anywhere close to the OAE.

Table 11.2 shows the sensitivity of the harvest, stock, and effort to changes in the unit cost of effort, assuming that the discount rate is 8 percent. We see that below a real cost of 4, the open access equilibrium will result in complete extinction of the stock, but not so with the social optimum. At a very high unit cost, above 30, no harvests are made in the optimal case and the fishery is at its maximum population level; but under the OAE, harvests still occur.

Table 11.3 shows that the actual open access harvests tended to fluctuate somewhat. The period from 1956 to 1959 and again from 1962 to 1964 would all be years of overfishing relative to the optimum (at each discount rate). In every year except

TABLE 11.2 **EFFECTS OF REAL COST OF EFFORT ON THE STEADY-STATE VALUES OF THE STOCK, HARVEST, AND AMOUNT OF EFFORT**

	Optimal values			Open access values		
Real cost of effort	**Stock**	**Harvest**	**Effort**	**Stock**	**Harvest**	**Effort**
0.00	13,790	10,533	1,085	—	—	—
4.00	21,200	10,423	765	4,460	7,753	1,926
6.00	24,530	10,039	675	7,450	9,254	1,544
11.84	33,450	8,321	425	17,725	10,625	897
14.20	36,950	7,437	350	22,250	10,320	729
16.00	39,260	6,800	306	23,200	10,210	697
20.00	44,850	5,111	207	33,100	8,404	433
30.93	59,156	—	—	49,000	3,731	140
40.00	59,156	—	—	58,850	118	4

NOTE: Numbers have been rounded up to the nearest unit.
Source: C. Gallastegui (1983). "An Economic Analysis of Sardine Fishing in the Gulf of Valencia (Spain)." *Journal of Environmental Economics and Management* 10, 146.

TABLE 11.3 **DATA FOR A SPANISH SARDINE FISHERY**

Year	**Catch (metric tons)**	**Effort**
1956	9,447	516
1957	10,269	551
1958	9,070	533
1959	9,932	627
1960	6,857	780
1961	5,192	756
1962	10,951	756
1963	11,100	804
1964	10,057	688
1965	4,060	492
1966	4,020	378
1967	4,092	503
1968	4,327	572
1969	5,289	878

NOTE: Numbers have been rounded up to the nearest unit.
Source: C. Gallastegui (1983). "An Economic Analysis of Sardine Fishing in the Gulf of Valencia (Spain)." *Journal of Environmental Economics and Management* 10, 140.

1966, the open access effort was far above that suggested by the social optimum for any unit cost above 11 pesetas (1 peseta equaled $0.0063 U.S. as of 1984). After 1964, the stock was apparently depleted enough that sardine effort was shifting toward other fisheries—specifically, anchovies.

Using these figures, Gallastegui computed the resource savings that would rise if the fishery were managed optimally. These savings are the reduction in effort needed to harvest the sardines net of the lower total value of the catch, assuming that the price of sardines remains constant. If the catch from this region has any impact on the sardine market, the price may rise as the harvests fall, and these revenue effects would not be as large. The saving in effort at a discount rate of 3 percent is about 54 million pesetas per year. The loss in revenue from decreased harvest is about 24 million pesetas, leaving a net gain of about 30 million pesetas. Effort must fall by 228 units, which would mean, if effort is immobile, forgone earnings of about 25 million pesetas. The *net* social gain from optimal management would then be about 5 million pesetas (about $300,000 U.S.) if all the unemployed effort was immobile and fully compensated for its loss.[6]

How could the optimum be reached? First, a three-year moratorium would be needed (assuming a perfectly elastic supply of effort) to build the stock of sardines up to the optimal level. The moratorium is the fastest way to rejuvenate the stock and can be shown to be the optimal dynamic path. Once the stock is at the optimal steady-state level, a tax on the catch or a tax on effort would be necessary to deal with the open access problem. It is unlikely that any property rights assignment would work in this case because of the pelagic nature of the fishery, and perhaps the difficulty of enforcing private property rights.

The tax on the catch must reflect the stock effect of the fish population and the difference between marginal and average cost at the optimum. Gallastegui computed the required tax to be 3,856 pesetas per ton. The 1971 price of sardines was 9,440 pesetas per ton, so the tax would mean a net price to fishing effort of 5.594 pesetas. Total tax revenue collected by the government would be over 31 million pesetas. Total revenue to the fishery would fall from around 100 million pesetas to 45 million pesetas, where these numbers are based on the OAE versus optimal equilibrium in Table 11.1 at a discount rate of 3 percent. Thus the total loss of revenue (as noted above) equals the reduction in total revenue to the fishers net of government tax revenues, 24 million pesetas.

The author does not discuss whether an optimal tax could be levied in practice. Given that all sardines harvested are landed at only two ports, a landing tax may be administratively feasible. Imposition of the moratorium may be more difficult, as 3 years is a long time to go without any fishing income. However, Gallastegui notes that if the supply curve of effort has a positive elasticity of 2, then the moratorium need last only 1 year, and no decline in effort is needed to obtain the optimum. Spanish policy makers would thus want to estimate this supply curve before implementing a moratorium. And as noted in Chapter 5, moratoriums have been imposed in other fisheries.

What regulations have been imposed on the sardine fishery? The Spanish government has in the past few years established some regulations for pelagic fisheries in the Mediterranean. In 1979, the number of hours each vessel can fish daily was restricted. Minimum vessel capacity was set at 25 gross registered tonnage. Previously, vessels of 10 to 15 tons were prevalent in the fishery. These regulations thus represent attempts to limit effort. The light intensity of lamps was limited to 2,200 candlepower, and fishing at depths below 25 meters was forbidden. Minimum size restrictions on the fish harvested were also imposed. These are measures to protect the species and reduce the harvest. Penalties for violating the regulations were introduced, but it is not known if these have been effective.

ENVIRONMENTAL FACTORS IN FISHERY BIOLOGICAL MECHANICS

There is no meaningful long-run, steady-state yield in many fisheries because the population in any period depends on ecological conditions—water temperature, currents, disease, new predators, pollution—that have prevailed over the life cycle of the species, not the population in the previous period. In each period, the population is determined largely by exogenous factors rather than biological mechanics. This means that at a particular point in time—say one fishing season—only short-run functions can be drawn for the fishery. Species whose biomass is greatly affected by environmental factors include shrimp and anchovies.

Suppose the stock can be measured at the beginning of the fishing season. It is them possible to analyze the optimal harvest *for that period.* The usual sort of total revenue and total cost curves can be drawn relating the harvest to the amount of effort used. But it may not be meaningful to analyze the fishery using the dynamic model. The stock must be reevaluated each period that harvesting is to occur, and a new set of short-run curves defined.

Moreover, if the fish feed on an erratic stock of another species, the harvest will also be highly variable. That is, if the cycles in the "food" are unpredictable, there will be stochastic variations in the population of the harvested species. If the cycles in the food are known, the optimal harvest of the commercial species is much simpler. The fish must then be harvested in different intensities over the cycle.[7]

The dangers from open access to a fishery with an unpredictable stock in each period can be substantial. Disease and fluctuations in water temperature, food supply, and presence of predators can lead to large swings in the stocks. If there are excessive amounts of effort at work harvesting the species and a bad year occurs, the population can be driven close to extinction. This occurred in the anchovy fishery off the coast of Peru in the early 1970s. The fishery was depleted because of open access and the unpredictable exogenous factors—namely, El Niño, a warm ocean current (see the next section).

Optimal harvesting practices require careful monitoring of the stock before each fishing season. If exogenous factors are such that a bad year for the stock occurs, effort should be curtailed. Regulating this type of fishery is difficult and costly, in part because of the different levels of effort that may be needed each year. But the costs of allowing open access and risking extinction may be even higher.

The Anchovy Crisis

An article by Idyll (1973) in *Scientific American* tells the story of the anchovy and the complex set of biological conditions that, combined with overfishing, led to its demise in 1973. The small Peruvian anchovy resides in a complex ecosystem off the coast of Peru. It is a key organism in an aquatic food chain that starts with microscopic diatoms and phytoplankton and goes on to small crustaceans; small fish, including the anchovy; and then larger fish and seabirds that feed on the anchovy. The anchovy was, however, the species that captured a very high proportion of the total energy from the food chain. The maximum sustainable stock of this anchovy is probably around 15 to 20 million metric tons.

Although anchovies can spawn at any time during the year, the peak spawning periods are from August to September and to a lesser degree in January and February. The natural life span of an anchovy is short—about 3 years. The female can reproduce when she is 1 year old and is capable of producing over 10,000 eggs. At 2 years, she can produce around 20,000 eggs. Life is not easy for an anchovy, however; natural mortality is high. Anchovies require food almost immediately upon hatching, and if environmental conditions are such that food is scarce, most new recruits will die. They are also preyed upon by copepods (who are themselves eaten by larger anchovies) and by seabirds known as guano. Only about 1 percent of all anchovy larvae survive 1 month after they hatch. This is why millions of eggs must be produced each period to ensure the survival of the species.

The anchovy's habitat is also somewhat precarious, because of periodic shifts in ocean currents. Most people are now familiar with the phenomenon known as El Niño, a reversal in the Pacific Ocean currents that happens periodically for unknown reasons. When El Niño hits the Pacific coast of South America, it greatly increases the water temperature and may lead to torrential rains in a normally very arid climate. These environmental changes spell disaster for the anchovy and many other species. It's not quite clear what exactly leads to the high mortality of the ocean species.

It could be the warmer water temperature that destroys the microorganisms upon which anchovies and other creatures feed. During conditions of El Niño, massive numbers of fish, squid, sea turtles, and even small sea mammals die. The guano birds that feed on these creatures also die or fly away. The decaying creatures release hydrogen sulfide from the water, and this leads to a phenomenon called El Pintor ("the painter"). The water becomes filled with microscopic plants called dinoflagellates, which turn the water to shades of red, brown, and yellow. This phenomenon is known elsewhere as *red tide*. At high concentrations, these plankton blooms are toxic. Why El Niño leads to El Pintor is not quite clear. It could be the higher water temperature or the sluggish current that does not disperse the plants as quickly as normal.

Anchovies are used in the manufacture of fish meal that is used to feed domestic livestock, and fish oils. They were a very valuable product for Peru. In the early 1970s, Peru was the world's largest fish-producing country, with fish products accounting for almost one-third of its foreign exchange earnings. The anchovy harvest was around 10 to 12 million metric tons per year until disaster hit in 1973. The industry was a classic case of open access. Although regulations had existed since the 1960s, they appear to have been designed merely to maintain the MSY anchovy stock. No limitations of effort appear to have existed (or to have worked, if they did exist). Idyll notes that the anchovy fleet off Peru was so large that it could harvest the equivalent of the annual United States catch of yellowfin tuna in *1 day,* or the United States salmon catch in $2\frac{1}{2}$ days. To harvest 10 million metric tons of anchovies annually, 75 percent of the fleet would be sufficient.

What happened to anchovies in 1973 illustrates the need to monitor environmental conditions and regulate effort accordingly. Because of the periodic presence of El Niño and the characteristics of anchovy reproduction and survival, *the stock of anchovies at any given point in time is not a good predictor of the growth of the species.* The number that survive in any season depends more on environmental factors than the biomass. This, combined with excessive effort and imprecise regulations, led in 1973 to the virtual extinction of the anchovy fishery. The story is simple, although some biological puzzles remain unexplained.

El Niño appeared in 1972. By June of that year, the anchovies had just about disappeared and the total harvest for the year was about 4.5 million metric tons, or about one-third to one-half of the harvests in preceding years. The stock was apparently only 1 to 2 million metric tons. El Niño continued until the spring of 1973. Anchovy harvests in 1973 were even less than in 1972, as shown in Table 11.4. Catches were far below the quotas set. Even with rapidly rising prices for fish meal (due to the "energy shock" and the commodity boom of the 1970s), there were not enough anchovies to warrant the use of effort in the fishery.

Idyll was unsure of the fate of the Peruvian anchovy over the long run. Table 11.4 suggests some recovery in the catch from 1974 to 1976, then a sharp decline in 1977–1978. If enough anchovies could survive both El Niño and the harvests, the species would rebuild if harvests were severely curtailed. But this required a change in the regulations, restrictions on effort, a more thorough monitoring of environmental conditions, and regulations that change quickly to reflect the environmental conditions. In the presence of El Niño, the appropriate policy would have been to curtail the harvest sharply or impose a moratorium. Even 3 to 4 million tons may have been too much. Without these regulatory responses, the anchovy fishery may not survive, and with it will go other species (the guano birds) and the livelihood of many people.

INTERACTION AMONG SPECIES

Biological interaction of different fish species can take place in many ways.[8] Each species can benefit from having more of the other on hand. This is called a *commensal* situation. Alternatively, each can suffer from a greater presence of the other. We then have a *competitive* situation. There can also be cross-effects, such as a predator-prey relationship in which one species benefits from the presence of the other (eats it), while the other species suffers (is eaten). From an economic perspective, the presence of another species can make harvesting more or less easy because the costs of harvesting a particular species may be affected by the presence of the stock of another species. If both species are valuable, harvesting one might yield the salable by-product—the other species captured simultaneously.

TABLE 11.4 **THE PERUVIAN ANCHOVETA FISHERY, 1959–1978**

Year	Number of boats	Number of fishing days	Catch (million tons)
1959	414	294	1.91
1960	667	279	2.93
1961	756	298	4.58
1962	1,069	294	6.27
1963	1,655	269	6.42
1964	1,744	297	8.86
1965	1,623	265	7.23
1966	1,650	190	8.53
1967	1,569	170	9.82
1968	1,490	167	10.26
1969	1,455	162	8.96
1970	1,499	180	12.27
1971	1,473	89	10.28
1972	1,399	89	4.45
1973	1,256	27	1.78
1974	—*	—	4.00
1975	—	—	3.30
1976	—	—	4.30
1977	—	—	0.80
1978	—	—	0.50

*Missing data not currently available.

Source: Colin W. Clark, "Bioeconomics of the Ocean." *Bioscience* 31, (3) (March 1981), p. 233, Copyright © 1981 by the American Institute of Biological Sciences.

A Predator-Prey Model

We examine the case in which two species interact in a predator-prey situation. We first consider the biological mechanics, then turn to the determination of an optimal harvesting program. There are many examples of predator-prey situations. For example, many species eat shrimp in their larval stage and can greatly affect important commercial harvests. Sea mammals such as sea lions, harbor seals, and killer whales feed on salmon. In this section, we look at a predator-prey model using sharks and tuna as our fictitious example. We choose these species for heuristic reasons—it is not difficult to remember which species is the predator and which is the prey.

Suppose, then, that we have two species—tuna and sharks. Tuna are a commercially desirable species, but they are eaten by sharks for which in general there is less commercial demand.[9] Tuna have a stock size of $X(t)$ and are eaten by sharks, which have a population of $Y(t)$. Sharks' natural mortality is at the exponential rate d. The change in the population of sharks over any two periods, t and $t + 1$, is defined by equation (11.17).

$$Y(t + 1) - Y(t) = Y(t)[-d + c'X(t)] \tag{11.17}$$

where c' is a parameter that reflects sharks eating tuna, and d is the "decay" of the shark species in the absence of tuna to eat. Tuna achieve a steady-state stock $X = a/b$ through their natural growth in the usual logistic pattern, but they are "harvested" by sharks by the amount $cY(t)X(t)$, given a stock size $X(t)$ and c, the parameter that measures the intensity of sharks "harvesting" tuna. The change in the tuna population over time is then given by equation (11.18):

$$X(t + 1) - X(t) = X(t)[a - bX(t) - cY(t)] \tag{11.18}$$

where a and b are the parameters of the biological production function for the tuna.

In an equilibrium without human predation, $X = d/c'$, and $Y = (a - bX)/c = (ac' - bd)/cc'$. In this steady-state equilibrium, the predator "harvests" cXY per period or $d(ac' - bd)/(c')^2$. Recall that sharks will die out without tuna, but tuna will grow to their carrying capacity in the absence of sharks. We have an equilibrium with sharks living off the net growth in the tuna at a stock size of $Y = (a - bX)/c$, which is equal to $(ac' - bd)/cc'$. We illustrate this in Figure 11.4. In Figure 11.4(a), we have our familiar single-species stock-sustainable yield schedule for the tuna, assuming that no predation occurs. When there is predation, the tuna stock will fall to d/c' and the sharks are eating $[d(ac' - bd)]/(c')^2$ each period—the vertical distance between the X axis and the $F(X)$ function at d/c'.

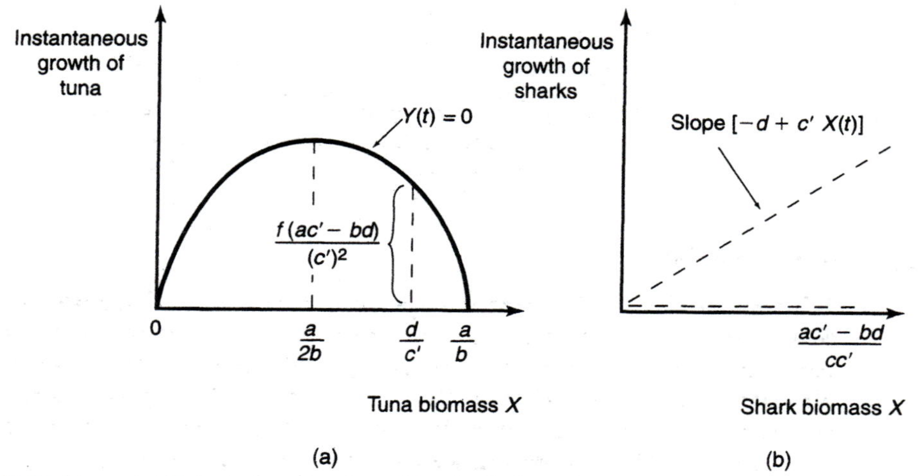

FIGURE 11.4 (a) Biological mechanics of the desired species when in isolation. (b) Mechanics for the preying species. With no human predation, a steady state emerges with the stock of Y at $\frac{ac' - bd}{cc'}$ and X at d/c'. The predator Y species consumes the net increment in the X species each period.

In Figure 11.4(b), we show the shark's biology. Sharks eat enough tuna to remain at a steady population. Tuna are also in equilibrium, with their net growth eaten by the sharks. That means when sharks are eating enough tuna, there is no growth in the stock of tuna. Natural increase and predation by sharks cancel out. In (b), no one harvests sharks, so there is no excess of births over deaths; no vertical part in (b) is positive. Births match deaths at the equilibrium stock size. The biological mechanics of the two species are quite different, but they interact to yield a steady state with both species having positive stocks.

We now introduce optimal fishing (by people) into the analysis. Assume that the tuna are commercially more valuable than the sharks. We will show that it will be socially desirable to harvest sharks so that the steady-state population of tuna will rise and more tuna can be harvested. This optimal solution requires that *the harvesting of sharks be subsidized—that a bounty be paid.* The government fisheries manager will try to maximize social welfare over time from the harvest of both species. The objective function the manager maximizes is given by equation (11.19):

$$\begin{aligned} W = {} & B^H[H(0)] - C^H[H(0), X(0), Y(0)] + B^L[L(0)] - C^L[L(0), X(0), Y(0)] \\ & + \beta\{B^H[H(1)] - C^H[H(1), X(1), Y(1)] + B^L[L(1)] \\ & - C^L[L(1), X(1), Y(1)]\} + \beta^2\{B^H[H(2)] - C^H[H(2), X(2), Y(2)] \\ & + B^L[L(2)] - C^L[L(2), X(2), Y(2)]\} + \cdots + \end{aligned} \tag{11.19}$$

where $B^H(H)$ = gross consumer surplus associated with a harvest of H tons of tuna—the high valued species

$B^L(L)$ = gross consumer surplus associated with a harvest of L tons of shark—the low valued species

$C^H(\cdot)$ = cost of harvesting H tons of tuna when the two stocks of fish are present at their indicated sizes

$C^L(\cdot)$ = cost of harvesting L tons of tuna when the two stocks of fish are present at their indicated sizes

β = discount factor, equal to $1/(1 + r)$, where r is the social discount rate

Let us rewrite the biological dynamics for each species in the more general form shown in equation (11.20):

$$\begin{aligned} X(t + 1) - X(t) &= G[X(t), Y(t)] \\ Y(t + 1) - Y(t) &= Q[X(t), Y(t)] \end{aligned} \tag{11.20}$$

Equation (11.20) shows general representations of the interactions between the two species. Previously, we had a specific case where sharks died at an exponential rate without tuna dinners. Now, the two species simply interact in some unspecified way. The harvests from fishing firms are then given by

$$\begin{aligned} H(t) &= G[X(t), Y(t)] - X(t + 1) + X(t) \\ L(t) &= Q[X(t), Y(t)] - Y(t + 1) + Y(t) \end{aligned} \tag{11.21}$$

We then substitute equation (11.21) for $L(t)$ and $H(t)$ in equation (11.19) to obtain a W that is to be maximized by choice of tuna and shark stocks (and hence, harvests) in each period, 0, 1, 2, . . . , that follows. This is readily done by differentiating equation (11.19) with respect to X and Y, then setting the resulting first-order expressions equal to zero. The solutions yield the relationships for an optimal extraction program over time.[10] Rather than write down the solution, which must hold at each point along the optimal path, let us assume that we have a steady-state equilibrium with positive values for X and Y. In the steady state, the stocks of tuna and sharks must satisfy equation (11.23) simultaneously

$$\begin{aligned}(p - C_H)(G_X - r) + (q - C_L)Q_X - C_H - C_L = 0\\(q - C_L)(Q_Y - r) + (p - C_H)G_Y - C_H - C_L = 0\end{aligned} \qquad (11.22)$$

where p and q are market prices for a ton of tuna and sharks, respectively; r is the discount rate; and the other terms are partial derivatives of the cost and production functions. For the following, we assume that q, the price of shark, is positive, but the analysis would be the same even if q were equal to zero.

For the *special case* of $G(X,Y)$ and $Q(X,Y)$ given by our predatory-prey biological dynamics above, and assuming that the total costs of harvesting each species are *not* interdependent—that is, $C^H(H,X) = wH/mX$ and $C^L(L,Y) = wL/nY$—then these two steady-state equations in (11.22) become, respectively,

$$\begin{aligned}p(a - bX) - pcY = (r + bX)[p - (w/mX)] - c'Y[q - (w/nY)]\\q(-d + c'X) = cX[p - (w/mX)] + r[q - (w/nY)]\end{aligned} \qquad (11.23)$$

Observe that the left-hand sides are steady-state harvests if multiplied by X and Y, respectively (in dollar terms). The terms $[p - (w/mX)]$ and $[q - (w/nY)]$ are the rent per ton from the harvest of tuna and sharks, respectively, where rent, as before, is the difference between price and marginal cost per ton. This indicates that $rX[p - (w/mX)]$ and $rY[q - (w/nY)]$ are the rental value of the respective stocks in flow terms multiplied by the discount rate. A steady-state solution must have the left-hand side of the first equation in (11.23) positive, because as we saw earlier in this chapter, rents are positive for a desired species in an optimally managed fishery.

To see what the steady-state stocks and harvests are in the optimal equilibrium, we solve equation (11.23) by inserting some assumed values for the parameters. These two equations can be combined to form a polynomial equation in X^3. For parameter values: $a = 0.5$, $b = 0.1$, $c = 0.6$, $d = 1$, $r = 0.05$, $w = 6$, $c' = 1$, $m = 6$, $n = 50$, $p = 1$, and $q = 0.5$. The two equations of (11.23) are plotted in Figure 11.5. Only the solution, $X = 2.24$ and $Y = 0.040$, is economically meaningful. The other positive solution for the steady-state stocks results in a negative harvest of sharks.[11]

We illustrate both the biological equilibrium without harvesting and the socially optimal equilibrium in Figure 11.6. The biological equilibrium is shown in (a); the optimal equilibrium with an active fishing industry is shown in (b). Without human predation, the stock of sharks is large and the tuna stock is small relative to the situation illustrated in Figure 11.6(b). The much smaller stock of sharks that occurs with human predation implies that the sharks are eating much less of the net growth in the tuna population (0.402 tons of tuna are consumed by sharks in the biological equilibrium versus 0.054 in the economic equilibrium). The larger sustainable stock of tuna that results with human predation on both sharks and tuna leads to a sizable commercial harvest of tuna: 0.564 tons per season. With commercial fishing, 0.05 tons of

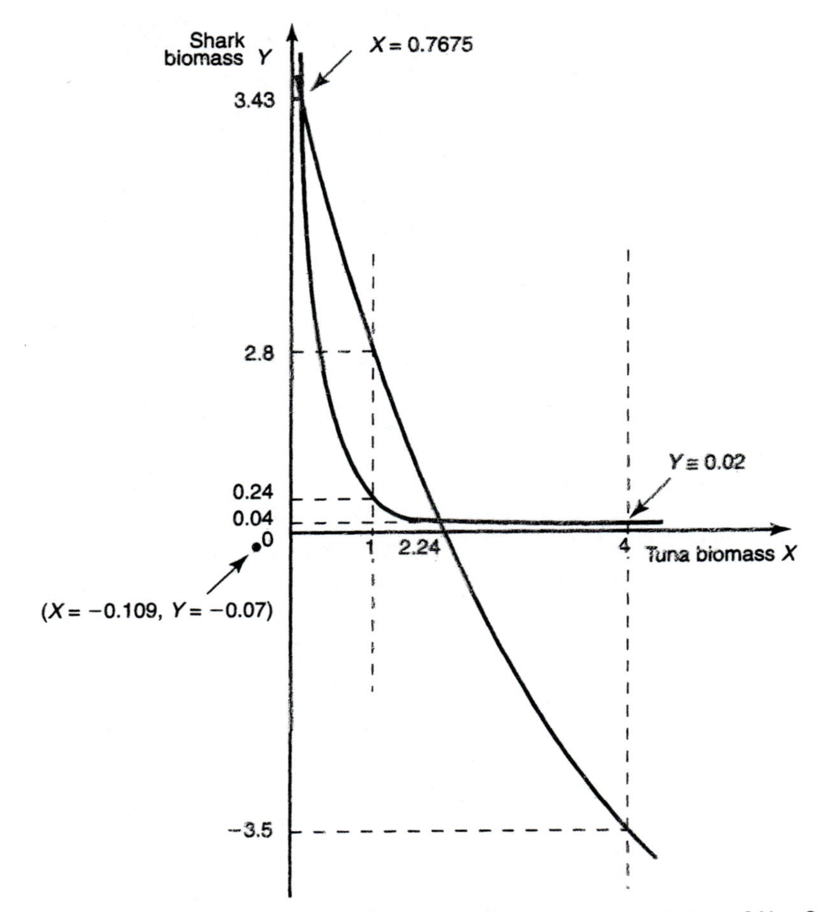

FIGURE 11.5 A sketch of the two equations in X and Y yielding our solution of $Y = 0.04$ and $X = 2.24$. Of the three sets of roots, only the one we have noted makes economic sense.

sharks are caught each season in order to keep that species from expanding and consuming tuna.

Because the commercial value of sharks is low, a subsidy or bounty will be necessary to have the shark species harvested under the socially optimal arrangement. The optimal value of the shark subsidy is the social value of the rent per ton from the shark harvest. The shark rent per ton is $[q - (w/nY)]$, or with our parameter values, -2.485. The negative sign indicates that a subsidy is necessary, because in an unregulated fishery no sharks would be harvested. The higher the price of sharks, of course, the lower the required subsidy. If the price exceeds the harvesting costs, no subsidy is required. To achieve the optimal harvest of tuna, a tax is required that is also set equal to the rent per ton of tuna harvested at the optimum. The tax is thus set equal to $(p - w/mX)$, which would be equal to 0.559 for our parameter values. (If the shark rent is

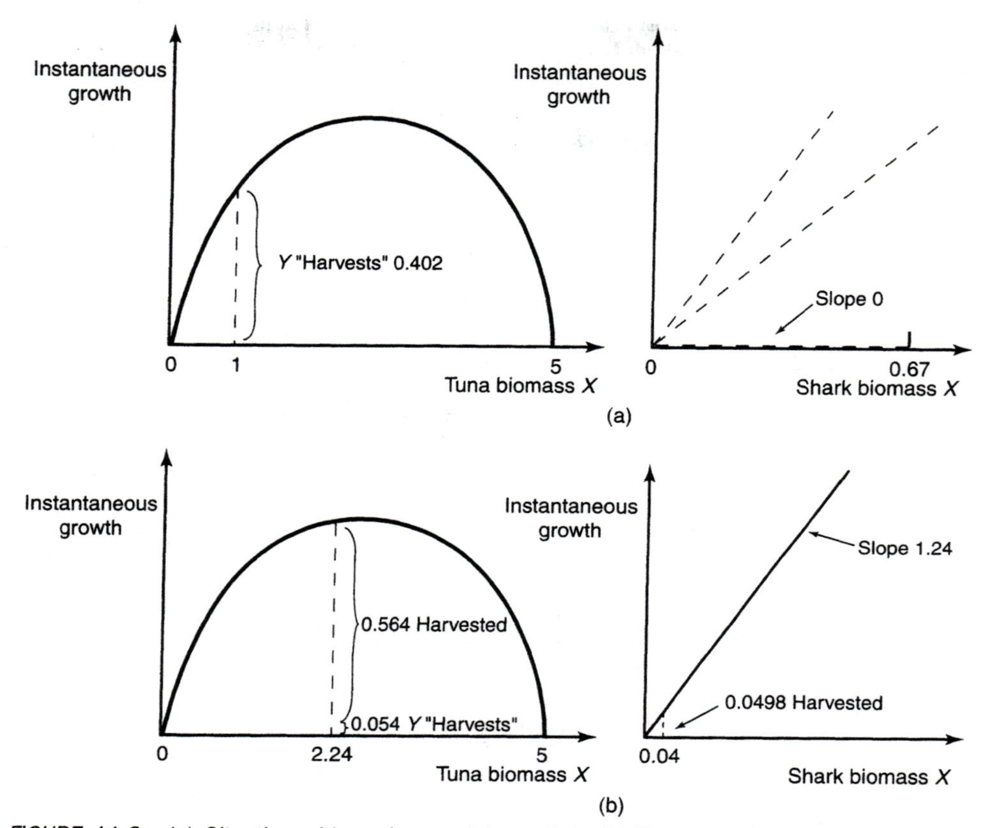

FIGURE 11.6 (a) Situation with no human intervention. (b) Humans harvest 0.564 of the *X* species and 0.0498 of the *Y* species. Observe the large changes in steady-state stocks after human intervention. The *Y* stock drops more than tenfold, and the *X* stock more than doubles.

positive, its harvests must also be taxed.) With our solution, the tax on the tuna yields revenues that exceed the subsidy to the sharks, so there is a surplus for the fishery managers that can offset administrative costs.[12]

Thus what the optimal policy does is subsidize the shark harvests to reduce their population and prevent sharks from eating as much tuna. The tuna population will then increase to a point where a sizable harvest can be taken by human fishing effort. Without the harvest of sharks, the available tuna harvest would be much lower, and although sharks would be better off, people would be worse off. In an optimally managed fishery, the rents per ton are "shadow prices" indicating the relative values of the different tons harvested at the optimum.

In practice, it would be very difficult to regulate a predator-prey fishery. In an open access setting, the regulator must first calculate the optimal solution and find the optimal tax and subsidy per ton. These taxes and subsidies must be levied on entering firms. The administrative and monitoring problems we examined in Chapter 5 will apply in this case as well. But the regulator cannot easily tell how changes in the fishing environment are affecting the equilibrium stocks without extensive recomputation. These computations are necessary in a single-species fishery as well, but with a predator-prey relationship the measurement is more complex.

But even if we leave aside the practical problems associated with imposing and enforcing optimal regulations over time, could the regulatory agency deal, even in theory, with changing economic conditions in the fishery? Suppose the social discount rate or the unit costs of harvesting fish rose. In the predator-prey model, would the regulator be able to determine the optimal response? In his analysis of this problem, Solow (1977) found that the effects of a change in the discount rate or unit costs on the optimal steady-state harvest (and fish stocks) could not be determined unambiguously for a general model. Algebraic investigations yielded results with different possible signs. Numerical values were needed to get definitive results. This awkward outcome led him to comment: "It's an excellent example of the conflict between complex ecology and simple economics."

Although we cannot get general comparative static results for the effect of changes in parameters on the steady-state equilibrium, we can calculate results for specific parameter values.[13] Given our "base equilibrium" from the parameters above, we changed separately the interest rate, r; a parameter in the cost function for harvesting tuna, m; and the similar parameter in the cost function for harvesting sharks, n. The results are shown in Table 11.5.

From our base equilibrium, an increase in the interest rate decreases the optimal tuna stock and tuna harvest while it increases the optimal shark harvest and stock. These results do not have much intuitive appeal and are quite different from the single-species case. Normally, an increase in the discount rate leads to an increase in the harvest and a decrease in the stock, because the present value of waiting for larger harvests in the future by letting the stock build up today is reduced. What appears to be happening here is that the decline in the tuna harvest makes more tuna available for shark food. Thus tunas decline and sharks rise, making more sharks available for harvest. But why the asymmetry between the shark and tuna harvests? Intuition is not always reliable when the number of interactions between variables increases. Simulation becomes necessary.

The cost effects are more straightforward and intuitively plausible. A rise in the

TABLE 11.5 **COMPARATIVE EQUILIBRIA IN THE PREDATOR-PREY MODEL**

	Change in			
Change in	**Tuna biomass**	**Shark biomass**	**Tuna harvests**	**Shark harvests**
Discount rate (r)	−	+	−	+
Cost of tuna harvests ($1/m$)	+	+	−	+
Cost of shark harvests ($1/n$)	−	+	−	−

cost of harvesting tuna decreases tuna harvests but increases shark harvests. Both stocks rise as a result. Firms shift to harvesting the lower-valued shark species as the rent per ton on tuna harvested falls. The tuna stock rises because fewer tuna are caught and more sharks are caught. The shark stock rises because there are more tuna to eat (even though more sharks are caught). Finally, a rise in the cost of harvesting sharks decreases the harvests of both species. A fall in shark harvests leads to a fall in the stock of tuna (more sharks remain to eat them). This results in a smaller tuna harvest and an increase in the stock of sharks.

We wish to emphasize that these results do depend on our parameters and will change when other values are chosen. An alternative equilibrium would be one with free entry and no subsidy for the harvesting of trash fish. In this case, the price of both species would equal their average harvest cost. For tuna, $p = w/mX$; and for sharks, $q = w/nY$. For our model and base-value parameters, $X = 1$ and $Y = 0.24$, with a tuna harvest of 0.256 and shark harvest of zero. These tuna values are slightly below half those for the socially optimal case. The shark stock is six times larger. The price of sharks might be zero in actual cases, and with no government intervention, the desired stock may be very low and the fishing activity quite small.

We have considered a detailed case of one type of biological interdependency: sharks preying on tuna. Other cases and numerical examples would change the results, although in general, we would expect human predation to increase the stock of the prey and reduce the stock of the predator. In our example, the tuna stock more than doubled in size when optimal human predation was introduced, while the shark population was reduced to about 1/17 of its original size. It's possible that for very low commercial value of the predator, extinction would result. There are examples of near extinction in predator-prey relationships among mammals as a result of human harvests of the predator. Wolves are known to prey on commercial species such as sheep and cattle when their "natural" prey such as deer are scarce. A bounty on wolves in some areas has depleted wolf populations. These actions may have been misguided ecologically and socially (preservation of species may have social value), but the actions were taken to increase the stock of the commercial species to increase their harvests. Other examples of this sort exist.[14]

Before turning to our next topic, note that we have analyzed only biological interactions. It is also possible that harvesting costs are affected by the presence of both species. For example, we assumed that the costs of harvesting tuna and shark were independent of the stock of the other species. Suppose instead that these costs were functions of each other's stocks. In our previous example, the total costs were wH/mX for tuna and wL/nY for sharks. If there are cost interdependencies, the functions could be written as wHY/mX and wLX/nY, respectively. In this situation, the costs of harvesting tuna are higher the larger the stock of sharks, and the costs of harvesting sharks are higher the larger the stock of tuna. Introducing such interdependencies complicates computation of our equilibria, but the model may then more closely capture the details of certain fisheries. The comparative static computations are no less complex. Anderson (1977) refers to these cost effects as technical interdependencies that may be present along with the biological interdependencies examined here.

BOX 11.1 Lamprey and Lake Trout

A profitable lake trout fishery in the Great Lakes (Ontario, Erie, Huron, Michigan, and Superior) was almost eliminated between 1930 and 1960 by the arrival of a predator species, the lamprey. The lamprey migrated from the ocean into the lower Great Lakes; a sea lamprey was first observed in Lake Erie above Niagara Falls in 1921. By 1946, they had migrated, in part by piggybacking on the hulls of ships, into the colder upper Great Lakes. Canadian and American harvests of 15 million pounds of lake trout annually fell to 300,000 pounds in the early 1960s as a result of the lamprey invasion. This is a case in which subsidized harvest of the trash species, the lamprey, was necessary in order to make harvests of the desired species, the lake trout, profitable.

"Harvesting" of the lamprey took the form of destroying the young lampreys, known as ammocoetes. Lampreys spawn only in certain streams. Once these were isolated, a specially tested toxicant, TFM (3 triflourmethyl-4 mitrophenol), was applied with special pumping systems. Of 2,000 Canadian streams tested for spawning, only 105 were used by lampreys. Large streams were first treated in 1959, and by 1962 only 20 percent of the early stock remained (see the figure). A large program of restocking of lake trout was initiated in 1958, with 20 million planted in Lake Superior by 1968.

Although not commercially exploited in North America, lampreys have been eaten for many years and are considered a delicacy in some parts of the world. Imports to North America have been taking place for many years. However, in the Great Lakes the lamprey was the trash species, and it was necessary to subsidize its harvest.

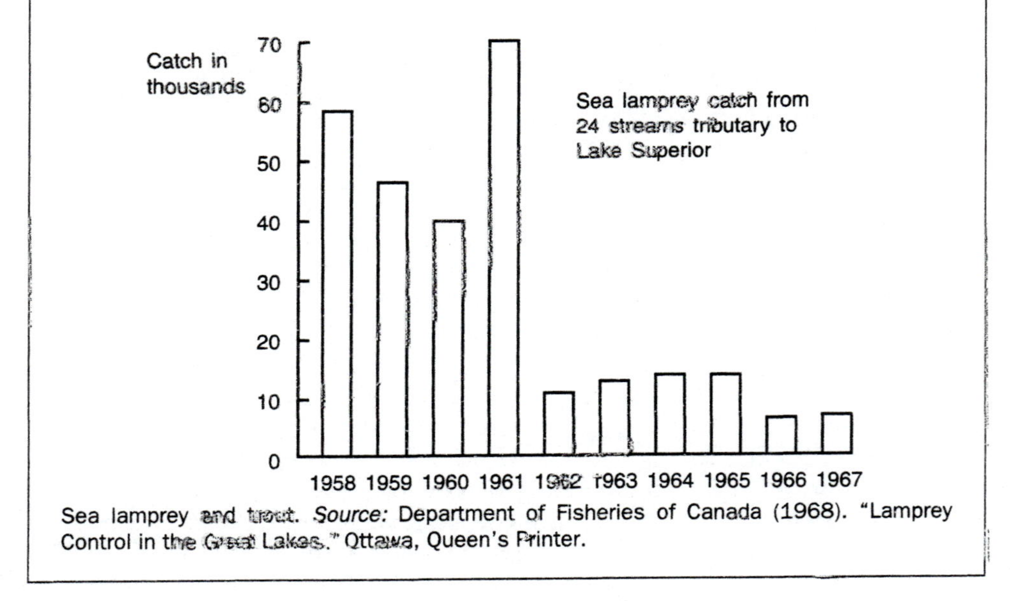

Sea lamprey and trout. *Source:* Department of Fisheries of Canada (1968). "Lamprey Control in the Great Lakes." Ottawa, Queen's Printer.

INTERNATIONAL FISHERIES

Until the 200-mile coastal boundaries were imposed by many countries in the late 1970s, most major fishing grounds were exploited by vessels from two or more nations. Under a regime of open access, the equilibrium should be the same as if one nation were in control. The flags on the boats would be of no importance—there would be too much effort and too small a stock size relative to the optimum results. Suppose, however, that a fisheries department in each nation wanted to control the number of boats used by its nationals in a fishing ground outside its territorial limits. What plan might it devise? How would this plan differ from a plan coordinated by all nations exploiting a particular fishery?

A Two-Country Model

Consider a two-country illustration with each government's fishing department acting in isolation. Suppose Iceland and Great Britain both fish for cod in the North Sea. Iceland makes an assumption about England's program of harvests into the indefinite future. That is, Iceland makes a conjecture about how much cod English boats will harvest period by period into the future. This is an abstract approach, but it introduces the concept of a *strategic game.* Games can be quite complex, especially when they occur in a dynamic environment such as our fishery model.

We assume that cod reside in a single-species fishery, so the biological environment is the same as our simple model of Chapters 4 and 5. The only difference is that the harvests are now divided between Iceland (I) and Great Britain (B). Several equilibrium concepts will also be introduced—a noncooperative equilibrium in which Iceland and Britain do not get together to plan their harvests, and a cooperative equilibrium in which they do. We first set up the social welfare problem each government manager solves, then show the differences between the two equilibria.

The steady-state relationship for the cod population is given by equation (11.24):

$$X(t+1) - X(t) = F[X(t)] - H^I(t) - H^B(t) \tag{11.24}$$

where $X(t)$ is the current stock of cod, $F[X(t)]$ is the natural growth in the stock, and $H^I(t)$ and $H^B(t)$ are Iceland's and England's current harvests, respectively. Suppose first that we are viewing the problem of determining the optimal harvest from the perspective of a fisheries manager in Iceland who believes that English harvests in each period are going to be at a particular level. This is a conjecture made about the competitive environment Iceland operates in. It must determine its own harvests, on the basis of its beliefs about English harvests. Iceland then selects its own harvests in all periods, $n = 0, 1, \ldots,$ to maximize the present value of cod harvests. Equation (11.25) shows Iceland's objective function:

$$\begin{aligned} W^I = {} & B^I[H^I(0)] - C^I[H^I(0), H^B(0), X(0)] \\ & + \beta\{B^I[H^I(1)] - C^I[H^I(1), H^B(1), X(1)]\} \\ & + \beta^2\{B^I[H^I(2)] - C^I[H^I(2), H^B(2), X(2)]\} \\ & + \cdots \\ & + \beta^t\{B^I(t)] - C^I[H^I(t), H^B(t), X(t)]\} \\ & + \cdots \end{aligned} \tag{11.25}$$

The variables are analogous to those defined above: $B^I(.)$ is the area under the demand curve for fish in Iceland; $C^I(.)$ is Iceland's cost of harvesting H^I cod *given* that England's cod harvests are H^B and the stock of cod is X; and β is the discount factor $1/(1 + r)$. Suppose that England's harvests are identical in every period. Then a steady state for Iceland must satisfy equation (10.10):

$$p^I - MCH^I = [MCX^I/(F_X - r)] \tag{11.26}$$

where we must also have $F(X) = H^I + H^B$—that is, the growth in the cod stock equals the harvests of both countries. The price of cod in Iceland is p^I, taken from the demand schedule for cod in that country; MCH^I is the marginal cost of harvesting cod in Iceland, given England's constant catch H^B and the stock size X; MCX^I is the effect of a marginal increase in stock size X on the cost of harvesting H^I by Iceland; and F_X is the effect on cod growth due to an increase in the stock size X. To have a steady state, the harvests of both Iceland and England must be constant over time. If the fisheries manager in England does the same calculation with the same demand and cost schedules, there will be the analogous relationship required for a steady-state equilibrium given by equation (11.27):

$$p^B - MCH^B = [MCX^B/(F_X - r)] \tag{11.27}$$

Both equations (11.26) and (11.27) should look familiar. They are very similar to the equation for a dynamic steady-state equilibrium presented earlier in this chapter. The difference is the dependence of each country's costs on the harvests of the other country.

We can now solve for the equilibrium stock size X and the harvests in each country. Suppose, first, that each country plans its harvests without consulting the other. If both countries assume that the harvest of the other is given and this indeed occurs, the steady-state equilibrium that results is called a Nash-Cournot or noncooperative equilibrium. There will exist a pair of harvests, H^I and H^B, such that equations (11.26) and (11.27) are satisfied simultaneously. A numerical example is presented below.

Now if the two countries coordinate their fishing plans by jointly determining the optimal harvest and stock of cod, the relationship for the optimal steady-state equilibrium becomes equation (11.28).

$$p^I + p^B - MCH = MCX/(F_X - r) \tag{11.28}$$

We can solve this for stock size X and harvests $H^I = H/2 = H^B$. For the case of a linear demand schedule that is identical in both countries, $p = A - BH$, and $F(X) = X(a - bX)$, and costs given by $C^I = [w(H^I + H^B)]/mX$ and $C^B = [w(H^I - H^B)]/mX$, we find that:

1. Rent from the fishing ground is always higher for the cooperative arrangement.
2. The stock size is always smaller for the cooperative arrangement, but it can be on either side of the stock corresponding to the maximum sustainable yield. The total harvest is generally higher for the cooperative solution. (Both solutions yield equilibrium stocks to the right of the stock corresponding to the maximum sustainable yield. See the Appendix to this chapter.)

3. Aggregate welfare is always highest under the cooperative arrangement.

The first two results are established by the algebraic solution for the noncooperative and cooperative problems. The last result holds because the cooperative arrangement jointly maximizes social welfare for two countries. There is no constraint operating on the objective function of each, where that constraint is the harvest of the other country. An unconstrained maximization problem always leads to at least as high a value of the variable being maximized as does a constrained problem. (Think about how high a consumer's welfare would be without a budget constraint.) In the joint problem, the countries are constrained by the biological mechanics and the usual marginal conditions, but they are not constrained by each other's independently chosen harvests.

The following example illustrates these points. Suppose the demand curve for cod in each country is linear and is given by $p = 1.4167 - H$. The total cost of harvesting cod in each country is $C = w(H^I + H^B)/mX$, with $w = 6 = m$. Marginal cost is w/mX. The biological mechanics are $F(X) = X(1 - .1X)$. Given these assumptions, the solutions are:

1. For the cooperative equilibrium: $X = 6$, and the total harvest is 2.4, with each country getting a harvest of 1.2 tons.
2. For the Cournot or noncooperative competitive equilibrium: $X = 6.588$, and the total harvest is 2.2478, with each country getting a harvest of 1.1239 tons.

The assumption that each party takes the other's harvest as fixed (the constraint) is a simple introduction to strategic behavior and merely provides a flavor of types of international conflict possible in fisheries. Other strategic settings might have one country dominant in the decision of how much to harvest. Highly aggressive strategies might result in cyclical activity in which one country is dominant, the other displaces it, and so on. Steady-state equilibria will be different in each situation.

It is not the case that the results obtained here will be repeated in other situations. If, for example, there are three countries exploiting a fish stock and only two of them coordinate their harvests, then it may not be the case that the welfare of the two cooperating countries rises compared with the noncooperative case. Similarly, it may not pay a country to cooperate, as it may do better by staying out of an agreement and "preying" on the other countries' harvests. The point is that each case of international fishing must be examined and the peculiarities of the situation incorporated into the model.

One final point. As with cartels in the nonrenewable resource sectors, it is very difficult to set up and enforce cooperative agreements in the fishery, especially if the species being harvested is pelagic and there are many ports where the catch is landed. Enforcement may be virtually impossible if any country has an incentive to cheat on the agreement. Countries have a very difficult time even setting up these agreements. Canada and the United States are still disputing fishing practices in the west coast salmon fishery. There is a growing literature on strategic games in the fishery that is interesting and complex.[15] Whether this analysis can be applied in its current state to international fisheries disputes is an open question.

SUMMARY

1. The optimal path to a dynamic fishery equilibrium is one where the harvest rate is chosen such that the net return to investing in the fishery equals the social discount rate. The net return to investing in fish incorporates the sum of: (a) capital gain from holding the stock from one period to the next; (b) stock externality; and (c) biological growth from one period to the next.

2. In a dynamic model, the steady-state harvest and level of effort occur where the rent from the fishery (price minus the marginal cost of the harvest or marginal revenue minus marginal cost) net of the stock externality equals the discount rate. In a static model, the optimal steady-state equilibrium will be to the right of the MSY stock. In a dynamic model, with a positive but not infinite discount rate, the equilibrium can be to the right or the left of the MSY. The higher the discount rate, the more likely an equilibrium is to be to the left of the MSY stock.

3. If the discount rate equals zero, the static and dynamic property equilibriums coincide. If the discount rate is infinity, an open access equilibrium exists and the static and dynamic equilibria are the same. Only if the discount rate is zero, harvesting costs are zero, and the price of fish is very high will the optimal equilibrium by the MSY harvest and biomass.

4. A study of possible dynamic paths of the fur seal industry in the late 1800s determines the open access equilibrium given assumptions about the fish population, its biological mechanics, and industry conditions (entry and exit). Dynamic models combine the behavior of the fish stock with the behavior of firms to find a path of harvests and fish stocks over time that is most likely.

5. In many species, exogenous factors, including the weather, water temperature, disease, and predators, can be a more important determinant of the total population at each point in time than the biomass. Short-run biological relationships are more meaningful than long-run functions. Optimal harvesting policies for this fishery must be flexible, allowing for large harvests in "good" years and small harvests in "bad" years. The possibility of extinction is high when there is unrestricted open access to this kind of fishery.

6. In a predator-prey model, the social optimum involves harvesting the predator to allow more prey to survive and be harvested by people. To achieve the optimum, a subsidy on the predator will be required when its commercial value (rent) is low. A tax on the prey is required to obtain the optimal harvest and amount of effort.

7. In a complex predator-prey model, comparative static results of a qualitative nature are difficult to obtain. Numerical simulation is required to get definitive results.

8. In a model where two countries compete for a particular fish stock, a cooperative fishing policy between the countries will lead to more rent from the fishery and higher aggregate welfare, but possibly a lower sustainable stock, than when the two countries compete for the fish (the noncooperative equilibrium).

DISCUSSION QUESTIONS

1. Explain the difference between the static and dynamic steady-state equilibriums of a fishery characterized by: (a) open access; (b) private property rights in a perfectly competitive market structure. Will a private property equilibrium ever be at the MSY biomass? Explain.
2. In a dynamic model with entry and exit of fishing effort as well as possible changes in the stock of fish, what conditions are necessary to extinguish the fish stock if the fishery is characterized by open access? Will extinction ever occur in the fishery if it is managed under private property rights?
3. In a fishery with a predator-prey relationship, is government intervention necessary to ensure an optimal harvest?
4. "International fishing organizations that plan global quotas on harvests are unstable. The more effective they are, the more advantageous it is for a single country to remain outside the organization." Evaluate this claim. Are there examples that come to mind?
5. "Ecological complexity is the principal barrier to planning appropriate harvests for fish. Once quotas are in effect, stock sizes are often quite different from those anticipated." Is this a valid contention, or might one instead contend that if binding quotas are maintained, the ecology will look after itself? Do examples come to mind?

NOTES

1. To solve the continuous time model, more advanced mathematics is required. We can solve the problem using the calculus of variations or control theory. We do not require these techniques here; those wishing a more complete mathematical treatment should consult Clark (1976) and Dasgupta (1982), and the references in those texts.
2. The term C_X will also be nonzero for nonrenewable resources when the marginal costs of extraction rise as the stock of the mineral declines. This is true in the case of, say, oil, where as oil is pumped from a well, the natural pressure remaining in the well diminishes and it will take more costly recovery methods (pumping in brine) to recover additional units of oil. The fundamental difference between minerals and fish is the growth term, $F'(X)$, which is not meaningful in the case of minerals.
3. There are conceptual difficulties with the harvesting function assumed in equation (11.11): No limit is placed on the harvest as additional units of effort are employed. But we know that, as X goes to zero, no amount of effort will yield a positive harvest. See Spence (1974) for a simple harvest function that eliminates this problem.
4. A variant of this path is the ever-cycling system. The boats and seals may simply cycle forever around the equilibrium point but never reach it.
5. There are many difficult empirical problems in the analysis, as one might expect. Data are sparse, and many simplifying assumptions had to be made. Nonetheless, the calculations show how the dynamic model can be used.
6. It should be noted that much of the effort is not likely to stay unemployed, because it can be used in another fishery—anchovies. Because anchovies are also harvested under open access, the Spanish authorities must be concerned not only about the sardine fishery but also about anchovies.

7. For an example of this type of fishery, see Flaaten (1983). Also see Blumo et al. (1982), who have developed a simulation model of the pink shrimp fishery in the Gulf of Mexico. Seawater temperature is taken into account in the biological mechanics. The growth of weekly age classes of shrimp is calculated. Optimal policies for the fishery are contrasted with existing regulatory practices proposed by the area's fishery management council.
8. Ecologists distinguish eight types of species interaction: (1) *neutralism*, no interaction between cohabiting species; (2) *competition*, mutual negative interaction, as in competing for scarce common feeding or breeding grounds; (3) *mutualism*, symbiotic relationships in which each species needs the other to survive (such as bacteria and host); (4) *cooperation*, an elected symbiotic relationship such as occurs for mutual defense against predators; (5) *commensalism*, in which one species benefits and the other neither benefits or suffers (phoresis is the transport of a small species by a larger one); (6) *amensalism*, in which one species suffers and the other, the inhibitor, is unaffected; (7) *parasitism*, in which one species, generally smaller, inhibits growth or reproduction of the host species; (8) *predation*, in which one species kills the other to obtain food. See Dajoz (1977), pp. 151–153.
9. Some consumers consider shark very desirable, but we will ignore this complication. In this example, we assume that sharks *only* eat tuna. If they don't eat enough tuna, the shark population begins to decline. This is not realistic, but it simplifies the analysis and allows us to illustrate the basic points in a predator-prey relationship using names of well-known species of fish.
10. The problem is analogous to that solved in the first part of this chapter.
11. See Solow (1977), pp. 217–220, for further comments on possible solutions. A steady-state solution need not exist for this problem.
12. Observe that the harvest of sharks exceeds stocks. This is both biologically and arithmetically possible. For example, if each pair of sharks has five offspring per period, then three can be harvested and the stock can remain constant.
13. Multispecies models are very difficult to analyze and interpret. With two interacting species, a four-dimensional nonlinear dynamical system is necessary to determine optimal management schemes. Multiple equilibria are likely, and some of these will be unstable. If an unstable equilibrium occurs, the comparative statics are not meaningful, because the fishery would never reach these outcomes. Our comparative static results are relevant in a stable or saddle-point stable equilibrium.
14. Clark (1976), pp. 303–311, presents a model in which every harvest of the two species caught results in quantities directly proportional to their stock sizes. The fishing firms cannot vary the mix of species caught. For an open access or common property solution, he argues that extinction of one species is a plausible outcome.
15. See, for example, Lewis and Cowans (1982), and Levhari and Mirman (1980).

SELECTED READINGS

Anderson, L. G. (1977). *The Economics of Fisheries Management.* Baltimore: Johns Hopkins Press.

Blumo, V. J., J. P. Nichols, W. P. Griffin, and W. E. Grant (1982). "Dynamic Modeling of the Eastern Gulf of Mexico Shrimp Fishery." *American Journal of Agricultural Economics* 64, pp. 475–482.

Clark, Colin (1976). *Mathematical Bioeconomics.* New York: Wiley.

Dajoz, Roger (1977). *Introduction to Ecology,* trans. A. South. London: Hodder and Stoughton.

Dasgupta, P. S. (1982). *The Control of Resources.* Cambridge, MA: Harvard University Press.

Flaaten, O. (1983). "The Optimal Harvesting of a Natural Resource with Seasonal Growth." *Canadian Journal of Economics* 16, pp. 447–462.

Idyll, C. P. (1973). "The Anchovy Crisis." *Scientific American* 228, pp. 23–29.

Levhari, D., and L. J. Mirman (1980). "The Great Fish War: An Example Using a Dynamic Cournot-Nash Solution." *Bell Journal of Economics* 11, pp. 322–334.

Lewis, T. R. and J. Cowans (1982) "The Great Fish War: A Cooperative Solution." Social Science Working Paper 448. California Institute of Technology.
Solow, R. M. (1977). "Optimal Fishing with a Natural Predator." In R. E. Grieson, ed., *Public and Urban Economics: Essays in Honor of William S. Vickery*. Lexington, MA: Lexington Books.
Spence, A. M. (1974). "Blue Whales and Applied Control Theory." In H. W. Gottinger, ed., *Systems Approaches and Environmental Problems*. Gottingen: Vandenhoeck and Ruprecht.
Wilen, J. E. (1976). "Common Property Resources and the Dynamics of Overexploitation: The Case of the North Pacific Fur Seal." University of British Columbia, Resources Paper No. 3.

Appendix to Chapter 11: Two Countries Competing for Harvests of Fish

Under the Cournot assumption that each country assumes the other country's harvests are fixed and constant indefinitely, we have the steady equations for each country.

$$p^I - C_H^I I = C_X^I/(g_X - r)$$
$$p^B - C_H^B B = C_X^B/(g_X - r)$$

where p^I = price in country I derived from the demand schedule in country I
$C_H^I I$ = marginal cost of harvest in country I and total cost is $C^I(X^I, H^B, X)$
C_X^I = impact on harvest costs in country I of marginal increase in stock size X
g_X = impact on births over deaths of the stock of a marginal increase in stock size X
r = interest rate

Terms for country B are similarly defined.

Under a cooperative arrangement between countries, total discounted welfare is maximized and the steady-state equation for the combined units is

$$p^I + p^B - C_H = C_X/(g_X - r)$$

where C_H = marginal cost of harvesting the total catch to be divided equally between our identical countries
C_X = impact on total harvesting costs of the combined harvest of a marginal increase in stock size X. The total cost function has the same form as the separate cost functions for each nation, but now $H^I + H^B = H$ is harvested in a centralized administration.
g_x and r are as defined above.

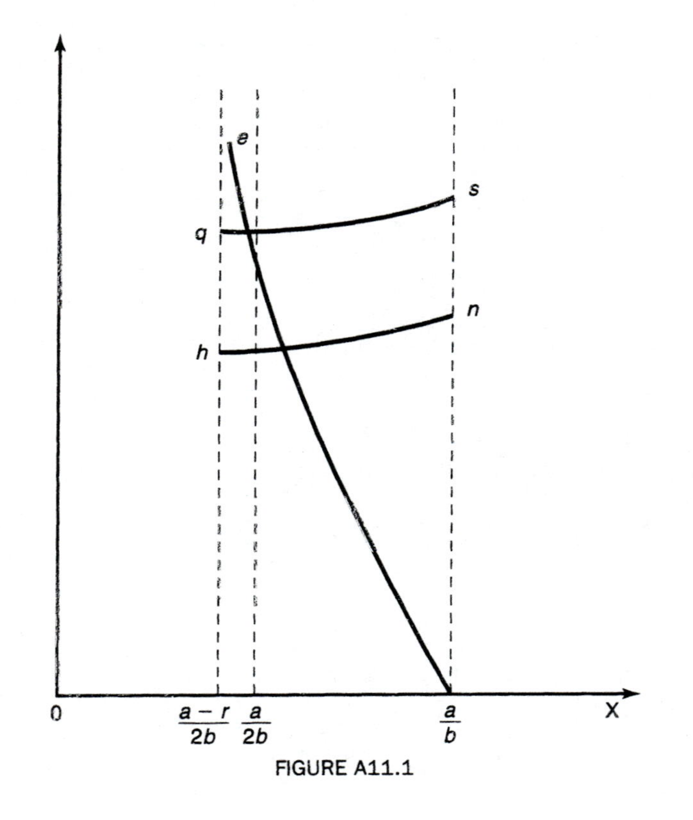

FIGURE A11.1

We make

$$C^I(H^I, H^B, X) = \frac{w(H^I + H^B)}{mX},\ C^B(H^B, H^I, X) = \frac{w(H^I + H^B)}{mX},\ C(H, X) = \frac{wH}{mx},$$

$$p^I = A - BH^I,\ p^B = A - BH^B, \text{ and } g(X) = X(a - bX)$$

Our equations above then become

$$\left[A - BH^I - \frac{w}{mX}\right] = \frac{w(H^I + H^B)}{mX^2[r - (a - 2bX)]}$$

$$\left[A - BH^B - \frac{w}{mX}\right] = \frac{w(H^I + H^B)}{mX^2[r - (a - 2bX)]}$$

$$\left[2A - BH - \frac{w}{mX}\right] = \frac{wH}{mX^2[r - (a - 2bX)]}$$

This latter is for the cooperative solution. In a steady state,

$$H = X(a - bX) = H^I + H^B \text{ or } H^I = \frac{X(a - bX)}{X} = H^B$$

Substituting in the above equations yields

$$A - \frac{B}{2}[X(a - bX)] - \frac{w}{mX} = \frac{w(a - bX)}{mX[r - (a - 2bX)]}$$

for each of the first two equations and

$$2A - B[X(a - bX)] - \frac{w}{mX} = \frac{w(a - bX)}{mX[r - (a - 2bX)]}$$

for the third equation representing the cooperative solution.

The left-hand side is price minus marginal cost and must be positive. For the right-hand side to be positive, $\frac{a - r}{2b} < X < \frac{a}{b}$. We sketch the right-hand side as in Figure A11.1. We plot $A - \frac{B}{2}[X(a - bX)] - \frac{w}{mX}$ as bn, and $2A - B[X(a - bX)] - \frac{w}{mX}$ as qs. The result is that the X in the cooperative solution is always less than X in the individualistic or Cournot competitive solution. For $r \cong a$, both steady-state stocks will be to the right of the stock corresponding to the maximum sustainable yield. For solution values of the Xs to the left of $X = a/2b$, "impatience" is dominant. Otherwise cost reductions for "high" stocks dominate. Rent, $p - mc$, is always positive and is always larger for the cooperative solution.

chapter 12

The Economics of Sustainability

INTRODUCTION

Sustainable development has come to mean different things to different people. Some use the term as a rallying cry for raising environmental consciousness. Some see it as an organizing principle for economic policy, a responsible alternative to the call for economic growth. Pessimists consider it self-contradictory: How can one have development (economic growth) in a sustained biosphere? Many people want the natural environment left alone—leave nature as you found it. A rather different view treats the natural environment as a larder to be drawn from to sustain human activity. Sustainability involves somehow keeping the larder stocked while still drawing from it.

Our purpose in this chapter is not to resolve this debate. Scientists and social scientists will continue to study our changing natural environment and the economies we live in. Our task is to lay out economic methods of analyzing sustainability. The central objective of our economic approach to sustainable development is to find paths of natural resource use that lead to *constant consumption paths per capita* as the specific target.

A constant consumption program provides a good reference point for the analysis of sustainability. It is a formalization of the stationary state made by J. S. Mill and other observers. With a constant population, it can be defined as an intergenerationally equitable path. Constant consumption paths focus on the balancing of disinvestment with positive investment to yield zero net investment. This is not a particularly difficult problem for renewable natural resources. For nonrenewable resources, however, the matter of sustaining constant consumption paths into the indefinite future is much more complex. A key factor is the degree of substitutability of one type of capital for another.

Some observers argue that constant consumption is too conservative a concept for sustainability. Asheim (1994) suggests that perpetual nondecreasing consumption is a better concept because it can, at a minimum, allow for an initial rise in consumption to a plateau. One can view this, crudely, as splicing together a constant consumption program and an early growth program. But in its more sophisticated rendering the approach can also be cast in terms of parents' altruism toward their children. If there is no technical progress, there are limits to growth, and the possibility of indefinitely declining consumption may be the best that one can hope for in certain circumstances. It was this scenario, of course, that preoccupied Malthus and many other observers, particularly those living before the industrial revolution. Notwithstanding these concerns, we press on with constant per capita consumption as the objective for sustainable development.

We begin with a review of the concept of sustainable yield in renewable resources. A steady-state equilibrium with renewable natural resources is sustainable by definition. Exhaustible resources present a challenge for sustainability. Can a natural resource that has a fixed stock that is depleted with extraction and use yield a sustainable flow of consumption over time? We will examine cases in which this is possible. We then turn to a discussion of how to calculate whether or not an economy is on a sustainable path. We look at how to measure changes in the value of all kinds of capital stocks (resource, machine, and knowledge). Next, we discuss how to modify national income accunting to incorporate measures of the stocks of natural and environmental resources. This builds on our introductory discussion of these topics in Chapter 2. The chapter concludes with observations on the difficulties of measuring the value of natural resources stocks and some implications for public policy.

At its heart, the economics of sustainable development integrates natural and environmental resources with the manufacturing and service sectors of the economy. The input base of traditional economics—land, energy, and produced capital—is expanded to include the services of natural resource and environmental capital: air and watersheds, minerals, forests, fish, and biological capital (biodiversity). By valuing natural inputs appropriately, one hopes the inputs will be used more efficiently. There will not be overuse of natural inputs. As aptly put in the Brundtland Report (1987, p. 43), "Sustainable development is development that meets the needs of the present without compromising the ability of future generations to meet their own needs."

SUSTAINABILITY IN ECONOMICS

Renewable Resources

The concept of sustainable yield has governed the use of renewable resources such as fishing and timber production for many years.[1] How does sustainable development relate to the concept of sustainable yield? As we saw in Chapters 4, 5, and 11, sustainable yield in a fishery is the annual catch (physical flow) from a fishing ground that can be taken year after year into the indefinite future. The stock from which the catch (flow) is drawn is in a steady state, which by definition implies a sustainable harvest year after year. This means that the economic use of the natural resource is also sustainable. It is also obvious that a nonsustainable yield is one that causes the resource to be depleted (the stock to be drawn down) and shrink year after year. Sustainability is rooted in notions of perpetual repetition or in steady states.

Steady-State Economies

The idea of sustainable development as an economy in a steady state has roots quite deep in the past. John Stuart Mill reflected on the nonexpanding, nondeclining economy in his *Principles of Political Economy* (1848, first edition). A steady-state economy can be conceived of in three parts: (1) flows of inputs, (2) the economic or production process, and (3) flows of outputs. We illustrate this for the case of a sustainable fishery in Figure 12.1. A steady flow of outputs requires: (a) maintenance of the economic or production process, which we later define more precisely as "replacement investment," and (b) a steady flow of inputs. Each input category in Figure 12.1 must be "set right" for the steady state to persist. Fish stocks must be preserved, i.e., not be overharvested. The selected yield must be sustainable. Somewhat analogously, capital in the form of fishing vessels and gear must be maintained so that it also is preserved. And to conceive of people experiencing a constant level of consumption, the population must be stationary.

Departures from the steady state are easy to envisage. As we saw in earlier chapters, if fish harvests exceed a sustainable yield, the fish stock will decline. This might occur because of population growth and a rising labor force.[2] Alternatively, technological change may induce overfishing because of large reductions in the cost of harvesting an ever smaller stock. We return to the link between technological change and sustainability below.

The haunting story of Easter Island is one of population growth in a fishing economy. The harvests from the sea were abundant enough to result in steady population growth, but harvesting required oceangoing canoes made from trees in the is-

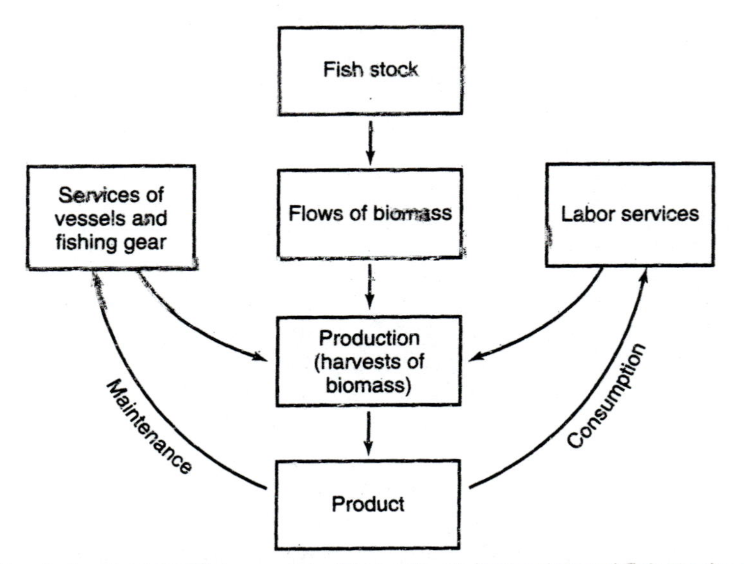

FIGURE 12.1 A steady-state "fish economy." Labor is not increasing and fish stocks are not decreasing.

land's forests. The food supply crashed when society exhausted its inputs for canoe production—trees. A population crash ensued. Archaeologists have unearthed the history of an island society developing, flourishing, and collapsing in the span of about 1,000 years. The final steady state in this case has been one of a small population with very low consumption levels on an "overgrazed" island. The story of Easter Island is a variant of Malthus's dismal scenario—population growth pushing consumption levels to subsistence and net population increases to zero.

People concerned about sustainable development cast Malthus's scenario somewhat differently today. We ask: If the world population levels off at, say, 10 billion in 2050, is the maintenance of a decent quality of life possible, given the nature of the economy that emerges at this steady-state population? Will people's utility be nondecreasing? As Figure 12.1 indicates, the fish harvest corresponds to per capita consumption. The maintenance of a constant harvest requires that the productive capital of the fish stock in this case remain intact or not be declining or degrading. The same concept applies to agriculture. As noted in Chapter 2, sustainable agriculture requires maintenance of the capital in the soil—its fertility. Degradation of land quality will ultimately shrink the size of the harvest. Nonshrinking productive capacity for all forms of capital, both natural and produced, is the important requirement for sustainability.

An Accounting Framework for the Steady-State Economy

The gross value of output in the fish economy in Figure 12.1 is simply pq, where q is the flow of fish harvested in tons and p is the price per ton. This gross value becomes net product when expenditures for capital are subtracted. Our gross figure is known as gross national product (GNP), and our net figure is net national product (NNP). The difference is output used to maintain boats, nets, and so on, and it is called capital consumption allowance (CCA)—a sum used to maintain produced capital goods (vessels, etc.).

The input side of the accounts values the services of labor (income to workers), produced capital (vessels, rent to boat owners), and rent to the owner of the fish stock. The sum of the values of these primary inputs is called value added in the economy per year. Accounting principles require that the value of inputs (here, labor, and capital in the form of vessels and fish) equal the gross value of output. A simple measure of how well a society is doing is the size of its NNP, given a constant population. This reduces here to the size of the consumption flow in this simple economy because there is no investment (new boats) other than the maintenance of boats. By definition, an accumulating society has positive value for net investment. A major issue in the economics of growth is how NNP is divided between net investment and current consumption. In our steady-state economy, this complicated topic does not have to be addressed.

We sketch the accounts for our steady state fishing economy in Table 12.1. On the right is the value of product summing to GNP, and on the left is the value of inputs: wL for labor L, zS for rent on the fish stock S, and rqK for gross rent on produced capital K. The term δ is the rate of depreciation or the rate of physical decay in K per year. In the steady state, per capita consumption will be unchanging. The fish

TABLE 12.1 **ACCOUNTS FOR A STEADY-STATE FISHERY**

Input	Output
$wL + (1 - \delta)\, rqK + zS$ (Value-added)	NNP
Economic depreciation: $rq\delta K$	Maintenance of boats (CCA)
	GNP

stock yields a constant harvest, and the resources of the economy produce the yield in a sustainable fashion. Sustainability here leaves the stock of fish S and the stock of capital K unchanged. Preservation of stocks is another view of sustainability of renewable natural resources.

Essential Exhaustible Resources

It is reasonable to separate the analysis of sustainable development into two parts—one dealing with renewable resources (as in our fish economy), and one dealing with nonrenewable resources. The preceding analysis focused on what a steady-state economy looks like. With nonrenewable resources, we know from Chapter 8 that there is no steady state. Extraction of the resource depletes the fixed stock. The key issue for sustainability is to find alternative sources of services for those that are shrinking as nonrenewable resource stocks shrink. As *oil* production declines, how can *energy* production be prevented from declining? Clearly, one must substitute a less exhaustible source of energy for a source facing imminent exhaustion. Or one must make current inputs to the energy sector "burn more efficiently," i.e., get more output per unit of time.

Exhaustible resources also include minerals and their products, metals. Metals are durable. If refined metal were perfectly recyclable, then one could imagine a steady state economy. But scientists emphasize that perfect recycling violates laws of physics. The use of metals degrades them. There are thermodynamic constraints on the percentage recyclable from period to period. Even if 98 percent were recoverable in period $t + 1$, the 2 percent "lost" implies that the stedy state is not achievable unless substitutes for the amount lost are discovered and made use of. Recall from Chapter 2 the investor's doubling rule: x doubles at y percent compounded in approximately $72/y$ periods. It is also true that x halves at -2 percent compounded in approximately $72/2$ periods. Thus a 2 percent loss each period represents a huge loss in only 36 periods.

Analysis of Sustainability with Nonrenewable Resources

The analysis of sustainability becomes much more complicated when energy and other inputs are not renewable. The whole concept of a steady state seems to crumble, and the question emerges whether a concept of sustainability can be rediscovered. The Brundtland Report had great difficulty in grappling with a world of nonrenewable inputs. Consider, then, sustainability or a new type of steady state when some flows (inputs) come from shrinking stocks.

Suppose that energy can be derived only from oil and that oil stocks are finite. How does one achieve steady-state consumption, given a constant population? The answer is, for a world with no technical progress, that one extracts and uses less and less oil each period and builds up extra produced or machine capital to maintain production levels (Solow, 1974). Machine capital is substituted for oil capital in a particular way, and oil use diminishes into the indefinite future (asymptotic decline). One uses less and less oil each period, but one never exhausts the stock. Machine capital is added to each period into the indefinite future. For example, one can think of covering deserts with solar collectors to generate energy with machine capital or producing fusion power generating stations. If this "replacement" of energy services by machine services is done correctly, output will remain constant and so will consumption. Thus our steady-state economy based on renewability can be generalized to a situation of a steady state deriving from an economy or production system with non-steady-state characteristics. On the production side, the services of machines exactly compensate for the loss of production that would result from the lower energy use period by period. The economy ends up moving along an isoquant (adjusted for a constant population–labor force) as in Figure 12.2.

In Figure 12.3, we sketch a steady-state economy with a depleting oil stock and shrinking flow of oil as input into production.

The key characteristic of this steady-state economy is that both the oil stock and the flow of the oil going as input into production are shrinking. In order to prevent this depletion effect from causing the economy (production) to shrink, machine capital must be accumulated sufficiently rapidly. One form of capital is substituted for an-

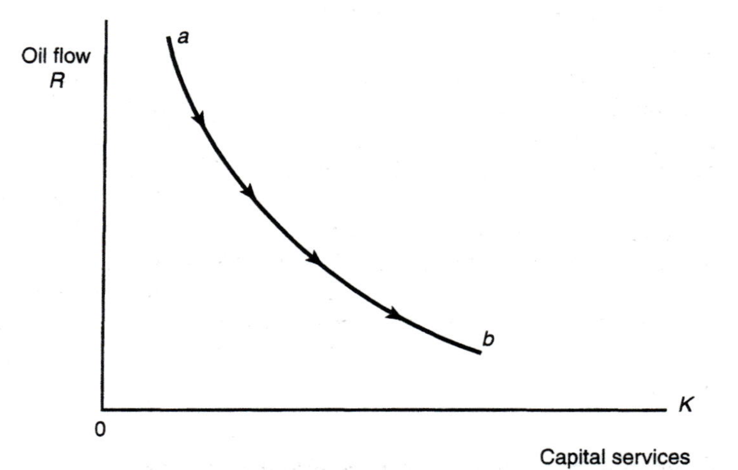

FIGURE 12.2 The economy moves along isoquant *ab* using less *R* (oil) and more *K* (machine capital) while output remains constant.

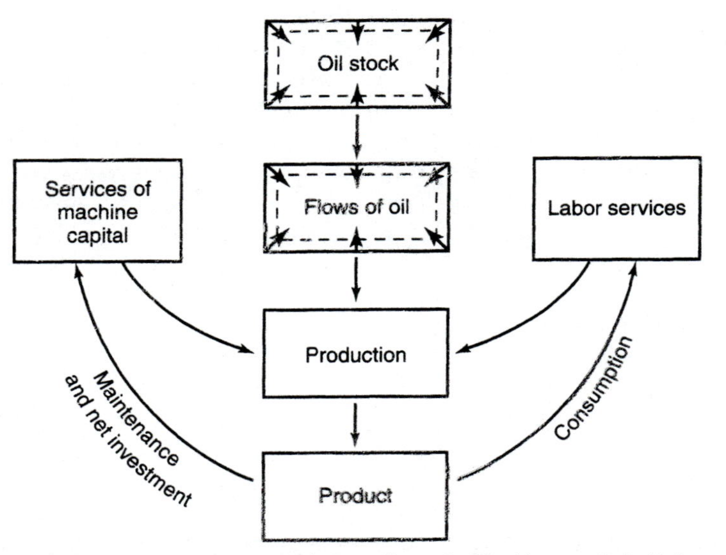

FIGURE 12.3 A "steady state" with a depleting oil stock. Machine capital, K, is accumulated sufficiently rapidly to balance off the shrinking service flow of the oil input.

other in such a way as to keep output constant. The way this is done involves interesting valuation relationships. The value of oil—the oil stock currently used up—equals the value of the net increment to machine capital. Roughly speaking, the sum of capital value is being held constant. More precisely, *net investment*, broadly defined, is *zero*. The accumulation of machine capital balances off the decumulation of oil capital.

In our steady-state fishing economy, harvesting was arranged so that the stock and the harvest remained unchanging. That is, capital in the form of fish stocks was kept constant by appropriate maintenance. In our economy with oil stocks, the combination of oil capital (the value of the stock in the ground) and machine capital is in a particular sense being held constant. Thus our economy with oil is a more complicated or generalized version of our fish economy. In each case per capita consumption and the technology are unchanging. In the economy with an exhaustible resource, a more subtle management of the two types of capital is required, but the parallels between the renewable and exhaustible resources are clearly discernible.

How much oil should this steady state economy extract and burn for energy each period, and how much output should be set aside to build more machine capital? As it turns out, the two rules that work are: (1) Draw down oil stocks at such a rate that the Hotelling r percent efficiency rule is always being satisfied; and (2) save and invest a part of current output that is equal in value to the rent on the amount of oil currently extracted and used up. Remaining output produced is left for consumption and will, given these rules, remain at a constant level. Thus if population and technical progress are unchanging, per capita consumption will be unchanging. Solow (1974) labels paths with constant per capita consumption as those satisfying intergenerational equity. Each generation enjoys the same level of consumption.

Table 12.2 shows an accounting for this economy with oil. This table differs from that for the fish economy (Table 12.1) in that part of NNP now is allocated to investment in machine capital, over and above maintenance (CCA). In the special case of a steady state, the amount of net investment in K equals the value of oil used up, this latter being equal to the decline in value of the stock of oil, S. Current oil used is R tons, equal to $-S$, the physical decline in the stock S. In our economy, the payment for oil used, zR dollars, equals the economic depreciation—the decline in value—of S. This latter value loss is $z\Delta S$ dollars. Recall that ΔS is the current decline in S.

We turn now to a more formal description of this steady-state (sustainable) economy. The economy's aggregate output Q is derived from labor L (equal to a constant fraction of the population), services of capital K and energy use R in $Q = F(K,R,L)$. If net investment is I, then consumption C equals $Q - I$. Energy R is equal to oil extracted from remaining stock $S(t)$. Thus the decline in the stock $dS/dt = -R$. This is "the economy" with its resources and materials balance requirements. Hotelling rent is then RF_R, where F_R is the price of a unit of energy. The rate of return (interest rate) is F_K. Thus Hotelling's rule is $(dF_R/dt)F_R = F_K$. One can show that when L is constant, investment I equals current oil rents, RF_R, and Hotelling's rule is being followed, then C remains constant.[3] In our earlier steady-state argument for the fishing economy it was given that if K remained constant, and L and R remained constant, then Q (as NNP or net of output used to maintain K) would be constant and C could be maintained equal to this net Q. So we have made a large extension to our earlier result because one of our inputs is now exhaustible. Per capita consumption can be sustained at a positive (constant) level over time even with energy being drawn from an exhaustible stock. Investing resource rents can be written as $\dot{K} + \dot{S}F_R = 0$ and has come to be referred to as *net investment equal to zero*, where net investment means the sum of changes in all stocks, weighted by their correct prices.

How long can this scenario persist? Does not exhaustibility eventually bite and result in declining output and consumption? The answer is "no" if the production function $F(\cdot)$ is of the form $K^{\alpha}R^{\beta}N^{1-\alpha-\beta}$ with $\alpha > \beta$ and β positive and less than one (Solow, 1974). The production function must be Cobb-Douglas (with unitary elasticities of substitution among inputs), and the capital input must have a coefficient larger

TABLE 12.2 **ACCOUNTING FOR AN ECONOMY WITH OIL**

Input	Output	
$wL + (1 - \delta)\ rqK + zR$ + profits	Consumption Goods	NNP
	Disinvestment in S $(= z\Delta S)$	
Economic depreciation in S $(= z\Delta S)$	Net investment in machine capital, K	
Economic depreciation in K $(= rq\delta K)$	Capital consumption allowance (CCA)	
	GNP	

than the coefficient for energy. Roughly speaking, capital must be more productive than energy. For this special case, Q and C will never decline even though R declines toward zero period after period. Not only must K be substitutable for R; the substitutability must be just right, and the "productivity" of K relative to R must be right also. Other sorts of production functions will not necessarily yield this outcome.

Is there a sense in which the composite stock of K and oil capital S is being kept constant? This can be answered from somewhat different perspectives. Investment in K (that is, $\dot{K}$) equal to disinvestment in oil stock $S(t)$ (that is, $-F_R\dot{S}$, equal to RF_R or Hotelling or resource rent) implies that the value of *net investment* equals zero. The value of capital (also known as wealth) measured at a specific date is $K + SF_R = W$. The change in wealth dW/dt, comprises quantity change, given by $\dot{K} + F_R\dot{S}$, and a value change, $\dot{S}F_R$. Investing resource rents (net investment set at zero) implies that the quantity change is zero but that the value change will be positive. Hence capital value or wealth is not constant, even though consumption is constant and investment in K equals disinvestment in S. The value change is, then, a wedge between net investment zero and wealth constant. In general, constant consumption programs are not constant wealth programs. It is true, however, that constant consumption programs are zero net investment programs.

Suppose one inquires about the interest flow on wealth—that is, $W(t)F_K$—in these constant conumption models. One does in fact get this flow equal to consumption C plus $\dot{W}(t)$. Here $\dot{W}(t)$ behaves like a generalized investment, as in the familiar $C + I$. The link between constant consumption and zero net investment is very general. For example, one could build up fish stocks to compensate for declining oil stocks to achieve constant consumption, or one could build up knowledge capital via research and development (R&D) activity to compensate for declining fish stocks. The principle is: *The sum of the value of all stock changes must be zero if aggregate consumption is to remain constant.* The value of positive stock change is investment, and the negative counterpart is disinvestment. Their sum is net investment, which when zero implies constant consumption over the period. Recent investigations in the area of constant consumption paths include Hamilton and Ulph (1994), who consider hydrocarbon extraction and use eroding the atmosphere with CO_2 emissions; and Dockner and Hartwick (1994), who examine the incomplete recycling of durable stocks such as copper. Becker (1982) considered the erosion of environmental capital caused by goods production. Robson (1980) investigated the building up of the stock of knowledge capital to compensate for the depletion of nondurable mineral capital, such as oil deposits. In fact, one can express constant consumption with many types of capital as interest from capital, each capital good with its own interest rate.

One can make a case that investing exhaustible resource rents in knowledge capital (new technology and useful science) is better than investing in, say, financial capital (as in a Heritage Fund). Later governments can raid the fund, leaving no extra capital to compensate later generations for depleted natural resource stocks. But knowledge capital cannot be depleted by a later government, which is not committed to compensating later generations for depleting the natural resource capital. One should not forget that returns from knowledge capital "leak" quite freely to competitors and the public in general.

Technical Progress Can Eliminate Scarcity

Building up the stock of knowledge requires investment. This is often labeled research and development (R&D) but can include education as well. Investment is clearly costly and in many cases quite risky, since the payoffs are often uncertain. Technical progress is the result of successful R&D. There is a tradition in economics of abstracting from the process side of creation of knowledge and focusing only on the net output, the technical progress. The term *exogenous technical change* describes a situation in which there is free augmentation of the knowledge stock that comes from many factors, not specific investment projects. If the rate of exogenous technical change is large enough, all standard input scarcities can be overcome. For example, if oil is an essential input, technical progress can allow any fixed quantity of it to become more productive period by period. It is in this sense that scarcity is overcome by technical progress.

Stiglitz (1974) examined what rate of exogenous technical progress was necessary to permit per capita consumption to grow in the face of both population growth and exhaustibility of mineral stocks. There always exists some rate, and this makes such investigations of limited interest. We do not deny that technical progress has been hugely significant in yielding economic growth; but when it comes to examining the impact of scarcity, the assumption that exogenous technical progress is zero allows one to focus on the constant consumption case. Another line of investigation is to make technical progress endogenous; then one deals explicitly with the investment needed to augment the knowledge stock or technical progress more generally. More technical progress is associated with more investment in knowledge and with less of something else. It is a world of explicit scarcity.

A more micro approach to technical progress involves more explicit substitution of a new technology for an old one. It is possible that someday fusion power will replace the combustion of hydrocarbons for energy. This is a case of a less input-intensive energy source replacing a more input-intensive source. It is an instance of technical progress and also can be viewed as a technology with an input in abundant supply replacing a technology with an input in short supply. One can argue that the analysis of the depletion of a stock currently being used is of less importance than that of the timing and cost of its substitute. The latter topic is often referred to as the economics of the backstop—a topic we discussed in Chapter 9.

Testing for Sustainable Development

Pearce and Atkinson (1993) have calculated broad changes in current capital values for a selection of countries in an attempt to provide an index of sustainability for them. Their results are reported in Table 12.3. Consider the case of Japan. It scores best on the Pearce and Atkinson's scale of sustainable economies. Clearly this is because its savings rate is high and its investment in new buildings, machines, roads, etc., is high. Moreover, it is not rich in oil, coal, and minerals and is thus not depleting these stocks rapidly. Hence its high score or large "net investment." However, Japan imports much oil, coal, and minerals and is thus contributing to depletion of its

TABLE 12.3 **TESTING FOR SUSTAINABLE DEVELOPMENT**

An Economy Is Sustainable If It Saves More Than the Depreciation on Its Human-made and Natural Capital

Sustainable economies	S/Y	∂_M/Y	−	∂_N/Y	=	Z
Brazil	20	7		10		+3
Costa Rica	26	3		8		+15
Czechoslovakia	30	10		7		+13
Finland	28	15		2		+11
Germany (pre-unity)	26	12		4		+10
Hungary	26	10		5		+11
Japan	33	14		2		+17
Netherlands	25	10		1		+14
Poland	30	11		3		+16
United States	18	12		3		+3
Zimbabwe	24	10		5		+9
Marginally sustainable						
Mexico	24	12		12		0
Philippines	15	11		4		0
United Kingdom	18	12		6		0
Unsustainable						
Burkina Faso	2	1		10		−9
Ethiopia	3	1		9		−7
Indonesia	20	5		17		−2
Madagascar	8	1		16		−9
Malawi	8	7		4		−3
Mali	−4	4		6		−14
Nigeria	15	3		17		−5
Papua New Guinea	15	9		7		−1

NOTES:
Y = gross national product
S = savings
∂_M = dollar depreciation of human-made capital (buildings, machines, etc.)
∂_N = dollar depreciation of natural resource capital
All numbers are percentages.
Source: David Pearce and Giles Atkinson (1993). "Measuring Sustainable Development" (mimeo).

trading partners' stocks. In isolation, Japan may be pursuing sustainable policies; but in partnership with its natural resource exporters, its claim to being sustainable is less compelling. Our open-economy results (below) indicate that for Japan, as an oil importer, to be on a constant consumption path, it must lower its consumption to provide for extra investment in machine capital in order to compensate for the continually rising prices of its resource imports. Japan's investment seems to be in part accounting for the depreciation of its trading partners' oil stock, depreciation which Japan "causes" by importing oil. The exporter need not cover off all of the depreciation in its oil stock because it is in part depleting its stock for Japan.

Pearce and Atkinson's calculations provide a limited indication of sustainability because they focus on the capacity of the productive system to be maintained. They do not proceed to examine whether per capita consumption is rising or declining. This would involve adjusting actual output for demographic change. Moreover, the net change in capital value does not translate into a notion of sustainability of productive capacity unless technical change or the change in the stock of knowledge more generally is incorporated in the calculation of change in capital value. The same growth in the value of capital goods measured at current prices may result in different changes in productive capacity, depending how much technical progress has been present. In some cases the prices used to sum the changes in all the types of capital will fully reflect technical progress, but this has to be fully analyzed.

MEASUREMENT OF SUSTAINABILITY

In this section, we look at concepts required to measure the sustainability of an economy. We then turn to specific measurement issues.

Measuring Changes in the Value of Capital

The measurement of sustainability involves measuring changes in various capital stocks to arrive at an index of decline or increase in the productive capacity of an economy. The term *economic depreciation* means decline in value of a capital stock. It is not sufficient to say that because we have 3 percent less oil in the ground, productive capacity has declined by 3 percent. We need to relate use of oil, production of goods, using the production function and current prices of inputs and outputs, and connect a decline in physical stock to a decline in productive capacity. Consider the case of a mine in use and its economic depreciation from current extraction.

Suppose output price, p, is constant and extraction costs, $C(q)$, increase with output, with the marginal extraction cost increasing. The selling price of the mine today is

$$V_t = \left[\frac{1}{1+r}\right][pq_{t+1} - C(q_{t+1})] + \left[\frac{1}{1+r}\right]^2 [pq_{t+2} - C(q_{t+2})]$$

$$+ \left[\frac{1}{1+r}\right]^3 [pq_{t+3} - C(q_{t+3})] + \ldots + \left[\frac{1}{1+r}\right]^n [pq_{t+n} - C(q_{t+n})]$$

where q_{t+i} is the owner's profit-maximizing extraction in period t. This level of q_i can be determined from Hotelling's r percent rule for defining profit-maximizing output strategies. Next year the selling price of the mine will be

$$V_{t+1} = \left[\frac{1}{1+r}\right][pq_{t+2} - C(q_{t+2})] + \left[\frac{1}{1+r}\right]^2 [pq_{t+3} - C(q_{t+3})]$$

$$+ \ldots + \left[\frac{1}{1+r}\right]^n [pq_{t+n} - C(q_{t+n})].$$

The decline in the *value* of the mine because q_{t+1} was removed from the stock is $V_t - V_{t+1}$, which is *economic depreciation.* Routine arithmetic shows that $V_t - V_{t+1} = pq_{t+1} - C(q_{t+1}) - rV_t$, or the loss in value of the mine from current extraction is profit earned on current extraction q_{t+1} plus interest on selling price V_t. We illustrate this in Figure 12.4. In Figure 12.4, the rectangle pq_{t+1} comprises, starting at the bottom, extraction costs, $C(q_{t+1})$; net profit, rV_t; and economic depreciation, $V_t - V_{t+1}$. A central result is that when extraction is being done in a profit-maximizing fashion (q_t, q_{t+1}, etc. are such that Hotelling's r percent rule on marginal profit is satisfied), then current rent or royalty equals economic depreciation, with a change of sign. Depreciation is a decline in value, whereas rent is a component of the extractor's income.

We see, then, that the mineral deposit's current value is its discounted future profit stream, and its decline in value from use (extraction) is economic depreciation,

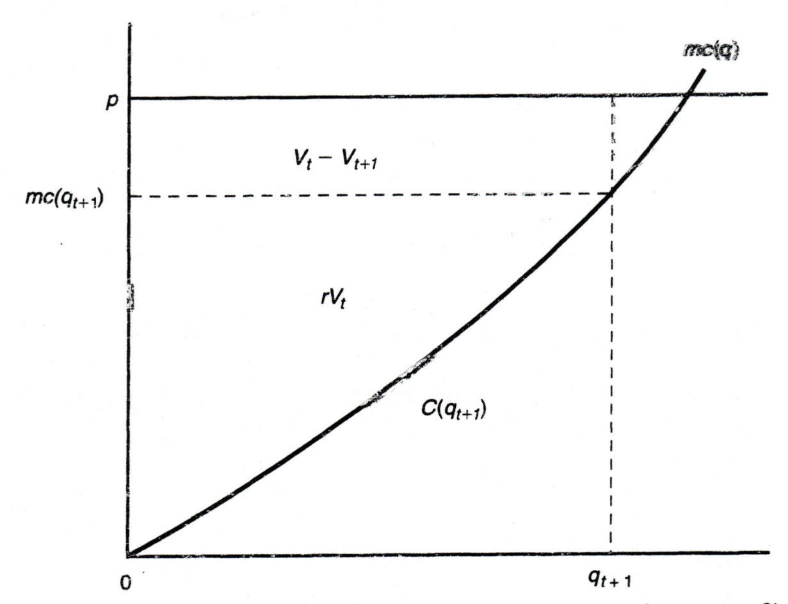

FIGURE 12.4 Total revenue from selling q_{t+1} of oil comprises extraction costs, $C(q_{t+1})$; net profit, rV_t; and economic depreciation, $V_t - V_{t+1}$. Economic depreciation equals Hotelling rent.

$V_t - V_{t+1}$. Observe that $V_t - V_{t+1}$ is marginal profit, $p - mc(q_{t+1})$, multiplied by q_{t+1}, the decline in the stock. This is the general measure of decline in stock value: a change in the stock's quantity multiplied by the marginal value of an additional ton of stock. Marginal value is typically output price of a unit minus the marginal extraction cost or is marginal profit per ton or rent on the marginal ton. If one incorporates exhaustible resources in a general equilibrium model of a competitive economy moving through time, one observes the same expression for economic depreciation of the stock of the exhaustible resource: $\Delta S_t \cdot [p_t - mc_t(q_t)]$ where $\Delta S_t = -q_t$, the current decline in stock size because extraction is ensuing. This economic depreciation term measures the loss in capital value of the current stock S_t and is *disinvestment* in natural resource capital, measured in dollars. One immediately thinks of compensating for this decline in capital value by building up capital value elsewhere in the economy—by investing in plant, equipment, and technical knowledge. Since one type of capital is not a perfect substitute for another in production, one cannot firmly link, preserving capital intact, to sustaining current productive capacity. However, preserving one's capital intact is a first step toward possible sustainability. But we have seen above that there are additional links to be checked between the notion of sustainable per capita consumption and preserving one's capital intact.

The simple expression "price minus marginal cost (called *net price*) multiplied by stock size change" is a universal expression for stock value revision (or economic depreciation when stocks are declining) in competitive, distortion-free economies not open to international trade. This expression or formula can be used to calculate capital value loss from declines in fish stock, timber stock, or water and airsheds. In the latter case, the decline in stock value corresponds to an increase in pollution stock. But the principle remains the same. We can then estimate current natural stock disinvestment in an economy by calculating a value for change in quantity of each type of capital and summing the values over types. These disinvestments can be compared with net machine and structure investment to arrive at net capital appreciation or depreciation in the economy.[4]

There is, in addition, an appreciation in the knowledge stock (as in R&D as investment in new useful knowledge) to consider. Estimation here is, of course, tricky. One can envisage a fraction of the wages and salaries of scientists and engineers as a measure of the growth in the knowledge stock, but this is just one of a variety of possible measures. Technical change is not something easily dismissed in a discussion of the depletion of natural capital.

Suppose that copper wires are made obsolete by glass fibers. Suddenly, copper stocks are much less in demand and command lower prices. The loss on the same stock, before and after the technical progress, will be reflected in a decline in stock value. Enthusiasts of technical progress suggest that we should generally depreciate natural resource stocks at low values because technical progress will make the stocks less valuable in the future. A reasonable characterization of this line of thought is that technical progress affects natural resource stock values crucially and precise quantification of technical progress is necessary for true capital stock valuation. In a world of perfect foresight on the part of economic agents, current prices of stocks and mineral outputs will accurately capitalize future technological shocks. This is the simplest case. It is the unanticipated shocks that pose the large problem in valuation of natural resource stock depreciation. One could envisage a risk adjustment in such cases. That is, one could argue that at current prices the value of the decline in, say, oil stocks overestimates economic depreciation because future unanticipated technological stocks will make oil less useful in the future. We must adjust economic depreciation downward (a smaller loss in stock value) because the current stock is commanding an artificially high net price.

Some observers would have very small values for the value of natural stock depletion because these people foresee much technical progress, freeing industrial society from the constraints posed by finite stocks of oil, copper, etc. This is an extreme view. Industrial society has surged on the crest of waves of technical progress, presumably mostly unanticipated. But this bounty may be finite, and we should not discount current stock values excessively because of past experience.

National Income Accounting and Depleting Capital

A major stimulus for reforming the national accounts was the observation by development specialists in the early 1980s that certain small countries were primarily living off their dwindling natural capital. By ordinary accounting calculations, these countries were "high-income," but clearly the measured national income was not sustainable When the natural resource stocks such as oil and timber were exhausted, there would be a crash in living standards and national income. Conventional measures of national well-being were misleading because they neglected the finiteness of the stocks that were supporting national well-being. There needed to be a focus on "national income" net of a measure of current depletion of natural resource stocks.

We observed the appropriate accounting above when we discussed an economy using oil in production. There, a part of gross oil income represented the decline in value of the stock. Thus a first step in the appropriate accounting is the separation of income to owners of natural capital (oil stocks, timber stocks, etc.) into an assignment for economic depreciation (decline in value from use) and a residual net income. In Figure 12.4, the upper rectangle, $-(V_{t+1} - V_t)$, is the assignment for economic depreciation and rV_t is the residual net income. The second step is the recognition that "traditional" NNP (the output side of the accounts) should include an assignment of product to cover off the decline in value of the natural stock or stocks. This key step implies that what has been viewed as output available for consumption is really output derived from depleting the economy's natural capital, a part of its productive base or capacity. Sustainable product is what is left after all declines in capital value have been taken into account. This is also *Hicksian income*, that is, what is left for prospective consumption after all capital stocks have been maintained intact.

Sustainable product (or Hicksian income) does not equal actual consumption in the economy. Society has to choose its level of consumption out of gross product. If it chooses to consume the sustainable product, then its value of capital is preserved intact (actually, its net investment is zero). Hicksian income and sustainable product are accounting entities. A society might choose to practice sustainable development and thus consume only its sustainable product, or it might choose a different consumption program.

Maintaining capital intact leads to tricky questions of measuring the diverse stocks in "capital," including questions of "quantity measurement" and "value measurement" under changing asset prices. However, NNP properly adjusted for "depletion" of natural capital is a much better measure of national well-being than traditional NNP, which considers only "depletion" of human-made capital such as buildings, machines, and roads. To incorporate disinvestment of natural capital in NNP, one takes the decline in the quantity of capital over the period and multiplies this by net price, unit rent, or net marginal value. Net price here is output price minus marginal "production" cost. In our simple case, marginal cost is marginal cost of extraction. In the next section we consider a situation in which net price has a term for pollution damage caused by the use of extracted minerals. In this case, as we know from Chapter 6, output price p exceeds true value because marginal pollution damage has not been netted out. For capital-using scenarios, the general approach is to start with NNP, then subtract the decline in the quantity of capital stock valued at its net price, rent, or marginal value. This deduction is the same as the decline in capital value over the period in question and is much easier to calculate than two capital values, one at the opening of the period and one at the closing. Discoveries of new stocks represent "investment" in natural capital and should be treated in the same way as disinvestments—include in NNP the quantity of stock increase weighted by its marginal value or net price. The lack of symmetry with disinvestment occurs because discovery is in general the result of costly exploration activity and the net price of discovered new stock incorporates marginal exploration costs.

If NNP is defined as the value of output left after capital is maintained intact, this sounds much like defining NNP as interest on capital. If capital is maintained at the same level for the next period, NNP resembles an interest flow arising from the capital. This can be made precise and was a key part of Weitzman (1976). One gets $NNP_t = \rho W_t$, where ρ is the social discount rate, acting as the interest rate, and W_t is capital, measured as the discounted flows of utilities of optimal consumption, into the infinite future.[5] It turns out that the unweighted sum of the value of past investments (including disinvestments in natural capital stocks) also equals W_t, and thus NNP can be viewed as interest on this more concrete notion of capital (see Solow, 1986; and Hartwick, 1996). Thus NNP viewed as income remaining after capital is maintained intact does have a precise interpretation as interest-on-capital. However, the level of "capital" is somewhat secondary in the analysis of sustainability. Measuring sustainability requires measures of consumption over time and aggregate net investment, including disinvestment in natural capital. Recall that Pearce and Atkinson (1993) have used aggregate net investment as a shorthand measure of the sustainability of a country's economic performance.

A traditional approach to greening the national accounts is to develop an inventory of valuable natural stocks in the economy. See, for example, World Bank (1997). Accountants attempt to measure the value of oil deposits underground, copper deposits, standing timber, land areas, fish stocks, and so on. This is called *wealth accounting*. Conceptually, this exercise is straightforward, but in practice it is burdened by basic estimation problems. How does one get reasonable estimates of fish stocks in coastal waters? Of unextracted mineral stocks? Regardless of the estimation method, there will be large residual uncertainty in the numbers for the physical values. Once one has the complete wealth accounts, one is supposed to graft *changes* in annual wealth values into ordinary national (flow) accounts. Our view is that the required changes in values are much easier to estimate. For oil, the physical decline is simply current annual use minus discoveries. Estimation of natural wealth, though interesting, seems to be extremely difficult to do accurately and should therefore be separated from a "greening" of the national accounts.

Open Economy Considerations

We noted in our discussion of Table 12.3 that though Japan was the most sustainable economy when treated in isolation, adjustments in the measure of sustainability were required, since Japan imports large amounts of natural resource flows such as wood, coal, and oil, to name a few. Japan may not be depleting its natural resource stocks rapidly, but it is depleting the natural resource stocks of its foreign suppliers. Asheim (1986) and Hartwick (1995) considered two countries, identical except that one had a slightly larger oil stock than the other. They found that the oil importer had to invest more than its own oil rents if it was to remain on a constant consumption path. This can be viewed as the oil importer building up its machine capital faster than the oil exporter because the importer is depleting both its own stocks of oil and its foreign supplier's stock. The opposite is true for the exporter. For it to remain on a constant consumption path, it need invest less than its oil rents in machine capital because its trading partner is, so to speak, covering off some of the value of the decline in the exporter's oil stocks. These results can be interpreted somewhat differently.

The oil importer is facing a rising price of its imports or a negative "terms of trade" effect. To keep consumption constant, it has to do "the standard thing" plus something extra because it faces adverse price effects. The something extra reduces to providing extra investment in machine capital, where "extra" is investment in excess of its own Hotelling oil rents (the "standard thing"). Conversely, the oil exporter benefits from the increasing price of its export and can do "something less" than "the standard thing." It need invest less in machine capital than the value of its own Hotelling oil rents in order to preserve its consumption constant. But the "terms of trade" effects also yield the result that the oil importer is investing as if it were assisting with covering off the value of the current decline in its partner's (the exporter's) oil stocks. Hence Japan's large net investment (the sum of the value of investment in machines and the value of disinvestment in own natural stocks) may not reflect above-average sustainability of economic performance. Its net investment figure must be adjusted downward because it is a major importer of natural stocks or a depleter of its supplier's stocks.

Accounting for Durable Exhaustible Resources

It is important to distinguish between extracted material that is immediately consumed, such as natural gas and oil, and extracted material that lasts and provides services for many periods, such as copper, gold, zinc, and iron. The latter are durable exhaustible resources, whereas the former are nondurable. Land as area is an infinitely durable resource; though its quality can be eroded. It is converted from one use to another but not used up. Thus the extraction of durable exhaustible resources can be viewed as changing them from storage in the ground to storage aboveground in use. If we could have infinitely durable resources (a physical impossibility), extraction would be purely value-enhancing, not stock-depleting, much like changing land from one sustainable use to another. This implies that mining very durable resources could end up in the investment part of NNP as a capital gains term, not an economic depreciation term, as with oil and other nondurable resources. (To the mine owner, extraction and sale correspond to a decline in the value of the mine, but the purchaser acquires good yielding service flows into the indefinite future.)

To the extent that a mined mineral is semidurable, it will have some aspects of depletability and some purely of "use change." Thus one cannot view extraction of semidurable minerals as simply depleting a stock period by period. There is a large component of relabeling from belowground assets to aboveground assets in use. Recycling can be seen as the process whereby durable resources get transferred from one use to another, aboveground. Since some material is inevitably lost in the recycling process, depletability is associated with recycling. Furthermore recycling requires energy, capital, and labor in addition to feedstock and is thus costly. This costliness will be capitalized in the price of the recycled material as it is circulated out of one use and into another. One can envisage a stage in which belowground sources are exhausted and recycling becomes the only source of certain durable materials such as steel and copper. Then one is dealing with a situation much like that with a nondurable exhaustible resource. Each period, some material is lost in the recycling process, so the aboveground stock is gradually depleted, period by period.

Accounting for Degradation of Environmental Capital

We discussed environmental issues in Chapters 6 and 7. In the context of sustainability and accounting for a sustainable economy, we can treat environmental resources (atmosphere, water, ecosystems) as capital goods yielding a flow of abatement services. If they are not overloaded, they do not become polluted. Once overloaded, they can often be renewed if the dumping of waste is greatly reduced, unless the pollutant has irreversible effects on the environmental resource. For decades, observers have recognized pollution as a by-product with negative value of goods. Although expenditures on pollution control enter the national accounts as "product" (like bicycles and stereos), observers felt that these expenditures should be subtracted because they reflected a negative "product"—pollution. Expenditures for pollution control are often referred to as "defensive expenditures."

Consider a simple example. Let the environment be represented by the level of pollution (a stock) it contains. This is a more easily measured dimension of the capital value of the environment. Nature abates the pollution. Suppose that use of oil pollutes the air (the environment). As we saw in Chapter 6, standard externality theory indicates that oil owner-extractors should be taxed for the damage their oil does to the air. The after-tax revenue to oil extractors is $(p - \tau_t)q_t$ where τ_t is the tax on oil. Taxes here are designed to reduce the oil extracted at any date and thus to leave the environment on average less polluted. In this world, with pollution, any ton of oil extracted is worth less than it was in a "no pollution" world because the extracted ton yields benefits, measured as $p-mc(q_t)$ and now damages, reflected in the tax. The net benefit of a ton of oil is reduced to $p-\tau_t-mc(q_t)$; and it is the percentage change in this entity that, when equated to the interest rate r, yields a profit-maximizing extraction path.

The central point is that economic depreciation from oil extraction will be *lower* period by period in a polluted economy because each ton of oil extracted is worth less than in a no-pollution world. The depletion effect of oil extraction includes a pollution effect but it is quite separate from the depletion effect of pollution on environmental capital. If pollution (degradation of environmental capital) is increasing as a result of oil extraction and use, then there is an additional term for depreciation of capital, this one for running down environmental capital. This is a straightforward extension of our argument that the depletion of oil stocks corresponds to economic depreciation of oil capital. Here, when environmental capital is depleted (more pollution is suspended), there is an economic depreciation term. But here also, the spillover of oil use into the degradation of the environment leads to a new expression for the economic depreciation of oil stocks.[6]

We have treated pollution as a stock-flow problem. Environmental capital is measured by the stock of pollutants it is burdened with. The flow of services from the stock is the current waste flows the capital can dissipate. Excessive waste dumping leads to the degradation of the capital (to stock depletion). One way to improve the quality of the environment is to reduce the dumping of waste. This gives nature a chance to renew the environment. One way to reduce the amount of waste dumped is to treat the waste before it is dumped, i.e., engage in pollution control. This is an example of a defensive expenditure that we examined in Chapter 7. Another direct approach is to clean up polluted sites. This corresponds to investing directly in environmental capital. A third approach is to change production technologies so that waste produced is less in either quantity or intensity of pollution. Waste with lower pollution intensity would be waste that is easier for the air or water to absorb or recycle.

Deforestation and Changing Land Use

We discussed deforestation at length in Chapter 10. In the context of green accounting, there are two ways to view the forest. It can be treated as a capital good like an oil deposit, that is, viewed as an exhaustible resource. An alternative approach is to treat the forest land as a capital good yielding a perpetual flow of crops. Then deforestation becomes a change in land use, and one arrives at the central result that if land clearing is costly and ownership of the land is secure in private hands, then deforestation must correspond to the replacement of a low-value use of the land with a higher-value use. If this were not the case, the owner would not be willing to incur the costs of clearing the land.

Suppose that an owner were to clear his or her land and sell off the timber cover. This makes sense only if there is no net loss in the activity. If the land is cleared, the timber sold, and the cleared land used for other activities, the owner must still not be in a loss position. In a smooth transition from forest to other uses of the land, we expect zero profit at the margin of land cleared—the value of trees cut and marketed on the marginal hectare equals the decline in the value of land. In this case there is no entry in the investment section of the NNP, since the downward revaluation on land cleared is exactly matched by the value of new product—trees cut and sold from the land cleared.

This view of deforestation implies that the land use change shows up as a revaluation or capital gains term in the investment part of the NNP. It enters as a quantity of land cleared in the current period multiplied by the marginal cost of clearing a hectare. This marginal cost corresponds to the difference in the value of a unit of land before and after clearing. Capital gains generally have no place in the calculation of NNP, but here they do have a place. The quantity of land (in hectares) remains unchanged over the period, but its value per hectare is changed by the clearing, and clearing is costly. One can imagine land in virgin forest yielding a small dollar flow being replaced by land in farming yielding a higher dollar flow. This is a benchmark case—with secure property rights (and no other distortions), land clearing must correspond to increase in land value; otherwise, the landowner would not agree to the change in land use.

As we saw in Chapter 10, inadequate property rights can lead to excessive land clearing, since underpriced land will be abused or overused in the same way that any underpriced input will be used in larger quantities than it would be under true scarcity pricing. This is the central pathology in resource allocation under open access arrangements, and a subject we have discussed at length throughout the book.

Forests have value beyond the marketable products they yield. Forests absorb carbon dioxide, provide oxygenation services to the earth, and can help stabilize local climates. A forest can also provide prospective ecotourism services. These services are not traded in a market and are not generally taken account of by landowners. Citizens of the world could be induced to pay for these services through a special levy and have the revenues transferred to land owners. D. Pearce (1991) estimated that in 1981 U.S. dollars, a transfer of about $3.5 billion per year would compensate Amazonian landowners for gains not realized from forest clearing. Deforestation would cease. Thus if the citizens of the world were receiving benefits in excess of this amount from forests about to be cut, they could get those benefits by buying off the landowners who would otherwise deforest the land in question. If these payments are not made, then privte ownership of the forest can lead to excessive use of trees, even in a sustainable pattern of harvests with reforestation. Too few trees will be standing at every point in time. The natural resource stock in the national accounts should be adjusted to reflect this lower level of the environmental stock.

Biodiversity and Natural Capital

The dwindling of biodiversity concerns many people, though the exact number of species on the earth is not known with any precision. We believe biodiversity is linked to the vitality of the ecosystem although there is still very little empirical work in this area. We do not know precisely which bits of biodiversity are most crucial to much of the viability of the ecosystem. Weitzman (1992) and Solow, Polasky, and Broadus (1993) have attempted to value a subspecies on the basis of its genetic "distance" from its nearest relative. More valuable bits of biodiversity are "more unique." From the viewpoint of green accounting, if we are willing to abstract from such important heterogeneity in the stock of biodiversity, we can view the stock much like the clean atmosphere. It yields a flow of services and when damaged yields less services. Loss of biodiversity is, then, a stock decline, a decline of very uncertain dollar value (economic depreciation). It seems appropriate to have an entry in the group of disinvestments in NNP for the economic depreciation in the stock of biodiversity. Given the difficulty in measuring (1) the decline in stock and (2) the value of each unit of stock, it seems appropriate to leave the entry blank until good measurements do become available. This protects the methodology against the criticism, "You forgot the depletion of important stock x." The list of stock declines could be long, and temporary blanks could be many, but the list need not be open-ended. Air, water, soil, and minerals cover the broad general categories of natural capital. Biodiversity can be viewed as a stock that renews air, water, and soil quality. There are complicated linkages here. Nevertheless, it is useful to pursue a comprehensive picture of stock declines and a valuation of these losses on a uniform basis.

Protection from a Catastrophe

The notion of some sort of collapse in the earth's system of supporting economic activity has common currency. We see here a variant of the Malthusian idea of an inevitable bottoming out of human living standards. Ecologists are trained to study biological systems that crash, as, for example, in rapid declines in certain fish stocks. Humans are subject to the biological constraints that may be associated with a sudden decline. It may be as simple as drought leading to mass starvation in a large area or as complicated as ozone depletion leading to desertification of the oceans and a snapping of a vital link in the earth's food chain. A crash in earth's support mechanisms, and hence in the economy, can be viewed as somewhat analogous to the sudden onset of illness or injury in an individual. The event cannot be wished away, but it can be guarded against. Thus a current reduction of carbon emissions from production activity can be viewed as guarding against a crash caused by the uncertain effects of global warming. Similarly, the reduction in the use of chlorofluorocarbons (CFCs) can be viewed as guarding against a crash caused by excessive depletion of the stratospheric ozone layer.

The economic argument is that an ecosystem catastrophe can be viewed as a future event with a large negative value to society. If that negative value is assigned a positive probability and incorporated into current valuation of social welfare, current actions that contribute to the crash will appear as very costly. A crash is labeled as irreversible, and increased prudence increases society's options for the future (Arrow and Fisher, 1974). The difference between a crash and a downturn seems to depend on the capacity of a system to bounce back. Crashes are linked to irreversible events, as in extinction of species. The more severe an anticipated decline, the more one is generally willing to pay to guard against the crash.

The clearing of forests to make way for farming, the damming of rivers to provide for electric power stations, and the "planting" of cities to provide for large-scale industrial activity have been celebrated as manifestations of human ingenuity. Today, however, there is the feeling that the pace of these activities should be slowed. The payoff from slowing down is a reduction in the impact human activity is having on the earth's natural systems, such as climatic and ecological balance.

IMPLEMENTING SUSTAINABLE DEVELOPMENT

Sustainability by Nations

The new elements in a sustainable development program are the careful monitoring of net investment (the sum of investment in human-made capital and disinvestments of natural capital stocks) and the targeting of nonnegative net investment in economic policy. It is not enough for a nation to save and invest vigorously in new buildings, machines, and R&D; it must also monitor the decline in natural resource stocks and balance off the economic depreciation of these stocks with investments in new buildings, machines, and R&D. Saving becomes broadly conceived partly as forgoing direct consumption out of current product but also as drawing on natural resource stocks in a prudent manner. A nation's policies can become more sustainable either because it accumulates more buildings, machines, and useful knowledge or because it reduces current depletion in its natural capital stocks.

To implement such policies, a nation needs high-quality estimates of the economic depreciation in its stocks. National accounting or accounting generally is needed in order to design policies. Then the familiar array of incentives—taxes, subsidies, and allowances—must be tailored to structure the correct policy. Pigovian corrective taxes are familiar components of a strategy of sustainable development and could be incorporated in a green national accounting. What is different about this approach to policy design, compared with existing approaches? The novelty is the integration of savings from current output and dissavings in natural capital into one expression for integrated savings. The economic depreciation of natural resource stocks is not either left out or put aside. It comes to be treated equally with traditional savings. We are aware that this policy approach is not a solution to the problem of maintaining good standards of living for all people into the indefinite future. Human-made capital and natural capital are imperfect substitutes, and we do not insure ourselves against a crash in the natural system by keeping net investment nonnegative.

This policy obliges us to measure key declines in the natural system and to value them carefully at each date. It represents a particular sort of conservation policy for the natural system on which we and our economy rely. Ultimately, one wants to see exhaustible sources of natural inputs replaced by renewable sources—solar power instead of power from burning hydrocarbons, fusion power instead of power derived from uranium fuel. Policies that encourage the substitution of renewable sources for depleting sources are, of course, desirable. In a steady state, renewable resource stocks yield a service flow and the stocks manifest no diminution or economic depreciation.

Thus net investment becomes positive when a renewable source of a service suddenly displaces an exhaustible source.

At the opening of this section, we mentioned "new elements" in policy design. Conventional policies still need attention. We have examined these policies extensively throughout this book. These include correct pricing for natural inputs or the correction for overuse of natural inputs such as the services of airsheds, watersheds, and fish stocks. Inadequate property rights are a principal problem in this area; and ill-defined property rights—as, for example, in many open access situations—result directly in underpriced resource inputs and the potential for nonsustainable use. These low prices are often manifestations of inefficiencies in natural resource use. The problem of underpricing is costly in two senses—it results in static inefficiency (people on unnecessarily low indifference curves), and it erodes dynamic efficiency (the development and implementation of resource-saving technologies). Efficiency prices reflect true scarcities and are also needed in calculating true measures of economic depreciation. For example, a "high" price for oil implies a larger economic depreciation of oil stocks in the relevant period. High or rising prices are often spurs to innovation or technical improvement. Technical change that saves natural resources is of course desirable, and any policy which fosters such innovation is praiseworthy.

The other conventional policy addresses population issues. Pensions, inheritance taxes, school taxes, and state funding of universities are some of the many policies that affect family size. Large populations make management of social life more difficult. It is difficult to imagine why a city of 6 million people is better for each citizen than a city of 2 million people, when the problems of managing public health, safety, pollution, welfare, and transportation are more difficult in huge cities. Recent estimates by the United Nations suggest a world of 560 cities with over 1 million people in 2015. In 1950, there were only 83. Tokyo, Shanghai, Bombay, Beijing, and Calcutta are in the top ten currently. Mexico City, Dhaka, Karachi, São Paulo, Jakarta, and Lagos are growing rapidly. The concept of an optimal population for a nation is not obvious, but the problems of very dense or large populations are quite clear. It is not unreasonable to link sustainability to a concept of manageable population growth, or in some cases to no population growth.

Sustainability by Regions and Sectors

Economic and geographic sectors require consideration on their own. People ask: What does sustainable development mean for my town, my region, or my economic sector? Regional economics addressed regional economic development before sustainable development became a concern. Attention was focused on investment in human-made capital as well as savings by regions and sectors. One can extend such analysis to disinvestments in natural capital by regions anad sectors. The sectoral flows will and should tally with the national figures as they are summed and account is taken of double-counting and overlaps in definitions of sectors and regions. The important question emerges: At what level should net investment be nonnegative? Should certain regions—for example, those concentrating in mining—not run deficits on net investment? In such regions economic depreciation of stocks will be relatively large, and earnings from the sale of mineral output to other regions will be large. These earnings allow the exporting region to undersave relative to zero net investment while keeping consumption in the region constant. Final goods will in part be imported from other regions that are importing minerals. The mineral-importing region must "oversave" to keep itself on a constant consumption path (Asheim, 1986, Hartwick, 1995). The exporters will, other things being the same, enjoy a higher constant consumption level. With labor mobility and identical workers, a quite different equilibrium would emerge, since one expects equalization of per capita consumption. However, the distribution of ownership rights in the different sorts of capital in each region is crucial.

Of importance at the regional level would be the correct scarcity prices—prices corrected for imperfections in property rights and externalities. People in the various regions would check that their local airsheds, watersheds, aquifers, and biodiversity stocks were not being abused—used that is, not being at low implicit prices. Given correct prices and the attendant use levels, one proceeds to calculate local economic depreciation of the diverse natural stocks and obtains a value for net investment for the region. The time trend in this measure could signal a move toward or from sustainability; but its level would have no special significance, since it would be a component of a set of diverse regional net investments. It would be instructive, of course, to compare net investment figures for similar regions. Guidance for reorienting policy could follow from such comparisons. Net investment by region brings to mind the trade balance of a region. The latter has been pondered on for decades but has proved difficult to draw policy guidance from. Regional net investment figures on their own are also hard to draw specific policy guidance from.

SUMMARY

1. Sustainability is a concept derived from the use of fisheries and forests, the economic of renewable resources. We have treated sustainability as an indefinitely maintainable consumption level. With no technical progress and zero population growth, this corresponds to a path of constant per capita consumption. Constant consumption per capita over time is a sound notion of intergenerational equity or fairness.
2. The simplest case involves renewable inputs and a steady-state "harvest" that can be perpetuated over time. The stock of the resource remains intact.
3. The more problematic case is that of a nonrenewable resource. We have seen how the combination of asymptotic depletion of exhaustible stocks and the accumulation of substitute stocks represents a way around exhaustibility. Under special assumptions, the steady-state outcome that we observed for the case of a simpler renewable input is restored. Prescriptions for sustainability with exhaustible stocks involve replacing the value of natural capital currently used up with an equal value

of new produced capital, as in machines, buildings, or new technical knowledge. Current investment must be sufficient at least to cover off current economic depreciation of capital, broadly defined. If current depreciation is more than covered by current investment, there is net capital accumulation.

4. The notion of replacing the loss in one capital stock (its economic depreciation) with an accumulation of another capital stock involves the methodology of measurement of changes in stocks and their values. This requires revisions to traditional national accounting.
5. The goal of "green accounting" is to measure how much "national income" is being derived from labor and human-made capital and how much is being derived from running down natural resource stocks such as oil reserves and valuable timber stands. These new approaches stand alone, independent of sustainability, as useful extensions to national accounting practice.
6. Measurement of natural resource capital (and values) is difficult, and work on these areas is in the formative stages.
7. Measures of net investment (the sum of investment in human-made capital and disinvestment of natural capital) are essential in establishing policies for sustainable development.
8. Economic models show that feasibility of sustainable policies depends on a variety of factors, including degree of substitutability between natural resource capital and produced capital, technology, and so on.
9. Secure property rights and efficient pricing of all resources are an essential component of sustainable development.

DISCUSSION QUESTIONS

1. Sustainable development is a concept, not an agenda for action. What is the concept?
2. Precisely what economic principles are involved in "conservation"? In "preservation"? Traditional policies toward the environment involve conservation and preservation. How do these policies fit into a framework of sustainable development?
3. What is economic depreciation? How is it measured? In what sense is economic depreciation an inherent part of sustainable development?
4. Is sustainable development associated with an optimal population? With a specific policy toward population growth?
5. Relate the extent of biodiversity to sustainable development.
6. How would you interpret the threat of a crash in the ecosystem in economic terms?

NOTES

1. Martin Faustmann laid out a formal model of sustainable timber production in 1849 and dealt in a modern way with present values (capital valuation).
2. Malthus popularized this scenario. His was an agricultural economy with land as the natural stock, but the analogy to the fish stock is accurate.
3. To see this, we differentiate with respect to time to get $\dot{C} + \dot{I} = F_K\dot{K} + F_R\dot{R} + F_L\dot{L}$. By assumption, $\dot{L} = 0$ and $\dot{K} = I = RF_R$ is the rule: invest resource rent. Differentiation yields $\dot{I} = \dot{R}F_R + R\dot{F}_R$. The Hotelling rule is $\dot{F}_R = F_K/F_R$. Substitute these into the first equation above and observe that $\dot{C} = 0$, or aggregate consumption is unchanging over time.
4. Asheim (1994) emphasizes that a current asset price—such as the price of copper or oil—reflects a current distinct view of the future by society. If society is not investing for sustainable development, current asset prices do not reflect a future course of sustainable development and thus should not be used to calculate current net investment. Thus the setting of current net investment at zero with current asset prices will not necessarily put society on a path of sustainable development. As a practical matter, it is, however, a large first step.
5. This concept of capital is associated with the economist Irving Fisher. It is the discounted flow of income period by period that stems from the capital good. In this case, the capital good is "the economy."
6. Details are provided in Hartwick (1993) or Hamilton and Ulph (1994). See also Becker (1982). Heal (1984) considers hydrocarbon extraction that causes air pollution in a framework that involves cumulative pollution leading to an uncertain catastrophe—a negative break in the capacity of the economy to produce output.

SELECTED READINGS

Arrow, K. J., and A. C. Fisher (1974). "Environmental Preservation, Uncertainty and Irreversibility." *Quarterly Journal of Economics*, 312–319.

Asheim, G. B. (1986). "Hartwick's Rule of Open Economics." *Canadian Journal of Economics* 19, 395–402.

Asheim, G. B. (1994). "Net National Product as an Indicator of Sustainability." *Scandinavian Journal of Economics* 96 (2).

Becker, Robert (1982). "Intergenerational Equity: The Capital Environment Trade-Off." *Journal of Environmental Economics and Management*, 9, 165–185.

Brundtland Report (World Commission on Environment and Development) (1987). *Our Common Future*. London: Oxford University Press.

Chichilnisky, G. (1993). "What Is Sustainable Development?" (mimeo).

Dockner, E., and J. M. Hartwick (1994). "Recycling, Constant Consumption, and NNP" (mimeo).

Faustmann, Martin (1849, 1968). "On the Determination of the Value Which Forest Land and Immature Stands Possess for Foresting," in M. Gane, ed., *Martin Faustmann and the Evolution of Discounted Cash Flow*, Oxford Institute Paper No. 42. Oxford: Oxford University Press.

Hamilton, Kirk, and D. Ulph (1994). "The Greenhouse Effect and Constant Consumption Paths" (mimeo).

Hartwick, J. M. (1977). "International Equity and the Investing of Rents from Exhaustible Resources." *American Economic Review* 66, 972–974.

Hartwick, J. M. (1978). "Investing Returns from Depleting Renewable Resource Stocks and Intergenerational Equity." *Economics Letters* 1, 85–88.

Hartwick, J. M. (1992). "Deforestation and National Accounting." *Environmental and Resource Economics* 2, 513–521.

Hartwick, J. M. (1993). "Notes on Economic Depreciation of Natural Resource Stocks and National Accounting," in A. Franz and C. Stahmer, eds., *Approaches to Environmental Accounting*. Heidelberg: Physica-Verlag, pp. 167–198.

Hartwick, J. M. (1994). "National Wealth and Net National Product." *Scandinavian Journal of Economics* 96 (2), 253–256.
Hartwick, J. M. (1995). "Constant Consumption Paths in Open Economies with Exhaustible Resources." *Review of International Economics* 3 (3), 275–283.
Hartwick, J. M. (1996). "Constant Consumption as Interest on Capital." *Scandinavian Journal of Economics* 98 (3), 439–443.
Hayek, F. A. (1941). *The Pure Theory of Capital.* London: Routledge and Kegan Paul.
Heal, G. M. (1984). "Interaction Between Economy and Climate: A Framework for Policy Design Under Uncertainty," in V. Kerry Smith and Ann Dryden White, eds., *Advances in Applied Microeconomics.* Greenwich: JAI, pp. 151–158.
Hicks, John R. (1939). *Value and Capital.* Oxford: Oxford University Press.
Hicks, J. R. (1942). "Maintaining Capital Intact: A Further Suggestion." *Economica* 9, 174–179.
Pearce, D. (1991). "Deforesting the Amazon: Toward an Economic Solution." *Ecodecision* 1, 40–95.
Pearce, D., and G. Atkinson (1993). "Capital Theory and the Measurement of Sustainable Development." *Ecological Economics* 8, 103–108.
Pigou, A. C. (1935). "Net Income and Capital Depletion." *Economic Journal* 45, 235–241.
Pigou, A. C. (1941). "Maintaining Capital Intact." *Economica* 8, 271–275.
Robson, Arthur (1980). "Costly Innovation and Natural Resources." *International Economic Review* 21, 1 (February), 17–30.
Solow, A., S. Polasky, and J. Broadus (1993). "On the Measurement of Biological Diversity." *Journal of Environmental Economics and Management* 24 (1, January), 60–68.
Solow, R. M. (1974). "Intergenerational Equity and Exhaustible Resources." *Review of Economic Studies* (Symposium), 29–45.
Solow, R. M. (1986). "On the Intergenerational Allocation of Resources." *Scandinavian Journal of Economics* 88, 1441–1449.
Stiglitz, J. E. (1974). "Growth with Exhaustible Natural Resources: Efficient and Optimal Growth Paths." *Review of Economic Studies* (Symposium on the Economics of Exhaustible Resources), 123–137.
Weitzman, Martin L. (1976). "On the Welfare Significance of National Product in a Dynamic Economy." *Quarterly Journal of Economics* 90, 156–162.
Weitzman, Martin L. (1992). "On Diversity." *Quarterly Journal of Economics* 107, 363–406.
World Bank (1997). *Expanding the Measure of Wealth.* Washington DC: The World Bank.

Index

Note: An italic *b*, *f*, or *t* following a page number indicates a box, figure, or table, respectively.